ABOUT THE PRODUCTION OF THIS BOOK

The Celestial Cycle was typed by electric typewriter directly on plastic plates, which were then run on a multilith press. Layout and specifications were prepared by the publishers; the typing was supervised and the plates proofread by the author.

The publication of this book, prohibitive in cost by ordinary methods, was made possible by the use of nomic (no-metal-in-composition) printing. A very large part of this saving resulted, of course, from the assumption of heavy editorial and production responsibilities by the author, whose expenditure of time and effort does not appear in the cost sheet. For his generous co-operation the publishers express their sincere gratitude.

THE CELESTIAL CYCLE

SOME BOOKS BY THE SAME AUTHOR

Victoria County Centennial History (1921)
International Aspects of Unemployment (1923)
European Elegies (1928)
The European Heritage (1930)
The Tide of Life (1930)
The North American Book of Icelandic Verse (1930)
The Magyar Muse (1933)
The Eternal Quest (1934)
A Canadian Headmaster (1935)
Canadian Overtones (1935)
A Golden Treasury of Polish Lyrics (1936)
The Death of King Buda (With Lulu Putnik, 1936)
Titus the Toad (1939)
Canada, Europe and Hitler (1939)
The Flying Bull and Other Tales (1940)
Twilight of Liberty (1941)
Seven Pillars of Freedom (1944)
The Quebec Tradition (With Séraphin Marion, 1946)
A Little Treasury of Hungarian Verse (1947)
The Humanities in Canada (With A.S.P. Woodhouse, 1947)

T H E   C E L E S T I A L   C Y C L E

The Theme of *Paradise Lost* in World Literature with Translations of the Major Analogues

by

WATSON KIRKCONNELL
President of Acadia University

Toronto
UNIVERSITY OF TORONTO PRESS
1952

University of Toronto Press
Reprinted 2017
ISBN 978-1-4875-9236-3 (paper)

PREFACE

This project was begun in January 1934 on the invitation of Professor A. S. P. Woodhouse, of the University of Toronto. The original plan was for a joint volume, to be entitled "The Theme of Paradise Lost", to which he would contribute an introductory essay, comparing the theological ideas and the treatment of Satan in Grotius's Adamus Exul, Andreini's L'Adamo, Salandra's Adamo Caduto and Vondel's Lucifer and Adam in Ballingschap with those in Milton's Paradise Lost, while I would undertake to edit English versions of the five analogues. For Grotius we would use the alleged English rendering by Francis Barham; for Andreini the Hayley-Cowper translation would do; and I myself was to furnish English verse translations of Salandra and Vondel. The authentic Latin text of Grotius (from a rare copy in the British Museum) was to be included, in view of the unfortunate accessibility of Lauder's adulterated version in several American libraries. A year or two would suffice for the whole undertaking.

We very soon had to raise our sights. Francis Barham's presumed version of Adamus Exul turned out, on collation with the Latin, to be no translation at all, but a piece of inflated Miltonese that omitted large sections of Grotius, improvised equally extensive passages that were not in the original, and garbled the rest (see below, p. 654). The Hayley-Cowper version of L'Adamo, while relatively faithful to Andreini's Italian, was nevertheless prone to stilted vagueness (e.g., where line 1443, Accuseria del Ciel cose sublimi, becomes Accuse the latent mysteries of heaven). It therefore seemed desirable that new translations should be made of these dramas as well. It was also decided that I should translate Avitus and the Caedmonian Genesis, and that excerpts from a number of other analogues (Valvasone, Fairfax's

Tasso, Andrew Ramsay, Phineas Fletcher, Sylvester's Du Bartas, etc.) should be included. Then followed my resolve to append a descriptive catalogue of all analogues in all languages, a decision that was to add at least twelve years to the time needed for the project. Nothing was to be taken at second hand. All works were to be tracked down and read in the original languages, except in the case of Sumerian, Babylonian, Arabic, Armenian, Syriac, Ethiopic and Old Church Slavonic, which lay beyond my linguistic orbit. So far as the libraries of the British Isles and Europe were concerned, the War years, 1939-45, were largely a blank; but I have since been able to secure numerous rare works in microfilm or photostat from libraries in London, Oxford, Paris, Göttingen, Lisbon, Madrid, Florence and Rome. Most of the North American libraries had been checked earlier.

Meanwhile Professor Woodhouse had withdrawn from our joint project. His share of the book had, like mine, grown beyond all expectation, and it now seemed wiser to plan for two independent volumes. My own is, however, much the poorer for the lack of his introductory essay. I have not attempted to duplicate its proposed comparison of ideas and in my own Introduction have merely dealt with some questions of evolution in form.

It ought perhaps to be emphasized that our interest from the beginning had not been in the threshing of old straw in the matter of Milton's "borrowing" from this or that specific source, but rather in the examination of the analogues as analogues. On the one hand, the nonsense uttered by an exclamatory source-hunter like Zicari (*see below*, PL-233) springs from his complete ignorance of a whole battalion of analogues marching across twelve centuries of literary activity, among whom Salandra borrows from Andreini and the *hexamera*, Andreini from Grotius and the *hexamera*, he in turn from Du Bartas, and the Fathers, and Du Bartas himself from St. Basil, St. Jerome, Georgius Pisides and still others. On the other hand, the varying treatment of the same subject-matter for dramatic, epic and didactic purposes by hundreds of authors of differing powers and personalities gives greater significance to the originality with which Milton shaped his own masterpiece out of almost identical materials. The denigratory school of critics has not dared to dismiss Shakespeare as a dishonest poetaster because he borrowed from North's Plutarch and Holinshed's *Chronicle*; but distaste for Milton's theme, style or *personality* has emboldened many little men, from William Lauder to the present day, to condemn Milton out of hand as a second-rate thief. If knowledge of the whole range of Miltonic analogues once becomes general, Milton's essential originality and greatness will dispose of these splenetic detractors once and for all. At any rate the present volume will make the most significant parallels to *Paradise Lost* accessible, in whole or in part, to all serious students of Milton.

The descriptive catalogue, although it contains over three hundred items, is not exhaustive. In the case of the hexamera, the chronicles and the mirror literature, where the relationship to *Paradise Lost* is one of subject-matter, rather than of artistic form, it seemed enough to list only a few typical and influential examples. The *Hermetica* and the *Zohar* have been omitted for the same reason. In general, notes on the translated analogues have been included, *sub nomine*, in the descriptive catalogue.

My thanks for counsel or suggestions go to Douglas Bush, James Holly Hanford, William B. Hunter Jr., Roy McKeen Wiles, Helen Darbishire, F. T. Prince, Molly Mahood, Malcolm Ross, Charles G. Osgoode, J. Milton French, William R. Parker, Theodore Silverstein, Harcourt Brown, and J. F. M. Sterck of the Vondel Museum, Aerdenhout-bij-Haarlem.

I should like to thank certain of my colleagues for their kindness in checking the final drafts of my translations with the originals: the late Dr. W. H. Thompson for the *Adamus Exul* of Grotius and Dr. H. W. Hilborn, now of Queen's University, for *L'Adamo* by Andreini and *Adamo Caduto* by Salandra. My *Vondel* translations have been read by Dr. W. L. Graff of McGill and by Mrs. Lyda van Delft Fraser of Sydney. To Professor Woodhouse, I am indebted for the original inception of the work and for the constant encouragement with which he has mitigated my eighteen years of academic "hard labour".

I should like to record my thanks to the Humanities Research Council of Canada for a generous grant in aid of publication. I am also grateful to the University of Toronto Press for its counsel and assistance in planning the issue of this volume.

WATSON KIRKCONNELL

Acadia University,
Wolfville, N. S.

CONTENTS

INTRODUCTION

The past forty years have seen a striking development in basic scholarship dealing with *Paradise Lost*, from the epoch-making hexameral thesis of F. E. Robbins[1] down to the penetrating analysis of B. Rajan[2]. The affinities of Milton's thought with that of his predecessors and contemporaries[3]

---

[1]Robbins, Frank Egleston, *The Hexaemeral Literature, a Study of the Greek and Latin Commentaries on Genesis*, University of Chicago Press, 1912.

[2]B. Rajan, *Paradise Lost and the Seventeenth Century Reader*, London, Chatto and Windus, 1947. Among the other works most relevant to the present study are Maury Thibaut de Maisières' *Les Poèmes Inspirées du Début de la Genèse à l'Époque de la Renaissance* (Louvain, 1931); George Coffin Taylor's *Milton's Use of DuBartas* (Cambridge, Harvard University Press, 1934); Grant McColley's *Paradise Lost: An Account of Its Growth and Major Origins* (Chicago, Packard, 1940); Maurice Kelley's *This Great Argument: A Study of Milton's De Doctrina as a Gloss upon Paradise Lost* (Princeton University Press, 1941); C. S. Lewis's *A Preface to Paradise Lost* (Oxford University Press, 1942); Douglas Bush's *Paradise Lost in Our Time* (Cornell University Press, 1945); Sister Mary Irma Corcoran's *Milton's Paradise Lost with Reference to the Hexameral Background* (Washington, Catholic University of America, 1945); Allan H. Gilbert's *On the Composition of Paradise Lost* (University of North Carolina Press, 1947), and Arnold Williams's *The Common Expositor* (University of North Carolina Press, 1948).

[3]In this connection see also A.S.P. Woodhouse's *Puritanism and Liberty* (London, 1938); W. Haller's *The Rise of Puritanism* (New York, 1938); and Arthur Barker's *Milton and the Puritan Dilemma* (Toronto, 1942).

have been traced with great diligence, and the fact has been established that most of his ideas are part of the warp and woof of a literary and intellectual tradition stretching back for more than a millenium. There is no longer any danger among serious Miltonists of regarding the identity of some commonplace idea (e.g. the felix culpa) in Milton and in some single earlier work as a proof of poetic borrowing by one from the other.

If any matter emerges from the present volume as worthy of special emphasis, it is the fact that Paradise Lost is an epic and as such is clearly distinguished in form and style from the great majority of its analogues. Thibaut de Maisières, for example, seems to imply that Milton's poem is a hexameron: "Tous les Hexamérons semblent s'unir dans une sorte de lignée généalogique pour fair éclore, après des générations d'efforts, cette oeuvre complète, qui les résume tous, qui les voue à l'oubli et qui étient leur race ayent atteint la perfection."[4] But there is as much difference between Paradise Lost and a hexameron as there is between a full-rigged ship and a timber-raft. They may be composed of similar materials, but their form and functions are fundamentally different. A condensed and stream-lined hexameron may be found in Paradise Lost, Book VII, 210-634, but even here it is subordinated to a larger pattern of epic narrative. Milton's models are Homer and Vergil, not St. Basil and St. Jerome.

The subject-matter of the epics and dramas dealt with in the analogues of Milton are those of the so-called "celestial cycle", comprising the Creation, the War in Heaven, the Temptation and the Fall of Man and its consequences, and finally the Redemption of the world by the Atoning sacrifice of God the Son. Different poets selected different

---

[4]Maury Thibaut de Maisieres, Les Poèmes inspirés du Début de la Genèse à l'Epoque de la Renaissance (Louvain, 1931), p. 119.

themes from this cycle of Christian story, just as the Greek epic poets and tragedians drew on the Trojan cycle or the Theban cycle. Where hundreds of authors dealt with the same range of ideas, the significant aspect in each is the architectural design and the power of language and imagination manifested in the individual work.

The first conscious development of such literary treatment appears to have begun in the 4th century A.D., when Apollinaris the Elder, of Syria, and his son, confronted by an edict of Julian the Apostate forbidding Christians to teach the classics, proceeded to turn the narrative portions of the Old Testament into Greek epic verse, the Psalms into Pindaric Odes, and the New Testament into Platonic dialogues. Virtually none of their work has survived to our own day, but the example proved a potent one for over a thousand years to come. Judging by the surviving material from the 5th, 6th and 7th centuries, the movement proved much more fruitful in Latin than in Greek. Aurelius Clemens Prudentius,[5] Valeria Faltonia Proba,[6] Hilarius Arelatensis,[7] Caelius Sedulius,[8] Prosperus Aquitanus,[9] Claudius Marius Victor,[10] Dracontius,[11] Cyprianus Gallus,[12] and above all Avitus,[13] bear witness to an active interest in the Vergilian tradition while the only even quasi-epic poem in Greek surviving from the same period is Georgios Pisides' Cosmourgia,[14] which is no more than a hexameron, versified in the iambic senarius. Generally speaking, the hexameron, or detailed description

---

[5]Descriptive Catalogue, 22-25.
[6]Descriptive Catalogue, 26.
[7]Descriptive Catalogue, 28.
[8]Descriptive Catalogue, 29.
[9]Descriptive Catalogue, 30.
[10]Descriptive Catalogue, 31.
[11]Descriptive Catalogue, 34.
[12]Descriptive Catalogue, 36.
[13]Descriptive Catalogue, 35. English translation on pp. 1-19.
[14]Descriptive Catalogue, 39.

of the "six days" of Creation, dominated the writing of the period. Some eighty specimens survive, almost all of them comparatively formless masses of erudite and discursive prose. Some of these, such as those by Saint Basil[15] and Saint Jerome,[16] achieve greatness of literary style, but their merit is to be found in texture and not in structure. The only surviving Greek hexameters of this age and theme are those of Gregorius Nazianzenus,[17] and they are avowedly dogmatic rather than narrative in purpose.

As the missionary influence of the Church spread northward and westward among the Teutonic peoples, the tradition of the Christian epic blended with a still active epic tradition in the Germanic vernaculars. Some of the results survive in the "Caedmonian" Genesis,[18] Christ and Satan,[19] the Old Saxon Genesis,[20] the Heliand (not relevant here) by the same author, Die altdeutsche Genesis,[21] Die Bücher Mosis,[22] and Die Schöpfung.[23] The most notable features of this poetry are the transposing of the Celestial Cycle into alliterative verse, the specific influence of Avitus on the Caedmonian Genesis-B, and a large measure of originality in the same poem (and its Old Saxon original) in dealing with Satan and the Temptation. A projection into the 14th century of the versifying of scriptural narrative appears in the Cursor Mundi[24] and in the equally prolix poetic paraphrase in French by Macé de la Charité.[25] Comparable likewise is the Saltair na Rann,[26] which

---

[15] Descriptive Catalogue, 8, 15, 16.
[16] Descriptive Catalogue, 15.
[17] Descriptive Catalogue, 14.
[18] Descriptive Catalogue, 41. English translation on pp. 19-43.
[19] Descriptive Catalogue, 42.
[20] Descriptive Catalogue, 47.
[21] Descriptive Catalogue, 51.
[22] Descriptive Catalogue, 55.
[23] Descriptive Catalogue, 56.
[24] Descriptive Catalogue, 74.
[25] Descriptive Catalogue, 71.
[26] Descriptive Catalogue, 48.

versifies Scriptural narrative, with many extra apocryphal details, in the intricate Celtic measures of Early Middle Irish.

Another literary form of the Middle Ages was the universal history, in prose, which opened with a detailed account of Creation and of the Fall. Practised most extensively by such Byzantine chroniclers as Syncellus,[27] Cedrenus,[28] Manasses,[29] Malalas, Georgios Monachos, Zonaras and Glycas, it also flourished among Christian Arabs,[30] and even came down as far as the *History of the World* (1614) by Sir Walter Ralegh.[31] Equally discursive, but encyclopaedic rather than chronological in its organization, was the type of treatise introduced by Gossouin's *Image du Monde*,[32] translated by Caxton,[33] and later represented in expanded form by *Batman upon Bartholome*[34] and Swan's *Speculum Mundi*.[35] Still other mediaeval genres in which the subject matter of Milton's theme was poured are the hymn,[36] the dream-allegory,[37] and the debate.[38]

---

27 Descriptive Catalogue, 43.
28 Descriptive Catalogue, 54.
29 Descriptive Catalogue, 58.
30 Cf. Descriptive Catalogue, 49.
31 Descriptive Catalogue, 198.
32 Descriptive Catalogue, 67.
33 Descriptive Catalogue, 98.
34 Descriptive Catalogue, 160.
35 Descriptive Catalogue, 219.
36 Cf. Descriptive Catalogue, 20 (St. Ambrose), 22 (Prudentius), 46 (Wandalbertus Prumiensis), and 57 (Abelard). Spenser's *Hymne of Heavenly Love* is a later glorified representative of the form (cf. pp. 87-95).
37 Cf. Descriptive Catalogue, 89, Federico Frezzi, *Il quadriregio*.
38 The type is best known from *The Debate of the Body and the Soul* and *The Owl and the Nightingale*. Jacobus Strassburgus, in his *Hypotyposis divini judicii contra lapsum hominem* (Desc. Cat. 146) presents just such a debate between Justice and Mercy

Drama as a vehicle for themes from the Celestial Cycle does not appear until the Middle Ages. The first, and indeed the only, hint of it in Greek is a brief 9th century mystery play on the Temptation, ascribed to Ignatius Diaconus.[39] In the vernacular mystery-cycles of France, England and Germany, the early events of Genesis took their due place in a rude dramatic sequence that ranged from the Creation to Doomsday.[40] Individual mystery plays by a man like Hans Sachs are found to re-emerge as folk-plays in Austria, Hungary and Czechoslovakia.[41] A variant of the foregoing type of play was the *processus prophetarum*, in which a whole sequence of Old Testament prophets is passed in review, usually to fall under the power of Satan, one by one, until the coming of Christ.[42]

As the Middle Ages passed into the Renaissance, the rediscovery of classical Latin and Greek dramas led to formal attempts to use them as models for new plays, either in Latin, as the common language of European scholarship, or in the vernaculars. So far as the subject-matter of the Celestial Cycle is concerned, the earliest and most significant of these is the Latin tragedy, *Adamus Exul* (1601), written at the age of eighteen by the Dutch scholar, Hugo Grotius.[43] It confines itself strictly to the episode

---

over the proper sentence for Adam and Eve; the same debate reappears in Giles Fletcher's *Christ's Victory in Heaven* (Descr. Cat. 190); while in Salandra's *Adamo Caduto* (Descr. Cat. 233) the arguments between Mercy and Omnipotence monopolize the play.

[39] Descriptive Catalogue, 45.

[40] Cf. Descriptive Catalogue, 76-81 (York plays); 87-88 (Towneley plays), 92 (*Mistére du Viel Testament*), 93-94 (Chester plays), 95 (Greban), 96 (Cornish Origo), 97 (Immessen), 101-102 (Coventry plays).

[41] Cf. Descriptive Catalogue, 119-125.

[42] Cf. Descriptive Catalogue, 64, 67, 68, 108, 113, 136.

[43] For the complete Latin text, facing an English translation, see pp. 96-220 below. Notes are under No. 178 in the Descriptive Catalogue.

in Eden, beginning with the arrival of Satan and ending with the expulsion of Adam and Eve. It is more closely related to Milton than is any other drama; and most of the parallels usually cited between *Paradise Lost* and plays in Italian and Dutch are to be found more convincingly in Grotius. The other chief pre-Miltonic analogues in drama are Andreini's mystery play *L'Adamo* (1613),[44] Lope de Vega Carpio's slight *Creacion del mundo y primera culpa del hombre* (1624)[45] Lancetta's prose drama, paralytic with rationalistic symbolism, entitled *La scena tragica d'Adamo ed Eva* (1644),[46] Salandra's ponderous morality play, *Adamo Caduto* (1647),[47] and Vondel's two stageworthy performances, *Lucifer* (1654),[48] dealing with the War in Heaven, and *Adam in Ballingschap* (1664),[49] based on *Adamus Exul*. A curious variant from the general pattern is the Latin Lucifer-play, *Parabata vinctus* (1595),[50] by Jacobus Augustus Aemerius Thuanus, modelled closely after the *Prometheus vinctus* of Aeschylus but with Lucifer as the martyred spirit in chains. A still more curious dramatic theme is that of the unlike children of Eve, repeated at least seven times[51] in Latin and German plays of the period.

In the full flood of the Renaissance interest in classical genres of all sorts, the subject-matter of the Celestial Cycle was poured into many different moulds. Thus elegiacs were freely used by Pontanus,[52]

---

[44]For English translation, see pp. 227-267, notes Descr. Cat. 197.
[45]Descriptive Catalogue, 208.
[46]Descriptive Catalogue, 226.
[47]For English translation, see pp. 290-349, notes Descr. Cat. 233.
[48]For English translation, see pp. 361-421, notes Descr. Cat. 238.
[49]For English translation, see pp. 434-479, notes Descr. Cat. 244.
[50]Descriptive Catalogue, 170.
[51]Cf. Descriptive Catalogue, 115, 118, 138, 139, 163, 173, 189.
[52]*De mundi creatione* (Descr. Cat., 103).

Husanus,[53] Gazaeus,[54] and Barlaeus,[55] and their use of the form had been anticipated by Hildebertus Cenomanensis[56] and Petrus de Riga.[57] Naogeorgus published five books of *Satyrae*[58] in the style of Horace, and Johannes Major's *Hortus Adami*[59] belongs in the same category. Cornazzano experiments with *terza rima*.[60] Henricus Harderus uses epigrams[61] in the tradition of Martial, a venture in which his forerunners were Prudentius[62] and Theodorus Prodromus.[63] Prose romances by Loredano[64] and Pona[65] were very popular. Even more favored, judging by their size and number, were purely didactic works, most of them in the tradition of Vergil's *Georgics* but some of them of great dimensions and highly philosophical character. Among them may be listed works by Pontanus,[66] Palingenius,[67] Palearius,[68] Mizaldus,[69] Hera y de la Vara,[70] Chrystopher Middleton,[71] Girolamo Zanchi,[72] Phineas Fletcher,[73] Thomas

---

[53]*Elegia de angelis* (Descr. Cat., 195).

[54]*Lacrymae Adami* (Descr. Cat., 215).

[55]*De creatione mundi*, *Adamus peccans*, and *Oratio Caini* (Descr. Cat., 227-230).

[56]*De operibus sex dierum*, *De ordine mundi* (Descr. Cat., 52-53.

[57]*Fragmenta ex Genesi* (Descr. Cat. 61).

[58]Cf. *Descriptive Catalogue*, 134-137.

[59]Descriptive Catalogue, 131.

[60]*De la creatione del mundo* (Descr. Cat. 107).

[61]*Epigrammatum libri tres* (Descr. Cat. 242).

[62]*Dittochaeon utriusque Testamenti* (Descr. Cat. 23).

[63]*Epigrammata* (Descr. Cat. 59).

[64]*Adamo* (Descr. Cat. 223).

[65]*L'Adamo* (Descr. Cat. 240).

[66]*Urania* and *Meteorum Liber* (Descr. Cat. 104-105).

[67]*Zodiacus Vitae* (Descr. Cat. 110, 143). Extracts from Googe's translation, pp. 44-47.

[68]*De animorum immortalitate* (Descr. Cat. 113).

[69]*Cosmographia* (Descr. Cat. 139).

[70]*Repertorio del mundo* (Descr. Cat. 166).

[71]*The Historie of Heaven* (Descr. Cat. 173).

[72]*De operibus Dei* (Descr. Cat. 175).

[73]*The Purple Island* (Descr. Cat. 216). Extracts on pp. 277-284.

Heywood,[74] Henry More,[75] and Joseph Beaumont.[76]

One didactic genre of the Renaissance calls for special treatment. This is the *hexameron*, which after apparently exhausting itself from the 4th to the 8th centuries, took on new vitality in the 16th. The impetus to the rebirth of the form came as the invention of printing made possible the publication of editions of the more important earlier *hexamera*. St. Ambrose was printed in 1490 and again in 1527, while the first Greek edition of St. Basil's *Hexaemeron* was printed in Basel in 1532 with a rhapsodic preface by Erasmus, for whom he surpassed all the orators of ancient Athens. Mingling with these prose works came likewise re-issues of some of the religious epic poetry of the same early period. Typical of this further enthusiasm was the printing in 1560 by Frédéric Morelle of a one-volume collection of the Latin verse of Dracontius, Hilarius Arelatensis, Marius Victor, Avitus and Cyprianus Gallus, and his further printing in 1584 of the Greek text of Georgios Pisides, with a Latin translation.

Significantly enough it was from this same printing press of Morelle that there appeared in 1578 a work which blended the two traditions and created an epic-length *hexameron* in French heroic couplets. This poem, *La Sepmaine, ou Création*,[77] by Guillaume de Salluste, Seigneur du Bartas, was one of the most popular books of any era, and ran through hundreds of editions, including verse translations into Latin and several of the vernaculars of Europe. A sequel followed in 1584. As noted elsewhere, Joshua Sylvester's English verse rendering[78] was a substantial

---

[74]*The Hierarchie of the blessed Angells* (Descr. Cat. 218). Extracts on pp. 287-290.
[75]*A Platonick Song of the Soul* (Descr. Cat. 232).
[76]*Psyche, or Love's Mystery* (Descr. Cat. 235). Extracts on pp. 350-357.
[77]Descriptive Catalogue, 153. Extracts 47-58, 62-79.
[78]*Du Bartas His Divine Weekes and Workes* (Descr. Cat. 182). Extracts are given below on pages 47-58,62-79.

volume in its own right and exerted a considerable influence on Milton in his youth. Imitations sprang up like mushrooms. Of these the most noteworthy are probably the poems of Camões,[79] Tasso,[80] Murtola,[81] Passero,[82] Gamon,[83] and Acevedo.[84]

The most important activity of the period from the point of view of the present study, was the direct emulation of the epics of Vergil and Homer. Thus the 16th and 17th centuries saw no fewer than three Latin "Christiads" or epics on the atoning death of Christ: the earliest and best by Vida[85], the second a sorry cento of Vergilian tags pieced together by Alexander Ross,[86] and the third and longest by the London-born Carthusian monk, Robert Clarke.[87] Vida seems to have set the fashion of describing a "great consult" in the Court of Hell, a feature that is caught up and reproduced in many other Renaissance poems, often with only a remote connection with Milton's theme.[88] Three extant epics, one in Italian by Valvasone[89] and the others

---

[79] Da creação e composição do homem (Descr. Cat. 158).

[80] Le sette giornate del mondo creato (Descr. Cat. 169).

[81] Della creatione del mondo (Descr. Cat. 184).

[82] L'Essamerone, overa l'opera de sei giorni (Descr. Cat. 185).

[83] La Semaine (Descr. Cat. 186).

[84] Creacion del mundo (Descr. Cat. 200).

[85] Descriptive Catalogue, 109, text pp. 43-44.

[86] Virgilii evangelisantis Christiados libri XIII (Descr. Cat. 211).

[87] Christiados libri XVII (Descr. Cat. 222).

[88] Examples may be found in Tasso's Gerusalemme Liberata (Descr. Cat. 159), Marini's Sospetto d'Herode (Descr. Cat. 188), Phineas Fletcher's Locustae and Apollyonists (Descr. Cat. 210-244); Robert Clarke's Christiad (Descr. Cat. 237), Masenius's Sarcotis (Descr. Cat. 239), and Abraham Cowley's Davideis (Descr. Cat. 241). Extracts are given below from Crashaw's translation of Marini (pp. 220-226).

[89] L'Angeleida (Descr. Cat. 167). For extracts see pp. 80-86.

in Latin by Taubmannus[90] and Valmarana[91] deal with the warfare of Satan and his wicked angels against the hosts of light. One of the least successful of the Latin epics is Sarcotis by Jacobus Masenius (1654),[92] which begins boldly with the theme of the Fall but peters out in allegory and the extravagances of the heroic romance. Much more direct and forceful is the work of Andrew Ramsey, Poemata sacra,[93] which needs only length to make it one of the more considerable forerunners of Paradise Lost. Portugal contributed two notable religious epics to the period, the one in Latin by Mellius de Sousa[94] and the other in Portuguese by Rolim de Moura.[95] The former is essentially still another "Christiad", but the first four books are devoted to the origin of man's fallen state. Thus Book III includes an idyllic picture of Eden, an infernal council in Hell, and the successful Temptation, while in Book IV Satan reports exultingly back in Hell and the evil consequences of the Fall multiply on earth. Canto I of Rolim de Moura's poem likewise covers the "great consult" and the Fall, but the rest of the poem is closer to Dante than to Milton. So far as poetry in English is concerned, the record of epic themes from the Celestial Cycle is limited to three third-rate poems in heroic couplets, by Thomas Peyton,[96] Joseph Fletcher,[97] and Samuel Pordage.[98] Of these only the work by Pordage is redeemed by flashes of imaginative insight and descriptive power; but on the whole he lacks a poetic

---

90 Bellum Angelicum (Descr. Cat. 180).

91 Daemonomachia (Descr. Cat. 206).

92 Descriptive Catalogue, 239. Translated extracts on pp. 358-360.

93 Descriptive Catalogue, 217. Translated extracts on pp. 1-19.

94 De Miseria hominis deque reparatione humana carmen (Descr. Cat. 201).

95 Os novissimos do homem (Descr. Cat. 207).

96 The Glasse of Time (Descr. Cat. 204-5). For extracts see pp. 267-272.

97 The Perfect-Cursed-Blessed Man (Descr. Cat. 213).

98 Mundorum Explicatio (Descr. Cat. 243). For extracts, see pp. 424-433.

competence to match his innate mental capacity.

Milton's epic towers above this nondescript array of forerunners. Of incidental interest is the fact that it is the first English epos to use blank verse, perhaps as a majestic equivalent for the unrhymed heroic hexameters of Latin and Greek, and that its subject-matter includes more phases of the Celestial Cycle than any other epic in any language. Some others might deal with the Creation or the War in Heaven or the Fall of Man or the Atonement, but Paradise Lost is unique in combining all four organically in a single poem. Not least in this respect could Milton legitimately employ the stock phrase that he was pursuing "things unattempted yet in Prose or Rhime". Of far more significance, however, is his superiority in structure and style.[99] At its most mechanical level, this is a matter of the symmetrical balancing of masses of material in the 12-book recension of 1674, which in this follows, with organic variations, the architectural technique of the Aeneid. Most of the epic analogues of Paradise Lost show little awareness of such structural principles. Vida's Christiad has six books, Ross's thirteen books, and Clarke's seventeen. Valmarana's Daemonomachia drags on through twenty-five. The only analogue in twelve books is Mellius de Sousa's De miseria hominis deque reparatione humana carmen, which subdivides these into three movements of four books each, the first movement dealing with the Fall, the second with the conception and birth of the Virgin Mary and of Christ, and the third with the Atonement. As each block of four has a centre of gravity at its midpoint, the epic may also be subdivided into a pattern of six units of two books each, or may even sustain

[99] Cf. Arthur Barker, "Structural Pattern in Paradise Lost", Philological Quarterly, XXVIII, 1, Jan. 1949, pp. 17-30; E.N.S. Thompson, Essays on Milton (1914); and B. Rajan, Paradise Lost and The Seventeenth Century Reader (London, 1947), pp. 42-52, 108-131.

a simple dichotomy into two sixes, with the Catholic poet's central pause at the birth of the Virgin. As Professor Barker has pointed out, a threefold movement is clearly marked in _Paradise Lost_, dominated respectively by Satan, by the Son, and by Man, and each pauses in its turn on a centre of gravity - as Satan turns from voyaging to earthbound conspiracy, as the Son turns from avenging justice to creation, and as Adam turns from sin to repentance. The midpoint of the entire poem is the shift, with Book VII, from Divine castigation to the creative power of Divine love.

As Mr. Rajan has emphasized, however, the rich unity of _Paradise Lost_ is achieved not merely by this skeletal pattern of structural organization but also by continual symbolic patterns of repetition and recurrence that knit the fabric of the epic together. Milton may have found most of the details of his poem ready to his hand in the _hexamera_, the commentaries, the plays and the epics of the general European tradition, but they existed there in abundant variety and his choice of one version rather than another, or even his decision to use an episode or a device at all, must find its poetic justification in his artistic design. Thus the frequently implied parallel between the sin of disobedience by which Satan aspired towards Godhead and the corresponding motif in the case of Eve and Adam stresses the fundamental identity of their offense, yet with the difference that Satan fell self-tempted and hence cannot look for mercy. The Trinity in Heaven finds its hellish counterpart in Satan, Sin and Death. The Council in Hell is paralleled by the Council in Heaven, each issuing in important decisions and in a volunteer who, after silence in each case, offers himself to carry them out. The Son, in Book VII, comes out from the gates of Heaven into Chaos and creates the terrestrial universe there; Satan's Daughter and Son, in Book X, come forth from the gates of Hell into Chaos and create a causeway from Hell to Earth. These correspondences and scores of others are the very nerves and sinews by which the epic is made a living organism; yet they had been rarely used in hexameral literature.

It is Milton's unique achievement to have used them as a major structural device, completely in harmony with his poetic material.

To all this he added syntax, diction and prosody of a sustained magnificence unequalled by any other English poet. As Dr. Johnson once vaguely suspected and as F. T. Prince[100] has recently demonstrated in great detail, Milton deliberately shaped his epic style on the poetic examples of della Casa's sonnets and Tasso's _Sette Giornate_ and on the epic theories of Tasso in _his Discorsi del Poema Heroico_. The chief principles called for were the long periodic sentence, with the suspension of the sense, the special use of conjunctions and prepositions, a frequent distortion of word-order, and the use of open vowels in the prosody. With della Casa the "magnificent" style was largely practised within the dimensions of the sonnet, while with Tasso it ran counter to the genius of the ottava rima in his _Gerusalemme Liberata_ and failed to redeem the ill-ordered and interminable versified borrowings from St. Basil, St. Ambrose, and DuBartas in his _Sette Giornate_ (cf. PL-169). With greater poetic imagination, more disciplined intellectual power, and the fresher resources of Elizabethan English to draw upon, Milton far outsoared the example of his instructors and produced an epic in which greatness of style, structure and theme all blended in a work of supreme originality.

Such was the finality of Milton's achievement that no serious epic treatment of his theme has appeared in English in the space of almost three centuries since he wrote _Paradise Lost_. Blackmore introduced a tabloid summary of the Creation, the Fall and the Atonement in Book II of his _Prince Arthur_[101] and Pollok does likewise in Book II of

---

[100] "The Influence of Tasso and della Casa on Milton's Diction." Oxford, _Review of English Studies_, Vol. XXV, No. 99, July 1949, pp. 222-236.

[101] Descriptive Catalogue, 249.

The Course of Time,[102] but these are only incidental inclusions. Blackmore's Creation[103] is a tedious descendant of the hexamera. There is nothing else in English; and in other languages the tenuous record includes slight but sincere works by Perrault,[104] Zachariä,[105] Lavater,[106] Reinoso,[107] Bilderdijk,[108] Njegosh,[109] and Macedo.[110] It is significant of a growing spirit of rationalistic revolt that Jens Baggesen could write a lengthy mock epic,[111] casting ridicule on the whole Eden-story. The same rationalism, in its more sober aspects, dominates the didactic poems of Haller,[112] Campailla,[113] and Byrom.[114]

With the Romanticism that succeeded the Enlightenment, two attitudes - sentimentalism and Satanism - dominated the treatment of the Celestial Cycle, both in narrative and in dramatic poetry. Interest and emphasis tended to shift from Adam to Cain or to Satan and to revel in defiant sympathy with these characters. Examples of the sentimental approach may be found in Klopstock,[115] Gessner,[116] Müller,[117]

---

[102]Descriptive Catalogue, 275.

[103]Descriptive Catalogue, 251.

[104]Adam, ou la création de l'homme (Descr. Cat. 250).

[105]Die Schöpfung der Holle (Descr. Cat. 259).

[106]Adam, Fragmente einer unvollendeten Epopee (Descr. Cat. 264).

[107]La Creacion (Descr. Cat. 267).

[108]De ondergang der eerste wereld (Descr. Cat. 272).

[109]Lucha Mikrokozma (Descr. Cat. 282).

[110]A creação (Descr. Cat. 296).

[111]Adam und Eva (Descr. Cat. 274).

[112]Ueber den Ursprung des Uebels (Descr. Cat. 254).

[113]L'Adamo, ovvero il mondo creato (Descr. Cat. 255).

[114]On the origin of evil (Descr. Cat. 260).

[115]Der Tod Adams (Descr. Cat. 257).

[116]Der Tod Abels (Descr. Cat. 258).

[117]Adams erstes Erwachen und erste seelige Nächte (Descr. Cat. 262).

Coleridge,[118] Stephens,[119] Lamartine,[120] Soumet,[121] and Hugo,[122] while the preoccupation with Cain or Satan appears in Alfieri,[123] Byron,[124] Cailleux,[125] Aird[126] J. E. Reade,[127] Leconte de Lisle,[128] Hugo,[129] Carducci,[130] Anatole France,[131] Cranch,[132] and Rapisardi.[133] A powerful modern version of Byron's Romantic protest is George Santayana's Lucifer,[134] in which the arch-fiend appears as "a purged and sublimated spirit, an atheistical saint".

Symptomatic perhaps of a lack of theological integration in modern thought is the extent to which Milton's great argument tends to be found today splintered into countless brief poems, chiefly lyrical in form, expressing only some fragmentary aspect of a once monumental whole. Representative specimens from Christina Rosetti,[135] George Meredith,[136] James Stephens,[137] Ralph Hodgson,[138] Humbert Wolfe,[139] and others, have been included in the Descriptive Catalogue.

---

118 The Wanderings of Cain (Descr. Cat. 268).
119 The Death of Cain (Descr. Cat. 270).
120 La chute d'un ange (Descr. Cat. 276).
121 La divine épopée (Descr. Cat. 280).
122 La sacre de la femme (Descr. Cat. 289).
123 Abele, tramelogedia (Descr. Cat. 266).
124 Cain: A Mystery (Descr. Cat. 273).
125 Le monde antédiluvien (Descr. Cat. 283).
126 The Devil's Dream (Descr. Cat. 284).
127 Cain the Wanderer (Descr. Cat. 277).
128 Qaïn (Descr. Cat. 286).
129 La fin de Satan (Descr. Cat. 288).
130 A Satana (Descr. Cat. 294).
131 La fille de Caïn, Lucifer, La révolte des anges (Descr. Cat. 293, 304, 317.
132 Satan (Descr. Cat. 298).
133 Lucifero (Descr. Cat. 300).
134 Descriptive Catalogue, 306.
135 Eve (Descr. Cat. 295).
136 Lucifer in Starlight (Descr. Cat. 301).
137 The fulness of time, etc. (Descr. Cat. 311-314).
138 Eve (Descr. Cat. 320).
139 Requiem (Descr. Cat. 322).

Among the few moderns who have revealed any new insights in an ancient theme are Ivan Franko, with his new interpretation of Cain,[140] Charles M. Doughty, whose direct experience of "Arabia Deserta" has passed into the primitive texture of his Adam Cast Forth[141] and Siegfried Lipiner, whose Adam[142] is a study of the striving of aboriginal man towards moral concepts. Two cases in which an intimate blending of influences from both Paradise Lost and Faust has resulted in new originality of a highly evocative sort are Imre Madách's Tragedy of Man[143] and Paul Valéry's Lust, la demoiselle de Cristal.[144] Both are profoundly pessimistic. The former ends, rather unexpectedly, by counselling faith and fortitude in life's tragic predicament; but the latter has nothing to offer. An age that has largely rejected the concepts of the Celestial Cycle has no comparable affirmations to set in their place.

---

140 Smert' Kayina (Descr. Cat. 303).
141 Descriptive Catalogue, 309.
142 Descriptive Catalogue, 315.
143 Az ember tragédiája (Descr. Cat. 292).
144 Descriptive Catalogue, 329.

PART ONE

A N A L O G U E S

ALCIMUS ECDICIUS AVITUS

Poematum de Mosaicae Historiae Gestis

Libri quinque[1] (A.D.507)

(a) I, 1-13

Whence various ills afflict the human race
And whence our mortal times assign to life
Its brevity - a lapse through character
Corrupted at its source by our first parents
And through the added trespass of ourselves
In that, though honour perished long ago,
We still persist in sinning - this my theme
I dedicate to Thee, Father of Life,
Who from the very seed of death dost rear
New living offshoots for a dying race.
And though Christ in Himself atoned for all
By His engraftment on the afflicted stock,
Yet through the fault of Adam, who incurred
The primal debt of death and sore disease
For him and all his seed, the fatal scar
Of mortal sin lives ever in the flesh.

(Avitus then describes the creation of the universe, plants and animals, but much more briefly than in Scripture and without proceeding by days. God gives a lengthy speech on the importance of creating man.)

(b) I, 73-130

And having deigned to touch the brittle earth,
He moistens dust and moulds it into mud
And with rich wisdom fashions a new body
Just as a workman whose artistic skill

1. Translation by Watson Kirkconnell.

Is to mould softened wax to yielding forms
And fill out faces with his hand or fashion
Bodies in plaster or compose the likeness
Of a statue in the lump, even so now
The Almighty Father kneads the yielding earth
That is to take on life, and the soft mud
He moulds to man. The citadel of the head
He marks upon the lofty summit, fitting
With senses rational the countenance,
And piercing it with seven apertures
Ready for smelling, hearing, sight and taste.
The sense of touch will be the only judge
That will be active through the entire body
And spread its consciousness through all the members.
The supple tongue is matched to the hollow palate
That modulated language may resound
Upon the smitten air, when it is forced
In the sound-chamber as by plectrum-stroke.
From the broad body, lower down, the breast
Extends stout arms, ending in fingered palms.
Below the gullet comes the midmost belly,
Which with soft covering on either side
Protects the vitals. Twofold is the leg,
In order that man's walking may proceed
By bending knees and alternating step.
But elsewhere, as the one Creator builds it,
The neck, extending down from the skull's base,
Adds structures of vast sinew. Stiff with knobs,
The spine in close communication spreads
A double wickerwork of ordered ribs.
The inward parts are framed for life's new uses;
A natural shelter for the heart is made,
Whose hanging mass amid the crowded vitals
Is hidden deep. The lung is added, too,
Which feeds upon thin air, when, being given
Nostrils of gentle breathing, it takes in
And renders back again the atmosphere,
And then once more new inhalation knows.
The right side of the liver holds a fountain
That must with blood be quickened; thence the veins
Spread a blind river through the viscera.
To the left part, the spleen's rule is assigned,
By which, they say, the hair and cut nails grow.
These in the living body have their source,

Yet when they are cut off, they feel no pain;
From the spleen's power they renew their growth.
After the image of this novelty
Lay there completed, and the moulded mud
Arrived at every feature, then the clay
Was turned to flesh and in the muscles' midst
The hardened bones acquired oozy marrow.
Blood in the veins is poured, and ruddiness
Touches the pallid lips with living colour;
Then from the body's length all pallor flees
And blushing paints the snowy countenance.
Thus the whole man to living grows accustomed
After the due completion of his members,
While the warm, steaming vitals only wait
To gain a soul. This the Creator brings
From a pure source, and to the upright limbs
Imparts as a directing principle.
Out of His everlasting mouth He pours
The gentle breath, and breathes into the man;
And as the latter takes and draws it in,
He learns the breezes of repeated breathing.
Then, when intelligence had realized
The experience of newborn consciousness
And the pure light of reason had shone forth,
The man arose, and walked upon the earth.

(The Creator warns Adam that he is to obey and worship God alone. On the sixth night, God imposes a heavy sleep on Adam and creates Eve from one of his ribs.)

(c) I, 160-169

A symbol of this sleep was manifest
In that death which the incarnate Christ endured
By His own choice. As He, about to die,
Was hanging bound upon the lofty cross,
Atoning for the sins of all the world,
A lictor thrust a spear into His side,
Out of the wound, straightway, gushed water forth,
A living bath for nations there outpoured;
Then also flowed a wave of blood, that sealed
His testimony. Then He fell asleep;
And as He lay at rest two nights, the Church,
Issuing from His breast, became His bride.

(God tells them to be fruitful, and faithful to one another.)

(d) I, 188-192

Thus in alliance everlasting joining
Their mutual vows, Marriage was making merry,
And with chaste modesty of mien she chanted
Angelic songs of blended harmony.
Their bridal chamber was this Paradise;
Their dowry was the glory of the world;
And the stars waved their torches of glad flame.

(Preparatory to locating Eden, a description of the Hindoos of the East is given.)

(e) I, 210-257

Beyond the Hindoos, where the world begins,
A sacred grove abides, whose citadel
Is inaccessible to mortal man,
Shut in by an eternal boundary.
Since Adam, author of the first sin, fell
And was expelled most rightly for his guilt
Out of the happy seat, this holy earth
Has had the angels as its ministers.
Here winter never comes with change of season,
Nor come the summer suns, replacing cold,
As the high circles of the sky bring back
The warm year or the meadows white with frost
And bitter freezing. Here a constant spring
Maintains the tender mildness of the sky;
The fierce south wind is absent; yielding clouds
Pass ever from the blue's perennial calm.
Nor does the nature of the place need showers,
Which never come, but the contented shoots
Are dow'red with their own dew. All of the ground
Is green forever, and the warm earth's face
Shines softly; grasses ever clothe the hills,
And leaves the trees; the trees are spread abroad
With flowers abundant and with juicy twigs.
Whatever a whole year with us begets,
There a brief month brings on to ripened fruit.
The lilies shine undrooping in the sun;

The violet from its heat endures no harm;
While the immortal favour of its face
Preserves the gentle beauty of the rose.
Thus neither winter nor the parching summer
Molest at all; mild autumn fills the year
With fruits; the spring with flowers; here as well,
Though rumour false assigns them to the Sabaeans,
Grow cinnamons, whose boughs the Phoenix gathers
When, at the end of life, he perishes
And then, his own successor, once again
Rises afresh from death that he has sought;
For, not content once only to be born,
His weary limbs renew their ancient power
And raise to youth the age by fire consumed.
The branches of this tree, exuding balms,
Provide an endless flow from its rich stem;
And if by chance a light wind stir its breath,
The whole rich forest, moved by whispering breezes,
Trembles throughout its leaves and healthful flowers,
Dispensing fragrant odours to the earth.
Here, from a lucent eddy, flows a spring
Whose gleaming light outshines the grace of silver
Or the chill beauty of the ice. Green pebbles
Sparkle upon the margins of the stems,
And all the gems that the world's ostentation
Gapes at with us lie scattered there as stones.
The fields in varied hues are decked, and paint
The meadows with a natural diadem.

(Avitus describes the four great rivers - Tigris, Euphrates, Geon or Nile, and Physon or Ganges - which have their source in Eden. God warns Adam and Eve not to eat of the fruit of the tree of the knowledge of good and evil. He ascends to Heaven. Book II. The state of innocence is described.)

(f) II, 35-276

Such blessings were the lot of these first creatures -
The sacred primogenitors of our race -
Until, in their first conflict, sin o'ercame them
Through a deceiving enemy. The latter
Had formerly been an angel; but in time,
Kindled by pride to arrogant endeavours,

On fire with his own crime, he came to think
That he had made himself, his own creator;
And so, conceiving frenzy in his heart,
He then denied his Maker, and declared:
"I shall achieve the title of a god
And set my seat eternal in the heavens,
Being in nature like the Most High God
And not unequal in omnipotence."
As he thus boasted, the Almighty Power
Hurled him from Heaven, stripped of former honours.
He, who had shone the foremost in the ranks
Of all created things, now foremost paid
The penalty of Judgement yet to come.
A heavier doom indeed to him is due,
At whose fall one may marvel, for the author
Enhances still the crime; in an unknown sinner,
The guilt is less; transgressions of the great
Incur with greater evil greater blame.
Since into hidden things he could project
A keen intelligence, and could foresee
Things yet to come, unlocking Nature's secrets,
Without a doubt there yet survives in him
An angelic essence as a fervent force.
He is a monster horrible to tell of,
And notable in portents. All dread deeds
Committed through the length and breadth of earth
Are taught by him; he guides the murderous hand,
The wicked weapon; like a hidden robber,
He carries on his fight through public crimes.
Often he now assumes the guise of men,
Now that of savage beasts, thus varying
With cunning wiles his strange appearances.
Sometimes he suddenly becomes a bird,
That falsely flies; and honorable forms
Again he takes; as a virgin fair in body
He lures warm glances on to joys obscene.
Often as gold he flashes to the greedy,
Kindling their souls with love of treacherous wealth
And then escaping their deluded grasp
Like a vain phantom. Warranty of faith
Or graceful form he grants to no man living.
But by whatever means he can succeed
To catch, and hold, and harm the human soul,
He assumes an outer semblance, false of face,

Most suitable for guile and hidden fraud.
To this cruel fiend, a greater power yet
Is granted: that he should present himself
A holy saint. Such is the force of nature
Bestowed of old on this created spirit,
Formed upright by its Maker but perverted
And turned to evil uses by itself.
Now when this fiend saw newly made mankind
Leading a happy life in a quiet home
Unvexed by dangers, ruling the subject world
Under accepted law with peaceful joy,
A spark of jealousy lit sudden passion
And fiery envy kindled into flame.
Recent in time, it happened, was the fall
In which he had been toppled from on high
And drawn his guilty followers headlong down.
Musing in heart on this his late defeat,
He mourns the more to mark that what he lost
Another now possesses. Then his shame
Is mixed with bitterness, and, from his soul
Unfolding woe, he sighs his anguish forth:
"What grief assails us that this sudden creature
Has risen here, and that a hated race
Grows greater by our downfall! Virtue once
Held me exalted; but behold me now
Rejected, driven out, while clay succeeds
To our angelic honour. Earth grasps heaven;
Dust, reared in a vile body, reigns, alas,
And power, transferred to man, is lost to us.
All is not lost, however, for pristine force
Of will survives, pre-eminent in valour
To accomplish evil. Neither does delay
Give any pleasure; I shall now advance
With joy to the assault on these, secure
In peace and ignorant simplicity
And hence unwary to oppose my weapons.
Better are they seduced while still alone,
Before they bring their fertile offspring forth
To spread through endless ages. Seed immortal
Must not be born of earth. Now at its source
Let the race perish, and its vanquished head,
Through his defeat, become the seed of death!
Let the beginnings of man's life bring forth
The risks of death! Let all in one be smitten!

The root that has been ruined will not make
A green and living tree-top. In my grief,
At least this consolation can remain:
That if I cannot mount to Heaven again,
Heaven can be likewise closed to humankind.
It will seem easier to have fall'n, if man,
God's new creation, shall be likewise lost.
Let him then be a comrade in my ruin,
My mate in punishment, and let him share
With all of us the flames that I foresee.
No hard sort of deception shall I seek;
I'll rather point him out the easy path
In treading which, once, of my own accord,
I tumbled headlong. The same arrogance
That cast me from the kingdom in the sky
Will drive man from the door of Paradise."
Thus spake he, and he closed his speech with groans.
It happened that the serpent, wise in heart,
Surpassed in subtlety all living things.
His form the Wicked One above all others
Decided to assume. His aëry body,
Changing to sudden serpent, he surrounds
With viperous flesh, a snake with outstretched neck,
Painting his gleaming throat to maculate,
Roughening the sliding spirals of his flanks
And arming all his back with bristling scales;
As when, in the opening months of early spring,
The summer in advance sends pleasant warmth
After the numbing cold, from the old year
The viper, now reviving, makes escape,
And sloughs the dry skin from its slender body,
And leaving its earthy covert, issues forth,
Dreadful of form, in beauty to be feared.
Its eyes flash awfully, as with sharpened sight
It grows accustomed to the hoped-for sun
And simulating mildness, in its throat
Whispers the hisses of incessant song
And from its mouth extends a triple tongue.
When therefore, bent on ill-persuading fraud,
The Deceiver had put on a serpent's form,
He hastened to the Garden; for by chance
The happy young folk from a leafy branch
Were plucking rosy apples. Then the serpent,
Fearing that he could not seduce the man

From the firm resolution of his mind
By sly injected poison, soon proceeds
With climbing coils to mount an upright tree;
And having reached Eve's ear in subtle wise,
With gentle voice he gains an easy hearing:
"O blessed maiden, O most beautiful,
The grace of all the earth, whose radiant form
The bloom of rosy modesty adorns,
Thou art the destined mother of the race;
The great earth waits upon thy motherhood.
Thou art the first and certain joy of man,
His comfort, without whom he were not great.
Thus thy sweet spouse, to whom, as is ordained,
Thou wilt bear children, is by love of thee
Rightly made captive. A deserved abode
Is thine upon the peak of Paradise.
The very substance of the subject world
Trembles before thee. Whatsoever sky
And earth create and all the sea brings forth
In its great gulf are destined for thy use
Nature denies thee nothing; see how power
Over all things is given to thy hand.
I envy not, indeed; I rather marvel.
As, none the less, free touch must be restrained
From one delightful tree, I long to know
Who with dread order has begrudged such gifts
And mingled hunger with the richest things."
These evil whispers formed a pleasing voice.
What folly closed thy mind with darkness then,
O woman, thus to parley with a snake,
Conversing with a brute? Is it not shameful
That beasts should speak as men? Dost thou endure
The monster, and vouchsafe him a reply?
When thus seductile Eve into her ears
Received the deadly poison and accepted
Praise without warrant, with vain lips she spoke,
Answering the snake: "O viper, with sweet words
Most charmingly endowed, thou art mistaken,
To think that God assigns us fasts, forbidding
To nourish these our bodies with rich food
Our Maker has most readily provided
All of these things to be enjoyed at will,
For He has loosened all the reins of life.
Only these apples must we handle not;

The rest can satisfy with ample diet.
For the Creator, swearing with dread voice,
Said that if harmful freedom broke His law,
We should atone straightway for our offense
With a certain death. That which He meant by death,
Do thou now willingly explain to me,
Most learned serpent; to the uninstructed,
The meaning of this matter is not known."
    Then did the cunning snake, master of death,
Gladly teach death and speak to captive ears:
"Woman, thou fear'st an empty term of terror.
The sentence of swift death shall touch thee not.
The envious Father has not given thee
An equal lot with His, nor granted knowledge
Of things supreme, reserved but for Himself.
For what can it avail to apprehend
Sheer beauty or perceive the universe,
While the blind soul is wretchedly imprisoned?
Nature has given equally thy senses
And open eyes to brutes; one sun serves all;
The beast is dowered with thy power of sight.
Take rather my advice; mingle thy mind
With those above in godhood, yea, extend
Aspiring, keen intelligence to Heaven;
Because this apple, which ye fear to touch,
As being a thing forbidden, will empow'r you
To know all things the Father has kept secret.
Restrain not then at all thy touch withheld,
Neither let captive pleasure long be bridled
By this His law. For when thou shalt have tasted
The juice divine, thine eyesight shall be purged,
Making thee equal to the gods in vision,
Knowing all holy things as well as harmful,
Discerning just from wicked, false from true."
    The credulous woman, with a yielding look,
Marvels upon him as he promises
Such gifts with whisper false. Now more and more
She hesitates, and turns her sense aside,
And sways uncertain thinking more towards death.
When he perceived that she was vanquished now
By an impending judgement, mentioning
Once more the name and station of the gods,
He pulled one apple down from all of those
Upon the fatal tree; enveloped it

In sweetest odour; recommended it
For pleasing sight; and offered it to her
As still she wavered. Neither does the woman,
Evilly credulous, reject the gift,
But takes the fatal apple in her hands,
With open lips and nostrils scents the fruit,
And ignorantly plays with death to come.
      How often, as the apple nears her mouth,
Does her right hand draw backward in remorse
And trembling with the weight of reckless evil
Retires and shuns the outcome of the crime!
Nevertheless, she would be like the gods:
The poison of ambition has crept in.
Opposing love and terror drive her mind
Now hither and now thither. Arrogance
Sometimes assails the law, and now the law
Comes to the rescue. Thus the dubious wave
Of a divided mind seethes in its struggles.
Nor does the instigating serpent cease
From his deception, and he shows the food
To her thus hesitating, and complains
At her delay, yet all the while rejoices
At a ruin hanging headlong, soon to fall.
      When she at length was vanquished, and had reached
The deadlier decision to essay
Eternal hunger through the food of crime,
To satisfy the serpent by the food
That she herself should take, she gave assent
To his dark ambush; greedily she bit
The apple then; sweet poison enters in,
And grim death is devoured as she eats.
Here first the cunning snake restrains his joy,
And savage victory conceals its triumph.
      Adam meanwhile, the deed unknown, returning
From elsewhere in the Garden, joyfully,
Through the broad meadow's grass, came seeking now
The embraces and chaste kisses of his wife.
And her he met, in whom then rashness stirred
Fell female frenzy in an audacious heart.
Thus she began to speak, for she still carried
The fatal fruit, half-eaten, in her hand
And offered it to her unhappy husband:
"Take food, sweet husband, from the seed of life,

Whose potency, perhaps, will make thee like
The Thunderer and equal to the gods.
I do not give this gift in ignorance,
But after due instruction. The first taste
Already lies within my vital parts,
With peril bold dissolving all debate.
Believe me willingly, it is a crime
For a man's mind to hesitate to do
What I, a woman, did. Thou wert afraid,
Perhaps, to go before me in this matter.
At least now follow me, and rouse thy spirits!
Why are thine eyes averted? Why delay
Successful enterprises, filching time
From all our honour that is now to come?"
Having thus spoken, she held out to him
The dish of conquering death; while perishing
In soul, they by their sin feed Death himself.
The unhappy man receives her whispered words
Of evil counsel and is quite dislodged
From his firm senses, nor does anxious fear
Smite him with trembling hands, not even as much
As when the woman shunned at first to taste.
Rather, he follows swiftly; from the mouth
Of her, his wretched wife, the unfirm man
Seizes with firmness on a poisonous dower
And fills his open throat with hostile food.
His horrid maw had scarcely touched the apple
With one bite, and its flavour scarce was tasted,
When a sudden light shone forth around his head
And gave him altered vision, drenched with sorrow.
Man was not blind by nature. Form's perfection
Owned not a face deprived of the use of sight.
For blinder will you be, if not content
To know alone the things a great Creator
Has wished that you should know. The power of seeing
Was given you for life. To gaze on death
Comes of your own accord. So thus they groan
Because their eyes are opened, for the fault
Was clear now to the rebels, and their bodies
Of obscene impulse had become aware.
Then for the first they saw their nakedness.
(Uncertain am I whether I should say
That modesty was blotted out or born.)

Now blushed a mind grown conscious of its guilt,
And an imparted law of carnal will
Fought in their members.

(A long passage narrates the parallel experience of Lot and his inquisitive wife.)

(g) II, 408-423

Then the victorious serpent, in glad triumph,
Swaying his scaly head's empurpled crest,
No longer hid his joy, till now concealed,
But heaped harsh insults on the vanquished pair
And railed against them thus: "Lo, there remains
The godlike glory that I promised you!
Believe me, all my knowledge is now yours;
For I have shown you all, and guided you
Through hidden ways; whatever cunning nature
Refused to give, I have ordained for you.
Hence I have consecrated you to me
By an eternal lot. Neither has God,
Although He formerly created you,
Rights in you any more. Yes, let Him keep
The body once created by Himself.
The soul, which I have taught, is surely mine.
Mine is the greater part. To your Creator
You may owe much; but to your master, more."
He spake, and left them trembling in the gloom,
And his false body vanished through the clouds.

(Adam and Eve sew garments of fig-leaves to cover their shame.)

(h) III, 27-65

Meanwhile the Father through the gentle walks
Of the green Garden came, to pleasure in
Soft breezes dropping dew from a clear sky.
Then presently the pair, with startled ears,
Became aware Jehovah was at hand;
And with sad eye they hate and fear the day
As a witness of their now detected sin.
For if, by chance, a deep, vast pit had opened,
Or earth had yawned before them with dark mouth,

They had not hesitated in their fright
To descend with a headlong leap. If doom of death
Were even then at hand, their eagerness
To cover up their shame would grasp at it.
To flames or water they would give themselves,
Or the avenging right hand would with sword assail
The breast with a cruel wound. The wretches thus,
As soon as they have earned it, yearn for death,
Although no formal sentence has imposed it.
So first things mark earth's last things, and
    foretell
How like grief will impend when earth's old age
Shall be consumed at last, when sudden brightness
Shall smite all things, when Heaven's trump shall
    peal,
At which a messenger shall terrify
The smitten world before the Judge shall come.
Then, when the Shepherd shall have sorted out
The pure lambs, He shall place the unlike goats
In another quarter, sundering them between
With Chaos, which an eddying gulf of fire
Shall fill with brimstone waves, a vivid lake,
Flooding with flame, from which a burning cloud,
Drawn in a storm, is said of old to have poured
Lightnings like raindrops on the sins of Sodom,
When the black night rained fires, and from the sky
Death fell on all sides through the sultry air.
Sent likewise from the fiery fount of Hell,
Grim rivers flowed in ages not their own.
But whom the Judge in that dread hour shall sentence
To live beyond mortality and burn
In everlasting torment, them a doom
Far heavier shall withdraw from hoped-for death.
And though it had been better for their bodies,
Dissolved in death, to take eternal rest,
The grave shall vomit forth the unwilling ones,
Whose sole desire would be to die again
And lose once more the sense of agony;
But in the fiery furnace they shall go,
Whose flame is destined so to burn its fuel
That it shall slacken not forevermore.

(God passes sentence on the serpent, Eve, and Adam, and foretells disasters to come.)

(i) III, 195-208

The Father clothed them then with skins of goats
And drove them from the seat of Paradise.
Together on the earth they fell in prayer;
Then rose, and entered on an empty world,
And made a rapid survey of all things.
And though they saw green fields and springs and rivers,
Blooms many-hued and fruits of many sorts,
Yet ugly seems the world when they compare
Its best with Paradise. They gaze in dread
At all they see, and, as man's custom is,
They love the more the blessings they have lost.
The soil is narrowed, and as they bewail
The waning of the earth, the world's dread end,
Though unperceived, now threatens none the less.
The day itself grows dim; they allege the light
Withdrawn from the very sun; in distant skies
The stars groan, and the firmament is seen,
Though it was formerly scarce apprehended.

(There follows the story of Dives and Lazarus. The unavailing repentance of Dives in Hell, like that of Adam, ought to be a warning to all of us.)

(j) III, 317-347

Then grim disease and various pain crept in;
Corrupted with dread rankness, earth infused
Some plants with deadly juices. Fierce wild beasts
Then first began to rage; then valour stirred
The fearful up to fight; claw, tooth, hoof, horn
To weapons turned; the very elements
Themselves broke primal laws, and all things strove
To violate their faith with mortal man.
The seas were blown upon by winds; waves rolled;
The angry ocean in new frenzy surged;
Then first in skies with horrid darkness hid,
Clouds, seeking to afflict man's painful toil,
Poured volleyed hailstones from the stormy heaven,
Begrudging harvests to the pallid earth.
Nay, earth itself, grown hostile to itself,
Changed for the worse the seed it had received.

These things the two first mortals then perceived.
As for the losses their posterity
Would some day bear, none could enumerate,
Not with a hundred tongues or a voice of iron,
Nor even if the poet Mantua bore
And Homer were to blend their varying strains.
For who could tell such tumult? Who, in short,
Could trace the floods of anguish that shall flow
Down through the centuries? Men rage in arms;
The earth is shaken with incessant fear;
Streams of blood flow, and more is thirsted for.
What shall I say of lofty cities, famed
For their inhabitants, now turned to deserts?
Of nations spilt by devastating rapine?
Of a torn earth made empty of its offspring?
Of masters humbled into servitude
And servants in their turn made masters, soon
To perish by the fate of war, the lot
The race has still ordained for famous blood?

(Avitus cites the parables of the potter, the lost coin, the lost sheep, the Prodigal Son, and the Good Samaritan as proofs of Christ's readiness to restore man to the Paradise lost by Adam. *Book* IV. The human race gives itself up to lawlessness and evil, thus developing the original sin of mankind. The story of the Flood. The Ark is symbolic of the Church in a world of sin. *Book* V. The story of the death of the Egyptians and the deliverance of the Israelites at the Red Sea is taken as symbolic of baptism.)

(k) V, 704-721

This mighty deed their famous general[1]
Has hymned in a solemn song, that now is sung
Throughout the world whene'er a mortal fault
Is purged with sacred baptism and the streams
Of that life-giving bath yield up new offspring
In place of the guilty ones that Eve brought forth.

---

[1]Moses, cf. *Genesis*, chap. XV.

Of her my slender page has made discourse
In the foregoing poem, while it told
The lamentable story of the Fall.
If, in that theme, my poor verse has been sad,
Let grief be swept away in this great wave
Of memorable triumph, in which joy
Breaks forth exultant, every wrong is ended,
The New lives, while the old life perishes,
Good things arise, iniquitous deeds are slain,
And the true Israel by the sacred sea
Bathes in salvation; a harmonious throng
Thus celebrates a glorious victory,
In limning which due symbols are supplied
By the devout prophet in five books of old,
Anticipating holy gifts to come.
His trumpet we have followed with our flute,
And now seek harbour for our slender bark.

ANONYMOUS

The "Caedmonian" Paradise Lost, being lines 1-964 of the Junius Manuscript.[1] Ca. 700-850 A.D.

For us it is well with words to praise
And in heart to love the Lord of Heaven,
The glorious Keeper and King of hosts.
He is full of power, the puissant Head

---

[1]Cf. PL-41 in the Descriptive Catalogue. The present verse translation by Watson Kirkconnell is based on the text given in The Junius Manuscript, edited by George Philip Krapp (New York, 1931), supplemented by The Later Genesis, edited by Fr. Klaeber (Heidelberg, 1931). There have been numerous earlier translations, but most of them are fragmentary or in prose. Special reference may be made to a complete prose version by Charles W. Kennedy, in The Caedmon Poems (London, 1916), and a partial prose rendering by Robert K. Gordon in Anglo-Saxon Poetry (London and Toronto, 1927). To

Of highest life, the Lord almighty.
Formed by none at the first of things,
He knows not death but endures forever
High in His majesty, mighty as Lord
Over the thrones of the throngs of heaven.
Strong and right, He has ruled those realms
Established afar by His force divine
For the kindred of glory, the keepers of souls.
The legions of angels felt love and joy,
Hailed their Maker with happy hearts.
Great was their bliss; and gladly in glory
His servants with praise their Prince adored,
Glorified God who governs all life.
Rich in blessings, unblotted by sin,
They lived in peace with their Prince forever.
Wrought they in heaven save right and truth
Naught, till the Archangel erred in his pride.
No longer they followed their life as before
But leaned aside from the love of God.
Boldly they boasted the abode of glory,
Wide and shining, to share with its Lord.
Pain came upon them then, pangs of envy,
Presumptuous zeal from that zealous angel
Who worked and wove this wickedness first,

---

the latter of these I am indebted for the frequent turn of a phrase.

In my translation, an attempt has been made to adapt the old alliterative line to the much less inflected character of Modern English and to the acquired habits of modern prosody. Thus, while preserving the strict rules of alliteration, the lines have been made predominantly dactylic and anapaestic rather than trochaic and iambic, in order to accomodate the sense to a more analytic language. A much greater uniformity of rhythmic pattern is also maintained; inversions and archaisms have been avoided as much as possible; and the hemistich-gap has been omitted in printing, as presenting the modern reader with a very real hindrance to free reading and appreciation, a sort of disconcerting visual hiccup in the middle of each line. Alliteration is by stressed syllable rather than by word.

When thirsting for strife he threatened to rear
Northward in heaven a home and a throne.
Then wroth was God at the radiant host
That erst He had dowered with honour and beauty.
As reward for their work, to the wicked ones
He made a prison, a murky dwelling,
Hell with its wailings and woes unnumbered.
Our Lord above, when He learned their sin,
Sentenced the keepers of souls to endure
Abodes of torment, abysses of pain,
Joyless tombs of eternal night
Filled with fire and fierce with cold,
Reeking with smoke and red with flame.
Terrors of torment He told to spread
Through that hopeless home in the hellish deep.
Crime against God had their guilt contrived;
Grim was the guerdon they gained for that.
They said in their zeal they would soon possess
The kingdom with ease. They were cozened then
By that lying hope when the Lord of heaven
Against their host His hand upraised.
False and reckless, they failed to share
In God's high power; the Glorious One
Ended their arrogance, awed their pride,
In His great wrath; He reft the sinners
Of glory and peace, of gladness and power,
Avenged His grief with a victor's strength,
Mastering His foes with His mighty power.
His spirit stern was strongly roused;
With hostile hands He held His foes,
Hot in His bosom broke them in wrath,
Reft of their home and their heavenly weal.
Then God, our Creator, grimly judged
The haughty race of rebel angels
And drove them from heaven; sent on distant journeys
The faithless host, the hostile legions,
With broken boast and bruised spirit,
Their glory battered and their beauty marred.
A weary while in woe they waited
With little cause for laughing loudly;
But haggard the torments of hell they endured;
Groaning was theirs and grief and sorrow;
Roofed with the dark, they were racked with anguish,
Stern retribution for striving with God.

Then, as before, there was found in Heaven
Peace, and the rule of perfect love;
Dear was the Lord to His legion'd hosts,
The King to His thanes; then throve the glories
Of the blessed ones in bliss with God.
The dwellers in Heaven, that home of glory,
Were strong in union; for strife had gone,
Enmity dark and angels' warfare,
After the foemen, fallen from glory,
Went forth from heaven. Behind them stood
Rich and wide through the realms of God,
Thrones of power and perfect grace,
Splendid and bright, yet bare and empty,
Since the cursed spirits, spent with pain,
Passed to prison, their place of exile.
Then mused in mind our mighty Lord
How to rebuild the bright creation,
Brilliant thrones for a better band
When boastful foes far forth had gone
Out of high heaven. Thus holy God
Planned the world and the waters wide
And the crowning sky and the creatures of earth
Under the spacious span of heaven,
To replace the foes He had plucked away,
Sent rebellious outside of His shelter.
Nothing was shapen save shadow of darkness
Here in the waste; but the wide land stood
Deep and murky, remote from God,
Empty and useless. With earnest eyes
The steadfast King then stared, and beheld
A joyless tract in eternal night,
Brooding mists beneath blackest heavens,
Gloomy and waste, till by word of power
The Master of Glory made the world.
Here first the Lord of life eternal,
Protector of all His teeming creatures,
Made with His hand the heavens and the earth,
Reared the firmament, fix'd this broad land,
Laid by His strength, the Lord Almighty.
Not yet green was the grass on earth,
Far and wide on the ways of gloom
The sea still moved in the murk of night.
Then bright on the waters, the Warden of Heaven's
Wondrous Spirit in speed was borne.

The Lord of Angels, Life's Dispenser,
Bade light come forth on the far-flung world.
The High King's bidding was quickly answered,
For a holy light illumined the waste,
Fulfilling the word of the wise Creator.
Then the Victor-Prince o'er the vastness of waters
Sundered shining from shadow and darkness.
Light was named, by the Lord's word, Day,
A brilliant creature of beauteous splendor.
At its honour'd beginning, its hour of birth,
The primal day then pleased the Lord.
Dim He had seen the darkened shadows
Over the breadth of the earth prevailing.
Then did the Lord, our life's Creator,
After the day had duly passed
Over the structure of earth new-shapen,
Kindle the flame of the first of evenings.
Black clouds in a throng came thrusting after;
Their darkness was known as Night to the King.
These by our Saviour were sundered wholly;
Eternal on earth for all time thereafter
They worked the will of the One who made them.
Another light dawned then, day after darkness
The Master of life then commanded the frame
Of the heaven to be made in the midst of the waters.
By its vault our Ruler divided the waters;
He made the firmament fast forever.
The powerful One, the Prince Almighty,
Reared it from earth by His regal word.
At His holy nod, beneath high heaven,
The waves were sundered, the waters from waters
Abiding under the bright, high roof.
Then the third bright morning came moving swiftly
Over the earth; but the ample lands
And their paths were useless as yet to God,
The earth stood wrapped in raiment of flood.
Then the Lord of Angels gave orders forthwith,
Called on the waters to come together
That now under heaven hold to their course
And establish place. Then straightway the ocean,
As the Holy One bade it, stood broad and united;
The sea from the land was severed wholly.
Then the Watchman of Life, the Warden of Hosts,
Beheld dry ground in grace outspread --

The King of Glory called it Earth.
Then to the waves, the waters broad,
He fixed due shores, the flood He fettered. . . .

- - - - - - - -

Then it seemed not well to the Warden of Heaven,
That Adam, the Keeper and King of the Garden,
New fashioned to life, should long be alone.
Then the lofty King, the Lord Almighty,
Made him a helpmeet; the Master of Life
Raised up a woman to wed the dear man;
Quickly He gave her. Cleaving the substance
Of Adam's own body, a bone He took,
A rib from his side with ready skill.
Fast in slumber and sleeping softly,
He knew no pain, no pang of anguish;
Nor from the wound was there welling of blood;
But the Lord of Angels loosed from his flesh,
Without wounding the man, a waxing bone,
And from it He fashioned the form of a woman.
He breathed in life, an everlasting soul;
She was like an angel, even Eve,
The bride of Adam, an embodied spirit.
Young were they both, in beauty fashioned
By God's own power to grace the earth.
They knew not enduring nor doing of evil,
But love in their breasts for the Lord was burning.
Then the King in His gladness, the God of all
creatures,
Bless'd the two fair ones, the first of mortals,
Father and mother, man and woman.
Freely He spoke: "Be faithful and multiply,
The green earth fill with your growing children,
Seed of your loins, your sons and daughters;
Set in your power, the sea shall abide
And every one of the world's new creatures.
Take your pleasure in prosperous days;
Joy in the fishes, the fowls of heaven.
Holy cattle and herds of the wild
Are placed beneath your power and rule;
All life that walks in the ways of earth,
All stocks of the living that stir the sea
And the sea's abyss, shall obey you two."
Then our Maker gazed at His many works,
The noble fruit of His new creation.

The Garden stood gracious and good and holy,
Filled with gifts and favours eternal.
Living water, a welling spring,
Graciously moistened the mild, fair land.
No driving rain-clouds, dark with wind,
Brought rain as yet to the roomy earth,
Yet the land with harvests stood laden richly.
Four noble rivers ran their course,
Pressing forth from that Paradise.
By the strength of God their streams were cleft
All from one that on earth He had made,
Sent into the world with waters fair.
One of these rivers the races of men,
The nations of earth, have now called Pison,
Encompassing with its crystal streams
The hinterland region of Havilah's realm.
In its native soil, both near and far,
Man's generations find gems and gold,
The best of both, as in books is written.
The second river surrounds the land
In the Ethiop's realm, a roomy kingdom.
Its name is Gihon. The noble Third
Is the Tigris, a stream of the strongest flood,
That circles the land of th' Assyrian folk.
The fourth of the rivers, Euphrates by name
To the sons of men, is Assyrian too.

\- - - - - - - -

(At this point the close paraphrase of *Genesis* is interrupted by a vigorous but very unscriptural version of the Fall of the Angels and the Temptation of Man -- lines 235-851 of the original.)

"All the rest you may taste, this tree avoid;
Beware of that fruit; you shall want no blessings."
They bowed their heads to the heavenly King,
Thanked him warmly for wisdom and counsel.
Then leaving them both the land to inhabit,
The holy Lord to heaven returned,
The strong-souled King. There stood His creatures
On the sand together, of sorrows unwitting
To be suffered in pain should they cease at length
To do God's will. They were dear to God
While yet they were willing His word to keep.

High and Almighty, the holy Lord,
Had moulded and made by the might of His hand
Ten angel-tribes that He trusted well
To serve his wishes and work His will.
Therefore did He, the holy Lord,
Endow them with minds when made by His hands.
He bless'd them well; but One above others
He made most strong and mighty of thought,
Next highest in sway to Himself in heaven.
So bright was he made by the Master of Hosts,
So fair in form was he fashioned in heaven,
That he shone as sheer as the shining stars.
His task it was to worship the Lord,
Justly to cherish the joys of heaven,
To thank his God for the gift He had given
The guerdon of light that had long been his.
But he wandered from faith into ways far worse,
Striving to stir up strife against God,
Heaven's high King on His holy throne.
He was loved by our Lord, but it little was hid
That His angel against Him began to be proud,
Exalted himself and was zealous in speech,
Braggart in boasting and bold against God.
He said that his body was bright in its beauty,
White in its hue. Nor in heart could he find it
Allegiance to give to the Lord most high.
It seemed to him then he exceeded in strength
The holiest God and His host of vassals.
The angel was wanton in words of presumption;
He thought through his strength to construct there a throne
More strong than the Lord's and more lofty in heaven;
He said that his heart was inciting him sorely
Westward and northward to work and to strive;
He set up a building, and said that it seemed
Doubtful that he should do duty to God.
"Why should I toil?" was his talk. "Yea, I need not
A master to have, for I may with my hands
Work wonders as many. My might will suffice
To gain me a higher and goodlier throne.
Am I so weak as to wait on His favour,
Bow down before Him and fawn as a vassal?
I can be God no less greatly than He.
Bold-hearted heroes stand bravely beside me;

Fellows, strong-armed, will not fail me in fighting;
Brave men, they choose me their chief and their lord.
With thanes of such merit a man may take counsel,
Carry it through with such comrades in war.
True are these friends of mine, trusty in heart;
I may thus be their ruler and reign in this realm.
It seems to me therefore a simple injustice,
That I, to seek favour, should flatter this Master.
No longer I'll live in allegiance to God!"
When now the Almighty was minded of this,
That His angel began with the greatest of pride
To challenge his Master and mouth in presumption
Arrogant words that were wild against God,
Then the traitor was doomed to atone for his deed,
Suffer war-torments, the toll of requital,
Penalties utmost in pang and in pain.
Such is their fate who would fight with their Ruler,
Waging in wickedness war with their Lord.
Then did the Mighty One, Master of Heaven,
Hurl him in wrath from the height of his throne.
Hate had he won from the heart of his Master,
Forfeited favour. Fierce was God's anger.
He sentenced him therefore to seek the abyss
And the hardest torture that hell could give;
A bitter reward for his war against Heaven.
God hid then His favour and hurled him to hell;
There, in deep dales, he the devil became,
The fiend with his followers. Fell they from heaven
Three nights and three days to the darkness of hell,
These angels our Master has altered to devils.
They would not honour His word and deed;
Therefore He set them, sorely vanquished,
In a darker place, in dusky hell,
Down under the earth. In the evening there
An infinite term of unending time,
All of the fiends feel fire fresh-flaming;
But there come at dawn winds keen with cold;
Frost or fire they feel forever.
Torment of toil is a task for some,
Dealt to them there as a due reward.
Their way of life was wanly changed:
Now first with His foes He filled the Pit.
Henceforth the heights of heaven were held
By the angels whose love and allegiance were sure.

The others as fiends in the fire lay,
Who before in such strength had had strife with
their Ruler
Torment they feel now, fierce flame of the furnace,
Murderous heat in the midst of hell,
Broadest flames and bitter fumes,
Darkness and smoke, for they dared to neglect
The service of God; deceived by their pride
And angelic presumption, they zealously scorned
To worship the word of the Warden of All.
Great were the pangs of their punishment then,
Fallen through folly to fiery depths,
Hurled down through pride to the hotness of hell.
They looked for a land that was lacking in light
Yet teeming with flame and the terror of fire.
The fiends were aware they had won as award
Torments past count, through their tyrannous hearts,
The might of the Lord, and their measureless pride.
Then spoke the proud king, once a spirit most
splendid,
Most lovely in heaven and loved by his Master,
Dear to God till they grew in folly,
And for their madness Almighty God
Sent him in anger to sigh in torment,
Brought him down to that bed of death.
Thereafter He gave him a grimmer name;
He bade that the highest be hailed as Satan,
Told him as prince of the pit of hell,
To cease to strive with the strength of God.
Satan spoke then, in speech of sorrow,
He who hereafter in hell must tarry,
And rule the abyss. He had been God's angel,
White in heaven till his heart betrayed him
And that primal evil, his pride, that scorned
To honour the word of the Warden of Hosts.
Pride within him pressed at his heart,
Hot within him was hellish torment.
These were his words: "This weary waste
Is a different world from the one we knew
In heaven's height, the home of our Lord.
Yet we could not hold and inhabit our kingdom
In the face of the reign of the Ruler of All.
He has done us a wrong in dooming us down
To the fiery bottom of blazing hell,

Ruined and reft of the realm of heaven.
For His purpose stands to restore with mankind
The gap we have left. 'Tis my greatest of griefs
That Adam, a wretch who is wrought from earth,
Shall sit on my throne and be set in bliss
While we must suffer these sorrows in hell.
Alas! could I only but loosen my hands,
Win free for an hour far out of this prison,
One brief winter hour, then I with this host --!
But fetters of iron are fastened upon me,
The manacles' chain; and my might is no more.
The hard bonds of hell have laid hold on me closely.
Vast flames are above me, vast fires below.
I never have looked on so loathsome a landscape,
Where flames ever fade not, still fierce throughout hell.
The links of my shackles, my shameful harsh fetters,
Have barred me and marred me from movement forever.
The portals of hell to all passage are shut;
Not the least can I loosen my limbs from these bonds.
Great bars of hard iron are battened about me,
Forged in the flame; and firm in their metal
The Almighty has fettered me fast by the neck.
So I know that He knew of the net I would weave Him,
That to Adam I'd cause, for the kingdom of heaven,
Strife, were I granted the strength of my hands.
But now we are touched by the torments of hell,
Flames and gloom in the grim abyss.
It is God himself that has swept us away
Into these mists of the murky deep.
Though He may not convict us of vileness of sin
Nor prove that we hurt Him in heaven's high land,
Lo, He has robbed us of light and has cast us
Into the utmost of anguish and pain.
We may not take vengeance, invade Him with evil,
For having so roughly bereaved us of light.
Now He has walled in a world and has wrought there
Man in His likeness, and looks to repeople
The Kingdom of Heaven with clean human souls.
Sorely we'll seek then to sate our revenge
On Adam and all of his offspring together,
If ever we may, to mar His desire,
By any plot we can plan or devise.
No longer I count on recovering that light,

That bliss that He hopes with his hosts to enjoy.
We can never succeed in assuaging God's wrath.
Let us seek then to turn from the sons of men
That heavenly kingdom that cannot be ours,
Cause them to leave their allegiance to God
And break the command that He made with His word.
Then He will rage at their wrong in His heart,
Send them from grace. They will seek then this hell
And walk these grim depths. Then we for ourselves
Shall have them as servants, the sons of men,
Firm in these fetters. Come, frame now our warfare!
If in days now gone I gave rich treasures
To any thane from my throne in heaven
While we dwelt in bliss in that blessed realm,
Never more timely than now could he pay me
Back for my gifts, if some bold retainer
Were willing to pass from the walls of this prison,
Had power to fly on pinions yonder,
Winging his way through the waste of clouds,
To where Adam and Eve on the earth now stand,
Wrought in that realm with riches around them,
While we hither are plunged in this Pit profound.
They are dearer now to their doting Lord,
And may own the wealth that once we possessed,
In the heavenly realm that is rightly ours.
Such is the fortune afforded mankind.
Sad is my mind and in sorrow my heart
That heaven henceforth should be held by these creatures.
If any of you can in aught contrive
To wean their will from the ways of God,
Hateful to Him will they haply be.
If they keep not His charge, He will change to anger;
Then their joy will be ended, their judgment prepared,
Some bitter pain. Therefore ponder this, all of you,
How ye may dupe them. That done, I shall rest here
At ease in my chains if we cheat them of heaven.
For him who shall work that, rewards will be waiting
Of all we may gain here of good in this fire.
He shall sit with myself, more soaring than all
Who may come to hot hell to declare they in shame

Have wandered away both in word and in deed
From allegiance and love of the Lord of the heavens.

(There is here a hiatus in the manuscript. Apparently one of Satan's loyal thanes volunteers to undertake the seduction of mankind on behalf of his captive master.)

The opponent of God prepared himself;
His harness was ready, his heart was evil,
He set on his head a helmet of hiding,
A headpiece whose witchcraft made wearers unseen;
Then fitted it firmly and fastened its clasps.
He was wise in speeches of wicked words.
Winging his way from the world of pain,
The devil passed through the doors of hell;
By the craft of the fiend the fire was cloven.
He sought to deceive the subjects of God,
To lure mankind by loathsome deeds,
Making them hateful to heaven's King.
So on he fared till by fiendish power
He found on the earth the face of Adam,
The creature of God, and his gracious wife,
Fairest of women, the work of wisdom;
For well they knew the ways of good
That the Lord of men had made for his vassals.
Trees beside them, two in number,
Were laden with fruit and fraught with plenty
As God Almighty, the Monarch of heaven,
Had planted them there in that place with His hands
That the children of men might choose between
The good and wickedness, weal and woe.
Unlike were their ways, for one was winsome,
Bright and beautiful, bland and worthy --
The Tree of Life. Whoso tasted its fruit
Could live in the world of life eternal;
Age and illness would irk him not;
Henceforth in bliss he could be forever,
Leading his life in the light of the favour
Of heaven's King in this kindly world.
Honours thereafter were owed him in glory,
High in the heavens, when hence he should go.
Black was the other tree, blotted and gloomy,
That was the Tree of Death, truly most bitter.

Each who should taste of that tree's fruit would
    know
Evil and goodness with grief in this world;
Living in torment and toil for ever,
Old age should rob him of resolute deeds,
Delights and lordship; at last he must die.
For a chill, brief space he shall cherish his life,
Then serve the devils for drudging ages,
The mightiest peril for mortal men.
The Fiend's sly envoy, who fought against God
In hostile wise, was aware of that.
He shifted then to the shape of a serpent;
Twined himself on the Tree of Death
With a devil's craft, and cropping the fruit
He passed again to the place where he knew
Stood the handiwork of Heaven's King.
Then the foe began to frame with lies
Questions to Adam: "Is aught still lacking
To thee from God? A greeting I bear
From afar in His name. It was not long since
That I sat with Himself; then He sent me forth
On a journey to tell thee to taste this fruit.
He said that thy might and thy mind and thy skill
Would be finer by far, and fairer thy form.
Nothing on earth were denied thee then,
Having granted His wish and gained His grace,
Serving with love to thy Lord's delight,
Endearing thyself to the Sovereign of Heaven.
I heard him commend in majestic glory
Thy speech and thy acts and speak of thy life.
Obey thou therefore the bidding brought
By His messenger's lips to this land below.
Wide in this world are the wastes of green earth.
God rules on high in the heavenly realm,
Enthroned in power. The Prince of Men
Desires not the trouble of taking this journey;
Instead of Himself, He sends His servant
To talk with thee truly. He told me to teach thee
The arts He has honoured. Be earnest to do them.
Let thy hand take this fruit; then fall to, and
    taste it.
Thy mind shall grow stronger, thy stature more
    stately.
Thy Sovereign Almighty hath sent thee this favour."

Then Adam made answer, on earth as he stood there,
A man without mother: "I marked the almighty
Victorious Lord speak in language severe;
He then bade me bide here, obey His commandments;
He gave me this woman, this wife full of beauty;
And bade me beware that my will should not wander
And fall in the power of the Perilous Tree,
Lured far astray and stricken with woe.
He said that the man who had sinned in his heart
Should abide in the depths of the darkness of hell.
I cannot be sure if thou comest with lies,
With secret intent, or art sent down from God.
Behold, I can grasp not one whit of thy orders,
Thy words or thy journey, thy ways or thy speeches.
I know what our Saviour Himself has assigned me,
The law that He left me when last I beheld Him.
He charged me to honour and cherish His mandate,
To look to His lore. Most unlike art thou surely
To any good angel that ever I saw,
Nor hast thou made certain by signs that my Master
Has sent thee to me as a mark of His favour.
I cannot obey thee; but bid thee begone!
Firm is my faith in the Father Almighty
Who fashioned me here with His fingers divine.
He from on high can enhance all my blessings,
Solace with gifts though He send not His servant."
Indignant in spirit, the demon then turned
Where he looked on the female, Eve, fashioned so fairly,
Standing on earth. And he stated in rage
That the greatest affliction would fall on their children:
"I know God Almighty will mantle with anger
When I myself bear this embittering message,
Bringing back word from my wide-ranging journey
That you two obey not each bidding He sends here
Out of the east on this errand of mine.
Now He Himself will come soon at your answer,
Since His herald has failed to enforce His command.
I know that His great heart will grieve at you both.
Yet, if thou, O woman, wilt willingly hearken,
Thou then canst be cautious to counsel thy husband.
Consider in soul that thy sense may yet save you

Both from your doom, as I duly shall show thee.
Eat of this fruit, and thine eyes shall be opened,
Able to see over all of the world,
Thread through all space to the throne of thy Master,
Favoured henceforth by the Father of All.
Given good will, thou shalt guide thy dear husband,
Tell him in truth, if he trusts in thy words,
Precepts of health that thou hast in thy heart;
Thus shalt thou meet the commandment of God.
Adam will cease from his answer of evil,
Turn from his strife if we two urge his welfare.
Earnestly urge him to act by thy counsel,
Lest ye grow loathsome, unloved by your Lord.
If, best of women, this work thou accomplish,
I shall hide from your Lord that thy husband spake insult,
Chattering ill. He has charged me with lies,
Calls me a messenger keen to work injuries,
Argues me never an angel of God.
Well do I know the true nature of angels,
The high vault of heaven, where hitherto warmly
I long served the Lord with the loyalest heart.
I am not like a devil, a demon from hell."

Thus he led her with lying and lured on the woman
With wiles to that wickedness; working within her,
The guile of the serpent began to well up
(Her Maker had framed her a mind that was feebler)
Till she yielded her heart to those hateful behests.
Against the commandment of God she received then
Death's tree's noxious fruit from the foe of mankind.
No deadlier deed had been destined for men.
The wonder is great that Lord God, the Eternal,
Should have let so many by lies be deluded,
When they sought for teaching. She tasted the fruit,
Flouting the mind and command of the Lord.
Then through the gift of her guileful betrayer,
She could see farther, she found, than before;
Heaven and earth seemed more ample in beauty,
This world and God's working more wondrous and worthy;
Yet not through the sense of man's sight did she see it:

The foeman betrayed her with treacherous ardour,
Gave her such semblance of sight that she seemed
Thus widely to gaze through the world of the sky.
Then the perjurer spoke in the spirit of spite;
No good thing he taught her: "In truth now, good Eve,
Thyself thou canst see (with no sermon of mine)
How beauty of form is transfigured for thee,
Since my words thou hast trusted, my teaching attended.
Now a light shines before thee, a lucid enchantment,
A beauty of beams that I brought down from God.
Lo, thou canst touch it. Go, tell now to Adam
What power of sight thou hast proved by my coming.
If even now he take note of my counsels,
Modest in conduct, my craft shall endow him
Amply with light, as allowed to thee likewise.
I spurn not the man for his speeches of evil,
Though he merit no grace for his guilt towards my person.
So shall his offspring live aptly hereafter:
When they fall into wrong they shall reap new affection,
Making amendment for mocking their Master,
Holding His favour henceforward forever."
Then forth went to Adam the fairest of women,
The comeliest wife that should come to this world,
Having been made by the Monarch of heaven,
Though she was darkly fordone by the devil,
Deluded by lies, to grow loathsome to God,
Through the devil's dark cunning, the craft of the fiend,
Be fallen from glory and favour in heaven
For many a season. Man shall know mourning
That he stayed not his hand while he still had the power.
One fruit in her hand, in her heart yet another,
She fetched the curs'd apple, the fruit of death's tree,
Disallowed her before by the Lord of lords.
The glorious Monarch commandment had given
Lest men as his servants should suffer sore death;
But the holy Lord gave a heavenly realm,
Bliss in abundance as boon to all men,

If they shunned the one fruit that the fatal tree,
Laden with bitterness, bore on its boughs.
Yea, he told them to touch not the Tree of Death.
He who in hatred was hostile to God,
To the Sovereign of Heaven, deceived them with lies,
Mastered Eve's heart, the weak mind of the woman,
Till she trusted his talk and attended his teaching,
Believed that he came with the counsels of God
Which he warily told her with words of persuasion,
Proving with tokens his trusty intent.
Then she spoke to her spouse: "My spirit's lord, Adam,
This fruit is most sweet, it assuages the breast;
This envoy so fair is the angel of God;
I perceive by his garb he is sent us from Heaven;
Let us wish his good will and not win his displeasure.
If today thou hast spoken a speech in despite,
He will grant us his grace if we give him our homage.
Where wilt thou stand through such strife with the envoy
Who comes in God's name? We have need of his favour;
For he can take news to Omnipotent God.
From here I can see where He sits by Himself;
To southeast in His seat who has set up this world,
Encircled with good. I can see all His angels
Wheeling about Him on heavenly wings,
The greatest of peoples, most pleasant of hosts.
Who could endow with such deep understanding,
Were it not sent by the Sovereign of heaven?
Wide can I see all the world's vast creation;
Far can I hear the loud high-day in heaven;
Such is the sight of my soul and my senses
Since the moment I fed on this fruit of the tree.
Now it is here in my hand, my good lord.
Gladly I give it thee; God is its sender,
As I believe, and His order ordains it,
Even as this envoy with anxious words told me.
This apple resembles naught else on this earth,
I am sure, as he says, it is sent us from God."
Often she spoke to him, ever kept urging him,
Pleading all day for a deed that was dire,
Even a breach of the bidding of God.
There stood the messenger, malice in heart,

Soliciting lusts and alluring with cunning,
Urging them frankly. The fiend was at hand,
He who with courage had come on this venture,
Trod the long path. For he plotted to cast men
Down to great death, to dupe and deceive them,
Until they abandoned the bounty of God,
The Almighty's grace and the guerdon of heaven.
Lo, the hell-foe knew well they would weep at God's anger,
Be fettered in hell, and perforce feel affliction,
When they had broken the bidding of God.
Duly with lies he seduced the fair woman,
The most winsome of wives to that wicked intent,
Till to Adam she spoke as the spirit desired.
In his crime he was helped by this creature of God.
Then the winsomest woman in words was abundant,
Till the mind of the man became mastered to trust in
The pledge that the woman kept plighting in words.
Yet she did it sincerely; she saw not the evils,
The hideous harms that it held for mankind,
The woe that should follow the will she conceived
In obeying the aims of the envoy of evil.
She thought she would foster the favour of God
By her speech to her spouse, where she spoke of such tokens
And pledged him her faith, till it followed that Adam
Turned the mind in his breast and was moved to her will.
Hell he received from her hand then, and death,
Though falsely misnamed as the fruit of a tree.
But the food that they took was the fruit of all evil,
The slumber of death and the sleights of the devil,
Hell and destruction for stricken mankind.
When Adam in tasting was touched to the heart,
The bitter-souled messenger, merry and glad,
Gave thanks to his lord for this loss to them both:
"Now have I worked out thy will and have won me
Thy favour as mine. Now for many a day
Mankind are ambushed, yea Adam and Eve;
The wrath of the Lord is their lot henceforward,
For forsaking His precepts and primal command.
No more may they hope for the heavenly kingdom;
To hell must they go by the gloomiest journey.

No more needst thou sorrow in soul where thou liest
Nor mourn in thy fetters that man shall inherit
A home in high heaven, while harm is our portion,
A land of darkness and deepest distress --
And many forsook through thy soaring ambition
Heaven's high halls and its handsome courts.
Angry was God; for He grieved at our grudging
To bow down our heads in obedience to Him,
The Sovereign of Heaven. But to serve such a master
Befitted us not; so in fury of heart
And with spirit severe, He expelled us to hell,
Hurling the greatest of hosts in that fire;
Then again with his hands in the heavenly kingdom
He set up the seats of the sanctified angels,
Assigning that realm to the sons of mankind.
Glad be thy heart, for two hopes are accomplished:
The children of men, being cheated of heaven,
Shall pass to thy place in the pangs of the fire;
And grief for His spirit to God has been given.
All that we suffer of sorrow and torment
Has been heaped upon man by the hatred of God,
With the ruin of souls in the rancour of death.
My mind then is healed and my heart is consoled.
Our wrongs are avenged and the ruin we suffered.
Once more shall I fly to the fires below,
Seeking for Satan in sable hell-shadows,
Shackled in Sheol with shame and disdain."
Then hell's bitter servant descended again,
Approached the broad flames and the portals of hell,
Seeking his master encircled with chains.
Then Adam and Eve in their anguish lamented,
Discourse of sorrow was dolefully spoken,
They feared for the hatred of heaven's high King.
To their minds it had seemed His command had been
    changed.
But the woman knew sorrow and sad lamentation
Perceiving the loss of God's love and instruction
When the light passed away which the liar had given,
A sign to deceive her; but suffering he brought them,
His counsels had sunk them in sorrows of hell,
In burdens past count. So grief burned in their
    hearts.
Sometimes the pair fell to prayer there together,
Hailing the Victor of heaven as good,

Turning to God in petition for pain,
Eager in spirit to undergo judgment
Since they had broken the bidding of God.
Then, too, they knew they were naked of body;
House they had none at their need in the land,
Nor could they conceive of the sorrows of labour.
Yet well could they live in the land if they always
Performed all the preaching and precepts of God.
Plaintive and often the pair spoke together.
Adam to Eve then did utter his anguish:
"Lo, thou hast marked now our lot with evil!
Behold'st thou not hell, so hungry and greedy?
Its roars can be heard even here where we stand.
Far other in kind is the kingdom of heaven;
Yet here is the loveliest land we might own,
As our Lord had designed, if thy zeal had not
listened
To him who has harmed us with hideous counsel,
So that we mocked the commandment of God.
Therefore in grief we may groan at His coming.
For God Himself charged us to guard against torment,
The greatest of harms. Now with hunger and thirst
My breast is beset, by whose suffering before
We never were touched in all times of the past.
How shall we live in this land now or dwell here,
If a wind comes from eastward, from west, south,
or north,
If with shadow of cloud comes a shower of hail
Flung headlong from heaven, or white lies the frost
That is chilling to men, or, it may be, the sun
Shines brightly and fiercely, a flame out of heaven
While naked we stand here and stripped of all
clothes?
We have nothing before for defence against tempests,
No store set aside to sustain us with food;
But the Strong God, our Ruler, has wrath in His
heart.
What will become of us? Coldly I grieve now
For having once pled with the Prince, the good
Ruler,
To frame thee and fashion thy form from my limbs,
For thou hast misled me and lost me my Lord.
I may sorrow for aye to have seen thee at all."
With words answered Eve, the most winsome of

women,
The fairest of wives and the work of the Lord,
Though swindled she was to the sway of the devil:
"Adam, my friend, thou mayst frown at my sin,
But no worse than myself canst thou sorrow in heart."
Then answer made Adam: "If I knew His will,
The penalty destined and due me from Him
(Hadst thou but seen quickly!), though the King should command me
To go hence on the sea and to sail on the flood,
No wave were so deep and no water so vast
That e'er I should doubt Him nor dive to the depths
In working God's will. I am weary of earth
And my service of faith, since I forfeit His favour
And may not possess it. But meet it is not
That we two thus naked should wander together.
Let us enter this copse and this cover of forest."
They both walked apart and in passion of sorrow
Went on their way in the woodland so green;
Sat there asunder and sadly awaited
Decrees from the Lord that no longer they held
The former good gifts of God the Almighty.
They covered their bodies with clothing of leaves,
Gowned them in foliage; no garments had they.
But both together they groaned in prayer;
Every morn to the Mighty One
They prayed that God should forget them not,
That the Lord would instruct them to live in the light.

- - - - - - - -

(At this point the paraphrase of Genesis is resumed.)

Then walking came the King Almighty,
The glorious Prince into Paradise
In the afternoon, as His object was;
Our Saviour, mild Father, would find and enquire
What His children did, the condemned poor creatures,
To whom He had given great good before.
Then they sought the shadows, shorn of happiness,
Sad in heart, they hid in the darkness
Hearing the holy behests of the Lord,
Frightened and pale. Then the Prince of heaven,

The Guard of creation, began to enquire;
The King bade His creature to come at once.
Then Adam answered in anguish of nakedness:
"Lord of my life, I am lacking in clothes;
I am garbing myself in a garment of leaves.
Guilty am I and great is my grief,
Dire is my spirit nor dare I come forth
Into Thy notice. Quite naked am I."
Speedy was God in His speech to Adam:
"Tell me, my son, why thou seekest in shame
The shade of the trees? For in truth, at the first
Thou wert given no shame but the surest of joys.
Why knowest thou woe and art naked with shame?
Why seest thou sorrow and servest thy body
With garments of leaves, and through grief about life
Loudly lamentest thy lack of all vesture,
Unless thou hast tasted the Tree's deadly apple,
The fruit I forbade thee with bitterest words?"
Adam to Him then made answer: "My Lord,
My bride, the fine wife, by Thee brought to my hurt,
Placed the fruit in my hand. Now I feel in myself
The proof of that sin. I know sorrow the more."
Then God, in His asking, of Eve made enquiry:
"What didst thou, my daughter, to dainties unnumbered,
The new works of Eden, the ample provision,
When hungry thou laidest thy hand on the Tree
And, breaking the fruit from the branches, didst take it,
Eat grief to thy harm, and then give it to Adam,
Fruit quite forbidden you both by my word?"
Then spoke the fair woman, the wife abashed:
"The serpent deceived me, unceasingly urged me
With fair words to crime and the craving of greed;
The worm with his wickedness won me to evil,
To devilish theft and a deed that was hostile.
In defiance of pledges I plundered the Tree
At the edge of the wood and I ate of its fruit."
Then our Saviour, the Lord, to the serpent spoke thus,
Condemning the sinner to sad, distant journeys:
"Thou shalt wearily go a long way on thy breast,
Thou shalt tread with thy bosom and travel forth

footless,
As long as thou livest and life is within thee.
Dust shalt thou eat all the days of thy life.
Evilly hast thou been author of sin;
Therefore this wife by the will of high Heaven
Shall tread thy foul head with the tramp of her foot.
In wait shalt thou lie with new war for her heel.
Between thine and her seed shall be set equal war
While the ball of this earth shall abide under heaven.
Evil foe of all souls, thou art certain indeed,
Thou knowest the life thou shalt lead in the land."
Then God unto Eve in anger spoke:
"Depart thou from bliss! In the power of man
I set thee henceforward, sorely oppressed
With fear of thy husband; thou'lt humbly atone
For thy wicked ways, and wait for death,
Conceiving in sorrow thy sons and thy daughters."
The infinite Lord, the Author of life,
Then uttered grim orders to Adam also:
"Naked and needy, another land
And a joyless abode I bid thee seek,
Exiled and stripped of Eden's glories.
Thy soul and thy body to sunder are fated.
Sin to the world thou hast wickedly brought:
Hence thou shalt labour; thy living on earth
With swink shalt thou gain and the sweat of thy brow,
Eat thus thy loaf as long as thou livest,
Till hateful disease grip thee hard to the heart,
Ills thou didst formerly eat with the apple.
Therefore to death art thou doomed without doubt."
Lo, we now hear how earth's harms have arisen,
Whence came the bitterest blows we must bear.
The Guardian of glory, our gracious Creator,
Clothed them with garments. Their God bade them cover
Their shame with a veil of new vesture provided,
When ordered from Eden to indigent living.
Behind them, their home of the happiest joys
An angel locked by the Lord's command
With a flaming sword; past that fire hereafter
No guileful may come, none guilty of sin,
For the guard is strong who greatly holds

That glorious life for the Lord's delight.
Yet the First of Fathers, earth's Founder almighty,
Did not deprive the primal pair
Of all of His mercies though erst they were rebels.
But He left to console them the solemn roof
Of heaven, studded with holy stars;
He gave them the widespread wealth of the soil,
And bade each sort in the sea and on land
To bring forth its fruit to favour the pair.
Then after their sin they settled down
In a sadder land, a sorrier home,
Less fertile of good than that first abode
From which they were shut by their shameful deed.

MARCO GIROLAMO VIDA

Christiados libri VI (1527)

From Book I[1]

Without delay, his Chiefs and train he calls,
A horrid Council! to his palace-walls:
And lo! the trump emits the piercing sounds,
Which the huge dome thro' all its cells rebounds.
Loud roars each cavern from its gloomy seat,
And earth vibrates beneath its pond'rous weight.
Instant the gate with various spectres swarms,
To day adverse, and strange with monst'rous forms;
Their breasts express the man, their wastes forsake,
And writhe with spiry folds into a snake:
Gorgons and sphynxes breathe an horrid air;
Some stalk a centaur, some a hydra stare;
These rise chimeras, spouting livid fires,
And Scylla's barking image those inspires.
Fiends clad in harpies swell the dreadful train
And realise the shapes, that mortals feign.
Above the rest, the form of towring size,
And flaming front of hell's grim tyrant rise:
With hundred hands the ambient air he cleaves,

[1]Translation by Edward Granan, London, 1771.

And his throat pours a hundred burning waves.
From all their mouths, and eyes, and nostrils stream
Dark gales of fume, and sheets of sickly flame.
Around their heads snakes bend into a wreath,
And dimpling down their necks in hisses breathe;
Each wields a trident, each a firebrand shakes,
That urge the guilty ghosts to burning lakes. . . .
All come with souls elate, in counsel strong,
And the roofs echo to th' infernal throng.
Till in the mid the King majestic rose,
And while he speaks, his hand with thunder glows:
"Tartarean Chiefs, whose births from ether spring,
Sad victims now, to Heav'n's inclement King;
Who (proudly weak, thro' lust to reign alone,
To bear each Equal, rival of his throne)
Against us roll'd his thunder big with fate,
And hurl'd us flaming from our native seat.
Should fame deny our conflicts to renew,
The woes that wait us, shall present to view
What wars we kindled in th' etherial plain;
What fury labour'd in each adverse train,
But now the Victor boasts the stars his prize,
And arrogates the sceptre of the skies.
How dire his vengeance our disasters tell:
Once brightness wrapt us, now the gloom of hell. . ."

MARCELLUS PALINGENIUS

Zodiacus Vitae (1531)[1]

Most glorious God, almighty King, thou Parent chiefe of name,
Whose wisdom great this wondrous world of nothing first did frame
And gouernes it and euermore preserues it daye by day,

[1]Translation by Barnabe Googe, The Zodiake of Life (1576). The extract given here is from the opening lines of Book XII.

The spring and end of that that be, to whom all
things obay,
Than whom more great, more good, or faire, is
nothing, nor more hie.
That blessed liuest for euermore, aboue the starry
Skie:
My minde desiring now to thee to clime doth nothing
neede,
Apollo, Muse, Parnassus hill, or springs that wont
to feede
The pratling Poets, fansies vaine when as they list
to write
Disguised tales, that frantike heads of countrey
Clounes delighte.
For, other ayde, and other grace it needful is to
haue,
And streames of other fountaines sweete I thirsty
now doe craue,
I thee beseech and humbly pray, on thee alone I
call,
That this my worke of late begonne and labour last
of all
Thou fauour wilt and graunt me grace, to touch the
appointed end:
O Lorde thy Holy Spirit vouchsafe into my heart
to send,
Wherewith inspirde, I may behould the secrets of
thy reigne
And others teach, and with my verse immortall
honour gaine. . . .

But in the State Diuine of God and Glorious
maiestie,
We must beleeue is nothing vaine since Godliest is
the same:
This God what so euer he could doe assuredly did
frame,
Least that his vertue were in vaine, and neuer
should ly hid.
But since he could make endlesse things, it must be
thought he did,
And all his power therein emploied so that there
did remaine,
In him no kinde of power or force that idle were
or vaine.

But learned Aristotle sayeth there can no body bee,
But that it must by boundes consist: to this do I
    agree,
Because aboue the Skies no kinde of body we do
    place,
But light more pure, of body voyde, such light as
    doth deface
And farre excell our shining Sunne, such light as
    comprehend
Our eyes cannot, and endlesse light that God doth
    from him send,
Wherein together with their King the Sprites that
    are more hie
Doe dwell, the meaner sorte beneath in skies doe
    always lie. . . .
For forme that can itselfe sustaine, without this
    matters hand,
Is perfecter than that which void, of matter cannot
    stand.
Therfore all void of matter there, things perfect
    are and pure,
And in despite of fretting age, and force of fate
    endure.
And store of goodly things are there, that in this
    worldly light,
God hath not made, from which proceedes, great
    ioyes & Saincts delight,
Such ioyes as toung of mortall man, can neuer full
    define,
Such ioyes as neuer can decay, with space of any
    time.
These incorporeall formes were known to minde of
    Plato hie,
Although the enuious sorte do scorne, his bookes
    full bitterly.
A fewe them finde to whom the LORD aboue, doth
    fauour showe,
And giues to them his light that they, these things
    may plaine beholde.
    In fine, there sprites and Angeles are, as
        many thousand folde,
As all the woods containe in leaues, or all the
    shores in sand,
Or all the Fishes in the seas, or starres in Skie

that stand,
Yea, number none can them containe. For since
that God could frame,
Them numberlesse, be sure he did, the more to
spread his name. . .

GUILLAUME DU BARTAS

La Sepmaine (1578)[1]

Day I

"The Chaos"

Thou glorious Guide of Heav'ns star-glistring motion,
Thou, thou (true Neptune) Tamer of the Ocean,
Thou Earth's drad Shaker (at whose only Word,
Th' Eolian Scouts are quickly still'd and stirr'd)
Lift up my soule, my drousie spirits refine,
With learned Art enrich This Worke of mine. . . .

Before all Time, all Matter, Form, and Place,
God all in all, and all in God it was:
Immutable, immortall, infinite,[2]
Incomprehensible, all spirit, all light,
All Majesty, all-self-Omnipotent,
Invisible, impassive, excellent,
Pure, just, wise, good, God raign'd alone (at rest)
Himself alone, selfs Palace, host, and guest. . . .

That first World (yet) was a most formless Form,
A confus'd heap, a Chaos most deform,
A Gulf of Gulfs, a Body ill compackt,
An ugly medley, where all difference lackt:
Where th' Elements lay jumbled all together,
Where hot and cold were jarring each with either;
The blunt with sharp, the dank against the drie,

---

[1]Translation by Joshua Sylvester, 1608.

[2]Copied verbatim by Milton in PL, iii, 373.

The hard with soft, the base against the high; . . .

This was not then the World: 'twas but the Matter,
The Nurcery whence it should issue after;
Or rather, th' Embryon, that within a Weeke
Was to be born: for that huge lump was like
The shape-less burthen in the Mothers womb,
Which yet in time doth into fashion com: . . .

The dreadful Darknes of the Memphytists,
The sad black horror of Cimmerian Mists,
The sable fumes of Hell's infernall vault
(Or if ought darker in the World be thought)
Muffled the face of that profound Abyss,
Full of Disorder and fell Mutinies: . . .

So did Gods Spirit delight it selfe a space
To move it selfe upon the floting Masse:
No other care th' Almightie's mind possest
(If care can enter in his sacred brest).
Or, as a Hen that fain would hatch a Brood
(Some of her own, some of adoptive blood)
Sits close thereon, and with her lively heat,
Of yellow-white bals, doth live birds beget:
Even in such sort seemed the Spirit Eternall
To brood upon this Gulf . . .

Reason it selfe doth overthrow the grounds
Of those new Worlds that fond Leucippus founds:
Sith, if kinde Nature many Worlds could clip,
Still th' upper World's water and earth would slip
Into the lower; and so in conclusion,
All would returne into the Old Confusion. . . .

No sooner said he, Be there light, but lo
The formless lump to perfect Form gan growe,
And, all illustred with Lights radiant shine,
Doft mourning weeds, and deckt it passing fine.
All-hail pure Lamp, bright, sacred and excelling;
Sorrow & Care, Darkness & Dread repelling:
Thou World's great taper, Wicked mens just terror,
Mother of truth, true Beauties only Mirror,
God's eldest Daughter: O! how thou art full

Of grace and goodness! O! how beautifull!
Sith thy great Parent's all-discerning Eye
Doth judge thee so: and sith his Majestie
(Thy glorious Maker) in his sacred layes
Can doe no lesse than sing thy modest prayse. . . .

Whether, <u>This-Day</u>, God made you, Angels bright,
Under the name <u>of Heav</u>'n, or of the Light:
Whether you were, after, in th' instant born
With those bright spangles that the heav'ns adorn:
Or, whether you derive your high Descent
Long time before the World and Firmament
(For, I nill stifly argue to and fro
In nice Opinions, whether so, or so;
Especially, where curious search, perchance,
Is not so safe as humble ignorance);
I am resolved that once th' Omnipotent
Created you immortall, innocent,
Good, faire, and free; in briefe, of Essence such
As from his Owne differ'd not very much. . . .

Even so some Legions of those lofty Spirits
(Envying the glorie of their Makers merits)
Conspir'd together, strove against the streame,
T' Usurpe his Scepter and his Diademe:
But He, whose hands doe never Lightnings lack
Proud sacrilegious Mutiners to wrack,
Hurled them in th' Aire, or in some lower Cell:
For, where God is not, everywhere is Hell. . . .

<u>Day II</u>

"The Elements"

For all that's made, is made of the First Matter
Which in th' old Nothing made the All-Creator.
All, that dissolves, resolves into the same.
Since first the Lord of Nothing made This Frame,
<u>Nought's made of nought; and nothing turns to nothing</u>:
Things <u>birth</u>, or death, change but their formal clothing. . . .

Others, amid the Starriest Orbe perceiving

A triple cadence, and withall conceiving
That but one natural course one body goes,
Count nine, some ten; not numbering yet (with
    those)
Th' empereall Palace, where th' eternall Treasures
Of Nectar flowe, where everlasting Pleasures
Are heaped-up, where an immortall May
In bliss-full beauties flourisheth for ay. . .

    O fair, five-double Round, Sloath's Foe
        apparent,
Life of the World, Dayes, Months and years own
    Parent;
Thine own selfs modell, never shifting place,
And yet thy pure wings with so swift a pace
Fly over us, that but our Thought alone
Can (as thy babe) pursue thy motion . . .

Transparent, cleer, light; law of this lowe Ball:
Which in thy wide bout, bound-less all dost bound,
And claspest all, under, or in thy Round,
Throne of th' Almighty, I would faine rehearse
Thy various Dances in this very Verse . . .

But know, what e'r thou be, that here I gather
Justly so many of God's works together,
Because by th'Orbe of th' ample Firmament
(Which round This Day th' Eternal Finger pent
Between the lower Waters and the higher)
I mean the Heav'ns, the Aire, and th' upper Fire,
Which separate the Oceans waters salt.
From those which God pour'd o'r th' Ethereal vault.
    Yet have I not so little seen and sought
The Volume, which our Age hath chiefest thought,
But that I know how suttly greatest Clarks
Presume to argue in their learned Works,
T' o'r-whelm these Floods, this Crystall to deface,
And try this Ocean which doth all imbrace . . .

Here, in the night appears a flaming Spire;
There a fierce Dragon folded all in fire;
Here, a bright Comet; there, a burning Beam;
Here, flying Launces; there, a fiery Stream;
Here seems a horned Goat, environ'd round

With fiery flakes, about the Aire to bound;
There, with long bloudy haire, a blazing Star
Threatens the World with Famin, Plague, and War;
To Princes, death; to Kingdoms, many crosses;
To all Estates, inevitable losses;
To Heard-men, Rot; to Plow-men, hap-less Seasons;
To Sailors, Stormes; to Cities, civill Treasons. . . .

I'le rather give a thousand times the ly
To mine own Reason, than but once defy
The sacred voyce of th' ever-lasting Spirit,
Which doth so often and so loud averr-it,
That God, above the shining Firmament,
I wot not, I, what kinde of Waters pent:
Whether, that pure, super-celestiall Water,
With our inferiour have no likely nature:
Whether, turnd Vapour, it hath round embow'd
Heav'ns highest stage in a transparent cloud:
Or, whether (as they say) a Crystall case
Do (round about) the Heav'nly Orb embrace.
And thou thy self, O Heav'n, didst set wide ope
(Through all the Marches in thy spacious cope)
All thy large Sluces, thy vast Seas to shed
In sudden spouts on thy proud Sister's head;
Whose aw-lesse, law-lesse, shame-lesse life abhor'd,
Only delighted to despight the Lord.
Th' Earth shrinks and sinks; now th' Ocean hath no shore:
Now Rivers run to serve the Sea no more;
Themselves are Sea: the many sundry Streams,
Of sundry names (deriv'd from sundry Realms)
Make now but one great Sea: the World itself
Is nothing now but a great standing Gulf,
Whose swelling surges strive to mix their Water
With th' other Waves about this round Theater.
The Sturgeon, coasting over Castles, muses
(Under the Sea) to see so many houses . . .

Day III

"The Sea and Earth"

My sacred Muse, that lately soared high
Among the glist'ring Circles of the Sky

(Whose various dance, which the first Moover drives
Harmoniously, this Universe revives)
Commanding all the Windes and sulph'ry Storms,
The lightning Flashes, and the hideous Forms
Seen in the Aire; with language meetly brave
Whilom discourst upon a Theam so grave:
But, This-Day, flagging lowely by the Ground,
She seems constrain'd to keep a lowely sound. . . .

All those steep Mountaines, whose high horned tops
The misty cloak of wandring Clouds enwraps,
Under first waters their crump shoulders hid,
And all the Earth as a dull Pond abid,
Untill th' All-Monarch's bounteous Majesty
(Willing t' enfeof man this Worlds Empery)
Commanding Neptune straight to marshall forth
His Floods a-part, and to unfold the Earth;
And in his Waters, now contented rest,
T' have all the World, for one whole day, possest.
As when the muffled Heav'ns have wept amain,
And foaming streams assembling on the Plain,
Turn'd Fields to Floods; soon as the showrs do cease,
With unseen speed the Deluge doth decrease,
Sups up it selfe, in hollow sponges sinks,
And 's ample arms in straighter Channell shrinks:
Even so the Sea, to 't selfe it self betook,
Mount after Mount, Field after Field forsook;
And suddenly in smaller cask did tun
Her Waters, that from every side did run . . .

When God, whose words more in a moment can
That in an Age the proudest strength of Man,
Had severed the Floods, levell'd the Fields,
Embas't the Valleys, and Embost the Hils;
Change, change (quoth he) O fair and firmest Globe,
Thy mourning weed, to a green gallant Robe;
Cheer thy sad brows, and stately garnish them,
With a rich fragrant, flowry Diadem . . .

No sooner spoken, but the lofty Pine
Distilling-pitch, the Larch yield-Turpentine,
Th' ever-green Box, and gummy Cedar sprout,
And th' Airy Mountains mantle round about . . .

The dainty Apricock (of Plums the Prince)
The velvet Peach, gilt Orenge, downy Quince
All-ready beare grav'n in their tender barks,
Gods powerfull providence in open marks.
The sent-sweet Apple, and astringent Pear,
The Cherry, Fibberd, Wal-nut, Meddeler,
The milky Fig, the Damson black and white,
The Date, and Olive, ayding appetite,
Spread every-where a most delightfull spring
And every-where a very Eden bring.
Heer, the fine Pepper, as in Clusters hung:
There Cinnamon and other Spices sprung.
Heer, dangled Nutmegs, that for thrifty pains
Yearly repay the Bandans wondrous gains;
There growes (th' Hesperian Plant) the precious Reed
Whence Sugar sirrops in abundance bleed;
There weeps the Balm, and famous Trees from whence
Th' Arabians fetcht perfuming Frankincense.
There, th' amorous Vine coll's in a thousand sorts
(With winding arms) her Spouse that her supports . . .

The fields of Corn, as Fields of Combat first;
And Ranks of trees, as Ranks of Souldiers yerst . . .

Day IV

"The Heavens, Sun, Moon"

Even so, some brain-sicks live there now-adaies,
That lose themselves still in contrary waies;
Prepostrous Wits that cannot row at ease
On the smooth Channell of our common Seas.
And such are those (in my conceit at least)
Those Clarks that think (think how absurd a jest)
That neither Heav'n nor Stars do turn at all,
Nor dance about this great round Earthly Ball;
But th' Earth it self, this Massie Globe of ours,
Turns round-about once every twice-twelve hours:
And we resemble land-bred Novices
New brought aboord to venture on the Seas;
Who, at first lanching from the shoar, suppose
The ship stands still, and that the ground it

goes. . . .

Arm'd with these reasons, 'twere superfluous
T' assaile the reasons of Copernicus,
Who, to solve better of the Stars th' appearance,
Unto the Earth a three-fold motion warrants:
Making the Sun the Center of this All,
Moon, Earth, and Water, in one only Ball. . . .

Dayes glorious Eye! Even as a mighty King,
About his Countrey stately Progressing,
Is compast round with Dukes, Earles, Lords, and
Knights,
(Orderly marshall'd in their noble Rites)
Esquires and Gentlemen, in courtly kinde
And then his Guard before him and behinde . . .

O second honour of the Lamps supernall,
Sure Calendar of Festivals eternall . . .
I think thy body round as any Ball,
Whose superfice (nigh equall over all)
As a pure Glass, now up, and down anon,
Reflects the bright beams of thy spouse, the Sun.

Day V

"The Fishes and Fowles"

In vain had God stor'd Heav'n with glistring studs,
The plain with grain, the mountain tops with woods,
Sever'd the Ayre from Fire, the Earth from Water,
Had he not soon peopled this large Theatre
With living Creatures: Therefore he began
(This Day) to quicken in the Ocean,
In standing Pools, and in the straggling Rivers
(Whose folding Chanell fertill Champain severs)
So many Fishes of so many features,
That in the Waters one may see all Creatures . . .
Shall I omit the monstrous Whirl-about,
Which in the Sea another Sea doth spout . . .

When on the Surges I perceive, from far,
Th' Ork, Whirl-poole, Whale, or puffing Physeter,
Me thinks I see the wandring Ile again

(Ortygian Delos) floating on the Main.
And when in Combat these fell Monsters cross,
Me seems some Tempest all the Seas doth toss.
Our fear-less Saylers, in far Voyages
(More led by Gain's hope than their Compasses)
On th' Indian shore, have somtime noted som
Whose bodies covered two broad Acres room . . .

Another haunts the shoar, to feed on foam:
Another round about the Rocks doth roam,
Nibbling on Weeds . . .

But, these are nothing to the Nightingale,
Breathing, so sweetly from a breast so small,
So many Tunes, whose Harmony excels
Our Voice, our Violls, and all Musick els. . . .

But (gentle Muse) tell me what Fowls are those
That but even-now from flaggy Fenns arose? . . .

The silver Swan, that dying singeth best . . .
I hear the Crane (if I mistake not) cry;
Who in the clouds forming the forked Y,
By the brave orders practiz'd under her,
Instructeth souldiers in the Art of War.
For when her Troops of wandring Cranes forsake
Frost-firmed Strymon, and (in Autumn) take
Truce with the Northren Dwarfs, to seek adventure
In Southren Climates for a milder Winter;
A front each Band a forward Captain flies,
Whose pointed Bill cuts passage through the skies . . .

There the fair Peacock beautifully brave,
Proud, portly-strouting, stalking, stately-grave,
Wheeling his starry Trayn, in pomp displayes
His glorious eyes to Phoebus golden rayes.
Close by his side stands the courageous Cock,
Crest-peoples King, the Peasants trusty Clock,
True Morning Watch, Aurora's Trumpeter,
The Lyons terror, true Astronomer,
Who daily riseth when the Sun doth rise;
And when Sol setteth, then to roost he hies. . . .

Thou happy Witness of my happy Watches,

Blush not (my Book) nor think it thee dismatches,
To hear about upon thy paper-Tables,
Flies, Butterflies, Gnats, Bees, and all the
    rabbles
Of other Insects (endless to rehearse) . . .

For, if old Times admire Callicrates
For ivory Emmets; and Mermecides
For framing of a rigged Ship, so small
That with her wings a Bee can hide it all . . .
Admire we then th' all-wise Omnipotence,
Which doth within so narrow space dispence
So stiff a sting, so stout and valiant heart,
So loud a voyce, so prudent wit and Art.
    For, where's the State beneath the Firmament,
That doth excel the Bees for Government?
No, no: bright Phoebus, whose eternall Race
Once every Day about the World doth pase,
Sees heer no Citie, that in Rites and Laws
(For Equitie) neer to their Justice draws . . .

Day VI

"The Beasts and Man"

Of all the Beasts which thou This-Day didst build,
To haunt the Hils, the Forrests, and the Field,
I see (as Vice-Roy of their Brutish Band)
The Elephant the Vant-guard doth command: . . .

    In a fresh Troup, the fearful Hare I note,
Th' oblivious Conney, and the brouzing Goat,
The sloathfull Swine, the golden-fleeced Sheep,
The light-foot Hart, which every year doth weep
(As a sad Recluse) for his branched head,
That in the Spring-time he before hath shed. . . .

Already howls the waste-full Wolf, the Boar
Whets foamy Fangs, the hungry Bear doth roar,
The Cat-fac'd Ounce, that doth me much dismay,
With grumbling horror threatens my decay;
The light-foot Tigre, spotted Leopard,
Foaming with fury doe besiege me hard . . .

But (Courage now.) Heer coms the valiant Beast,
The noble Lion, King of all the rest . . .

Alas, why didst thou on This-Day create
These harmfull Beasts, which but exasperate
Our thorny life? O! wert thou pleas'd to form
Th' innamel'd Scorpion, and the Viper-worm,
Th' horned Cerastes, th' Alexandrian Skink,
Th' Adder, and Drynas (full of odious stink)
Th' Eft, Snake, and Dipsas (causing deadly Thirst):
Why hast thou arm'd them with a rage so curst? . . .
And, in the Childehood of the World did bring
Th' Amphisbena, her double banefull sting. . . .

Now of all Creatures which his Word did make,
Man was the last that living breath did take . . .

All th' admirable Creatures made beforn,
Which Heav'n and Earth, and Ocean doe Adorn,
Are but Essays, compar'd in every part,
To this divinest Master-Piece of Art. . . .

Admired Artist, Architect divine,
Perfect and peer-less in all Works of thine,
So my rude hand on this rough Table guide
To paint the Prince of all thy Works beside,
That grave Spectators, in his face may spie
Apparent marks of thy Divinity.

Yet, not his face down to the Earth-ward bending
(Like Beasts that but regard their belly, ending
For ever all) but toward th' azure Skyes
Bright golden Lamps lifting his lovely Eyes;
That through their nerves, his better part might look
Still to that place from whence her birth she took.
Also thou plantedst th' Intellectuall Pow'r
In th' highest stage of all this stately Bowr,
From thence it might (as from a Cittadell)
Command the members that too often rebel. . . .

For, soon as ever he had framed thee,
Into thy hands he put this Monarchy;
Made all the Creatures know thee for their Lord,

And come before thee of their own accord . . .

So, God empal'd our Grandsires lively look,
Through all his bones a deadly chilness strook,
Siel'd up his sparkling eyes with iron bands,
Led down his feet (almost) to Lethe Sands;
In briefe, so nummed his Soule's and Bodie's sense,
That (without pain) opening his side, from thence
He took a rib, which rarely He refin'd,
And thereof made the Mother of mankinde:
Graving so lively on the living bone
All Adams beauties; that, but hardly, one
Could have the Lover from his Love descry'd,
Or known the Bridegroom from his gentle Bride:
Saving that she had a more smiling Eye,
A smoother Chin, a Cheek of purer Dye,
A fainter voyce, a more enticing Face,
A Deeper tress, a more delighting Grace,
And in her bosom (more than Lillie-white)
Two swelling Mounts of Ivory, panting light.
    Now after this profound and pleasing Transe,
No sooner Adam's ravisht eyes did glance
On the rare beauties of his new-come Half,
But in his heart he 'gan to leap and laugh,
Kissing her kindly, calling her his Life,
His Love, his Stay, his Rest, his Weal, his Wife,
His other-Selfe, his Help (him to refresh)
Bone of his Bone, Flesh of his very Flesh.
    Source of all joyes! sweet Hee-Shee-Coupled-One!
Thy sacred Birth I never think upon.
But (ravisht) I admire how God did then
Make Two of One, and One of Two again.
    O blessed Bond! O happy Marriage!
Which dost the match 'twixt Christ and us presage!
    O chastest friendship, whose pure flames impart
Two Soules in one, two Hearts into one Heart!
O holy knot in Eden instituted . . .
By thee, we quench the wild and wanton Fires,
That in our Soule the Paphian shot inspires;
And taught (by thee) a love more firm and fitter,
We find the Mel more sweet, the Gall less bitter. . . .

TORQUATO TASSO

Gerusalemme liberata (1581)

From *Book IV*[1]

1

While thus their worke went on with luckie speed,
And reared rammes their horned fronts advance,
The ancient foe to man, and mortall seed,
His wannish eies vpon them bent askance;
And when he saw their labours well succeed,
He wept for rage, and threat'ned dire mischance,
He chokt his curses, to himselfe he spake,
Such noise wilde buls, that softly bellow make.

2

At last resolving in his damned thought,
To find some let, to stop their warlike feat,
He gave command his princes should be brought
Before the throne of his infernall seat,
O foole! as if it were a thinge of nought
God to resist, or change his purpose great,
Who on his foes doth thunder in his ire,
Whose arrowes hailestones be, and coles of fire.

3

The drearie trumpet blew a dreadfull blast,
And rombled through the lands and Kingdoms vnder,
Through wastnes wide it roard, and hollowes vast,
And fild the deepe, with horror, feare and wonder,
Not halfe so dreadfull noise the tempests cast,
That fall from skies, with storms of haile and thunder,
Nor halfe so lowd the whistling winds doe sing,
Broke from the earthen prisons of their King.

---

[1] Translation by Edward Fairfax, entitled *Godfrey of Bulloigne* (London, 1600).

4

The Peeres of Plutoes realme assembled beene
Amid the pallace of their angrie King,
In hideous formes and shapes, tofore vnseene,
That feare, death, terror and amasement bring,
With ouglie pawes some trample on the greene,
Some gnaw the snakes that on their shoulders hing,
And some their forked tailes stretch forth on hie,
And teare the twinkling stars from trembling skie.

5

There were Cilenos foule and loathsome rout,
There Sphinges, Centaures, there were Gorgons fell,
There howling Scillaes, yawling round about,
There serpents hisse, there seu'n-mouth'd Hydrayes yell,
Chimera there spues fire and brimstone out,
And Poliphemus blinde supporteth hell,
Besides ten thousand monsters therein dwels
Mis-shapt, vnlike themselves, and like nought els.

6

About the Prince each tooke his wonted seat
On thrones red hot, ibuilt of burning brasse,
Pluton in middest heav'd his trident great,
Of rustie iron huge that forged was,
The rockes, on which the salt sea billowes beat,
And Atlas tops, the clouds in height that passe,
Compar'd to his huge person, mole-hils be,
So his rough front, his hornes so lifted he.

7

The tyrant proud frown'd from his loftie cell,
And with his lookes made all his monsters tremble,
His eies, that full of rage and venome swell,
Two beacons seeme, that men to armes assemble,
His feltred lockes, that on his bosome fell,

On rugged mountaines briers and thornes resemble,
His yawning mouth, that fomed clotted blood,
Gapte like a whirlepoole wide in Stygian flood.

8

And as Mount Etna vomits sulphur out,
With clifts of burning crags, and fire and smoke,
So from his mouth flew kindled coales about,
Hot sparks and smels, that man and beasts would choke,
The gnarring porter durst not whine for dout,
Still were the Furies, while their soveraigne spoke,
And swift Cocytus staid his murmur shrill,
While thus the murdrer thundred out his will.

9

Ye powres infernall, worthier far to sit
Above the sunne, whence you your ofspringe take,
With me that whilome, through the welkin flit,
Downe tombled headlong to this emptie lake,
Our former glorie, still remember it,
Our bold attemptes and war we once did make
Gainst him, that rules above the starrie sphere,
For which like traitors we lie damned here.

10

And now in stead of cleere and gladsome skie,
Of Titans brightnes, that so glorious is,
In this deepe darknes loe we helplesse lie,
Hopelesse againe to ioy our former blis,
And more (which makes my grieves to multiplie)
That sinfull creature man, elected is,
And in our place, the heavens possesse he must,
Vile man, begot of clay, and borne of dust. . . .

15

Oh, be not than the courage perisht cleene,
That whilome dwelt within your haughtie thought,
When, arm'd with shining fire and weapons keene,
Against the Angels of proud heav'n we fought,

I grant we fell on the Phlegrean greene,
Yet good our cause was, though our fortune nought;
    For chance assisteth oft th' ignobler part,
    We lost the field, yet lost we not our hart. . . .

18

Before his words the tyrant ended had,
The lesser devils arose with gastlie rore,
And thronged foorth about the world to gad,
Each land they filled, river, streame and shore,
The Goblins, Fairies, Feends and Furies mad,
Ranged in flowrie dales, and mountaines hore,
    And vnder everie trembling leafe they sit,
    Betweene the solid earth and welkin flit. . . .

GUILLAUME DU BARTAS

La Seconde Semaine (1584)[1]

Day I, Part i

"Eden"

GOD (supreme Lord) committed not alone
T' our Father Adam, this inferiour Throne . . .
But also chose him for a happy Seat
A climate temperate both for cold and heat,
Which dainty *Flora* paveth sumptuously
With flowry *VER's* inameld tapistry;
Pomona pranks with fruits, whose taste excels;
And Zephyr fils with Musk and Amber smels:
Where God himselfe (as Gardner) treads the allies,
With Trees and Corn covers the hils and valleyes,
Summons sweet sleep with noise of hundred brooks,
And Sun-proof Arbours makes in sundry nooks:
He plants, he proins, he pares, he trimmeth round
Th' ever green beauties of a fruitfull ground;
Heer-there the course of th' holy Lakes he leads,

[1]Translation by Joshua Sylvester, 1608.

With thousand Dies he motleys all the Meades. . . .

If there I say the Sun (the Seasons stinter)
Made no hot Sommer, nor no hoary Winter,
But lovely VER kept still in lively lustre
The fragrant Valleys, smiling Meads, and Pasture:
That boistrous Adams body did not shrink
For Northren winds, nor for the Southren wink:
But Zephyr did sweet musky sighes afford,
Which breathing through the Garden of the Lord,
Gave bodies vigour, verdure to the field,
That verdure flowrs, those flowrs sweet savor yeeld:
That Day did gladly lend his sister, Night,
For half her moisture, half his shining Light:
That never hail did Harvest prejudice,
That never frost, nor snowe, nor slippery ice
The fields en-ag'd: nor any stormy stowr
Dismounted Mountains, nor no violent showr
Pov'risht the Land, which frankly did produce
All fruitfull vapours for delight and use:
I think I lye not, rather I confess
My stammering Muses poor unlearnedness.
If in two words thou wilt her praise comprise,
Say 'twas the type of th' upper Paradise . . .

Yet (over-curious) question not the site,
Where God did plant his Garden of delight;
Whether beneath the Equinoctiall line,
Or on a Mountain neer Latona's shine,
Nigh Babylon, or in the radiant East.
Humble content thee that thou know'st (at least)
That, that rare, plenteous, pleasant, happy thing
Whereof th' Almighty made our Grand-sire King,
Was a choice soil, through which did rowling slide
Swift Ghion, Pishon, and rich Tigris tide,
And that fair stream whose silver waves do kiss
The Monarch Towrs of proud Semiramis. . . .
A certain place it was (now sought in vain)
Where set by grace, for sin remov'd again,
Our Elders were: whereof the Thunder-darter
Made a bright Sword the gate, an Angel Porter . . .

Now of the Trees wherewith th' immortal Powr
Adorn'd the quarters of that blissfull Bowr,

All served the mouth, save two sustain'd the mind:
All served for food, save two for seals assign'd.
God gave the first, for honorable stile,
The tree of Life: true name (alas the while!)
Not for th' effect it had, but should have kept,
If Man from duty never had mis-stept.
For, as the ayre of those fresh dales and hils
Preserved him from Epidemick ills,
This fruit had ever-calm'd all insurrections,
All civill quarrels of the crosse complexions;
Had barr'd the passage of twice-childish age,
And ever-more excluded all the rage
Of painfull griefes, whose swift-slow posting pase
At first or last our dying life doth chase.
The Tree of Knowledge, th' other Tree behight:
Not that it selfly had such speciall might,
As mens dull wits could whet and sharpen so
That in a moment they might all things know.
'Twas a sure pledge, a sacred signe, and seal;
Which, being ta'en, should to light man reveal
What ods there is between still peace, and strife;
Gods wrath, and love; drad death, and dearest life;
Solace, and sorrow; guile, and innocence;
Rebellious pride, humble obedience. . . .

Sometimes by you, O you all-faining Dreams,
We gain this good; but not when Bacchus streames
And glutton vapours overflowe the Brain,
And drown our spirits, presenting fancies vain:
Nor when pale Phlegm, or saffron coulour'd Choler,
In feeble stomacks belch their divers dolor,
And print upon our Understandings Tables;
That, Water-wracks; this other, flamefull fables:
Nor when the Spirit of lies, our spirit deceives,
And guileful visions in our fancy leaves . . .

And yet far higher is this holy Fit,
When (not from flesh, but from flesh cares, acquit)
The wakefull soule it selfe assembling so,
All selfly dies; while that the body though
Lives motion-less: for, sanctified wholly,
It takes th' impression of God's Signet solely;
And in his sacred Crystall Map, doth see
Heav'ns Oracles, and Angels glorious glee:

Make more than spirit, Now, Morrow, Yesterday,
To it, all one, are all as present ay. . . .

But above all, that's the divinest Transe,
When the Souls eye beholds Gods countenance;
When mouth to mouth familiarly he deales,
And in our face his drad-sweet face he seales . . .

Now, I beleeve that in this later guise
Man did converse in Pleasant Paradise
With Heav'ns great Architect, and (happy) there
His body saw (or bodie as it were)
Gloriously compast with the blessed Legions
That raign above the azure-spangled Regions.
ADAM, quoth He, the beauties manifold
That in this Eden thou dost heer behold,
Are all thine, onely: enter (sacred Race)
Come, take possession of this wealthy place . . .
I only ask one Tree: whose fruit I will
For Sacrament shall stand of Good and Ill.
Take all the rest, I bid thee: but I vow
By th' unnam'd name, where-to all knees doe bow,
And by the keen Darts of my kindled ire
(More fiercely burning than consuming fire)
That of the fruit of Knowledge if thou feed,
Death, dreadful Death shal plague Thee & thy Seed.
. . .

Most mighty Lord (quoth Adam) heer I tender
All thanks I can, not all I should thee render
For all thy liberall favours far surmounting
My harts conceit, much more my tongues recounting.
. . .

But since thy first Law doth more grace afford
Unto the Subject, than the Soverain Lord:
Since (bounteous Prince) on me and my Descent,
Thou dost impose no other tax, nor rent,
But one sole precept, of most just condition
(No Precept neyther, but a Prohibition);
And since (good God) of all the fruits in EDEN
There's but one Apple that I am forbidden,
Even only that which bitter Death doth threat,
(Better, perhaps, to look on than to eat)

I honour in my soule, and humbly kiss
Thy just Edict (as Author of my bliss):
Which, once transgrest, deserves the rigor rather
Of sharpest Judge, than mildness of a Father.
    The Firmament shall retrograde his course,
Swift Euphrates goe hide him in his source,
Firm Mountains skip like Lambs; beneath the Deep
Eagles shall dive; Whales in the Air shall keep,
Yer I presume, with fingers ends to touch
(Much less with lips) the Fruit forbad so much.

Day I, Part ii

"The Imposture"

O who shall lend me light and nimble wings,
That (passing Swallows, & the swiftest things)
Even in a moment, boldly daring, I
From Heav'n to Hell, from Hell to Heav'n may fly?
O! who shall show the countenance and gestures
Of Mercy and Justice? Which fair sacred sisters,
With equall poiz, doe ever balance ev'n
Th' unchanging Projects of the King of Heav'n.
Th' one stern of look, the other milde-aspecting:
Th' one pleasd with tears, the other blood
    affecting.
Th' one bears the sword of vengeance un-relenting:
Th' other brings Pardon for the true-repenting.
Th' one, from Earths-Eden, Adam did dismiss:
Th' other hath rais'd him to a higher Bliss. . . .

WHILE Adam bathes in these felicities
Hell's Prince (sly parent of revolt and lies)
Feels a pestiferous busie-swarming nest
Of never-dying Dragons in his brest,
Sucking his bloud, tyring upon his lungs,
Pinching his entrails with ten thousand tongues,
His cursed Soule still most extreamly racking,
Too frank in giving torments, and in taking:
But above all, Hate, Pride, and Envious spight,
His hellish life do torture day and night,
For th' Hate he bears to God, who hath him driv'n
Justly for ever from the glittering Heav'n,
To dwell in darknesse of a sulph'ry clowd

(Though still his brethren's service be allow'd):
The Proud desire to have in his subjection
Mankind inchain'd in gyves of Sin's infection:
And th' Envious hart-break to see (yet) to shine
In Adams face Gods image all divine,
Which he had lost; and that Man might atchieve
The glorious bliss, his Pride did him deprive;
Grown barbarous Tyrant of his treacherous will,
Spurs-on his course, his rage redoubling still.
To vent his poyson, this notorious Tempter
(Meer spirit) assails not Eve, but doth attempt her
In fained form: for else, the soule divine,
Which rul'd (as Queen) that Little-worlds designe,
So purely kept her Vow of Chastity,
That he in vain should tempt her Constancy.
Much like (therefore) some theef that doth conceive
From travellers both life & goods to reave,
And in the twi-light (while the Moon doth play
In Thetis Palace) neer the Kings high-way
Himself doth ambush in a bushy Thorn;
Then in a Cave, then in a field of Corn,
Creeps too and fro, and fisketh in and out,
And yet the safety of each place doth doubt;
Till, resolute at last (upon his knee
Taking his levell) from a hollow Tree,
He swiftly sends his fire-winged messenger,
At his false sute t' arrest the passenger:
Our freedoms felon, fountain of our sorrow,
Thinks now the beauty of a Horse to borrow;
Anon to creep into a Haifer's side,
Then in a Cock, or in a Dog to hide;
Then in a nimble Hart himself to shroud;
Then in the starr'd plumes of a Peacock proud;
And lest he miss a mischiefe to effect,
Oft changeth minde, and varies oft aspect.
At last, remembring that of all the broods
In Mountains, Plains, Airs, waters, wilds, & woods,
The knotty Serpents spotty generation
Are filled with infectious inflammation . . .
He crafty cloaks him in a Dragon skin
All bright-bespect; that, speaking so within
That hollow Sagbuts supple-wreathing plies,
The mover might with th' Organ sympathize.

For, yet the faith-less Serpent (as they say)
With horror crawl'd not groveling on the clay,
Nor to Mankinde (as yet) was held for hatefull,
Sith that's the hire of his offence ingratefull.

. . .

The Dragon then, Mans Fortress to Surprise,
Follows some Captains martiall policies,
Who, yer too neer an adverse place he pitch,
The situation marks, and sounds the ditch,
With his eyes levell the steep wall he metes,
Surveies the flanks, his Camp in order sets;
And then approaching, batters sore the side
Which Art and Nature have least fortifi'd:
So, this old Souldier, having marked rife
The first-born payrs yet danger-dreadless life;
Mounting his Canons, subtly he assaults
The part he finds in evident defaults:
Namely, poor Woman, wavering, weak, unwise,
Light, credulous, new-lover, giv'n to lies.
Eve, Second honour of this Universe!
Is't true (I pray) that jealous God, perverse,
Forbids (quoth he) both you and all your race
All the fair Fruits these silver Brooks embrace;
So oft bequeathed, and by you possest,
And night and day by your own labour drest?
With th' air of these sweet words, the wily Snake
A poysoned air inspired (as it spake)
In Eves frail brest; who thus replies: O! knowe
What e'r thou be (but, thy kind care doth showe
A gentle friend) that all the fruits and flowrs
In this earths-heav'n are in our hands and powrs,
Except alone that goodly fruit divine
Which in the midst of this green ground doth shine;
But, all-good God (alas! I wot not why)
Forbad us touch that Tree, on pain to dy.
She ceast; already brooding in her heart
A curious wish, that will her weal subvert.
As a false Lover, that thick snares hath laid
T' intrap the honour of a fair young Maid,
When she (though little) listning ear affords
To his sweet, courting, deep-affected words,
Feels some asswaging of his freezing flame,

And sooths himself with hope to gain his game;
And rapt with joy, upon this point persists,
That parley'ng Citie never long resists:
Ev'n so the Serpent, that doth counterfeit
A guilefull Call t' allure us to his net;
Perceiving Eve his flattering gloze digest,
He prosecutes, and jocund, doth not rest,
Till he have try'd foot, hand, and head, and all,
Upon the Breach of this new-battered wall.
No fair (quoth he) beleeve not, that the care
God hath, mankinde from spoyling death to spare,
Makes him forbid you (on so strict condition)
This purest, fairest, rarest Fruits fruition:
A double fear, an envie, and a hate,
His jealous heart for ever cruciate;
Sith the suspected vertue of This Tree
Shall soon disperse the cloud of Idiocy,
Which dims your eyes; & further, make you seem
(Excelling us) even equall Gods to him.
O Worlds rare glory! reach thy happy hand,
Reach, reach, I say: why dost thou stop or stand?
Begin thy Bliss, and do not fear the threat
Of an uncertain God-head, onely great
Through self-aw'd zeal: put on the glistring Pall
Of immortality: doe not fore-stall
(As envious stepdame) thy posteritie
The soverain honour of Divinitie.
This parley ended, our ambitious Grandam,
Who only yet did heart and eye abandon
Against the Lord, now farther doth proceed,
And hand and mouth makes guiltie of the deed.
A novice Thief (that in a Closet spies
A heap of Gold, that on the Table lies)
Pale, fearfull shivering, twice or thrice extends,
And twice or thrice retires his fingers ends,
And yet again returns; the booty takes,
And faintly-bold, up in his cloak it makes,
Scarce finds the door, with faultring foot he flies,
And still looks back for fear of Hu-on cries:
Even so doth Eve show by like fear-full fashions
The doubtfull combat of contending Passions;
She would, she should not; glad, sad; coms & goes:
And long she marts about a Match of Woes:
But (out alas!) at last she toucheth it,

And (having toucht) tastes the Forbidden bit.
Then as a man that from a lofty Clift,
Or steepy Mountain doth descend too swift,
Stumbling at somwhat, quickly clips some lim
Of some deer kinsman walking next to him
And by his headlong fall, so brings his friend
To an untimely, sad, and sudden end;
Our Mother, falling, hales her Spouse anon
Down to the gulf of pitchy Acheron.
For, to the wisht Fruits beautifull aspect,
Sweet Nectar-taste, and wonderfull effect,
Cunningly adding her quaint smiling glances,
Her witty speech, and pretty countenances,
She so prevails, that her blind Lord, at last,
A morsell of the sharp-sweet fruit doth taste.
Now suddenly wide-open feel they might
(Siel'd for their good) both soules and bodies sight;
But the sad Soule hath lost the Character,
And sacred Image that did honour her:
The wretched Body, full of shame and sorrow
To feel it naked, is enforc't to borrow
The Trees broad leaves, whereof they aprons frame,
From Heav'ns faire eye to hide their filthy shame.
Alas, fond death-lings! O! behold how cleer
The knowledge is that you have bought so deer:
In heav'nly things yee are more blinde than Moals,
In earthly, Owls. O! think ye (silly soules)
The sight that swiftly through th' Earth's solid centers
(As globes of pure transparent crystall) enters,
Cannot transpearce your leaves? Or doe ye ween,
Covering your shame, so to conceal your sin?
Or that, a part thus clouded, all doth lie
Safe from the search of Heav'ns all-seeing eye?
Thus yet, mans troubled dull Intelligence
Had of his fault but a confused sense:
As in a dream, after much drink it chances,
Disturbed spirits are vext with raving fancies.
Therefore, the Lord, within the Garden fair,
Moving betimes I wot not I what ayre,
But supernaturall: whose breath divine
Brings of his presence a most certain signe:
Awakes their Lethargie, and to the quick,

Their self-doom'd soules doth sharply press and
prick:
Now more and more making their pride to fear
The frowning visage of their Judge severe:
To seek new-refuge in more secret harbors
Among the dark shade of those tufting arbors.
Adam, quoth God, (with thundring majesty)
Where art thou (wretch!) What dost thou? answer
me
Thy God and Father; from whose hand, thy health
Thou hold'st, thine honour, and all sorts of wealth.
At this sad summons, wofull man resembles
A bearded rush that in a river trembles:
His rosie cheeks are changed to earthen hew;
His dying body drops in ycie deaw;
His tear-drown'd eyes, a night of clouds bedims;
About his ears, a buzzing horror swims;
His fainted knees, with feebleness, are humble;
His faultring feet doe slide away and stumble:
He hath not (now) his free, bold, stately port;
But down-cast looks, in fearfull slavish sort.
Now, nought of Adam, doth in Adam rest;
He feeles his senses pain'd, his soule opprest:
A confus'd hoast of violent passions jar;
His flesh and spirit are in continuall war:
And now no more (through conscience of his error)
He hears or sees th' Almighty, but with terror:
And loth he answers (as with tongue distraught)
Confessing (thus) his fear, but not his fault.
O Lord! thy voyce, thy dreadful voyce hath
made
Me (fearfull) hide me in this covert shade.
For naked as I am (O most of might!)
I dare not come before thine awfull sight.
Naked (quoth God)? Why (faith-less renegate,
Apostate Pagan) Who hath told thee that?
When springs thy shame? What makes thee thus to run
From shade to shade, my presence still to shun?
Hast thou not tasted of the learned Tree,
Whereof (on pain of death) I warned thee?
O righteous God (quoth Adam) I am free
From this offence: the wife thou gavest me,
For my companion and my comforter,
She made me eat that deadly meat with her.

And thou (quoth God) O! thou frail
treacherous Bride,
Why, with thy self, hast thou seduc'd thy Guide?
Lord (answers Eve) the Serpent did intice
My simple frailty to this sinfull vice.
Mark heer, how He, who fears not who reform
His high Decrees, not subject unto form,
Or stile of Court: who, all-wise, hath no need
T' examine proof or witness of the deed:
Who for sustayning of unequall Scale,
Dreads not the doom of a Mercuriall;
Yer Sentence pass, doth publicly convent,
Confront, and hear with eare indifferent
Th' Offenders sad: then with just indignation,
Pronounces thus their dreadfull Condemnation.
Ah cursed Serpent, which my fingers made
To serve mankinde: th' hast made thy selfe a blade
Wherewith vain Man and his inveigled wife
(Self-parricides) have reft their proper life.
For this thy fault (true Fountain of all ill)
Thou shalt be hateful 'mong all creatures still:
Groveling in dust, on dust thou ay shalt feed:
I'le kindle war between the Woman's seed,
And thy fell race; hers on the head shall ding
Thine: thine againe hers in the heel shall sting.
Rebell to me, unto thy kindred curst,
False to thy husband, to thy self the worst,
Hope not, thy fruit so eas'ly to bring-forth
As now thou slay'st it: hence-forth every Birth
Shall torture thee with thousand sorts of pain;
Each artire, sinew, muscle, joynt and vein,
Shall feel his part: besides foul vomitings,
Prodigious longings, thought-full languishings,
With change of colours, swouns, and many others,
Eternall fellows of all future mothers:
Under his yoak, thy husband thee shall have,
Tyrant, by thee made the Arch-tyrants slave.
And thou disloyall which hast hearkned more
T'a wanton fondling, than my sacred lore,
Henceforth the sweat shall bubble on thy brow:
Thy hands shall blister and thy back shall bow:
Ne'r shalt thou send into thy branchie veines
A bit, but bought with price of thousand pains.
For, the earth feeling (even in her) th' effect

Of the doom thundred 'gainst thy foul defect;
In stead of sweet fruits which she selfly yields
Seed-less and Art-less over all thy fields,
With thorns and burs shall bristle up her brest:
(In short) thou shalt not taste the sweets of rest
Till ruth-less Death by his extreamest pain
Thy dust-born bodie turn to dust again.
Heer I conceive that flesh & blood will brangle,
And murmuring Reason with th' Almighty wrangle,
Who did our parents with Free-will indue,
Though he fore-saw, that that would be the clew
Should lead their steps into the wofull way
Where life is death ten thousand times a-day:
Now all that he fore-sees, befals: and further
He all events by his free powr doth order.
Man taxeth God of too-unjust severity,
For plaguing Adams sin in his posterity:
So that th' old years renewed generations
Cannot asswage his venging indignations
Which have no other ground to prosecute,
But the mis-eating of a certain fruit.
O dusty wormling! dar'st thou strive and stand
With Heav'ns high Monarch? Wilt thou (wretch) demand
Count of his deeds? Ah! shall the Potter make
His clay, such fashion, as him list, to take?
And shall not God (Worlds founder Natures Father)
Dispose of man (his own meer creature) rather?
The supreme King, who (Judge of greatest Kings)
By number, weight and measure, acts all things,
Vice-loathing Lord, pure Justice, Patron strong,
Law's life, Right's rule; will he do any wrong?
Man, holdest thou of God thy frank Free-will,
But free t' obey his sacred goodness still?
Freely to follow him, and do his best,
Not Philtre-charm'd, nor by Busiris prest?
God arms thee with discourse: but thou (O wretch!)
By the keen edge the wound-soule sword dost catch;
Killing thy selfe, and in thy loins thy line.
O banefull Spider (weaving wofull twine)
All Heav'ns pure flowrs thou turnest into poyson:
Thy sense reaves sense: thy reason robs thy reason.

For thou complainest of Gods grace, whose Still
Extracts from dross of thine audacious ill,
Three unexpected goods; praise for his name;
Bliss for thy self; for Satan endless-shame:
Sith, but for sin, Justice and Mercy were
But idle names: and but that thou didst erre,
CHRIST had not come to conquer and to quell,
Upon the Cross, Sin, Satan, Death, and Hell;
Making thee blessed more since thine offence,
Than in thy primer happy innocence. . . .

Now, Adams fault was not in deed so light,
As seemes to Reason's sin-bleard Owlie sight:
But 't was a chain where all the greatest sins
Were one in other linked fast, as Twins:
Ingratitude, pride, treason, gluttony,
Too-curious skill-thirst, envie, felony,
Too light, too-late belief; were the sweet baits
That made him wander from Heav'ns holy straights.

Day I, Part iii

"The Furies"

Rebellious Adam, from his God revolting,
Findes his yerst-subjects 'gainst himselfe insulting:
The tumbling Sea, the Aire with tempests driv'n,
Thorn-bristled Earth, the sad and lowring Heav'n
(As from the oath of their allegeance free)
Revenge on him th' Almightie's injury. . . .

So soon as God from Eden Adam drave,
To live in this Earth (rather in this Grave,
Where raign a thousand deaths) he summon'd up
With thund'ring call the damned Crew, that sup
Of Sulph'ry Styx, and fiery Phlegeton,
Bloody Cocytvs, muddy Acheron.
Heer first comes DEARTH, the lively form of Death,
Still yawning wide, with loathsom stinking breath,
With hollow eys, with meager cheeks and chin,
With sharp lean bones pearcing her sable skin . . .
Insatiate Orque, that even at one repast,
Almost all creatures in the World would waste . . .

Next marcheth WAR, the mistriss of enormity,
Mother of mischiefe, monster of Deformity:
Laws, Maners, Arts, she breaks, she mars, she chaces:
Bloud, tears, bowrs, towrs, she spils, swils, burns, and razes. . . .
Feare and Despaire, Flight and Disorder, coast
With hasty march, before her murderous hoast. . . .

Heer's th' other FURIE (or my judgement fails)
Which furiously mans wofull life assails . . .
Blinde, crooked, cripple, maymed, dear, and mad,
Cold-burning, blistered, melancholike, sad . . .
So this fell Fury, for fore-runners, sends
Manie and Phrenzie to suborne her friends . . .
And now the Palsie, and the Cramp dispose
Their angry darts; this bindes, and that doth lose
Mans feeble sinews, shutting up the way
Whereby before the vital spirits did play.
Al-ready th' Asthma, panting, breathing tough,
With humors gross the lifting Lungs doth stuff . . .
And feeble Age is seldom-times without
Her tedious guests, the Palsie and the Gout,
Coughs and Catarrhs. And so the Pestilence,
The quartan-Ague with her accidents. . . .

Who alwaies murder and revenge affect,
Who feed on bloud, who never do respect
State, Sex, or Age: but in all humane lives
In cold Bloud, bathe their parricidiall knives;
Are stiled Valiant. Grant, good Lord, our Land
May want such valour whose selfe-cruel hand
Fights for our foes, our proper life-bloud spils,
Our Cities sucks, and our owne Kindred kills.

Day I, Part iv

"The Handicrafts"

Rein-searching God, thought-sounding Judge, that tries
The will and heart more than the work and guise,
Accepts good Abels gift: but hates the other
Profane oblation of his furious brother;

Who feeling deep th' effects of Gods displeasure
Raves, frets, and fumes & murmurs out of measure.
. . .

But, one day drawing with dissembled love
His harm-less brother far into a Grove,
Upon the verdure of whose Virgin-boughs
Bird had not pearcht, nor never Beast did brouz;
With both his hands he takes a stone so huge,
That in our age three men could scarcely bouge,
And just upon his tender brothers crown,
With all his might he cruell casts it down.
The murdred face lies printed in the mud,
And lowd for vengeance cryes the martyr'd blood . . .

While through a Forrest Tubal (with his Yew
And ready quiver) did a Boar pursue,
A burning Mountain from his fiery vain
An yron River rowls along the Plain:
The witty Huntsman, musing, thither hies,
And of the wonder deeply 'gan devise. . . .

But Adam guides, through paths but seldom gone,
His other Sons to Vertues sacred Throne:
And chiefly Seth (set in good Abel's place)
Staff of his age, and glory of his race. . . .

While on a day by a cleer Brook they travell,
Whose gurgling streams frizado'd on the gravell,
He thus bespake: If that I did not see
The zeal (dear Father) that you bear to mee . . .
I should misdoubt to seem importunate . . .
But your milde Love my studious heart advances
To ask you further of the various chances
Of future times: what off-spring spreading wide
Shall fill this World: What shal the World
betide? . . .

With sacred fury suddenly he glowes,
Not like the Bedlam Bacchanalian froes . . .
But as th' Imperial airy peoples Prince,
With stately pinions soaring-hy from hence . . .
So Adam, mounted on the burning wings
Of a Seraphick love, leaves earthly things,

Feeds on sweet Aether, cleaves the starry Sphears,
And on Gods face his eyes he fixtly bears:
His brows seem brandisht with a Sun-like fire,
And his purg'd body seems a cubit higher . . .

O strange to be beleev'd! the blessed Race,
The sacred Flock, whom God by speciall grace
Adopts for his, ev'n they (alas!) most shame-less
Do follow sin, most beastly-brute and tame-less,
With lustfull eyes choosing for wanton Spouses
Mens wicked daughters; mingling so the houses
Of Seth and Cain; preferring foolishly
Frail beauties blaze to vertuous modesty.
From these profane, foul, cursed kisses sprung
A cruell brood, feeding on blood and wrong;
Fell Gyants strange, of haughty hand and minde,
Plagues of the World, and scourges of Mankinde.
Then, righteous God (tho ever prone to pardon)
Seeing his mildness but their malice harden,
List pleade no longer, but resolves the Fall
Of man forth-with, and (for mans sake) of all:
Of all (at least) the living creatures gliding
Along the ayr, or on the earth abiding.
Heav'ns crystall windows with one hand he opes,
Whence on the world a thousand Seas he drops:
With th' other hand he gripes, and wringeth forth
The spungie Globe of th' execrable Earth,
So straightly prest, that it doth straight restore
All liquid floods that it had drunk before:
In every Rock new Rivers doe begin;
And to his ayd the snowes come tumbling in:
The Pines and Cedars have but boughs to show,
The shoars do shrink, the swelling waters grow.
Alas! so many Nephews lose I heer
Amid these deeps, that but for mountains neer,
Upon the rising of whose ridges lofty,
The lusty climb on every side for safety,
I should be seed-less: but (alas!) the Water
Swallows those Hils, and all this wide Theater
Is all one Pond. O children, whither fly-you?
Alas! Heav'ns wrath pursues you to destroy-you:
The stormy waters strangely rage and roar,
Rivers and Seas have all one common shoar,
(To wit) a sable, water-loaden Sky

Ready to rain new Oceans instantly.
O Son-less Father! O too fruitfull hanches!
O wretched root! O hurtfull, hatefull branches!
O gulfs unknown! O dungeons deep and black!
O worlds decay! O Universall wrack!
O Heav'ns! O Seas! O Earth (now Earth no more)
O flesh! O bloud! Here, sorrow stopt the door
Of his sad voyce; and, almost dead for wo,
The prophetizing spirit forsook him so.

Day II, Part i

"The Ark"

If now no more my sacred rimes distill
With Art-lesse ease from my dis-custom'd quill:
If now the Laurell, that but lately shaded
My beating Temples, be dis-leaved and vaded:
And if now banisht from the learned Fount,
And cast down head-long from the lofty Mount
Where sweet Urania sitteth to endite,
Mine humbled Muse flag in a lowly flight:
Blame these sad Times' ingratefull cruelty,
My houshold cares, my health's infirmity,
My drooping sorrows for (late) grievous losses,
My busie suits, and other bitter crosses. . . .

Day II, Part iv

"The Columnes"

If ever (Lord) the purest of my Soule
In sacred Rage were rapt above the Pole . . .
Father of Light, Fountain of learned Art,
Now, now (or never) purge my purest part . . .
That (purg'd from passion) thy divine address
May guide me through Heav'ns glistering Palaces;
Where (happily) my dear URANIA'S grace,
And her fair Sisters I may all imbrace . . .

Day III, Part iii

"The Law"

Then (zealous) calling on th' immortall God,
He smote the Sea with his dead-living Rod:
The Sea obey'd, as bay'd: the Waves controul'd,
Each upon other up to Heav'n doe fold;
Between both sides a broad deep Trench is cast,
Dri'd to the bottom with an instant blast:
Or rather, 'tis a Valley, paved (else)
With golden sands, with Pearle, and Nacre-shels;
And on each side is flanked all along
With wals of Crystall[1], beautifull and strong.
This floud-lesse Foord the Faithfull Legions passe,
And all the way their shoe scarce moisted was. . . .

Day III, Part iv

"The Captaines"

Stay, stand thou still, stand still in Gibeon;
And thou, O Moon i' th' vale of Ajalon[2] . . .

Day IV, Part iv

"The Decay"

So all at once the Isaacian Souldiers threw
Floods, Flames and Mountains on these Engins
new . . .

---

[1]Cf. P.L.,xii, 197.
[2]Verbatim in P.L., xii, 266.

ERASMO DI VALVASONE

L'Angeleida[1] (1590)

(a) Canto I, 1, 2, 4; II, 6

The ancient war in heaven shall I sing,
Through which the ways of conflict first arose,
Whence human kind on land know battle's sting
And even on the sea exchange their blows;
He who was author of the evil thing
Lies vanquished in the Abyss, in endless woes,
While everlasting palms of pure delight
Grace the glad victors in the holy Height.

Spirit, third Person in the God triune,
By whom all things are nourished in their prime,
Thou who didst see the evil forces strewn
By holy armies in that ancient time,
Deign with Thy sacred grace my heart to attune
To Thy pure knowledge of a theme sublime.
To Thee, not to the Muses, do I turn,
For they of that far war have still to learn.

A great attempt it were to set one's feet
In paths untrodden, of the primal age,
And yet devout audacity is sweet
With strange, new frenzy and with joyous rage;
With lesser escorts, I have borne the heat
Of long hard roads; and if my heart engage
A better guide from Heav'n, I may aspire
To a high work of disciplined desire.
Spirit divine, O holy Love, inspiring
Our will and knowledge past all human test,
Form Thou my song, control Thou my desiring,
Unlock the ardent utterance of my breast,
That I may rear on earth in song untiring
The story of Heaven's warfare all unblest.
Thou knowest; Thou hast seen; from Thee alone
I seek my tale of evil overthrown.

---

[1]Translation by Watson Kirkconnell. *Ottava rima*, as in the original.

(b) Canto II, 20

Valvasone appears to have been one of the first poets[1] to describe in detail the invention of artillery by the evil angels:

Another placed a nitrous, sulphurous dust
Inside an iron tube, and then with fire
Touched it within and caused it to combust
And burst abroad with crashing din most dire;
And as it flashed, a bullet forth was thrust
That sped at any mark with burning ire,
A cruel shaft that sought to imitate
The sky-hurl'd thunderbolt of God most Great.

(c) Canto II, 28-32

In his description of Lucifer, Valvasone is far inferior to Milton in sublimity. He makes the Devil a blend of Briareus, Virgil's *Fama* and the beasts in Revelation - a monster with one hundred arms, one hundred wings, seven heads, serpent locks, and a long bull's tail. To study the grotesque of the Italian's portrayal is to realize more fully the imaginative achievement of Milton in picturing Satan as not "less than Arch Angel ruind". Valvasone has simply heaped up attributes of dreadfulness, and the result is a baroque absurdity:

Amid the rest, an impious giant tall,
The cruel Leader, hundred-armed, arose;
His breast is cloaked with mail, a steely wall;
He raises fifty shields athwart his foes;
And fifty spears he wields in war's fierce brawl;
In him alone mixed lineaments disclose
A blend of all wild, wicked forms of wrong -
Sole Monster mid the monsters of his throng.

He stood above them like an Alpine peak

[1]The idea is expressed in the same year (1590) by Spenser, *Faerie Queene*, Bk I, vii, 13, and goes back to Ariosto in *Orlando Furioso*, ix, 9.

With countless shapes of horror on its back,-
Tall oaks and hollow caves and summits bleak,
Harsh torrents, and the glacier's icy track,
Gaunt rocky passes, twisted paths oblique,
Terrors and toilsome hazards, deep and black,
Fierce beasts, and, where the pathway sinks or
    soars,
A silence broken by appalling roars.

Above his black and boundless trunk there shone,
On seven heads, a cruel crown of gold,
And yet its hue seemed scorched, its brightness
    gone,
And like the Moor's dark visage to behold;
As for his back's broad base, there hung thereon
A great bull's tail, in length a thousandfold,
That drew a third part, trailing on the ground,
Of all the stars that had in heaven been found.

The seven caverns of his mouths exhaled
A cruel stench, from slimy slaver reeking;
In fourteen eyes a deadly anger flailed,
Beneath his bristling eyebrows fiercely speaking;
Across his livid cheeks stray flushes trailed
And scornful shadows, all his visage streaking,
Within whose midst dark Sorrow had her house;
While locks of writhing snakes enwreathed his brows.

Above the shoulders of his hundred arms
(I know not how) a hundred wings fulfil
His dark behests, as soaring high he charms
The weight of that great body at his will;
No wind so fierce and stormy with alarms
Darkens the ocean's billowy face with ill
As that which, as the shadowy plumes are stirred,
Blows from the evil wings of such a Bird.

(d) Canto II, 121-124

The combat between Michael and Lucifer resembles Milton's version in the sword-wound given to the latter and in the flow of angelic blood:

Then, as he spoke, the mighty sword, that flashed

More than the lightning out of heaven flung,
Into the mass of that dread body slashed
And, pausing not an instant as it swung,
Through all that it encountered cleft and gashed,
Through wing and arm and far into the lung,
Which from its deep and hideous wound outpoured,
Instead of blood, infernal gouts abhorred.

What more defense can the fierce spirit make?
Against the sword-blade that unwearied wheels
His desperation finds no arms to take
But the insensate anger that he feels,
And he is dazzled by the flames that wake
From his foe's blazing armour, and he reels
With eyes as sorely pained as if the sun
Were burning out his eyeballs, every one.

Damned to dense darkness in the shadowy deep,
He had begun at last to fear a light
That far outshone his own; he could not keep
His trembling strength before a power so bright;
So, at the deadly sword's unceasing sweep
That drove him towards the confines of the night,
He yielded, to despair at last a prey,
And, as an angry loser, fled away.

He flees; and what a countenance he shows
As he departs! His face is pale with fear;
Yet in that fear his indignation glows;
Terror and rage are mingled in his sneer;
From his fierce breast dark frenzy breathes its
woes
With heavy, red-hot breath and scalding tear.
With scorn he marvels in himself to scan
No mark of what he was when he began.

(e) Canto II, 125-131

His followers, now broken in the fight,
When they beheld him flee, ran after him;
Many had fled before, and in their flight
The troops kept not their ranks secure and trim;
They only hope, deep down, where it is night
And where the air is ever lost and dim,

To hide themselves, exempt from hostile eyes,
Far from the day and from the shining skies.

The swift-winged victors hasten on behind,
Raining continual pain from bows and slings,
And from their squadrons of celestial kind
The golden trumpet loud in gladness rings,
Till the remotest realm and farthest wind
Reëchoes with their joyful trumpetings.
Even in striking they could not refrain
From praising God in song with joyful strain.

The shattered host of evil, having lost
All their rash hopes, in desperate lament,
Had reached a region where their path was crossed
By a deep gulf that headlong earthward went;
Dazed were their faces, gazing to their cost
Down the great void of horrible descent.
A silence from lament comes swiftly o'er them
To see so stark an obstacle before them.

The swift recoil, all unforeseen and blind,
Made by the first who that dread chasm found
Smote on the face of those who came behind
And toppled many backward on the ground;
While those to rearward still, unwarned in mind
That thus the path was broken, hemmed around
With urgent pressure those who sought to keep
Their footing on the edge of that great deep.

The cruel sight of that dread precipice
That yawned in awful darkness at their feet,
Perhaps had made the impious throng dismiss
Their thought of flight, and warfare fierce repeat;
But as they paused before the black abyss,
The stern Creator, watching their retreat
And rallying ranks, rose up in wrath divine
And gave the world a formidable sign.

A sudden, fearful sound of crashing smites
From top to bottom that celestial land;
Then from its cloudy quiver in the heights
The lightning flashes at His dread demand;
A thing of terror, trailing fiery lights,

The flaming weapon leaves the great Right Hand,
And falls, and burns, and shatters all delay
Of the curs'd wretches on their downward way.

Struck down on every hand in that fierce war
By angels and by God, no longer brave,
The wicked Leader with his wicked corps
Leaped downward from the height; they sought to
save
Themselves far off; and like a beckoning door
The fearful earth yawned open with a cave;
Earth's centre then they sought, to hide their sin;
And the cleft surface closed, and shut them in.

(f) Canto III, 8-9, 17-19, 26-29, 37, 38

But the sad King, seeing disaster whelm
The good that once was his upon the Height,
Now turned his thought to founding a new realm
Among those coasts devoid of any light;
Thick shadows wreathed a garland round his helm
As he stood up his project to indite;
Swelling with lordly rage his hairy cheeks,
Out of his seven mouths he hoarsely speaks:

"O ye who once were known a heavenly race,
Noble and fair, but now a base, low throng,
Since we have lost the stars, our dwelling-place,
Domains that did of old to us belong,
'Twere well in this dim land of our disgrace
To found a new dominion, broad and strong.
Though Heaven be lost, let our fierce indignation
Make the infernal court its peer in station! . . ."

So spake he; and the gloomy prince of hate,
Holding his rusty sceptre, stern and proud,
Sat down upon his throne in royal state
And all Tartarean things before him bowed;
Yet one there was who sought to moderate
In vain his anxious heart, and cried aloud:
"Proud Sir, you have no cause to grieve for dearth.
If Heaven be lost, yet there is gain on earth.

"Nay, grieve not, for your fortune is not spent,

Though Heaven be lost, where you took second place.
Here, in the confines of your banishment,
Rule now another world as first in grace.
And if one view the land with good intent,
Its merits can all Heaven's good outface.
Here you are far more favored, it is plain:
In Heaven you served a King, but here you reign.

"You are the King of Earth; within its breast
Are gems and iron, copper, silver, gold,
To make the world more pleasant and invest
Its ways with wealth through labours manifold.
It will have valleys too, the mountain-crest,
And shores where herbs and flowers deck the wold.
It will have seas, and fish, and forests deep
Where countless birds and beasts will roam and
sleep." . . .

Roused by a speech where malice sought to grope,
The cruel Emperor raised his heart again
And fed his impious sin with impious hope
That surged within his soul in endless pain;
For though he dreams of wealth of royal scope,
His agonies of torment still remain;
He hears his promised fortune, and is glad,
Yet all his joy more suffering seems to add.

Eternal are his torment and the fire
Which, though it sears his flesh, destroys him not;
Eternal are the storms and tempests dire;
Peace never comes to soothe his sighings hot;
His great ambition and his deep desire,
His work, his will, the anguish of his lot
Are rage eternal, which still feeds unblest
Eternal woe, yet never fills his breast.

But meanwhile, through the gloomy countryside
Of the Abyss, the fallen legions wait
To rear a power in Hell whose pomp and pride
For the lost weal of Heaven may compensate;
A lofty town amid the sulphurous tide
On cliffs impregnable they build in state,
Whose gates are adamant, whose walls they seal
With triple battlements of stubborn steel.

The holy angels, who with ranging flight
Amid the elements had onward flown
To chase their broken foemen from the height,
Now that the victory was clearly known
And they were laden with the spoils of fight,
Halt at commands upon the bugles blown;
And all the squadrons through the skies retire
Triumphant to the great celestial Sire.

There the celestial Siren stood to praise
With holy harmony of sweetest notes
Her Maker, as on silver wheels she sways
The first orb in a circle as it floats,
Shedding a gracious influence down through space,
And the moist weal of the dry earth promotes.
She, at the passing of the conquering folk,
Hailed them with honour, and exultant spoke:

"Hail, O true scions of the most high God,
Unwearied valour and unvanquished skill!
Hail, and when up to Heaven ye have trod,
Whence ye have barred your brethren for their ill,
Rejoice and triumph with approving nod
As due rewards your merits shall fulfil;
For there your Father with His hand shall lay
Upon your brows a wreath of deathless bay."

EDMUND SPENSER

An Hymne of Heavenly Love (1596)

Loue, lift me vp vpon thy golden wings,
From this base world vnto thy heauens hight,
Where I may see those admirable things,
Which there thou workest by thy soueraine might,
Farre aboue feeble reach of earthly sight,
That I thereof an heauenly Hymne may sing
Vnto the god of Loue, high heauens king.

Many lewd layes (ah woe is me the more)
In praise of that mad fit, which fooles call loue,

I haue in th' heat of youth made heretofore,
That in light wits did loose affection moue.
But all those follies now I do reproue,
And turned haue the tenor of my string,
The heauenly prayses of true loue to sing.

And ye that wont with greedy vaine desire
To reade my fault, and wondring at my flame,
To warme your selues at my wide sparckling fire,
Sith now that heat is quenched, quench my blame,
And in her ashes shrowd my dying shame:
For who my passed follies now pursewes,
Beginnes his owne, and my old fault renewes.

Before this worlds great frame, in which al things
Are now containd, found any being place
Ere flitting Time could wag his eyas wings
About that mightie bound, which doth embrace
The rolling Spheres, and parts their houres by space,
That high eternall powre, which now doth moue
In all these things, mou'd in it selfe by loue.

It lou'd it selfe, because it selfe was faire;
(For faire is lou'd;) and of it selfe begot
Like to it selfe his eldest sonne and heire,
Eternall, pure, and voide of sinfull blot,
The firstling of his ioy, in whom no iot
Of loues dislike, or pride was to be found,
Whom he therefore with equall honour crownd.

With him he raignd, before all time prescribed,
In endlesse glorie and immortall might,
Together with that third from them deriued,
Most wise, most holy, most almightie Spright,
Whose kingdomes throne no thought of earthly wight
Can comprehend, much lesse my trembling verse
With equall words can hope it to reherse.

Yet O most blessed Spirit, pure lampe of light,
Eternall spring of grace and wisedome trew,
Vouchsafe to shed into my barren spright,
Some little drop of thy celestiall dew,
That may my rymes with sweet infuse embrew,
And giue me words equall vnto my thought,

To tell the marueiles by thy mercie wrought.

Yet being pregnant still with powrefull grace,
And full of fruitfull loue, that loues to get
Things like himselfe, and to enlarge his race,
His second brood though not in powre so great,
Yet full of beautie, next he did beget
An infinite increase of Angels bright,
All glistring glorious in their Makers light.

To them the heauens illimitable hight,
Not this round heauen, which we from hence behold,
Adornd with thousand lamps of burning light,
And with ten thousand gemmes of shyning gold,
He gaue as their inheritance to hold,
That they might serue him in ęternal blis,
And be partakers of those ioyes of his.

There they in their trinall triplicities
About him wait, and on his will depend,
Either with nimble wings to cut the skies,
When he them on his messages doth send,
Or on his owne dread presence to attend,
Where they behold the glorie of his light,
And caroll Hymnes of loue both day and night.

Both day and night is vnto them all one,
For he his beames doth still to them extend,
That darknesse there appeareth neuer none,
Ne hath their day, ne hath their blisse an end,
But there their termelesse time in pleasure spend,
Ne euer should their happinesse decay,
Had not they dar'd their Lord to disobay.

But pride impatient on long resting peace,
Did puffe them vp with greedy bold ambition,
That they gan cast their state how to increase
Aboue the fortune of their first condition,
And sit in Gods owne seat without commission:
The brightest Angell, euen the Child of light,
Drew millions more against their God to fight.

Th' Almighty seeing their so bold assay,
Kindled the flame of his consuming yre,

And with his onely breath them blew away
From heauens hight, to which they did aspyre,
To deepest hell, and lake of damned fyre;
Where they in darknesse and dread horror dwell,
Hating the happie light from which they fell.

So that next off-spring of the Makers loue,
Next to himselfe in glorious degree,
Degendering to hate, fell from aboue
Through pride; (for pride and loue may ill agree)
And now of sinne to all ensample bee:
How then can sinfull flesh it selfe assure,
Sith purest Angels fell to be impure?

But that eternall fount of loue and grace,
Still flowing forth his goodnesse vnto all,
Now seeing left a waste and emptie place
In his wyde Pallace, through those Angels fall,
Cast to supply the same, and to enstall
A new vnknowen Colony therein,
Whose root from earths base groundworke shold begin.

Therefore of clay, base, vile, and next to nought,
Yet form'd by wondrous skill, and by his might:
According to an heauenly patterne wrought,
Which he had fashiond in his wise foresight,
He man did make, and breathd a liuing spright
Into his face most beautifull and fayre,
Endewd with wisedomes riches, heauenly, rare.

Such he him made, that he resemble might
Himselfe, as mortall thing immortall could;
Him to be Lord of euery liuing wight,
He made by loue out of his owne like mould,
In whom he might his mightie selfe behould:
For loue doth loue the thing belou'd to see,
That like it selfe in louely shape may bee.

But man forgetfull of his makers grace,
No lesse then Angels, whom he did ensew,
Fell from the hope of promist heauenly place,
Into the mouth of death, to sinners dew,
And all his off-spring into thraldome threw;
Where they for euer should in bonds remaine,

Of neuer dead, yet euer dying paine.

Till that great Lord of Loue, which him at first
Made of meere loue, and after liked well,
Seeing him lie like creature long accurst,
In that deepe horror of despeyred hell,
Him wretch in doole would let no lenger dwell,
But cast out of that bondage to redeeme,
And pay the price, all were his debt extreeme.

Out of the bosome of eternall blisse,
In which he reigned with his glorious syre,
He downe descended, like a most demisse
And abiect thrall, in fleshes fraile attyre,
That he for him might pay sinnes deadly hyre,
And him restore vnto that happie state,
In which he stood before his haplesse fate.

In flesh at first the guilt committed was,
Therefore in flesh it must be satisfyde:
Nor spirit, nor Angell, though they man surpas,
Could make amends to God for mans misguyde,
But onely man himselfe, who selfe did slyde.
So taking flesh of sacred virgins wombe,
For mans deare sake he did a man become.

And that most blessed bodie, which was borne
Without all blemish or reprochfull blame,
He freely gaue to be both rent and torne
Of cruell hands, who with despightfull shame
Reuyling him, that them most vile became,
At length him nayled on a gallow tree,
And slew the iust, by most vniust decree.

O huge and most vnspeakeable impression
Of loues deepe wound, that pierst the piteous hart
Of that deare Lord with so entyre affection,
And sharply launching euery inner part,
Dolours of death into his soule did dart;
Doing him die, that neuer it deserued,
To free his foes, that from his heast had swerued.

What hart can feele least touch of so sore launch,
Or thought can think the depth of so deare wound?

Whose bleeding sourse their streames yet neuer
    staunch,
But stil do flow, and freshly still redound,
To heale the sores of sinfull soules vnsound,
And clense the guilt of that infected cryme,
Which was enrooted in all fleshly slyme.

O blessed well of loue, O floure of grace,
O glorious Morning starre, O lampe of light,
Most liuely image of thy fathers face,
Eternall King of glorie, Lord of might,
Meeke lambe of God before all worlds behight,
How can we thee requite for all this good?
Or what can prize that thy most precious blood?

Yet nought thou ask'st in lieu of all this loue,
But loue of vs for guerdon of thy paine.
Ay me; what can vs lesse then that behoue?
Had he required life of vs againe,
Had it beene wrong to aske his owne with gaine?
He gaue vs life, he it restored lost;
Then life were least, that vs so litle cost.

But he our life hath left vnto vs free,
Free that was thrall, and blessed that was band;
Ne ought demaunds, but that we louing bee,
As he himselfe hath lou'd vs afore hand,
And bound therto with an eternall band,
Him first to loue, that vs so dearely bought,
And next, our brethren to his image wrought.

Him first to loue, great right and reason is,
Who first to vs our life and being gaue;
And after when we fared had amisse,
Vs wretches from the second death did saue;
And last the food of life, which now we haue,
Euen himselfe in his deare sacrament,
To feede our hungry soules vnto vs lent.

Then next to loue our brethren, that were made
Of that selfe mould, and that selfe makers hand,
That we, and to the same againe shall fade,
Where they shall haue like heritage of land,
How euer here on higher steps we stand;

Which also were with selfe same price redeemed
That we, how euer of vs light esteemed.

And were they not, yet since that louing Lord
Commaunded vs to loue them for his sake,
Euen for his sake, and for his sacred word,
Which in his last bequest he to vs spake,
We should them loue, and with their needs partake;
Knowing that whatsoere to them we giue,
We giue to him, by whom we all doe liue.

Such mercy he by his most holy reede
Vnto vs taught, and to approue it trew,
Ensampled it by his most righteous deede,
Shewing vs mercie, miserable crew,
That we the like should to the wretches shew,
And loue our brethren; thereby to approue,
How much himselfe that loued vs, we loue.

Then rouze thy selfe, O earth, out of thy soyle,
In which thou wallowest like to filthy swyne
And doest thy mynd in durty pleasures moyle,
Vnmindfull of that dearest Lord of thyne;
Lift vp to him thy heauie clouded eyne,
That thou his soueraine bountie mayst behold,
And read through loue his mercies manifold.

Beginne from first, where he encradled was
In simple cratch, wrapt in a wad of hay,
Betweene the toylefull Oxe and humble Asse,
And in what rags, and in how base aray,
The glory of our heauenly riches lay,
When him the silly Shepheards came to see,
Whom greatest Princes sought on lowest knee.

From thence reade on the storie of his life,
His humble carriage, his vnfaulty wayes,
His cancred foes, his fights, his toyle, his strife,
His paines, his pouertie, his sharpe assayes,
Through which he past his miserable dayes,
Offending none, and doing good to all,
Yet being malist both of great and small.

And looke at last how of most wretched wights,
He taken was, betrayd, and false accused,
How with most scornefull taunts, and fell despights
He was reuyld, disgrast, and foule abused,
How scourgd, how crownd, how buffeted, how brused;
And lastly how twixt robbers crucifyde,
With bitter wounds through hands, through feet
and syde.

Then let thy flinty hart that feeles no paine,
Empierced be with pittifull remorse,
And let thy bowels bleede in euery vaine,
At sight of his most sacred heauenly corse,
So torne and mangled with malicious forse,
And let thy soule, whose sins his sorrows wrought,
Melt into teares, and grone in grieued thought.

With sence whereof whilest so thy softened spirit
Is inly toucht, and humbled with meeke zeale,
Through meditation of his endlesse merit,
Lift vp thy mind to th' author of thy weale,
And to his soueraine mercie doe appeale;
Learne him to loue, that loued thee so deare,
And in thy brest his blessed image beare.

With all thy hart, with all thy soule and mind,
Thou must him loue, and his beheasts embrace;
All other loues, with which the world doth blind
Weake fancies, and stirre vp affections base,
Thou must renounce, and vtterly displace,
And giue thy selfe vnto him full and free,
That full and freely gaue himselfe to thee.

Then shalt thou feele thy spirit so possest,
And rauisht with deuouring great desire
Of his deare selfe, that shall thy feeble brest
Inflame with loue, and set thee all on fire
With burning zeale, through euery part entire,
That in no earthly thing thou shalt delight,
But in his sweet and amiable sight.

Thenceforth all worlds desire will in thee dye,
And all earthes glorie on which men do gaze,
Seeme durt and drosse in thy pure sighted eye,

Compar'd to that celestiall beauties blaze,
Whose glorious beames all fleshly sense doth daze
With admiration of their passing light,
Blinding the eyes and lumining the spright.

Then shall thy rauisht soule inspired bee
With heauenly thoughts, farre aboue humane skil,
And thy bright radiant eyes shall plainely see
Th' Idee of his pure glorie, present still
Before thy face, that all thy spirits shall fill
With sweete enragement of celestiall loue,
Kindled through sight of those faire things aboue.

H. GROTII

Adamus Exul[1]

Tragoedia

Eius interlocutores

Sathan
Chorus
Angelus
Adamus
Eva
Vox Dei

Argumentum

Post rerum creationem, et Angelorum lapsum homo in Paradiso constitutus est, datum ei in inferiorem orbem Imperium, vetitumque, ne arboris quae scientiae boni et mali symbolum erat, fructum carperet. Sathan ut contra praeceptum fieret primum hominem marem simulata amicitia aggreditur, deinde foeminam serpentis figura, quae educta virum ad peccati societatem impellit. Unde uterque horto expulsus est, et morti miseriaeque mancipatus. Salus restituta spe, et fide venturi Messiae. Scena est in Hedene Babyloniae regione, ubi erat hortus, ad ripam Euphratis. Chorus est ex bonis spiritibus, quos Angelos vocamus. Sathan προλόγιζει.

---

[1]Because of the rarity and importance of this item, the original Latin is given here, facing an English translation. The text is that of the first edition (1601), from a copy, apparently now unique, in the library of the British Museum, London. American libraries report only a corrupted reprint (1750) edited by the Jacobite Milton-hater, William Lauder, who dishonestly interpolated passages from Milton's Paradise Lost in Latin translation in order to "prove" that Milton had stolen these passages from Grotius. For a general note see PL-178 in the Descriptive Catalogue.

HUGO GROTIUS

The Exile of Adam (1601)[1]

A Tragedy

Dramatis Personae

Satan
Chorus
An Angel
Adam
Eve
The Voice of God

Argument

After the primal Creation and the fall of the Angels, man is set in the terrestrial Paradise. He is given authority over this lower world but forbidden to pluck the fruit of a tree which symbolizes the knowledge of good and evil. Satan, in order to cause him to violate this condition, first assails the man under the guise of friendship and then the woman in the likeness of a serpent. The latter, having been persuaded, urges her husband on to partnership in her sin. Thereupon they are both driven out of the Garden and delivered over to death and misery. Their ultimate salvation is assured by hope and faith in a coming Messiah. The scene is in Eden, in the region of Babylon, where there was a Garden on the bank of the Euphrates. The chorus consists of those good spirits whom we call angels. Satan speaks the prologue.

---

[1]Translation by Watson Kirkconnell. Since the English blank verse line is too short to contain a line-for-line rendering of the Latin senarius, recourse has been had to the "free Alexandrines" of Robert Bridges' *Testament of Beauty*.

ACTUS PRIMUS

Trimetri Iambici

Sathan. Saevi tonantis hostis, exul patriae
Caelestis, adsum, Tartari tristem specum
Fugiens, et atram Noctis aeternae plagam.
Odium bonorum sede me infausta extrahit,
Diros scelesta mente versantem dolos.
Terribile iniquum, triste, formidabile,
Quod et ipse Sathan horream, quaero scelus.
Hac spe per omnes Orbis ibo terminos,
Hac spe citatus clausa littoribus vagis
Transibo maria, saevus ut rictu Leo
Patulo timendus per locorum devia
Quaerit quod avido dente dilaniet pecus.
Hac spe, quod unum maximum fugio malum,
Superos videbo. Fallor? an certe meo
Concussa Tellus tota trepidat pondere?
Bene est. Abunde est. Fiat hoc, fiat, nefas
Quod Mundus horret. Ecce, quae petitur, prope
Apparet Heden: proxima Auranitidos
Amoena cerno: Lambit hic Babylonios
Narmalca campos, Susianes intimis
Fugiens ab agris, Bdellii qui fertiles,
Ubi sub profundo nascitur terrae specu
Fulvum metallum, plurimusque ubi Sardonyx
Latet in fodinis: parte labitur altera
Arvis rigandis aptus unda Narsares,
Solaris ignis conscius qui fervidas
Succingit oras: propius his a partibus
Phoebi sub ortum lubricas curvans aquas
Non largus undis alveus tangit tuas
Assyria Cauchas, praeviumque in Tigridis

ACT ONE

(Iambic Senarii)

As the scene opens, Satan is discovered standing alone on an eminence commanding a wide prospect of The Garden of Eden.

Satan. The savage Thunderer's foe, exiled from
heaven, my home,
I hither come in flight from Tartarus' grim cave
And the black wilderness of everlasting Night.
Hatred has drawn me forth from that unblest abode,
Planning in wicked mind dire plots against the good.
Some awful wrong I seek, most terrible and grim,
A crime that even I, the Devil, tremble at.
In this hope, I shall go through all the Globe's
wide bounds;
Spurr'd by this hope I'll cross the seas, hemm'd in
By wandering shores; just as a cruel lion seeks
Through wandering ways, with formidable open jaws,
Some hapless flock that he may rend with greedy
fangs.
By this hope, fleeing from the greatest ill of all,
I shall attain to Heaven! Can I be wrong? Or does
The whole earth truly tremble, smitten by my
weight?
'Tis well. It is enough. Come, let this wrong
be done,
Shaking the Universe. Lo, Eden shows near by,
The object of my search; I see the neighborhood
Of pleasant Auranitis; here Narmalca laves
The Babylonian fields, fleeing the innermost
Confines of Susa, rich in Bdellium and gold,
Where in deep-bosom'd subterranean caves is born
The tawny metal, where Sardonyx lurks in quarries
Most abundant; on the other side there flows,
Apt with its waves for irrigating fields, Narsares,
That, conscious of the sun's consuming fire, girds
round
The burning coasts; still nearer, on this side,
a stream,
Fronting the dawning East, meandering as it goes,
Touches thy Cauchae, O Assyria, and falling

Delapsus amnem Persicos fugit ad sinus.
Regione dextra medius Euphrates fluit,
Et amne pingues diluit glebas suo,
Paludibusque prodigus Chaldaicis
Participat undas: Parte ab illa, quae videt
Solis renatum surgere Oceano jugum,
Iucunda sancti forma se latissime
Distendit horti, cujus in gremium fluit
Sectus quaternis tumidus Euphrates vadis.
Hic densa tenuis languidos Zephyri sonos
Arbusta referunt, silvaque arguto tremens
Ludit susurro: semper hic placido nitet
Solare vultu lumen: arridet favor
Constantis aurae: dulce adulatur dies
Firme serena fronte non nubes loco
Impendet, atri non ab irato Polo
Funduntur imbres, nec trisulci fulminis
Timet ista telum, nec tonitruum murmura
Beata novit regio: solvit frigora
Tepor benignus, Verque perpetuum gravem
Defendit hyemem: nullus horrenti fremit
Boreas ab Arcto: nullus aetherias aquas
Minatur auster. Quicquid est optabile,
Gratumque in unum pariter adfluxit locum,
Iusso exulare, quicquid est alibi, malo.
Quaecunque visus arbor, aut gustus juvat
Convenit: omneis iste delicias locus,

With narrow channel into Tigris' mightier flood,
Merges its waters till it finds the Persian gulf.
Amid the right-hand tract the broad Euphrates flows,
Washing the fertile clods with its life-giving stream,
And shares its waves, most generous, with marsh and pool
Across Chaldea; on that side which contemplates
The Sun's resurgent crest arising from the sea,
A sacred Garden's pleasant form spreads far and wide,
Into whose leafy bosom the Euphrates flows
And pours its swelling flood through fourfold arteries.
Here the dense groves give back the languid harmonies
Of the light Zephyr; and the woods all tremulous
Sport with melodious whisper; ever the sunlight here
Shines with calm countenance; a constant breeze's grace
Smiles on it; day fawns in delightful constancy
With peaceful brow; above that spot no shadowing cloud
Hangs hostile; nor does dark rain shower down in wrath
Out of an angry sky; the blessed region fears
No fiery bolt of three-fork'd lightning, neither knows
The rumblings of the thunder. Kindly warmth dissolves
All touch of chill and cold; perpetual spring wards off
The war of winter. Here no north wind rages loud
Out of the shuddering Arctic; nor do South winds threaten
A rainstorm from the sky. All things desirable,
All things that please and charm have flow'd into one spot;
All else goes otherwhere, to exile and to ill.
Whatever tree seems good, with fruit of grateful taste,
Has gather'd in this place; all sweet things, all delights

Et amoena servat, quem beatae prodigus
Sortis colendum tribuit Adamo Deus.
Postquam ille coeli Machinam candentibus
Astris repletam, fertilisque effecerat
Telluris orbem, jamque roseis per polum
Invecta bigis sexta fulgeret dies,
Quo nil sub astris majus Orbis cerneret
HOMINEM creavit, pulveremque ignobilem
In justa finxit membra, et inflata pater
Vegetavit aura, nec tamen vitam dedit
Sensusque solos, propriae sed imaginis
Expressit altum mente in humana decus,
Docuitque eundem qualis, et cuia manu
Formatus esset nunc, prius qui non erat.
Quaecunque volucris aerem, terram fera,
Vel Piscis undas habitat, illius omnia
Parent habenis tota qua tellus patet
Unius ager est quaeque possideat sola
Nec ipse novit dominus; et quicquid vago,
Quae varia lucis non suae alternans vices
Refugit in orbem, Luna continet ambitu,
Saevo Tyrannus unus imperio premit.
Tantique regni generis ut serie suus
Superesset haeres, uxor Adamo data est.
Ex osse fictam masculino foeminam
Miratus Orbis stupuit, et Titan novus
Vidisse nil tam meminit admirabile
Post se creatum: nunc uterque in florido
Spatiatur horto nudus: omnis abest Pudor
Rudibus malorum: fraudis expers, et doli
Sincera virtus colitur, et grato Deus
Celebratur ore: nulla securos mali
Vexat cupido: mortis ambo vulnera
Impune temnunt: Morbus, et Lethi dolor,

The spot preserves, which God, most bountiful in good,
On Adam hath bestow'd, that he may cultivate.
For after He had made the Frame of heaven, fill'd
With shining stars, and wrought the globe of fertile earth,
And now across the sky on rosy chariot-wheels
The sixth day issued forth in gleaming majesty,
He fashion'd MAN, than whom, beneath the stars, Earth saw
No thing created greater; from the ignoble dust
The Almighty Father shaped the human form and quickened
The body with His breath; nor gave He life alone
And lively sense, but deep within the human mind
He stamped at last the glorious image of Himself.
And taught that same Man who he was and by whose hand
He had been fashion'd, who before had had no being.
And whatsoever fowl inhabits air, what beast
Or fish inhabits earth or sea, all these obey
His human rule. All earth, however wide it spreads,
Is the sole territory of a single master
Who knows not his own realm; all that the roving Moon,
Who with her changing aspects of a borrow'd light
Wheels in a circle, environs in her wandering,
Yields to the harsh authority of one stern lord.
In order that an heir to imperial realms so vast
In sequence might succeed, a wife was giv'n to Adam.
At woman rarely fashion'd from the bone of man
Earth marvell'd in amaze, and the primordial Sun
Could think upon no creature more endow'd with grace
Since he himself was made; now both in flowering garden
Walk wholly naked, for no sense of shame have they,
To evil uninitiate; virtue is cherish'd,
Exempt from fraud and guile, and there with grateful lip
They give their Maker praise; no itching lust disquiets
Those free from evil; with impunity both scorn
The wounds of Death; Disease, and deadly Pain, and Fear

Ipsoque vel dolore deterior metus
Fugiunt ab illis. Sorte, Proh, quantum mea
Sors distat ista! Nos rotanti sidera
Coelo coaevi, non vel ignis proditi
Fervente flamma, vel tepore volatili
Humentis aurae, non aqua, aut Terrae gravis
Torpente gleba, sed sine ulla corporum
Compage facti maximo aequales Deo
Mancipia poenae vivimus, nec vivimus.
Mors una, quam nec novit humanus timor
Mihi summa voti est, nec, quod extremum est malis,
Licet perire. Media quo tellus loco
Subsidit, ad se gravia quo trahit, et duos
Spatio remotos spectat aequali Polos,
Hic ora solvit Tartari invisi domus,
Ignota radiis Solis: immensis hiat
Caverna tenebris: ambitu obscuro patet
Tristis vorago: spissa caligo specum
Occupat inanem: vastus hic horror silet,
Et ampla vacuo spatia laxantur loco.
Mersum profundis omne Sathanum genus
Latet sub antris: quicquid infensi dare
Potuit Tonantis ira, nos vexat malum.
Sedet repostum mente sub memori scelus,
Animosque duros stimulat, et serus pudor
Semper quietem conscio cordi negat.
Luctus pavorque regnat, et certus timor,
Et herilis ira sequitur: interdum dolor
Mutatur odio, poenae et impatiens reus,
Ut saevus hostis, ardet, et summum putat
Inferre nulli posse, quod patitur, malum,
Miserosque non sic esse, quam solos, dolet.
Poenam levabit socius: Hedenis licet

(Itself more horrible than all the pangs of Pain)
Flee from them. Ah, how different is that lot of theirs
From my harsh lot! We who were stars, coeval made
With all the wheeling sky, unharm'd by the fervent flame
Of white sidereal fire or by the fluid chill
Of clammy air or water or the numbing clod
Of heavy earth, -- we, without bond of bodies made
The spiritual peers of Him, the most high God,
Now scarcely live as slaves; our life is less than life;
Extinction, which the fear of mankind knows not yet,
Is my supreme desire; and -- utmost of my ills --
I may not perish. In that spot where midmost earth
Sinks darkly down, and draws within itself things heavy,
And gazes from an equal distance at both Poles,
Here hated Tartarus' subterrane opes its maw,
By suns unlit; immeasureable shadows fill
The yawning cavern, and a murky whirlpool gapes
With circuit grim; thick darkness floods the emptiness
Of that vast pit; here silent horror broods unplumb'd,
And termless spaces here grow yet more infinite.
Plunged in these sunless deeps, the whole Satanic race
Is hidden in earth's entrails, and whatever ill
Th' offended Thunderer's wrath can give, harasses us.
Still cherish'd in the memory our crime remains
And goads our harden'd hearts, and shame, now learn'd too late,
Eternally denies the conscious soul all peace.
Grief reigns, and Panic, and the sceptre of sure Fear,
And God's wrath still pursues us; but at times our pain
Is turn'd to hatred, scorns the penalties of guilt,
And, burning in dire wrath, thinks the extremest woe
Can add no anguish to its present sufferings.
We grieve to think ourselves alone in punishment:
Companionship would lighten it. Let Adam till

Colat arva felix, speque non dubia meum
Super astra sibi promittat Adamus locum,
Tutoque conjunx perfruatur gaudio,
Non sic abibunt odia: nec vivax dolor
Deponet iras: Pace sublata procul
Perpetua bella pertinax animus geret.
Violenta certam mens aget discordiam
Malum datura. quod malum? quicquid boni
Aetherea servat aula, vel Tellus creat
Amica, quicquid Pelagus, aut aër habet
Gratum, ejus omne est. Bella contemnit mea,
Hostemque dedignatur: in risus suos
Mea vertit odia: certus, et fisus Deo
Iamjam parata tendit ad coelum via.
Hoc, hoc videndum est, regna ne summa occupet,
Qui jam tenet terrena. tum demum Poli
Fugisse ab arce pudeat imbellem exulem,
Si, ut dentur alii, regna deserui mea,
Locumque generi pulsus humano dedi.
Perge ira, perge, magna conantem opprime,
Adsitque ab alto Tartari fundo excitum
Quicquid profunda conditur caligine.
Fauces Averni, et Noctis aeternae Chaos
Adversa superis regna, sociique impii
Una ruina simul in hostem emittite,
Quodcunque nostrum est. Veniat ignotum Scelus,
Cujusque nos didicimus experti malum
Parere jussis imparata Superbia.
Adsit rebellis maximo impietas Deo,
Gravis adsit Error, adsit Ambitio nova
Rerum novarum cupida; non illex gulae
Desit libido, vana nec falsi fides,
Levitasque rebus credula in non cognitis.
His his ministris noster utetur dolor.
Quaecunque pestis Tartaro obscuro sata

In bliss the fields of Eden, and in confidence
Promise himself my place above the stars. Let him
A husband, revel in safe hymeneal joys,
Yet will my enmity remain, enduring grief
Will not lay down its anger. Peace having been renounced,
My soul importunate shall wage perpetual wars,
And my fierce mind shall stir up certain discord, thus
Intent on working ill. What evil? All things good
That Heaven's court possesses or the kind Earth brings forth,
All things delightful in the Sea or in the Air --
All, all are Adam's. And he scorns my rivalry,
Despises me as foe, and turns my enmity
Into his laughter. Trusting constantly in God
He presses on towards heaven by the path prepared.
This, this must be withstood, lest he who now rules earth
Should seize a throne celestial! Then might I indeed
Blush to have fled, a coward exile, from the sky,
If I but left my realms that others might possess
And in defeat bestow'd my place on humankind.
Come, Anger, come! And smite the rash pretender down!
Aroused from the abysmal gulf of Tartarus,
Let all the brood of Darkness rally to my cause!
Maw of Avernus, gape! Chaos and timeless Night,
Realms hostile to the Highest, impious mates of mine,
Yea, all that name my name, now issue on the foe
In one fell charge of ruin! Let Sin come, unknown
To man as yet, and Pride, that scorns to heed commands,--
Pride that ourselves, expert in evil, well can teach!
Let red Impiety against the Most High God
With leaden Error come, and raw Ambition, eager
For violent revolt; nor let the Belly's Lust
Be lacking to our cause, nor empty Faith in Lies,
Nor Levity that puts its trust in things unknown!
These, these shall be the servants that our pain employs!
Ah, let some pest, begotten in dim Tartarus,

Blando Cerastas lubricos vultu tegis
Hoc agite: poenas poscite exilii graves,
Ruptoque Averni carcere, et nigri specus
Portis ahenis, latiorem invadite
Telluris orbem: pectus Adami malis
Concutite, cesset nulla peccato manus.
Ubi laetus hortum lambit Euphratis latex,
Quocunque spectes media ramos exserit
Arbos, opacis lumen admittens comis.
Ubique grato poma pendent pondere,
Curvantque matrem: fulvus his auri color
Delectat oculos, spemque non vanam facit
Placere gustu posse: sed vetuit Deus
Tangi, nec ulla passus est carpi manu,
Scientiamque tam malorum, quam boni
Poenam severus statuit, et sanxit minis:
Nam mancipatus nunc homo virtutibus
Ignorat omne crimen; in medio tamen
Utriusque positus, cum volet, flectet viam.
Quocunque vento flante poterit libera
Pelli uoluntas: parte dimidia nocens,
Qui velle potuit, esse coepit. Spem mea
Capit ira: recta si recedens semita
Semel caducos devium per tramitem
Gressus movebit, gemina et animae, et corpori
Decreta mors est. Poma si vetitae arboris
Gustabit unquam, subito in exitium ruet,
Poenasque socius, Tartari et novus incola
Pro perpetrato scelere communes dabit.
Accingere ira: si moveri vir potest,
Tentetur ipse: si moveri non potest,
Tentetur eius uxor: hoc prosit mihi
Non esse solum: Foeminae ingenium leve,
Negligere jussa facile, nee coepti tenax
Variatur ultro, plurimum indulget sibi,
Majora semper spe superba praecipit,
Amatque solum, quo caret: prae incognitis

Concealing slimy snakes beneath a kindly face,
Assume this task! Exact strict penalties for exile,
And having burst the brazen prison-doors of Hell
And issued from its melancholy cave, invade
Earth's broader sphere; smite Adam's breast with
    evil plagues,
And let no hand retreat from havoc and offence!
Where the glad water of Euphrates laves the Garden,
Where'er you gaze amid the trees thick branches
    grow,
Admitting dappled light through shady foliage.
In every place the apples hang with pleasing weight,
Bending the mother-tree. Their yellow tint of gold
Delights the eye, and rouses an effectual hope
That they can please the taste; but God forbids
    to touch,
Nor is a human hand permitted e'er to pluck.
Knowledge of evil and of good He has assign'd
Strictly as penalty, and ratified by threats.
For man, in utter servitude to virtues now,
Is ignorant of crime; placed none the less between
Alternate choices, he may freely turn his course.
By any wind that blows, his liberty of will
May be deflected; half already lost to grace,
He who can wish to sin, begins to be a sinner.
My wrath takes hope. If once he leaves the path
    of right,
And moves with wicked steps by a mistaken road,
A double death, of body and of soul as well,
Has been decreed him. If he ever taste the fruit
Of the forbidden tree, he will rush straight to
    ruin,
And will, as Hell's new inmate and my sworn ally,
Share in our common penalties for sin and crime.
My Anger, gird thyself! If Adam can be moved,
Let him be tempted! But if naught can sway his
    faith,
Let us essay his wife! Let this advantage me,
That he is not alone. The female mind is light;
Prone to neglect commands, fickle in undertakings,
She varies willingly; wanton in self-indulgence,
She reaches ever in proud hope for greater gain,
Loves only what she lacks, and finds familiar
    things

Antiqua sordent: displicet, quod non novum est.
Sortis beatae taedium, inconstantia,
Spes vana, Pomi dulcis aspectu color,
Gustus cupido, quod volo spondent mihi:
Spondet sine illis Mulier, apta author malis.
Sed audietne, quem sibi infensum putat,
Mihique vacuas hostis aures porriget?
Pax offeratur: mente depositum pia
Simuletur odium: qui palam laedit, juvat.
Gestare nescit odia, quisquis non tegit.
Facile est amorem fingere, atque optans sibi
Mentitur ipsi. Credula est spes improba.
Dicam futuros Numini summo pares,
Novosque Divos. Forte non possent capi,
Nisi magna vellent capere: stat facilis fides
Sequuta votum. Si tamen firma in bonum
Haeret voluntas, si mihi facilem negat
Inimicus aurem, forma sumetur nova.
Non oculus ullus Daemonum cernit genus,
Non aliqua tangit dextra: nil sensus suum
Reperit in illis. Forma materie carens
Simplexque species alia quaevis corpora
Assumit, et sic sensui foris obvia
Dat se videndam. Consili sapiens mei
Serpens minister fiat: animal callidum
Servire fas est spiritus vafri dolis.
Anguis per horti lubricum repens solum
Ignotus ibo: lingua sermones seret
Trisulca: verbis virus inflabo meum,
Et qui venenum maximum spirat draco
Majus loquetur: utraque tentanda est via,
Fallamque gemina fraude sub amico virum,
Evam sub angue. Stabo et urgebo scelus,
Regamque edentis ora, carpentis manus.
Quid adhuc moramur? ista quae lucet dies

Tarnish'd, and strange things fair. What is not
new displeases.
Her blest lot's tedium, her frail inconstancy,
Vain hopes, the color of the sweet-appearing fruit,
Her lust to taste -- all these assure me my desire.
Woman, apt source of ill, is sure without the rest.
But first, will Adam hear me, whom he deems his foe?
Will he, my enemy, vouchsafe a willing ear?
Let peace be offer'd; and let hatred, set aside,
Be cloak'd; for open enmity assists one's foe.
Who cannot hide his hatred, cannot gain its ends.
Love's easy of pretence; and he who deigns to hope
Lies to himself. Base hope is ever credulous.
I'll say that they will be the peers of God Most
High,
New deities. Perhaps they cannot be enticed
Unless they wish great things. Faith that pursues
an aim
Is easy of access. But if his will clings firm
To what is good; if he, my enemy, denies
An easy hearing, I shall alter then my shape.
No eye of humankind can see the race of Demons,
No hand can touch their substance, nor can senses
find
Aught of their own in them; but unsubstantial form
And empty semblance can be turn'd to any shape
And proffer itself forth abroad to be beheld
By human sense. In this, the snake, who knows my
wile,
Shall be my servant; for a cunning animal
Serves best the dark contrivance of a subtile spirit.
Thus I shall pass unknown, a serpent crawling sly
On the moist Garden's floor. My three-fork'd
tongue will sow
Most cunning discourse, breathing poison with my
words.
So shall the snake, most venomous of things created,
A greater venom speak. Both issues must I try,
By two-fold fraud: Adam seduce in guise of friend,
Eve, as a snake. I'll stand and fan the flames of
crime.
I shall control the eater's mouth, the plucker's
hand.
Why do we yet delay? This very day that dawns

Homini parem me reddat, aut hominem mihi.

CHORUS

Anapaestica Dimetri et Monometri

Quisquis ab alto culmine rerum
Infra se humili sede locatos
Despicit audax, videat ne mox
Urgente suam mole ruinam
Pondere sidat: gravior semper
Casus ab alto est. Levius contra
Leviora cadunt. Sequitur major
Cura beatos, quo plus nactos
Plura timentes.
Qui modo magni civis Olympi
Aurea coeli templa tenebat
Nunc occlusus tristique specus
Conditus umbra poena nunquam
Pereunte perit, soloque Deo
Ante inferior, dum minor uno
Esse recusat, nunc supra se
Omnia cernit.
Quanto praeceps cecidit lapsu
Qui prius alma luce coruscus,
Quique aetheria splendidus aura
Stabat in ortu! Talis Eoa
Parte diei fax Luciferi
Praevia Solis grata sereno
Lumine fulget, quae mutato
Nomine surgens dux tenebrarum,
Noctis et atrae signifer exit
Hesperus idem.
Quid in exitium ruiture tuum
Rerum authori parere negas,
Cumque obtigerit res quae potuit
Maxima, frustra majora paras?
Hoc esse, quod est solus, qui te
Facit esse cupis. Pugnas illi
Cui nihil obstat.
Extimus orbis complectentis
Caetera coeli, quem felices
Habitant turmae, celebransque suum
Sub mille Choris vox grata Deum,

Shall make me peer to man or draw man down to me.

CHORUS

Let him who, from the Heaven's height,
On those below in humbler flight
Looks boldly down, beware lest he
By his own weight fall presently
In ruin down; for the descent
Is graver to the eminent.
While lighter things more lightly fall,
Intenser cares the blest enthral
With fears proportion'd to their gains.
He who but now in Heaven's domains
And golden temples of the sky
Resided, in the Pit must die
With pain undying and the gloom
Of that deep dungeon of his doom.
Erst was he less than God alone;
Now less than all things lies he prone,
Since he disdain'd that second place.
     How headlong fell he in disgrace
Who used to shine with gracious light
And at his rising in the height
Stood radiant forth, whether at dawn
As Lucifer his glory shone,
The Sun's serenest harbinger,
Or changed in title would recur
And rise as Hesperus again
And lead the shadows from their den
As standard-bearer of black Night!
     O thou so swift thy fate to blight,
Why dost thou not in grace obey
Th' omnipotent Creator's sway,
And why, when thou so high art set,
Wouldst thou, in vain, soar higher yet?
Thou wouldst be that which only He
Can be who has created thee.
With weapons impotent and dull
Thou fightest the Invincible.
     That farthest sphere, that heavenly shell,
Where hosts of happy spirits dwell,
And from a thousand choirs raise
To God a grateful voice of praise,

Quem nec celeri turbine versat
Lex redeuntis certa diei,
Nec qui Lunae variat formas
Menstruus ordo, nec qui celeres
Tempestatum labente vices
Digerit anno, sed perpetua
Tenet immotum statione quies,
Prope tunc visus nutare loco est,
Dum male Sathan movet aetherias
Transfuga sedes, bellumque ciet.
Sensit turbas Sphaera rebelles,
Totusque nefas horruit aether,
Geminique Poli tremuere malis,
Nec bene firmus substitit axis,
Et Naturae facie versa
Metuit tingi Cynosura salo,
Metuere graves Aras aquilones,
Heliceque Notos.
Ipse inciperet mox Aegoceros
Laxare diem, Cancerque breves
Ducere noctes, Solque in tenebras
Capiens regnum tradere lucis
Jura sorori, nisi magna Dei
Jussa capessens sumpserat audax
Arma Michaël. Ille rebelles
Domuit turmas: Ille tenaci
Compede vinctas jussit superis
Migrare locis, et praecipites
In Tartareas depulit umbras.
Illius armis prostrata jacet
Furiosa cohors, quae poenarum
Monet exemplo potiora sequi.
Eheu satis est. Haec mala finem
Dent criminibus, dent suppliciis,
Nec quem in bivio dubium versat
Vitii labes, haerensque pio
Pectore virtus deflectat HOMO
Trepidum recto de calle gradum,
Possit ut illo sata progenies
Tandem coeli vacuum exilio
Supplere locum.

That sphere which sure diurnal laws
Wheel not in motion, neither draws
In monthly sequence there of change
The Moon's bright phases through their range,
Nor does the passage of the year
Receive its seasons from that sphere:
That realm, which rather seems to stay
Unmoved in endless peace alway,
Was almost shaken in its place
When Satan, traitor to his race,
Stirr'd up foul war the sprites among.
The Sphere perceived the rebel throng;
All aether shudder'd at the sin;
The Poles with trembling fear did spin;
Nor did the Axis steadfast hold;
The pole-star, seeing manifold
The change in nature, fear'd the Ocean;
The Altar fear'd the north wind's motion;
The Great Bear fear'd the south wind's force.
Then Capricorn had changed earth's course
With lengthening days, and Cancer's sleights
Had been the lead in shorter nights,
The Sun had gone to rule the dark
Leaving the day to Luna's spark,
Had Michael not, at God's command,
Made fearless war on Satan's band.
He tamed their rebel regiment,
He bade them, into fetters pent,
To realms celestial bid farewell,
And hurl'd them headlong down to Hell.
Prostrate in arms those raging hosts
Now lie and by their shatter'd boasts
Warn us to seek for better things
Than black ambition's murmurings.
May heavenly punishment no more
Find other crimes to punish sore;
Nor may the wreck of vice dismay
MAN still uncertain of his way,
Nor may he, pious still at heart,
From virtue's pathway e'er depart!
So may the offspring he begets
At length throng Heaven's parapets,
And fill the heavenly fields left bare
By rebels exiled in despair!

ACTUS SECUNDUS

Adamus Angelus

Trimetri Iambici

Dies tenebras legis aeternae vice
Fugans resurgit: Certus ordo temporum
Solis reducit aureum terris caput.
Stellis fugatis majus exoritur jubar;
Nox jussa luci cedit, et Phoebo soror.
O quantus ille est, cujus ingenti manu
Coeli rotatur axis, et turbo celer
Refert Olympum duplici fultum Polo,
Vastumque mundi pondus aequalem trahit
Retrahitque in orbem! Sidera authoris sui
Secuta legem temperant anni vices,
Titan coruscis explicat lucem comis,
Et Luna ducens mille stellarum choros
Tenebrosa noctis rumpit. Aetherei sacer
Sonus ille motus cantat artificem manum,
Omnesque stellae celeris ad coeli modos
Plaudunt choreis: Ipse nos Mundus monet
Servire rerum conditori, nec sinit
Haerere terris: supera nos rapit in loca,
Mentesque proprium ducit ad primordium.
An. O te beatum, cujus in Praecordiis
Imago magni nobilis fulget Dei,
Et cui, quod unum maximum et summum bonum est,
Rationis usus cum Dei cultu datur.
Adame, quantum cerne praestes caeteris
Rebus creatis: Saxa et hos lapides vide:
Sunt ista, qua tu maximi authoris manu
Formata: nullos sed quibus tribuit parens
Natura motus: Arbores quas aspicis
Foliis virescunt, et suos fructus ferunt,

ACT TWO

In the Garden of Eden. Adam and an Angel are engaged in solemn but friendly converse.

Adam. Day, rising in the course of everlasting law
Drives Night away once more. Fix'd sequences of time
Bring back to earth the Sun's resplendent head of gold;
His greater radiance, rising, puts the stars to flight;
Night and the Moon at God's great bidding flee away.
Behold how great is He, in whose gigantic Hand
The Sky's vast axle turns, as its swift wheeling brings
The heavens about, supported on a double Pole,
And draws and draws again the universe' vast weight
In a due circle! Loyal to their Author's law,
Th' obedient stars control the changes of the year,
The Sun shakes out white glory from his glittering hair,
And the Moon leads a thousand choruses of stars
To break the gloom of Night. The ethereal motion's sound
Sings holily the hand of the Artificer,
And all the stars dance to those measures of the sky
In swift delight; The Universe itself exhorts us
To serve God the Creator, not to cling to earth;
Its voice would speed us rather to the realms above
And lead our minds back to their own high origin.
Angel. Blessed art thou, within whose human breast there shines
The high and noble image of Almighty God,
To whom is given that sole and highest good of all --
The use of reason join'd with piety towards God!
Perceive, O Adam, how thou dost surpass the rest
Of things created! For behold these rocks and stones,
Form'd like thyself by the supreme Creator's hand:
To these, their parent Nature has assign'd no life,
Nor aught of movement; and the trees thou dost perceive
Grow green with foliage and bear their several fruits;

Annisque crescunt, rursus et senium mora
Patiuntur aevi: nulla delectat tamen
Plantam voluptas, nullus excruciat dolor.
Pisces, feraeque, et alitum altivolans genus
Vident colores, audiunt vocem et sonos,
Capiunt odores, pabulum gustu probant,
Munusque in illis tactus exercet suum:
Nocitura discunt fugere, quae prosunt sequi.
Sensu trahuntur: Non habent mentem ducem,
Nec cogitata mutuis sermonibus
Capiunt, feruntque: nulla Relligio Deum
Demonstrat: omnis in brevi vita est salus.
Tibi praeter illa mortis expers et mali
Anima tributa est imperatrix sensuum.
Laudum suarum te Deus testem sacris
Parere jussis voluit, haec lex est data:
Tibi benignus reliqua, te fecit sibi.
Ad. Deus est profecto, cujus et terra, et fretum,
Et utraeque Phoebi sentiunt Numen domus.
Praesentia illi cuncta: principio carens
Fini carebit, ipse principium simul
Finisque rerum: cuncta mille a seculis
Futura cernit: Fecit omnia, et omnibus
Factis opifera prospicit prudentia:
Non corpus illum claudit, aut servat locus:
Sed ubique vivit, omnis expers termini:
Origo veri, Fons boni, Sapientia
Regina mundi, quae potest quicquid cupit.
Coelum ille in orbem versat, et Terram suis
Firmat columnis: ille quodcunque est grave

These grow through many years, but then again decline
And suffer age; but pleasure can delight no plant,
No pain can lacerate its senses to the quick.
Fishes, again, and beasts, and birds' high-flying race
See colours, hear the voice, hearken to sundry sounds,
Perceive the smells of things, and prove their food by taste,
And touch with them performs its function; they have learn'd
To flee from things that harm and follow after good.
But they are drawn by instinct, lacking Mind as guide,
Nor do they, as in mutual conversation, grasp
And render rational thought. Religion shows them not
That God exists. All weal for them is in brief life.
To thee, beyond these, is assign'd a soul, exempt
From death and sin, and mistress of the body's senses.
God has ordain'd thee as a witness to extol
And serve His will; has given this law; all other things
He kindly made for thee, but made thee for Himself.
Adam. 'Tis God assuredly, whose godhead land and ocean
And both the abodes of Phoebus know full well. In Him
All things have their subsistence. Uncreated God,
He perdures without end; He is Himself beginning
And end of things; throughout a thousand centuries
He sees whatever shall be; He has made all things
And cares for His creation with kind providence.
No body hems Him in, no habitation holds Him,
But He lives everywhere and knows no bounds at all.
He is the source of Truth, the Fount of Good, and Wisdom,
Ruling the Universe, accomplishing its will.
He turns the heavens on their round, and stablish'd Earth
Upon her many pillars; He it is that thrusts

Depellit: idem quod leve est sursum trahit,
Motuque motus ipse principium caret:
Nunquamque variat unus: attamen in tribus
Subsistit unus. Est enim rerum parens,
Is qui potenti cuncta moderatur manu:
Est natus ipso patre ab aeterno satus,
Divina ratio, Mens patris: Lex Omnium,
Sermoque, cuius incomprehensa fuit
Virtute factum quod prius fuerat nihil:
Utrumque Sancti Spiritus Concordia
Amorque jungit: Tresque sunt Unus Deus.
An. Quam multa paucis, Magna parvis vocibus
Satis explicasti, quantaque ingenii tui
Mensura summum pectori insculpsit Deum,
Quem novimus pro parte: perfecto modo
Deus ipse novit, seque dum capit, et cupit
Pleno, quod aliis dividit, fruitur bono.
Deus ipse Mens est, universum quae replet
Superatque mundum: caepta nullo tempore
Nulloque desitura: Quod verum est videt
Etiam ante, quam sit: vult bonum, caussa est boni.
Procul hinc remoti, proximi certe tamen,
Sumus per illum nos ministri coelites,
Animaeque vestrae. Quippe respondet locis
Pars nulla nostri: dividi nec possumus:
Tamen hic, vel illic esse recte dicimur,
Non simul ubique: et anima vobis quamlibet
Infusa membris tota inhaeret singulis,
Qua corpus illud, non et ulterius patet.
Nostrae actioni temporum non competit
Mensura, semper non idem facimus tamen:
Incipimus, et desinimus: Haec absunt Deo.
Ab eo creati mortis immunes sumus.
Non vera scimus integre, non omnia,
Nihil futuri. Nostra rebus de bonis
Pendet voluntas: Mente ab illius bonum.
Adame nobis maxima est foelicitas
Hoc velle solum, quod Deus vult, et facit:
Parere jussis, sponte rectori obsequi,

All that is heavy down and raises what is light.
First Cause of Motion, He Himself moves not at all.
One is He, without variation, yet in Three
That One subsists: there is a FATHER of all things,
He who controls the universe with mighty hand;
There is the SON, born of that same eternal Father,
Reason divine, the Father's Mind, the Law, the Word,
By whose incomprehensible command was made
A universe where heretofore was utter nothing;
These essences the Concord of the HOLY GHOST
Combines in sacred Love: these Three are but One God.
<u>Angel</u>. How many weighty things in these few words and slight
Hast thou set plainly forth! With what sagacity
Hast thou engraved the Most High God within thy heart! --
Him whom we know in part; but only God Himself
Can know that Self entire, which knowing and desiring
He tastes that perfect good, given else in moieties.
God is Himself a Mind, that fills the universe
And dominates it all -- an Essence uncreated
And destined to endure. That which is true He sees,
Even before it is. He wills, and causes good.
Remote from Him, yet truly very near, through Him,
Are we, the ministering spirits of His heaven,
Yea, and your human souls. Doubtless no part of us
Is match'd with Him in space. We cannot be divided;
Yet we are rightly said to be now here, now there,
Not everywhere at once. Likewise thy soul, though spread
Through individual members, in one frame inheres,
Lives wholly in one body and extends no further.
No measurement of time is adequate to gauge
Our action, yet our action does not stay the same:
For we begin, and end. These limits God transcends.
Fashioned by Him, we angels are exempt from Death.
The Truth we know not fully, no, nor everything,
And nothing of the future. Upon good our will
Is all dependent; on His Mind all good depends.
It is, O Adam, our supreme felicity
Only to will the thing that God may will and do,
With swiftness to obey our Master's governance,

Laudare justum, patrem amore prosequi,
Et discere illum quem nihil rerum latet.
Vis conditorem nosse? rebus conditis
Utere magistris; quicquid est index Dei est.
Ad. Cum nil fuisse tot feras, pisces, aves,
Ipsumque me, Telluris, et Coeli globos,
Solemque, Lunamque, ante perpaucos dies,
Tacitus revolvo totus extra me feror,
Stupidusque rerum miror artificem Deum.
Age, si vacabit, (scire nam perfectius,
Quae facta fuerint ante me factum potes:)
Narra petenti, quo modo, quoque ordine,
Tam magna numeris machina impleta est suis.
An. Gemina ante tempus omne, cum solum foret
Nil praeter ipsum, corpora effecit Deus,
Moli priori conditae simplex erat
Materia: partes mutuo aequales sibi,
Perfecta species, orbis in justi modum
Rotunda, nullis angulis protuberans
Ne discreparet finis a primordio.
Natura nullas motuum patiens vices,
Secura lethi, non timebat deteri,
Tantum revolvi prona, nec mutans locum,
Referebat orbes sempiterno turbine
Dimensa tempus: Magna coeli Machina
Pendebat axi fulta, cui gemini procul
Fines utroque terminabantur Polo.
Concava profundae Molis intra viscera
Latebat expers Lucis, et formae Chaos,
Quod cuncta possis dicere, et possis nihil.
Depressa nondum gravia tunc secesserant,
Nec levia superos evolarant ad locos:
Sed mixta liquidis sicca, frigida fervidis,

To praise His justice, worship Him with holy love,
And learn of Him whom nothing in Creation hides.
Wouldst thou thy Maker know? Use as thy teachers then
The things that He has fashion'd. All are guides to God.
Adam. When I recall in silence that a few days since
None of these beasts existed, fish, nor birds, myself,
Nor Earth nor globes of Heaven, nor shining Sun nor Moon,
In wonder I am wholly rapt beyond myself
And marvel at the God that fashion'd everything.
Come, if the time permit, (for thou more fully knowest
The things that were created ere myself was made)
Tell me, I pray, in what succession and what wise
So great a System into number'd order came.
Angel. Before all time, when He alone existed, nor
Was aught but God in being, He made bodies twain.
The mass first form'd, with simple substance He endow'd,
Its parts reciprocally equal, and in form
Perfection, a round globe in perfect measure shaped,
Projecting with no angular discrepancy
Lest the beginning should not balance with the end.
Primordial Nature, that endures no change of motion,
Exempt from taint of death, fear'd not to change to worse,
Only inclined to turn but not to change its place,
Brought back its circuits in eternal revolution,
Meting out time; there heaven's great Mechanism hung,
Supported on an axle which at either end
Far distant terminated in a skyey Pole.
Within the hollow viscera of the Deep Mass
Lurk'd Chaos, destitute of Light or any form,
Chaos, which one may term "all things" and "nothing" too.
Things heavy had not yet been separated out;
Light things had not yet risen to their higher station.
Dry things were mix'd with wet, frost blent with

Confusa magnis parva, duris mollia
Cumulo latebant: cuncta quae sunt effici
Ex mole poterant, cuncta formis perfici.
Ad. Iacuitne inanis illa materies diu?
An subito species rebus effulsit sua?
An. Non illud una singulis formis opus
Perfecit hora: quippe lapsu temporum
Digesta varios cuncta ceperunt gradus.
Pars ista medio, quam tui calcant pedes,
Confinis axi pondere oppressam suo
Terram recepit: illa primo turbidis
Submersa in undis delitescebat salo
Cincto tenebris. Subito divina manu
Formatus aër cursibus liber vagis
Incubuit undae. Flamma tantum splendidae
Ministra lucis deerat: Umbrae Machinam
Densa tenebant conditam caligine.
Itaque ex capaci Mole luciferum Deus
Secedere Ignem jussit, et jusso obsequens
Secessit ignis fervidus, siccus, levis.
Quaterna nondum ceperant sedes suas
Principia: nondum clauserat littus Mare,
Aerve terram concavi specie globi:
Natura nondum proximo Lunae loco
Ignem locarat: qui simul in auras Chao
Abiit relicto, non in excelsum fuit
Redactus orbem, flamma sed massam in rudem
Coacta tanquam temere Eois aetheris
Partibus adhaerens, et citato turbine
Correpta coeli mobili luxit face:
Rursumque bissex tracta praecipiti rota

fervent heat,
Small things confused with great, soft things with hard lay hid
In that colossal heap; all things that could be wrought
And fashion'd into forms were latent in that Mass.
Adam. Did all that substance lie in that confusion long?
Or did their own forms suddenly shine forth in things?
Angel. One single hour did not achieve that work in all
Its individual forms; doubtless through lapse of time
All things in order there assumed their various ranks.
That midmost part of all, on which thy feet now tread,
Adjacent to the axis, received Earth, oppress'd
By its own weight; those things submerged in turbid waves
At first lay hidden in an ocean girt about
With murky darkness; suddenly the atmosphere,
Form'd by the Hand divine, free in its wandering courses,
Brooded upon the wave. The ministering flame
Of radiant light was lacking. Shadows the Machine
In densest pall of darkness held impenetrable.
And so God bade light-bearing Fire withdraw itself
From the capacious Mass. Obedient to command,
The Fire withdrew -- an essence hot and dry and light.
Not yet had the four Elements assumed their seats;
Not yet had shores hemm'd in the immitigable Sea;
Or Air the Earth with semblance of a hollow globe.
Nature had not yet station'd Fire in its place,
Hard by the Moon, Fire which had risen out of Chaos
But had not mounted upward to the highest place.
Driv'n in an orbit-circle, compacted as flame
Into a rude mass, held at random in the East
And caught in the swift wheeling of the firmament,
It shone in molten glory as a moving torch.
And the same light again, propell'd on headlong wheel

Eadem per horas pristinas parti alteri
Tenebras reduxit, alteri lucem novam.
Sic temperanda noctis alternae vice
Primi diei fuit opus primum dies.
Ad. Quibus illa, si fas scire, disposita est modis
Rerum parens quadriga, quae nunc mutuo
Complexa sese parte ab omni convenit,
Vastumque inane cuncta complendo fugat?
An. Redeunte rebus luce praecepit Deus
Inania auris spatia repleri vagis,
Vastumque vacuis aëra expandi locis,
Qui medius undis separaret ab inferis
Superos madores: ille mandati tenax
Diffusus ultro in alta secum pendulos
Vexit liquores: ivit ad Coelum vapor,
Ubi nunc librantur onere praecipites suo
Nubes, et imbrem ventre parturiunt gravi.
Non una regio est Aeris: trina occupat
Distinctus ille spatia: supremum coquit
Contigua flammae fervidae vicinia:
Ibi, qui malorum posteris utinam tuis
Nunquam sit index nuntia cladis face,
Fulget Cometes: ille siccos halitus
Locus, ille servat siderum labentium
Coelo figuram: Media qua regio patet,
Ibi frigus, humorque habitat, et varii vage
Pendent vapores. Patria haec pluvias parit,
Celerisque venti spiritum, cum despuit
Fervor liquorem, frigus aut medii loci
Praecludit altum flatibus calidis iter.
Ibi tonitruum murmur, et vis fulminis
Corusca magna nascitur discordia.
Ibi tristis imber algido strictus gelu

Through twice six hours, brought back its pristine dark once more
To the one part, and gave a new light to the other.
So, by an order'd change of alternating night,
The first work of the primal day was Day itself.
Adam. Tell me, if one may know, in what due fashion came
Our fourfold Parent, that, reciprocally
Itself embracing, from all sides now comes together
And filling all things puts the vast inane to flight?
Angel. When dawn returned to Earth, God gave divine command
That empty space be occupied with wandering winds
And that the vast air should be spread in hollow places,
That in the midst they might cut off the floods above
From waters here below. Air hearken'd to His voice,
And spreading of its own accord across the heights,
It bore suspended moisture. Vapour soar'd aloft
Where now the headlong clouds are poised by their own weight
And bring forth teeming rain from out their pregnant bellies.
Air holds no single region: three distinct domains
Its essence occupies. The uppermost by flame
In an adjacent neighborhood of fire is scorch'd.
There gleams the Comet -- may it never be hereafter
For thy posterity a harbinger of doom,
A gleaming sign of evil! That division holds
Dry exhalations and the forms of gliding stars
Across the lofty sky. Where the mid region opens,
There cold and moisture dwell, and wandering vapours hang.
This realm engenders rains and the swift tempest's breath,
When fervent heat spews down fierce moisture from on high,
On the cold essences that roam the middle tract
And bar the lofty highways of the genial breeze.
There thunders mumble and the flashing levin-bolt
Is born amid the pangs and anguish of the air.
There too the gloomy shower, shackled by the cold,

Aut in nivem duratur, aut in grandinem.
Inferna sedes quae repercussae trahit
Flammae calorem crassior, nebulas graves
Roremque purum proximo immittit solo.
Sic aeris transire septum duplices
Inter madores alter aspexit dies.
Cumque hac eadem luce compulsu Dei
In maria, et amnes se recepissent aquae,
Et destitutis quos inundarat locis
Littoribus iret clausus, et ripis liquor,
Coeloque nudum Terra monstraret sinum,
Fructus sequenti jussa produxit die.
Quodcunque germen floridos campos tegit,
Et herba succo quae salutifero viret
Tunc jussa primum crescere est, et vividum
Ejicere semen. Tempore ex illo arbores
Alimenta Terrae matris infixa bibunt
Radice, semperque Aëris genitabili
Vegetantur aura, traditisque in viscera
Crescunt ab undis: sede sublimi trahunt
Ignis foventem cuncta vitalis facem,
Genusque totum planta ne secum auferat
Moritura formae proferunt similes suae.
Ad. Verene quarto credimus factas die
Stellas, et ipsas Solis, et Lunae faces?
An. Cum per quaternas Mundus aetherius vices
Repetisset unde caeperat volvi locum,
Orbis figura subjugem Coeli globo
Aptavit ignem, quodque vacuum liquerant
Aether et aër Circulo spatium suo
Media occupavit flamma: post haec siderum

Is chill'd to crystal snow or hardens into hail.
The heavy lowest region of the air, which draws
The heat of mirror'd flame, bestows oppressive mists
And the pure dew upon the ground adjacent to it.
Thus did the second day perceive a barrier
Of air divide the two-fold waters from each other;
And when on this same day, compell'd by Might divine,
The waters of the Earth were form'd to seas and streams,
And having left those regions which they erst had flooded,
Moved on, hemm'd in by banks and circumscribed by shores,
Then Earth reveal'd her naked bosom to the sky.
Upon the following day, God's edicts brought forth fruits:
Whatever leafy shoot bedecks the flowering fields,
Whatever grass springs green with health-inducing sap,
These then at His command began to grow, and cast
Their live seed forth. From that time shady trees began
To drink their nurture from the breast of Mother Earth
With thirsty clinging root; and ever are they quicken'd
By fruitful breezes, and by moisture do they grow,
Drawn into vital parts; while their tall branches seek
That touch of vital fire that nourishes all things;
And lest the mortal plant should perish, with its kind,
Each duly brings to birth those like to it in form.
Adam. Shall we indeed believe that during the fourth day
The stars and torches of the Sun and Moon were made?
Angel. When through four revolutions the high Universe
Had sought again the spot whence it began to turn,
A sphere was yoked beneath the topmost firmament,
Furnish'd with gleaming fire; and in the space left void
By air and ether, flame then enter'd in the midst

Opus secutum est: illa non humili ex Chao
Formata noris, melior et sublimior
Materia genuit astra, naturam parem
Sortita Coelo, cuius infixa in globis
Noctem, diemque lumine illustrant vago,
Horas tenebris, et diei dividunt,
Tollunt vapores coelicae attractu facis,
Serena, et imbres, et procellas praemonent,
Annoque partes, partibus tribuunt dies.
Bina astra lucent ex solo spectantibus
Majora reliquis: Phoebus ignis fervidi,
Terris calorem reddit in speculi modum,
Rector diei, cujus immensum jubar
Obscurat alia lapsa coelo sidera:
Sed Luna noctis domina fraternum sibi
Furata lumen splendet aliena face,
Cumque alma Phoebe Solis opposita viae
Regione vadit, lumen adversum bibit,
Seseque in orbem redigit, ut plenus nitor
Rumpat tenebras: Solis at complexibus
Cum soror inhaeret, Nox ut illunis silet.
Quantoque propius lumen est Titanium
Majora Lunam damna cornigeram manent.
Haec praeter ambo plura Sphaeris sidera
Infixa variis quarta conspexit dies.
Bis quattuor sunt astra portantes globi:
Sideribus horum summus innumeris nitet,
Sphaerisque in aliis singulae lucent faces.

With circling orbit. The creation of the stars
Next follow'd, nor from humble Chaos were these form'd
As you may know; a better and a loftier stuff
Begot the ethereal stars; for they achieved a nature
Equal to Heaven itself, set in whose wheeling spheres
They shine with moving radiance on day and night,
Divide the hours for darkness and for day, and banish
The fogs by the attraction of their heavenly torch;
Fine weather they foretell and likewise rains and tempests;
They give the year its seasons, and those seasons, days.
To those who gaze aloft from earth, two stars shine forth
Greater than all the rest: the Sun's perfervid fire
Bestows heat on the earth as might a flashing mirror;
It rules the day and with refulgence most immense
Obscures the other stars that glide across the sky.
The Moon, however, mistress of the night, herself
Purloins her brother's rays and shines with borrow'd brightness;
And when she walks in grace athwart the lofty path
Of the bright Sun, she drinks the opposing glory in
And grows to rounded radiance, till her fullest splendor
Shatters the gloom with beauty; but when the sister clings
In the strong Sun's embrace, the moonless night is dark;
And ever as she nears his bright Titanic arms
Her horned form pines dwindling fast away.
Besides these twain, the fourth day saw more stars infix'd
In various spheres of heaven; twice four are these that bear
The flashing constellations through the vasty void;
The uppermost of these shines with unnumber'd stars,
The other several spheres bear single luminaries.

Orbe in supremo fasciae latae via
Bissena gestat signa, quae Sol permeans
Nunc Noctis aequat, et diei terminos,
Nunc liberali prorogat lucem manu,
Nunc laxat umbras. Illa habet geminos domus
Septentriones, illa pluvias Suculas,
Verisque, et Autumni indices Atlantidas.
Illic procellis tumidus Orion furit,
Flagratque anhelo fervidus mento Canis.
Septem vagantes qui ferunt stellas globi
Istum sequuntur: omnibus motus duo.
Nam concitatus maximi lapsus Poli
Quanquam diurno turbine invitos trahat,
Tamen coactis cursibus contrarii
Ultro moventur: namque supremi diem
Vis rapida Mundi parte ab Eoa trahit;
Illos reducit lentus adversos gradus
Ab occidente ad Solis ortivi domum.
Nec una cursus spatia: nam senas quater
Mundus per horas inferos secum globos
Convolvit: illi proximo torpet gravis
Saturnus astro, qui suam bis quindecim
Tarde per annos destinat Caelo viam.
Inferior illo Jupiter ter quattuor,
Vicinus annos Mars sibi indulget duos.
Sol sequitur illos annuo cursu suum
Mensurus orbem: certa nec Solis comes
Lucifera stella, parva nec fax Mercuri
Majora poscunt spatia; quis cunctis subest
Contenta Phoebi menstruo cursu soror;
Haec cum videret opera, qui fecit Deus
Laudans probavit.
Ad. Quae feras, Pisces, aves,
Jumenta, et angues vidit effingi dies?

Across the topmost sphere, a broad celestial band
Bears twice six signs, among which the Sun's
    wanderings
Now measure equal bounds for earthly day and night,
And now extend the darkness. That abode the Bears,
Both Great and Small, possess, the rainy Hyades,
And the Pleiades, bright signs of autumn and of
    spring;
There too Orion rages, arrogant with storms,
And the hot Dog-star blazes with plutonic jaw.
Thereafter come the seven heavenly spheres that
    bear
The wandering planets. Each possesses motions
    twain:
For while the violent wheeling of the empyrean
Draws them unwillingly in daily revolution,
Yet of their own accord they move in ways opposed
To their forced courses. For the Universe draws on
The day in rapid might from out the Eastern quarter;
But gradual regression brings the planets back
From out the west to where emergent Phoebus dwells.
Nor have their courses equal distances, for though
Through four and twenty hours the universal frame
Swings all the rest, the sphere next outermost
    bears Saturn,
Numb and inert, who asks for thirty tedious years
To consummate his ponderous orbit through the
    heavens;
The next in order, Jupiter, takes three times four;
Next lower neighbor, Mars, concedes himself but two;
The Sun comes next, destined to mete his circuit out
In one strict year; nor do his sure companions
    Venus,
That fair light-bearing star, and Mercury's small
    torch
Demand a greater orbit; less than all of these,
The Sun's fair sister is content with one brief
    month.
When God who made them all, beheld these works of
    His
He praised them and approved.
Adam. What day beheld the
    beasts,
The birds and fishes, and the herds and serpents

An. Ubi secundam Phoebus accendit facem
Jussit per amnes, Numen, et vitreos lacus,
Lunaribusque reflua momentis freta
Natare Pisces: Jussit et volucres citis
Secare pennis aëris liquidi vias.
Ergo creavit monstra foecundi maris
Immensa cete; et omne squammigerum genus,
Alisque fultum: mille species singulis,
Faciesque generum mille Natura suos
Prodente luxus: singulis anima est data,
Quae forma princeps corporum est viventium,
Quae sentit, auget, vegetat, alit, et procreat.
Nam cum videret magnae opus dextrae Deus,
His allocutus comprobavit vocibus:
Alimenta in usus quaeque sumentes suos
Majore mole crescite, et numeros quoque
Augete vestros sobole, et ovis insitas
Excludite animas, quaeque mistis sexibus
Deposita in alma condidistis viscera,
Servate justo redditura in tempore,
Innumerae ut ab humo suspici possint aves,
Vastique Pisces impleant undas sali.
Sequente luce, sexta quae Mundo fuit
Tertiaque Phoebo, caeteris animantibus
Tibique prima, Conditor jussit Deus
Centum cavatis ire serpentes viis,
Centum veneni genera, si Numen sinat,
Vitanda cautis. Jussit incultis feras
Errare silvis, pascere et viridantibus
Armenta campis, cuncta spectant patriam
Quae prona terram, nec suos audent Pole
Monstrare vultus, atque coelestes domos

made?
Angel. When the transplendent Sun kindled his
second fire,
The Deity bade fish, in streams and glassy lakes
And seas drawn to and fro by lunar tides, to swim;
Likewise he bade the fowls on fleeting pinions
cleave
The high and pathless region of the liquid air.
Then he created monsters of the teeming sea,
The mighty whale, and all the scaly breeds that go
Supported upon fins: a thousand kinds to each,
Form'd in a thousand different types and shapes
He made
Through fertile Nature's gift. To each a living
soul --
First principle of living bodies -- was assign'd,
A soul that feels, grows, quickens, nourishes,
begets.
For when God saw the work of His almighty hand,
He voiced divine approval with this utterance:
"Go, take the food you need, each for his proper
use;
Grow greater yet in bulk, increase and multiply
With offspring, hatch out living souls that lodge
in eggs,
And that which after mingling in the act of sex
You store away to nourish in the pregnant womb,
Preserve, that in due season you may bring them
forth,
In order that unnumber'd birds may spring from
earth
And countless fish may fill the waves of the vast
sea!"
The following day, which for the Universe was
sixth,
Third for the Sun, but for the rest of living things
And thee thyself the first, God the Creator bade
A hundred serpents go by low and hollow ways,
A hundred kinds whose venom dark, if God permit,
The cautious must avoid. He bade the wild beasts
wander
In the untill'd woods, and herds their food to seek
In the green fields; all these look steadfast down
On earth as their due home, and dare not raise

Contra tueri fixa perpetuum solo.
Adame tantum est haec quod a te differant,
Quem vultus ipse destinat majoribus,
Te, cum creasset imagine imbutum sua
Deus, quievit septima sancta die
Fecisse fassus ultimo majus nihil.
Sed ad te euntem conjugem video tuam
Abibo, quo me munus appellat meum.

Eva Adamus
Trimetri Iambici

O Sempiterno foedere auspiciis Dei
Mihi juncte conjunx longius praesentia
Tua carere justa me pietas vetat,
Amorque sancta corda succendens face.
Ad. Consors cubilis cui meis ex ossibus
Composuit ossa, cui maritali Deus
De carne carnem finxit, ut redeat suum,
Quod inde natum fuerat, ad primordium,
Quam bene putavit, nulla quem fugiunt Deus,
Non posse vera me frui sine compari
Felicitate: semper animos dulcior
Tangit voluptas, sorte quam gratus pari
Socius frequentat: ista natura est boni,
Communicari gaudet, et multis suo
Prodesse fructu: nemo participi carens
Vivit beatus. Solus et felix dolet.
Cum liberali cuncta rerum Conditor
Mihi bestiarum genera tribuisset manu,
Quibus arbitratu nomina imposui meo,
Deesse visa est socia, quae solo foret
Diversa sexu. Tunc Dei immissus manu
Omnes mihi artus altus invasit sopor.
Somno jacebam pressus, et torpor gravis
Sensus ligabat, spiritusque ex intimo
Pectoris anhelans capitis officiis dabat
Vacationem: dumque securum quies
Profunda tenuit, ultimo dorsi loco
Succincta geminis terga qua lumbis patent,
Hac parte costam corpori eripuit meo,

their eyes
To front the heavens and the abodes above the sky,
Nay, all their glance is ever fix'd upon the earth.
This, Adam, is their primal difference from thee
Whose very countenance predestines greater things.
When God had made thee in the likeness of Himself,
He rested then upon the holy seventh day,
Proclaiming that His last creation was the best.
But now I see thy wife draw near to where we stand.
I shall depart, whither my duty calls me forth.
(Exit Angel. Enter Eve.)
Eve. O husband, join'd to me by everlasting compact
And the auspices of God, devotion and true love,
Kindling my tender heart with flame and yearning fire,
Bid me no longer to be barren of thy presence.
Adam. O consort of my bed, whose bones from out my bone
God fashion'd, and whose flesh the Deity created
Out of a husband's flesh, so that it might return
To embrace that body whence it had its origin,
How well has God, whom nothing can escape, consider'd
That I without a mate could not enjoy a true
Felicity! Spirits are ever touch'd more sweetly
By that delight which kindly comradeship redoubles
With equal lot. This is the nature of true good;
It joys in being shared, and blessing with its fruits
The lives of many. None who lacks a confidant
Is happy. And the lonely man of wealth is sad.
When the Creator of all things with lavish hand
Had given to my custody all tribes of beasts,
To whom I render'd names according to my judgement,
I seem'd to lack a comrade who should differ from me
Only in point of sex. Then deep and heavy sleep,
Sent from the hand of God, invaded all my limbs.
I lay o'ercome with slumber; heavy numbness bound
My every sense; my spirit panting from within
My inmost heart gave to the duties of the brain
Vacation absolute; and while profoundest sleep
Then held me fast, God from the soft base of my back,
Where girt about with double loins my waist extends,
Tore out a bloody rib from that part of my body,

Vacuumque hiatum carne supplevit Deus.
Ubi recreata membra, qui primus fuit,
Somnus reliquit, ex meis, uxor tua
Formata membris astitit species mihi,
Quam cum viderem, languidos artus adhuc
Stupor occupavit, flamma quem solvit nova,
Et amoris ignis. Postea omnipotens Sator
Conjugia verbis nostra firmavit sacris.
Augete, misti, dixit, Humanum genus
Imago nostra: terra quam late patet
Vestra regatur sobole: quas Tellus feras,
Aërque volucres gestat, aut Pisces mare
Imperia vestri sanguinis discant pati.
Ev. Felicitatis magna pars, aut unica
Vir est maritae: dulce nunc quicquid mihi est
Te sine nocebit.
Ad. Sic amoris mutui
Ut duret ardor, utque communi bono
Aevum fruamur, nosque deliciae beent
Hedenis almi munus egregium Dei,
Ipsum colamus omnis authorem boni,
Primumque amemus, quasque nobis praecipit
Leges sequamur pariter, ut vetitae arboris
Vitare gustum, caeteris liceat frui.
Iucunda quae vox auribus sonuit meis?
Sanctus supremi Regis aetherius Chorus
Laudes celebrat: ex propinquo succinam.

CHORUS

Ex vario Carminum
genere.

Artifex rerum, tibi grata laudes
Mens novo celebrabit hymno,
Testemque magnitudinis
Mundi domum citabit.
Majestas tua gloriam
Induta fulget, laudisque amictu
Decorata sancto lumine splendet:

And fill'd the vacant cavity again with flesh.
When I was thus made whole once more, the former sleep
Deserted me, and thy form, O my wife, stood by,
Fashion'd in beauty from my proper flesh and blood;
And when I saw thee, sweet amazement seized upon
My still inactive limbs; a new flame melted me
With all the fires of love. Then the Almighty Father
Confirm'd our marriage with approving holy words:
"Unite in flesh!" said He. "Increase the human race,
O ye who bear Our image! And let ample Earth
By all your heirs be ruled! Let all the beasts Earth bears
And all the birds of Air and fish within the Sea
Learn to endure the empire of your progeny!"
Eve. Her husband, to a wife, is happiness' chief part,
Her one true joy. Whatever now in me is sweet,
Without thee would be bane.
Adam. In order that the ardour
Of mutual love may endure, and that we may enjoy
A life of good together, blest with the delights
Of Eden, that consummate gift of gracious God,
Let us give worship to that Author of all good,
Him love the first, and follow equally the laws
His wisdom hath ordain'd, to avoid the fatal taste
Of the forbidden tree, and feast on all the rest.
What pleasant voice but now has sounded in my ears?
Th' ethereal chorus of the Most High King now chants
His praises. I from close at hand shall sing with them.

CHORUS

To thee, Creator, grateful souls we raise;
A new-wrought hymn of worship we rehearse;
And shall, as witness to Thy power and praise,
Summon Thy Universe.
Thy Majesty indued with raiment bright
Of laud and honour gleams with glory's rays
And shines with holy light.

Aeris vasti cujus expandit
Dextra cortinam, nitidaeque velo
Aureo flammae vestiit orbem.
Tu nubes pluvia graves
In conclavia dividis, rapidis et instans
Auriga loris flatibus imperas
Vectus alite vento.
Tibi Legati munere fungentes,
Silvarum quatiunt superna Cauri.
Sentit Ortus, sentit Occasus
Flammae ministrae vim genitabilem.
Tibi nos ministri, nec minus ventis
Agiles, nec igni rapimur jussa
Exsequi proni tua.
Te tellus tibi fixa tremit: quae turbine circum
Diverso aetherios passa rapi globos,
Ullis ipsa trahi curriculis negat.
Illam prima dies gurgite viderat
Obscuro, et pelagi fluctibus obrutam.
Coelum littus erat: summaque montium
Cinctorum tenebris condiderat juga
Exlege Oceanus vado.
Tu subito verbis Deus altitonantibus undam
Cedere jussisti: vix-jussa recesserat unda.
Tunc parentes Domino fluctus
Fugere procul: liquere solum
Telluris aquae, quae praecipiti
Lapsae pulsu vertice ab alto
Inter valles humili primum
Sedere loco, donec jussos
Tenuere sinus.
Inclusum est a te praescriptis finibus aequor
Sublimi ne rursus humum sub gurgite condat,
Terraque delapsis siccum caput extulit undis.
Natos jugis in altis
Iubes salire fontes,
Quos cum feris bibentes
Sitim levent Onagri:
Ad quos aves sedentes
Dulci canant susurro
Sub arborum coma.

Thy right hand spread aloft the vast expanse
Of th' Empyrean and did clothe the same
With veils of golden flame.
The pregnant clouds Thy glance
Divides into their chambers; and the blast
Thou as a swift-rein'd Charioteer directed hast,
Borne on the wind's dark wings in Thy sublime
advance.
The North-west Winds, Thy messengers, fulfil
Their tasks and stir the tree-tops as they go;
The Sun, Thy minister, from dawn to sunset glow
Feels the deep force of Thy creative will.
We are Thy servants; not less swift than air
And fire we hasten headlong here and there
To do Thy bidding still.
Earth, grounded in Thee, dreads Thee; though
the ethereal spheres
It grants in course diverse to whirl about,
It will not yield itself to join their swift careers.
The First Day saw it in the dim gulf jutting out,
Half-hidden with the billows of the sea.
The sky was then its shore; the mountains' highest
heap,
Girt round with darkness and the sea, ordain'd by
Thee,
Drown'd in its watery deep.
Thou, God, with sudden, lofty-thundering word
Didst bid the wave retire: it went straightway;
Obedient to the Lord they heard,
The billows fled afar; from earth's wet clay,
With headlong rushing and tumultuous spray,
Down from the lofty peaks they swept
By valleys ever lower, till they pass'd
Into the sea's great gulf at last,
And its abysses kept.
By Thee the Ocean within bounds was shut,
Lest it again should overwhelm the earth,
Whose dry head from the waters now did jut.
In the high mountain's dearth
Thou bad'st the living fountains forth to burst
And quench the thirst
Of the wild ass and creatures of Thy hand,
That perching birds might sing
With fluted murmuring

Humores pluvios super alta cacumina fundis,
Et procul ex magno despectans infera coelo
Participas terrae depressum e nubibus imbrem,
Ebria quo fructus genetrici prodit ab alvo.
Inde, quo vivunt pecudes, gregesque,
Nascitur foenum: generantur herbae
Mitibus succis, meliorque pastus
Pinguibus crescunt segetes in arvis:
Inde procedent Oleae nitentes
Quoque vis cordis satiata gaudet
Palmitis humor.
Te succos tribuente suos in montibus altis
Fertilibus Cedri crescent ad sidera ramis,
Quas habitet passer, tremuloque ciconia rostro:
Saepe etiam summa pendentes abiete nidi
Emittent trepidis pullos super aëra pennis.
Montium alta cacumina
Esse perfugium facis
Capreis silvestribus:
Te jubente cuniculi,
Te jubente vagi petunt
Concito lepores pede
Scrupeae abdita rupis.
Luna tua formata manu est, quae mensibus annum
Distinguat, reparansque levis dispendia formae
Nunc gemino cornu, nunc pleno fulgeat orbe.
Ipse etiam certis fulgor Titanius horis
Occidit, et priscae terras cum tradidit umbrae
Ex antris prodire genus monet omne ferarum.
Fulvae feroces tunc catuli leae
Praedae manentes pabula rugiunt,
Potus, et escam voce famelica
Deum rogantes: Lucida cum dies
Coelo refulsit silvicolum cohors
Omnis ferarum nescia conspici
Arboreum redit ad cubile.
Ipse homo, siquid habet quod agat, ne ignavus oberret,
Invigilat curis intenta mente diurnis,

In the foliage of a rightly water'd land.
Thou pourest holy showers on the rocky height
And gazing from afar on things below,
For Earth Thou pressest from the clouds the rain's delight
That from her fruitful womb rich fruit may flow.
Thence grass is born, by which the lowing herd
And fleecy flock may live; and herbs come forth,
With mellow juice and ample yield conferr'd
On pastures fat and fields of fertile worth;
Thence follows too the shining olive-tree
And vines whose juice makes strong the heart with mirth
And jovial jollity.
As Thou vouchsafest sap in lofty hills,
The Cedars starward point with fruitful boughs
In which the little sparrow hath her house
And the tall herons with their slender bills.
Often the birds' nests on the fir-tree top
Launch fledgelings on the air with trembling wings.
Through Thee, the wild goats safely crop
The grass beside the mountain springs.
At Thy command, the coney weak,
At Thy command, the wandering hare
Both seek a refuge on the peak,
Amid the rocky ramparts bare.
Thy Hand prepared the Moon, that metes the years
In months, that, oft replenishing her light,
Now with two horns and now a globe appears.
The Sun himself at fix'd hours yields to night;
And when to pristine darkness he surrenders earth,
He bids the wild beasts from their coverts issue forth.
The fierce cubs of the tawny lioness
Awaiting prey, roar fiercely for their food;
For meat and drink, in clamour and distress,
With hungry voice they cry aloud to God;
But when bright dawn shines radiant in the air,
Then the shy cohort of the forest-dwelling breed
Seeks out its leafy lair.
And Man, if he have aught to do, some busy quest,
And works with earnest mind throughout the anxious

Quas solvit veniens securo lumine Vesper,
Somnum olli requiemque ferens. O maxima Mundi
Regnatrix lataeque opifex Sapientia terrae,
Tu coelumque solumque regis: tua maxima (quanquam
Nec facunda satis) cantat praeconia Tellus.
Te te velifero sub gurgite
Magna et parva gerens animantia,
Piscesque innumeros celebrat mare.
Illic luminibus Pistris micat,
Squammigero et fluctus dorso subit,
Ludentique secat tergo freta
Artificem testata manum.
    Sic quicquid tuus Orbis habet
Pendet a dominae gratia dextrae:
Ad tuos pendent animantia nutus:
A te rapaci destinata morti
Amittunt vitam.
Justis temporibus pabula bestias
Nutriunt tua tribuente dextra,
    Quae sua cum bona liberali
Dividit cumulo satiantur omnes
Pecudes, feraeque. Simul opiferam
Avertes faciem, difficilique vultu
Intueberis, recedet
Spiritus vacuas in auras,
Destituetque inane corpus,
    Quod repente agitari
Reciprocanti desinet halitu,
Tenuemque sese in pulverem vertet:
Rursumque tui Numinis aura
Favente gravidis foetus ab alvis
Nascentur, quae suum
Non sinant genus interire,
    Terra recentes
Ut pro interemptis capiat colonos.
Donec Sol reparator Eoi
Variis vicibus saecula volvet:
Donec obscura nocte micantes
Cingent rotatum sidera Mundum,
Numinis laudes resonabit Orbis.

day,
Finds that the light of Hesper takes his cares away
And brings him sleep and rest.
O Wisdom, mightiest King and Maker of all things,
Thou rulest earth and heaven; and Thy most high praise
Earth, though deficient in her eloquence, now sings;
Thee, Thee, the Ocean worships all its days,
That bears beneath its vessel-dotted streams
Live creatures great and small and fish past counting;
There the Leviathan with fierce eyes gleams,
Diving with scaly back, in glory mounting,
And cleaves with playful chine the waves at Thy command,
Thus bearing witness to the great Creator's hand.
Thus all things in the universe of God
Depend upon the favour of their Lord.
All living creatures wait upon Thy nod;
Destined to Death abhorr'd,
They die in mute accord.
Food granted in due season by Thy grace
Sustains the life of beasts that look to Thee:
When Thou dispensest nurture bounteously,
All herds and beasts are sated for a space;
But when Thy quickening glance
Thou turnest quite away,
Or when Thou gazest with stern countenance,
The spirits into empty air depart
And leave the senseless bodies in dismay;
So, suddenly the heart
Is still'd, the lung knows not its vital gust,
And soon the flesh is but a little dust.
But when again Thy Godhead's breath
Is breathed into the body's glooms,
New seed is born from pregnant wombs
And guards the mortal race from death;
And thus shall Earth new tenantry
Receive in turn for those that died
As long as Earthly dawns shall see
The ceaseless change of time and tide;
And while the stars that sparkle through the night
Girdle the wheeling Universe with light,
So long in Heav'n shalt Thou be glorified!

Divina Scilicet
Nullis majestas interibit annis;
Ipsum, ipsum capiunt gaudia cum videt
Machinam tantam, quam magnus opifex
Ante septimum effecit diem.
Illius Tellus concussa nutu
Trepidat, tactique montes
Piceo fumo
Aera involvunt: nebulasque vertex
Halat, et crassos agitat vapores.
Astra dum septem libero cursu
Coelum rotabit, non desinemus
Rerum parentis celebrare nomen
Vaga septisoni carminis Harmonia.
Aeternumque modis sacris
Indulgere juvabit,
Gaudioque maximo
Tollere in astra Deum.
Si quid erit malorum
Benignus ille tollet,
Sanctorumque Chorus modulabitur omnis ALLELVIA.

ACTUS III

Sathan Adamus

Trimetri Iambici

Hostem superbis pedibus adversos mihi
Gressus moventem video: jam Tempus meis
Se praebet iris: obvius tandem mihi
Adamus ultro venit, et solus quidem.
Coelicola monitor liberum socio latus
Deseruit, odiis commodus nimium meis.
Nodis inextricabilis fallaciae
Vinctum tenebo: rite disposui plagas:
Amore ficto facilis ambiguo dolo
Quaeratur aditus. Lentus inimicum vides
Sathan, nec illum dente discerpis fero?
Fraenum recusat impotens animi sui.
Sic ille magni summus armenti metus
Quoties bovem scrutatur, et longe lupus
Vestigiorum perlegit tacitus notas

Never, forsooth, shall any years suppress
The splendor of the Majesty Divine.
Himself, Himself shall certain joy possess
When gazing on the cosmic loveliness
Wrought in His vast design.
His nod the earthquake doth invoke;
The mountains, smitten by his stroke,
Are wrapp'd in pitchy smoke;
So long as in the sky each several Planet swings,
Each in the path and orbit that to it belong,
We shall not cease the Parent of all things
To hail with seven-toned harmony of song.
I, too, shall sing and shall rejoice
To hail the Eternal One in sacred measures;
To praise Him to high heaven with my voice
Will e'er surpass the rarest of all pleasures.
If there in me be aught of ill,
May He remove it by His gracious will,
While all the heavenly host sing "Hallelujah" still!

ACT III

Enter severally Satan and Adam.

Satan. I see my enemy advancing towards me now
Upon disdainful feet; now opportunity
Is furnish'd to my anger; of his own accord
Adam at last to meet me comes; alone moreover --
His heavenly mentor has departed from his side,
Obligingly has left it open to my malice.
Soon shall I hold him bound in nets of fallacy
Inextricable; I have duly set my snares.
Now by pretended love let apt approach be sought
For double-dealing guile! O Satan, dost thou see,
Sluggish, thy foe, nor rend him with wild tooth
asunder?
He only spurns restraint, who cannot rule himself.
For thus the wolf, that mortal terror of the herd,
Whene'er he seeks for kine and silently afar
Examines signs of footprints in the yielding soil,
He gives no sound, but pausing, checks his rapid
pace;
Then, when his prey stands near before his eyes,

Silet, et citatum sustinet tardus gradum:
Ubi praeda rursum propior ante oculos stetit,
Majore cursu sequitur, et villos quatit,
Rictuque pandit ora, nec patitur moras.
Ubi spes refulsit, ira difficilis tegi est.
Tamen est tegenda: semper armatos minus
Provisa feriunt tela: simuletur fides.
Terrestris orbis rector, et princeps freti
Adame, dextram liceat amplecti tuam.
Quo saeva torques lumina, et gratos mihi
Avertis oculos? Renuis oblatam fidem?
Et me Tonantis dextra tibi non disparem
Formavit, et me fulgidus civem suum
Conspexit aether. Testor immitem mihi,
Tibique amicum, forte nec semper, Deum,
Mihi mille amicos, cum beatus viverem
Fuisse, quem nunc tota destituit cohors
Secuta sortem. Tu, rogo, clementior
Miserere miseri; supplicem dextram vide
Securum amoris pignus, aeternum mihi
Promitte foedus. Quid sacrum quassas caput?
Ad. Deo rebellis, perfide, execrabilis,
Procul nefandos corpore a puro amove
Tactus: amicus est mihi quisquis Deo.
Tu sempiternis propter horrendum scelus
Damnate poenis procul ab aspectu fuge
Pii, et beati. Sa. Gerere quid tandem juvat
Inimica semper odia? Si nescis, malum
Est mentis ira, pervigilque animi dolor:
Invidia, luctus, cura, tristitia, et metus,
Odiumque nullos ista felices premunt.
Miseros perurit ista carnificum manus,
Et pertinaces: Semper in melius trahi
Sors est beati. Pone nunc iras truces.
Ad. Seges ante multo mergite in coelestibus

He runs with greater speed and shakes his shaggy
mane,
Opens his hungry mouth and suffers no delay.
When hope has dawn'd again, anger is hard to hide.
Yet must we hide it. Shafts that are foreseen
will ever
Bring less harm to the arm'd. Good faith be our
pretence!
O Adam, ruler of the globe terrestrial
And emperor of ocean, let me clasp thy hand!
Why dost thou roll stern eyes and turn thy gracious
glance
Away from me? Dost thou reject my proferred faith?
Me, too, the right hand of the Thunderer created
Not less than thee, and gleaming ether gazed on me
As its high citizen. I call to witness God --
Savage towards me, a friend to thee, perhaps not
always --
A thousand friends were mine when once I lived in
bliss,
I whom the whole celestial throng has now deserted,
Scorning my lot. Do thou, I pray, in kindlier wise
Pity my wretchedness! Behold my suppliant hand,
Sure pledge of lasting love: wilt thou not promise
me
Eternal faith? Why dost thou shake thy holy head?
Adam. O rebel against God, thou execrable traitor,
Remove thy sinful touch afar from my pure body!
Whoever is a friend to God, is friend to me.
O thou who on account of horrid sin art damn'd
To everlasting torment, flee afar from one
Now blest and dutiful!
Satan. What pleasure can there be
In hoarding hostile hatreds? Know'st thou not that
wrath
Within the mind and wakeful grief of soul are evil?
Envy and grief and care, sorrow and fear and hate --
These things upon the blessed lay no injury.
But wretched souls, and stubborn, does that
torturing band
Burn without ceasing. It is blessed spirits' lot
Ever to seek the better. Lay aside grim wrath!
Adam. Sooner will harvest sheaves be reap'd in
fields of heaven,

Metetur arvis, Terra sidereas faces
Rotata tollet, proferet flammas mare,
Dabit ignis undas, ante vel caput in suum
Sursum relapsas volvet Euphrates aquas,
Vel pronus amnis Tigrin in fontem feret,
Quam Pax, amor, fidesque cum Coeli exule
Mihi sit ulla. Qualis agnos cum lupis
Concors societas jungit, inter nos erit,
Dum lucis ortu vecta purpureis rotis
Aurora surget, Noxque dum stellas feret,
Dumque ego beatus, tuque dum infelix eris.
Sa. Fortis potenti pugnet: in miseros potest
Qui bella gerere, spiritus humiles gerit.
Princeps ferarum nunquam in imbelles Leo
Desaevit agnos: non boves rictu petit.
Adversus urso bellicas tollit jubas,
Orisque hiatum pandit, et dentem asperat.
Nocere tibi me posse si credis, metu
Depone bellum: si minus credis, tamen
Depone bellum, nec tuis dignum puta
Odiis, sed ultro pacis oblatae fidem
Suscipe: clientem perditum felix fove.
Ad. Non esse dignum te meis odiis puto,
Sed minus amore es.
Sa. Non ita abjecti sumus
Adame, nec te vana fallat opinio,
Ut non amicis mente, consilio, aut ope
Prodesse liceat: abstulit sortem Deus
Quam potuit, animis pristinum mansit decus,
Et cor profunda providum sapientia.
Sunt reliqua nobis regna, sunt vires suae,
Multa et potestas. Deus ab aetheria tonans
Se jactet aula. Melius imperium tibi
Tellus fretumque cessit: at nobis loca
Inferna parent. Subditum pedibus tuis
Regnum tenemus. Regitur umbriferum Chaos
Sceptris sacrorum Daemonum. Tua sic meis

Sooner will Earth wheel skyward, bearing starry lights,
Sooner will Ocean bring forth ardent flames, or fire
Roll on in watery waves, or the Euphrates turn
Its down-pour'd waters backward to their primal source,
Or headlong Tigris flow back to its mountain springs,
Before I offer peace or love or trust to thee,
Exile of Heaven! Between us there shall be the sort
Of sympathetic pact that links the lamb and wolf,
As long as Dawn arises, born on shining wheels
From out the East, as long as Night bears gleaming stars,
As long as I am blest and thou shalt be unhappy!

Satan. Let the brave fight against the powerful. But he
Who wars against the wretched must be mean of soul.
The lion, king of beasts, is never known to rage
Against the timid lamb, nor does his maw crave kine.
Rather against the bear he rears his warlike mane
And opes his gaping mouth and gnashes his grim teeth.
If thou believest I can harm thee, then with fear
Abandon war. If thou believest not, lay war,
Nevertheless aside. Think me not worth thy hate,
But rather, freely take my pledge of proferr'd peace.
In thy good fortune help a hopeless suppliant!

Adam. I cannot think thee worthy of my hatred, yea,
And much less of my love.

Satan. We are not so cast down,
O Adam, nor let vain opinion cozen thee,
That we cannot advantage friends with wit, advice,
Or active aid. God, as He could, has stol'n away
My heavenly lot; but all my former pride still lives
And a foreseeing heart of penetrating wisdom.
Some remnants of my rule remain, and my own strength,
And mighty sway. God from His court ethereal
Boasts thundering. To thee He has assign'd a realm
Better than mine, even the earth and sea; yet us
Th' infernal tracts obey. An empire we possess
Hidden beneath thy feet. Demonic Spirits wield

Imperia sunt vicina, regnemus simul.
Ad. Quod Terra Sceptris paret et Pontus meis
Donum est Tonantis, mutua qui me fide
Sibi obligavit: non ego illius cliens
Alios clientes quaero, non socios mihi,
Contentus ista sorte quam tribuit Deus,
Damnumque censens omne cum vitio lucrum.
Sa. Oblata ab aliquo quis recusat munera?
Ad. Quemcunque non tam dona, quam donans juvat.
Sa. Perpetua gerere bella prodest nemini.
Ad. Mihi quid nocebit? nil timens, spero nihil.
Sa. Misero quod est necesse, felici expedit.
Ad. Relligio quod permittit id solum expedit.
Sa. Ferire foedus ecqua relligio vetat?
Ad. Communionem criminis foedus vocas?
Sa. Quodcunque nostrum est fiat hoc pariter tuum.
Ad. Vestrum daturus, nil potes praeter malum.
Sa. Nunquam nocebo: qua licebit prodero.
Ad. Hoc ita futurum quis fidem faciet mihi?
Sa. Primitto, polliceor, paciscor, spondeo.
Ad. Desertor, exul, perduellis, perfidus.
Sa. Jurabo magni Numen aeternum Dei.
Ad. Qui jam, quod in te est, aetheris regno caret.
Sa. Si fallo, semper ira me illius premat.
Ad. Paenum [sic!] timebis, qui nihil pejus times?
Sa. Juvare socios soleo.
Ad. Sic, simul ut ruant.

Their sceptres over shadowy Chaos. Since thy realm
Is neighboring to mine, let us bear sway together.
Adam. That land and sea obey my sceptre is the gift
Of God the Thunderer, who with a mutual pledge
Has bound me to Himself. I, as His client true,
Seek not for other clients or allies of mine,
Content with that same lot that He has given me
And judging but as loss all profit gain'd by sin.
Satan. What man rejects a gift that anyone may bring?
Adam. He whom the giver pleases less than does the gift.
Satan. It is no one's advantage to wage endless war.
Adam. What thing can harm me? Fearing naught, I wish for naught.
Satan. That which the wretched need, may help the fortunate.
Adam. That which Religion grants, alone can bring advantage.
Satan. Does any scruple bar the forming of alliance?
Adam. Callest thou comradeship in crime alliance fit?
Satan. Let all things that are mine be thy possessions too.
Adam. Proposing to bring gifts, thou canst give naught but evil.
Satan. Ne'er shall I harm: where'er permitted, I shall help.
Adam. Who shall assure me that this will indeed be so?
Satan. I promise, give assurance, pledge, sincerely plight.
Adam. Deserter, exile, public enemy, and traitor!
Satan. By the eternal godhead of great God I swear.
Adam. By Him whom thou hast striv'n to drive from off His throne.
Satan. If I deceive thee, may His anger ever rend me!
Adam. Wilt thou fear punishment, that canst fear nothing worse?
Satan. I'm wont to please my friends.
Adam. Yes, to their utter ruin.

Sa. Quia pertinaci fretus insipientia
Pacem recusas, odia nunc primum mea,
Irasque disces. Semper immites dolos
Versabo: semper hostis instabo tibi:
Nullus vacabit fraude, vel bello dies,
Nec coeptus unquam cedet ex animo furor,
Ut qui negasti foederis consortium
Patiare poenae. Parta, jam parta ultio est.
Ad. Saevi, feroci, dum libet, nec bellicas
Leges recuso, nec tuas metuo minas,
Cui sagittis cor tuis impervium
Divinus ambit triplici scuto favor.
Deum timere, nec aliud tutissimum est.
Exul, recede!
Sa. Vos quoque exilium manet.

CHORUS

Asclepiadei

Euphrates Capoten nate sub ultimum
Montana Armeniae Qui peragrans loca
Tauro nubifero laberis obvius,
Qui vires reparans Cappadoce in solo,
Primum flumineo victus ab impetu,
Praeceps occiduas qua ruis in plagas
Invitum pluvios diripit ad Notos,
Ripis non alibi nobilioribus
Inclusum poteras volvere gurgitem,
Quam qua deliciis sacra perennibus
Heden quadruplici lambitur alveo,
Tellus pinguis ubi, glebaque densior
Amnis temperie diluitur tui.
Mundi illic opifex dextera fertile
Ornavit variis arboribus nemus.
Pendent de gravidis pomo parentibus,
Et ficus virides, prunaque mitia,
Et cum Crustuminis castaneae piris.
Nux illic bifido tecta putamine
Incumbit foliis, junctaque amygdalis
Insultant rubidis mespila frondibus.

Satan. Since, trusting in thy pertinacious foolishness,
Thou spurnest peace, learn now my hatred and my wrath
For the first time; for I shall ever meditate
Pitiless wiles and ever threaten thee as foe.
No day henceforth for thee shall lack its plot and war,
Nor shall my fury, so aroused, cease from my soul;
Thus thou who wouldst not share my pact and company
Shalt share my penalty. Revenge, revenge is born!
Adam. Rage, while thou mayest, fierce one! I do not refuse
Thy terms of warfare, neither do I fear thy threats.
About my human heart, impervious to thy shafts,
The favor of my God hath placed a triple shield.
The only true salvation lies in fearing God.
Go, exile, get thee hence!
Satan. Exile awaits thee too.

CHORUS

O fair Euphrates, born of mountain rills
On far Capotes, 'mid Armenian hills
Flowing to meet tall Taurus' cloudy crest,
Then gaining strength in Cappadocian soil
First conquer'd by thy waters' eager broil
Where thou dost hurry headlong to the west
And turn unwilling to the rainy south, --
Sure, nowhere canst thou roll thy flood shut in
By nobler banks than where eternal youth
In holy Eden's pleasures without sin
Is water'd by thy current's fourfold course,
There where a richer earth and thicker sod
Are made yet richer by thy streams' divorce.
There the creative handiwork of God
Has deck'd a fertile grove with divers trees;
From heavy parent-limbs bright apples grow,
Green figs, and mellow plums; and chestnuts show,
With Sabine pears, their rare sapidities.
The walnut cover'd with its two-cleft shell
Lurks in the leaves; medlars with almonds dwell
And match the ruddy foliage in hue,

Sunt mites cerasi, fragaque moraque
Ambo purpureis tincta coloribus.
Horti sed medii qua regio patet
Binas Omnipotens condidit arbores:
Vitam haec perpetuam denotat, altera
Praesignat duplicem planta scientiam:
Quam carpi vetuit, ne meritam trahat
Mortem culpa gravis: nam dolor, et labor,
Cum curis miseris, et senium grave,
Ac mors, ac aliud, si quid erit mali,
Contingi vetito cortice delitent.
Adamus platani suppositus comae,
Et vinctus viridi tempora laurea,
Nudus cum tenera conjuge, cum libet
Ripis Assyrii fluminis assidens,
Sacro dulcisoni carminis alite
Divinae celebrat mira potentiae.
Auditis volucres cantibus advolant:
Certant dulce sequi carmen aëdones:
Euphrates tacito murmure consonat,
Quotquot sunt fluviis sorte beatior.
Non illum superat Nilus in aequora
Qui septemgemino funditur ostio,
Exundante Pharum gurgite qui rigat:
Non telo citior currere missili
Tigris contiguo proximus alveo.
Non qui per calidam labitur Indiam
Ganges aurifero flumine nobilis.
At vos o homines, (si bene pergitis
Felices nimium!) parcite, parcite
Jussum legiferi spernere Numinis,
Nec fructus vetita carpite ab arbore
Omnis matre mali. Magna rebellibus
Semper poena comes. Cernite Tartari
Clausos sollicito carcere Daemonas
Depulsos patrii finibus aetheris.
Si sunt grata Dei munera, si timor
Non deest in Dominum, non amor in patrem,
Aeternum dabitur vivere; sic genus
Vestrum perpetua sorte beabitur:
Sic et cum geminis pacta parentibus
Contingent similes foedera posteros:
Transcurret Domini gratia perpete
Haeredum serie, nec minor est Dei

Ripe cherries, too, and strawberries as well,
And mulberries bright-tinted to the view.
But where the middle of the Garden lies,
The Hand Omnipotent two trees hath set:
The one, life everlasting can beget;
The other, twofold knowledge signifies.
This He forbids to pluck, lest condign death
Avenge the fault that He admonisheth:
For Pain, and Toil, and wretched Care and Age,
And Death, and every other ill of life
Lurk hidden in the fair, forbidden bark.
There Adam lies beside his tender wife
Naked beneath a plane-tree's foliage
Save for a wreath of laurel; in that Park,
He sometimes sits beside th' Assyrian stream
And celebrates the wonders of God's might
With sacred poetry and song supreme.
To hear that music, come the birds in flight,
And nightingales with him in chaunting vie;
Euphrates murmurs the soft melody,
More blest in lot than all the streams that flow,
Surpassing Egypt's River that doth go
With sevenfold debouchure to the sea
And laves the Pharos with its foaming flood;
Nor is the Tigris greater, though it be
Swifter than any arrow as it runs,
Nor noble Ganges, with its golden mud,
Flowing through Hind beneath the tropic suns.
But ye, mankind, (if over-fortunate
Ye prosper mightily) forbear, forbear
To scorn the ordinance of God All-Great!
Pluck not forbidden apples of despair,
The source of every evil! Punishment
To rebels as a comrade e'er is sent.
Behold the sorry demons, shut in Hell,
And driven from the Heav'n they loved so well.
If God's good gifts are pleasing, and if fear
And love for God, your Father, fail you not,
An everlasting life will be your lot
And your descendants will be blessed here.
Thus the agreement with the parents made
Will likewise bless their due posterity;
God's favoring Hand will evermore be laid
Upon successive heirs; His care will be

Prospectura piis cura minoribus.

ACTUS IIII

Eva Sathan

Trimetri Iambici

Quod illud animal tramite obliquo means
Ad me volutum flexili serpit via?
Sibila retorquet ora setosum caput,
Trifidamque linguam vibrat: oculi ardent duo.
Arrecta cervix surgit, et maculis nitet
Pectus superbis: caerulis picti notis
Sinuantur orbes, tortiles spirae micant
Auri colore: lubricos longos sinus
Tendit volumen, terga se in gyros plicant.
Nunc se reclinat flexile in collum caput,
Retroque spectat, quodque caudae proximum
Nodatur agmen lumine adverso videt.
Quodcunque tandem est, propius huc ad me venit,
Pronos propinqua fundit anfractus via,
Longosque tractus pedibus advolvit meis:
Attollit ora: miror an queat et loqui.
Sa. Utilia certe proloqui, et possum tibi,
Et non omittam. Gratulor vestris ego
Cessisse regnis, quicquid immenso ambitu
Spatiosus aer claudit: Omnes bestiae,
Quas Terra, vel quas pelagus aut aer habet,
Gaudemus illa sorte: res est maxima
Parere natis non feros dominos pati,
Sed jussa capere humana: si quando regit
Ratio regentes, servitus est libera.
Miramur unum hoc, omnis authorem boni
(Nam sic vocari gaudet) istis fructibus
Vetuisse vesci. Tanta quae menti sedet

Upon their pious seed eternally.

ACT FOUR

Eve (alone). Satan approaches in the guise of a serpent.

Eve. What is that creature, moving with a slantwise path,
That crawls by winding ways and writhes along to meet me?
Its flat and scaly head twists back a hissing mouth
And shakes a three-fork'd tongue; its two eyes gleam like fire;
Its rampant neck arises and its clammy breast
Shines with proud spots; painted with azure markings,
Its coiling spirals twine, and twist, with hue of gold
Resplendent; in long slippery volutes it extends,
And folds its back in many a sinuous labyrinth.
Its swaying head now rests a moment on its neck,
It backward gazes and with rearward-looking eye
Now contemplates the knotted column next its tail.
Whatever it may be, it hither draws more near,
Pouring its prostrate windings by a closer path,
And rolls its lengthy undulations to my feet.
It rears its head. I wonder whether it can speak.
Satan. Things profiting to thee I can most surely speak,
Nor shall forebear. I bring congratulations
That all that spacious air in its vast range encloses
Has yielded to your sway. All we beasts indeed
Whom earth and sea and air possess within their bounds
Rejoice in our good fortune. 'Tis a privilege,
For those born to obey, not to endure wild tyrants
But to receive the clemency of human sway.
When reason rules the rulers, servitude is free.
We marvel only that the Author of all Good
(A title He delights in) has forbidden you
To feed on yonder fruits. Does such great envy dwell

Invidia? qui Telluris imperium dedit
Is vos nec uno patitur horto perfrui?
Ev. Quascunque plantas istud arbustum gerit,
Quoscunque fructus, usibus nostris gerit.
Hortum per omnem, queis libet, vesci licet.
Sed arbor una, qua Nemus medium patet,
Vitanda ramis poma curvatis gerit.
His abstinere Lex monet magni patris,
Ne forte vitae consequamur terminum.
Sa. Ne crede pomi unius ob dispendium
Debere certam protinus mortem sequi.
Perire poterunt, perpeti vitae Deus
Quos destinavit? Fata res omnes agunt:
Praevisa tantum facimus, et ab alto venit
Quodcunque patimur. Scripta divina manu
Decreta durant semper, et recto suis
Connexa caussis cuncta vadunt tramite.
Ratus ordo, series certa, dia necessitas
Futura cogunt. Si volunt ea vos mori
Effugere non est: si negant, decerpere est
Impune fructum, nullus impendet metus.
Negant profecto: nulla vos lethi manet
Conditio. nullus imminet mortis dolor.
Mors ipsa nihil est, si mihi credis, nisi
Mutationum perpetes semper vices.
Quidquid creatum est ut sit, id nunquam perit,
Peritque semper: Lethifera quaevis dies,
Natalis eadem est rursus: haec contraria
Pugnant per omne tempus, et vincunt simul.
Mors ipsa vitam, et ortus interitum trahunt.
Quod rere poenam id esse Naturae scias.
Metuere lethum non decet: poteris mori
Certe, et renasci in melius: haec lex corporum est,
Perfectiorem semper ad sortem trahi.

Within His mind? Does He who has bestow'd on you
The rule of Earth not suffer you to use one garden?
Eve. Whatever kinds of plants this wide plantation
    bears,
Whatever kinds of fruits, it raises for our use.
Through all the Garden we may eat whate'er we like.
Only one tree, where spreads the middle of the
    Garden,
Bears, on its curving branches, apples we must shun.
The law of the Great Father warns us to abstain,
Lest we perchance be smitten and should surely die.
Satan. Do not believe that through the loss of
    one small apple
Thy certain death must straightway be the consequence!
How can those perish whom to everlasting life
God hath predestined? For the Fates control all
    things.
We merely do that which has been ordain'd, and
    suffer
That which comes down from heav'n. Writ by the
    Hand divine,
Decrees endure forever. By a path direct,
All things, link'd with their certain causes, still
    proceed.
Due order, sequence fix'd, divine necessity --
These rule the future. If they will that ye should
    die,
Ye cannot then escape. If they do not, the fruit
Can with impunity be pluck'd; no fear impends.
Surely they will it not. Condition of sure death
Does not await you, nor does pain of dying threaten.
Nay more, believe me, death itself is nothing but
An everlasting chain of metamorphoses.
That which is made in order to exist, dies not
And yet is always dying. Every day brings death,
And yet likewise brings birth once more. These
    opposites,
Struggling eternally, are both victorious;
For death itself brings life and birth induces
    death.
Thus what thou deemest punishment is part of Nature.
To fear death is not meet; for thou canst surely die
To live in higher state; this is a law of bodies,
Ever to be drawn on towards a more perfect lot.

Sed forsan animam morte plectendam putes.
Deterius erras: Anima non didicit pati,
Sed agere tantum. quod perit sensim perit
Membris solutis: anima nec partes habet,
Nec ulla damna temporum patitur moris.
Subsistit in se, nec foris vitam petit,
Quam tribuit: ipsa sola principium sibi est.
Nec mihi profecto facile persuadebitur
Damnasse inusu poma perpetuo Deus.
Nam quis negarit opera divinae manus
Merito probanda? Quicquid est, etiam bonum est:
Gratosque rebus singulis fines dedit
Natura cur sint, esse nil frustra jubens.
Rebus creatis si putes uti nefas
Hanc, quae cavenda fecit, accusas manum.
Ev. Incerta jussi causa: sed certum tamen
Parere jusso. quicquid est vetuit Deus.
Memini, recordor, ista conditio fuit
Praescripta nobis tradita Nemoris sacri
Possessione, ne boni simul, et mali
Magistra nostras planta pollueret manus
Dare quenque jus est muneri legem suo.
Sa. Cur non et illam muneris legem dedit,
Cum Terra vestris, cum juberetur salum
Parere Sceptris? aliqua magnae portio est
Telluris arbos, dona quae facit irrita.
Si licet, et aequum est muneri semper suo
Detrahere partem, nulla tandem gratia est.
Totum redire dona repetenti potest.
Mutare factum parte nec minima decet,
Si liberalis semper, idemque est, Deum.
Perpende cuncta: majus et secretius
Aliquid necesse est subsit: indubie subest.
Invidit illud, quod latet fructu, bonum,

Perchance thou thinkest souls are punished thus by
death;
This is a worse mistake. The soul has never learn'd
To suffer; it but acts. And that which dies, dies
slowly,
With a decay of members. No parts hath the soul,
Nor can it suffer any loss by Time's delays.
Subsisting in itself, its own sole principle,
It seeks not otherwhere the life that it con-
tributes.
Nor will God easily persuade me, I am sure,
That He has damn'd these apples to complete disuse.
Who will deny that all works of the Hand divine
Are rightly to be tried? Whatever is, is good.
To each thing pleasant ends and uses are assign'd
By Nature, that asks nothing to exist in vain.
If thou think this a crime among created things,
Thou dost accuse this Hand that made things to be
shunn'd.
Eve. The cause of the command is doubtful. This
is sure,
We must obey. Whate'er it is, God doth forbid.
For I remember that condition was prescribed
When we were giv'n possession of the sacred Grove --
The holy plant, mistress of good and ill alike,
Was not to bring pollution to our reckless hands.
'Tis right that one should join conditions to his
gift.
Satan. Why did He not impose that same restraint
of gift
When He commanded Earth and Ocean to obey
Your sceptres? For the tree forbidden is a part
Of the great earth, whose ample gifts He thus
makes void.
If it be fair and right ever to take away
Some portion of His gift, at length no grace is
left.
Wholly can gifts return to Him who seeks again.
It is not fit that God change in the least His deed,
If He is ever bounteous and unchangeable.
Consider everything. Some greater, more mysterious
Intent must lie behind. Undoubtedly it does.
He grudges you that good that lurks within the
fruit;

Scientiamque, quae bonum miscet malo,
Servare soli conditam voluit sibi:
Pro servitus odiosa, famulatus gravis,
Curari ab illo, sola cui cura est sui!
Malus est vocandus, qui sui causa est bonus.
Utrum videtur, prospicitne, an despicit,
Qui cuncta largo gloriae pretio facit,
Sibi summa servans? O jugum intolerabile!
Quam satius est non esse, quam non liberum?
Centum fideles militum coelestium
Turmas, beata sors quibus crimen fuit,
Et invidendum robur, et paritas minax,
Pepulit Tyrannus, et gravem indixit fugam,
Coelique alumnos inferae densis specus
Damnavit umbris: Quicquid orent supplices,
Culpamque, si qua est culpa, fateantur suam,
Aures reorum precibus inclemens negat,
Non desituro puniens miseros malo.
Si nunc recentis imperi primordiis
Altum elevatos gravius iterum deprimit,
Quid faciet olim? quam putas subdent facem
Animo insolenti tempus, et regni mora?
Bonum est cavenda discere alieno ex malo.
Si vos amaret, mortis auferret metum:
Si non, quod unum restat, excusso jugo,
Vos vindicate. statis in vestro solo.
Aetherea non hic aula, non exercitus
Coelestis isto castra disposuit loco.
Accingere animo: Servus aufugiat metus.
Nullum periclum sine periclo vincitur.
Cum res sit anceps certa res audacia est.
Ev. Procul absit: absit hunc ut invidiae putem
Stimulis peruri, et angi ab alieno bono,
Qui tribuit ipse, quique quod libitum est, habet.
Telluris ergo dominus, et dator arborem

And that deep knowledge, that blends evil truth
    with good,
He has desired to keep, stored in Himself alone.
Ah, hateful servitude, detested slavery,
Cared for by Him whose care is only for Himself!
Bad must he be, who only for himself is good.
Which does it seem now? Does He favor you or
    scorn you,
He who does all things for a heavy price of praise,
Keeping the best Himself? O yoke unbearable!
Were it not better not to be, than not be free?
A hundred faithful squadrons of celestial knights,
Whose only crimes were lots of too great happiness
And enviable strength and threatening parity
The Tyrant hurl'd down and inflicted grievous
    flight
And damn'd the children of the sky to a low cave
And densest darkness. Though as suppliants they
    beseech,
Confessing Him their fault, if any fault there be,
He now denies a hearing to His victims' prayers
And punishes the wretches with unending evil.
If He smites down again in heavy tyranny
Those raised on high with prelude to imperial power,
What will He do hereafter? What flame, dost thou
    think,
Have time and rule's delay hid in His tyrant heart?
Learn from another's ill what things are to be
    shunn'd!
He, if He loved you, would remove the fear of death.
If He does not, one course remains, shake off His
    yoke;
And vindicate yourselves. Ye stand on your own
    soil.
The court of heaven is not here, nor has the host
Celestial pitch'd its shining bivouac in this place.
Gird up your spirits now! Let servile fear depart!
Without due peril is no peril overcome.
In doubtful issues, boldness is the safest course!
Eve. Far be it from me! Let me not think that He
Is gall'd by Envy's spurs and grieved by others'
    good,
He who has giv'n, and owns, whatever He has pleased!
Shall the great Giver of the earth be envious

Invideat unam? Dira Sathanum suae
Rebellionis quod luat poenam cohors,
Nihil illud ad me: sed tamen justum puto.
At tu, recense, cujus ingenium feras
Exsuperat omnes, quod putes vetito bonum
Latere fructu. Sa. Nomen hoc ipsum docet.
Animae est voluptas scire, res cognoscere
Bonas malasque: nam malum non est malum
Qua scitur: una haec mentis est felicitas
Species in aliis quae renident singulis
Congerere in unum, et intus oculis integrum
Perspicere Mundum, cuncta cum causis simul
Insculpere animo, maximum cujus bonum est
Notitia veri certa, falli nescia.
Nam perspicaci mentis intellectui
Patet universum, tendit ad finem vigor
Rationis istum, quoque plus invenerit
Minus quiescit id quod ultra est quaerere.
Ita semper animum cura discendi quatit,
Nunquamque quod habet respicit, sed quo caret.
Deus unus omnes nec laborans vindicat
Sibi notiones, sponte quae sese offerunt,
Cunctas scit artes, cumque non discat sapit:
Socium recusat: caeteris animantibus
Mentem aut negavit, aut, quod aeque injurium est,
Mancam, atque mutilam tribuit, et sapientiae
Condit molesta studia sollicitudine.
Ipsisque vobis, quos sibi promiserat
Similes futuros, istud invidit bonum.
Arripite pacti jura: promissum dari
Ipsi occupate: quod tenax renuit Deus
Dabit arbor ista, numen arcanum gerens.
Equidem sciebat ille, qua primum die
Comesta succum poma vitalem darent,
Cessuram ab animo protinus caliginem,
Caecasque tenebras, nilque distantes Deo

Over a single tree? That the dread soldiery
Of devils suffers castigation for revolt,
Does not concern me; though I think their sentence just.
But tell me, thou, who in intelligence surpassest
All living beasts, what mystery of good doth lurk
In the forbidden fruit.
Satan. Its very name may teach thee.
It is the soul's delight to know, to learn of things
Both good and evil; for things bad their badness lose
When they are known. This is Mind's one felicity,
To bring together into one all traits that shine
In individual things, to see with inward eye
All things as one great Whole, by causes bound together,
Within the mind, that seeks thus its supremest good,
Sure knowledge of all truth, unable to be duped.
For to the keenness of the penetrating mind
The universe lies open; towards that self-same end
The force of reason presses, which, the more it finds,
The less it rests from seeking that which lies beyond.
Anxiety for learning ever shakes the soul,
That never recks of what it knows, but what it lacks.
God only, without toil, claims for His Self Divine
All concepts; for spontaneous they come to Him.
He knows all arts, and, without learning, He has wisdom.
Companionship He spurns; to other living things
He has denied a mind or, what is equal wrong,
He has assign'd a maim'd and mutilated one
And clogg'd fair Wisdom's study with vexatious care.
To you yourselves, promised by Him similitude
To His celestial self, He has begrudged this good.
Break the agreement's terms! Seize with your own fair hands
That which He promised you! What niggard God denies
Is found in yonder tree, that offers secret power.
You may be sure He knew that on the very day
When first sweet eaten apples gave their vital juice
All intellectual darkness would at once depart,
All undiscerning shades, and ye, not far from God,

Vos cognituros, quicquid aut nocet, aut juvat.
Hinc illa lex est quae sacro fructu frui
Vetat: hinc inanis mortis injectus timor,
Mala ut timentes abstineretis bonis:
Mihi tu monenti crede: nulla ad jus sui
Sibi vindicandum negligenda occasio est.
Quod non habes tibi quaere, ne perdas tua:
Nunc ille forsan mobilis rector Poli
Eripere, quicquid ante tribuit, cogitat:
Tu fac, quod ille cogitat: fraudem occupa.
Difficilis est res gloriae custodia
Nisi vetera servans semper acquiras nova.
Concessa nisi quis usque sustineat bona
Ducet ruinam pondus, et dominum premet.
Captare lucrum, maxima est damni fuga.
Quae res agatur cerne, si quicquam vides:
Ex homine morsus unus efficiet Deam.
Ev. Adeone et alia praeter hominum pectora
Ratio occupavit? bruta namque haec bestia est,
At bruta certe verba non visa est loqui.
Ferme ut prohibitos edere fructus audeam
Facerent et eius pervicax persuasio,
Et mea cupido. Forte melius sensuum
Tamen est dolosas illecebras vincere,
Quam se ut voluptas vera nobis subtrahat.
Sa. Permitte vanis ne superstitionibus
Te fascinandam, neve naturae tuae
Demens rebella: si quid est placitum tibi,
Puta licere, quoque te sensus rapit
Sequere, nec ipsi praelium indicas tibi.
Natura tutrix, et parens animantibus
Sensus magistros tribuit, ut rerum foris
Percepta facies intimarum virium
Illas moneret; profuturae si forent,

Would know whatever harms and what delights.
Hence comes that law that bars you from the sacred fruit;
Hence was the empty fear of death injected in you,
That, fearing evil, you might not enjoy the good.
Believe my warning, for no opportunity
Of laying claim to one's own rights should be neglected.
Thyself seek what thou hast not, lest thou lose thine own!
For even now, perchance, the King of the wheeling heavens
Makes plans to snatch away what He bestow'd before.
Do thou, then, what He plots to do. Forestall the fraud.
The custody of glory is a thorny thing,
Unless, while guarding old gifts, you gain ever new.
The good things granted one must be maintain'd
Or their mere weight must bring fell ruin on their lord.
To grasp at profit is the chief escape from loss.
If thou canst see at all, see what is to be done!
One bite will alter thee from human to divine.
Eve. Can this be so? Does reason dwell indeed in breasts
Other than man's? Surely this creature is a brute,
But never has a brute been known to utter words.
His resolute persuasion and my own desire
Doubtless would almost make me dare to eat the fruit
Against commandment. But perhaps 'twould better be
To quell the guileful fascination of the senses
Than that true pleasure should withdraw itself from us.
Satan. Let not thyself be cozen'd by fond superstitions,
Neither against thy nature foolishly rebel!
If anything has brought sweet pleasure to thy mind,
Consider it permitted; where thy senses lead,
Follow straightway, nor join in war against thyself.
Nature, thy guardian and parent, has assign'd
Senses to living things as teachers; outward shows
That they perceive in things thus bring them warnings sure
Of inner powers, in order that the appetite

Ut appetitus visa sequeretur bona,
Sin obfuturae, fugeret: haud temere insita
Menti cupido fertur ad finem suum.
Odore, visu, quicquid aut gustu placet
Naturae amicum est: nanque [sic] odos, color, et sapor,
Et si quid istis simile, non per se juvant,
Sed appetitum res ad optandas trahunt,
Desideratis perfrui dantes bonis.
His ducibus utens conde visceribus tuis
Cupita merito poma: continge arborem:
Decerpe pendens aureum ramis onus.
Jam restat ori tantum ut admoveas tuo.
Minimum est, quod unum facere te magnam potest.
Ev. O dulce pomum, quam tua haec species meis
Arridet oculis, quam vel olfactus juvat?
Utinam soluto te metu possem frui,
Tuosque succos discere, et magnas mihi
Vires, vel uno hoc, quod sub aspectu latent.
Satisne ratio docuit, interitum pati
Corpus nec animum posse, sed vanum metum
Torquere mentes? satin, et invidiam Dei
Lex illa monstrat quae vetat pomo frui?
Nonne illud etiam patuit aequalem Deo
Me cognituram quicquid aut gratum juvat,
Aut triste laedit? nonne sensus praecipit
Gustare magnam commodi faciens fidem!
Quid hoc quod artus horror incussit meos,
Et ima gelidus ossa perrupit tremor?
Causam timoris nescio: timeo tamen.
Placet admovere poma, sed renuit manus
Parere, dextra pondus accusat suum,
Alioque fertur. Fructus a labris fugit,

May seek things seen as good, if it should profit
them,
Or flee things profitless. Desire, wisely placed
Within the mind, leads on to its own proper end.
All that delights thee by its odor, sight, or
taste,
Is Nature's friend; for fragrance, hue, and taste,
and all
The like fair attributes, please not in their own
selves,
But lure the appetite to things desirable,
Permitting us to savor long'd-for benefits.
Led by these guides, grant straightway to thy
wistful throat
Apples deservedly desired! Touch the tree!
Pluck down the golden burden hanging from its
boughs!
And now thou only needest to apply thy mouth;
Only that little act remains to make thee great.
Eve. O sweetest apple, how thy heavenly beauty
smiles
And charms my eyes, and how thy fragrance raptures
me!
Would that, discarding fear, I might enjoy thee
now,
And learn to know thy juices and thy mighty powers,
That virtue above all that lurks beneath thy
beauty!
For does not Reason teach assuredly that soul
And body cannot suffer death? That empty fear
Torments the mind? Does not the law forbidding us
To enjoy the fruit reveal the envious heart of God?
Has not this creature shown that I, divinely
changed,
Shall know whatever good thing can be pleasureable,
What grim thing hurt? Do not the senses, making
faith
In my own daring useful, teach me how to taste? --
What is this horror, that has smitten all my limbs?
What trembling shudder penetrates my inmost bones?
The cause of fear I know not; yet I surely fear.
I long to pluck the apple, but my hand refuses
To do my will, accuses its reluctant weight,
And elsewhere moves. The fruit flies from my lips,

Et fixa pigris ora sub malis stupent.
Arborque trepido tota subsiluit solo.
Quid agere tentas mulier? authorem boni,
Qui cuncta fecit, te beavit commodis,
Unamque rebus anteposuit conditis,
Hunc tu paras deserere? res brutas duas,
Hoc reptile animal sequeris, et sensus tuos?
Meliora praefer monita: si nil te movet
Timor ille mortis, dona sed moveant Dei.
Nihil ista prosunt? at mali moveat metus.
Perpende utrumvis. Cogita praesens bonum,
Malum futurum. Pendula est sententia.
Mens ipsa dubio trepida consilio labat.
Quid tamdiu haeres anime, quid te interrogas,
Quid te lacessis, atque consilium diu
Tam facile torques? Vince: nodos disseca.
Diffringe quicquid obstat, et tete expedi.
Expende quantum praemii secum ferant
Arcana pomi: Quicquid est rerum scies,
Novumque fies Numen: audendum puto.
Humana morsu pendet ex uno salus.
Non sola tua res agitur: hac hora potes
Prodesse mille saeculorum posteris
Servosne parere an liberos melius putas,
Homines, Deosne? sors utra est felicior?
Ignoscet ipse forte si videat Deus,
Mihi videri melius esse nihil Deo.
Quod si severus crimini veniam meo
Non est daturus, hoc quoque vocabit nefas
Tam prope fuisse: magna delicti mei
Jam pars peracta est: arborem vetitam attigi,
Pomumque carpsi, quodque dicet pessimum
Deliberavi: constat accusatio,
Faciamque nil ut pejus, inscribet dicam

And my dull mouth, fixt beneath sluggish cheeks,
    is dazed.
The whole tree seems to quiver in the trembling
    soil.
Woman, what wouldst thou do? Art ready to desert
The Author of all Good, Creator of all things,
Who blest thee with his benefits, preferr'd alone
Above all things created? Wilt thou follow brutes --
This reptile animal and thine own appetite?
Choose better counsellors! If nothing move thee
    else,
Be caution'd by the fear of death, the gifts of God.
Are these of no avail? Stop at the fear of evil!
Weigh both considerations: think on present good
And evil that may come. Decision is uncertain.
The hesitating mind in doubtful counsel wavers.
Why wait so long, my soul? Why question with
    thyself?
Why thus afflict thyself and crucify so long
A plan so easy? Come! Conquer, and cut the knot!
Shatter whate'er opposes thee, and free thyself!
Weigh out how much reward the secrets of the tree
Can bear with them. Thou wilt have knowledge of
    all things,
Thou wilt become divine. I think this must be
    dared.
The welfare of mankind depends upon one bite.
Not thy lot only is at stake; for by this hour
Thou canst enrich a thousand ages yet to come.
Shall thy race then obey as slaves or live in
    freedom?
Shall they be men, or gods? Which lot is happier?
Perhaps God will forgive, if He may chance to see.
It would seem better that it should escape His
    notice;
But if, in His severity, He will not grant
Pardon to my offence, this also will He blame,
That I have been so close. A great part of my
    crime
Already is committed: I have touch'd the tree,
Have pluck'd the apple, and, what He would call the
    worst,
Resolved to do it. Thus the accusation stands.
Should I do nothing worse, I know that He will

Quod paene feci. Quid juvat cum ceperis
Labare retro trahere pendentem pedem?
Res est inepta, et stulta peccati modus.
Culpam per aliam tuta fit culpae via.
Aut me superni lege spreta Principis
Divina faciet laesa Majestas ream,
Aut crimine ipso criminis felicitas
Absolvet: hoc, hoc potius eligere est meum.
Jam dextra manus perfice, atque ori admove,
Jamdudum hianti, quicquid hoc pomo latet:
Tuque os beata recipe fructum ex arbore,
Ut mox receptum ventris immittas cavo.
O persuavis gustus, o tenero sapor
Gratus palato, quam tuus succus juvat,
Quam me beasti! restat hoc unum modo,
Tanti ut maritus particeps fiat boni.
Sa. Fiat profecto: plurimum dices meis
Debere monitis, cum, quod est res, senties.
Scies bonum, sciesque, ne dubita, malum:
Hanc auferet tibi nulla notitiam dies,
Similesque matri liberos paries suae,
Jam se recludent lumina, et quod nunc latet
Dabitur tueri: Quid, precor, majus petas?
Et ecce, (primum sortis indicium tuae)
Commoda maritum duxit huc occasio.
Ego ad latebras tacitus abrepam meas.
Ad delicatam tu virum invita dapem.

Adamus Eva

Iambici Trimetri

Lente per omnem, saepe sustento gradu,

charge me
With what's already done. What boots it, when
thou'st taken
The fruit, to falter and draw back a lagging foot?
Sinning in moderation is a foolish thing.
Another crime makes safe the highway of offence.
Either th' offended Majesty of Heaven's King
Will hold me guilty of contempt for His great law,
Or else my crime's felicity will set me free
From crime itself. This, this is rather mine to
choose!
Now, O my hand, perform thy task! Present my mouth,
Long-gaping, with whatever lurks within this fruit!
And thou, my mouth, accept fruit from the blessed
tree,
In order to remit it straightway to my stomach.
(She eats).
O most sweet taste, O flavor to the tender palate
Above all else delicious, how thy juice delights,
How thou hast blest me! Now one privilege remains:
To make my husband sharer in so great a good!
Satan. In sooth it shall be so. Thou shalt declare
thyself
Debtor to my advice when thou hast learn'd the
truth.
Thou shalt know good and -- doubt it not! -- thou
shalt know evil.
No day shall take away from thee this certain
knowledge,
And children shalt thou bring forth like the dam
that bore them.
Now shall thine eyes be open'd that thou mayest see
Things that lie hid. What more, I pray thee, dost
thou seek?
And now behold (first omen of thy happy lot)
Fit opportunity has led thy husband hither.
I to my lair shall creep away in silent haste;
Do thou invite thy husband to the dainty feast.

(The serpent slips silently away. Enter Adam, in evident anxiety, and for a time does not notice Eve.)

Adam. Now having slowly walk'd through all the
Garden ways,

Spatiatus hortum, repeto vix sero locum,
Primum unde nostrae fuerat auspicium viae.
Ab arbore ista sumpseram primordium
Non desiturae sacra quae vitae nota est.
Exinde lato, ripa qua jacet, ambitu
Reliquas pererrans singularum fructibus
Satiatus isthuc redeo: nam nusquam obvia
Mihi facta conjunx dubito quo lateat loco,
Et quo petacem prandio expulerit famem.
Fallorne, an ipsam video? prope sistam gradum.
Ubi tamdiu haeres? cujus alimento dapis,
O socia thalami, corporis vim sustines?
Ev. Haec ipsa viridem gramine imposito thorum,
Haec arbor umbram tribuit, haec etiam cibum.
Ad. Quid video? nonne haec illa, quam Deus imperat
Vitare, cujus fructibus pasci vetat?
Ev. Adame, sic est: vetuit attingi arborem,
Fructum caveri jussit: hoc ipsum fuit
Cur non caverem: Cerne quam rutilus color
Praestringat aciem luminum: Ecquid tu putas
Intus latere, si foris tantum est boni?
Ad. Gelidus per artus vadit excussos tremor,
Exanguis asto, crinis erectus riget.
Vix ipse valido spiritus gemitu viam
Perrupit: omnis adsit huic miraculo
Spectator Orbis: ipse homo gemit, et tremit.
Quod facinus aures pepulit? haud vanas Dei
Percipio leges: Ipse jam videor mori.
Ev. Non est, marite, crede, cur trepides: nihil
Est perpetratum, quod citet suspiria.

With often lagging step, I seek again that spot
Whence all our ineffectual wanderings first began.
From yonder Tree, which is a sacred sign, I took
Th' inauguration of a life not due to cease.
Wandering from thence, by a broad circuit, through the rest,
And sated with the fruitage of the several trees,
I hither come again, for nowhere in my walks
Has my wife met me. Where she hides I do not know,
Nor by what diet she has driv'n out eager hunger.
Am I deceived, or do I see her? Near I'll stay.
(Addresses Eve)
Where hast thou linger'd long? Upon what banqueting,
Bed-fellow mine, dost thou sustain thy body's strength?
Eve. As I lay stretch'd upon a verdant couch of grass,
This self-same Tree has given me both shade and food.
Adam. What do I see? And is this not the Tree that God
Bids us avoid, whose fruits are quite forbidden us?
Eve. Yes, Adam. He did warn us not to touch the Tree;
He bade us shun its fruit. And this same cause it is
Why I have disobey'd: See how its ruddy colour
Intrigues the eye! Think you that aught but good can lurk
Within, when on the outside it appears so fair?
Adam. A frosty trembling runs through all my smitten limbs;
Bloodless I stand, with hair erect and terrified;
My very breath, with mighty groan, can scarce breathe forth.
Let the whole Universe be present to behold
This fatal marvel! Man himself now groans and quakes.
What ill deed smites my ears? For I anticipate
God's edicts not in vain. I seem, myself, to die.
Eve. Believe me, husband mine, thou hast no cause to tremble.
Nothing has here been done to summon up thy sighs.

Quin potius aude tu quoque, atque hilaris cape
Tibi conjugali traditum pomum manu.
Ad. Egone ut supremi jussa contemnens Dei
Purus profanam te sequar, vir feminam?
Ev. Cum judicaris velle quidquam est dignius,
Quam cum volueris caeca judicia exsequi.
In arbitrando crimen est properatio.
Tu me immerentem voce condemnas tua
Praejudicatam proferens sententiam.
Fecisse fateor: jure non factum nego.
Ad. Herile jussum jure contemni putas?
Ev. Si sceptra iniquo rector imperio tenet.
Ad. Si dominus aequus est, ames; si non, feras,
Ev. Servire et ipso turpius letho putes.
Ad. Servire magno est summa libertas Deo.
Ev. Quin hoc laboras potius ut fias Deus?
Ad. Ex homine Numen effici ratio negat.
Ev. Dabit illud arbor, quam tuis oculis vides,
Omnis magistra quae boni est.
Ad. Eadem et mali est.
Ev. Mala scire gaudet ipse, quem laudas, Deus.
Ad. Ut careat: at tu experta percipies malum.
Ev. Procul absit omen: me facinoris non piget.
Ad. Peccare nolle prima virtutis via est,
Pudor secunda: facta didicit reddere
Infecta nullus: alterum superest iter.
Revertere illuc, unde fuerat tutius
Abiisse nunquam. Vix enim ad mores bonos
Sero reditur. Quem malorum paenitet,
Pudetque vere, est innocenti proximus.
Spes aliqua veniae est, si potes resipiscere.

Nay, rather, dare thou also, and with gay delight
Take from my wifely hand the apple that I give!
Adam. Shall I despise the ordinance of God Most High,
And, a pure man, take counsel from a wife unholy?
Eve. Worthier is it to let one's wish follow decision
Than to let blind decisions follow after wishes.
It is a crime to make decisions hastily.
Thou with thy voice condemnest me, though innocent,
Giving a verdict thou hast settled on beforehand.
I, who admit this deed, deny it wrongly done.
Adam. Dost thou then think our Master's edicts justly scorn'd?
Eve. Yes, if the Ruler holds His sway in unjust rule.
Adam. If He's just, thou shouldst love Him; and if not, endure.
Eve. Thou shouldst consider servitude more base than death.
Adam. Service to God Almighty is the highest freedom.
Eve. Wouldst thou not rather toil that thou shouldst be a god?
Adam. Reason denies that man can rise to deity.
Eve. That is the gift of this Tree that thine eyes behold,
Revealer of all good. . . .
Adam. And likewise of all evil.
Eve. God, whom thou praisest, takes delight in knowing evil.
Adam. That He may shun 't: but thou shalt know it by thine act.
Eve. Far be it from me! I'm not sorry for my deed.
Adam. Unwillingness to sin is the first step in virtue;
The next is modesty; no one has learn'd to make
Ill deeds once done undone. Another course remains:
Thither return whence it were better far that thou
Hadst ne'er departed. For hardly and late shalt thou
Regain lost goodness. He who repents of sinfulness,
In true contrition, is not far from innocence.
There is some hope of pardon, if thou canst repent.

Ev. Quantum moveri nescius sedeat Deo
Amor ultionis poena Sathanum docet.
Ad. Quae spes tibi est residua?
Ev. Desperem ut nihil.
Ad. Deus est timendus.
Ev. Temere quis metuit parem.
Ad. Moriere.
Ev. Vivam.
Ad. Digna poena es.
Ev. Proemio.
Ad. Quid misera fies?
Ev. Diva.
Ad. Quo tandem modo?
Ev. Virtute pomi.
Ad. Quo frui vetuit Deus?
Ev. Quia invidebat.
Ad. Maximum hoc reri est nefas.
Ev. Per conjugalem te precor supplex fidem,
Tuos per oculos, et per amplexus meos,
Per, si quid unquam dulce fuit ex me tibi,
Ne me relinquas: junge te socium mihi,
Ut nuptialis pacta serves foederis.
Si consequatur vota successus mea,
Felicitatis te esse participem decet.
Si non, (quod absit) miserias opus est tuum
Meas levare vocis alloquio tuae,
Socio labore, consili sapientia.
Utriusque sortis inita si communio est,
Neutram recusa ferre. Quin potius metus
Omnes omitte: prospero res in statu est.
Felix mihi animus sorte divina viget:
Te quoque beabo: profuit pomi mihi
Gustus vel unum hoc maxime, quod sentiam
Sine labe posse, quicquid est, carpi, et capi.
Sed me fidelis cura sollicitat tui,
Quod scrupulorum mole te infestus graves.
Collo superbum cum Superstitio jugum
Imponat, hoc tibi tute servitio places.
Dum te beatum credis, iritas malum,
Donumque sponte, renuis ablatum, tua,

Eve. The punishment of devils demonstrates to us
How a remorseless love of vengeance dwells in God.
Adam. What hope is left thee then?
Eve. That I should not despair.
Adam. God must be fear'd,
Eve. Who recklessly has fear'd an equal?
Adam. Thou'lt die!
Eve. Nay live.
Adam. Thou'rt worthy punishment.
Eve. Reward!
Adam. What wilt thou be, poor wretch?
Eve. A goddess!
Adam Ah, but how?
Eve. By virtue of the apple. . . .
Adam. Which God bade thee shun.
Eve. Because of envy.
Adam. To imagine this is sin.
Eve. As suppliant I beg thee, by our nuptial love,
Thine eyes that love my body, and my own embraces,
And whatsoever has delighted thee in me,
Forsake me not! Join me as an ally, to save
The sacred contract of our matrimonial bond!
If my ambitions should achieve felicity,
'Tis very fit that thou shouldst share my happiness.
If not (which God forbid!), it then becomes thy duty
To soothe my anguish by the discourse of thy voice,
Companionable toil and wisdom of advice.
If we begin with comradeship in either lot,
Be willing to bear either! Nay, then, cast aside
All fears; for we are destined to prosperity.
My happy soul grows strong in destiny divine.
Thee likewise shall I bless. The apple's pleasant taste
Has brought me this chief good: I know that without blame
The fruit, whate'er it is, can be pluck'd off and eaten.
But loyal care for thee distresses me, since thou,
In hostile fashion burdenest thyself with scruples.
When superstition lays its proud yoke on the neck,
Thou takest pleasure in this captious servitude.
Thou thinkest thyself blest, but stirrest evil up,
And of thine own accord, worthy to be without it,

Carere dignus. Quid necas magnam indolem,
Et te ipse torques? Natus es majoribus.
Effunde habenas mentis, et laxa impetum,
Quem male coerces: non quid habeas, sed vide
Quid habere possis. hoc erit vere tuum,
Quod, non ab alio traditum, debes tibi.
Metu vetaris? hoc timere ipsum time.
Ad. Non est pavere fortis: odium criminis
Probo, quam timorem. Sed amor adversus Deum
Me deligatum retinet aeterna fide.
Ev. Amare stultum est quempiam, tanquam effici
Non possit hostis: sic amicum dilige
Olim nocendi ne sit inimico locus.
Sin juvat amoris candidi ductum sequi,
Nec hoc vetabo: quid maritali fide
Prius esse oportet? huc se amor vertat tuus,
Quo sacra thalami jura, quo foedus vocat.
Quod facinus unquam tale, quod tantum nefas
In te, marite, caepi, ut in dubium meam
Fidem vocares? Me beatam nuncupo,
Suspecta quae sum conjugi? vere mala,
Mala sim necesse est, si nec Adamo proba.
Ad. Quid est agendum? lubricas agitant duo
Curas amores: hinc Dei, atque hinc conjugis:
Uterque magnus: illa suspectam mihi
Se male putabit, ille contemni arguet.
Grave est et hoc, et illud: utinam cogerer!
Eligere durum est; haereo, animi pendeo.
Sicut reciproco littus alluitur mari
Fervente fluctus semper alterna vice,
Sic totus agitor, refluoque aestu feror.

Rejectest a fair gift. Why slay a noble nature
And rack thyself? For thou art born for greater
things.
Slacken the reins of thy bold mind, and loose that
course
That thou art wrongly checking. See, not what thou
hast
But what thou canst possess. That will be truly
thine
Which thou shalt gain by thine own act, and not
by gifts.
Art thou held back by fear? Fear but to be afraid!
Adam. It is not brave to tremble: crime's odium
I'd choose
Rather than know fear. But my faithful love towards
God
Still holds me bound in permanent fidelity.
Eve. Surely 'tis folly to love anyone as if
He could not be a foe: so love thy friend that
there
May never be occasion for a foe to harm.
But if it pleasure thee to take pure love as guide --
Nor this shall I forbid -- what should take
precedence
Over connubial faith? Hither turn thy regard,
Where holy rights of bed and contract summon thee!
When, O my husband, have I ever done offense
Against thee, by what crime so monstrous and so
great
That thou shouldst doubt my faith? Shall I myself
call blessed,
If doubted by my husband! I am truly bad,
Wicked indeed, if Adam doubts my honesty!
Adam. Alas, what shall I do? Uneasy cares arise
From two conflicting loves -- of God and of my wife --
Each a great love. She thinks that I suspect her
faith
In evil error; He would charge me with contempt.
Both have important claims. Would that my choice
were ordered!
To choose is hard. My spirit wavers in suspense.
Just as a beach is beaten by a tidal sea
That fumes with endless alternation as it flows,
So am I smitten and dragg'd backward by the tide.

Pars utra vincet? Magne te testor Deus,
Hactenus in ipsa conjuge haud aliud mihi
Placere, quam te; cujus illa umbram refert.
Sociae bonorum, vita quo auxilio mea
Sustenta floret, una quae mecum caro est.
Quid huic negandum? vilis unius tibi
Iactura pomi est. Ut ne contemnam boni
Legem parentis? Fallor? an voluit Deus
Conjugis amores anteferri caeteris
Etiam parentum? Voluit: huc Pomum mihi.
Ev. Vox Homine digna. Sume secretum bonum
Ādame, sume: Quicquid est usquam mali,
Bonique disce. sentiat Deus aemulum,
Socium recusans. Nos quoque expectant preces.
Sed quid tibi ambit languidas pallor genas,
Caputque nutat? omne ruat in me malum,
Si quod futurum est: Parcat, o, parcat viro.

CHORUS

Sapphici cum Adoniis

Lugeat tristi revoluta motu
Aetheris sedes, celeresque moestum
Naeniae cantum meditentur Orbes.
Lugeat moerens miseros alumnos
Terra, et humanam doleat ruinam
Pontus insuetis agitatus undis:
Tuque qui curru rutilo diurnum
Promis, et celas decus alme Titan,
Fac tuos condant tenebrosa vultus
Nubila, invitus mala ne tueri
Tanta cogaris, nitidumque Coelum
Contrahat nubes pluvias, ut aër
Tristia Adami mala lachrymantes
    Exprimat imbres.
O miser vere, miser ipse nescis
Obrutis quantis jaceas periclis.
Heu tibi qualis cumulus laborum
Imminet! quantis agitaris undis
Nescius sortis! tibi jam patescet

Which side will conquer? Thee, Almighty God, I call
To witness that thus far naught in my wife has pleased me
But Thee Thyself, whose image she has mirrored back.
To the companion of my blessings, by whose aid
My glad life is upheld, who is one flesh with me,
What is to be refused? To Thee one apple's loss
Is surely trifling! Am I to despise the law
Of the Good Parent? Am I wrong? Doth God not will
That love of wife should be preferr'd above all others,
Even of parents? 'Tis His will. Give me the apple!
<u>Eve</u>. Words worthy of a man! Take, Adam, take and eat
The secret good! Learn all that there is anywhere
Of ill and good. Let God, who scorns thee as ally,
Feel thee His rival. We too look for worshippers.
But why does sudden pallor blanch thy languid cheek?
Why droops thy head? If an evil is to follow,
Let it all fall on me; but spare, ah spare my man!

CHORUS

Now, with sad motion wheeling, let the sky
Lament and mourn, and let the coursing spheres
Prepare a song of tristful agony!
Now let Earth weep the hapless mutineers,
The ruin of her race; and let the Sea
With wild, unwonted billows shed its tears!
And thou, O gracious Sun, whose chariot
Brings forth and takes away thy daily light,
Make shadowy clouds thy shining face to blot,
Lest thou be thought upon so foul a sight
To gaze complacent; let the shining Height
Assemble all its clouds that it may press
Out of their vapours tear-drops of distress
To mourn man's sinful plight!
O wretched, truly wretched, even yet
Thou knowest not the perils of thy fate.
A grievous load of toil, alas how great,
Above thee hangs! By what vast waves beset,
Thou sitt'st in ignorance! Thee doth await

Corporis nudi pudor, hunc amictu
Stulte frondoso, foliisque tectum
Rere ficulnis: male sanus error
Sopit interni stimulum pudoris.
Quis status mentis tibi, cum videbis,
Conscius tanti sceleris, sequelam
Vindicis poenae, meritoque tandem
Te tua agnosces periisse culpa?
Mille te pestes miserum sequuntur:
Criminis luctus memor, et malorum
Pertinax sensus: tibi mors severis
Instat a tergo metuenda telis.
Occidis magni decus ante mundi,
Cujus et Tellus prius et profundi
Gurgites regnum metuere ponti.
Illa fictorem referens imago
Occidis: tecum series minorum,
Spesque tam magni generis peribit.
Quanta delicti fuit execrandi
Culpa, quae necdum genitos peremit?
Si Deus tristem tibi mortis horam
Proroget clemens veniaque largus,
Quam tua in longum mala proferuntur?
Languor instabit, maciesque turpis
Corpori, aerumnis comes imminebit
Morbus, et morbo gravior Senectus.
Semper urgebunt alii labores,
Cura te semper nova, pessimumque
     Vita malorum.
Posteros omnes Hominum novercae
Ira Naturae sequitur, malique
Criminis seros amor in nepotes
Transit a primo comitatus ortu.
Laedet haeredes sceleris paterni
Dira contages, animique morbum
Nulla delebit mora saeculorum.
Dicet infami vitio parentum,
Dicet Adamo generata proles
Unius morsu cecidisse pomi.
Dicet infelix soboles: scelesta
Omnium matrem simulatus anguis
Fraude decepit: Mulier maritum
     Capta fefellit.

Shame for thy naked body; for this net
Of foolish fig-leaves thou shalt execrate
And feel dishonour thou canst ne'er forget.
Unhealthy error numbs thy conscience now.
What wilt thou think hereafter, conscious grown
Of crime so vast and of a sequel shown
To punish crime, and realize that thou
Hast perish'd through no error but thine own?
A thousand plagues shall cling about thy brow:
Grief that remembers crime, and conscious moan
For sin that will not die, and at thy back
Strides death most dreaded with his arrows black.
Thou, heretofore the glory of the World,
Whose reign imperial the Earth revered
And even the deep gulfs of Ocean fear'd,
In whom the image of thy God appear'd
Thou and thy progeny to doom are hurl'd;
The hope of thy great race is lost indeed!
How great the fault of such a curst offence
Destroying generations yet unborn!
If God, long-suffering and gracious, heed
Thy sighing, and delay thy going hence,
How long shalt thou in torturings be torn?
Thou shalt grow weary, and thy flesh decay,
Disease shall haste, with Hardship by its side,
And Age shall come, more grievous still than they.
Yet other ills shall press upon thy pride,
Ever new cares, a life to pain giv'n o'er,
With still worse woes in store.
Nature, the grim stepmother of mankind,
Shall harry all thy progeny with ire;
And in thy children's children shall she find
Transmitted evidence of foul desire.
The dread contagion of ancestral sin
Shall harm thy heirs; no passage of the years
Can rid their spirits of the stain within.
Descendants sprung from Adam, in their tears,
Shall to their parents' sin trace back their woe,
To stolen fruit, the source of their sad fate.
Thy hapless race shall say a serpent-foe
With cursed fraud seduced their mother in his hate,
And that sad woman, by his wiles brought low,
Deceived her sorry mate.

ACTUS QUINTUS

Sathan

Trimetri Iambici

Cessere voto cuncta: sublimem meo
Superis superior vertice exaequo Polum.
Nunc regna Terrae teneo, nunc Sceptrum maris.
Aeria spatia sub meum misi jugum.
Iam poena me delectat, exilium juvat,
Laetetur Acheron omnis, omnis gaudeat
Phalanx Averni: Vindicem agnoscant suum,
Regumque Regem. Iam satisfeci et mihi:
Quin multa restant: nondum Homo, nondum mala
Suprema sentis: fertile hoc horti solum
Deserere jussus profugus ignotas procul
Inquire terras: verte, quo cupies, gradum:
Quocunque curres regna percurres mea.
Ego te per omnes pertinax latebras premam,
Furiisque tradam: nulla restabit fuga,
Nec tempus unquam faciet aerumnas leves:
Longa malorum sensus accrescet die.
Errabis agris semper incultis, egens,
Exul, pavens, invisus, et dubii Laris,
Tibique soli sors mea invidiam dabit:
Atque anima multis fessa vix tandem malis
Inferna viset regna: non tecum mea
Morientur odia: liberos gignes mihi.
Ita perge Sathan: omne perturba genus:
Certetur omni scelere: nil vetitum sibi
Putet ira: frater dirus in fratrem ruat.
Majore rursus scelere mulctetur scelus.
Crescat furor cum sobole: paeniteat Deum
Hominis creati: nec suorum pignorum
Aspicere nutrix Terra sustineat nefas,

ACT FIVE

Enter Satan alone.

Satan. My hopes are all fulfill'd. Higher than all things high,
I now shall smite the stars with my triumphant head!
Now I possess Earth's rule, the sceptre of the Sea,
And I have placed the realms of Air beneath my yoke.
Now punishment delights me, evil pleases me:
Now let all Acheron rejoice, and all the phalanx
Of damn'd Avernus! Know Thy avenging Nemesis,
Thou King of Kings! Now I have satisfied myself.
But many things remain. Not yet, O man, not yet
Dost thou know utter evil! From the fertile soil
Of this fair Garden driven, seek, in exile, lands
Far off, unknown! Turn wheresoever thou dost wish, --
Where'er thou runnest, thou shalt run through realms of mine.
Ruthless, in every covert I shall trace thee out
And throw thee to the Furies. There is no escape,
Nor will the lapse of time e'er lighten thy sore load.
The consciousness of sin will grow with the long day.
Ever through untill'd fields thou'lt wander, destitute,
An exile, fearful, hated, lacking fix'd abode;
To thee alone will my lot furnish cause for envy.
At length thy soul, worn out by evils, will behold
My hellish realms. Nor will my hatred die with thee.
Children thou wilt have borne for me to curse in turn.
And so, proceed, O Satan! Harry the whole race!
Let all crimes serve thee! And let rage consider naught
Forbidden it. Let ruthless brother slaughter brother.
Let sin be recompensed with greater sin; and Fury
Increase with all her offspring, until God repent
Of man's creation, nor may Earth, his nurse, endure

Redire ut iterum tentet ad priscum Chaos,
Seseque, et illos vindice immergat salo.
Adame, quantum est haec quod ignoras mala?
Sed et hoc peribit: cuncta non uno impetu
Simul patebunt: corporis te dedecus
Primum movebit: consues frondes tibi,
Nec sic abibit, ille qui tegitur, pudor.
Tacitus deinde consciis praecordiis
Flagrabit aestus: stabit ante oculos tui
Imago sceleris: illa te quatiet metu.
Tunc incitatus semet accendet dolor,
Vultusque in omnes ibit, et sententiam
Sibi dicet ipsi: candidum exosus diem
Pudor ille mentis abditas quaeret specus.
Spes fugiet: animus turbidus sese obruet.
Libet videre crimen agnoscens suum
Quos det colores, membra quis teneat stupor,
Aut primus in quae verba prorumpat dolor.
Videre miserum non juvat: dum fit miser
Conspicere cupio: Subdoli anguis commodam
Servabo formam, simul ut intuear duos
Neutri videndus: Ibo, et allabar prope.
Sed ecce rapido motus Adamus gradu
Prosiluit amens: omnis in facie est color.
Stetit furenti similis, et certe furit.
Abit, haeret, errat, sistit: ardescunt genae
Mutatur habitus: pallor ardorem fugat.
Trepidat, resultat, queritur, exclamat, gemit.
Tacitos dolores ore turbato exerit.

The spectacle of all her children's felonies,
So may she try to turn again to ancient Chaos
And plunge herself and them in an avenging sea!
How strange, O Adam, that of this thou knowest
naught.
But this will pass; though all things will not be
reveal'd
By one swift act of God. Shame for thy naked body
Will move thee first; thou wilt sew leaves to
clothe thyself,
But shame which is thus cover'd will not thus
depart.
A silent tide of passion in thy conscious heart
Will fiercely burn. An image of thy lustful crime
Will stand before thine eyes and shudder thee with
fear.
Then all thy stirr'd-up grief will kindle of
itself,
Thy countenance will turn towards all; and on
itself
Will utter its own sentence; hating the bright day,
That shame of mind will seek far caves. Hope will
depart;
And the distracted spirit will o'erwhelm itself.
I shall delight to watch him realize his sin,
To see what hue he shows, what numbness grips his
body,
Or in what words his first cold anguish will burst
forth!
It is no sport to see a wretch; but I desire
To watch him become wretched. I shall keep the
form
Of a sly serpent, that I may observe them both
Yet be beheld by neither. I shall nearer glide.
But lo, with rapid step of movement Adam leaps
Infuriate forth, with all his colour in his face!
He stands like one demented, and is surely mad.
He leaves, he lingers, wanders, halts, his cheeks
aflame;
Then, with changed visage, pallor drives away his
flush.
He trembles, he leaps back, complains, cries out,
and groans,
And from his frenzied mouth pours forth profoundest

Adamus Eva

Iambici Trimetri

Quis sum? quid egi? quo feror? quod me solum,
Quae regio tantis cernit oppressum malis?
Inopemne servat dives Hedenis nemus,
An tristis Acheron? dira Furiarum loca
Aspicere videor: Mors quid a tergo mihi
Crudelis instas? pectus hoc, pectus feri.
Miseranda coniunx agmen infernum vides?
Ego video: dirum Noctis obscurae genus
Me circum oberrat: ducit omnem exercitum
Scelus, et rebellis fastus, et facti pudor.
Hinc pallidorum longa morborum cohors,
Turpisque egestas sequitur, et duri labos
Sudoris author: parte ab hac luctus venit:
Tremulo senectus tarda procedit gradu
Vicina lethi. Turba curarum ingerit
Se parte ab omni: nec procul tristi Fames
Metuenda vultu ducit aerumnas graves,
Bellique nutrix impotens Discordia
Tollit, cruentas sanguine innocuo, manus.
Perspicere nequeo: semper ulterius malum est.
Ev. Quae fingis amens spectra? quis te agitat furor?
Quove aestuantes huc et huc vultus refers,
Acieque falsas turbida species vides?
Compesce sensus: comprime affectus truces,
Parumque sanae mentis affectum doma.
Resipisce, et animos ipse pacifica tuos.
Comprimere primos impetus si non potes,

griefs.

(Satan lurks in the background as Adam and Eve enter, the former desperate, the latter arguing more calmly against his desperation.)

Adam. Who am I? What's my deed? Where am I borne? What soil,
What region sees me overwhelm'd with such great ills?
Is it rich Eden's grove that holds me hopeless here,
Or doleful Acheron? I seem to see th' abode
Of the grim Furies. Why, O cruel Death, ah why
Dost thou behind me stalk? Strike, strike this breast of mine!
O wretched wife, dost thou behold their hellish train?
I see them. Round me wander the insensate brood
Of sable-vested Night: Sin marshals all their host,
And hot rebellious Pride, and melancholy Shame;
Thereafter come long, livid Legions of Disease,
And squalid Poverty, and Toil that still engenders
Swooning and Sweat. From that same quarter issues Grief;
And tardy Age, the neighbor of pale Death, advances
With tottering step. A multitude of Cares draws near
From all directions; while from close at hand dread Hunger,
With grim, malignant face, brings grievous sufferings,
And Discord, the outrageous nurse of wanton War,
Lifts hands bedabbled with the blood of Innocence.
I cannot look: ever worse evils lie beyond.
Eve. What phantoms of delirium oppress thy brain?
In what hot frenzy dost thou glower to and fro
And see illusive semblances with blood-shot glance?
Control thy senses! Damp these wild emotions down,
And tame thy spirit, that just now is far from sane!
Come to thy senses, pray, and calm thy soul thyself!
If thou canst not suppress thy novel impulses

Novusque mentis raptus ignorat modum,
Recolligendo tempus indulge tibi,
Rationis usu spiritum indomitum exue.
Ad. Quin parte ab omni rector astrorum tonas?
Quin motus ira bella ventorum undique
Immittis: omne nubibus coelum horridis
Convolvis: imbres cadere collectos jubes?
Oppono cuivis vile supplicio caput.
Intende dextram: vindices flammas Poli
Iaculentur ambo: Stelliger subita cadat
Mundus ruina: non potest in nos gravis
Errare lapsus: me, vel hanc Coelum premat,
Utriusque merito.
Ev. Sana meditari incipe,
Et imprecari ne velis demens tibi
Decreta si qua est poena non tarde venit.
Ad. Quaecunque fuerit, sera ventura est mihi.
Iamjam decebat stare in inferno specu
Utrunque nostrum: sustines sceleris reos
Gestare Tellus? concavos aperi sinus.
Cur non dehiscis, aut in Acherontis plagam
Te, nosque mergis? gemina compages soli
Pateat revulsa, quaque stamus noxii
Opaca Tellus corpora absorbat duo.
Sin forte terra pondus ignavum jacens
Nescit moveri, veniat e silvis fera
Saevam minaci fronte concutiens jubam,
Quae lacera toto membra dispergat solo,
Aut aliqua rostro viscera haec curvo rapax
Perfodiat ales: Conscia aut sceleris mei
Impellat Heden integrum lapsu Nemus,
Totamque silvam. caudicum pondus grave,
Truncosque supra corpus excipiam meum,

And this new frenzy of the spirit knows no bounds,
Grant thyself time to gain self-mastery back once more
And shed this untamed violence by using Reason!
Adam. (disregarding her) Why, Ruler of the stars, dost Thou not everywhere
Thunder, and send in anger on all sides the winds
To battle? Why not enwrap the sky in dreadful clouds?
Why not command the gathered rains to fall on me?
To any penalty I offer my vile head.
Stretch forth Thine hand! Let both Poles straightway fling
Avenging flames! Let the star-bearing Universe
In sudden ruin fall! Against us, that collapse
Would do but justice. Let God crush out me, or her!
We both deserve that fate.
Eve. Begin to think sane thoughts,
Nor madly curse thyself! If any penalty
Has been decreed for us, 'twill not be slow to come.
Adam. Whatever it may be, for me 'twill come too late.
Already both of us within the pit of hell
Ought to be standing. Canst thou, O Earth, support us,
Guilty of heinous sin? Open thy hollow gulfs!
Why dost thou not gape open and to Acheron
Plunge us forthwith? Let the strong structure of the soil
Be torn asunder and where we now stand in sin
Let the dark Earth engulf two guilty carcasses!
But if perchance the earth, laid prone with heavy weight,
Cannot be moved, let some wild beast from out the woods
Come forth, shaking a savage mane with threatening brow,
And scatter our torn bodies all across the ground;
Or let some ravening eagle rend our vital parts
With his curv'd beak; let Eden, conscious of my crime,
Precipitate its Grove, cast down its woods entire
Upon me; on my body may I then receive
The heavy weight of wood and all the trunks, and

Hortique tumulo condar, atque istam arborem,
Quae passa scelus est, in meum vertam caput.
Ev. Meliora, conjux, loquere: nemo sic perit
Ut non salutis spe foveri debeat.
Ad. Quae spes salutis post nefas tantum mihi?
Heu, quos dolores, quos miser questus dabo,
Vocesque quas? quae verba sufficient mihi?
Periere virtus, jus, fides, felicitas,
Et qui redire perditus nescit decor.
Nostram supremi Numinis legi gulam
Praetulimus, animae corporis stimulos bono,
Hortoque pomum. Nulla conspiciet dies
Pulsa miseria pristinis nos gaudiis
Iterum fruentes. Instat aeternus dolor,
Poenaeque tristes: deseruimus nos Deum,
Et nos Deus deseruit. O dirum nefas,
O scelus iniquum, triste, et auditu horridum!
Mens illa soli nata famulari Deo
Emancipari gestit, et sese abdicat:
Sui esse juris voluit, et vili arbori
Servire caepit: Animus almo debitum
Parenti amorem vertit in se, nec malo
Contentus isto devio res infimas
Gressu secutus isto praefecit sibi,
Quibus imperabat, passus et contagium
Rerum minorum sponte decrevit sua.
Relinque corpus, qui reliquisti Deum
Crudelis anime, et eripe hoc cruciatibus
Vivum cadaver. quid juvat poenas tuas
Proferre? possum, debeo, cupio mori.
Ev. Supplicia votis aggravas demens tuis.
Mortalitatem pateris, et mortem petis.
Ad. Pereo ante mortem: spiritum exemit dolor.
Infamis author sceleris, exosus Deo,
Miserque, jam sum sine sepulcro mortuus.

heap
The Garden up in one great mound, and take that Tree
That suffer'd my dark crime, upon my guilty head!
Eve. Husband, speak better words! No one is so
far lost
That he should not still hope for some deliverance.
Adam. What hope of grace have I, after so great
a sin?
Alas, what griefs, what outcries, what complaints
shall I
In sorrow utter? Ah, what words shall serve my
need?
Virtue is lost, and justice, faith, felicity,
And honour, which once tarnish'd cannot shine again.
We have preferr'd our gluttony to God's great law,
Set carnal appetites above the soul's true good,
The fruit above the Garden. Sunk in misery,
Never, on any day, shall we delight again
In former joys. Eternal sorrow is at hand,
And penalties austere; we have deserted God,
And God abandons us. How dire this sin of ours,
A grim, unjust offence and horrible to hear!
The mind, once born to serve great God alone,
Is eager to be free, and abdicates its lot.
Wishing its own authority, it turns to serve
A common tree. The soul, directing towards itself
Love due our gracious Father nor with that offence
Fully content, has sought out with a wandering step
The lowest things of all, and set above itself
Those things which once it rules, and with
deliberate will
Now suffers the contagion of inferior things.
O cruel soul, that darkly hast forsaken God,
Leave now the body, snatch this living corpse from
pain!
What pleasure is there in prolonging punishment?
I can, indeed I ought, and so desire to die.
Eve. Madman, thou dost make worse thy doom by
these thy prayers!
Having been shown mortality, thou seekest death.
Adam. I perish before death, for grief destroys
my soul.
Disgraceful author of this crime, hateful to God
And sick, I am already dead without a tomb.

Longas omittam languidae poenae moras,
Nec aeger ultra funus extendam meum.
Quodcunque vitae restat, abrumpam manu
Juste severa. quid mihi exsequias nego?
Quid pereo vivus? quid meos Manes moror?
Ibo, ibo solus, qua rapax amnis cadit,
Ubi prona tumidus ducit Euphrates vada,
Fluvioque mersus procul Erythraei ad maris
Provolvar undas. Tu manus potius veni
Ministra poenae, quae fuisti criminum:
Perfringe guttur ictibus, pomum prius
Cui tradidisti, concitatis pulsibus
Dirumpe ventrem, viscera infausta extrahe,
Dapesque iniquas, corque delicti capax
Evelle: nusquam corpore in toto tuum
Vulnus peribit. Morte sanandum est scelus.
Ev. Quod odit auget, scelere qui punit scelus.
Dignum esse vita monstrat hoc, dignum nece
Quod te putaris. Majus isto crimine
Crimen relinquet vita, si mortem petis.
Non vincla rumpens anima corpus deserat,
Sed corpus animam. si tuam expectas diem,
Iam praestitutum tempus aderit, spiritum
Cum lassa sponte membra dimittent sua,
Iugumque solvat arbiter vitae Deus:
Illo jubente morere. nunc insania
Rogo ne subactus fata praecipites tua.
Ad. Non ita pudorem caecus extinxit furor,
Ut, quicquid usquam est, impio aspectu fugem.
Pisces, volucres, cumque jumentis feras
Sentire video criminis poenas mei:
Ea cuncta clamant: Morere, decede, occide,
Et exsecrandi capitis intuitu leva

I shall forego the long delays of lingering pain
Nor further, nauseate at heart, postpone my death.
What still remains of life, I justly shall cut off,
Remorseless. Why should I deny myself a grave?
Why do I perish living? Why delay my ghost?
Alone, alone I'll go, where falls the greedy river,
Down where the swol'n Euphrates pours his headlong
waves;
Drown'd in that stream, to the far Erythrean Sea
My body shall be borne. O thou, my hand, come
rather,
My minister of punishment, as once of crime!
Rend with thy blows asunder this foul throat, to
which
Thou didst commit the apple; burst my belly too
With eager force, and drag my luckless vitals forth
With their unholy meal! Tear out my sinful heart;
Yea, nowhere in my body let thy wound be sated!
The sin I have committed must be heal'd by death.
Eve. He who pays crime for crime, increases what
he hates.
That thou dost think thyself deserving death but
shows
That thou deservest life. For if thou seekest
death,
Thou wilt but aggravate thy sin by further sin.
Let not the soul burst from its bonds and leave
the flesh!
Rather let flesh leave soul: if thou wilt wait
thy day,
That time will soon arrive when of their own accord
The wearied members will dismiss thy soul, and God,
The Arbiter of life, will take away thy yoke.
Die when He biddeth thee, but do not now, I beg,
Hasten along thy fate in this insanity.
Adam. Blind frenzy in me has not so extinguish'd
shame
That I, with impious countenance, should flee from
aught.
I see that fishes, birds, wild beasts, and cattle
feel
The fatal consequences of my awful crime.
All these cry out to me: "Die! Perish! Pass away!
Let not the earth and sky behold thy cursed head

Coelum, atque terram: spiritum nocuum expue.
Paremus: orbem hunc integrum purgabimus.
Minime resistam: Vota conveniunt bene.
Cur animam in ista luce detentam morer
Mihi causa nulla est: omnia amisi bona,
Regnum, salutem, gaudium, mentem quoque:
Nunc vita restat: hanc quoque amitto libens.
Ev. Quo te ipse conjunx impiae morti ingeris?
Quo pergis amens? forte post vitae moram
Moriere melior. Temporis longo potes
Proficere tractu: quicquid errasti hactenus,
Mea culpa certe est. poena me meritam manet.
Ego te fefelli misera. Iam facies scelus
Ultro, atque certus? unicum hoc aufer malum.
Mihi crede conjunx.
Ad. Credidi semel, et nimis.
Ev. Perimesne memet?
Ad. Nolo, ne possim, occidam.
Ev. Ratione quamvis careat, et flecti dolor
Magnus recuset, pauca miserandae precor
Verba ut maritae mente pacata audias,
Quae potius ad me tute deberes loqui.
O Fata! mulier misera soletur virum,
Et ipse leges sexus invertat suas!
Quin refice monitu femina hunc, monitu tuo
Quem perdidisti. melius alloquium incipe.
Non nunc ut omnes cordis affectus domes
Peto, vel dolores mente tranquilla ut feras,
Vincasque temet (licet et hoc fuerat viri
Superare luctus, nec malis tergum dare)
Adame, tantum vivere ut cupias precor.
Tu fortis esse credis, atque animi gravis
Mortem minacem spernere: ego contra puto

From this time forth, we pray! Spew forth thy
guilty spirit!"
I shall obey, and wholly purify this globe.
I offer no resistance, for it suits me well.
There is no reason why I should detain my spirit
Amid the upbraiding light. For I have lost all
good:
My kingdom, my salvation, joy, and intellect;
Now only life remains, and this I'll gladly lose.
Eve. Whither to impious death betakest thou
thyself?
Where madly tendest thou? Perchance after delay
Thou'lt find a better death. By a long lapse
of time
Comes gain. Whatever error thou hast made thus far
Is my fault surely. Condign punishment awaits me.
Sadly I had deceived thee. Wilt thou now commit
A conscious further crime? At least avoid this
evil!
Believe me, husband.
Adam. I believed thee once too often.
Eve. Wilt thou destroy me then?
Adam. Nay, rather would I die.
Eve. Although thy heavy grief lacks reason, and
refuses
To change its course, I beg thee that with calmer
mind
Thou'lt hear a few words from thy pitiable wife,
Consoling words that thou shouldst rather speak to
me!
O fates! then let a wretched wife her husband
comfort,
And let sex undergo reversal of its laws!
Yet, woman, save by thy advice this man whom thou
By thy advice hast ruin'd! Better discourse use!
I do not now petition that thou shouldst subdue
All thy heart's passions or with calm mind bear
thy griefs
Or rule thyself (though fit it had been for a man
To overcome his grief and not give way to ills).
I only beg thee, Adam, to desire to live.
Thou dost believe that he who's brave and strong
in soul
Will spurn the threat of death; but I think he may

Timidum vocari jure, qui vitam timet.
Contempsit ille, qui nec optavit mori.
Virtute fretus mascula adversa impetu
Perfringe solido, nec tuas damna manus.
Quodcunque querere, est error: immerito cadis,
Nisi te ipse perimens jure te perimi facis.
Ad. Unde illa virtus tanta tantis in malis
Emersa lucet? aliquis etiamnum sapit,
Et recta suadet? multa, quae memoras, scio
Ratione fulta, sed dolor cogit sequi
Etiam improbata: fertur in praeceps sciens
Animus, negatque sana consilia exsequi.
Furore teneor: ille me insontem potest
Iam facere solus: ille me absolvit reum.
Socia malorum desere infaustum virum,
Deliberatas luere me poenas sine.
Ev. Per sancta thalami sacra, per jus nominis
Quodcunque nostri, sive me natam vocas
Ex te creatam, sive communi patre
Ortam sororem, sive potius conjugem,
Ne me relinquas: nunc tuo auxilio est opus,
Cum versa sors est. unicum lapsae mihi
Firmamen, unam spem gravi afflictae malo
Te mihi reserva dum licet, mortalium
Ne toto soboles pereat unius nece.
Si te miserae, si tuae clades movent,
Hoc cogitato: summa tetigisti mala:
Auferre quidquid mors potest, vita abstulit.
Nil pejus ultra restat: in tuto es loco.
Ad. Bona mors futura est, quae tot extinguet mala,
Aut non molesta, si nihil pejus dabit.
Placet interire, parce vanis vocibus.

rightly
Rather be styled a coward who's afraid of life.
He who hopes not for death, has shown his scorn of death.
Trusting in thy male valour, rout thy obstacles
With obstinate attack, and do not lose thy hands!
To grieve of aught is wrong. Thou fallest undeserving
Unless thy murderous act shall justify thy murder.
Adam. Whence does this splendid virtue of my wife emerging
Shine forth 'mid such great evils? Is she truly wise?
Does she urge wisdom? I know many things which thou
Dost cite are based on reason, but my grief compels me
To follow things unproven. Headlong my conscious soul
Is carried, and refuses to take healthy counsels.
I am possess'd by frenzy. God alone can now
Hold me unguilty and absolve me from my sin.
O comrade of my ills, forsake thy hapless man,
And let me expiate them as I have resolved.
Eve. By our bed's holy rites, and by whatever name
Gives me a claim on thee, whether thou call me daughter,
Created from thee, or thy sister, springing from
A common father, or that best of names, thy wife,
I beg thee, leave me not! I need thy succour now,
When thus our lot is overthrown. But while thou mayst,
In this my fall preserve for me my one support,
One hope in my adversity ---- let not, I pray,
Our progeny all perish through the death of one!
If a poor woman's misery move thee, and thine own,
Think upon this: thine ills have reached their climax now;
What death can take away, life has already taken.
Nothing can touch thee further; thou art safe indeed.
Adam. Death will be good, since it blots out so many evils;
Nor grievous is it, if it bring me nothing worse.
I have resolved to die. Cease from thy vain harangue.

Ev. Ergone vacuos vidua, deserta, et vaga
Curram per agros, mistaque errabo feris?
Si, Adame, pietas vera quaerenda est tibi,
Me perime meritam: si tibi ignotum est scelus,
Ego sum magistra: sive tu jugulum petis,
Praebebo jugulum, sive adhuc sterilem cupis
Invadere uterum, dirue anfractus cavos
Sinuantis alvi. Facere me quicquam mali
Authore dubitas? Non soles. Dextram para.
Si tu recusas feminae facient manus
Opus virile. Non ego insons occidam.
Non si ipse Coeli rector in mea viscera
Vertat coruscas fulminis trifidi faces,
Poenas rependam sceleribus tantis pares
Scelerata conjunx: non sat est quod sum nocens,
Feci nocentem: nec sat est: nisi mors vetat,
Pariam nocentes. ego duplex feci nefas,
Cum fallor, et cum fallo: restat tertium.
Quid trepida cessas? Luere quid doctrix mali
Poenas recusas? Anime, quid torpes adhuc?
Luctus, dolores, lachrymas, planctus, mala
Innumera patior: ista debebam Deo.
Quid dabo marito? Nil, nisi ut moriar prior.
Utcunque miserum est, moriar Adami tamen
Conjunx, nec ullus nocte depulsa dies
Viduam videbit. Stare in ancipiti tuam
Marite causam disce. non est tertium,
Aut vivis, aut occidis. An placuit scelus?
Aliud paratum est. Non veto. monstro viam.
Non vivo sine te: sed mori mecum potes.
Unum in duobus statue: nil sine me facis.
Mori volentem praeeo, viventem sequor.

Eve. Shall I then, widow'd and deserted, run
Wandering through empty fields and mingling with
    wild beasts?
If, Adam, thou wouldst seek to do thy duty now,
Slay me, who merit it! If crime's unknown to thee,
I shall instruct thee. If thou seek'st a throat
    to cut,
I shall present my throat; if thou wouldst rip a
    womb
As yet unpregnant, I now beg thee to destroy
The hollow labyrinths of mine. Dost thou, with me
To prompt, shun any deed? Thou art not used?
    Prepare!
If thou refusest, with my female hands I'll do
A man's stark work! I shall not fall in innocence.
Even if heaven's own Ruler turn'd against my vitals
The flashing torches of His three-fork'd thunderbolt,
The penalty would still not match my fearful crime.
Curst consort that I am! My own sin not enough,
I made my husband sin. Nay more, if death forbid
    not,
I shall bring sinners forth. Mine was a two-fold
    crime,
Deceived and then deceiving. And a third remains.
Why dost thou stay, my soul? Why, since thou
    urgedst evil,
Dost thou reject thy doom? Why art thou slow to
    act?
Sorrows, pains, tears and wailings, ills innumerable
I suffer: these I owe to God. What to my husband?
Nothing, except that I precede him in my death.
However foul it is, I'll die the wife of Adam,
Nor will any day hereafter, as the night retreats,
See me a widow. Learn, my husband, that thy case
In a dilemma stands: thou livest or thou slay'st
    me.
There is no third alternative. Has thy crime
    pleased thee?
Another waits thee. I assent and show the way.
I cannot live without thee. Thou canst die with
    me.
Choose one course for us both. Without me thou'lt
    do nothing.
In death I'll go before, in life I'll follow thee.

Ad. Iam parce conjunx, parce, parebo tibi,
Parebo rursus. Vincis affectus meos
Aequos, iniquos: sola tu mentem domas.
Eat dolores hic quoque ad reliquos dolor,
Non interire. quid tibi, conjux, negem?
Iubente te vel jussa contemnam Dei,
Iubente te vel sustinebo vivere.
Ev. Quis ille strepitus? audio ventos truces
Late furentes: audio murmur grave,
Quod gravia minitans aëre ex summo cadit.
Repente longo terra mugitu fremens
Concussa caecos egit ad coelum sonos,
Retroque cessit: capitibus nutans Nemus
Fragore vasto tonuit: omnes arbores
Concussit horror, silvaque erexit comam.
Ad. Pavet animus: horret corpus: insedit meos
Torpor per artus: frigidus sanguis coit.
Ultor nefandi sceleris, Edicti memor,
Vindexque spretae legis, adventat Deus.
Fugiamus illuc, qua frequentes arbores
Lucem recusant: Abditi densis comis
Lateamus: iterum criminis nostri dolor,
Me stimulat: iterumque erubesco, et palleo,
Foliisque tectus non satis videor mihi.
Aspicio nudum corpus: Heu! quid cingula
Frondosa prosunt? Intus est, intus pudor.
Quae poena, Mulier, crimini par nos manet?
Moriemur ambo. Iam tuae pereunt preces.

VOX DEI

Adamus Eva

Iambici Trimetri & Trochaici
Tetrametri

Adame, quas nunc te in latebras proripis?
Quae te recondit umbra? cernentem omnia,

Adam. Enough, enough, my wife. I shall obey thy word.
Again shall I obey. Thou conquerest my heart,
For, right or wrong, thou art sole ruler of my thought.
Now let this pain be added to my other griefs,
Never to perish! What would I deny thee, wife?
At thy behest, I'll even spurn the words of God;
At thy behest, I even shall endure to live.
Eve. What is that uproar? I hear savage hurricanes
Raging from far and near; I hear a murmur deep
That falls with threat of fatal ruin from on high;
Earth, raving with long ululations, suddenly
Is smitten and sends muffled outcries up to heaven,
And then subsides again; the Grove, with nodding head,
Has thunder'd with vast crashing: all the trees are struck
With horror, and their leafy hair stands all erect!
Adam. My soul's afraid; my body trembles; numbness dwells
Through all my members and my blood is curdled cold.
God, mindful of His edict comes, the Punisher
Of our dread crime, th' Avenger of His slighted law.
Let us flee thither where the crowding trees shut out
Th' accusing light. There let us shield ourselves and hide
In the dense foliage. Again our crime's sharp pain
Pricks at my heart; again I redden and turn pale
And seem to find the leaves an insufficient screen.
I see my nakedness. Alas, of what avail
Are leafy girdles, for our shame's within, within!
What doom, O woman, waits proportion'd to our crime?
We both shall perish. Now thy hopes are at an end.

(The Voice of God, Himself unseen, fills all the Garden with its terrible majesty.)

Voice. Adam, into what lurking-place hurriest thou?
What shadows hide thee? Wilt thou hide from Him

Praesentem ubique, cuncta cui rerum patent,
Huic delitescis? Ipse te appello Deus,
Quem rapidus aether trepidat, et Tellus gravis
Iustae potentem judicem sententiae.
Ego te creavi, te creatum maximis
Muneribus auxi. Natus ausculta patri,
Cliens patrono, nunc hero servus tuo.
Fugitive prodi.
Ad. Pareo: audivi truces,
Metuende rector, per nemus sacrum sonos;
Venti severum murmur aptum gaudiis
Commovit hortum. membra concussit pavor,
Tremuique totus: illa majestas tui
Insueta vultus me fugavit territum.
Ingenuus istis, et verecundus pudor
Accessit: ecce nudus obscoenos male
Velatus artus ad forum sistor tuum.
Talem creasti.
Vox. Nuditatis conscius
Per quem fuisti? nullus in terris fuit
Qui te doceret. Sed pudor crimen sequi
Solet, et malorum conscio habitat pectore.
Fatere veram judici caussam tuo.
Defensiones, ne tuum crimen gravent,
Omitte vanas. Nonne pomum ex arbore
Vetita comedere es ausus, et legem meam,
Poenamque mortis spernere, infidum caput?
Ad. Mea culpa non est. Crimen hujus feminae est,
Quam mihi dedisti sortis auxilium meae,
Pellace quae me voce, et exemplo suo
Cepit: comedi.
Vox. Conjugi conjux nocens
Dic, causa tantae quae fuit dementiae?
Ev. Serpens, Creator, dextera fictus tua

who sees
All things, who everywhere is present, and to whom
All earth lies open? I, God, summon thee. 'Tis I,
At whom swift Ether and the heavy Earth both quake
As at a Judge, author indeed of just decrees.
I made thee, and endow'd thee, after thy creation,
With gifts magnificent. Child, hear thy Father now!
Client, attend thy Patron! Slave, obey thy Lord!
Come forth, thou fugitive!
Adam. I will. O awful Ruler,
I heard horrific sounds throughout the sacred Grove,
And all the Garden, seat of blessed joys, was stirr'd
With winds' dread murmuring. Then panic smote my limbs,
I trembled utterly; th' unwonted majesty
Of Thy great countenance put me to flight in terror.
A natural and modest shame assail'd my soul.
Behold with obscene members ill conceal'd I stand
In carnal nakedness before Thy holy presence.
Thus Thou didst make me.
Voice. And through whom didst thou become
Aware of this thy nakedness? For none on earth
Was there to teach thee. But Shame's wont to follow Guilt
And to inhabit breasts grown conscious of their sin.
Confess the truth of thy behaviour to thy Judge!
Omit all vain excuses, lest they aggravate
The trespass of thy crime. Hast thou not, faithless one,
Been bold to eat the fruit of the forbidden tree
In scorn for all my law and penalty of death?
Adam. The crime is not my own, but springs from this my wife
Whom Thou didst give me as the helpmeet of my lot.
She won me with persuasive voice and her example;
And I ate.
Voice. O woman harmful to thy husband's soul
Expound to me the cause of thy demented act!
Eve. The serpent, O creator, which Thy hand has made,

Astu fefellit simplicem, atque insons ego,
Quam sexus ipse perviam fecit dolis,
Seducta pomum gutturi admovi meo.
Vox. Fraudibus nimis apte Serpens, quem creatrix dextera
Usui hominum destinarat, quos inique subdola
Sceleris infandi minister perdidisti machina,
Bestiis invisus aliis ibis, atque animantia
Cuncta fugies, et fugabis: virus horrendum vomes;
Triste spirabis venenum mortis atrae nuntium,
Signa divinae notanda praeferens sententiae:
Praeque jumentis, ferisque, poena queis instat gravis,
Poena te gravior manebit: ista per se insontia
Sentient luctus heriles: Fraude tu meritas tua
Semper aerumnas dolebis: utque te mentem duce
Haec homo ad terrena flexit rebus a coelestibus,
Tu quoque in summa natabis terra, et infixus solo
Ventre serpes, non rapaci subriges corpus pede.
Tanta victus comparandi difficultas te premet,
Ut tenebrosa cavatae conditus terrae specu
Pulvere hibernas per horas pauperem pellas famem:
Dum tibi reciprocantem vita ducet spiritum
Commode nullus voracem pascet esuriem dies.
Tu ferox homicida Sathan, angue qui tectus latens
Perfidis effascinasti feminam mendaciis,
Non vice hac una rebellis, sed priori crimine
Aetheris damnatus exul ultimas poenas pati,
Iam malo crudeliori non reliquisti locum.
Spes tamen te vana fallet: non enim voto tuo
Inferi Regis dominio mancipabo feminam,
Quae licet mereatur illud, tu mereri non potes
Cujus infido est subactus sequior sexus dolo.

Deceived with cunning my simplicity; and I,
Made by my very sex susceptible to wiles,
Was cozen'd in my innocence, and ate the apple.
Voice. Vile Snake, too fond of fraud, whom thy Creator's hand
Had destined for the good of man, whom thou instead
Hast subtly ruin'd as a minister of crime,
Hated by other creatures shalt thou go, and flee
And put to flight all beasts. Thou shalt spew out dread poison,
And breathe out venom, a black messenger of death,
Bearing upon thy back grim signs of Heaven's doom.
For thee, before all herds and beasts, whom pains await,
Worse penalties impend; for they, though guiltless, share,
Through thee, their master's woe. But condign pangs for fraud
Shalt thou endure forever. Since, with thee as guide,
Man has withdrawn his eyes from Heaven to earthly things,
Thou on the surface of the earth shall crawl, with belly
Set on the soil, nor rear thy body on lithe feet.
In gaining food, such hardships shall afflict thee, that,
Laid in dark wintry caves of hollow earth
With dust as food, thou'lt drive away thy squalid hunger.
As long as life shall grant thee ebb and flow of breath,
No day shall grant thy greedy maw sufficient food.
And thou, fierce murderer Satan, who conceal'd within
The serpent didst bewitch the woman with base lies,
Rebel not thus alone, but for an earlier crime
Condemn'd in exile to endure the utmost doom,
Thou hast now left no place for a more cruel crime.
Vain hope, however, shall deceive thee; I shall not,
As thou dost wish, enslave the woman to the King
Of griesly Hell, deservedly perhaps, but he,
Whose lying guile undid her sex, cannot deserve it.

Lucis antiquae favillam, quae salutis praevia est,
Mente in humana fovebo, nec sinam cinere obrui.
Bella, sempiterna bella mulier, et tu perpetim
Mutuis odiis geretis: ipse succendam faces:
Ipse cordi feminino, cujus una est indoles
Mente conceptum tenaci gravius odium prosequi,
Inseram hostiles furores, et simultates dabo
Quas datas alat impotenter, nec sinat frigescere.
Proferam certamen istud cuncta late in saecula,
Illius proles ut armet se genus contra tuum,
Invicemque bella vexent posterorum posteros.
IPSE veniet, ipse carnem sumet humanam Deus,
Non viro genitus, sed uno feminino ex semine,
Virginali natus alvo, generis humani Salus,
Qui Triumphator superbum conteret tibi verticem,
Et feri victor veneni tempus utrunque opprimet.
Illius ductu piorum coetus armata manu
Spolia referet saepe opima, vimque superabit tuam.
Non tibi tuto licebit Marte aperto cernere,
Non in os prodire contra: semper aversos petes,
Ausus inflixisse tantum caeca calci vulnera.
Proditrix mulier mariti, quae dolosis vocibus
Te nimis facilem dedisti, multa te expectant mala.
Mille te novi dolores mille cruciabunt modis,
Cumque materna sub alvo conditum foetum geres
Aegra languebis, nec ipsis imperabis sensibus
Passa varios appetitus sana quos mens respuat,
Vsque dum te terminatis praestitutis mensibus
Onere maturo levatam solvat immitis dolor.
Te manent uteri labores, te puerperium grave,
Teque sobolis educandae cura praesertim premit,
Quam reges licentiosa mollis indulgentia:
Pressaque aerumnis ad unum misera te vertes virum.
Ille erit tibi refugium, spesque praesidium, et salus,

In human minds I'll cherish sparks of former light,
Forerunners of salvation, cover'd by no ashes.
Wars, everlasting wars, the woman and thyself
Shall wage with mutual hate; that fire myself shall
    kindle;
I, in the female mind, whose nature is to hold
With dark tenacity a hatred deep conceived,
Shall thrust in hostile frenzies and sow bitter
    feuds
That she shall nourish fiercely nor allow to cool.
I shall prolong that conflict down throughout all
    ages,
So that her heirs may arm themselves against thy
    race.
And wars of her posterity vex thine in turn.
HIMSELF shall come, for God shall take on human
    flesh,
By mankind not begotten, yet from woman's seed,
Born of a Virgin's womb, the Saviour of mankind,
And He as Conqueror shall bruise thy haughty head,
And tramp triumphantly on both thy venom'd temples.
Often, with Him their Head, the just, with armèd
    hand
Shall bring back *spolia opima*, routing thee.
Nor shall I suffer thee to strive in open warfare,
Nor meet them face to face. Ever behind thou'lt
    lurk,
Venturing nought but hidden ravage on their heel.
    Woman, betrayer of thy husband, since to guile
Too easily thou yieldedst, many ills await thee,
A myriad new pains to rack in myriad ways,
And when in womb maternal thou shalt bear thy young,
Thou shalt in sickness faint, and fail to rule thy
    will,
And suffer appetites that the sane mind rejects,
Until, when thy predestined months have been
    fulfill'd,
Raw pain at last relieves thee of thy ripen'd load.
The labors of the womb await, and child-bed's pangs;
Most care of all thou'lt find in rearing up thy
    young,
Whom thou with soft indulgence shalt control in vain.
Oppress'd by evils, to thy husband shalt thou turn:
And he will be thy refuge, hope, protection, saviour --

Ille, quem tu perdidisti. Subdita illius jugo
Iussibus parere disces, ille te imperio reget.
Cape tuas, Adame poenas, quem ducem, non asseclam
Esse oportuërat maritae, quique culpam feminae
Praepedire debuisti mascula prudentia,
Non inire perpetrati criminis consortium,
Quique muliebri lepori posthabens legem meam
Vetita persuasus profana poma violasti gula.
Terra propter te dolebit sterilis, effoeta, arida:
Sponte lolium, sponte tribulos, sponte progignet rubos,
Non nisi compulsa fruges. Insativis fructibus
Fervidam pasces orexim. Panis aerumnis tibi
Plurimis constabit emptus: opere defessos gravi
Defluet sudor per artus testis aegri corporis:
Solis et quoties per orbem lumen orietur novum
Multa perpesso renatus alter exsurget dolor,
Vsque dum lethalis hora reddat Adamum solo.
Nam suum sese resolvet corpus in primordium,
Cumque sis pulvis, necesse est te reverti in pulverem.
Poteram repente crimen infandum intuens
Vtrunque mortis impetu prosternere,
Animasque vestras procul ad infernos specus
Deprimere poteram: praetuli clementiam
Iuris rigori, nec malis solatium
Tantis negavi, vos sacro sub foedere
In spem salutis erigens: vitae quoque
Proferre volui spatia, et humanum genus,
Quod omne vestris inditum membris latet,
Servare: nomen indet uxori suae
Adamus Evae: prima nam mortalibus
Parens et altrix illa victuris erit,
Similesque sorte gignet et forma sibi.

He whom thou hast betray'd. Beneath his yoke thou'lt learn
His orders to obey; and he shall be thy lord.
Adam, accept thy punishment, for thou in truth
Shouldst be the leader, not the follower, of thy wife,
And with male prudence shouldst have check'd a woman's fault,
Not entered into partnership in acts of crime.
And thou, who thought my edicts less than female charm,
Wert moved with greed to violate forbidden fruit.
Through thee the Earth shall mourn -- sterile, exhausted, dry.
Cockles and thorns and brambles shall it freely bear,
But shall refuse thee fruits unless compell'd by toil.
Thus shalt thou feed thy appetite. Bread must be bought
With utter hardship. Witness of an ailing frame,
Hot sweat will flow down limbs fatigued with heavy toil.
Whenever a new dawn shall rise, another grief
Shall wake, new born, for one who has endured so much,
Until the hour of death restore thee to the ground.
For to its first beginnings shall thy flesh dissolve;
Since thou art form'd of dust, to dust must thou return.
Gazing on your dread crime I could have overwhelm'd
The pair of you with sudden gunnery of death,
And sent your souls far down to seek the cave of Hell.
And have preferr'd to show you clemency, and not
The rigours of my law, nor amid such great ills
Have I denied you comfort and a second pledge
That bids you hope salvation; I have also will'd
To extend the limits of your lives, and to preserve
The Human race that now lurks wholly in your loins.
And now let Adam give his wife the name of Eve,
For she to all the mortals that shall be hereafter
Shall be the primal mother and the kindly nurse,
And she shall bear those like to her in lot and

Sed ut pudori consulam vestro simul,
Et sanitati, corpori tegmen dabo,
Quod induatis, pinguis exuvias ovis,
Ne gravibus auris, atque coeli injuria
Superatus animae fomes intereat calor.
Ad. O dura sors! o poena peccati minax!
O longa misero vita, languenti gravis!
Ah quam dolenda multa vivendo diu
Semper redibunt! quam malum est tarde mori!
Quam dura res cum miseriis fieri senem!
Scelerate Sathan, gentis humanae lues,
Quo nos tulisti! quod nefas commisimus!
Ex corde culpae conscio suspiria
Mihi jam trahantur: tristis hos vultus gravet
Imber, fluantque turbidis lachrymae genis.
Nec flere satis est, nec licet: durus malis
Lacrymare nescit oculus. ipsum non levi
Feriatur ictu pectus, et planctu sonet,
Pronaeque ab omni capite lacerentur comae.
Heu jure quanti sceleris actus sum reus,
Meoque vidi crimine iratum Deum.
Vox. Adamus, ecce (qui prius speraverat
Boni malique gnarus aequalis mihi
Futurus esse, similis aeterno Deo)
Nunc qualis astat? nunc quis in vultu est color?
Majora quaerens pristina amisit bona.
Sed jam videndum est ne sua carpens manu
Vitale pomum, Nemore sub medio sita
Quod peperit arbos, speret indictam sibi
Effugere mortem, luce et aeterna frui.
Vos ergo Cherubi coelites, mihi quos ego
Legi ministros, ite, et horto pellite
Par istud hominum: sacra deliciis loca
Miseri relinquant, alia Telluris sola,
Glebasque quaerant, et parentem exerceant.

beauty.
But, that I may take counsel for your shame and health
Alike, I shall assign your bodies covering,
The fleeces of fat sheep, that you may put them on
Lest haply overcome by scathe of savage winds
And of the sky, the heat within your souls may fail.
Adam. O doom severe! O threatening penalty of fate!
O life, long to the wretched, heavy to the faint!
How many lamentable things must still return
To me who must live long! How ill to perish late!
How hard a lot to grow old in one's miseries!
Accursed Satan, thou destroyer of our race,
Where hast thou brought us now! And what a sin is ours!
From out a breast too conscious of its guilt
My hapless sighs are drawn. Let sad rain drench these faces!
Let tears flow down our cheeks in their disquietude!
'Tis not enough to weep; nor may we: for an eye
Harden'd by evil cannot weep. With no light stroke
Let my cold breast be smitten and resound with grief
And let the hair be torn in sorrow from my head!
Alas, how justly am I doom'd for awful crime
And have beheld my God made angry by my sin!
Voice. Look now at Adam (who once hoped to be my peer,
Acquainted with all truth, the evil and the good,
Equal in intellect to everlasting God)
What is his plight? What colour now is in his face?
In his ambition, he has lost his pristine blessings.
But now we must take care lest, plucking with his hand
An apple from that tree of everlasting Life
That grows amid the Garden, he may hope to shun
The death decreed for him and taste Eternity.
Go therefore, heavenly Cherubim, ye whom I chose
To be my ministers, drive forth that human pair
Out of the Garden! Let the wretches leave resorts
Sacred to pure delight; let them seek other soils
And other fields of Earth, and let them till the ground.

Vos state in aditu nemoris, Ortivam ad plagam,
Et impedite flammeo versatilis
Mucrone teli, ne quis infigat pedem.
Ev. Quis subitus ardor iste, quae lux emicat?
Corripuit hortum flamma, et excelsae arbores
Ardent sine igne, fervidumque incendium
Trepide vagatur, qualibus coelum nitet
Illustre facibus: integrum flagrat nemus,
Haec digna thalamis taeda praelucet meis.
Hominum propago patriam hac discet nota.
Ad. Fugiamus aestus: ista divinae manus
Sunt opera, quae nos ire in exilium jubet.
O magne rector, o gubernator Poli
Non jam resisto. volo, volo discedere
Suffulta pigris membra sed genibus labant,
Retroque, quoties gradior, abreptus feror.
Quo miser abibo? quem locum profugus petam?
Vbi morabor, quamque tellurem excolam?
Monstra latebram quaeso longinquam, abditam,
Vbi nulla signa pristini restent boni,
Vbi nil in animum perditam Hedenem mihi,
Pomosque revocet, cum meis mergar malis.
Nemus beatum, verque perpetuum loci,
Felixque regio, cujus heu frustra mihi
Concessus usus tempore interiit brevi,
Arborque vitae, cujus effectu frui
Vetat altera arbor luridae pestis parens,
Valete; tuque quae quatergemino alveo
Alluere tellus, dulcia Euphratis vada
Felicitatis conscia, atque animi mei
Quem saepe vobis cantico prompsi sacro,
Et quicquid hortus iste servavit boni
Nunquam videndum rursus, aeternum vale:
Hoc vos supremum tueor. En fugio, exeo:
Mortifera vitia, dira morborum lues,

Stand at the entrance to the Grove, that fronts the East,
And with your wheeling sword-blade's scintillating edge
See ye prevent all souls from setting foot therein.
Eve. What sudden gleam is that? What light shines fiercely forth?
A flame has caught the Garden and the lofty trees
Are burning without fire, a gleaming conflagration
That wanders hastily; as when the bright sky shines
With cometary lights, the whole Grove is ablaze.
These torches shine forth worthy of my marriage-bed.
By this sign let mankind discern from whence it came!
Adam. Now let us flee the flames! These are the holy works
Of the Divine Hand, bidding us go forth to exile.
O mighty Ruler, Thou great Governor of Heaven,
No longer I resist. I will, I will depart.
But still my body totters on reluctant knees;
And when I walk, I stagger back against my will.
For what place shall I seek in exiled wretchedness?
In what spot shall I stay, and what soil shall I till?
Show me some far, sequester'd hiding-place, I pray,
Where no signs of our former fortune may remain,
And nothing, when in evils I am wholly plunged,
May there remind me of lost Eden and its fruits.
O ever-blessed Grove, place of perpetual spring,
O happy region whose use granted me in vain,
Alas, has perish'd in a fleeting space of time,
And O thou Tree of Life, to enjoy the effect of whom
The other Tree, parent of livid plague forbids --
Farewell! And thou too, that with fourfold effluence
Dost water all this region, sweet Euphrates' stream,
Witness of all my happiness and all my heart
That I pour'd often forth to thee in sacred song,
And all things that that Garden held for me of good,
Good never to be seen again -- farewell for ever!
This last time I behold you. Lo I flee, depart.
But come ye mortal faults, Disease's dread destruction,

Languor caducus, horridus febrium tremor,
Labor, dolorque, et cumulus instantis mali,
Vos ite mecum tristis exilii duces.

Translation:

And swooning Langour, Fever's horrid paroxysms,
And Toil and Pain and storm clouds of impending Woe,
Come ye along with me, guides of my mournful exile!

(Exeunt Adam and Eve.)

GIAMBATTISTA MARINI

La Strage degli Innocenti (1610)[1]

5.

Below the Botome of the great Abysse,
There where one Center reconciles all things;
The worlds profound Heart pants; There placed is
Mischifes old Master, close about him clings
A curl'd knot of embracing Snakes, that kisse
His correspondent cheekes: these loathsome strings
Hold the perverse Prince in eternall Ties
Fast bound, since first he forfeited the skies.

6.

The Iudge of Torments, and the King of Teares:
He fills a burnisht Throne of quenchlesse fire:
And for his old faire Roabes of Light, hee weares
A gloomy Mantle of dark flames, the Tire
That crownes his hated head on high appeares;
Where seav'n tall Hornes (his Empires pride) aspire.
And to make up Hells Majesty, each Horne
Seav'n crested Hydra's horribly adorne.

---

[1] Extracts from Book I in the translation of Richard Crashaw (London, 1646).

7.

His Eyes, the sullen dens of Death and Night,
Startle the dull Ayre with a dismall red:
Such his fell glances as the fatall Light
Of staring Comets, that looke Kingdomes dead.
From his black nostrills, and blew lips, in spight
Of Hells owne stinke, a worser stench is spread.
His breath Hells lightning is: and each deepe grone
Disdaines to thinke that Heav'n Thunders alone.

8.

His flaming Eyes dire exhalation,
Vnto a dreadfull pile gives fiery Breath;
Whose unconsum'd consumption preys upon
The never-dying Life, of a long Death.
In this sad House of slow Destruction,
(His shop of flames) hee fryes himselfe, beneath
A masse of woes, his Teeth for Torment gnash,
While his steele sides sound with his Tayles strong lash.

9.

Three Rigourous Virgins waiting still behind,
Assist the Throne of th' Iron-Sceptred King.
With whips of Thornes and knotty vipers twin'd
They rouse him, when his ranke Thoughts need a sting.
Their lockes are beds of uncomb's snakes that wind
About their shady browes in wanton Rings.
Thus reignes the wrathfull King, and while he reignes
His Scepter and himselfe both he disdaines.

10.

Disdainefull wretch! how hath one bold sinne cost
Thee all the Beauties of thy once bright Eyes?
How hath one blacke Eclipse cancell'd, and crost
The glories that did guild thee in thy Rise?
Proud Morning of a perverse Day! how lost
Art thou unto thy selfe, thou too selfe-wise

Narcissus? foolish Phaeton? who for all
Thy high-aym'd hopes, gaind'st but a flaming fall.

11.

From Death's sad shades, to the Life-breathing Ayre,
This mortall Enemy to mankinds good,
Lifts his malignant Eyes, wasted with care,
To become beautifull in humane blood.
Where Iordan melts his Chrystall, to make faire
The fields of Palestine, with so pure a flood,
There does he fixe his Eyes: and there detect
New matter, to make good his great suspect. . . .

18.

Strucke with these great concurrences of things,
Symptomes so deadly, unto Death and him;
Faine would hee have forgot what fatall strings,
Eternally bind each rebellious limbe.
Hee shooke himselfe, and spread his spatious wings:
Which like two Bosom'd sailes embrace the dimme
Aire, with a dismall shade, but all in vaine,
Of sturdy Adamant is his strong chaine.

19.

While thus Heav'ns highest counsails, by the low
Footsteps of their Effects, hee trac'd too well,
Hee tost his troubled eyes, Embers that glow
Now with new Rage, and wax too hot for Hell.
With his foule clawes hee fenc'd his furrowed Brow,
And gave a gastly shreeke, whose horrid yell
Ran trembling through the hollow vaults of Night,
The while his twisted Tayle hee gnawed for
spight. . . .

25.

While new Thoughts boyl'd in his enraged Brest,
His gloomy Bosomes darkest Character,
Was in his shady forehead seen exprest.
The forehead's shade in Griefes expression there,
Is what in signe of joy among the blest

The faces lightning, or a smile is here.
   Those stings of care that his strong Heart
      opprest,
   A desperate, Oh mee, drew from his deepe Brest.

26.

Oh mee! (thus bellow'd hee) oh mee! what great
Portents before mine eyes their Powers advance?
And serves my purer sight, onely to beat
Downe my proud Thought, and leave it in a Trance?
Frowne I; and can great Nature keep her seat?
And the gay starrs lead on their Golden dance?
   Can his attempts above still prosp'rous be,
   Auspicious still, in spight of Hell and me?

27.

Hee has my Heaven (what would he more?) whose bright
And radiant Scepter this bold hand should beare.
And for the never-fading fields of Light
My faire Inheritance, hee confines me here,
To his darke House of shades, horrour, and Night,
To draw a long-liv'd Death, where all my cheere
   Is the solemnity my sorrow weares,
   That Mankinds Torment waits upon my Teares.

28.

Darke, dusty Man, he needs would single forth,
To make the partner of his owne pure ray:
And should we Powers of Heav'n, Spirits of worth
Bow our bright Heads, before a King of clay?
It shall not be, said I, and clombe the North,
Where never wing of Angell yet made way
   What though I mist my blow? yet I strooke high,
   And to dare something, is some victory.

29.

Is hee not satisfied? Meanes he to wrest
Hell from me too, and sack my Territories?
Vile humane Nature means he now t' invest
(O my despight!) with his divinest Glories?

And rising with rich spoiles upon his Brest,
With his faire Triumphs fill all future stories?
   Must the bright armes of Heav'n, rebuke these
        eyes?
   Mocke me, and dazle my darke Mysteries?

30.

Art thou not Lucifer? he to whom the droves
Of Stars, that guild the Morne in charge were given?
The nimblest of the lightning-winged Loves?
The fairest, and the first-borne smile of Heav'n?
Looke in what Pompe the Mistresse Planet moves
Rev'rently circled by the lesser seaven,
   Such, and so rich, the flames that from thine
        eyes,
   Oprest the common-people of the skyes.

31.

Ah wretch! what bootes thee to cast back thy eyes,
Where dawning hope no beame of comfort showes?
While the reflection of thy forepast joyes,
Renders thee double to thy present woes.
Rather make up to thy new miseries,
And meet the mischiefe that upon thee growes.
   If Hell must mourne, Heav'n sure shall sympathize
   What force cannot effect, fraud shall devise.

32.

And yet whose force feare I? have I so lost
My selfe? my strength too with my innocence?
Come try who dares, Heav'n, Earth, what ere dost
        boast,
A borrowed being, make thy bold defence.
Come thy Creator too, what though it cost
Mee yet a second fall? wee'd try our strengths.
   Heav'n saw us struggle once, as brave a fight
   Earth now should see, and tremble at the sight.

33.

Thus spoke th' impatient Prince, and made a pause,

His foule Hags rais'd their heads, & clapt their
hands.
And all the Powers of Hell in full applause
Flourisht their Snakes, and tost their flaming
brands.
Wee (said the horrid sisters) wait thy lawes,
Th' obsequious handmaids of thy high commands.
Be it thy part, Hells mighty Lord, to lay
On us thy dread commands, ours to obey.

34.

What thy Alecto, what these hands can doe,
Thou mad'st bold proofe upon the brow of Heav'n,
Nor should'st thou bate in pride, because that now,
To these thy sooty Kingdomes thou art driven.
Let Heav'ns Lord chide above lowder then thou
In language of his Thunder, thou are even
With him below: here thou art Lord alone
Boundlesse and absolute: Hell is thine owne.

35.

If usuall wit, and strength will doe no good,
Vertues of stones, nor herbes: use stronger charmes,
Anger, and love, best hookes of humane blood.
If all faile wee'l put on our proudest Armes,
And pouring on Heav'ns face the Seas huge flood
Quench his curl'd fires, wee'l wake with our Alarmes
Ruine, where e're she sleepes at Natures feet;
And crush the world till his wide corners meet.

36.

Reply'd the proud King, O my Crownes Defence?
Stay of my strong hopes, you of whose brave worth,
The frighted stars tooke faint experience,
When 'gainst the Thunders mouth we marched forth:
Still you are prodigal of your Love's expence
In our great projects, both 'gainst Heav'n and Earth.
I thanke you all, but one must single out,
Cruelty, she alone shall cure my doubt.

37.

Fourth of the cursed knot of Hags is shee,
Or rather all the other three in one;
Hells shop of slaughter shee do's oversee,
And still assist the Execution.
But chiefly there do's shee delight to be,
Where Hells capacious Cauldron is set on:
   And while the black soules boile in their owne
        gore,
   To hold them down, and looke that none seethe
        o're.

38.

Thrice howl'd the Caves of Night, and thrice the
        sound,
Thundring upon the bankes of those black lakes
Rung, through the hollow vaults of Hell profound:
At last her listning Eares the noise o'retakes,
Shee lifts her sooty lampes, and looking round
A gen'rall hisse, from the whole Tire of snakes
   Rebounding, through Hells inmost Cavernes came,
   In answer to her formidable Name.

39.

Mongst all the Palaces in Hells command,
No one so mercilesse as this of hers.
The Adamantine Doors, for ever stand
Impenetrable, both to prai'rs and Teares,
The walls inexorable steele, no hand
Of Time, or Teeth of hungry Ruine feares.
   Their ugly ornaments are the bloody staines,
   Of ragged limbs, torne sculls, & dasht out
        Braines.

40.

There has the purple Vengeance a proud seat,
Whose ever-brandisht Sword is sheath'd in blood.
About her Hate, Wrath, Warre, and Slaughter sweat;
Bathing their hot limbs in life's pretious flood.
There rude impetuous Rage do's storme, and fret:

And there, as Master of this murd'ring brood,
Swinging a huge Sith stands impartiall Death,
With endlesse businesse almost out of Breath.

GIAMBATTISTA ANDREINI

L'Adamo (1613)[1]

Dramatis Personae

The Eternal Father
Chorus of Seraphim, Cherubim, and Angels
The Archangel Michael
Adam
Eve
A Cherub, Guardian of Adam
Lucifer
Satan
Beelzebub
The Seven Deadly Sins
The World
The Flesh
Hunger
Fatigue
Despair
Death
Vain Glory
The Serpent
Volano, a messenger of Hell
Chorus of Hobgoblins
Chorus of Spirits of Fire, Air, Water, and Hell.

The scene is set in the Earthly Paradise.

---

[1]Translation by Watson Kirkconnell. Loose canzone-measure in the dialogue of the original has been replaced by blank verse in English. Rhymed lyrics retain their rhyme.

Prologue: Chorus of angels singing the glory of God. (lines 1-20).

Act I, Scene I

Enter the Eternal Father and a Chorus of Angels.

Etern. F. Raise from dark horror thy appalling brow,
O Lucifer, grieving at so much light;
Be dazzled at the gleaming stars' white lamp,
Pant at the radiance of a sun not hot:
Read in the shining volumes of the sky
The mighty marvels of the heavenly Hand;
Wonder, O rebel, madman, how to me,
The Architect of all the universe,
It were an easy enterprise to rear
The thresholds of the lofty Empyrean,
Raising the humble thither whence there fell
The proud in spirit. Thence with bitter grief
(O mole of horrors, hell's black salamander)
Let the stiff-necked and obstinate observe,
(Despairing of my grace and his escape)
His proper ruin in another's safety,
Heav'n closed to him but wide to others' feet;
Till heaving from his inmost heart a sigh
He give me grudging glory as he says:
Ah, miserable me, I well perceive
That the supreme Creator has no need
Of any force or essence but Himself
To give due order to all things that are.
Seraphim. O glorious preparation
With Sun and Moon as radiant decoration,
Sweet in the angel chorus
And in the Spheres sonorous,
O how thou goest awaking
Mankind to be spectator
Of Love in the Creator!
Cherubim. Across the great page of the sky
The sovereign Hand divine
Using its finger as a pen,
As letters stars that shine,
Wrote his best works' fair story line by line:
And man in wonder at the sight

Goes mounting upward in the height;
Though veiled in flesh, such vision is he given
That though his foot's on earth his head's in
heaven.
Etern. F. Descend from heaven, O angels. With
you comes
One who brings Heaven to earth. Let each who views
His works sublime see, humble and devout,
Earth changed to flesh, mud fashion'd into man,
Man elevated as a sovereign lord
And a soul waxing in angelic strength.
Seraphim. Let us now cleave the sky on wings of
gold,
Let earth be Paradise,
Since from the lofty skies
The King of Heaven descends to tread its mould.
Let us now cleave the sky on wings of gold.
Flow'rs, weave a carpet for His foot divine:
Rivalling the stars you shine,
The spheres acclaim you fine,
Ye gems of heaven, in beauty manifold.
Let us now cleave the sky on wings of gold.
Etern. F. Behold, ye new-made herbs and primal
flowers,
The Foot that used to tread among the stars
And the great shining pathway of the Sun
Begins today beside a woody bank
To set its heavenly footprints in the clay.
On humble substances I lay my hand
In order to achieve a work sublime.
(He proceeds to fashion Adam out of clay.)
Angels. Wail, grieving angel, wail indeed
Thou rebel to God's grace!
Lo, he shall rise with sudden speed
Who brings more glory to thy former place.
In folly thou wert proud
Considering thy birth
But he will drive away all pride,
Formed of the humble earth.
So it will come to pass, humility
Will gain for him what you by pride have lost;
Since the first Lord of lodgings in the sky
Welcomes the humble and ejects the high.
Etern. F. Rise quickly, Adam, now that into thee

I've breathed a soul with warm and loving breath;
Rise, primal man! Let the great world with joy
Embrace the microcosm in its arms!
Adam. O marvels new, O sacred, everlasting
And holy object of the angelic cohorts,
Why have I not indeed as many tongues
As the sky now has stars? Do I behold
Before a thing so earthy and so small
The heavenly Author of the Universe?
O great and peerless Monarch, if this tongue
Fails to frame thanks to match my obligations,
Behold in the affection of my heart
An ampler language than my lips express,
A fuller worship than my knees that kneel.
Already, Lord, in ecstasy devout
My mind flies upwards, soars beyond the clouds,
Past every sphere, yea, enters even heaven
And there beholds the stars, a throne for man.
Thou, Lord, who in true love all things dost turn
To flame in Thee: merge me into Thyself
That I, a part of Thee, may utter praise
More worthy of thy everlasting name.
Angels. Turn to this pleasant Paradise with mirth
Great demigod of earth!
Yonder like murmuring spheres
Clear circling waters charm the ears;
There tuneful choirs of birds
Sing like the angelic powers;
Legions of scattered flowers
Are there the living stars;
The white rose like the silver moon is shod,
The helianthus is the golden Sun.
Dower'd with fair corporeal form, this earthly god,
What should he crave, what more should he wish
given,
If in the midst of earth he finds a heaven?
Adam. But what sweet slumber, O ye tuneful birds
And pomp of lovely flowers, shuts my eyes?
Behold, I lay me down. Farewell, pure light
Of the transcendent Sun. Sweet air, farewell.
(Adam lies down and falls asleep. God proceeds to extract a rib and form Eve.)

Etern. F. Adam, I come to thee, belovèd child,

Son of a loving Father. Lo the hand
That never works in vain, the hand that knit
The elements to order and upreared
The heavens in their spheres, that made the stars,
Gave the moon light, and laws to rule the sun,
Today sustains the world and has provided
The solid ground on which thy weight may rest.
Now from thy rib, I plan, O sleeping Adam,
To draw the substance that shall bear the name
And all the form and loveliness of Woman.

Angels. O deathless works of an immortal Maker,
O trophies fortunate, O works designed
For the high and blessed coasts
Of the fair world, the boasts
Of starry realms beyond the reach of mind!
O power and might
That out of shades and horror made the sun's clear
light!

(The newly created Eve rises and looks around.)

Eve. What heavenly melody pervades my heart
Before it strikes my ear? And what invites me
To gaze at marvels? Ah, what do I see?
What change is this? Has earth been changed to
heaven?
Do I behold the radiance of Him
Who humbles still the Sun with His high splendour?
Am I the handiwork of Him who made
From nought the Angels and the Empyrean?
High Lord, whom reverently I adore,
So tender an affection stabs my heart
That while the tongue would venture to discourse
The words that falter from my lips remain
Suspended in a tide of tears and sighs.
Dear love of a celestial Deity
That deigns to show His glory upon earth,
And to the world descends today to form
Out of the substance of a little mud
The emperor of all created things,
Thou who canst plumb the holy, hidden depths
Of human hearts, with proofs of warmest love,
Cause even my poor tongue to answer Thee
That these dear valleys and these woods may hear

The thanks, O Lord, that I should render Thee.
But if my tongue be mute, let my heart speak.
Etern. F. Adam, awake! Cease to enjoy thy dream
Of hidden things made manifest on high
And the deep secrets of the Trinity.

(Adam rouses himself and looks about him.)

Adam. Where have I been? Where am I? What threefold
Intensity of light beyond the sun
Withdraws from sight? Where has it vanished now?
O holy miracles of heavenly faith,
Of such bright suns that, diverse in their nature,
Form one sole ray of glory infinite
Embellishing all Heaven, making fair
Each winged being: Most mysterious light
That from the Summum Bonum issuest
He alone sees thee well who mounts to thee
As strong as a great eagle in his faith.
What white and sacred rose in Heaven's garden
Wet with empyreal dews have I beheld
Open its bosom to these suns? Or rather,
What sun emparadised in its soft bosom
And in a moment after (O high wonder!)
Rise like a lily in a flood of light
From the fair virgin breast? Are the suns lilies?
Are lilies children of the virgin rose?
Etern. F. Heav'n is too high for thee to understand,
The world too low. It is enough that man
With humble intellect should plumb in vain
The ocean of creative deity.
Embrace now with the arm of thy affection
The virtuous bosom of thy fair companion
Who is called Woman and whose name is Eve.
Adam. My dear companion, helpmeet of my life,
Pride of my heart and power of my pulse,
Flesh of my flesh and bone of my own bone,
With holy love I clasp thy bosom now.
Etern. F. Children, I leave you now. Abide in peace.
I bless you. Be ye fruitful and increase
Until the world is small for man's fair race.

May man have lordship over all that now
The sun warms and the sea bathes. Give a name
To every beast that runs or flies or swims.
But let a changeless prohibition sink
By way of ear to soul: listen, O Adam,
Let thy wife hear it and in both your hearts,
Where love now dwells, cherish the words divine.
Of whatsoever fruits each fertile tree
Can offer to your lips with branchy hand,
Of whatsoever fare of pleasant dainties
Is yielded by this garden of delights,
This paradise of flowers, this joy of man,
This treasury of earth, terrestrial miracle
And glorious handiwork of the Creator,
I say to you, O children, you may taste.
But of the tree revealing Good and Evil,
On pain of death to him who knows not death,
The fruit is here forbidden by decree.
I leave you now and through the aëry ways
Forsaking earth, I journey back to Heaven.
Seraphim. Let every cloud above descend to earth
And white and clear
Mount up with God as to the glowing sphere.
Then let the stars come down,
The moon and sun come bright,
Forming a stairway to the Empyreal height.
Let each rejoice that God, Monarch past thought,
Today is walking where His hand has wrought.
(Exeunt God, Seraphim, Cherubim and Angels.)

Adam. O glorious spectacle, at sight of which
I find all God's high glories yet more fair,
How through my eyes you satisfy my heart!
Behold, my fairest wife, how at one nod
Of the eternal Master, fire flames forth
Obedient as fire, the sea is sea,
The sky becomes the sky, the earth the earth,
And air is air where formerly there stood
Nor fire nor sky nor air nor earth nor sea.
Behold the azure of the sky, where oft
A lovely shining star shall wake the dawn,
A heavenly brightness, harbinger of day,
To illuminate the vastness of the morn.
Then the bright sun, to make the world more glad,

Shall scatter forth the light of his great lamp;
And when he tires of gazing at the earth,
The pure white moon and all the tiny stars
Will make procession in nocturnal pomp.
Lo, fire is bright above all elements
And in its lightness takes its seat aloft.
See the pure brightness of the limpid air
Support the pinions of the painted birds
That guide the happy hours with tuneful notes.
See the broad bosom of the fecund earth
Adorned with flowers and with ripened fruits.
See, on her verdant hair she wears a crown
Of lofty hills; and tall trees are her sceptre.
Behold the fair, blue prairie of the sea,
That from its moist sands and its valleys deep
And from its silent scaly tribes below
Rolls over gold and beds of precious pearls
And crimson corals, raising to the sky
Its billowy head, adorned with dulse and moss.
No glory could be greater
From the Supreme Creator.
Eve. Such power comes direct
From the High Architect.
Adam. Yonder, my consort, let us go where other marvels,
Framed by my Maker to delight me,
A legion infinite, invite me.
(Exeunt Adam and Eve.)

Act I, Scene II

Enter Lucifer alone.

Luc. Who calls me from my dark abyss to see
Excess of light? What further miracles
Dost Thou reveal to me today, O God?
Hast Thou perhaps grown tired of Thy home
In Heaven above, that Thou hast made on earth
This paradise? Why hast Thou fashioned then
These two terrestrial gods in human flesh?
Tell me, vile Architect, who out of clay
Hast formed Thy handiwork, what will become
Of this poor man, this solitary weak
Naked inhabitant of woods and forests?

Perhaps he dreams of treading on the stars?
I am the cause that Heaven is made poor:
I glory in the ruin I have wrought.
Let God weave star with star, join sun to moon,
And tire Himself in patching the bright sky,
For at the last, in obloquy and scorn,
His work will be in vain, and vain His sweat.
From Lucifer alone came ample light
That shone through Heaven in a thousand rays;
But these His fires are shadows now and smoke,
Mere bastard candles to my greater lights.
I do not wish to know what Heaven may be,
Nor care to know the nature of this man;
Too obstinate and hard is my resolve
To show myself implacable and stern
Towards Heaven, Man, th' angelic host, and God.

Act I, Scene III

Lucifer as before. Enter *Satan* and *Beelzebub*, who at first converse without noticing *Lucifer*.

Satan. To the light rear we our foreheads, to the light
Brows crowned with horns that tell the haughty power
And noble pride that lodges in our breast!
Should we then suffer outrage such as this?
Shall we not rather with these talon'd hands
Tear out the stars that sparkle in the sky
And take the sun and moon to blaze in hell
As tokens of our glorious victory?
For we are those who in great feats of arms
Caused the pale face of Heaven to twitch in fear
In the star-studded battle-ground on high.
To arms, most dread Beëlzebub, to arms,
Ere it be noised abroad throughout the spheres,
To our great loss and memorable scorn,
That from the race of man (who is vile clay)
The stars once more have someone to exalt.
Beëlzebub. I burn with such great flame, so foul a wave
Of venom floods me that from inward frenzy
My sighs seem thunder and my glances lightning,

My tears a fiery rain. Thus from my brow
The hissing vipers that obscure my face
I needs must push aside, that I may see
God's mighty works and the new demigods.
Be silent, silent -- now that this Man is made --
Whoever thinks to imitate his voice,
Saying perhaps: Satan most sorrowful,
Unhappy spirits, how are ye miserable!
From being first, ye sink to second place,
Alas, supremely wretched! The Heaven above
Was once your station, the bright stars your seat,
And God your high Creator. Now, ye wretches,
Since ye have lost the everlasting dawn
And every light celestial, ye are called,
On lips above, the dark and doleful throng.
Instead of walking in the sun's glad paths,
Ye tread the prairies of eternal night.
Instead of golden hair and angel faces,
Your hair is snaky and your glance is grim,
The wrathful visage wears a sombre mien,
Each mouth is heavy now with blasphemy
And cursing issues forth in sulphurous cloud
Of foulest fire and mephitic slaver.
You have an eagle's claw, a goat's cleft foot,
A bat's dark wings, and as your last abode
A dismal Tartarus, profound and black,
Whose theatre of anguish ever turns
Its horrid back upon the sun's bright rays;
For the Angel born to suffer no offense,
To ruin Heaven and to upraise Hell,
Ought to be bloody and in brow to mirror
The dreadful standard of the horrid deep.
Satan. Although our beaks are hook'd, our talons sharp,
Our tresses snaky and our glances grim,
Our feet now cloven hooves, our bodies winged
And horrible, and though our place is now
The abyss of pitchy darkness and deep horror,
Yet we are angels still, and worthier far
Than all the others as the lofty Lord
Is worthier than the humblest soul that serves Him;
So that, if far from Heaven we spread our wings,
They may remember still that we are lords,
That they are slaves, and that if we have left

A little seat in heaven, in its place
We have erected here a royal throne,
Immense and massive, where the first champion
Among us all lifts up his countenance
More than a mountain towering in the sky,
And there, invoking anger against God,
Defies the stars, our constant enemies,
And bears an awful sceptre, tipped with fire,
Which, while he wheels it, coruscates and burns
More than the brightest brilliance of the sun.
Lucifer. (Aside) The time is ripe to show myself.
(Aloud) My brave ones!
O angels great, courageous, born with strength
For waging war, I know the grief that plagues you
In living death is to see man upraised
To such exalted station in the world
That every thing created bows to him;
Because you fear this pair will rise one day
With all the horde of their posterity
Up to the lofty seats of blazing glory,
Our riches once and our renounced splendour.
Satan. Great Monarch of the grim infernal Pit,
I bow to you and bare my harsh deep pain,
Which, through this man, grows hourly more bitter,
Fearing the Incarnation of the Word.
Lucifer. And is it true that from so little dust
A God shall rise, that flesh, that very God,
The Power that forces us to dwell below?
Can it be true that He whom angels worship
Will veil Himself in this vile clay of earth,
He who is worshipped now by all in Heaven?
Shall angels do obeisance then to Man?
Shall impure flesh give the angelic nature
A higher form? Can this indeed be true?
Does it surpass our powers to imagine
The way of it, we who at such a cost
Have bought the right to boast that we are wise?
Yet I am he indeed who would not suffer
That your high natures once above in heaven
Should suffer outrage when a mad desire
Came to the Tyrant of the starry courts
That you should fall in worship of the Word
Incarnate in the flesh. Yes, I am he
Who armed a noble mind on your behalf

Boldly to dare, and led you to the North,
Far from the crazy purposes of Him
Who boasts Himself creator of the Heavens.
Ye are yourselves; I recognize you well
Who gave me by your daring and your valour
A triumph almost sure in any heaven.
Up, then, let noble glory kindle you,
Set you on fire! And let it ne'er be heard
That He you scorned to worship up above
Now has your adoration down in Hell.
For thus you swore to aid me, by the might
Of your unconquer'd worth -- worth, ah, so great
That Heaven was unworthy to possess it.
The outrage is too great, the loss too heavy,
If we are not impatient to avenge it.
Already I see flaming in your faces
Your hearts' high zeal, your kindled eagerness.
Already in the air I see you spread
Your wings to smother earth, to scale the sky,
That hurling all in ruin to the abyss
You bring this human upstart to his end,
Wounded as soon as born, brought to his grave.
Satan. Ah, give me orders now! Ask what you will!
Speak with a hundred tongues! What do you bid?
And forthwith in a hundred works for you
Will Satan pant and Hell perspire with zeal.
Lucifer. Behold, a God in vain in human form
Appears incarnate to prepare their way,
To smooth for them the steep and craggy path
By which they hope at last to mount to Heaven.
Too easy a device for human ruin
The ancient God has offered the new Man;
Since Nature wills too much, she ev'n compels
This man, if he would live, continually
To eat of various foods; and so to me
It seems a matter of the greatest ease --
Since bitter ruin lies in dainty sweets --
That he today should taste the Forbidden Fruit,
Whence by the road of Death he may return
To nothing, as he nothing was before.
Beëlzebub. O mighty thought of a most mighty
angel!
Lucifer. Nay, but a greater fire of nobler thought
Enkindles me to speak: That God perhaps,

Scornful today that He has put His hands
In clay and stained them both, and having learn'd
An angel's nature and the state of man,
And then repenting fully of man's dainties
Has issued from deliberate deceit
This prohibition, so that when man sins,
He may with right, although tyrannically,
Make him become destroyer of this earth
And turn the clay once more to filthy mire;
And having thus uprooted altogether
The Word's due Root, open a sure approach
To high Olympus (grieving for His error)
To the most great first Ornaments of Heaven.
Satan. Pardon, O pardon, if with humble thought
Born on my tongue I may offend your ear
Too much perhaps! As long as this man lives
And breathes on earth, we must endure raw war
And live in constant terror of the Word.
Lucifer. This man may live, and breathe, and sin, and die.
This human nature may fill all the earth
And rule the beasts; his soul may be immortal,
Made in God's image; but for the Word divine
To incarnate itself, I deem it vain.
Beelzebub. O dear angelic words I longed to hear,
O words to heal our hearts, however wounded!
Lucifer. Let this man sin, yea let him sin; for sinning
He forms a fault that shall be real in man
And shall be then declared original
In his posterity. Thus as man lives,
And ever sins, and dies at last in sin,
And then is born in like depravity,
The Word can scarce incarnate human sin
Of which it is so great an enemy.
Now then, arise from the great dim Abyss
All ye who ought in duty to make sure
That man shall be a sinner, doomed to death!

Act I, Scene IV (lines 559-596)

The devils Melecano and Lurcone, summoned from Hell, are to assume the roles of Pride and Envy and to assay Adam and Eve, especially the latter.

Act I, Scene V (lines 597-651)

The devils Ruspican and Arfarat are similarly assigned the roles of Anger and Avarice.

Act I, Scene VI (lines 652-721)

The devils Maltia, Dulciato and Guliar are given the roles of Sloth, Lechery and Gluttony.

Act II, Scene I (lines 722-886)

Fifteen angels, jointly and severally, hymn the greatness of God the Father, the purity of the Incarnate Word, the woe of the fallen angels, and the happy lot of man.

Act II, Scene II.

Enter Adam.

Adam. O mighty Lord of the great things on high,
Supreme Creator, infinite in love,
To me, Thy humble servant, dost Thou give
Such ample favours from Thy bounteous hand,
That wheresoe'er I look, I am revered?
Draw near me now, wild beasts, and you, dear birds,
Fold now your painted wings; for I am Adam,
Yea, I am he who shall assign the name
To every thing that God has formed for man.
Praise, praise Him then who has created me
And who has made you all! Rejoice with me
All lovingly in His transcendent love!
But what do I behold? O happy me,
See where my dear, my sweet companion comes
To bring me showers of blossoms and enwreathe
My brow with woodland honours. Go, proud lion,
And you, rhinoceros, impenetrable
And scaly monster, vaunted conqueror
Of the unvanquished elephant, and you,
Hot-mettled horse, go gallop through the fields
And shake the skies and valleys with your neighing,
You, camel, too, and all ye birds and beasts,

Withdraw in deference to Eve, who comes.

(The beasts and birds withdraw, Eve enters.)

Eve. What greater pleasure than my company
Draws Adam far from me? O gentle flowers,
Where is his foot's dear print upon you seen?

(Enter Lurcone and Guliar, unobserved)

Lurcone. Behold the Man and Woman. Hide and watch.
Adam. Weary your eyes no more. Make no more
 lightnings
With these your living lamps. Turn the clear sky
Of your dear face on one who loves its light.
Behold your Adam, sweet beloved one.
For are not you alone the world's delight,
The only love and paramour of man?
Lurcone (aside). Fear your impending loss!
 Guliar (aside). Fear guile of Hell!
Eve. My tongue is tied with my supreme content;
But still my face becomes most eloquent
To voice the rapture of my silent heart.
Adam. O my dear consort!
 Lurcone (aside). Soon perhaps your foe!
Adam. O sweetest life!
 Guliar (aside). Perhaps your bitter death!
Eve. Accept, my gentle Adam, these my flowers.
They are my gift; I twine them in your hair.
Adam. O snowy privet, ivory jessamine,
White lily, purest hue, the meadows' milk,
O lovely rose, nurse of the rarest colours,
Consort of dawn, the fresh dew's paramour,
The hedgerow's treasure and vermilion gem,
Dear harbinger of April, here alone
Fair flower amid flowers, floral Empress,
You frame a fragrant garland for my hair
So that the perfume even spreads to Heaven.
With holiest embraces, O my dear,
Let us so intertwine ourselves that we may seem
An interwov'n acanthus of the hedge!
Lurcone (aside). Fetters of hellish toil will
 soon enfold you
In such a fashion that no mortal striving

Will serve you to untie the subtle knot.
Eve. Now that with flowers so lovely we have both
Adorned our hair, let us on reverent knees
Give humble praises to the great Creator;
For this my heart cannot refrain from worship.
Adam. At such dear words, at your heart's fair desire,
I gladly kneel among the grass and flowers.
Lurcone. Now must I surely from this humble act
Flee furiously away and leave the sun.
Guliar. And I, alas, must follow you in flight,
Encumber'd with immeasurable grief.
(Exeunt Lurcone and Guliar.)

Act II, Scene III (lines 1052-1095)

Lucifer, disguised as a serpent with a female head, bosom and arms, explains to Satan and other spirits his plan of campaign against Eve.

Act II, Scene IV (lines 1096-1130)

Volano, a messenger from Hell, brings word to Lucifer that the chieftains there wish him to conquer Man or to acknowledge the latter as victor.

Act II, Scene V (lines 1131-1192)

Lucifer (as Serpent) welcomes Vain Glory as an ally, and together they take their posts in the Forbidden Tree.

Act II, Scene VI

(The Serpent and Vain Glory as before, concealed. Enter Eve.)

Eve. Handmaiden of a lofty Lord, a low
And humble servitor, I ought to kneel
With reverent knees upon the ground to praise
The love divine and measureless of Him
Who made me queen of all the Sun surveys.
But if I raise my eyes and heart to heaven,
Is it not clear to Eve that she was made

For everlasting and celestial marvels?
So that in soul or veil'd in mortal flesh,
Enjoyment should be hers in highest Heaven
Or on this earth. Yonder the leafy tree,
Weaving its foliaged arms to rival Heaven,
Desires above my tresses to spread out
A rich sky of green leaves. If I betake me
Among the grasses and the flowers, I see
That those on which I tread show still more
charming.
Even the buds come open, garlanding
The grassy tresses of a thousand meadows.
Other new charming flowers that stand remote,
Gather'd in groups, battalion'd in the valleys,
Turn their glad eyes on me and seem to say:
"Let neighbouring flowers rejoice to be a carpet
Beneath your feet, but we, like eagles proud,
Gaze from afar but to behold your face,
A humble image of the Face divine."
Still other flowers, other plants, desiring
That I should sit among them, seem to rise
Beyond their native habit so that they
From charming flowers form a fragrant hedge.
Still others in a thousand gentle knots
Weave with such skill a secret snare of herbs
That the unwary scarcely shall escape --
The hand that frees the foot itself is caught.
If I should wish for food or drink, behold,
Ready for me are fruits, milk, honey, manna,
And from a thousand springs, a thousand rills,
Water pours clear as crystal, cool and sweet.
If I wish music, lo the tuneful birds
And banded angels sing their matchless songs.
If it is lovely day or night I wish,
Behold the Sun, behold the moon and stars.
If for a friend I ask, Adam responds.
If God I would invoke, behold in Heaven
The eternal Maker hearkens to my prayer.
If I crave subject creatures for my rule,
Behold a thousand creatures at my side.
What can I wish for more? What more obtain?
Nothing more, Lord. Eve's cup of honour's full.
But what do I behold? Am I awake,
Or do I dream? Surely among the branches

I see a human face, a charming one.
How then do other folk besides ourselves
View the bright Sun? O thing miraculous!
Ev'n at this distance I can see it plain:
For arms and hands it has, a human bosom,
And all the rest appears but trailing serpent.
How the sun, gilding with his rays those scales,
Flashing with fair hues, dazzles both my eyes!
I wish to draw more near.
Serpent (aside to Vain Glory). Now then you see
That I have taken just the shape to wreck her.
Eve. The nearer I approach, the greater charm
He shows to view, sapphire and emerald
And ruby now and amethyst and now
All jasper, pearl and jacinth is each fold
By which his tail clings to this leafy tree.
Serpent (aside). I will assail her.
(To Eve). Hey, to view me better,
You vanquisher of eyes, charmer of souls,
Darling of hearts, fair maiden, pray approach me!
Lo, I disclose myself. Behold me here,
Yea, all of me, and sate your eyes with gazing:
View me with care, you who are total beauty,
You the chief ornament of all the world,
You Nature's show-piece, micro-paradise,
To whom all things on earth bow down in praise.
Whither alone thus far from your friend Adam
Are you now straying? Where are those bright bands
Of angels who are lovers of your charms?
How fortunate am I, a thousand times,
That it has fallen to my happy lot
With just two eyes to marvel at that beauty
That Heaven scarcely sees with all its eyes!
Believe me, if the radiance of Heaven
Should wish to veil itself in human form,
What dwelling-place sublime could it elect
But your fair breast. How well, how well I see
That she who has your swift and nimble feet
Walks now in Heaven's expanses, laughing there
With your fair mouth to cheer those blessed spheres;
Moreover with your lips she breathes and speaks
And pauses; with your eyes, in fine, enhances
The beauty of the skies, the grace of earth.
Eve. Who are you? Why so eager in my praise?

My eyes have never seen a form like yours.
Serpent. Shall I be silent? Too much am I spurred
To be acceptable to the fair beauty.
Know then, that when the world was first derived
From nothing, and the fertile Garden likewise,
The Tiller of the fair celestial meadows
Installed me here as gardener to tend it.
Here gladly do I rear myself to see
That no rapacious bird should dare assault
A fruit so gracious. Hence comes my delight
(Though everything is marvellously fair)
To wreathe the lilies or weave rose with rose;
Here giving contour to a fragrant hedge,
Or causing there a crystal rill to flow
In flowers' bosoms and by tiny herbs.
What sweet displays all round shall I disclose
To the fair vision of so fair a maiden!
Return now, if you can, to view some spot
That has attracted you, that you may marvel
How I enhance its charm with flowers and myrtles.
This is the wondrous power that your Creator
Gave me, to guard the blossoms and their fragrance.
Eve. You who are courteous as you are wise,
Ah, tell you name to me, reveal it now,
Unless indeed I seek to know too much.
Serpent. My name is Wisdom; although sometimes too
I am called Life. The twofold name arises
Because of the two natures I possess,
The one all serpent and the other human.
Eve. Strange things I hear today! And why have you
A serpent body joined to human form?
Serpent. I'll tell you that indeed. Almighty God,
When seeking to make everything of nothing,
In order to weigh all things with due balance
The Wise One of Olympus would not pass
From one extreme to its sheer opposite
Without establishing a mid-way mean.
Hence it has pleased Him to create in me
A kind of serpent between brute and man:
And even this participates in reason
And power of speech, as it has human face.
But who ought not to be a willing subject
To you, great demigoddess of the earth?
If to your beauty or the worth of man

There had been added equally the gift
Of supreme knowledge, I doubt not that you
Would be in all things marked as lofty gods;
Because the value of such mighty knowledge
Is of the first and greatest attributes
Of deity itself. Ah, were it so,
How would I, sliding down to seek the base
Of this delightful tree, bow down to you
And worship you, a goddess beyond question!
Eve. What do you mean? Perhaps it seems to you
Man's knowledge is but little? Knows he not
The lore of herbs and plants and flowers; of gems
And minerals; of fishes, birds and beasts;
Of earth and water; of the air and fire;
And the most secret power of the heavens --
Of sun and moon and stars?
Satan. Ah, that is nothing.
It serves you only to make known the things
Of empty nature. Even I, though still
Of rank inferior enough to man,
Can these enumerate to the last one.
But how much worthier of you would it be
To know of good and evil: this indeed,
This is the height of all intelligence,
A knowledge of sublime and lofty secrets
That here on earth would make you even as gods.
Eve. That which alone is able to reveal
Both good and evil with conspicuous power,
And yet with deadly anguish, is the Tree,
That same Forbidden Tree where you are sitting.
Serpent. And why, pray tell me, is a law so bitter
Derived from fruit so sweet? Where is that wisdom
That you just now acknowledged so sublime?
Think if it can be just, that a man so strong,
And worthy, too, a man who rules the world
With learned hand, whom it pleased God to frame
As He made mighty marvels of the earth
And the vast heavens, should at last be ruined
For such a trifling fruit, his whole creation
Thus brought to nought or lasting but a moment!
No, no, repel the doubt! Colour your cheek,
Return the vanish'd crimson to your lip.
Speak. But I know the heart within your breast
Voices the selfsame language that I speak.

Eve. The Lord already has ordained for me
That I taste not; and gladly I obey.
Serpent. Ah, if He has forbidden you to taste
Of such an apple, it was for this cause:
He did not wish that man should be a god.
Give ear, you who are gracious to my words,
And answer me: If the Creator wished
You so obedient that you could depend
Only on His command to guard your ways,
Perhaps Faith, Hope and Love and their high laws
Were not enough to rule you. Why, O Lady,
Are laws for man so multiplied past need,
Outraging with such yoke your liberty,
Making you slaves, not lords, inferior
To the wild beasts, to whom He gave no law?
Who does not know that by imposing thus
Such precepts on you, He has greatly lessened
The happy life in which He set you first?
Perhaps he fears you both would equal Him
In knowledge, or in godhead? 'Tis not so.
For even if you took on deity
By such a means, yet a great difference
Would be between you: your divinity
And knowledge would be but derivative,
The far effect of the First Cause above.
Also can it be true that He would slay --
His hand of life commit a deed of death?
Oh, if you would but taste! How you would hasten
To meet your Lord! How with Him talking then
Your tongue would name the lofty things of Heaven!
For other flowers, other plants and fields,
New elements and spheres, new suns and moons
And other stars above differ from those you see,
Gazing aloft from your low station here.
Near are they to you now, behold how near,
Only as far from grasping as this apple.
Extend your hand, be bold and stretch it out!
Alas, what are you doing? Pausing yet?
Eve. What should I do? Who counsels me, O God?
Hope quickens me and terror straightway slays me.
But tell me: How can you know that there are
Such great things and such goodly things above,
And that on earth one makes oneself the peer
Of God Himself by eating of the apple,

If you yourself have never been in Heaven
Nor has it been your lot to taste the fruit?
Serpent. In very truth, I would deny you nothing
To make you happy. Hearken to me then
When your supreme Creator made me here
The guardian of the Garden, He expounded
To me the selfsame story as to you.
Then opening the everlasting bosom
Of Heaven with all its great celestial glories,
He made me sate my eyes; then said to me:
"Serpent, You have enjoyed your paradise.
No more shall you behold it. Now preserve
The memory of Heaven down on earth
By ever feeding on such fruit as this.
The heavenly land is due to man alone,
Being the home of beauty. Since you are
Thus doubly natured, man and also beast,
Your lodging is on earth, because the World
Is the due habitation of all beasts."
He added then: "It ought not to displease you,
Man-serpent, to lodge ever on the earth,
Since you already, in your human part,
Have fully tasted of your joys above."
Eternal thus I live, feeding myself
On this choice fruit; and Heaven ever opens
Before my eyes by reason of the knowledge
That this sweet good communicates to me.
Eve. Alas, what should I do? To whom apply?
What counsel do you offer me, O heart?
Serpent. Your sovereign Monarch has imposed on you,
In truth, on pain of death, a prohibition
Of this sweet fruit. To keep you utterly
From eating of the fruit, He set me here
As wakeful guardian of the pleasant tree.
And so, if I assent, the Man and you,
O charming one, Lady most beautiful,
May raise yourselves with joy to rival God.
Alas, it is too true that to partake
Of common food and drink with the wild beasts
Renders us like them. It can not be just
That you two, creatures of a high Creator,
The mighty children of Almighty God,
Should in the vilest and most humble state,
Alone in woods and forests lead a life

On the same level as the lowest beasts.
Eve. Ah, why are you so anxious that I eat
The food forbidden?
Serpent. Would you have me tell you?
Eve. I don't choose otherwise. It is my wish.
Serpent. Now listen to me. Arch your brows in wonder.
For two high benefits for me myself
More than for your sole good, I make this offer --
Swearing to maintain silence at your theft
Of the forbidden fruit. The one, to avenge
The indignity that God inflicted on me,
Making me thus, for Heaven deems me refuse,
By reason of the scaly serpent part
That I trail ever on the earth behind me.
My other grievance is, He should have made me
Sole master of the world, to rule the beasts,
Not merely be among them. But my rule
Over such great things was mere vassalage
While Man drew vital air; for Man alone
Was chosen lord of this supernal marvel,
Raised up today to lordship out of nothing.
But when the fairest of the fruits of Eden
Are seized and tasted, you may justly both
Abandon earth and mount to higher spheres.
Thus to inaugurate myself as lord
Of every beast on earth; I dare to take
A wise advantage of your human error.
Know that to rule is pleasing and delightful.
It pleases God and Man, a serpent too.
Eve. I fain would eat! Alas, what am I doing?
Serpent. Rather, what do you fail to do? Be bold,
Seize it! Ah, make yourself a god in heaven
And me a deity on earth as well.
Eve. Alas, I feel cold tremors through my bones!
They turn my heart to ice!
Serpent. Your mortal part
Begins to weaken; the diviner half
Rises in power now above your tresses.
Behold the lovely plant, richer and fairer
Than if it lifted boughs of gold to heaven,
With leaves of emerald, with roots of coral,
With trunk of silver. See the gemlike fruit
That causes one to be a god forever.

How fair it is! How it keeps altering
In the sun's living radiance like the sheen
Upon the painted peacock's rainbow tail
Athwart the sun, its thousand eyes alight.
See, how it draws you. All is grace and sweetness.
The senses are not liars. Your eye sees it.
Now take it, while I see no angel's looking.
Will you not take it yet? Up, once again
I guide you. Now you have the victory!

(Eve plucks the apple.)

Eve. Behold me mistress of a fruit so fair!
But why, alas, does all my forehead drip
With chilling sweat that overwhelms my heart?
Serpent. The reason, lovely maiden, is indeed
That high felicity is bought with sweat.
But who will wipe away the mighty sweat
That suddenly has mantled my own brow?
Who will destroy the fear that stabs my heart?
Eve. Tell me, what do you want? Or what afflicts you?
Serpent. Fear of your Lord. Therefore I do implore you,
After you both have tasted of the sweet
Forbidden Fruit, becoming deathless gods,
That you will shield me from the wrath of Heaven.
For He who is called God may with due cause
Blame me for having had you taste the apple
In violation of His high command.
Tell Him that the desire that I should be
An emperor on earth while Man arose
To be a god in Heaven kept me silent
While Eve reached out her hand to pluck the fruit.
Eve. The gift that I have had through you, O serpent,
Constrains me never to dispute with you.
Serpent. In these green leaves I now conceal myself
Till you glad voice recalls and reassures me.
Eve. Hide then. I promise you that I shall be
Your sure defense against God's great displeasure.
O what sweet odour! Sure, so pleasant is it,
It must give fragrance to all charming flowers.

These dewy leaves appear to be besprinkled
With manna and not dew. 'Twill surely be
So sweet a fruit was born to give man life
And not stand idly in the wind and sun.
Nothing, indeed, of any harm to man
Has the eternal hand of God created,
Because His love for man is so immense.
Now I shall taste it! (She eats.) Oh, how sweet
it is!
How all the flavours of all other fruits
Are met in this alone! Ah, where is Adam!
Adam! Dear Adam! Nay, he answers not.
I must go speedily to seek him out.
But I must hide this fruit in leaves and flowers,
Lest angels, seeing it, should interfere,
Commanding Adam not to taste at all
Or change his mortal nature to a god. (Exit Eve.)
Serpent. Blot out thy radiance in the sea, O sun,
And shine no more! Thus decrees Lucifer,
And thus the apple. Man is vanquish'd, vanquish'd!
Vain Glory. (Sings, to the accompaniment of many
sounds):
O happy day! O day of joy for Hell
And scorn for Heaven! Eve has tasted now
The fatal apple and is all determined
That man shall taste it too. Behold at last
With guilty lot Life changes into Death.
Therefore I gladly sing and so depart
Exulting hence, because the boast of man
Is beaten down, his day is turned to night.
(Exeunt Serpent and Vain Glory.)

Act III, Scene I

Enter Adam and Eve.

Adam. O my belov'd companion, O true heart,
Dear life of this my life, have you then gone
In such great haste and eager pilgrimage
To seek your Adam wandering alone?
Here is he. What's your bidding? Speak your will.
Ask without hesitation what you come for.
Eve. O dearest Adam, O my guide and escort

Who ever comforts me and soothes my heart,
You only have I longed for, you alone
Have I been seeking in these pleasant shadows.
Adam. Fairest companion, Eve, since it has pleased
you
To name me source and root of all your joy,
If you will come with me, my dear, I wish
To show you something that you have not seen,
A thing so charming you will arch your brows
In wonder at the sight. Look, gentle spouse,
In the direction of that dense, green grove
Where all the birds resort, and as you gaze
Those two white doves fly down in open flight.
There you will see a marvel, 'mid soft flowers
A living brook arising that flows forth
So hastily with winding course that you,
Delighted with its ways, might say to it:
"Stop, pretty rivulet, and wait for me!"
Then, pleased to follow it, you follow on,
And it, as if it wished to sport with you,
By a thousand hidden ways of leaf and flower
Known only to itself, moves on concealed;
Then, when it hears you grieve because you've
lost it,
It lifts its watery hair and seems to say,
Gurgling with taunting laughter, "Follow, follow
My gentle course. If you delight in me,
I'll sport with you." And so with sweet
allurement
At last it guides you to the farthest edge
Of a blooming meadow; then with sudden stay
It cries out: "Wait. Farewell. For now I
leave you."
Then it leaps downward where no human foot
Can follow it. Only the eye can follow.
And there you see a mighty store of water
Penned in a strait enclosure in a deep
And fruitful valley, crowned with orange-trees,
Laurel and olive, cypress and tall pines.
In the sun's radiance that clear water seems
The purest crystal. In its lovely depths,
In the wave's crystalline, rich sands of gold
You may see shining, and the moving silver
Of fish innumerable. With harmonious notes

White swans make sweetest sojourn on the wave
And seem to tell the breezes in their trilling:
"Here let him stay his going who desires
A joy complete." And so, my dear companion,
To come with me would please you, I am sure.
Eve. So well your language has revealed to me
What it would show me, that I see the brook
Sporting in flight and hear it murmuring.
Yet pleasant also is this spot where now
We sojourn happily and where perhaps,
More than elsewhere, the lovely lily whitens,
The budding rose grows crimson; here as well
Are tiny dewy plants, painted with flowers;
And here the leafy trees extend their shade
And proudly reach in rivalry towards heaven.
Adam. Now to the shade of all these lovely trees,
And to the charm of meadows, hues of flowers,
And music of the waters and the birds,
Let's yield ourselves with joy.
Eve. Here am I seated.
In truth how I rejoice that I can see
Not only all these flowers, plants and trees
But Adam my dear lover! You are he
Through whom the meadows seem more dear and fair,
The fruits more coloured and the springs more clear.
Adam. These lovely flowers that adorn the fields
Afford me less joy than the fairer flowers
I gaze at in the garden of your face.
Forgive me, ye fair flowers! My words are true.
Ye may be sprinkled with ethereal dew,
Make glad the humble earth at one sole blaze
From the enkindled sun, but with the evening
Ye also vanish; but the living flowers
Of my dear Eve stay fresh continually
In the warm dew she scatters in her joy,
Praising her Maker; while beneath the rays
Of two terrestrial suns in her brow's sky
They rise and do not fall as they bedeck
A lovely face's blessed paradise.
Eve. Ah, seek not, Adam, with sweet eloquence
To charm my ear, saying, "O Eve, I love you."
My heart, that burns with pure and holy ardour,
Is confident you love me. O beloved,
Take therefore in exchange this rosy gift.

You know it well. This is the blessed fruit,
This the forbidden Apple.
Adam. Woe is me!
What do I see? Alas, what have you done,
Stealing the fruit our great Lord has forbidden?
Eve. It would be tedious to tell you all
The occasion that induced me to purloin it.
Let it suffice that I with it have gained
The means to fledge you wings to soar to Heaven.
Adam. Ah, may it not be true that I, to oblige you,
Should show myself a rebel against Heaven
Ungratefully, and in obeying women
Should disobey my high Creator, God.
Did not the threatened penalty of death
Make your cheek pale with terror at the thought?
Eve. And do you then believe that if the Apple
Had been the food of death the mighty Gard'ner
Would rear it here where life is everlasting?
And had the Apple been the source of error,
Would he have made it flourish in this air,
So fruitful and so fair to human eyes?
Indeed, had that been so, He would have given
Great cause for our offense, because kind nature,
Preceptress wise, ordains that man should eat
That he may live, and that he should believe
All viands which are beautiful are good.
Adam. If the celestial Gardener who sowed
The stars across the fairest fields of Heaven
Has placed the forbidden Apple among so many
Superb and fruitful plants as the most fair,
It is because He seeks thus to make trial
Of man as a wise observer of His will
And gives him thus the means to merit well;
Since he alone has earned the name of brave
Who rules himself and curbs his own desires.
Man would have cause to sin here if the Garden
Had had few fruits; but it abounds in them,
Thus many and thus sweet, to prove that man
Ought not to stray from the commands of God.
Eve. Is this the way you love me? Ah, henceforth
Let me not call you my delight, my life!
I shall go wandering in loneliness
Away from you, with sighs and lamentations,

Hating myself and hiding from the sun.
Adam. Eve, my sweet love, my spirit and my heart,
Ah, dry those tears, since all the grief is mine
That wets that cheek and moistens thy white bosom.
Eve. Alas, my sorry state, I who have said
And done so much to raise this man to Heaven!
Does he then love and trust in me so little?
Adam. Grieve not, my love. I mourn to see you sad.
Eve. I know you only wish my tears and sighs,
And so I render them as bitter tribute,
Paid to the winds and seas.
Adam. My heart is breaking.
I cannot tell now what I am to do.
If I consider Heaven, then I feel
A chill that slays me wandering through my bones;
I only wish to obey the eternal edicts.
But if I look upon my fair companion,
I sorrow at her tears, sigh at her sighs;
Refusal to obey her rends my heart.
My love for her makes me extend my hand
To take the Apple quickly; but my soul,
Anxious within my bosom, closes it
And draws it back again. O wretched Adam,
How many mixed desires throng your heart!
One makes you sigh, another gives you joy;
Nor is it given you to know if now
You will be bent by sighs or moved by joy,
Obedient to this woman or to God.
Eve. (Aside) He still deliberates, and in his thinking
Wishes that Eve would cease from happiness
In elevating man to deity --
Yet here I hold the Apply of all glory.
Adam. So mute yet eloquent your glances are,
My dear, alas, that what you ask, yea all
I grant you; naught do I withold from you.
Before the tongue can speak, let heart concede it.
Suns of my soul, sweet eyes, let the brow's sky
Be no more darkened. Turn, alas, to expel
The clouds that mar those cheeks. Lift, lift the brow
From the mass'd, golden hair that frames that face,
Disclose those glances, fetters of my heart,
Light of my eyes. Make your fair tresses now

Sport wandering in the air, reveal your face,
The garden of the glory of my heart.
I will obey you; for your prayers to me
Are my commands. Up, up, and light a smile
Within your glances and upon your lips,
And dry your weeping!
Eve. Ah, distrustful Adam,
Now make yourself the courteous receiver
Of the fair fruit. Hasten, O hasten now;
Extend your hand to touch the blessed symbol
Of beatifying food.
Adam. Sweetest companion,
See your dear lover; drive out from your heart
The Syrtis of harsh grief, and turn to him
The stars desired in a precious sky.
Show me the pleasant apple you are hiding,
O cunning plunderer, amid leaves and flowers.
Eve. Here is the Apple, Adam. What's to fear?
For I have tasted it and am not dead.
Ah, it will make us live, equal to God
In Heaven above. But it is fitting first
That the whole apple should be shared between us,
And after it is eaten, the glad angels
Will then in flight escort us to assume
A beauteous throne of light, a throne of stars.
Adam. Give me the stolen fruit, obliging thief.
Give me the pleasant fruit. 'Tis meet to obey
The one who toiled and wept to make me a god.
(He eats.)
Alas, what have I done? What bitter pain
Pierces me to the heart with sudden pang?
Alas, what drowns me in a sea of grief?
Eve. Ah, woe is me! What do I now behold?
O bitter recognition, novel sight!
Is everything prepared for human ruin?
Adam. O dearest liberty, where art thou gone?
Eve. O dearest liberty, dread slavery!
Adam. Has this sweet fruit caused so much bitterness?
Tell me, alas, why have you thus betrayed me?
Why have you robbed me of all hope of Heaven?
Why have you taken me from innocence
Where I was happy? Why subjected me
To the harsh arms of death -- you, once my life?

Eve. I was a sightless mole to all my good,
But far too keen of sight in seeking evil.
I was a foe to Adam; against God
A rebel; and for daring to exalt
Myself to Heaven's gates, I am cast down
Even to the threshold of deep Hell itself.
Adam. Alas, what holy spear with kindled flame
Seems to be waving in the awful sky?
Eve. What scourge, alas, hangs over us? Alas,
Naked am I! And do I speak with Adam?
Adam. And do I too stand here in nakedness?
Who will conceal me? I depart. (Exit.)
Eve. I fly. (Exit.)

Act III, Scene II (lines 1946-1956)

Volano exults, and invites all Hell to celebrate.

Act III, Scene III (lines 1957-1968)

Volano urges celebration on a crowd of devils, with flags and infernal instruments of music.

Act III, Scene IV (lines 1969-2036)

The Serpent, Vain Glory, Satan, Volano and other evil spirits all exult. Canoro sings a song of victory.

Act III, Scene V (lines 2037-2079)

As they celebrate, a blast of heavenly trumpets and a burst of heavenly light send them all in dismay down to hell.

Act III, Scene VI (lines 2080-2155)

God the Father enters, interrogates Adam and Eve, and passes sentence on them and the Serpent.

Act III, Scene VII

Adam and Eve as before. Enter an Angel.

Angel. Ah, Eve, how much you now have lost,

forgetting
The words of the great Monarch! You have sinned,
O Adam, you have sinned, and with you Eve
Sinning in concert, you have both shut fast
The doors of Heaven and opened those of Hell.
Seeking sweet life, you have tasted bitter death;
And brief joy brings you countless lingering pains.
And how much better it had been for man
To say: "I have sinned. Pardon, O Lord, I pray
Thee!"
Than to accuse his spouse and she the Serpent.
Now let these shaggy skins become to each
A humble cloak; and let each learn that God
Approves the meek and punishes the proud.
Adam. O man! O earth! O fate of sin and death!
Eve. O woman, greedy source of naught but woe!
O tempting fruit! O vile, deceitful snake!
Angel. Now let these skins you bear foretell to you
The hardships you must bear. The skins are rough;
And you from that can learn you must endure
Harsh anguish in the field of life till Death
Reaps you at last. Then mourn and sigh, cry out
To God for mercy, for 'twill ever be
That Heaven beholds the supreme Creator mild,
Earth sees Him kind, and man will find Him gracious
If in humility he learns to weep
As formerly in pride he learned to err. (Exit Angel.)
Adam. Where hast thou fled? Where dost thou leave
me lonely?
Alas, too bitter Apple, if you make
Mankind thus hateful to an angel presence!
My fall is from a place so high that yet
It has not found the bottom. Wretched Adam,
If you have fallen, who will lift you up
If those eternal Hands that hold the sky,
The earth and man, are closed to all your good
And open to your loss? Alas, how much
I ought to say, but sorrow ties my tongue,
Pierces my heart. Alas, my sin! Ah, terror!
Eve. Adam, my Adam, whom I still call mine
Though I have caused your ruin, hapless Eve
Confesses, mourns, and sighs at her mistake,
And looks upon you with profound distress.
Would that my tears could wash away the stain

You have upon your brow! O Adam, Adam,
Do you not answer? And I suffer pain,
Seeing you pale, distraught, with hands entwined
In a tightened knot. If even deed of mine
Has given you eternal cause for silence,
Answer me still. Though that I merit not.
A woman, only evil do I merit.
Eve has discovered grief, has met with pain --
Toil, sweat, fear, horror, death, and lastly, Hell.
Adam. Rejoice, O woman, at my fall and death!
Or banish me for loving you too much!
If you were greedy for my tears, stretch out
Your hand and catch the torrents that I shed!
If it was sighs you wanted, hear my sighs;
If you desired my anguish, see that anguish;
Or if you sought my blood, pray take it now, --
You may with ease deliver me to death,
Since I through you no longer merit life.

Act III, Scene VIII

Adam and Eve as before. Enter the Archangel Michael.

Michael. Why do ye tarry? Quickly up, depart,
Ye rotted buds, out of the glorious
And pleasant paradise on earth below!
Do ye then dare so much, ye putrid worms!
Up! Depart quickly! For I order you
Armed with a whip of fire.
Adam. Ah, I am dead
At the high stroke of the great castigant!
Eve. Alas, I feel my soul is scarce alive
When smitten with the awful scourge of fire!
Michael. Your naked feet must tread these stony plains
And not fair blossoms since your crazy folly
Forbids your sojourn in the pleasant Garden.
Know now that I am punisher of all
Who disobey our Lord. Therefore have I
Put on these brightest and most dreadful arms
That render me resistless. I am he
Who in celestial conflict, entering
The regions of the North, crushed Lucifer,
Proud general of the accursed spirits,

Hurling his whole host headlong down to Hell,
Vanquished and shattered. So it seems but right
To my tremendous Chief that with this sword
Of fiercest fire I drive from this fair spot
Man, who is grown a rebel against God.
(Exeunt Adam and Eve.)
Depart now, all ye angels, and with me
Unfold your wings for Heaven. It has been
Your custom here on earth to rejoice with me
In company with man, once demigod
And now but clay. Hereafter, armed with steel,
Steel that breathes fire, let Cherub strong and swift
Assist you to protect these pleasant gates.
(Exeunt.)

Act III, Scene IX (lines 2276-2285)

A chorus of angels sympathizes with the outcasts and foretells ultimate joy for them if they repent and turn to God.

Act IV, Scene I (lines 2286-2323)

Volano, the messenger, summons the spirits of fire, air, earth and water to consult with Lucifer.

Act IV, Scene II (lines 2324-2622, with translation from 2599 ad finem)

Lucifer and the spirits debate in great detail the meaning of God's words to Adam and Eve. The other spirits think that man is doomed, but Lucifer perceives that man's soul may yet be saved and raised to Heaven. Briar protests:

Briar. Shall Briar hold his tongue? Not so, my Lord,
Do not believe this man shall mount to Heaven!
His wings are weak. Should he grow otherwise,
I shall be ready, all alone, to slay him,
Armed with a heavy cudgel or a stone,
Even if I alone be damn'd for it

To all the evils of blind Hell. Thereafter,
In gloating on the glory of my deed,
The pangs of Hell would seem the joys of Heaven.
Lucifer. O generous ardour! Sure, a noble heart
That yearns for fame is worth a victory.
But let us be prepared to stay in Hell,
Since there is more content to live in freedom,
Even though damn'd, than live in blessedness
The subjects of another. Spirits, up!
Let now a black and sulphurous mass be raised
From foul infernal pitch to greet this light,
For so the Captain of Damnation wills.

Act IV, Scene III (lines 2623-2677)

Lucifer, summoning the infernal Cyclopes, has three monsters shaped of dark elements and transforms these into three human likenesses: a wealth-laden man (the World), a fair damsel (the Flesh), and an icy skeleton (Death). These are to aid in a further campaign against Adam and Eve.

Act IV, Scene IV (lines 2678-2803)

Adam mourns, relating the bloody savagery that now animates the brute creation.

Act IV, Scene V (lines 2804-2823)

Adam and Eve take refuge in a cave from beasts of prey.

Act IV, Scene VI (lines 2824-2879)

Adam and Eve as before. Enter Hunger, Thirst, Fatigue and Despair.

Hunger. In vain, vile sprouts, ye seek to escape
our talons,
Yea, and a thousand other dread disasters
With which Heaven threatens you. Seek not to flee;
It is in vain! -- Guard the ways round about,
My comrades, watch their pathway. -- I am Hunger,
Who now today disclose myself to man
In such a hideous form to make it clear

How eagerly I make his sweet things bitter;
And from this inauspicious semblance shown
To you this day, well do you recognize
How the sharp shaft of Hunger shall assail you,
More than all other creatures. As I thus
Devour these tendrils of the tender vines
And suck the sweet juice in my awful thirst,
So from your weary and decrepit bones,
By sinning made infirm, I shall tear off
The flesh and suck the blood from out your veins.
And this fell monster that you here behold
Seeking to sate its thirst at that clear spring
And, not succeeding seeking to befoul
The pool with greedy foot, is known as Thirst.
In such a semblance, horrible and fierce,
It would reveal to you how thirstily
And rudely you shall suffer from its pangs.
This next form is Fatigue, which here today
Pours mighty streams of sorrow on your heart.
Behold her melting in a wave of sweat
In lifting on her back that heavy stone!
O Adam, she will make you so exhausted
That in cold pallor you will drip with seas
Of copious sweat; yes, she will so molest you
That you will fain abhor your very life.
Thence it must come to pass that both of you
Shall walk by bitter and unwonted ways
To meet at last this fierce, tremendous monster
Who bears the hopeless title of Despair.
See how he writhes, and screams, and tears his hair,
Gnashes his teeth, rends himself with his claws,
And makes his breast re-echo with his blows.
This fearsome monster will afflict you so
That you will wish to seek a wretched end.
If you perchance may think that I am lying,
See who appears from regions dark and deep
'Mid clouds of smoke and sulphurous balls of fire!

Act IV, Scene VII (lines 2880-2935)

Death, with his sickle, comes and announces their ultimate doom and fate in Hell.

Act V, Scene I (lines 2936-3154)

The Flesh, in fair female form, seeks in vain to seduce Adam.

Act V, Scene II (lines 3155-3269)

Lucifer, disguised as a grey-bearded man, professes to be Adam's elder brother and urges him to embrace the temptress. He wavers.

Act V, Scene III (lines 3270-3470)

Adam, with the aid of Cherubim and his guardian angel, exposes and routs his tempters.

Act V, Scene IV (lines 3471-3580)

The World, in man's form, soliloquizes on his power to seduce mankind with gold.

Act V, Scene V (lines 3581-3823)

The World rears a palace for Eve and offers her royal robes. She refuses.

Act V, Scene VI (lines 3824-3877)

As the World continues his solicitations, Adam enters and exposes the fraud. The World then summons the forces of Hell to seize Man.

Act V, Scene VII (lines 3878-3903)

Lucifer, Death and demons enter armed.

Act V, Scene VIII (lines 3904-4054)

Adam, Eve, the World, Death, Lucifer and demons as before. Enter Michael and chorus of angels in arms.

Michael. Tremble, thou son of wrath, before the flash

Of this sharp spear, the stroke of Heaven's captain!
Not against mightiest God dost thou wage war
But still against thyself and in thy onslaughts
Thou harmest but thyself. Fall into darkness,
O sad and erring spirit, who art wholly
Deprived of light angelic. Blind thyself
In gazing at the empyrean brightness
Bestowed upon my form by light's Creator.
The dazzler of the sun can put to flight
The tainted host of God's dark enemies.
Let not a whirlwind breathing out of Hell
Blacken this day the shining life of Man!
Thy hiss, O snake of Hell, will no more deafen
With its shrill sibilation, since transfixed
And gasping thou shalt languish utterly,
Infected and destroyed by thine own venom.
Lucifer. Loquacious messenger of Heav'n, with more
Of levity than courage in thy breast,
Effeminate creature of the unwarlike sky,
Angel of soft repose and solemn ease,
With heart a nest of meekness and of peace,
A warrior but in name, whose face is fear,
Whose bosom throbs with panic, spread thy wings
And seek the breast of God. There He will shield thee
And comfort thee, for too ill-matched would prove
The fight between my valour and thy fear
When warrior meets with weakling, when the strong
Confronts the infirm, the fatal fight, in fine,
Of worthy Lucifer and worthless Michael.
But if temerity has fired thy heart
To seek to rescue from this warrior hand
Today this man, this thing of flesh and mire,
Mere animated dust, I warn thee well
Of harsh and deadly fray, whence presently
Thou mayst behold this strong avenging hand
Wipe out the whole vast family of God.
Michael. O Devil, furious and desperate,
Sad was the victory thou once didst have
Over both Heav'n and man, when thou didst dupe
And overcome him; but the vanquished now
Conquers in turn, the bound is free, and thou
Art taken in thy snare. Let it be clear
To thee what sort of palms of victory

Thou'rt like to garner here. Against thee now,
A faithless spirit, see how Michael's arm
In mercy becomes cruel.
Lucifer. If at first
When war broke forth, if at the first encounter
A mighty warrior like myself was able
To tear a third of all the stars in ruin
Hellwards, behold in what short order now
I shall destroy the palace of Jehovah.
Be dazzled by the martial rays I shed,
The lights I flash from under brows of death,
While bloodily I wheel these cloudy comets
That on my forehead brood! See, see how Heaven
No longer is a refuge for the angels,
Now that a way auspicious opens up
To a happier lot for me and seems to say:
Fly, fly ye frighted angels, flee from Heaven!
The once-damn'd Warrior seizes now the sky!
Michael. Why delay longer to abate the boasts
Of this hot, reckless rebel? Presently
With pen of iron and in words of blood
The fame of thy defeat shall be inscribed
In dark Damnation's everlasting book.
To arms, to arms now! At the overthrow
Of foul Avernus mankind shall rejoice,
All Heaven shall laugh and Hell lament in vain.
Lucifer. It rarely happens that a froward tongue
Is matched by equal bravery of the hand.
To arms, to arms! Fight thou with me, I pray.
And all ye others here, my matchless soldiers,
Transfix and put to flight this craven crew,
Unwarlike followers of a feeble captain!

(They fight, and Lucifer is overthrown.)

Alas, after brief grace and endless sorrow
In Heaven above and here on earth today
Brief power indeed after long aspiration,
A stroke celestial smites me through and through
And sends me headlong to the blind abyss!
Justice has here decreed that I who lost
This battle, lose the sunlight. Ye have conquered,
Angel and God, at last ye here have conquered,
Here Lucifer is punished, and his army

Forsakes the day and falls to endless night. (Exit.)
Michael. Fall now, yea fall, wounded and vanquish'd one,
Monster of darkness, fall to lie among
The horrors of perdition, there to die
An everlasting death, nor ever hope
To wing thy way to Heaven, since for thee,
Desperate and unrepenting, such a wish
Is far too bold. Now thou at last art fallen,
Most haughty monster, just as deep in pain
As thou hadst thought to soar aloft in joy.
Again thou learnest, smitten by the thunder,
To fall into the tenebrous Abyss.
Fool, thou hadst hoped to make this man thy captive,
And the deep dungeon is for thee alone.
Wounded and humbled, falling to Avernus,
Thou now art borne by everlasting wrath
To a Hell made ten times hotter than before.
O fool, proud liar, thou hadst hoped to rout
A pure archangel, but confronting him
Thou hast recoil'd and fled on winged feet.
It was thy hope, moreover, with thy flames
Here to consume the whole vast world to ashes,
As at thy zealous breath and evil blasts
Clouds, lightnings, thunders, tempests, swept the skies,
Shaking the hills and making loud the valleys.
But now, behold, across the lucid sky
The spheres wheel on, with added harmonies,
The sun adorns the azure with his rays,
The calm sea shimmers -- from its Persian waves
It gladly pours its pearls and corals forth,
While sportive fish glide through its sapphire waves.
See how these pleasant valleys raise their brows,
Green and beflower'd. Hear the gracious voices
Of every feather'd minstrel, citizen
Of the sky's domain, who wandering through the glades
Makes grove and vale melodious with song.
Now as all things are glad at such a day
Of triumph, to the shame and scorn of Hell,
Let each white ensign flutter to the breeze
And let the golden bells peal out on high,

Re-echoing the victory of Heaven!

Act V, Scene IX (lines 4055-4278)

Adam and Eve welcome their rescuers. In a closing interview, Michael exhorts Adam and Eve to prayerful submission and faith in God, assuring them that by penitence they will attain to Heaven. The play ends with a hymn of praise by the angelic chorus.

THOMAS PEYTON

The Glasse of Time (1620, 1623)

Part I

1.

The author first, doth Gods assistance crave,
Throughout the worke that he his help may have:
The sacred Sabbaoth, Satans envious gall,
The woman fram'd, and mans most dismal fall:
The tree of Life protected from the Brute,
The tree of Knowledge with her fatal fruit:
For feare the world should be finally ended,
Gods dearest Daughters down in hast descended.
The flaming sword the tree of Life which guarded,
The Cherubims upon the Wall that warded.
The land of Eden is described at large.
Heavens judgement just to all mens future charge.
. . .

5.

O glorious God inspiror of my Muse,
Grant that thy word my soul may daily use.
And that what learning painfully is got,
Still from the truth may never swerve a jot
That in her spring, beginning and in her bud,
May sing thy glory to the churches good. . . .

7.

O that my muse might once but rest in peace,
Then would she sing divinely, never cease,
But worke out Truth within her holy Rimes,
Gliding along descending to our times,
And dear Urania Soveraigne of my verse,
Should heere the glory of this world rehearse,
Unfolding still to Gods immortall glory,
The heavenly sweetness of a sacred story. . . .

9.

Adam what made thee, wilfully at first,
To leave thy offspring, to this day accurst;
So wicked foul, and overgrown with sinne;
And in thy person all of it beginne?
That hadst thou stood in innocency fram'd,
Death, Sin, and Hell, the world and all thou hadst tamed.
Then hadst thou been a Monarch from thy birth;
Gods only darling both in Heaven and Earth . . .
Curst be that Devill that first thy sense belied;
Oh God! to purchase with that bloody cost,
Our soules redeem'd when they were fully lost.
Here is a love that farre surmounts the skies,
My senses wrapts and dazles both mine eyes. . . .

65.

But now thy God hath perfect made thy state,
Linckt thee in marriage with so choice a mate,
Himselfe the Priest which brought her to thy hand,
And knit the knot that ever more must stand,
Ring'd her with virtue, glorious beauty chaste,
Upon thy self and no man else to waste,
Made her the Tipe our senses all to rouse,
Of Christ himselfe, and of the Church his spouse:
And charged the angels for thy fence and guard,
Of nothing now, but one thing thou art bar'd. . . .

67.

But Lucifer that soard above the skye,

And thought himself to equal God on high,
Envies thy fortunes, and thy glorious birth,
In being fram'd but of the basest earth,
Himself compacted of pestiferous fire,
Assumes a Snake to execute his ire,
Winds him within that winding crawling beast,
And enters first whereas thy strength was least. . . .

69.

At another time thy nimblenesse and flight
Above the clouds, will be an angel bright,
And though the air close in a fiery waggon
Thou'lt sometimes mount as monstrous as a Dragon,
And when thou list Thou any shape canst take,
Even from an angel to an ugly snake. . . .

72.

And watching time when Adam stept aside,
Even but a little from his lovely bride,
To pluck perhaps a nut upon the trees,
Or get a combe amongst the honey bees:
Or some such thing to give his welcome spouse,
Even just to Eve thou dost thy body rouse,
And questions with her of much idle prattle,
As women they delight to talke and tattle,
What they may not, and what it is they eate,
And what is best, within that pleasing seat,
What tree it is that was to them forbidden
They dare not eat, for fear they may be chidden. . . .

74.

But thou againe that ever didst devise,
In nothing else but execrable lies,
Straight told the woman that they need not feare,
To eat the fruit that pleasant tree did bear:
For in the day that they should thereof eat,
The Gods themselves they would indeed defeat,
Attaine much knowledge, farre above mans reach,
And all the Gods in many things would teach.
To think of death they need not fear at all.
For why, their eyes should opened be withall:

The goodly fruit would breed this wondrous odds,
Never to die, but ever live as Gods.

75.

O cursed, damned, execrable Devil,
Delighting best in that thing which is evil!
What made thee now thy baneful speech to blow,
Out of that canckerd, venom'd mouth below?
Thus to entice by thy allurements working,
Within so sly and ugly creature lurking
That Eve must reach, and in her hand to grapple
So fair a fatal curst bewitching apple:
And not content herselfe thereof to eate,
But reacht another as a daintie meate,
And in her sweet delightful lovely hands,
Runs to her Lord, where all alone he stands
Plaining and greiving that he had her mist,
Takes her in 's armess, and both together kist.

76.

Then she began (in smiling wanton sort)
To shew that apple, which before in sport
She late had taken from that fatal tree,
The better now to make her eyes to see:
And in the hands of her beloved Lord
The same she put, according to her word,
And mild persuasions, gentle speeches plaine,
In hope much knowledge by the same to gaine,
The gawdy looks and curious pleasing sight,
He takes the same and so of it doth bite.

114.

Adam what made thee fearfully to hide?
(Entangled in the allurements of thy bride,)
Thyselfe from God, who by his sacred voice,
Amongst the trees within the garden choice
Repaired now as often times before . . .

115.

Adam (quoth God) why dost thou hide thy face?

What is the cause thou art so poore and base?
That thou shouldst thus with simple shifts begin,
Asham'd of me to cover now thy skin . . .
O heavenly God, then Adam answered strait
I was intrapt with such a pleasing baite,
That made my reason, sense and all to yield,
My strength but weeke within so strong a field . . .

123.

Accursed Devil, thrice damn'd is all thy race,
Thy wicked plots and secret actions base:
What made thee wind within this winding Snake,
The shape of serpent in thy mind to take? . . .
To creepe to Eve, as if she were thy Aunt,
And fawne on others like a Puritant.
What hast thou got for all thy villany? . . .

126.

And but beginning of Eves dismall speech,
When suddenly she began to cry and screech:
When in an instant from the holy skies,
Mercy comes down and into Eden hies:
Prostrated falls upon her bended knees,
But God himself his daughter dear that sees,
With weeping eyes before his face to crave,
That but on Eve he would compassion have:
Began to stay his minde, to alter cleane,
And to the woman thus began to leane:
But that hard by stood Justice in the place,
And urg'd him much to prosecute the case:
When all the reason Mercy well could render,
Was that herselfe was of the female gender. . . .

Part II

1.

Urania soveraigne of the muses nine
Inspire my thoughts with sacred worke divine
Come down from heaven, within my Temples rest,
Inflame my heart and lodge within my breast,
Grant me the story of this world to sing,

The _Glasse of Time_, upon the stage to bring,
Be _Aye within me_ by thy powerful might,
Governe my Pen, direct my speech aright,
Even in the birth and infancy of Time,
To the last age, season my holy rime. . . .

65.

Medusa, damn'd, in foul black ugly cloathes,
That all the world most deadly hates and loathes,
Swolne like a Toade, her lookes cast downe to Hell,
Where none but fiends, and hateful monsters dwell,
Whose cursed hair, about her shoulders falls,
Powdred with Serpents full of poisoned galls,
Hissing and crawling round about her head,
Hatcht by a viper in her wombe that bred . . .

PHINEAS FLETCHER

The Locusts, or Apollyonists (1627)

Extracts, lines 64-198, 271-289, 343-351

When lo, a sudden noise breaks th' empty air,
A dreadful noise which every creature daunts,
Frights home the blood, shoots up the limber hair;
For through the silent heaven hell's pursuivants,
Cutting their way, command foul spirits repair
With haste to Pluto, who their counsel wants.
  Their hoarse bass-horns like fenny bitterns sound;
  Th' earth shakes, dogs howl, and heaven itself,
      astound,
Shuts all his eyes, the stars in clouds their
      candles drowned.

Meantime hell's iron gates by fiends beneath
Are open flung, which framed with wondrous art
To every guilty soul yields entrance eath;
But never wight but He could thence depart,
Who, dying once, was death to endless death.
So where the liver's channel to the heart

  Pays purple tribute, with their three-forked mace
  Three Tritons stand and speed his flowing race,
But stop the ebbing stream, if once it back would
    pace.

The porter to th' infernal gate is Sin,
A shapeless shape, a foul deformèd thing,
Nor nothing, nor a substance, as those thin
And empty forms which through the air fling
Their wand'ring shapes, at length they're fastened
    in
The crystal sight; it serves, yet reigns as king;
  It lives, yet's death; it pleases, full of pain;
  Monster! ah who, who can thy being feign,
Thou shapeless shape, live death, pain pleasing,
    servile reign!

Of that first woman and th' old serpent bred
By lust, and custom nursed, whom when her mother
Saw so deformed, how fain would she have fled
Her birth and self! But she her dam would smother,
And all her brood, had not He rescuèd,
Who was his mother's sire, his children's brother,
  Eternity, who yet was born and died;
  His won creator, earth's scorn, heaven's pride,
Who th' deity enfleshed, and man's flesh deified.

Her former parts her mother seems resemble,
Yet only seems to flesh and weaker sight,
For she with art and paint could fine dissemble
Her loathsome face; her back parts, black as night,
Like to her horrid sire, would force to tremble
The boldest heart; to th' eye that meets her right
  She seems a lovely sweet, of beauty rare,
  But at the parting, he that shall compare,
Hell will more lovely deem, the devil's self more
    fair.

Her rosy cheek, quick eye, her naked breast,
And whatsoe'er loose fancy might entice,
She bare exposed to sight, all lovely dressed
In beauty's livery and quaint device;
Thus she bewitches many a boy unblest,
Who, drenched in hell, dreams all of paradise;

Her breasts his spheres, her arms his circling sky,
Her pleasures heav'n, her love eternity;
For her he longs to live, with her he longs to die.

But he that gave a stone power to descry
'Twixt natures hid, and check that metal's pride
That dares aspire to gold's fair purity,
Hath left a touchstone erring eyes to guide,
Which clears their sight and strips hypocrisy;
They see, they loathe, they curse her painted hide;
Her as a crawling carrion they esteem;
Her worst of ills, and worse than that they deem,
Yet know her worse than they can think or she can seem.

Close by her sat Despair, sad ghastly sprite,
With staring looks, unmoved, fast nailed to Sin;
Her body all of earth, her soul of fright,
About her thousand deaths, but more within,
Paled, pined cheeks, black hair, torn, rudely dight,
Short breath, long nails, dull eyes, sharp-pointed chin;
Light, life, heaven, earth, herself, and all she fled.
Fain would she die, but could not, yet half dead,
A breathing corse she seemed, wrapped up in living lead.

In th' entrance Sickness and faint Langour dwelt,
Who with sad groans toll out their passing knell,
Late fear, fright, horror, that already felt,
The torturer's claws, preventing death and hell.
Within, loud Grief and roaring Pangs, that swelt
In sulphur flames, did weep and howl and yell.
And thousand souls in endless dolors lie,
Who burn, fry, hiss, and never cease to cry,
Oh, that I ne'er had lived; oh, that I once could die!

And now th' infernal powers through th' air driving,
For speed their leather pinions broad display;
Now at eternal death's wide gate arriving
Sin gives them passage; still they cut their way,
Till to the bottom of hell's palace diving,

They enter Dis' deep conclave; there they stay,
  Waiting the rest, and now they all are met,
  A full foul senate, now they all are set,
The horrid court, big swoll'n with th' hideous
    council sweat.

The midst but lowest (in hell's heraldry
The deepest is the highest room) in state
Sat lordly Lucifer; his fiery eye,
Much swoll'n with pride, but more with rage and hate,
As censor mustered all his company,
Who round about with awful silence sate.
  This do, this let rebellious spirits gain,
  Change God for Satan, heaven's for hell's sov'reign;
Oh, let him serve in hell, who scorns in heaven to
    reign!

Ah, wretch, who with ambitious cares oppressed,
Long'st still for future, feel'st no present good,
Despising to be better, wouldst be best,
Good never, who wilt serve thy lusting mood,
Yet all command; not he who raised his crest
But pulled it down, hath high and firmly stood.
  Fool, serve thy tow'ring lusts, grow still, still
    crave,
  Rule, reign, this comfort from thy greatness have,
Now at thy top, thou art a great commanding slave.

Thus fell this prince of darkness, once a bright
And glorious star; he willful turned away
His borrowed globe from that eternal light;
Himself he sought, so lost himself; his ray
Vanished to smoke, his morning sunk in night,
And never more shall see the springing day.
  To be in heaven the second he disdains,
  So now the first in hell and flames he reigns,
Crowned once with joy and light, crowned now with
    fire and pains.

As, where the warlike Dane the scepter sways,
They crown usurpers with a wreath of lead,
And with hot steel, while loud the traitor brays
They melt and drop it down into his head, --
Crowned he would live, and crowned he ends his days;

All so in heaven's courts this traitor sped,
  Who now, when he had overlooked his train,
  Rising upon his throne, with bitter strain
Thus gan to whet their rage and chide their
    frustrate pain:

See, see, you spirits, I know not whether more
Hated or hating heaven, ah, see the earth
Smiling in quiet peace and plenteous store.
Men fearless live in ease, in love, and mirth;
Where arms did rage, the drum and cannon roar,
Where hate, strife, envy reigned, and meagre dearth,
  Now lutes and viols charm the ravished ear;
  Men plow with swords, horse-heels their armors
    wear;
Ah, shortly scarce they'll know what war and armors
    were. . . .

But me, O never let me, spirits, forget
That glorious day when I your standard bore,
And scorning in the second place to sit,
With you assaulted heaven, his yoke forswore.
My dauntless heart yet longs to bleed and sweat
In such a fray; the more I burn the more
  I hate; should he yet offer grace and ease,
  If subject we our arms and spite surcease,
Such offer should I hate, and scorn so base a peace.

Where are those spirits? Where that haughty rage
That durst with me invade eternal light?
What? Are our hearts fallen too? Droop we with age?
Can we yet fall from hell and hellish spite?
Can smart our wrath, can grief our hate assuage?
Dare we with heaven and not with earth to fight?
  Your arms, allies, yourselves as strong as ever;
  Your foes, their weapons, numbers weaker never.
For shame, tread down this earth! What wants but
    your endeavor? . . .

And now you states of hell give your advice,
And to these ruins lend your helping hand.
This said, and ceased; straight humming murmurs
    rise;
Some chafe, some fret, some sad and thoughtful stand,

Some chat, and some new stratagems devise,
And everyone heaven's stronger power banned,
  And tear for madness their uncombèd snakes,
  And everyone his fiery weapon shakes,
And everyone expects who first the answer makes. . . .

PHINEAS FLETCHER

The Purple Island (1633)

From Canto I

39

When that great Power, that All, farre more then all,
(When now his fore-set time was fully come)
Brought into act this undigested Ball,
Which in himself till then had onely room;
  He labour'd not, nor suffer'd pain, or ill;
  But bid each kinde their severall places fill:
He bid, and they obey'd; their action was his will.

40

First stept the Light, and spread his chearfull rayes
Through all the Chaos; darknesse headlong fell,
Frighted with suddain beams, and new-born dayes;
And plung'd her ougly head in deepest hell:
  Not that he meant to help his feeble sight
  To frame the rest, he made the day of night:
All els but darknesse; he the true, the onely Light.

41

Fire, Water, Earth, and Aire (that fiercely strove)
His soveraigne hand in strong alliance ti'd,
Binding their deadly hate in constant love:
So that great Wisdome temper'd all their pride,
  (Commanding strife and love should never cease)
  That by their peacefull fight, and fighting peace,

The world might die to live, and lessen to increase.

42

Thus Earths cold arm cold Water friendly holds,
But with his drie the others wet defies:
Warm Aire with mutuall love hot Fire infolds;
As moist, his dryth abhorres: drie Earth allies
   With Fire, but heats with cold new warres prepare:
   Yet Earth drencht Water proves, which boil'd
      turns Aire;
Hot Aire makes Fire: condenst all change, and
      home repair.

43

Now when the first weeks life was almost spent,
And this world built, and richly firnished;
To store heav'ns courts and steer earths regiment,
He cast to frame an Isle, the heart and head
   Of all his works, compos'd with curious art;
   Which like an Index briefly should impart
The summe of all; the whole, yet of the whole a
      part. . . .

48

Look as a scholar, who doth closely gather
Many large volumes in a narrow place;
So that great Wisdome all this All together
Confin'd into this Islands little space;
   And being one, soon into two he fram'd it;
   And now made two, to one again reclaim'd it;
The little Isle of Man, or Purple Island nam'd it.

54

That old slie Serpent, (slie, but spitefull more)
Vext with the glory of this happy Isle,
Allures it subt'ly from the peacefull shore,
And with fair painted lies, & colour'd guile
   Drencht in dead seas; whose dark streams, full
      of fright,
   Emptie their sulphur waves in endlesse night;

Where thousand deaths and hells torment the
damned sprite. . . .

56

That deathfull lake hath these three properties:
No turning path, or issue thence is found:
The captive never dead, yet ever dies;
It endlesse sinks, yet never comes to ground:
Hells self is pictur'd in that brimstone wave;
For what retiring from that hellish grave?
Or who can end in death, where deaths no ending
have?

57

For ever had this Isle in that foul ditch
With cureless grief and endlesse errour strai'd,
Boyling in sulphur, and hot-bubbling pitch;
Had not the King, whose laws he (fool) betrai'd,
Unsnarl'd that chain, then from that lake
secur'd;
For which ten thousand tortures he endur'd:
So hard was this lost Isle, so hard to be recur'd.

From Canto VI

24

But who (alas!) shall teach my ruder breast
The names and deeds of these heroick Kings?
Or downy Muse, which now but left the nest,
Mount from her bush to heav'n with new-born wings?
Thou sacred maid, which from fair Palestine
Through all the world hast spread thy brightest
shine
Kindle thy shepherd-swain with thy light flaming
eyn.

25

Sacred Thespio, which in Sinaies grove
First took'st thy being and immortall breath,
And vaunt'st thy off-spring from the highest Jove,

Yet deign'dst to dwell with mortalls here beneath,
   With vilest earth, and men more vile residing;
   Come holy Virgin in my bosome sliding,
With thy glad Angel light my blindfold footsteps
      guiding.

26

And thou dread Spirit, which at first didst spread
On those dark waters thy all-opening light;
Thou who of late (of thy great bountyhead)
This nest of hellish fogges and Stygian night
   With thy bright orient Sunne hast fair renew'd,
   And with unwonted day hast it endu'd,
Which late both day & thee, and most it self
      eschew'd:

27

Dread Spirit, do thou those severall bands unfold,
Both which thou sent'st a needfull supplement
To this lost Isle, and which with courage bold
Hourely assail thy rightfull regiment;
   And with strong hand oppresse & keep them under:
   Raise now my humble vein to lofty thunder,
That heav'n and earth may sound, resound thy
      praises wonder. . . .

41

Within the Castle sit eight Counsellers,
That help him in this tent to govern well:
Each in his room a severall office bears;
Three of his inmost private Counsell deal
   In great affairs: five of lesse dignitie
   Have outward Courts, and in all actions prie,
But still referre the doom to Courts more fit and
      high.

42

Those five fair brethren which I sung of late,
For their just number call'd the Pemptarchie;
The other three, three pillars of the state:

The first in midst of that high Tower doth lie,
(The chiefest mansion of this glorious King)
The Judge and Arbiter of every thing,
Which those five brethrens poasts in to his office bring.

45

Ev'n so the first of these three Counsellers
Gives to the five the power of all-descrying;
Which back to him with mutuall dutie bears
All their informings, and the causes trying:
For through strait waies the nimble Poast ascends
Unto his hall; there up his message sends,
Which to the next well scann'd he straightway recommends.

46

The next that in the Castles front is plac't,
Phantastes hight; his yeares are fresh and green,
His visage old, his face too much defac't
With ashes pale, his eyes deep sunken been
With often thoughts, and never slackt intention:
Yet he the fount of speedy apprehension,
Father of wit, the well of arts, and quick invention.

47

But in his private thoughts and busy brain
Thousand thinne forms, and idle fancies flit;
The three-shap't Sphinx, and direfull Harpyes train,
Which in the world had never being yet:
Oft dreams of fire and water, loose delight;
And oft arrested by some ghastly sprite,
Nor can he think, nor speak, nor move for great affright.

From Canto VII

9

Tell me, oh tell me then, thou holy Muse,

Sacred Thespio, what the cause may be
Of such despite, so many foemen use
To persecute unpiti'd miserie:
   Or if these cankred foes (as most men say)
   So mighty be, that gird this wall of clay:
What makes it hold so long, and threatned ruine stay?

10

When that great Lord his standing Court would build,
The outward walls with gemmes and glorious lights,
But inward rooms with nobler Courtiers fill'd;
Pure, living flames, swift, mighty, blessed sprites:
   But some his royall service (fools!) disdain;
   So down were flung: (oft blisse is double pain)
In heav'n they scorn'd to serve, so now in hell they reigne.

11

There turn'd to serpents, swoln with pride and hate,
Their Prince a Dragon fell, who burst with spight
To see this Kings and Queens yet happy state,
Tempts them to lust and pride, prevails by slight:
   To make them wise, and gods he undertakes.
   Thus while the snake they heare, they turn to snakes;
To make them gods he boasts, but beasts, and devils makes.

From Canto XII

27

The first that crept from his detested maw,
Was Hamartia, foul deformed wight;
More foul, deform'd, the Sunne yet never saw;
Therefore she hates the all-betraying light:
   A woman seem'd she in her upper part;
   To which she could such lying glosse impart,
That thousands she had slain with her deceiving art.

The rest (though hid) in serpents form arayd,
With iron scales, like to a plaited mail:
Over her back her knotty tail displaid,
Along the empty aire did lofty sail:
The end was pointed with a double sting,
Which with such dreaded might she wont to fling,
That nought could help the wound, but bloud of heav'nly King. . . .

31

Yet fair and lovely seems to fools dimme eyes;
But hell more lovely, Pluto's self more fair
Appeares, when her true form true light descries:
Her loathsome face, blancht skinne, and snakie hair,
Her shapeless shape, dead life, her carrion smell,
The devils dung, the childe and damme of hell,
Is chaffer fit for fools their precious souls to sell.

32

The second in this rank was black Despair,
Bred in the dark wombe of eternall Night:
His looks fast nail'd to Sinne, long sootie hair
Fill'd up his lank cheeks with wide-staring fright:
His leaden eyes, retir'd into his head,
Light, heav'n, and earth, himself, and all things fled:
A breathing coarse he seem's, wrapt up in living lead. . . .

64

The Dragon, wounded with this flaming brand,
They take, and in strong bonds and fetters tie:
Short was the fight, nor could he long withstand
Him, whose appearance is his victorie.
So now he's bound in adamantine chain;
He storms, he roars, he yells for high disdain:
His net is broke, the fowl go free, the fowler ta'ne.

65

Thence by a mighty Swain he soon was led
Unto a thousand thousand torturings:
His tail, whose folds were wont the starres to shed,
Now stretcht at length, close to his belly clings:
   Soon as the pit he sees, he back retires,
   And battel new, but all in vain, respires:
So there he deeply lies, flaming in icie fires. . . .

ANDREW RAMSAY

Poemata Sacra[1] (1633)

(a) The exordium

What high creative Power at the first
Shaped the rude mass primordial and assigned
To each of things his place, cleft land from sea,
Framed orb in orb concentric and enchambered
O'er all the lofty roof-tree of the sky,
And how the soul of man, endued from Heaven
With God's own breath, conceived in Paradise
The seeds of mortal sin, for which God's Son
Forsook the shining temples of the Height
That to that heavenly citadel once more
He might restore us (a great argument,
Worthy the flights of an exalted mind),
I purpose to unfold. O Holy Father,
Who built the walls of the world, and reared the sky
With flaming arch, assist my effort now!
Aid me, O Son, Redeemer of mankind,
Ready at suppliants' prayers! And thou, O Spirit,
Abiding both in Father and in Son,
Inspire my mind and glide into my soul!
The Muses and Apollo move me not,
Nor Cirrha, nor earth's futile deities.

[1] Selections translated by Watson Kirkconnell.

O gracious Trinity, control my heart,
That I may consecrate the acts of God
In holy numbers for posterity,
Unfolding a great theme with fitting praise.

(b) Satan's speech of envy

We, though immortal spirits who were born
In Heaven's height, have been expelled from thence,
And, dwelling in the realms of darkness, pay
To an avenging Deity, alas,
Unending penalties; while now this Adam,
Who is a very son of clay, possesses
The coasts of earth, and in his vaunting hopes
Grasps at the towers of Heaven. Do we fall thus,
We spirits, while a son of dust stands firm?

(c) The Serpent approaches Eve

As one, perchance, who, foiled by adverse winds
From making harbour, turns askance his spars
And linen sails and, where he cannot go
With course unswerving, cleaves the azure sea
With veering track, the Snake of Tartarus
In such a fashion, skilled in devising wiles
And cheating with false semblances of things,
Seeing himself frustrated of his goal
Upon his first attempt, changes his course
And strives for victory by a path oblique.

(d) The Serpent flatters Eve

"O ruler of the earth and of the sea,
And queen of all things underneath the heavens,
Worthy to grasp the sceptre of the sky
And hurl Jove's jagged lightnings from Olympus!
What humble lands are these that you inhabit?
Or, if you are a goddess, ruling earth,
Why are you thus excluded from its fruits?
Will He who has begrudged such slender fare
As a cheap apple, grant you to recline
Some day at Heaven's feasts? Be sure He will not.
And if some different thought possess your mind,
Alas, vain faith and empty hope delude you!"

Thus spake the Serpent, nor in fruitless wise
Wafted his words on air.

(e) The universe feels the Fall

Then Heaven appeared to melt, all things to
tremble -
The Styx and Acheron and Phlegethon
And Chaos and the sunless realms of Dis.
Hell's gates on grating hinges open wide
And vomit flames, and in the sudden tumult
The universal frame is rent with war.

(f) Adam's grief and sense of guilt

"O Judge, a novel and unlooked-for state
Fills me with fear; vile stains and naked shame
Of body pain me, and my heart is grieved,
Racked with harsh pangs. Wild horror drives me on.
Green meadows please me not, nor crystal springs,
No, nor the golden temples of the sky
Nor anything at all beneath the sun.
The words of God, my Judge, affright me sore
And my sick heart is rent with guilty sorrow.
Oh, were it granted me to end my life,
And shun my doom by any sort of death!
Would that the deeps of Mother Earth herself
Might yawn for me! That I might be thrust down
To pitchy shadows and infernal realms,
The sombre shades of Hell and utter night!
Or that I might be whelm'd by heaped-up hills
And all the streaming wreckage of the sky,
Before I see Thy face, Thy flaming face,
Almighty God, and Thy celestial power!"

THOMAS HEYWOOD

The Hierarchie of the Blessed Angells (1635)

Inspire my Purpose, favour mine Intent,
(O thou All-knowing and Omnipotent)
And give me leave, that from the first of daies,
I (Dust and Ashes) may resound thy praise . . .

He is without beginning, and yet gives
A First, to each thing that subsists and lives:
Who hath made all things changeable; yet He
Stable, and free from mutabilitie.
Himselfe without place; all things else instating;
Without materials, all his works creating . . .

I will not bring Philosophers to brall
And quarrell 'bout the Worlds originall.
Of which, their curious Censures some have past,
That this was ever, and shall ever last.
Others, That many worlds have been before;
And this bee'ng ended, wee shall still have more.
. . .

A little further let my Muse aspire,
To take myne eyes from Earth, to looke up higher,
Unto the glorious Hierarchy above;
The blest degrees in which the Angels move.
In this, the best Theologists assent,
That they are Substances Intelligent,
Immortall, Incorporeall, moving still;
Assisting Man, observant to Gods will.
In three most blessed Hierarchies th' are guided,
And each into three Companies divided:
The first is that in which the Seraphims bee,
Cherubim, Thrones; distinct in their degree.
The Seraphim doth in the word imply,
A Fervent Love and Zeale to the Most High.
And these are they, incessantly each houre
In contemplation are of Gods great Power.
The Cherubim denotes to us the Fulnesse

Of absolute Knowledge, free from Humane dulnesse,
Or else Wisedomes infusion. These desire
Nothing, but Gods great Goodnesse to admire.
The name of Thrones, his glorious Seat displaies;
His Equitie and Justice these still praise.
The second Ternion, as the School relates,
Are Dominations, Vertues, Potestates.
Dominions, th' Angels Offices dispose;
The Vertues (in the second place) are those
That execute his high and holy Will;
The Potestates, they are assistant still,
The malice of the Divell to withstand:
For God hath given it to their powerfull hand.
In the third order Principates are plac't;
Next them, Arch-Angels; Angels are the last.
The Principates, of Princes take the charge,
Their power on earth to curbe, or to enlarge;
And these worke Miracles. Th' Arch-Angels are
Embassadors, great matters to declare.
Th' Angels Commission hath not that extent,
They only have us Men in government. . . .
Some would allow them Bodies: and of them,
Tertullian one; another, Origen.
From Genesis: The Sonnes of God ('tis there)
Seeing Mens Daughters, and how faire they were,
Tooke them to be their wives. Now both agree,
That these no other could than Angels be.
Who if they married, must have bodies; those
Compos'd of Forme and Matter, to dispose,
Else how should they have Issue? And againe,
How are bad Spirites sensible of paine,
In Hells eternall torments, if there faile
That Substance on the which Fire may prevaile. . . .

Now when the Great and most Divinely Wise,
Did the rare Fabricke of the World devise,
And did by vertue of his Word create
The Heav'n and Earth in their so goodly state;
He made the Angels in the first of Time,
Of Substances most noble and sublime.
Amongst which Lucifer was chiefe; and hee,
As he might challenge a prioritie
In his Creation, so above the rest
A supereminence, as first and best:

For he was chiefe of all the Principalities,
And had in him the three stupendious qualities
Of the most holy Trinitie, which include
First, Greatnesse, Wisedome next, then
Pulchritude. . . .

In this their wonder at th' inscrutabilitie
Of such great things, new fram'd with such
fecilitie,
To them, just in the end of the Creation,
He did reveale his blest Sonnes Incarnation:
But with a strict commandement, That they
Should (with all Creatures) God and Man obey.
Hence grew the great dissention that befell
'Twixt Lucifer and the Prince Michael. . . .

In Hell is Griefe, Paine, Anguish, and Annoy,
All threatning Death, yet nothing can destroy . . .
Of Fire nor Light no comfortable beames,
Heate not to be endur'd, Cold in extreames.
Torments in ev'ry Artyre, Nerve, and Vaine,
In ev'ry Joint insufferable paine.
In Head, Brest, Stomake, and in all the Sences,
Each torture suting to the foule offences,
But with more terror than the heart can thinke:
The Sight with Darknesse, and the Smel with Stinke;
The Taste with Gall, in bitternesse extreme;
The Hearing, with their Curses that Blaspheme:
The Touch, with Snakes & Todes crauling about them,
Afflicted both within them and without them. . . .

Of the Rebellious there be Orders nine,
As corresponding with the Spirits Divine.
In the first eminent place are those install'd
As would on earth be worshipt, and gods call'd.
As he that did his Oracles proclaime
In Delphos, Shadow'd by Apollo's name:
He that the Pythian Prophetesse inspir'd,
As likewise those th' Aegyptians so admir'd,
Ascribing to themselves Honour and Feare;
And those in sundry Idols worshipt were:
And of these Belzebub is Lord and Master. . . .

Next, touching the rare knowledge which insists

In them by nature; Some Theologists
Affirme them pregnant in Theologie,
Philosophie, Mathematicks, Astrologie,
In Musicke they are skill'd, expert in Physicke,
In Grammer, Logicke, and Arithmeticke.
Nay, he that is among them the most low,
Contemn'd and vile, more than weake Man doth know.

Nor are their reasons vaine; for in respect
A Spirit is but a mere Intellect,
Not burden'd with a body, of agilitie
Nimble and quicke; therefore with much facilitie
In all materials he acquainted is,
From the Earths superficies, to th' Abisse. . . .

They waking trouble us, molest our sleepe;
And if upon our selves no watch we keepe,
Our bodies enter, then distract our braine,
They crampe our members, make us to complaine
Of sicknesse or disease, and in strange fashion
They cause us to exceed in Joy or Passion . . .

SERAFINO DELLA SALANDRA

Adamo Caduto (1647)

THE FALL OF ADAM[1]

Dramatis Personae

The Goodness of Heaven
God
Omnipotence
Mercy
An Angel
Adam
Eve

[1]Abridged translation by Watson Kirkconnell. Loose canzone-measure in the original has been rendered by blank verse. Rhymed choruses retain their rhyme.

Cain) - Sons of Adam
Abel)
Calamana) - Daughters of Adam
Delbora)
Life)
Innocence) - Free Gifts
Simplicity)
Earth)
Water) - Subordinate elements in the scene
Air)
Fire)
Sin)
Death) - Effects of the Fall
Guile)
Serpent, with a human face
Lucifer)
Benemoth) - Devils
Belial)
Megaera - A Fury of Hell
Lamech - Slayer of Cain, and of
Cintio, his servant.
Chorus of Angels
Chorus of Devils
Echo

Prologue (lines 1-110)

The personified Goodness of Heaven summarizes the argument of the drama: the creation of Adam and Eve, their temptation by the Serpent, and their lamentable fall.

Act I, Scene I (lines 111-198)

Personified Omnipotence enters, dressed in cloth of gold, carrying a sceptre, and crowned with a triple crown. She soliloquizes, describing the creation by God, through her, of the universe, from Nothing, and of Man, the highest of created things, bearing the image of the triune Deity. From Man's side Woman has come.

Act I, Scene II (lines 199-265)

The style of the morality play continues. Personified Mercy enters. She is described as a young woman, with wind-dishevelled hair, slow of foot, almost naked with poverty, and carrying in her hand a withered palm-branch. In a long dialogue with Omnipotence, Mercy laments how small a part she has to play in a world still sinless; but she goes on to hint mysteriously that, if man should disobey God, she might yet reign on a throne as high as that of Omnipotence.

Act I, Scene III

Enter God, Adam, Eve, Earth, Water, Air and Fire.

God. Thou seest, Adam, with what gifts and worth,
Beyond all creatures else beneath the sky,
Or ardent spirits underneath the spheres
That have their motion given by my hand,
Thou art endowed today, in state sublime
So high that, though thou art in human guise,
Praises and glories shall be given thee.
Adam. Sir, I perceive that the Almighty hands
Drew me and formed me from the humble mire,
The vile stench of the earth; and through Creation
I recognize my origin as vile --
Though then they formed such and so mighty works
That I must marvel and within my mind
Must largely fail to comprehend myself;
And yet with gazing fill my heart with joy.
God. I formed thee of the earth. The stamp divine
That shines upon thy form, thou hast from me;
For such a gracious likeness could not issue
In any other way from such vile stuff.
Of earth I formed thee, that thou mightest know,
If disobedient to my holy laws,
The end will be reduced to the beginning
And thou'lt return to earth whence thou didst rise.
Of earth I formed thee that thou mightest know
The humblest born are apt for highest rule,
For so the sceptre may be rightly thine.
Of earth art thou: and ne'er could the World consent

To reverence thee, of vilest substance born,
If I had failed to set upon thy form
The image of my venerable self.
My graft divine upon so vile a trunk
I placed, in order that it might dissolve
The juices of the earth, and so the fruits
Might not be human but in truth divine.
Then from a portion of thy body's flesh
Into like form and semblance, as thou seest,
I made thy helpmeet, Woman, like to thee,
With difference of sex but not of soul.
Eve. O supreme Lord, Creator everlasting,
I know that from Thy hand proceeds the work
That past our merit prodigally moves
To high rewards and grandeurs, gifts and graces,
Until at length the soul and body come
To the full consummation of all virtue.
Earth. I, Adam, whom thou seest thus beautiful
And noble, so that others may refresh
Their faces in my presence if they will,
A seated matron whose delightful mantle
Is decked with flowers, herbs, and golden apples,
With which it comes embroidered; and besides,
In my right hand I hold an apple sphere,
A flowing horn of plenty in my left;
Lo, I am EARTH, the greatest Element,
And occupy the space between the Poles;
The weight within myself is my support,
For all alone I stand about my centre.
To serve thee, Adam, the high King of Heaven
Drew me already out of utter nothing.
These animals that in their mien seem fierce,
Such as the lion, leopard, bear, and lynx,
Tiger and dragon, greyhound, bull, and wolf,
Stag, horse, and elephant, camel and boar,
Will profit thee; nor will the need arise
To guard thyself against their hostile onsets.
They will be ready to obey thy nod
As if thou wert their lord, will do obeisance
And arm them to defend thee; though indeed
There lives no creature that could do thee harm.
Adam. O gracious God, how freely hast Thou wrought!
Water. I, Adam, who have garlanded my hair
With marshy reeds, bearing in my right hand

A noble sceptre, with cerulean veil
Adorning all my body with delight,
About my waist a zone of wrought sea-beasts
And with all these an urn of gushing brooks
To fructify the seed of the great Earth,
Lo, I am WATER, summoned into being,
For thy true service, by our common Maker.
These monsters of the sea, dolphins and lampreys,
Mollusks and salmon, pike and cormorants,
Seals, sea-calves, divers, cachalots and mermaids,
Glide in my watery bosom but to serve thee.
Adam. I thank my Maker for so fair a work.
Air. I, too, O Adam, whom thou seest dishevelled
With tangled tresses tossing in the breeze,
Seated amid the clouds and by the rainbow
Girdled about with variegated hues
That likewise gleam upon my golden hair;
I who am shod with linen and bear wings
That I may fly like bands of tuneful birds,
Lo, I am AIR, by breathing which thou livest;
And all the birds that I assemble here,
The eagle, halcyon, dove, swan, and crane,
Falcon and phoenix, pheasant, partridge, owl,
Geese, grouse, gerfalcon, goshawk, magpie, kite,
Jackdaws and kestrels, peacocks, grackles, bees,
Chickens and ravens and a thousand more,
Will always, Adam, be at thy command,
Ever prepared to hearken to thy voice.
Eve. But adders, hydras, basilisks, and asps?
Earth. All these will place their head beneath
thy foot.
Eve. The vipers, scorpions, and serpent dark --
Will these attack the issue of my womb?
Earth. Never, if thou obeyest God's commands.
Adam. And is it then my destiny to rule
Over the mighty whales, the strong swift dolphins,
The savage lions, the fleet-footed horses,
The ponderous elephants, the eagles proud,
The ruthless serpents, the misshapen camels,
The inhuman tiger-tribe, the foam-white swans,
The biting dogs, the spiny porcupines,
The treacherous vultures, and whatever else
The Elements may gather in their bosoms?
Fire. And, Adam, I am here, girdled about

With flashing sparks of ever-kindled flame;
In my dark tresses gleams the crescent moon;
I am the highest element; my foot,
Uplifted, is most nimble; on my head
The Phoenix stands, that burns and is consumed;
The lightning is the weapon of my hand;
My flaming limbs are cloaked in purple vesture;
Lo, I am FIRE, enkindled in thy service.
Adam. O gracious Giver! Let my mouth, O Lord,
Not vilify Thy gifts whose highest worth
Is past my mind's conceit, should I presume
To name them to Thee; for what human tongue,
Though formed of God, can praise God's utter marvels?
Thy works, O Lord, will sooner bring to birth
Silence than words; and greater silence still
My awe must feel in their great Maker's presence.
And so, my Lord, if I declare Thou art
Greater than all the greatest, 'tis the least
That can be granted to Thy spacious grandeur.
To say, Lord, Thou art better than the best,
That is but little to Thy lofty goodness.
The greatest attributes my mind can frame
Could ne'er express Thine awful sovereignty.
Yet to the limit of my soul and strength,
I thank Thee, Lord, I praise Thee, and adore Thee.
God. Thou thinkest little, if thou turnest not
Thy thoughts to something worthier of my making.
Adam. What is it, Lord? What further can the voice
Utter of adoration, or the heart
Offer Thee hour by hour continually?
God. Your highest praise lies in resembling me.
Be thou like me, though formed of substance vile.
Adam. Adam like God? The creature like his Maker?
Can the Artificer then make Himself?
Can the work bear the likeness of the Workman?
Eve. In what way, Lord? I do not understand
How human clay can possibly resemble
The Uncreated One that fashioned it.
God. Man is like God, but only in the soul,
Which, if its life be single, figures forth
The undivided Unity Divine.
Soul has indeed three Powers, with their acts,
That have a real distinction in themselves
Yet have their Being in a single Essence.

In so far then as man is made a spirit,
He bears a trace of God, being a spirit
One-minded, true, and good -- as God is One,
The son of the paternal mind is True
And th' inbreath'd love of both of them is Good.
Eve. And am I then, O Lord, vile though I be,
Not unlike God? When can I ever render
My thanks and adoration adequate
For benefits so rare and singular?
God. Where gifts are greater, stricter reckoning
Must be imposed. To forfeit greater good
Is to know greater woe and greater loss.
Adam. When shall I be unmindful of the gifts
Thy hand bestows, Lord? May it never be
That I prove false! Let my heart ever be
Intent on God, who made it from the mire!
What thing could I presume to offer Thee
Of which Thou art not Master and Creator?
Yet it is true the Workman takes delight
In His own works; therefore I give myself
And offer Thee the work of Thine own hand
While I preserve the imprint of Thine image.
Naught greater than Thy likeness I possess.
Accept the gift, O Lord! Receive Thine own!
God. Adam, I like thy heart's delirium
Of love and zeal. To man I have prescribed
No law for the enjoyment of his love
Except the dictates of his own free will.
That is a great gift, but I give a greater;
And may you both enjoy its happiness!
Adam. What is it, Lord?
Eve. What is it?
God. That you be adorned
With what I value highest under Heaven,
With Innocence, a virtue lacking which
No soul can be acceptable or pleasing.
The gift is granted not alone to you;
But all of your descendants upon earth
Will still enjoy it likewise, if thou knowest
In spite of all to guard the gift from harm.
Adam. Who would not guard a treasure such as that?
Eve. Most foolish would a man be if he lost it.
God. It can be lost if man grow sensual.
Adam. I shall defend it then by every art.

Eve. And I, O Lord, shall all my wit employ.
God. Speaking is useless if it prompt no action.
Adam. I'll arm myself with zeal against the thief.
Eve. And I shall take the shield, although unwarlike.
God. Arming is helpful when the foe assails.
Adam. I strongly hope to have a trophy from him.
Eve. Unconquered, I'll defend my breast from blame.
God. The greedy heart is often prone to fall.
Adam. Arming my heart, I shall not fear assaults.
Eve. I can avoid a dart that is foreseen.
God. All will go well with him whose heart is firm.
Adam. I think I shall not wander from the path.
Eve. I shall be valorous 'mid hostile swords.
God. Who thinks to conquer may be overcome.
Adam. Yes, if his hand in peril be not armed.
Eve. A man unarmed would leave his breast exposed.
God. Stand therefore, one in heart and strong in will.
Adam. I shall prepare myself to avoid the ambush.
Eve. And in the fight I shall be thine ally.
God. Come now, for I await the end of this.
And further, give ye ear to these my words.
Among all things on earth 'neath heaven's mantle
(But now described), man hath the primacy.
Come, therefore, Adam. I create thee here
The first, high Emperor of the Universe.
Thou hast the sceptre, thou the crown and rule
Over the vast blue sky, the earth, the sea;
Rule then, reign over with thy high command
The beasts, the fishes, and the winged birds.
I have set all things underneath thy feet
That they may render thee their vassalage.
Adam. So great a gift? Dost Thou exalt me thus?
God. Adam, I would give more.
Adam. And what, O Lord?
God. Seest thou this charming and delightful spot?
Adam. I do my Lord.
Eve. And it is fair and pleasant.
Earth. Peach-trees, pines, ash-trees, myrtle-trees, and palms,
The laurel, the fair juniper, the beech. . . .
Eve. What beauty here! And what extreme delight!
Earth. The apple, the fair cherry, acorns, nuts,

Dates, figs and laurel-berries, almonds, grapes,
And every fruit that's pleasant to the taste.
Adam. O what a habitation full of joy!
Eve. My spirit could desire nothing greater.
Earth. The plain is decked with violets and roses,
With lilies, fair narcissus, privet white,
Acanthus, jessamine, and hyacinth,
Crocus, and the immortal amaranth
Which form a garland for your Paradise.
God. And, Adam, all are thine; be thou the master.
I give them as pure gifts. For thee alone
I set their beauty here with mine own hand.
Adam. The gift is all the greater, in that we
Ourselves supply no merit, while the Giver,
No past or future servitude imposing,
Has lavished treasures of such amplitude.
Eve. What is it that I see? What do I see?
And with what greater joy could I be filled?
Each hour that fills my bosom with such flowers
Equals the rapture of a thousand years.
It seems each calls to you to adorn with it
Your hand and breast, and says: "O gather me!
'Tis for your sake I stand upon my stem!"
God. Adam, come here and take possession now;
Survey the site, the beauty marvellous
That in the bosom of this garden lies.
Adam. O what a work, my Lord, from what a hand!
Eve. Happy past measure is this gracious spot
Transcending past conception the deserts
Not only of us to whom by grace 'tis given
(While the gift comes before the inward act
That any mind could frame by way of merit)
But of whatever creature else could work
Works that are pleasing to the taste of God.
God. And as for thine own taste? Art thou content
With everything, O Adam?
Adam. Greater joy
My heart could not conceive than this delight.
God. Out of Damascus' rough and thorny field,
Thy primal fatherland and natal place,
To this place whose delights must still outdo
The utmost of the human heart and eye,
I have conveyed thee, Adam, that thou may'st learn
The gulf between thy fatherland and this,

And view both places with unequal love.
Earth. Thou mayest sport thee here with full
delight,
For here thou wilt not suffer heat nor cold,
Nor will the spring or summer cause thee pain.
Here lamentations will not enter in;
All groans and grief and martyrdom are banned.
In such a garden thou shouldst know content.
Adam. O blessed Adam! Now thine eye can see
The peerless gifts with which thou art endowed
Without desert.
Eve. O blessed Eve, enjoy
The gracious gift to full satiety!
God. Adam, guard well the plenitude of fruits
That here thou findest.
Adam. I see them and enjoy them.
Earth. They are at thy command, to serve thee here
With all their charm and graciousness of view.
Eve. Lord, may I eat of this fruit that I see
Surpassing all in beauty and in goodness?
God. Of that one above all, because that fruit
Is of the Tree of Life.
Eve. How fair an apple!
I long to taste it now without delay.
Adam. O Lord, why is it called the Tree of Life?
God. Adam, although thou art a worthy work
Formed by so great a Hand and rarely framed,
Yet art thou mortal, liable to death.
Adam. Then can I die, surrounded by such joys?
God. Truly thou canst. Yet thou wilt never die
(Weary and bent with age, with ancient flanks
Trembling, and every power failing quite)
If of the Tree of Life thou still shalt eat.
It will give restoration to thy frame
And all the years shall seem to touch thee not,
Transmuted by the virtue of the Fruit
Into the fresh condition of thy youth
In strength and force, in firmness and in vigour.
Not only shall it work such deeds in thee,
But all the trees and plants and herbs and flowers
In paradise shall at the sight of it
Be ever verdant without withering
And fertile without failing for one hour.
And therefore I have placed here in the midst

The Tree by which man lives and plants may grow.
Eve. And shall our life then be eternal here
While we have such a cure to heal our strength?
God. Eternal, but not here; for I shall come
One day (not sundering your soul and body)
To carry you to heaven, to enjoy
The empyrean, which exceeds this place
In splendor more immeasurably noble
As the Creator must excel his handiwork.
Adam. Lord, may I eat the other kinds of fruit?
Eve. Why shouldst thou not, if God has given them all?
God. Adam, observe with care what I shall say:
Thou shalt partake of all, except one only.
Except one only, Adam -- mark'st thou that?
Thou understandest, Adam?
Adam. Yes, my Lord.
God. In order that thy sense be not surprised
By the blind love of blameful appetite,
I shall supply a rein to draw it back
From the wrong path, and turn it to the right.
So, Adam, I thy Lord command that thou
Shalt not eat of that Fruit. Thou understandest?
Adam. I do, my Lord.
God. And in no circumstance
Thou wilt forget this strictest of injunctions?
Adam. Never, O Lord, shall my firm purpose fail.
Eve. And I, my Lord, shall keep it constantly.
God. Right there it is -- thou seest? And its name is
The Tree of Knowledge, both of Good and Evil.
Adam. What is the evil that would issue from it?
God. What is the evil? Loss. And ruin too.
If thy rash hand in folly steal that Fruit,
Thou shalt become first liable to Death,
The greatest of all ills and sum of them.
If thou shalt bite the Fruit, that moment Death
Shall set his horrid tooth-bite in thy heart,
Nor in thine only (thus the ill were slight)
But all the future offspring of thy loins
Will also know irrevocable death.
Earth. If thou shalt eat it, Adam, thou shalt turn
Earth upside down, likewise the sky and sea
And all things that their fruitful bosom bears.

Fire. The sky against thee will make battle then
With lightning-flashes and with thunder-bolts.
The friendly stars will then in wrath send down
A baneful influence to pervert the mind.
The sun, by freezing absence, will create
A rigid winter, while the summer he
(As penalty for sin) shall scorch with fire.
Earth. And I, the earth, shall be thy greatest foe,
In that, to gain thy necessary living,
Thou shalt toil long and hard with my stiff clods.
These animals, now most obedient,
Shall plot against thee and may cause thy death.
Water. The Ocean, bellowing, shall rear its billows.
Air. More than one body then, more than one soul,
Driven by winds, shall founder in the deep.
Subject to every penalty and woe,
Infirmity and travail and ill fortune
Thou wilt go ever sadly, full of grief.
God. And causing all this trouble to thyself,
Thou wilt loathe life and long at last for death;
What is now sweet to thee, shall then be bitter;
And what is thine will plunder be for others.
In short -- pray mark me, Adam! -- thou wilt be
A target for all sorrow and all travail.
O most unhappy Adam! -- if thou eat.
Adam. Thunder and lighten at my folly, Lord,
With angry sky, if ever I do that.
Eve. When will the human hand be e'er so bold
As merely to come near that deadly fruit
If Thou forbid it, Lord, with stern command?
God. Thy words have little worth without the deed.
Adam. I hope that speech and action will agree.
Eve. And all the more since Thy command is light.
God. It will seem heavy, through mere prohibition.
Adam. Restraining sense, the heart will choose
the best.
Eve. Who will remove Thine edict from our thought?
God. Forgetfulness, and itching appetite.
Adam. Commands so novel cannot be forgot.
Eve. Not only novel but so advantageous.
God. The rebel Angel has more guile than you.
Adam. Created prudent, I shall face the risk.
Eve. And all the more, since each beholds it near.
God. But unforeseen assault may dim the eye

And blind the heart with quick oblivion,
Quite unaware of my avenging hand.
Lo, I predict it, Adam.
Adam. Yes, my Lord.
God. Adam, beware, beware! Arm, arm thy breast!
Adam. Lord, I shall be obedient without fail.
Eve. Is it so hard then not to eat a fruit?
I wouldn't touch it if I knew I'd die.
God. To thee, my mere commandment should suffice.
Exit God.
Adam. My lady, hast thou heard the gravity
Of God's great ordinance and its penalties?
Eve. Adam, to tell the truth, the Tree is pretty.
Adam. Turn thy glance elsewhere and regard it not,
For appetite descends from eye to heart
And could evoke unworthiest desire.
Eve. It has a hidden power that draws one to it
Even in sheer despite of one's desire.
Fair though it be and charming to behold,
I shall stay fasting, so that cruel death
May not have victory and triumph o'er us.
Adam. There is no need to waver here, or risk
A grievous misadventure. Let us often
Recall the great command of the great God,
Thankful to Him who gives us so much else.
Exeunt.

Act I, Scene IV (lines 730-926)

Three maidens, Life, Innocence, and Simplicity, meet on earth and debate the cause of their having left Heaven. An angel enters and explains their relationship to newly created man. Innocence and Simplicity are needed to defend Life (in man) from spiritual enemies.

Act I, Scene V (lines 927-981)

Mercy soliloquizes on her coming hour of triumph, if man should fall and have need of the Divine mercy.

Act I, Scene VI (lines 982-1155)

Mercy and Omnipotence have another long argument

over the possibility of the Fall and the part they may play.

Act I, Scene VII

Enter Adam and Eve.

Adam. As God, the Maker of the world, disclosed
The sun amid the darkness, and the eye
Turns to that light more than to all things else
Friendly to man and ready in his service,
So among things created he revealed,
As a light amid the shadows, thee my mate,
Eve, my sweet helper, to whose face I turn
My glances more than to the sun above.
The sun is one light only in the sky
But under thy twin eyebrows I admire
Two eyes more ardent and more luminous
Than that same sun.
Eve. Thou shouldest praise Him then
From whom thou hast received a work so dear.
But oh, what brush, unless it were divine,
Could on so vile a canvas draw the essence,
The deep, inmost Idea of His mind?
Adam. O dearer portion of my own true self,
Bone of my bone and flesh of my own flesh,
To whom the rapture of my spirit turns!
Dear Eve, when thou appearest, Paradise
Is quickly dimmed, though charming and adorned.
The flaming crocus fades before the gold
Of thy fair hair; the red rose languishes
Beside the live vermilion of thy cheeks;
At thy white brow, the snowy privet darkens;
The hyacinth grows pale before thine eyes;
The jessamine is brown beside thy breast
And its pure ivory; the lily's white
Is dingy by the whiteness of thy hand.
Eve. Yet praise God only; for a common rib,
However fair to see, could give thee nothing.
In such a work, all honour is the Maker's.
Adam. If I had not been sure that God's great hand
Had shaped thee from my flesh, assuredly
Enravished by thy beauty I should think
Thou wert no woman but a goddess rather.

Thus I deny not (and I thank God for it)
That I behold on earth another heaven
More charming than the regions of the sky.
That is inanimate, while this has life.
I seek the sun, and lo it is thy face;
I seek the silver moon, it is thy body;
Stars are thine eyes; and rainbows are thy brows;
Thy radiant forehead is the Milky Way.
The sea has beauties, but they are dispersed;
In thee, my lady, they are joined in one.
Thy mouth's a precious shell; thy teeth are pearls;
Thy lips are coral, and thy face a calm
Surrounded by soft waves of rippling hair;
Thy low, sweet accents are the siren's song;
Thy constancy in good is marble rock.
Eve. I likewise see that Nature in thy body,
Dear consort, is not grudging with her gifts,
But has bestowed upon thee prodigally
Authority in action, majesty
In all thy bearing, gravity in voice,
Prudence in discourse, sanity in counsels,
And wisdom in the conduct of affairs.
I praise God and give thanks that He has opened
His heavenly treasury so wide that while
We are united and thus intermingled,
Both in one heart, one will, one soul, one body,
Thou art the fate predestined for my heart,
Soul of my spirit, spirit of my soul,
The fragrance of my sighs, my one desire,
The habitation of my thoughts, the target
Of all my knowledge, centre of my love,
Harbour of hope and polestar of my steps,
The fountain of my good, my only life.
Adam. I recognize that sons born of our loins
In distant generations will abandon
Father and mother and a home's due comfort
To follow her who is to be their spouse;
Still more the frailer sex drawn from my side
Will follow and love who loves and follows her.
From that sweet nuptial knot that binds a pair
Within the lodging of a single breast
Neither the soft lure of the silver sea
Nor joy in tracking beasts through the dense woods
Will e'er again be able to release them.

Eve. But that fair knot ought but to bind thee more
With which God binds us to His love divine,
Even the ordinance that He has given.
Adam. 'Tis true enjoyment when the will of man
Is one with God's. Therefore, my dearest Eve,
Thy thought is wise! Let there between us be
One heart, one soul, one will; and let our union
Be dedicated utterly to God.
Eve. Only by help divine the mind is saved.
Therefore he does not fall who clings to God.
Adam. A man who walks the true path does not wander.
Eve. And he who leans on Truth is justified.
Adam. He must shun death, who wishes for true life.
Let then a constant fear of death provide
The strongest rein to hold us in restraint.
Eve. Moreover, I believe not that this Fruit
Has primacy of taste among them all.
Adam. O foolish fair one, banish from thy mouth
Not its taste only, but its very name!
Eve. Art thou so timid as to fear its name?
Adam. He who loves, fears; he who desires, procures.
He who would shun a fall, avoids encounters.
And he who would not lose, holds fast his own.
Therefore let eyes and thoughts avoid the Fruit.
Eve. I think of it, but not of acting ill.
Adam. Minds once debauched are ready then for action.
Eve. The sense could not so quickly be depraved.
Adam. The impure will can make the senses slaves.
Eve. Quite true, if reason were not there to guide.
Adam. Can reason matter, if the will prevail?
Eve. Then he who guides will lead himself astray.
Adam. False he may be, yet sees his ruin well.
Eve. So reason meets this fate by his own will?
Adam. He has no will, but serves the will of others.
Eve. How can he serve them, if he is their leader?
Adam. He helps the others to learn good and evil.
Eve. Can he teach good, and learn it not himself?
Adam. He is not master over what he knows.
Eve. How can he not control what is his own?
Adam. Research is the true property of mind.
It weighs whatever is, and values it.

But in all human choice, the will determines
Fidelity to duty -- or betrayal.
Therefore, sweet helpmeet, value present good
And fear the evil that is still unseen.
That heart is foolish which, desiring good,
Neglects to bar the entrance to all evil,
Standing on armed guard to defend the way.

(A Chorus of Angels then sings a hymn, lines 1308-1331, in praise of "The Age of Gold", with its joys of innocence and obedience.)

Act II, Scene I

Enter Lucifer, Belial, Benemoth and Chorus of Demons.

Lucifer. And didst thou hear?
Belial. And didst thou hear?
Benemoth. I heard.
What think ye now? Are we, high worthy spirits,
Removed from Paradise?
Belial. And what is worse,
Penn'd in the blind Abyss.
Benemoth. And now is man
Master of Heaven? Shall he be lord of Heaven?
Lucifer. We are God's first creation, nobly born,
Sublime in worth, immortal in our form,
Bright flames and flashing stars, fair burning fires,
Strong columns of the fair and lofty Hill,
White lilies, mirrors of the empyrean,
Mermaids and swans in heaven's harmony,
Strong warriors in all lofty enterprise,
Unwearied movers of the ample spheres,
The governors of all the elements,
Alien to matter that is low and vile
And rather formed alone of purest essence.
We who are bright and nimble, swift and speedy,
Prudent and wise, alert and penetrating,
Resolute, free, cunning and beautiful --
Shall we lose Paradise? Alas, that loss
Is my most frenzied penalty in Hell!
Belial. God's hand with all its power can create
No punishment more bitter than that loss.
Yes, Lake Avernus and the Stygian waves

Without our envious thoughts of Paradise
Would be more sweet than April and the Spring.
Benemoth. Is man so greatly honoured? Does that mire,
The abominable effluvium of Earth,
Born of the foulest and most savage spot,
The vile Plain of Damascus, all-obscene,
Receive the likeness and the stamp of God?
Lucifer. So vile is man that from his place of birth
He moves elsewhere to rule; and thus the birth
Of man is surely judged obscure and coarse.
He could not stay there and be hailed as prince,
For there his swaddling clothes were too well known
And he is ill served that is basely born.
That is the creature that so pleases God
That, placed o'er me, humbly I must adore it
Or else lie deep in the abyss of Hell.
To worship such a man, I should be like
An ass, an ox, an insect. Paranymph
Of Heaven is he indeed, who has such merit
That little could be added to his grandeur
Unless the Creator too should worship him.
Benemoth. Too much thou boastest. Heaven bids me tell thee
That thy o'erweening pride has brought thee here --
Pride that presumed to raise thy throne too high.
Lucifer. Thou speakest like a fool, and such thou art.
Benemoth. Inspired by Heav'n, no tongue is ever silent.
Listen, proud sir, how little are thy powers.
Deliberately thou saidst: "I will ascend
High in the North!" So thou wert given a fling
So fast and free that thou resembledst lightning --
O speedy lightning that was soon extinguished!
Lucifer. Can I endure all this? Restrain myself?
Benemoth. Thou art unmoved, as the Prime Mover wills.
Then thou didst call to witness that high mountain
Where thou hadst planned to enthrone thy arrogance,
But ruin followed fast that invocation.
Lucifer. And shall I not take vengeance for these words?

Belial. Thy purpose proved a plague; therefore thereafter
(We pestilential ones having been first
In haste removed, lest we infect the rest)
In Heaven it was not found.
Lucifer. Who thwarts me now?
Who will restrain my arm?
Benemoth. The hand of God.
Thy will was poison, therefore like a Dragon
With tail importunate thou dragg'dst us down,
A third of all the stars, most bright and fair.
Lucifer. Descend, descend like lightning, my right hand!
Benemoth. Thou wert called Light, but why thou wert so named
Is somewhat vague. The Sun in darkness goes
Into the shadows of the evening West,
But presently in rising, at the dawn,
Has joy in light. A rising once was thine;
But thou hast set, and that eternally.
Belial. A plant may languish in the frosts of winter,
Yet in the Spring it smiles upon its stem.
But in these icy shadows of despair
Eternal lamentation is thy lot.
Lucifer. How can I bear my cruel destiny?
Benemoth. The rivers seek the sea from which they rose;
But exile borne of everlasting shame
Will hold thee back from Heaven eternally.
Belial. The bird toils on the wing, but after flight
His pleasant nest at last will welcome him;
But thou, after thy single flight beneath the earth,
Wilt never soar to see the sky again.
Benemoth. That's why your habitation is called Hell:
'Tis not a swift and constant torrent's flow
But a foul lake of fire, in keeping with
The place's adamant stability.
Belial. Thy flame of torment is perpetual;
For as the grass on which the gentle sheep
Feed day by day is daily yet renewed,
So fire about us grows continually.
Benemoth. God's Justice operating here in hell,
Is like a gladiator who behind

The back of his spent foeman plies his sword;
The latter, open to unseen attack,
Hopeless and helpless, has no choice but death.
Belial. Unhappy Salamander, who 'mid heats
Of Hell art still consumed, yet diest not!
Lucifer. Shall I, unmoved, be weak at such assaults?
Benemoth. Why, thou stout warrior, did great Michael's arm
Tear thee invincibly away from Heaven,
As the North Wind tears off a rotten branch,
With infinite contempt, to thy great shame?
Lucifer. I won't admit that. For had Michael power
Against my traitorous heart and traitorous breast,
Unbreakable in anger and in daring?
By my sheer will I could have blotted out
Michael and all his host and Heaven too;
But for this reason I restrained myself:
I did not wish to win. There my own will
And not another's brings me. Here I came
To baulk God of His pleasure in my safety.
In this it pleased me more to displease Him
Than if I had displaced Him from His throne.
Fool, dost thou think to err in this account?
Here I am Head and Leader, here the Prince
Of a thousand legions that obey my nod.
This I enjoy, and soon Man, in his frailty,
To God's great sorrow, will become my slave.
And hast thou, in thy folly, so far loosed
That lying tongue of thine?
Belial. O my dear Leader,
I do not understand. How is it true
That (as thou sayest) thou art so high and great
When here in Hell thy majesty is humbled,
Thy wealth is all impoverished and destroyed,
Thy lofty beauty quite deformed and black,
Thy ample power curtailed and subjugated?
Thy wisdom, too, so utterly derided?
Thy strength is weakness, when upon us all
Supremest misery has settled down.
Lucifer. Thou ribald thief, lie prone upon the earth
For I shall trample on thy carping mouth
With my strong foot, and place thy unworthy tongue
Beneath my heel.
Belial. Pity! Alas, my Prince!

Lucifer. Dost thou seek pity for impiety?
Ask for wrath rather, scorn, and flame, and fire,
Outrage, and infamy, and wrong, and sorrow,
Torments and injuries and villainies,
Cruelty, ruthlessness, revenge and rage,
Blood, strife, and death. Is pity asked by thee
Of the most ruthless one that girds the earth?
(Stamps on the face of the prostrate Belial)

Belial. Ruthlessness, cruelty, revenge, and rage.
Lucifer. What sayst thou, Belial? Did Michael beat me?
Belial. I say not.
Lucifer. Why?
Belial. I else should be a liar.
Lucifer. And did my eminence fall down in ruin?
Belial. Rather it rose upon a higher throne.
Lucifer. Shines anyone in Heaven more than I?
Belial. Beside thy brightness, all are but a spark,
As thou, great Sire, out of the darkness comest,
O Treasure, Gem of light, enkindled Lamp,
Illuminator of the dayspring-hour,
Ruler of rays, sole Phoenix among lights,
Transcendent Beacon of the Universe,
In whose fair presence every eye delights.
Lucifer. O my dear Belial, I shall make thee Head
Of all my host and under thy command
Shall place the legions of the most sublime
Spirits that Hell now holds. Stand on thy feet now.
Let now be sung the worth of my great realm.

Chorus of Demons

As kingdom, I rule the Abyss;
My throne is of rock, fire-cloven;
My sceptre, a pale torch a-hiss;
My crown is of snakes interwoven;
My robes are thick clouds from Hell's trench;
My court is the Stygian nation;
My incense is sulphur's foul stench;
My mirth is prolonged lamentation;
My music is uproar's harsh fit;
My song knows dark grief's overcasting;
My hall is the gulf of the Pit

And my rest is unrest everlasting.

Lucifer. As for our task, what shall we do with
man?
What say'st thou, Benemoth?
Benemoth. I never know
How to conspire best against that fellow,
If God is still his guide, if the world serves him,
If God has fixed his eyes and guards his purpose
So that he may not wander from his path.
Lucifer. Time has a way of settling mighty issues.
Let us go down into the Abyss together
And sound the sackbut loud in Tartarus.
An impious council shall we hold together,
That Man may yet become a foe to God
And glut my fury as the prey of Hell.
Exeunt.

Act II, Scene II (lines 1531-1688)

As Innocence and Simplicity wander timidly through a terrestrial forest, they see and overhear two ugly demons, Sin and Guile. The virtues and vices meet, and argue at great length over their respective abilities to persuade Man.

Act II, Scene III (lines 1689-1741)

The Fury Megaera soliloquizes, describing with enthusiasm the horrors of hell and her own evil nature. She has just summoned, by the trumpet, an assembly of Hell's leaders to encompass the ruin of Man.

Act II, Scene IV

Scene the same. Enter Lucifer.

Lucifer. Rancours and hates and scorns, my potent
helpers,
Through whom my eyes are blood-shot, my mouth
foaming,
My heart and veins swollen with confidence,
My blood a-boil, my breast on fire with wrath,

These have decided on the dreadful ruin
That they'll inflict on man. Now I shall say
What I intend to do. Ho there, Megaera!
Meg. Here am I, in thy presence, to command.
Luc. Kindle the flames of sulphur in my breast!
Meg. I shall enflame thee into one sheer fire.
Luc. Lay now thy Stygian hand upon my head;
Crown it with fire, and make me furious;
Apply my unjust heart to shameful deeds
Proper to so inexorable a breast.
I swear by this my Head, I swear by Hell,
That I shall bring on loss irreparable.
Ho there! Ho there!

Enter Belial, Benemoth, and Chorus of Demons.

Ben. We are all ready, Sire.
Luc. Let each contrive calamity and death.
Bel. Who would not scorn the very thought that God
Should grant to man what He denies to us? --
To man, who had derived his origin
Out of the vilest stuff that earth possesses.
Ben. To him God promises (besides His likeness)
Rule over all the earth and sky and sea,
And vows to place beneath his human feet
All of the circumambient universe.
Meg. Is vigour in your foolish ones extinct?
And will you ne'er rise up? Do you like babes
Avenge such harsh atrocious grief with weeping?
You stir a thousand frenzies in my breast.
Luc. I sought to rise up at a single bound
Upon the throne of God (my curses on Him)
And match myself with Him while Heaven contained
No greater than myself. From thence He tried
Without avail to follow me down here
Whither my will alone has drawn and thrust me.
Meg. You, great-souled Sire, will you not now display
Indomitable pride against this man
Whose size of body is contemptible,
Surely the kin of brutes and not of spirits.
Ben. If one surveys his animate machine,
One sees but flesh and skin, the sort of stuff
He has in common with the sensual beasts.

Has God exalted him? Has He desired
To give him domination over angels?
Luc. I shall not bow myself to such vile clay,
Nor was it folly when I made the endeavour
To elevate my place and subjugate
Both Earth and Heaven; nor yet do I wish
To find myself eternally in Hell.
(To the Chorus)
But come now with quick songs and lively voices
And raise my spirit from such woes and griefs.

CHORUS

No spirit can ever conceive
The thrill of unspeakable pleasure
I find when in plotting I weave
Strife, rancour, and hate beyond measure,
Iniquity, faithless and false,
Plague, discord, and bitter traduction;
My purpose ne'er weakens or halts
In compassing man's dark destruction.
I am the corrupter of souls,
The planner of evil and folly:
In Hell, 'mid the flaming of coals,
I find evil thoughts very jolly.
If I ask for a voice of complaint,
If groans and laments I require,
Then ravings and sighs past restraint
Rush forth to fulfil my desire.
There torrents of tired lament
Come mingled with horrible hisses;
Grim faces, hot furies are blent
In the flame of the sordid abysses;
And yet it is true that, though wild they may be,
They never have seemed the least bother to me.

Luc. One pain alone my heart feels, one alone, --
That a man wishes to contend with me
In dignity, in honours, and in worth.
But I shall plan with care, I shall weave snares,
That he may fall at last into my net.
Ben. We shall contrive that at thy fair eyes' flashing
The mind of man shall stupid grow and dull;

That at the tossing of thy radiant hair,
His heart shall grow affrighted and dismayed;
That at the flaming of thy shining face
All warmth in man shall freeze with rigid cold;
That at the reddening of thy dawning light
He may be darkened in his shuddering soul;
That at the turning of thy countenance
His glance may fall, confused and motionless.
Bel. Thou shouldst try every method, every way:
Kindle his honour, threaten him in ire,
Make equal use of prayers and flattery,
Break down his arguments, advance strong reasons,
Propose things good to him, propose things evil,
Praise and exalt him, so that he may plunder
The deadly Apple to his own destruction.
Meg. With heart intrepid and with fearless face,
In battle staunch, in zeal unquenchable,
Fearless and firm, strong and unvacillating,
I now present myself for this great war.
I, nurse of anger, alien to peace,
Close friend of hatred, shall now slake thy thirst
On man's vile blood. These snakes within my hair
Have not as much of sulphur, flame and stench
And venom as I have within my heart.
Luc. Up now, my servants! Let us come to action.
Which one among you all is brave enough
To lure Man to the Apple and his fall?
Ben. To tell the truth, I admit myself too weak
To undertake so difficult a deed.
Fresh in his mind is God's great ordinance;
And man with so much favour is endowed
That it were hard to urge him on to evil.
Luc. Is it from zeal like mine that thou hast learned
This fear and sloth? Thou weak and craven spirit,
Is it so hard to undertake this task?
Ho, now, my men! Hoist him upon your shoulders!
This fellow must be lashed to stir his blood!
(Benemoth is scourged.)
Ben. Ah, I am dead! Alas, no more, my Prince!
I do repent, and am prepared for war.
Luc. He still lacks heart. Redouble all those blows!
(They flog him again.)

<u>Meg</u>. Coarse, savage Spirit, well would I know how
To give thyself rewards to match thy merits.
<u>Luc</u>. I go, in evil hour. Surely this task
Fits mine own hand. But you, my fellow-fiends,
At my attempt, with flattering human voice
Will whisper further lying thoughts to man.
Thou, Benemoth, with thy battalion, hide
In yonder shady thicket and be silent.
Mellow the flavour and delight of taste.
Thou, with thy legions, Belial, hide here.
Open man's eyes to see, that the appearance
Of the fair fruit may quite entice his sense.
Fly, thou Megaera, into yonder Pit
And rouse all Hell to flaming indignation,
Rancour and rage, that in the unholy hour
In Eden every tree and branch and flower
May be an abode for devils.
<u>Meg</u>. I am ready.
I take my leave, fulfilling thy command.
<u>Luc</u>. Now for good counsel. Sure, the plan is safe
That I assail the weaker partner first,
And having conquered there, o'erthrow the other.
Yes, I shall tempt the Woman, that she eat;
And cause her then to undertake her husband.
A feigning female friend will dupe him better.
If he resist, I'll turn her eyes to weeping;
And he, in order to console her grief,
Will eat, to his damnation and my joy.
To serve me as my spokesman, I desire
This very serpent, whom I have beheld
Playing with Eve and gathered in her bosom.
Within its twining shape I hide myself,
Dissolving first my form ethereal.
Thus I lie here in secret and in silence.

Act II, Scene V (lines 1921-1987)

An ingenious scene, in which an Echo lures Adam away in futile search, thus leaving Eve alone and unprotected.

Act II, Scene VI

Scene the same. <u>Eve</u> alone.

Eve. While Adam elsewhere follows that far voice
I shall be able here with straying steps
To gaze with joy upon these trees and flowers.
O what variety, what great delight
Of fruits and plants, of grasses and of leaves!
Then, gathered in one army, I behold
The animals, who, in their regiments
To me, for whom Heaven's King created them,
Ever make low and reverent obeisance.
Among the others, in cool branches' shade,
I see the shining serpent wound in coils;
It has a woman's head, a reptile body.
Oh, art thou there, my pet? And art thou cool,
Twined on the trunk, enjoying thy fair ease?
Oh, thou art beautiful, delightful, charming,
With such variety that thou appearest
Another starry sky, enamelled earth.
In truth, thou bear'st the boast among them all;
And if thou hadst from Nature gifts of speech,
Instead of being silent as thou art,
Thou wouldst be quite complete and all adorned.
Speech is thy only lack.
Serpent. I, too, have speech.
Eve. What do I hear? Thou speakest? Serpent dear,
Do not disdain to join in conversation
And give me (for to that end thou wert made)
Some sport and consolation with thy jests.
Serp. For such a purpose came I, and am zealous
In that desire; since that is dear to me
Which pleases thee and brings joy to thy breast.
Eve. O serpent, what could anyone desire
Better and dearer than the things we have,
Blessings perpetual and infinite?
Serp. All other gifts indeed that could be given
I do consider as surpassed already.
The favours that God grants with open hand
Could not be heaped in bounty any higher.
Only one doubt remains for me: and that,
To tell thee truly, seems more than a marvel.
Eve. What doubt is that?
Serp. I do not wish to say.
Eve. Yet tell me.
Serp. No, not now.
Eve. I prithee, tell me.

Serp. Another time.
Eve. I'm going to know it now.
Serp. 'Tis very odd.
Eve. Thou inflam'st me all the more.
Serp. I'll tell thee something else.
Eve. No, only that!
Serp. I'll tell, but thou wilt falter for reply.
Eve. I'll have a good reply for all thou sayest.
Serp. What I would say is, that it seems most strange
That God with open hand has given so much
And emptied all the treasury of Heaven,
And then forbids you to eat one fruit only.
It is just that. And amongst all the others
That fruit is the most charming and most gracious.
Eve. Talk not to me of that, if thou'rt a friend.
This is the will divine; I know no other.
I must do only as my Lord requires.
If thou hadst listened here not long ago,
Thou'dst heard not only warnings but commands --
That I should eat it not and touch it not,
And I thereto gave promise of obedience.
If I should do the opposite, He told me,
In that same hour should I be doomed to death.
Serp. Thou wouldst not surely die. Thou art a fool.
And yet I am not telling thee to eat it.
Eve. How should I die not? Make me understand.
Serp. I should appear to lie, or weave deceit.
Hence I keep silence and refuse to tell thee.
Eve. Thou sayest that if I eat I shall not die.
That is not truth but vain imagining.
Serp. I ask not that thou touch it. But I know
So fair an Apple has no death in it.
I shall not tell thee secrets such as these.
Eve. What secrets dost thou mean?
Serp. I'll tell them rather
To a more virile listener, thy husband.
He, with more courage and more wit than thou,
Will listen fearlessly to all my counsel,
Which has utility and helpfulness,
And he will bind it to his breast as wise.
Eve. But tell it to me too, my noble Serpent.
Serp. I shall not tell thee. Thou art not my friend.
Eve. From thee I have received no slight or wrong.

How shall I be a foe to one so dear?
Serp. This charming fruit . . .
Eve. Oh God, thou grievest me!
Speak not of that now, as thou lovest me.
Discourse thou rather on some other theme.
Serp. I've nothing else to say. Lo, I am gone.
Eve. But stay, don't go.
Serp. Thou call'st on me to speak,
And then thou wilt not hear what profits thee.
Eve. What thing can profit me?
Serp. Listen, my lady,
If thou wert only willing, thou couldst be --
I know not what.
Eve. What other thing indeed
Could I become?
Serp. This fair fruit . . .
Eve. Dost thou still
Prate to me of that fruit? And yet observe
Thou giv'st me pain. What dost thou then desire?
(Yet keep thy theme of discourse from the fruit.)
Serp. This gracious fruit God has forbidden thee
Has been forbidden for the simple reason
That precious things are always thus forbidden.
Eve. I still must hear what yet displeases me.
Serp. The fruit is not death-bearing, as He said.
And if He has preserved it by such threats,
It is because He knows its hidden virtue.
Eve. Its hidden virtue is the curse of death.
Serp. That is not true. It ministers to life;
And this is a small part. (O glorious Apple,
Who could declare the virtues of thy fruit?)
One quality it has among the rest
Dearer to me than I am to myself, --
The power to unseal thine eyes and make thee see
All good, all evil, knowing everything.
Note well, I am not telling thee to eat.
Eve. My eyes are open now and can perceive
Without the Apple.
Serp. That is self-deception!
Only thy body's eyes are open yet
And in thy spirit's vision thou art blind.
What God alone can see, thou canst not see;
If thou wouldst touch the Apple thou wouldst know,
Yet without eating it.

Eve. What dost thou tell me?
Serp. What do I tell? I've told thee nothing yet.
Thou couldst have listened to a greater thing
If thou hadst not been heedless of my speech.
Let me depart.
Eve. Oh stay!
Serp. I have said too much.
Eve. What greater thing could be than thou hast said?
Serp. The greatest thing that could be thought or uttered.
Eve. I am curious to hear so strange a thing.
Serp. What benefit is hearing without action?
Eve. Yet tell me what it is that has such value.
Serp. Listen, dear lady, and let then thyself
Be judge whether a greater could be uttered.
God has not banned it without mystery
Because He knows the Apple has such power
That at a touch thou wouldst become a goddess.
Eve. How dost thou know that, if I know it not?
Serp. From those with power to profit is it hid.
'Tis known to me, because 'twould serve me not.
Eve. Thy speech is hard to credit or believe.
Is deity then harvested from plants
Even as their fruits and flowers are collected?
Serp. God can engender such a quality.
If He forbids it thee, thou mayst be sure
It is because the Great scorn to have equals.
The sceptre is not carried well by two
And good divided never sates the heart.
Therefore His seat is still declared a throne
Because it is His will to sit alone.
Eve. Wouldst thou deny that nothing can resist Him?
Serp. Of course not. He is Lord of all the world.
Eve. Then, if thy speech be not completely false,
He would destroy the tree, or plant it not,
Rather than let His sceptre find a rival.
Serp. 'Tis true that God would not have planted it,
Had He not will'd it so, to set you both
Under a yoke of rigid ordinance.
Hence He applied the name of Good and Evil.
The Evil is to shun it, and be slaves;
The Good, to touch it and be free from law.
Eve. Thou liest, if thou sayest such a thing.

The Good is not to eat it, and to live;
The Evil is to eat it, and to die.
Serp. And dost thou think it good to serve another?
I'd give all Heaven just to loose myself
One hour from servitude! A harsher thing
Cannot be suffered than the impious yoke
Of servile fear. God treats you worse than brutes,
For to the beast He issues no such law;
It drinks of every stream, eats every herb.
Tell me then, what restrains thy noble will
Except false reverence for a common branch?
What bough ought man to fear, to venerate?
Eve. When brutes and all the world obey my rule,
It matters little that this plant does not.
I am quite satisfied and wish no other.
Serp. The whole world cannot satisfy the heart,
Which in its outline is triangular.
The world is spherical, and, placed entire
Upon the heart of man, can never fill it.
Eve. How can that be done?
Serp. Only another form
Triangular in shape can fill it quite.
Eve. And what is that?
Serp. It is the triple God's
Divinity here hidden in the Apple.
Eve. I halt 'twixt Yes and No. But tell me, friend,
How have I merited thy love so much
That thou shouldst open ways for me to gain
So great a gift as to become divine?
Serp. It is thy peerless beauty that impels me
To make thee greater still, if that might be.
Eve. Unless thy tongue is luring me to woe,
Why dost thou not thyself take this advice,
Dispensed to me with so much prudent zeal?
Serp. A lover keeps back nothing for himself
But pours out all his wealth on her he loves.
Eve. Thy offering is much too bountiful.
Try thou it first; that I may do it then.
Serp. 'Tis only inability prevents me:
Beast that I am, I cannot reach that high.
Eve. Well do I know thou teachest and couldst tell
me,
After thy doctrine, to know good and evil.
Serp. Such a result is far beyond my power;

But thou dost have it ready at thy hand,
Since thou dost bear God's image and art like Him.
Eve. And, as thou say'st, a touch would be enough?
I do not wish to touch what God forbids.
Serp. I marvel at such simpleness of speech.
God has forbidden eating but not touching.
Hast thou forgotten in so short a time?
Eve. Then I can touch it, and obey Him still?
Serp. Who tells thee not to touch it? God did not.
Eve (touching an apple). I touch it! Yet I am
not made a goddess.
Serp. But touching it, lo, thou art not yet dead:
And hence thou mayst perceive I do not lie.
Death (entering at side, unperceived).
Softly, softly, without her seeing me,
With this my mighty sickle in my grasp,
At the motion of her hand, at every turn
I draw near and retire.
Eve. Alas, my heart.
It trembles. Wouldst thou have me touch again?
Serp. Yes, without fail thou wilt become a goddess
If without fear thou touch it once again.
Eve. Thou sawest it before, how nothing happened.
Serp. No great end is accomplished at one step.
Eve. And should I then approach it without fear?
Serp. So have I said.
Eve. I draw near, and I tremble.
If I but touch again, I'll be a goddess?
Serp. Yes, if thou pluck it from its proper place.
Eve. Oh no, not that!
Serp. What dost thou fear?
Eve. To die.
Serp. Sure, deity knows not mortality.
How shalt thou be a goddess and then die?
Eve. Pray let me go and call my husband first.
Serp. O simple one, dost thou not know that Adam,
Created ere thou wert, preceded thee
In all the gifts that Nature gave to him?
By thy proposal, you would both be gods.
But if thou take it first, thou wilt precede
Thy husband in becoming thus divine;
And if he was created the first man,
Thou wilt become the first divinity.
Eve. Thy speech is wise. I grasp the fruit again.

Serp. Bend the branch more, and tear it from the trunk.
And be not slow in undertaking this.
Eve. Behold, I take it, pull it from the branch.
Where is my godhood? Am I still a woman?
Serp. Dost thou not know, beauty is hid within?
All that possesses power is always hid,
And so the Apple's virtue is inside,
Not in the skin.
Eve. Alas! Thou saidst I would become a goddess
At just a touch; but that word was not true.
I plucked it, but thy promise still was vain.
Thus I believe thou liest in the rest.
Serp. I said that no one could become supreme
All in such headlong haste as thou supposest.
Slowly do what I say, and all is thine.
Eve. Behold, with trembling hands I thus divide it.
Serp. My gentle lady, thou must know right well
And thou indeed dost teach me once again
That changing common substance into noble,
As woman into goddess, must begin
By changing into deity that part
Which in the body is most noble, then
Transform the rest, the much less worthy part.
Eve. The heart is the most worthy part of man.
Serp. Then should the glorious Fruit first touch thy heart.
Eve (touching the apple to her breast).
Behold, it touches it, and I perceive
I am unchanged in nature, as before.
Serp. Thou art deceived. 'Tis too remote to touch
Or yield its power by this outer contact
Its virtue cannot work unless it pass
Within the breast and join thy very heart.
Eve. Wouldst thou then have me gash my breast wide open?
Serp. Ah, that exactly, that thou gash thy breast
And pass the Apple through the opening;
But first let's see if there's some other way
Of entry without opening thy breast?
I think, and think again, and see naught else.
Canst thou think, lady, of another way
More natural that will not hurt thy heart?
I cannot, for my life, think up another.

Eve. Surely the natural way is through the mouth.
Serp. In truth, I never should have thought of that.
Thou hast thought well. Wiser art thou than I,
O lady (goddess, rather), and more cunning.
Come then, and introduce it to thy heart!
Eve. And will the end be even as thou sayest?
Serp. I swear by God that thou wilt be divine.
Eve. O happy me! I eat without delay. (She eats.)
Serp. Swallow it down at once then! O brave lady!

Enter Death, Belial, Benemoth, Lucifer and Megaera.

Eve. Alas! What do I see? O traitor serpent!
Death. I have caught thee in the act, unhappy lady.
Thou art already set beneath my rule.
Bel. Ah, victory is ours, and palm, and triumph!
Ben. (to Lucifer). A stroke so fine as surely to seem thine!
Eve. Alas, I am but dead. O cursed serpent!
Death. Thou'rt dead indeed. Dominion now is mine
Upon thee, but I do not seize thee yet.
Luc. Let every hand bind my triumphant head
With dusky garlands of Tartarean myrtle!
And let the circuit of the black Abyss
Ring with our lewd and loud-resounding laughter!
Eve. Where is the godhood that thou promised me?
Death. Thou wert a fool to credit such a lie.
Death, death hast thou begotten in the world.
See with what zeal thou stripp'st the leafy trees,
Striving to shun the shame of nakedness?
Meg. Ho, come before the throne of Lucifer!
Bow down before the King and give him glory,
While all the abyss joins in his retinue,
Crying out "Victory, ho, Victory!"
(Exeunt all but Eve and Death.)
Eve. Who would have thought of such a strange mishap?
Death. Thyself did think it, hesitate, and choose.
Eve. Begone, and don't annoy me any more.
Death. Where should I go but in thy company?
Eve. Turn now thy angry weapon somewhere else.
Death. Fearest thou this, that thy hand gave to me?
Eve. When was I maker of the hooked sickle?

Death. When thou didst make thine iron heart the anvil,
Kindling the coals of thine own vanity
With the keen fire of thy wicked will;
The bellows were the hissing of the serpent.
Yea, thou wert then the smith of thine own death.
Eve. Must I obey thee, though I wish it not?
Death. Once thou hadst power to avoid my rule.
Now thou art bound and wholly in my hands.
Eve. Oh, bitter sequel to the sweets I've lost!
I yearn supremely for my former life.
Wilt thou not leave me if I bid thee go?
Can loss so great as this be e'er repaired?
Death. As final sentence, it has been decreed
That thou shalt place thy head beneath this blade.
Eve. Alas, what shall I do amid such pains?
I run in haste to hide among the branches,
Seeking to shun a sight so horrible.
(Exit Eve.)
Death. O woman, thou mayst flee in haste away
From all things else on earth, but not from me.

Act II, Scene VII (lines 2319-2381)

Death, in a soliloquy, rejoices in his coming dominion over the human race. All the young, the mighty, and the beautiful of earth will descend into the grave and be but a little dust.

Act II, Scene VIII (lines 2382-2504)

Lucifer instructs his followers that the fall of Eve is not enough, for Adam still remains. He has foreknowledge of their ultimate defeat by Jesus, the son of God and Mary, but is nevertheless constrained to achieve the necessary fall of Adam. He will make Eve his tool in the overthrow of her husband.

Act II, Scene IX

Enter Eve.

Eve (soliloquizes). Alas, unhappy me, where have I come?

Girt with what evils do I see myself!
In what snares am I caught, past all release!
Most evil spectacle! Ah, wicked serpent,
Is this the deity that I was promised?
Alas, to what strange state hast thou reduced me,
O faithless plotter and disloyal serpent!
But dost thou blame him? Blame thyself alone,
For giving credence to his lying faith.
Alas, thou tyrant slayer of thyself,
In thine own hand thou took'st this deadly shaft,
Then bent the bow, then shot it, struck thyself,
And compassed thine own death. Now dost thou blame
The serpent and thy destiny? Thyself,
A woman, thought to be a goddess. How
Could one created vile, infirm, and frail
Ever be changed to the Creator's essence?
Alas, what do I feel? Does yet the tempter
Faithless again assail me, and within,
As openly he tempted me but now,
Whispers the lying thought to me that I
Should tempt my husband, that he too may eat?
I do not want that, for it would be rash
If I should lead my husband on to sin.
What then? If I alone eat, and God blames me
For sins already done, shall I alone
Be caught, with blushes on my guilty face?
I'll make him eat too, so that I, a woman,
May be less blamed if Adam, being a man,
Eat likewise. Thus his fault were my defense.
But if he falls into the same dark error,
Will not the world be ruined through my act?
If I am lost, I little reck of others.
But no! because the life of me must be
Subordinated to the general weal.
That's if I had a share in other's good.
What greater sin than disobeying God?
Little I care, since I have done it too.
Would I have Adam die, so dear to me?
If I am dead, 'tis well that he dies too.
And shall I suffer God to curse my husband?
I, too, am cursed, and so can bear his lot.
And shall I have the heart to incur from God
Adam's exile from hence? How shall I not?
I outside and he inside? Certainly

I shall secure an equal loss for both.
Shall I subject him then to heavy toil?
Neither can I be idle, if I'd eat.
But I should think that I shall place in doubt
The everlasting safety of his soul.
What's that to me? I too have no assurance
That I shall gain salvation for myself.
But Adam is not guilty in my sin.
He too has guilt, because he left me here.
Did I not bid him go across the Garden?
But even so, he ought not to have gone.
Now take the deadly Apple, and go meet him!
But if I venture him with this sad face,
Will not my sin be openly betrayed?
In all my sorrow, I shall feign delight.
O foolish one, where art thou going now?
Do not these leafy twigs about thy waist
Give guiltily assurance of thy fall?
I strip myself, and know my nakedness,
Yet shall pretend to be all innocence.
Up now, and off! And tarry here no longer!
Alas, what do I do? How cold I am
And slow to undertake another's harm,
Yet glad and prompt I was to work my own!
But go now without fear and take this apple.
Did I not say, to me it was a dart
Wounding my breast? Then am I impious.
More impious was I to strike myself.
Behold, he comes. I gird me to the task.
And if I sinned, I'll cause him, too, to fall.

Act II, Scene X

The Same. Eve as before. Enter Adam.

Adam. Ah, how much I have wandered in the Garden
In search of him who called, and certainly
Sought him in vain, because I was deluded
By the murmur of the wind and of the wave.
How now, my consort, do I see thee glad?
What grieves thee? Or has grieved, a little since?
Troubled in countenance? Art thou not she
Whom here I left contented, more than merry?
What grievous thought is shadowing thy face?

What heavy sorrow weighs upon thy heart?
Eve. Although I don't perceive it, yet perhaps
My countenance has altered at thy absence.
Adam. But now, on my return, that troubled pallor
Ought from thy face to pass away at once
And all thy natural colour be restored.
Eve. So lost was it that it could not return
All in one instant to revive my cheeks.
Adam. If God were with thee here -- the primary joy
Of eye, affection, and devoted heart --
What could afflict thee, though I walked apart?
Eve. Then dost thou not desire me to love thee?
Adam. Yes, but with slower love than that for God.
Eve. And thus thy mighty love for me is spent?
Adam. It still is great, yet less than that for God.
Eve. Love has no limits when it always burns.
Adam. Heaven's love is infinite, but earth's is
finite.
Eve. Love is a flame of still-advancing fire.
Adam. But must not burn on till it loses God.
Eve. I wish to make a proof of this thy love.
Adam. What better is that than my plighted word?
Eve. Unless I test it, I am not content.
Adam. Hast thou no faith then in the words I speak?
Eve. I wish to see the thing that I believe.
Adam. I have no need to prove, if thou art sure.
Eve. I know that well, yet I should like to see it.
Adam. What proof of love is this that thou wouldst
see?
Eve. I fear denial of the thing I ask.
Adam. I shall deny thee nothing that is just.
Eve. I would not have my wishes trouble thee.
Adam. How could the thing thou wishest trouble me?
Eve. Adam, for love of thee I here would die.
Adam. To die is folly, if it help not others.
Eve. Do I not well, to show my great desire?
Adam. To what end is all this? Conclude the rest.
Eve. And wilt thou promise to comply at once?
Adam. Make known thy thought. I shall consider it.
Eve. Consider what? Obey me, and be silent!
Adam. As though I were without both brain and sense?
Eve. My dearest Adam, dost thou see this fruit?
Adam. I see it; it is from the Tree of Life.
Thou speak'st of it?

Eve. Of course.
Adam. What wouldst thou say?
For thou canst eat without my helping thee.
Eve. The fruit is fair, but we have fairer here.
Adam. But not at our disposal, as is this.
Dost thou cast eyes at the forbidden Tree?
Eve. What evil would it be to take a taste
And praise its sweetness greater than the rest?
Adam. What sayest thou? Hast thou the hardihood
To think of such a deed?
Eve. I've thought of it,
And I have plucked the Fruit and eaten it.
Behold, here is thy half awaiting thee.
Adam. Alas, what do I see? Art thou not dead?
Ah, woe is me that I am come to this!
And hast thou not this hour been blotted out
According to God's awful declaration?
Eve. Thou seest I am not sundered from myself.
Adam. Not dead?
Eve. I speak not, since thou seest it,
And me more strong and brave and beautiful.
I'd have thee eat it.
Adam. It may never be
That I should touch or eat that fatal fruit!
Eve. That is a clear sign that thou lov'st me not.
Adam. I love thee much, thou know'st. This is forbidden.
Eve. As proof thou lovest me, eat now the Apple!
Adam. How would it profit thee if I should eat?
Eve. Enough to know that such is my good pleasure.
Adam. Enough to know that it displeases God.
Eve. Thou shouldst consider only pleasing me.
Adam. And so neglect God's pleasure and His will?
Eve. A single time is not a great excess.
Adam. Is it not better to avoid God's wrath
Once only, than to die a thousand times?
I shall know how to clothe my face with strictness;
I shall know how to arm my heart with scorn,
Woman, against thy evil conversation.
Mayest thou be content for one brief hour
To have done evil! How then shouldst thou shun
To find companions for thy evil deed!
Wicked is he who sins; but guiltier far
Is he who leads another into ruin.

Eve. Art thou so strict? If, after all God's threats
No blow has fallen, the rest will not be true.
Adam. Ah, what unseemly speech! Is God a liar?
Why art thou angry, my dear wife? Sure he
Who does not punish others' faults, approves.
He who condemns not evil, yearns for it;
And he who blames not, treasures up the fruit.
Not more unjust is he who has done evil
Than he who urges sin and praises it.
Eve. Am I then dead? And yet I ate the Apple.
Adam. But to thy doom.
Eve. Damnation winks at me.
Adam. Thou'lt feel it presently.
Eve. Know'st thou the future?
Adam. I know the future by what God has spoken.
Eve. Did He fulfil it?
Adam. He did.
Eve. And I yet live?
Adam. Thou'rt dead, for Death is victor over thee.
Slave, dost thou joy in such dark tyranny?
Eve. In any case, the brave heart does not tremble.
Adam. Fear that is felt towards God is truly brave.
Eve. But let us pass from argument to action.
Adam. If I fear God, I'll not do such a deed.
Nor must I add a further sin to thine.
Eve. Come back to that. What evil have I done?
Adam. No greater could be acted or conceived.
Eve. (Aside) I'll see if flattery can move his heart.
(Aloud) Sweet Adam, tell me if thou lovest me,
Even as I love thee more than my life.
Adam. 'Tis more distress she gives me than advice.
Eve. I love thee as the idol of my heart;
Thou know'st that for thy love I'd lose myself
Wholly and utterly, without reserving,
That which for all the world must not be lost.
Now dost thou see how much I love thee, Adam?
Thou art the light of my sad eyes, my hope,
My precious treasure; then if it be true
Thou hast a spark of love, however small,
Truly thou then wilt not delay to eat.
Adam (aside). She moves me partly, softening my heart,

But love of Heaven masters me yet more.
Eve (aside). I'll seek to draw him to my will
with tears.
Adam (aside). She still creates new thoughts and
new occasions.
Yet stands the heart perplexed, the fight uncertain.
(To Eve) Dost thou not trust I love thee without
that?
Eve. Honest affection rather works than talks.
Such speech as thine brings doubt into the heart.
Adam. And thou wouldst have me eat it?
Eve. 'Tis my wish.
Adam. Thy wish is wickedness, if God forbids.
But calm thyself, e'en though I eat it not,
And end the doubt whether I love and prize thee.
Eve. Dost thou deny my one, my first request?
How shall I ever fix my hopes in thee?
Sure, I shall burst in tears, and ever lead
My life in wailing most disconsolate.
Adam. Weep not, my dear, it pains me to the heart.
Eve. If thou didst care, thou then wouldst do my
pleasure.
Adam. Ask any other proof of love than that.
Eve. Alas, my spouse is void of sympathy!
I shall go far away, see thee no more.
Adam. Alas, my treasure, do not leave me thus!
Eve. Thy voice may flatter, but thy heart is hard.
Adam. Ah, do not go, my dear!
Eve. Stay by thyself.
Adam. I shall do all thou wishest. Only stay!
Eve. What more dost thou desire of me? Wouldst
thou
Kill my kind spirit with discourtesy?
Adam. To comfort thee, I take it, though I fear.
Eve. I would not have thee eat it. Yes, no more
Do I request that. Wilt thou leave me now!
For if I am not thine, what dost thou want?
My only grief is that I love thee still.
I should know comfort if I loved thee not.
Adam. Thou knowest well my reasons. Do not grieve.
Eve. I know thee well, for I am in thy breast.
Unhappy Eve, to whom is thy heart lost?
Adam. Do not be angry.
Eve. Nay, I am not angry.

I would be angry, but my heart refuses
For still I dote on him that hates me so.
These eyes are rivers. Can they move thee not?
Adam. Weep not, my love!
Eve. Why dost thou not remove
The occasion for my tears? For if thou canst
Allow that, thou canst bear my weeping too.
Adam (pretending). To appease thee, lo, I take
the fruit and eat.
Eve. Truly? I do not like these jests of thine.
As far from her that loves thee is thy heart
As that untasted apple from thy mouth.
Adam. Gladly I'd do it, but my heart's afraid.
Eve. Since thou art ice where I, for thee, am fire.
Adam. Thou'lt have me eat it?
Eve. Trouble me no more.
How could he show more plain his lack of love?
Ah, wretched me! As I've a faithful heart,
I'll tear this hair, I'll quite destroy myself.
Adam. Stop, hold thy hand, Eve, if thou lovest me!
Eve. Dost thou, unripe in loving, speak of love?
Prevent my hand no more!
Adam. My sweetest dear,
Desist from weeping, tear thy hair no more.
Behold I promise thee to eat the Fruit.
Eve. A promise is a luke-warm lover's gift.
Adam. My darling, look, as I too eat the Fruit.

(He eats. Enter Sin, Guile, and Death.)

Ah, I am naked! Ah, what haughty monsters!
Sin. I am the greatest and most impious Tyrant
That e'er shall bind the bosom of the earth,
The Seven-headed One, thy fear and dread.
Guile. See with what haste the trees and plants
are stripped
To cover what's indecent to the eye!
Eve (looking at Guile). Alas, who is it that with
various skins
Changes her colour in such changing shapes?
From what Cave hast thou come to my damnation?
Guile. I have risen from the Cavern of thy heart.
Adam (to Sin). From whom hast thou so quickly
been begot?

Sin. Thou hast begotten me. Dost thou not know
 me?
And this shape so deformed (pointing to Death) is
 my dear daughter
Engendered in the world by me but now.
Eve (to Guile). Dost thou pursue me, ugly phantom?
 Lo,
I flee thee in the forest, yet, alack,
Dost thou not cease pursuit! (Exit Eve.)
Guile. Where wilt thou go
That I shall not pursue thee to the end.
(Exit Guile, pursuing.)
Adam. How is that from bodies not united
There comes an offspring that is born of both?
Sin. It yet is true that without mating flesh
Thou art my father and fair Eve my mother.
Adam. Could she bring forth so hideous a son?
Sin. Then I too made her pregnant and begot
Yonder grand-daughter of her sinful loins.
Adam. I see no sign of any due resemblance.
How is it true that thou art born of us?
Sin. I cannot tell thee further; but with thought
Thou wilt regard my statement as the truth.
Adam. Deformed and foolish monster, where in thee
Mirrors itself the amiable grace
Of Eve and me? If parents should be found
Moulded once more within their children's face
By Mother Nature's laws of generation?
Sin. The case is worse when the first living issue
Is so deformed and monstrous that the man
Who has begot it thinks it is not his.
It is not true then that thy first-born child
(For I indeed am thine) resembles thee.
Would he were like the father that begot him!
Deformity is mine, and that I prize --
For if I had been beautiful and charming
I should not be existent in the world,
Because my essence is impure and ugly.
Adam. Who art thou then? Oh, tell me clearly, thou
That, to keep up my great anxieties,
Hast now appeared in such peculiar form
And dost with brute invincibility
Confound the thinking and oppress the heart?
Sin. He am I who now girdles thee with branches

And loads thy bosom with atrocious pain.
Death. And I am she whom thy offense has sent
Into the world, more rapid than the whirlwind,
Horrid beyond all horror, furious
Beyond all fury, raw beyond all rawness,
And cruel past all cruelty, in form
Dressed in no human shape. Regard me well.
Adam. My own hand made this girdle; nor did I
Send thee into the world, misshapen Monster.
Death. Thou liest, by that word. For I lay buried
Deep in oblivion, and thou didst wake me
When proudly to the high forbidden Fruit
(First plucked in folly from its fatal tree)
Thy hand was stretched, weakened by lamentation.
Adam. Now I should like at last to learn your names.
Sin. I am foul Sin.
Death. And I am cruel Death.
Adam. Woe is me! Sin and Death? I flee away
Because I cannot bear your horrid faces. (Runs off.)
Sin. Vain is thy thought in thinking to escape me;
Closer to thee am I than to myself.
Death. And me, who shall unfold my wings at length
In Heaven itself to strike God's only Son,
How wilt thou manage to escape from me?
What man by chance, by fortune, or by lot
Shall e'er escape the sickle of pale Death?
(Exit Death.)

Act II, Scene XI (lines 2838-2904)

Sin soliloquizes, glorying in the wide range of activity now open before him, especially in his seven deadly aspects of pride, avarice, lechery, wrath, gluttony, envy and sloth.

Act II, Scene XII (lines 2905-2922)

Eve, trying in vain to escape from Guile, learns with shame the latter's identity and intimate place in her own life.

Act II, Scene XIII (lines 2923-3013)

Guile, in a long soliloquy, analyses the infinite variety and resourcefulness of female wickedness. Woman is completely saturated with guile, deceit, falsehood, and depravity.

Act II, Scene XIV (lines 3014-3159)

A dialogue between Mercy and Omnipotence. Mercy has laid aside her former rags and has now "in hope put on green and beautiful garments." She rejoices in Adam's "fortunate fault", and is upbraided by Omnipotence for being glad at the pain and ruin of another. Mercy prophesies that a day will come when, through a Death on a Cross, she will call the dead to life. A Chorus of Angels then laments the depravity of Eve and its calamitous consequences.

Act III, Scene I

Enter Adam and Eve.

Adam. Whence have we fallen so unhappily?
From the first happy state of innocence
Into the greatest sum of woe and grief.
Ungrateful Adam, hast thou changed thy lot?
By thy own greedy will, thou art deprived
Of whatsoever good things thy Creator
Bestowed upon thee in that first, fair hour
When into thee He breathed the breath of Heaven.
Eve. Oh evil accident, untimely fate!
What refuge have I from such penalties?

Enter Omnipotence, left, unobserved.

Omn. (aside). Laments and weeping do I hear near by.
Who might those persons be attired in leaves?
But if their converse is about the Fall,
They will be Eve and Adam. It is they.
I'll stand aside to hear what's in their hearts
And to observe their actions and their words.
Adam (addressing himself). Vain, arrogant, most

wanton, and most proud,
Didst thou not turn thine eyes back to the promise,
Considering how unequal in its essence
Is man's foul frailty compared with God?
And how it is quite contrary to reason
For clay to match the Uncreated One
From whom it has its being and its moving?
Eve. Already we had seen the impious One
Who wished to raise his throne as high as God's,
Whence he and the companions of his fall
Were purged from Paradise. Was his example
(Fools that we are) no adequate restraint
To hold the hand back from its poisonous act?
Omn. (aside). How sorrowful and doleful and half-
dead
Are now the hearts and breasts and eyes of both!
Vanished is all their friendly gaiety,
And jest and joke and laughter, quip and song.
Adam. Had such a change from man to deity
Been possible, as it, the serpent said,
It would itself have taken its advice.
If otherwise, did not the arrogance
That it made manifest, affronting God,
Reveal it as a vile and wicked thing?
Omn. (aside). If my companion, Mercy, were but here
And hear these heavy accents and laments,
Sure she would blush in shame with both her cheeks.
Eve. Alas, he well said that our eyes would open:
But only to shed tears, to see the traces
Of a thousand ills and how deformed is evil.
Adam. Oh, how diverse and different in thee
The outcome from the intention, for those means
Which lifted thee in pride have brought thee down,
Reducing thee (unripe, alas, and wanton)
From mighty lord to something less than slave!
God (at first a distant voice, gradually approaching).
Adam, where are thou?
Adam. Hark, I'm good as dead!
My Master seeks me. What am I to do?
God. Adam! Adam!
Adam. Dost hear that still, small voice?
Eve. What should we do, alas, if God thus calls us?
Adam. Ah, woe is me, alas!
Eve. Into this thicket!

Come, let us flee to hide ourselves from Him.
<u>God</u>. Where art thou, Adam?
<u>Eve</u>. Answer not a word.
Under this fig-tree's shadow let us flee
And crouch in utter silence, though He call us.
<u>God</u>. Adam, where art thou?
<u>Eve</u> (to Adam). We are hidden here.
<u>God</u> (entering). O Adam, dost thou hide thyself from me
Among those branches, and avoid my face?
Come here, thou ingrate, quickly! Dost thou shun me?
<u>Adam</u>. I heard Thy voice, Lord, in the garden now,
And as I was ashamed, being thus naked,
I ran in haste to hide among these branches.
<u>God</u>. And who has told thee, Adam, thou wert naked?
Who opened wide thine eyes to shame and scorn?
Who taught thee thus to cloak thyself with branches?
Unless it be the Tree that only now
I did forbid thee. Hast thou eaten, wretch?
And did I not foretell thee thy perdition?
What blindness led thee to commit such evil?
<u>Adam</u>. The woman that Thou gavest me as mate
Gave me the Apple, and in madness, I,
Forgetful of Thy strictest ordinance,
And softened further by her constant weeping,
Ate it, unhappy man, and sought my death.
<u>Omn</u>. (aside). A greater evil and a greater loss
Could not have come upon him in this world.
<u>God</u>. And thou, inconstant woman, why didst thou
Despising my command, stretch out thy hand
To steal the fatal Apple and to eat it?
<u>Eve</u>. Alas, my Lord, the soft insidious serpent,
Peaceful and ever gentle in appearance,
Was found by me filled full of fraud within.
In aspect it appeared devoid of guile,
But with an unsound heart and crooked mind.
In speech it seemed all candour and all truth,
But at the last its tongue proved poisonous.
It seemed to take much joy in others' good,
But speech and spirit did not correspond.
With flattery it offered many hopes,
But they were lies and phantoms, every one.
This faithless creature, Lord, beguiled my heart.

Omn. (aside). This is the pleasant fruit of bootless sin --
Sighing and lamentation, pain and grief.
God. Since thou hast done this much, O evil serpent,
Cursèd art thou amongst all animals.
Crawling upon the earth, thy evil breast
Shall bear thy evil body's heavy weight;
Nay more, the base and ever-dirty earth
Shall be thy filthy food; in a vile cave
Thou'lt lead thy life, never to rise again.
Omn. (aside). Behold the harvest of unworthy sin!
Sagacious Mercy, my companion, now
At such a time of flood escapes in haste.
God (to the Serpent). Since thou didst join with Eve to my disgrace,
Between her seed and thine I shall decree
Such hatred, such hostility and scorn,
That thou, by very aspect, shalt benumb
The blood within her veins; if thou advance
Thyself insidiously against her ankle,
Thou'lt cause her death, and she shall bruise thy head
Under her foot. (To Eve.) Further to thee I add
Grief upon grief, O woman, pain on pain,
And place thee in the arms of Evil Fortune.
She with false hopes and fear most genuine
Will nourish thee in bitter and fierce pain.
More than one child shalt thou conceive; but sad
Wilt thou in long protracted child-bed be.
Before thou wrapp'st thy babe in swaddling clothes,
Thou'lt plunge thyself in blood and lamentation.
I shall subject thy proud and faithless head
To the harsh mastery of this thy husband;
Restricted to the pale of his commands,
Thou canst not ever take a step beyond;
And this harsh yoke is admirably designed
To curb thy arrogance, O haughty woman.
Omn. (aside). I feel my heart melt and my bosom split
That my companion Mercy is not here
To learn the sad effects of her desire.
God. Adam, since thou didst hearken to her voice
And since her weeping and her feignèd sighs

Did break thy heart and vanquish thee with crying,
And since, spurred on by her pretence of love,
Thou yet didst eat of the forbidden Tree,
Curs'd shall the soil of Earth be for thy sake,
Through all the days of all thy troubled life,
Which shall be only murky, foul, and black.
Like a coarse beast shalt thou devour the grass;
And though, tired out and panting, thou employ
Iron to plough the earth, it stubbornly
In thy despite shall yield thee thorns and brambles;
And only after copious sweat has flowed
Down from thy burning face, shalt thou eat bread.

Omn. (aside). Oh, these are bitter mouthfuls to digest --
Toil, scorn and hatred, and, to end them, death.

God. And since, O ingrate, thou hast dared too much,
Begone from out the Garden!

Adam. O my Lord,
The woman made me err. 'Twas not my fault.

God. Depart, thou rebel, without more delay.

Eve. The Serpent, Lord, was the cause of all this evil.

Omn. (apostrophizing absent Mercy). Perceive, my good Companion, pray perceive,
Thou who didst jest in folly to the winds.

God. Depart outside, I say!

Adam. Have pity, Lord!

(Exit God.)

Angel (entering with flaming sword).
Lo, I shall smite thee with this sharp-edged sword
If thou delayest longer. Go at once!
First take and cloak your bodies with these skins,
And then depart, returning here no more.

Adam. Where shall I go, alas?

Eve. What road is this?

Angel. Go, for you still could make yourselves Immortal
By feeding on the deathless Tree of Life.

Adam. Ah, woe is me!

Eve. Alas, where shall we go?

(Exeunt Adam and Eve.)

Omn. My comrade Mercy in some spot, I'm sure,
Finds pleasure for herself on this occasion;

And while she jests among delights and comforts,
She has no feeling for the pangs of others.
Angel. With sword in hand I tarry here, that none
May enter. Well I guard the way that seeks
The Tree of Life, so that no mortal man
May pluck its fruit and taste Eternity.

Act III, Scene II (lines 3338-3508)

Mercy dances and sings for joy, much to the indignation of Omnipotence. They meet Adam and Eve, led in chains by exultant Death, Sin, and Guile. Mercy is still joyful, and foretells the Incarnation and Atonement.

Act III, Scene III

Enter Lucifer, Belial, Benemoth and Megaera.

Luc. Hurrah!
Bel. How glad we are!
Ben. No other triumph
Has ever been more splendid in our times.
Meg. I have been happy to enlarge my Kingdom.
Luc. How has the end been equal to my hopes!
Who ever had expected from a woman
Such arts, deceits, frauds and duplicities?
'Tis well for me that I have found her such.
In my high enterprise, I shall not want
More warriors than her, nor shall I often
Use other weapons than her subtle tongue.
Saw you her circumspect and crafty ways
While she concealed the arrow of my power?
And oh, what crooked snares and plots she plied
So that, as I her, she, the sly seductrix,
Might vanquish him -- and I might win them both!
No means she left untried to influence him
To lay a thieving hand upon the Apple.
Now she seemed faint and pale and languishing;
Now loving, now unloving, flame and frost,
One look avoided him, the next pursued him,
Now she would have this, then she'd have it not,
Now showed a grim face, now a merry one.
Up, up, Megaera! Come, so fair a work

Deserves the recompense of our rewards!
Meg. They know right well that cruel Hell's rewards
Are blows, and its caresses naught but shame;
That he who plunders most is most the prey
Of that consuming flame that never fails.
Who makes most profit shall acquire most torment;
He who slays, dies; the conqueror is conquered;
Who arms himself with hatred, wrath and scorn,
Shall in abundance find those very things;
He who does evil, gains more evil still.
Luc. Benemoth, tell us of the work thou didst.
Ben. A wondrous thing, and thou, my Prince, didst hear it.
Laying aside this spiritual body,
I stood within her mouth and made her say
With that soft, flattering and faithless voice:
"Adam, thou art my life. I die for thee
Thou art my treasure dear and all my joy!"
Touched in his heart, he then put forth his hand,
And took the Apple from her. Now consider
If such a deed deserve not a reward.
Luc. Why not? Thou shalt enjoy thy labor's fruit.
Come here, Megaera.
Meg. Ready and quick am I.
Luc. Thou heardest his achievements. What reward
(For thou art now the treasurer of Hell)
Hast thou for this one, paying him in full?
Meg. Among my treasures yonder in the Pit
For those whose mouths hiss hideous infamies,
I keep a boiling cauldron on the fire,
Filled to the brim with sulphur, pitch, and poison.
Pouring this blazing brew into a goblet,
I'll have him drink a deep and grateful toast
Unto Your Highness.
Luc. Surely I should like
From my belovèd, faithful Benemoth
To enjoy just such a toast.
Meg. I promise now
To give him such good measure, so abundant,
That it shall overflow the great Cup's lip.
Wait. I shall go, and come without delay.
(Exit Megaera.)
Luc. I understand now well that in mankind
The worst of evils is the power of love

That opens up the pathway of the heart
To amorous flattery from a loving woman.
Love was wrapped up in folds of lying speech
To serve the impulse of my dire attack.
For when she arched her brows and turned on him
Crude glances, lifting up her voice to Heaven
In vehement profession of devotion,
All was for me a subtle form of guile.

Enter Megaera with Devils bearing cauldron.

Meg. Support the cauldron well, so that the sweetest
Nectar of Hell may spill not nor be spoiled.
Make firm your shoulders underneath the pot.
Do ye turn eyes away to shun the smoke?
Can ye be steeped in reek, and yet evade it?
He who is used to pain should feel it not.
Stand firm thus, while I take the mighty urn.
Do thou here pinion both the drinker's arms;
And let another bring the liquor rare
And prop it to his mouth, that he may drink.
Behold the Cup! A health to toast the Prince!
Ben. A toast, my Prince.
Luc. Drink it, for thy heart's good.
Meg. (to Ben.) Stand still, thou beast! Why dost thou shake and shift?
Ben. No bitter wormwood more! Alas, I'm dead!
No more black gall! No more, it tortures me!
Ah, change the drink, and keep this brew for others!
Meg. Each one who sins must have his penalty.
Come, taste again! Perhaps it will be sweet.
Dost thou, ungrateful, flee from my caress?
Ben. Cruel Megaera, wilt thou never stay
Thy tireless hand? Alas, stop but a moment.
Unfortunate are we: we shun one reef
But strike on others with a greater wreck.
For if thou art not hot to do the will
Of Lucifer, such rage is his that scourges,
Wielded by hands of his dread ministers,
Rain down upon thy back and new misfortune
Is added to thine ancient, evil pains.
If then with evil doing thou floutest Heaven,
Thou feel'st the bitter hand of this one, working
So torturous that Hell, compared with her,

Is but a flowering garth, a fair abode.
Lo, I, that erst refused before the Prince
To tempt this Eve, then had my back well broken;
And now, for helping her to ruin Adam,
God smites me, through Megaera, beyond measure.
Meg. Since thou didst bait her tongue with
sweetest words,
So that Eve's speech surpassed all honey sweetness,
I shall cut out thy tongue. Lo, I have cut it,
And turn it on the point of my grim knife.
Ben. It has been torn away. Do I still talk?
Meg. Hear a deep mystery: to eternalize
Eternal pain in thee, thy tongue's destroyed,
But, born again in perpetuity,
Destroyed anew, it rises up anew,
And though it dies in pain a thousand times,
Revives a thousand times to taste the fire.
Ben. O wrath implacable! Eternal pain!
Meg. What other fiendish bosom makes its boast
In flattery? Why ought that gallant Belial,
Who likewise had a great part in the fight,
Remain without reward? I'd be discourteous
If I should fail to honour him as well.
Luc. (to *Bel*.) Narrate thy dark devices in due
order.
Bel. Through the man's constancy that, full of
Heaven,
He showed in stout defense, the victory
Already was despaired of, in that Eve,
After those preludes fair of jest and sport,
Was fain to cease from fight, as one defeated.
Then did I help her in her weakest part
(But which, to cast to earth, is strongest still);
I entered at her eyes, and softening
The marble heart of Adam with false weeping,
I moved his heart and lifted up his hand
To take the Apple, then, grown stronger, raised it
To meet his mouth, then opened it and placed it
Within his jaws. He ate it, and was lost.
Luc. Megaera, didst thou hear his merry deed
And victory? Now ponder the reward.
Meg. It has been pondered and is all prepared.
Through eyes he won; in eyes is his reward.
Down in the everlasting Pit I keep

A spit so sharp and charming to behold
That it were merry now to prove its point
In honouring his eyes. Now wait you here!
I shall descend and bring it hastily
In this my red and burning right hand. Wait!
Bel. That victory should mean my punishment
(In due fulfilment of the law divine
That he who wrongs mankind should merit pain),
I suffer all unwilling; yet I must,
For I am powerless. Behold Megaera
Come fiercely, like the Fury that she is,
Rushing with dagger, spit, and hookèd irons.
Meg. I am here, Belial.
Bel. May thy black neck break!
Meg. I shall gouge out thy eyesight with this iron.
(To her devils.) Bind him, bind him with ropes, lest he escape!
Bel. Alas, what pain! Art thou not glutted yet?
Meg. Now I am satisfied. The eye is out.
Behold it, cut and bloody on the spit.
Is the left eye (that wrought its evil too),
Shut in its socket, to stay unrewarded?
It, too, I shall require to drag out.
Give me that iron hook. It's good for that.
Dost think to soften with evasive shrinking
The iron or my arm? That were in vain.
Bel. Alas, abate the iron! Ah, just outrage!
Meg. One slow slash in, one slithering gouge out,
And I'll relieve thee of the weight of eyes.
Bel. Ah, what atrocious penalty of Hell
Is harder than the ruthless hand of God!
Meg. Thy grievous cries cannot persuade high Heaven
To extinguish at its ministers' just hands
Its ruthless wrath. Behold, here is the eye.
I have pulled it out to punish thee for sin.
Bel. O Heaven, thou art vengeful, strict and harsh!
I rather would endure a thousand hells
Than thy most passionate and awful wrath.
My two eyes are torn out, and yet I see --
Reborn and then extinguished in new pangs,
The flame alike their mother and their tomb,
The fire at once their father and their bier!
Begotten from dead eyes, they see again.

Luc. Ah, mad fool that I was! What should I do,
Who have perverted heart and mind and senses
That Eve might pass to death, fatal first cause
And first occasion of all ill success?
Am I to suffer blows and penalties?
Of what sort will my hellish torments be?
Ho there! Ho there, my men! (Thus Heaven commands.)
Even I, a rebel, impious and proud,
Cannot, alas, escape the wrath of God.
Then gather hastily, with the hoarse sound
Of the Tartarean trumpet, each who walks
Beneath the hollow concave of my kingdom,
The darkest, fiercest, and most evil spirits,
And let the rudest and the strongest of them
Drag hither straight my Stygian chariot,
That I victoriously may mount upon it
With triumph and with palm-branch, as befits
The elevation of so vast a power
As baffled God and mastered mortal man.
Meg. Up, up, with treasures and with ornaments,
With gems, these pearls and carbuncles and gold,
With all the equipage Hell gives her own
And gladly decks the chariot of her Prince!
Why do ye tarry? Are ye indolent?
Here at the brink I wait, and if delay
Impede you further, I shall come in wrath
And make your punishment still more severe.
Ben. Each one advances with the greatest speed,
And none delays his hand in idleness.
Bel. The chariot is begirt, as is our wont,
With flaming garnets; let the street be gay
With flowers beyond measure; here and there
Let blushing purple and vermilion gleam.
Meg. Are all things ready?
Ben. Nothing remains undone.
Meg. (to the devils, severally)
Thou, with the shrilling trumpet, shalt go first;
And ye, as battle-chargers, draw the chariot.
Thou shalt be charioteer. Ye four in front,
Sing loud the madrigal of the Abyss
And march in front, leading the merry dance.
I, the avenging servant of God's wrath,
With this red fire burning in my breast,
Shall to the Prince and to you all together

Redouble, for your double victory,
My fires. Behold us here before the Throne.
The haughty Prince may mount his chariot.
But first of all, go crown his head with fire!

(They place a crown of flame on _Lucifer's_ head.)

Luc. Ah, luckless one! What fatal victory!
The sky has not so many shining stars,
The sea has not so many salty drops,
Earth's bosom does not bear as many seeds,
Nor are there grains of sand so numerous
As I feel pangs of anguish in this hour!
Yet, being the foul cause of deadly pain,
Should I not look to suffer even more?
Meg. Lo, I, who am elected to this office,
Kindle the flames still more about thee here.

Chorus of Devils

O Stygians, come with thunders
Of praise to greet your King
And celebrate the wonders
He wrought in vanquishing
Man to his black damnation
Through treason to his Lord.
Come, all Hell's population,
To witness his reward!
His prize is pain eternal
Amid the searing flame,
Since he with guile infernal
Brought man to death and shame.

Luc. Grief have I now forever, boundless grief;
Solace for others will enhance my pain.
Ah, the irrevocable scorn of Heaven!

Chorus of Devils

At his redoubled wailing,
Come forth and view him well,
Drawn by Might all-prevailing
Right to the throat of Hell.
That is his nest forever;

Thence came he, to man's pain;
And now, from his endeavour,
Behold he comes again.
In triumph comes the victor;
And yet, another's sin
Binds him in torment stricter
Than man shall taste herein.
(Exeunt omnes.)

Act III, Scene IV (lines 3773-3896)

Adam, in sad soliloquy, reproaches the serpent, the woman, the apple, and finally himself.

Act III, Scene V (lines 3897-4090)

The four Elements (Earth, Water, Air, and Fire) recount to Adam the disastrous effects of the Fall so far as they severally are concerned.

Act III, Scene VI (lines 4091-4223)

Mercy meets the penitent and disconsolate Adam and Eve, and consoles them by foretelling the salvation that is to come through Christ, their descendant, the incarnate Son of God.

Act III, Scene VII (lines 4224-4306)

Adam and Eve are comforted and reaffirm their confidence in God. They decide to seek abundant progeny through wedded union, in order that their divine Descendant may come all the sooner.

Act III, Scene VIII (lines 4307-4339)

Death in soliloquy complains that no one has died yet. She is still unfed.

Act III, Scene IX (lines 4340-4449)

Lucifer and his lieutenants, aware of the promised Atonement of Christ, plan to pervert the Learts of mankind so that His sacrifice will be rejected. They will instigate such horrid sins as fratricide, and estrange man from God.

Act IV, Scene I (lines 4450-4517)

Adam assigns to his sons, Cain and Abel, the duties of farming and of sheep-tending respectively.

Act IV, Scene II (lines 4518-4629)

Eve's two daughters, Calamana and Delbora, quarrel and tear each other's hair, Eve lamenting the while these effects of her fall. She rebukes them and finally beats them.

Act IV, Scene III (lines 4630-4835)

Cain is grieved because God favours Abel and not himself. Abel piously explains that the fault is in Cain's own heart. This explanation does not improve Cain's disposition.

Act IV, Scene IV (lines 4836-4915)

Adam relates to Eve a dreadful dream. A fierce wolf murders a lamb. Later an archer shoots the wolf and also a foolish servant.

Act IV, Scene V (lines 4916-5103)

Megaera, Sin, Guile and Death plan further their campaign for destroying mankind. Sin will cause Cain to murder Abel.

Act IV, Scene VI (lines 5104-5285)

Adam entreats Cain to love his brother Abel, explaining that God accepts Abel's sacrifice because it is offered with the heart while Cain's is not. Cain questions the existence of God and asserts all to be from chance and nature. He declares his hatred for Abel.

Act IV, Scene VII (lines 5286-5448)

Cain murders righteous Abel. A chorus of angels comes to escort Abel's soul to Heaven. Cain hides the body.

Act IV, Scene VIII (lines 5449-5493)

God curses Cain and drives him into exile.

Act IV, Scene IX (lines 5494-5622)

Adam and Eve lament their murdered son, and reproach themselves for this consequence of their own primal disobedience.

Act IV, Scene X (lines 5623-5864)

Lamech and his servant Cintio discuss the unhappiness that women bring to men. They decide to go hunting.

Act IV, Scene XI (lines 5865-5937)

Cain now an old man, is led back by Sin and Death to the spot where he murdered Abel. Cain longs for death, and is told to hide in a thicket.

Act IV, Scene XII (lines 5938-6116)

Lamech, misdirected by Cintio, shoots Cain by mistake. Enraged at the stupidity of his servant, he kills the latter as well. The second part of Adam's dream is thus fulfilled.

Act V, Scene I (lines 6117-6188)

Mercy assures Omnipotence that she will ultimately outdo her, and that man will be raised to Heaven.

Act V, Scene II (lines 6189-6408)

Lucifer and his court plan to teach mankind

the hellish arts of war and so estrange man further from God.

Act V, Scene III (lines 6409-6512)

Adam and Eve, grieving over the consequences of the Fall upon mankind, decide to petition God for mercy for their posterity.

Act V, Scene IV (lines 6513-6561)

Mercy accosts Sin, Guile, and Death. They are insolent and defiant, but at her word they fall with dismay into Hell.

Act V, Scene V (lines 6562-6776)

Mercy is dressed in lacy robes, wears a crown, and carries a sceptre and a green olive branch. Omnipotence is still unconvinced that God will show clemency to man.

Act V, Scene VI (lines 6777-6817)

An Angel comes and reconciles Omnipotence and Mercy as equal attributes of one and the same Deity. In the first creation each had a share; for Omnipotence 'produced it from nothing', but Mercy bestowed it as a gift. So too with the work of redemption.

Act V, Scene VII (lines 6818-7023)

Adam and Eve, in the presence of God, ask Him to punish them but to be merciful on their posterity. God declares His delight in them, and announces that His love, through the Atonement, will ransom Adam and all his race.

Act V, Scene VIII (lines 7024-7049)

The Goodness of God epilogizes, proclaiming the infinity of God's compassion in opening to man, through the Cross, the gates of Heaven and eternal life.

JOSEPH BEAUMONT

Psyche, or Love's Mystery (1648)

I, 6.

A MYSTERY, which other Shades beset;
Substantial Shades, made up of solid Hate;
Born in the Deep, which knows no bottom, yet
Vent'ring to block up Heaven's sublimest gate:
   Whilst Belzebub, in blackness damn'd to dwell,
   Plots to have all things else as dark as Hell.

7.

For He, th'immortal Prince of equal spight,
Abhors all Love in every name and kind;
But chiefly that which burns with flames as bright
As his are swarthy, and as endless find
   Their living fuel: These enrage him so,
   That all Hell's Furies must to council go.

8.

For (as the wounded Lyon frights his Den
By roaring out his grief;) his shatter'd heart
Vomits a hideous groan, which thundring in
His hollow realm, bellow'd to every part
   The frightful summons: all the Peers below
   Their King's voice by its sovereign stink did
      know.

9.

Nor dar'd they stay their tails vast volumes to
Abridge into a knot's Epitome;
Or trim their hoofs foul cleft with iron shoe,
Or their snarl'd snakes confusion unty;
   Only their paws they fill with Rage, and bring
   That desperate subsidy to their mad King. . . .

16.

His awful Horns above his crown did rise,
And force his fiends to shrink in theirs: his face
Was triply-plated Impudence: his Eyes
Were Hell reflected in a double glass,
   Two Comets staring in their bloody stream,
   Two Beacons boyling in their pitch and flame. . . .

20.

I yield not yet; Defiance Heav'n, said He,
And though I cannot reach thee with my fire,
Yet my unconquer'd Brain shall able be
To grapple with thee; nor canst thou be higher
   Than my brave Spight: Know, though below I dwell,
   Heav'n has no stouter Hearts than strut in
      Hell. . . .

22.

Courage my Lords; ye are the same, who once
Ventur'd on that renown'd Design with me
Against the Tyrant call'd Heav'n's righteous Prince.
What though Chance stole from us that Victory?
   'Twas the first field we fought; and He being in
   His own Dominion, might more easily win. . . .

31.

Was't not enough, against the righteous Law
Of Primogeniture, to throw us down,
From that bright Home, which all the World do's know
Was by most clear Inheritance our own:
   But, to our shame, Man, that vile Worm must dwell
   In our fair Orbs, and Heaven with vermin fill?. . .

VI, 115.

All things at first was God, who dwelt alone
In his unbounded self: but bounteous He
Conceiv'd the form of this Creation
That other things by Him might Happy be.
   A way to ease his streams his Goodness sought,

And at the last into a World burst out.

116.

Which World at first was but one single step
From simple Nothing; yet that step was wide:
No Power but His, or could, or yet can leap
Over to Something's bank from Nothing's side.
If you those Distances compare with this,
The East and West are one, the Poles will kiss.

117.

This Something, Son of Nothing, in the gulf
Of its own monstrous Darkness wallowing lay.
And strangely lost in its confounded self
Knew neither where to go, nor where to stay,
Being hideously besieg'd on every side
With Tohu's and with Bohu's boundless Tide. . . .

123.

Forth flew th' Eternal Dove, and tenderly
Over the floods blind tumult hovering,
The secret seeds of vital Energy
Wak'd by the virtue of his fostering Wing:
Much like the loving Hen, whose brooding care
Doth hatch her eggs and life's warm way
prepare. . . .

221.

Eve, Topstone of the goodly-fram'd Creation,
The Bliss of Adam and the Crown of Nature;
Eve, who enjoys the most removed station
From ugly Chaos; Eve that final Creature,
In whom th' Almighty Lord set up his rest,
And only spar'd to say He'd done his best.

222.

Her spatious polish'd forehead was the fair
And lovely Plain where gentle Majesty
Walk'd in delicious state: her temples clear

Pomgranate fragments, which rejoyc'd to lie
   In dainty ambush, and peep through their cover
   Of amber-locks whose volumes curled over. . . .

232.

Her blessed Bosom moderately rose
With two soft Mounts of Lilies, whose fair top
A pair of pritty sister Cherrys chose,
And there their living Crimson lifted up.
   The milky count'nance of the Hills confest
   What kind of Springs within had made their nest.

233.

So leggiadrous were her snowy Hands
That *Pleasure* mov'd as any finger stirr'd:
Her virgin waxen Arms were precious Bands
And chains of Love: Her waste it self did gird
   With its own graceful Slenderness, and ty
   Up *Delicacy's* best Epitomy. . . .

252.

In this condition did they live and love,
And by perpetual interchange of hearts
Fairly transcribe our blessed life above
Where through his eye his Soul each Angel darts
   In his fellow's breast, that all may be
   In common blest by one felicity. . . .

255.

To *Paradise* he rush'd, and brought his Hell
Into that earthly Heav'n, whose dwellers he
With anxious eye survey'd and mark'd, until
A Creature brisk and spruce he chanc'd to see
   Upon a bank of floury pleasures spred,
   But far more sweet and beauteous than its bed.

256.

It was the *Serpent*, whose illustrious skin
Play'd with the Sun and sent him back his beams

With glorious use: that Wealth which glisters in
The proudest strand of oriental Steams,
   Salutes Aurora's cheek with fewer raies
   Than this bright robe did all heav'ns highnoon
      face.

257.

His sharpest Eyes sparkled with nimble flames,
The light by which his active Soul was read:
Wisdom and Art, with all their plots and frames
Chose their chief shop in his judicious head.
   Above his fellows on Crafts wings he flew;
   All Beasts but he to that dull Name were true.

258.

This Agent Belzebub approv'd; and as
He fed upon his couch, mix'd with his meat;
Which ambush help'd him his Lips guard to pass,
Where (having taught his bane to relish sweet)
   He eas'ly won the Entry of his Throat
   And down into his bosom's centre shot. . . .

267.

The wary foe thus plants his Battery
Against the Castles female weakest side;
Judiciously hoping that if he
Can there but make a breach, the fortify'd
   And well-mann'd Posts will soon appalled be,
   And yield up all their strength for company. . . .

271.

Unhappy Error that, which could invite
The jealous Tempter to be bold, since she
Had robb'd her self of all her Spouse's Might
By starting from his holy company.
   But all the way the spightful Serpent went,
   He put on looks of contrary Intent.

272.

For Love and Friendship smiled in his eyes,
Fair on his face sate Tenderness and Care:
His flattering Neck he bowed thrice, and thrice
His silent homage he presented her:
   And then, fair Queen of Paradise, said he,
   Why must the Prince be bound, and Subjects
      free? . . .

274.

Admiring Eve, who had presum'd till now
That Speech had been Man'd privilege alone;
Thought fair respect to this new Talker due,
And freely join'd communication:
   Right glad withal to meet another here,
   Who with Discourse could entertain her ear.

275.

Nay courteous Serpent, she replyed, we
Have large Commission, and our God is kind:
He gives us leave to feast on every Tree,
And pick and choose and freely please our minde;
   Bate but that one of Knowledge, on whose boughs
   Death, certain Death (for so he tells us)
      grows. . . .

283.

For yesterday, when first I 'gan to taste
The sprightful Fruit, flames kindled in mine eyes;
My Soul awak'd, and from my bosom chas'd
Those Mists of Ignorance, whose thick disguise
   Muffled my thoughts, and kept me down a beast
   As dark and dull as any of the rest. . . .

292.

Up went her desperate hand, and reach'd away
The whole world's Bliss whilst she the Apple took.
When lo, with paroxisms of strange dismay
Th' amazed Heav'ns stood still, Earth's basis shook,

The troubled Ocean roard, the startled Air
In hollow grones profoundly breath'd its fear.
. . .

298.

Her Heart, till now soft as the Turtles sighs,
Forgets its heav'n-inamoring Tenderness,
And with the stubborn Parian Marble vies:
Her Thoughts, before all Sons of Love, profess
No trade but Mischief, deeply plotting how
To propagate that Death she liv'd in now.

299.

Nor fears her Rage to play the Serpent too,
Mad at her innocent Husband's blessed state,
And him with sweet-invenom'd kindness woo
To taste of Hell, and swallow down his fate;
Wherefore the goodliest Apples having cull'd,
Her treacherous hands with those fair baits she fill'd.

300.

Thus with a loving Glance, and modest smile,
(Those mighty Arms by which all females fight)
She charg'd his eye; and seconded that Guile
By trying at his ear this vocal sleight:
O wellcom, wellcom, since I now have here
A banquet fit to entertain my Dear.

301.

Soul-fatning Cates, seeds of Divinity,
Edible Wisdom, and a mystic feast
Of high Illuminations. Ask not why
Our jealous God injoin'd us not to taste
Of that whose most refining energy
Would raise us to be Gods as well as He.

302.

As for the bugbear Threat of Death, behold

Its confutation in still-florid Me
Since I have been thus fortunately bold,
Shall needless Dread a Coward make of Thee!
   Fall to, my joy; I have thy Taster been.
   Think not the seeking thine own Bliss, a sin.

303.

So spake insidious Eve. But he agast,
Deeply agast, reply'd with groans and sighs:
Sadly he shak'd his head, and smote his breast,
And roll'd to heav'n his lamentable eyes.
   Alas no need, no need was there of arms
   Him to secure against his Consort's charms. . . .

305.

In aw a while it kept it: but at last
Commiseration of his Spouse's case
Grew to such strength in his too tender breast
As, to himself all pity to displace.
   Eve sate so near to his uxorious heart
   That rather he with heav'n than Her will
      part. . . .

309.

Thus Adam yields; and eats and tears his great
Creator's Law: in rending which he tore
His health, his life, his happiness, and that
Fair robe of pureness which till now he wore:
   And thus Eve's woful consort grew no less
   In nature, than in shameful nakedness. . . .

XV, 44.

The Lakes of Sulphure boiled with new heat;
Each Grief and Pang and Torment hotter grew;
Despair afresh at every bosom beat;
Upon the next feinds face each fury flew;
   And every Devil scratch'd and tore his brother,
   Wreaking their madness upon one another.

45.

The Snakes their hisses and their poison spit,
And in a thousand knots ty'd and unty'd
Their woful selves: the frighted Gorgons split
Their raving Throats hot furnace; and the wide
   And fiery-mouthed Dragons howling loud
   Whole torrents of their flaming venome spew'd.

46.

The Peers of Hell curs'd their unhappy King
Whose Pride betray'd them to this Anguish; they
Had hopes the Light of Heav'n would never spring
In their black Clime, to pour on them Dismay;
   But now they saw't in Jesus eyes, it more
   Vex'd them than when they fell from it before.
      . . .

XVIII, 154.

But O what Man's, or Muses tongue can tell
The other Monsters which were hissing there!
Huge Snakes, preposterous Amphisbaena's, fell
And fiery Basilisks discover'd were
   With angry Hydras, Scorpions, Dragons, and
   Of foul Chimaeras many a marshall'd band. . . .

JACOBUS MASENIUS

Sarcotis[1] (1654)

(a) Argument and Invocation

The origin of guilt, sprung from the Prince of Hell,
And what dire fates oppress the progeny
Of wretched man with servitude of sin
And penalties of crime, we now unfold.

---

[1]Translation by Watson Kirkconnell.

O goddess, queen of sacred poesy,
Who once controlled the harp-strings and the art
Of Jesse's son, grant my song ready strength!
Pierian nymphs and Cirrha's cool retreat
And Phoebus' laurel and Minerva's olive,
The spring of Pegasus and all the dreams
Of all earth's ancient bards now please me not.
A heavenly Parent takes the Muses' place;
A mightier Olympus there will be
In place of Cirrha's peaks; a kindlier Grace
Will pour her waves on me; and God's own Wisdom
Will overmatch the deity of Pallas.
Favour, O goddess, this my enterprise!
Direct my task with unoffending course
Through Earth's first age! Where'er thou leadest
me,
I follow, full of zeal. With thee as guide,
All things lie bare. Thou seest all hidden things,
And thou, O first Creator, wert the first
To gaze upon the ruin of mankind.
Am I thus heard? Behold in easy flight
I soar across the void, above the earth,
Above the sightless breezes of the sky,
Beyond the paths of Boreas and the birds.
And now in thought I stride beyond the stars,
I pass the clouds' high dwelling and the court
Where sleeps the lightning, on, beyond the poles
And flashing fires, and with audacious feet
I trample on the stars and take no harm.

(b) The description of Eden

There is a place that lies beyond the Dawn,
The rosy couch of Tethys, and the cradle
Of her bright son Apollo, where he lay.
The natal soil it is of our first father,
The field where first he played and tasted joys
In innocence of life. The pride of gardens
Is surely here; the grace of charming fields
Is green in harmless beauty undespoiled.
All that may soothe with scent of Persian balm,
And please the eye, and win the praise of Spring
The Graces here have set; 'tis Zephyr's home,
Who ever through the sunny silence flits

On gentle wings. Winter is exiled hence.
Here sleeps the rose, unvexed by any gale,
And paling at no storm from birth to death;
No dog-star heat may stifle her sweet breath,
Or wither the moist sap within her veins. . . .
Here in the midst the garden's soil is soft,
And never-failing springs of water flow
To moisten the earth's bosom far and wide
And give the thirsty meadows welcome draughts.

(c) Speech of the Arch-Fiend

"Chieftains of Hell, whose power unknown thus far
Is hidden in the pitchy Cave of shades,
We live, the scorn of God and man alike,
Nor are we reverenced yet by any rites.
Only a mighty weight of punishment,
The menaces of Fate and hungry flames
Oppress us with an everlasting death.
Why do we linger thus without due vengeance,
An idle throng? Wherefore in vile Avernus
Remain we torpid? Though the Powers above
Have seized upon the Heavens, let them not hold
The nether sky as well. This might of ours,
Though trodden on, is far from feeble yet.
Valour of soul is ours, and dark deceit,
And cause for working evil on our Foe!! . . .
He spoke no further. And at once in arms
The threatening legions roared; through Tartarus
With sword and torch they drove, with sulphurous
clouds
And thunderbolts to pour upon the earth.
A multitude past numbering, they rush
Through the vast Cave, dark squadrons up the steep.

JOOST VAN DEN VONDEL

Lucifer, Treurspel (1654)

"Praecipitemque immani turbine adegit."

LUCIFER. A TRAGEDY.[1]

Argument.

The Archangel Lucifer, highest and most illustrious of all the angels, being proud and ambitious for his own honour, was jealous of God's infinite greatness and of man, created after the image of God and endowed in the terrestrial Paradise with dominion over the earth. He was the more jealous of God and man when Gabriel, God's herald, declared all angels to be ministering spirits and revealed to them the mystery of God's future incarnation, in which, through a passing-by of the angelic host, human nature, united with Divinity, would inherit like power and majesty: wherefore the proud and envious Spirit, endeavouring through his accomplices to establish himself as the peer of God and to keep man out of heaven, stirred up innumerable angels in arms and led them, in spite of Raphael's warning, against Michael, heaven's Field Marshal, and his troops. At last, defeated and worn out by fighting, he ruins man and all his descendants in him in revenge; and being cast with his rebels into Hell, he is damned forever.

Dramatis Personae.

Beelzebub)
Apollyon) rebellious captains
Belial)

[1]Translated from the Dutch by Watson Kirkconnell. The original dialogue in rhymed Alexandrine couplets has been rendered by blank verse. The strophes of the choruses retain the original rhyme-patterns.

Gabriel, herald and interpreter of God's mysteries
CHORUS of Angels
Lucifer, the Viceroy (under God) of the heavenly Realm
Luciferists, rebellious spirits
Michael, Field Marshal of the Heavenly Host
Raphael, guardian angel
Uriel, squire to Michael

The setting of the drama is in Heaven.

ACT ONE

Enter Beelzebub.

Beelz. Yonder along the sky went Belial
On fleeting wings, in order to spy out
Where our Apollyon might be tarrying.
Prince Lucifer despatch'd him, fit by nature
To journey earthward in reconnaissance
Of Adam's bliss and state, in which th' Almighty
Of late establish'd him. 'Tis time indeed
That from beneath he hither should return.
He must be near, for vigilant is he
To fly at his lord's bidding, and devoted
To stay his master's throne with neck and shoulder.

Enter Belial.

Bel. O Lord Beelzebub, thou counsellor
Of Heaven's Viceroy, hither mounts Apollyon
Steeply from sphere to sphere, into our view.
Outstripping winds, he leaves a trail of light
And radiance behind him, where his wings
Cleave through the clouds. And now he scents our
air
In other daylight and a fairer sun
Whose rays are mirror'd in the crystal blue.
The wheeling spheres below behold his flight
Astonished at his speed and godlike mien;
He seems no angel, but a flying flame,
Swifter than any star. Here now he comes,

Bearing a golden bough, that speaks success
In his far journey up the shining steeps.

Enter Apollyon.

Beelz. What brings Apollyon?
Apol. Lord Beelzebub,
I have, as keen-eyed as I could, explored
The lower lands, and offer you its fruits,
Grown far below, beneath another sun
And other skies. Judge, by the fruits, the land
And the blest Garden, planted there by God
For man's delight.
Beelz. I see the golden leaves,
Soft with ethereal pearls, the silver dew.
How lovely smells the bright-hued foliage!
How glows the laughing fruit of red and gold!
'Twere shame to desecrate it with one's hand.
Its aspect tempts the mouth. Who would not lust
For these terrestrial luxuries? He would spurn
Our manna, who could pluck the fruits of earth.
For Adam's court, we'd curse our Paradise:
Th' Angelic bliss must yield to that of man.
Apol. Is it not so, Sir? Although Heaven seems high,
It lies indeed too low. What I have seen
With mine own eyes forsooth deceives me not.
Earth's fields and their delight now beggar us,
And Eden quite outdoes our Paradise.
Beelz. Speak on, and we shall listen to thy tale.
Apol. I say nought of my journey forth -- how fleet
I sank descending through the ninefold Spheres,
That, as they wheel, outstrip the arrow's flight,
The wheel of thought, revolving in the mind,
Turns not more swift than I, below the moon
And clouds, shot down; then hover'd for a space
To gaze across Earth's surface to the east.
There the tumultuous Ocean wash'd about,
Stirr'd by sea-monsters of a thousand sorts;
Far off, I saw a mountain-peak peer forth,
From which a waterfall, four rivers' source,
Foam'd down a valley. Then I dived again
And coasting steeply, lighted on the crest
Of that high mountain and could see more clear

The happy realms of earth and all their wealth.
Beelz. Picture for us the Garden, and its shape.
Apol. Round is it, like the circuit of the world.
Its centre is that peak, from which descends
The vocal stream, dividing into four,
And waters all the land, its trees and meadows,
Where brooks, as clear as crystal, babble on,
And spread abroad, and quicken all the soil.
Here onyx-stone and bdellium are found.
As bright as heaven gleams with glittering stars!
Here constellations of bright gems are strewn
Across the bosom of the kindly Earth,
And gold, more fair than stars, gleams in her veins.
Here Nature heaps all treasures in one lap.
Beelz. What serves as air, by which Earth's
creatures live?
Apol. No angel here has half so sweet a breath
As the fresh atmosphere that greets mankind
And with embraces blesses everything.
There swells the bosom of the land with life --
A myriad hues of bud and leaf and flower
And every sort of sweet perfumery,
Refresh'd by dews at night. Their appointed time
The rising and the setting sun observe
With such full knowledge that to each plant's need
They temper so their mighty rays that flower
And fruit alike are in one season found.
Beelz. Tell me the nature and the mien of man.
Apol. Who would desire to assume our angelhood
Instead of man's estate, when one had seen
These creatures who surpass all things that are,
And 'neath whose sway all other beings stand?
I saw th' assembly of a myriad beasts
That tread the earth or revel in the air
Or swim in stream and sea as each is wont,
Each living in its own due element.
And who could judge the essential kind of each
But Adam! For he gave to each its name.
The mountain-lion fawn'd, and wagg'd his tail,
And laughed allegiance. At man's royal feet
The tiger purr'd; the bull bow'd down his horns,
The elephant his trunk; the bear grew mild;
Gryphon and eagle listen'd to the man,
As did the Dragon and great Behemoth

And that vast shape, Leviathan himself.
Nor should I fail to state what twitterings
Of praise were sung to Adam by the birds
That thronged the branches of his pleasure-bower.
Sometimes the zephyrs play'd upon the leaves,
The brook upon the shore, both murmuring
A never-cloying music to the heart.
Had but the duties of Apollyon's task
Already been fulfill'd, I had forgotten
Our heavenly kingdom in the realm of man.
Beelz. What is thy judgement of the human Pair?
Apol. No heavenly creature has so pleased my eyes
As these two on the earth. Who can so twine
With subtlety a body and a soul,
Creating double angels out of clay?
The body, beautiful of shape, bears witness
To the Creator's art, whose glory glows
Most in the face, the mirror of the mind.
Upon the face is stamped the soul's bright image,
That lights the countenance, and makes life fair
With godlike glances out of human eyes,
The rational soul set in a human face.
Man only, while the dumb, unreason'd beasts
Gaze at their feet, holds up his head in pride
Toward God in Heav'n and praises his Creator.
Beelz. And not in vain, to whom such realms are given.
Apol. Godlike he rules, whom everything must serve.
The soul, in its invisibility,
Of spirit is in essence, not of matter.
It rules in every limb; the brain's its court;
Its home is in Eternity, and fears
No rust nor violation. It is past
All comprehending; while knowledge, prudence,
Virtue, and freedom are its true possession.
Before its glory, Spirits are amazed.
Ere long, the world will swarm with humankind;
It waits, from little seed, rich grain of souls;
For this cause, man was wedded to a mate.
Beelz. What thinkest thou of his beloved wife?
Apol. I cover'd with my wings my burning vision
To curb my counsels and my eyes' delight,
When first she filled my gazing, as her spouse
Led her across the meadows by the hand.

At times, he stood and gazed; and as he viewed
The naked beauty of her, a holy fire
Began to kindle swift in his pure breast.
Then he embraced his bride, and she her man;
Then went their nuptials forward, with a flame
Of mutual love, that beggars all expression,
A higher happiness, that Angels lack.
How poor our single state! We know no pair
Of twofold sex, a maiden and a man.
Alas, we are ill-treated, lacking marriage
And mating, in a Heaven without women!
Beelz. And will the world be peopled in due time?
Apol. Yea, through a pleasure in the beautiful
Imaged in human minds and printed deep
With power of senses keen. This holds the pair
In fruitful union, living but to love
And to be loved again, in mutual delight
Ever indulged, without extinguishing.
Beelz. Picture this bride before me, to the life.
Apol. That would demand no less than Nature's
brush,
The palet of the sunlight. Man and maid
Are both well-shaped, equally beautiful
From top to toe. While Adam wears by right
The crown of male supremacy, made tall
In stature and majestic in his mien,
As one ordain'd for kingship of the earth,
Yet all that Eve has, pleases his demands;
Her tenderness of limb, soft skin and flesh,
A friendly blush, blue loveliness of eyes,
A gracious mouth, speech whose enrapturing power
Consists in noble music, and twin breasts,
Consummate fountains of white ivory,
And that which it were better not to mention,
Lest it should lead a spirit to temptation.
The fairest Angels that our realm contains
Are but deform'd beside this radiant girl.
Beelz. You seem to burn with passion for the
creature.
Apol. I singed my feathers in that pleasant fire.
Heavy it seem'd to mount up from the Earth,
And fly to reach the top of Angel-town.
Departing, yet with pain, three times I gazed
In lingering longing back, and sure it seem'd

No Seraph in the holiness of Heaven
Were fair as she, in gold of hanging hair
That rippled in its beauty from her head
And down her back. As out of light she came,
And gladden'd all the daylight with her face.
Let pearl and nacre promise purity:
Her whiteness far surpasses any pearl.
Beelz. What profits all the glory of mankind,
If its beauty melts away and withers out
Like flowers of the field that soon must die?
Apol. As long as naught prevents the Garden there
From bearing fruit, the happy pair shall live
By apples that are nurtured in the midst
Of the fair forest, water'd by the stream
By which their tree's root lives. This wondrous
plant,
Is called the Tree of Life. Its inmost nature
Is incorruptible, and man, through this,
Enjoys eternal and immortal being,
Becoming like his kin, the Angel host,
Yea, in the end surpassing them; his power
And kingdom shall be widen'd over all.
How can his wings be shorten'd? For no Angel
Has power, from out his loins, to sow his seed
In myriad hosts of countless progeny.
Consider what shall issue from this thing!
Beelz. Mighty is man, to rise above our heads.
Apol. His increase will soon startle us indeed.
Although as yet his domination lies
Much lower than the moon, with stinted sway,
In time he will mount upward, without check,
To set his throne above the highest Heaven.
If God does not prevent it, how can we?
God favors man, and for him made all things.
Beelz. What do I hear? A trumpet? Sure, betimes
A proclamation follows. Look thou forth,
While we wait here to learn thy prompt report.
Apol. Th' Archangel Gabriel, with Heaven's choirs,
Approaches in the Name of the Most High,
As Herald, under orders from the throne,
To promulgate what has been bidden him.
Beelz. It pleases us to hear what he proclaims.

Enter *Gabriel* and *Chorus of Angels*.

Gab. Listen, ye Angels! Hark, ye folk of Heaven!
The highest Goodness, from whose bosom flows
All that is good and holy, never wearied
In His well-doing, nor impoverish'd
By lavish'd mercy, apprehensible
By no conceiving of created things --
This God, in His own likeness, fashion'd man,
And also made the Angels, that together
They might possess with Him His ageless Kingdom,
Of good compact, through their supporting zeal
And due obedience to His laws ordain'd.
This wondrous Universe He also built,
And framed the World, meet both for God and Man,
That man, set in his Garden, there might rule
And multiply, and ever, with all his seed,
Acknowledge God, and serve Him, and adore, --
So may he mount upon the world's high stairs
Up to the throne of uncreated Light,
The beatific Brightness. Though the realm
Of Angels seems all others to surpass,
God has determined, from Eternity,
To raise the lot of Man above the Angels,
Leading him upward to a radiance
Of light that differs not from the Divine.
Ye shall behold the everlasting Word,
Clothed in the flesh and blood of humankind,
The Lord's Anointed, Head and Judge of all,
Angels and men alike, judge from His throne
In an unshadow'd Kingdom. Now the throne
Stands consecrated in the midst of Heaven.
Let all the hosts of Angels honour Him
When he rides in, triumphant, having made
The form of Man exalted o'er our own.
Dark seems the bright flame of the Seraphim
Beside that human light and godlike lustre.
Thus Grace eclipses Nature and her splendours.
Take this as an immutable decree.
Chorus. Whatever God ordains, shall please his
Angels.
Gab. Now take good heed enduringly to serve
Both God and man, since the Divinity
Himself of man is mindful. Honouring Adam,
You win the heart of Adam's Father, God.
Both Man and Angel, sprouted from one stem,

Are brothers, chosen comrades, sons and heirs
Of the Most High, without a stain. One love,
One undivided will should be your law.
Ye know th' Angelic host has been disposed
In nine due Orders, threefold in their kind:
Highest are Seraphs, Cherubim, and Thrones,
Confirming in God's Council His decrees;
In the mid ternion, Dominations, Virtues,
And Powers wait upon God's secret will
For mankind's benefit and general good;
The third and lowest ternion, consecrated
In Principalities, Archangels great,
And Angels, to the bidding of the second
Must stoop, and let themselves be freely used
Beneath the vault of purest crystalline,
Taking mankind within their special charge
As widely as the starry heavens shine.
When the world spreads its limits further forth,
Each of these spirits will be separated
Into his several region; ye will know
Each his own city and the house and soul
Entrusted to his care, in Heaven's name.
Go hence then faithfully, immortal Spirits,
Obedient, under Lucifer, to God.
Further His honour in the human race,
Each in his ward, and each upon his watch.
Let some raise before God the censer's praise,
Bring to His throne the offerings of men,
And sighs and prayers and hallelujahs sung,
That through His joyful court the sound may spread.
Let others turn the star-lit Spheres of heaven,
Or urge the day along, or hold the air
Shut in with clouds, to bless the hills below
With sunshine or fresh showers of honey-dew
And manna, where in their first innocence,
The pair adore their God in Eden's bowers.
Let those who range through earth or air or fire
Or water, each in his own element,
Control his pace as Adam may desire,
Or lay the lightning-flash in leaden chains,
Bridle the storm or tame the raging sea.
Let another strike the branches from man's path,
Where'er he wanders. The Divinity
Has number'd all his tresses, to a hair.

Let him by the hand be led, so that his foot
May stumble not. Let an envoy now be sent
To Adam, Prince of Earth, requiring him
To do the duty of his empery.
So runs my charge, to which God binds you all.

CHORUS OF ANGELS

Who is it, that so high can be,
   So deep in the unfathom'd light,
Unbounded by eternity
   Or any Sphere, but, in His right,
With His own counterpoise endued,
   Rests unsupported, quite alone,
And in His nature can conclude
   All that, to tottering unknown,
In endless wheeling course can roll
   About that Centre of all things,
The Sun of suns, the Life and Soul
   Of all that your imaginings
Conceive of, or can e'er conceive;
   The Heart, the sacred Source, from whence
All blessings flow, as we believe,
   From mercy and omnipotence
And wisdom, and in Him subsist,
   Created by Him out of naught
Ere this high palace did exist
   Or was in all its radiance wrought;
Here, where with wings we cloak our eyes
   Before the glory of His crown,
And sing His praise in heavenly wise
   And fall in adoration down
With swooning fear before His face?
   Who is it? Name that Joy of joys!
With seraph's quill His likeness trace --
   Or does it shatter thought and voice?

'Tis GOD. O everlasting Essence (Antistrophe.)
   Of all that has existence here,
Forgive us, praise-deserving Presence
   In all that lives, in every Sphere,
Thou whose Estate can ne'er be spoken,
   Forgive us, and assoil from blame,
Since no high fancy, tongue, nor token

Can tell Thee. Evermore the Same
Thou dost abide. All Angel-learning
And speech, that impotence impairs,
Are desecration, undiscerning,
For each his own due title bears
Save Thee Thyself, for who can name Thee
By Thy great Name? Who is so pure
That he may praise Thee and proclaim Thee
Who solitary dost endure,
Known to Thyself alone? No sages
Can know Thy Nature as Thou art,
Glory and Source of all the ages.
What creature could that Light impart?
In whom is that great Light implanted?
To see it, greater bliss entails
Than has to us by Grace been granted;
It oversteps the bounds and pales
Of our own strength. The years distort us;
They drag us down, but never Thee.
Ever Thy Being must support us.
Sing homage to the Deity!

Holy, holy, once more holy, (Epode.)
Three times holy: praised be God!
In Him is salvation solely.
Holy is His regal rod.
Let His mysteries be binding;
May obedience in us dwell,
Angels all their pleasure finding
In what faithful Gabriel
In his proclamation bade them.
Let us honour God in Adam!
All that pleases God, is well.
(Exeunt omnes)

ACT TWO

Enter Lucifer and Beelzebub.

Luc. Ye hasting Spirits, stay my chariot now.
All the high pleasure of God's Morning Star
Is past its zenith: now must Lucifer
Stoop at the coming of this double star
That from beneath assails the upward way

To tarnish Heaven with an earthly light.
Embroider no more crowns upon my robes!
Gild not my forehead with the light of dawn's
Bright star to which Archangels bow the head!
Another radiance now rises, lit
With glory from the Deity Himself
That dulls our light, as when the sun by day
Extinguishes the stars, to earthly eyes.
Now is it night for Angels and the stars:
For man has won the heart of the Most High,
In a new Paradise. He is God's friend,
And we but slaves. Go hence, rejoice and serve
And honour this new race in mean subjection.
Men have been made for God, but we for man;
And now his feet shall tread on Angels' necks,
Yea, we must guard him, draw him by the hand,
Or bear him on our wings to thrones on high.
Our birthright goes to him, the favorite son,
Who violates our primogeniture.
The youngest son, in face so like the Father,
Obtains the crown; and there is given him
The sceptre before which the first-born bow
And tremble greatly. No denial avails;
For ye have heard what Gabriel trumpeted
Before the golden gate of Heaven's court.
Beelz. O Governor of God's supernal realms,
We heard it all too well, and 'mid the joys
Of chanting choruses that edict seem'd
A sound to check the everlasting feast.
The charge of Gabriel is clear. No tongue
Of Cherubim among us need expound it.
Nor was there need of late to send Apollyon
In downward flight to gain a nearer view
Of Adam's realm, so low beneath the moon;
For now we see with what magnificence
Man has been blest by God, yea by a guard
Of myriad spirits to defend his state,
With all the service of th' Angelic host
As if he were their monarch. Heaven's gate
Stands open wide to welcome Adam in.
An earthworm, creeping from a clod of clay,
Defies thy power. Thou shalt see this creature
Raised high above thee, and upon thy knees,
With downcast eyes and dull humility,

Thou'lt hail his might and majesty and power.
Man, glorified by God's omnipotence,
Shall sit by God Himself upon a throne;
And see his rule, amid th' eternal Spheres
Roll on, bound in by neither time nor place,
With God its centre and its orbit set.
What clearer insight do we need, to know
That man will be exalted, we abased?
That we are born to serve, and man to rule?
Lay down the sceptre henceforth from thy hand,
For an inferior will snatch the crown
Away ere long. Strip off thy diadem
Of morning light before this rising sun,
Or else be sure with song to lead him in,
With triumph glad and dignity divine!
Soon shall we see our Heaven changed in state.
The stars look forth; with longing they retire
To welcome this new light with due respect.
Luc. That shall I check, if it is in my power.
Beelz. There I hear Lucifer, and see the star
That drives away the night from Heaven's face!
For where he shines, day gloriously begins.
His crescent radiance, brightest next to God,
Shall never wane. His word's a high command,
His will and nod a law that none transgresses.
In him, the Deity is served and worshipp'd,
Extoll'd and fear'd; and shall a lesser voice
Now thunder from God's throne, worshipp'd above him?
Should God a younger son, from Adam's loins,
Exalt still higher? That were a breach of rights
Of the most utter sort, thy throne to tarnish,
For next to God, none is as great as thou.
God set thee once most glorious at His feet.
Let none make bold our Orders to uproot
And desecrate sworn rights, without a reason:
Else will all Heaven in arms wage civil war!
Luc. Thou hast good understanding: this concerns
The justice of Dominions, not at all
So freely to let slip their legal rights;
For to His own high law the Power Supreme
Is bound in duty. He should change the least.
I am a Son of Light, a ruler, too,
In realms of Light, and shall defend my own.
I yield before no Power nor Tyranny.

Submit who will: I shall not yield a foot.
Here is my Fatherland; and neither curse,
Calamity, nor any evil course
Shall curb us or affright us. We shall perish,
Or make port round this darkest cape of all.
If it should be my fate to fall, bereft
Of honour and of station, let me fall,
If I but bear this crown upon my head,
This sceptre in my grasp, attended still
By my strong guard of trusted warrior-spirits
And all the thousands that embrace my cause.
Yea, it were honour and unfading glory
To perish thus. Better it were by far
To be the first Prince in a lower Court
Than second, or still less, in heaven's Light.
So I submit to chance, defying fear.
But here comes God's smart Herald, with the book
Of mysteries committed to his care.
It were not inadviseable, I think,
Further to question him. I will descend
From this my chariot, and go to meet him.
(Exit Beelzebub)

Enter Gabriel.

Gab. Hail, Governor! Where lies thy journey now?
Luc. To thee, good Herald of the heavenly Court.
Gab. Methinks I read thy thoughts upon thy brow.
Luc. Thou who revealest through the light of Reason
The murky grounds of God's deep mysteries,
Enlighten me!
Gab. What is it troubles thee?
Luc. God's counsel and decree, by which He values
Our Heaven lower than the stuff of earth,
Oppressing us and lifting up the world
From an abyss, through all the stars, to set
Man on the throne of Angels, whom thus robbed
Of their primordial rights He bids to sweat
And slave for human profit. Shall our race,
Sworn in as officers of Heaven's court,
Stand henceforth at the bidding of a worm,
Crawl'd meanly out of dust, and meanly grown?
And shall we wait on him and watch his race
Increase above us all in rank and numbers?
Why does His Grace degrade us thus so early?

What Angel has been tardy in His service?
How, too, can Deity be mix'd with man?
How could He pass His chosen Angels by
And pour His Essence in a human body,
How knit the finite with the Infinite,
The Highest with the lowest thing of all,
The great Creator with the creature made?
Who can make any sense of this decree?
Shall the eternal Light be now obscured
In the world's darkness? We, the governors
Of God's authority, be ask'd to kneel
Before this puppy in his borrow'd power?
Shall countless bodiless and godlike Souls
Bow down before this dull, slow Thing of earth
On which God prints His majesty and Being?
We Spirits cannot grasp such mysteries.
Do thou, who hast the keys of God's dark counsels,
Unfold, if that thou mayest, this dispute,
From thy seal'd Book: explain God's will to us!
Gab. I will, so far as 'tis permissible
To unlock these leaves. Although to have much knowledge
Seems sometimes partly profit, partly harm;
For He reveals His will imperfectly.
His Light excessive blinds the Seraphim;
And Wisdom Absolute conceals its will
In prudent part and shows us but the rest.
It thus befits the subject to conform
And rule his conduct by the law assign'd;
For he is bounden to his Master's charge.
The reason of it all, for which we wait,
When, through the sequence of a race of heirs,
That Lord, at once born human and divine,
Shall bear the sceptre and extend His rule
Over the stars, earth, sea, and all that lives --
This, Heaven has hidden. Time will show that Heir.
Heed then God's trumpet. Ye have heard His will.
Luc. And shall a worm, this stranger, exercise
Supreme authority in Heaven's realm
With foreign rule above the native-born?
Shall man enjoy a seat that rivals God's?
Gab. Content thee with thy lot, and still maintain
The dignity conferr'd on thee by God.
God set thee over all the Hierarchies,

But not to envy others' rise to greatness.
Rebelliousness breaks its own head and crown,
Whenever it opposes God's commands.
'Tis from His power thy visage draws its light.
Luc. Only to God have I yet bow'd my crown.
Gab. Then also bow thyself before His word,
Who has directed to a certain end
All things that are or shall hereafter be,
Although we Spirits comprehend it not.
Luc. For man to share the Light of Deity,
To sit with God divinely on His throne
And see the censer swung before him hymn'd
By myriad thousands in harmonious chorus,
Dims all the majesty and diamond rays
Of our bright Morning Star, that shines no longer
And causes Heaven's joy to pine with grief.
Gab. Our happiness consists in duty done
In calm obedience to the will of God
And adaptation of ourselves to Him.
Luc. The majesty of God will be impair'd
In case His nature mingles with man's blood
In vital union. We, the Angel host,
Have closer kinship with the Deity,
Sons of one Father, and resembling Him --
If one may be permitted to compare
The transient with the Eternal, the finite spirit
With all the powers of Infinitude.
Suppose the sun should wander from his course
And cloak itself in mist, to light the earth
Bedimm'd by murk and vapour; how the joy
Of earth would perish, and the earthly race
Miss light and life! And do I say the Sun
Might lose his orbit and his majesty?
I see the heavens dark, the stars confused,
Chaos and foul disorder wreck the cosmos,
If the great Source of light should sink Himself
In this morass of clay. Excuse me, Gabriel,
If I thy trumpet or God's high command
Oppose or seem a little to oppose.
Zealous for God's own honour, I grow bold
To vindicate His rights and dwell thus far
Outside the track of my obedience.
Gab. The glory of God's name affects thee rarely!
But pray consider that Himself should know

Far better than do we the point in which
His honour is involved. This checks thy quest.
But God in man incarnate shall Himself
Unlock this Book of holy mysteries,
Seal'd with its seven seals. Thou tastest not
The pith as yet, and seest but the bark.
Then shall we see the cause, the reason why,
In all His mysteries, and know the depths
Of holy counsels. Now 'twere best to stoop,
To worship this new dawn, employ ourselves
With gratitude until full knowledge given
Drives away doubting as the sun the night.
Now learn we by degrees to meet God's wisdom
In modest reverence, till by degrees
The dawn of comprehension shall arise
And each, upon his watch be subject to it.
Rest in this, Governor. Be thou the first
To guard this law. I go where God has sent me.
(Exit Gabriel)
Luc. It shall be tended to with vigilance!

Enter Beelzebub.

Beelz. Now hast thou heard the trend of the decree
That Gabriel's horn so proudly has proclaim'd.
He gave thee a keen smell of God's design
To clip the wings of thy authority!
Luc. 'Twill not be easy. Nay, I shall prevent it.
Let no inferior thus dream to rule
Over his betters here.
Beelz. He issues threats
Of force to crush the spirit of revolt.
Luc. Now swear I by my crown to hazard all
Upon one cast, and set my throne on high
Above the heavens, through all starry Spheres!
The firmament shall one great palace be,
The rainbow be my throne and earth my foot-stool,
Amid fair star-shine in my halls of state.
Thence in a cloudy chariot, high and swift,
I'll drive along the air and with my levin
I'll shatter everything, above, below,
That may oppose us, were it Michael's self.
Yea, ere we yield, this azure vault of heaven,
So proudly built, with its translucent arcs,

Shall burst to pieces and be blown away,
The mutilated Earth shall be a trunk
Misshapen, and the wondrous Universe,
Turning again to chaos, shall become
A wilderness of utter desolation!
Come, let us see who'll dare to challenge us.
Summon Apollyon.
Beelz. Here he comes uncall'd.

Enter Apollyon.

Apol. O Governor of God's unbounded realm,
Chief in the Council of the lesser gods,
I offer you my service at command.
What labor would your Majesty desire?
Luc. It pleases us to understand thy thought
In an important cause that must not fail.
We plan to pluck out Michael's proudest plume
So that our onset on his power may win.
He musters, with his arm, as many orders
As ever God has with His hand writ down
In everlasting adamant. Behold
Man raised up now to Heaven's pinnacle,
Hence through all Spheres, and see th' Angelic race
So low, so deep beneath, that now they swarm
Like worms beneath the carpet that he treads on.
I purpose, therefore, to assault the Throne
With violence, and by that overthrow
To set up, at one stroke, whatever State
My rank and star and crown can institute.
Apol. Praiseworthy venture! May thy crown increase!
And in that noble growth, I count it honour
To counsel, under thee, so brave a deed;
For be it right and well, or ill beset,
The will deserves all praise, howe'er it thrive.
But, lest we rashly strive without a plan,
How does one best essay this bold emprize?
How with most safety fight against God's purpose?
Luc. We can with guile devise opposing counsels.
Apol. There's much in that. To weigh our borrow'd strength
In the same scale with God's Omnipotence
In open trial, makes His weight prevail.
Watch for thy crown then, for our side's too light!

Beelz. Yet not so light, but that the scale may
waver.
Apol. Who shall begin th' attempt, and how, and
where?
These plans offend God's majesty already.
Luc. We'll hold it unoffended, and with skill
Storm the steep slopes, the cliffs impregnable.
Our skill and courage can defy all dangers.
Apol. But not Omnipotence: draw not too near
Lest with repentance one should learn too late
That vassals to their Sovereign must submit.
Luc. Out of thy reckoning leave Omnipotence!
Set equals and equality together.
Then let us learn whose weapon weighs the more.
I see our foes in flight, the battlements
Of Heaven clear'd by our first cannonade,
Our armies loaded down with glorious loot;
Then we'll take counsel as to further action.
Apol. Thou know'st the strength of Michael, God's
great Marshal:
God's regiments stand pledged to his command;
He bears the key to Heaven's armouries;
The Guards are faithful to him; and he keeps
A wakeful eye on all of Heaven's faithful,
So that no star of all the heavenly host
Dare lag or wander from the march ordain'd.
Rashly we may begin, but to achieve
Success in such a war is past our strength
And draws a lingering train of difficulties.
What tools, what implements of siege have we
To assail and overthrow the walls of Heaven?
Although the gates of adamant stand open,
The Castle fears no ambush or surprise.
Beelz. Let but the sword support our resolution,
And Lucifer, defiant 'neath our flag,
Shall change the state and empery of Heaven!
Apol. Michael, the Marshal, bears defiantly
And proudly in his banner's shining field
The wondrous Name of God, the Sun above it.
Luc. Though writ in light, what profit's in a name?
Heroic parts, like this, are not achieved
By pomp and titles, but by bravery
And cunning, hatch'd from subtlety and reason.
In craft thou art a master, skill'd to play

On angels' minds and dupe them at thy will.
For thou canst ruin the most honest Spirit
In all the Guard of Heaven, and aptly teach
That heart to doubt that never thought of doubting.
Begin! We see God's army rent in twain;
The sever'd heads and members rage and quarrel;
The greatest power already blind and deafen'd,
And captains meanwhile calling for a leader.
If thou entice a fourth part to our side,
Thy scheming shall be crown'd with honour'd office.
Go hence, deliberate on this with Belial.
It must be dark, where he shall go astray!
His smooth face, varnish'd with hypocrisy,
When he in his deceitful masquerade
Engages, none can recognize, and flee.
I mount my chariot, and leave you two
To think on this. My Privy Council's met.
Already comes the guard to summon me.
Ye shall be welcomed with us, when ye come.
(To the officer of the Guard)
Colonel, you'll guard the court-door with your troops.

(Exit Lucifer and Beelzebub)

Enter Belial.

Bel. The Governor makes much use of us two.
Apol. We both fly, like twin arrows from his bow.
Bel. And aim at one mark, dubious to hit.
Apol. Stand fast, and Heav'n will crack at our assault.
Bel. Let crack what will: the venture must go forward.
Apol. How may we undertake it with success?
Bel. Weapons we need, and first must gain the troops.
Apol. The leaders first, and win the boldest over.
Bel. With promise of a project fair and bright.
Apol. Give thy design a name! I fain would hear it.
Bel. Let them maintain the realm that Angels hold,
And vindicate their rights and rank and honour,
And choose a Head, on whom each may rely.
Apol. That is most bravely put! And I could wish
No fairer cause, no seed of mutiny
So quick to stir our citizenry up

Against the court, and draw the battle on.
Each is resolved to guard his honour'd rank
And primal rights of law, which the Most High
Has stol'n with violence and giv'n to man,
The sorry creature of a later birth.
The heavenly Court was our inheritance!
Spirits, who soar thus high on shining wings,
And, free from any body, sink not down
Are better suited to these realms than men,
Whose nature is ill fitted for the Spheres.
Here falls the daylight far too stark and strong,
Their eyes endure not light, our custom'd joy.
Then let man keep to his own element,
Like other animals, and be content
With the due limits of his kingdom's court!
The circling sun metes out his earthly days,
The moon his months, and the bright starry Spheres
His annual seasons. Let him be content
With Eden's fruits, the fragrance of its flowers,
And turn himself to east, west, north and south.
Be that his recreation, as is fit;
But here we shall not know an earthly ruler.
Or so say I! Express my thought more briefly.
Bel. We'll shut man out of Heav'n eternally.
Apol. That will sound wondrous well in Angels' ears,
And fly like flame from choir on to choir
Through all nine Orders of the Hierarchy.
Bel. So shall we best feign indolence, although
The safety of our venture hangs on speed.
Apol. Not less on cunning and on bravery.
Bel. These will increase as countless warriors join us.
Apol. They murmur busily. One might fly down
And mingle secretly among the throng
And nurse their grievance into open fire.
Bel. Then would Beelzebub great service render,
Being a prince of great authority,
To set his seal upon their legal claim.
Apol. Not suddenly, but by discreet degrees.
Bel. The Governor would, by his presence, give
A strong direction to so bold a venture.
Apol. Here in the Council we shall learn his thought
And project. He'll dissemble for a space,

But in the end will show us how to use
This mutiny that only needs a head.
Bel. On that head, all depends. Whate'er we
    promise,
They will not march without a general.
Apol. One need not win what is already won.
He who is most offended in his honour
Is most concerned. He will go forward still
And rally friends in myriads to the cause.
Bel. All equity of speech would honour him
With leadership. But ere we deeper tread,
Let us first weigh the danger, and dare nothing
Unless all Councillors affix their seals.
(Exeunt)

CHORUS

Why glows the Court's façade so ruddy? (Strophe)
   Why streams the holy light of grace
   So red upon each face
Through clouds and murky haze so bloody?
   That smoke has now profaned
   The pure and never stain'd
   Translucent sapphire height,
   The fire, the flame, the light
Of the Almighty's presence?
   Why does that Light that once could blind
   Now seem so dark incarnadined,
Though not long since its radiant Essence
   Rejoiced all eyes? The cause of this
What Angel Spirit has discover'd
   Of those in these high realms of bliss
Who have in holy anthems hover'd,
   In fragrance and in light array'd
   Along high Heaven's colonnade
Beneath the golden vault and choir,
Enrapturing with celestial fire
   All creatures that in Heav'n are found?
   Who can this prodigy expound?

When we, at Gabriel's proclamation, (Antistrophe)
   Stood trembling, and in novel ways
      Wrought humbly, to God's praise,
The rose-beds and the vegetation

In Heaven's paradise
Rejoiced with hue and spice
To hear our chorus peal;
But Envy seem'd to steal
Among us in sad measure.
For many of the Spirits stood,
A wan and silent multitude,
And wept in dark displeasure;
The brow hung blighted on the eye,
Scowls wrinkled out each smiling dimple,
The doves of Heaven, here on high,
Erst plain and upright, kind and simple,
To murmurs and to groans did fall
As if our courts were far too small
Since Adam gain'd the throne of Heaven
And such a crown to man was given.
This blemish irk'd the eye of Light
And lit these flames in God's stern sight.
We, out of love, shall mix in their society,
To bring this tumult back to peace and piety.

ACT THREE

Enter Luciferists and Chorus.

Lcsts. How could we be so cozen'd in our thought!
And now, how all is changed! We prized no Order
As happier than ours in God's new kingdom,
Yea, deem'd our state like that of the Most High,
Unchangeable and blest above things human;
But Gabriel met us with God's proclamation
And from the golden portals troubled us
With this decree that robs th' angelic Host
Of their superior lot, bestow'd on them
By primal right from the full lap of God.
Too low we lie, and see the sparkling glory
Of all our honour and our splendor quench'd,
Our Hierarchy in confusion thrown,
And man so proudly raised in state and power
That we must cringe like slaves before his sceptre.
O unexpected blow and change of state!
Alas, companions in this pain, sit here
Together in a circle; help us grieve

And sigh. 'Tis time to rend our festal garments
And make lament. None can forbid us that.
Our happiness now pines at sight of sorrow.
Alas, alas, our brothers, choirs of Heaven,
Lay down your diadems, and liveries,
And cheerfulness of mien, in utter mourning!
Seek darkness, as do we. Grief shuns the day.
Follow our voice and anxious lamentation.
Drown in lamenting. Sink in grievous thoughts.
Weeping relieves the anguish of the heart,
And groaning heals the fever of our wounds.
Now call out with one voice and cry together:
Alas, alas, where has our joy departed!

CHORUS

What wailings do we hear? Unpleasant tones
Make the air shudder. Heaven is not used
To hear a dirge of lamentation ring
Through the triumphant vault. Palm-wreaths and
    harps
And songs of triumph suit us. Who are these
That in a circle here, with hanging heads,
Sit destitute and downcast and forsaken?
Who gives them cause for grief? Who can explain?
Follow, my choir-companions! We must ask
After the source of their distress, these throes
Of sorrow that bedim our radiant splendor
And darken the eternal festival.
Heav'n is a court of wealth and joy and peace.
Sorrow has never nested 'neath its eaves.
Follow, my comrades! Comfort their distress.

Lcsts. Alas, alas, where has our joy departed!
Chorus. Comrades in weal and rapture, how is this?
Sons of the Light, why are ye grieved in spirit?
Who gives you reason to lament and mourn?
Ye had begun to lift your heads to heaven,
To blossom in the radiance from God's face.
He fashion'd you to wing from court to court,
From pinnacle to pinnacle, to hover
In the unshadow'd light, happy to live
In one continual festival, and taste
The manna of God's immortality

In one calm fellowship of feast-companions.
How now? For this befits no citizens
Of the Angelic City, nay, it suits
Neither Dominions, Powers, Thrones, nor aught
That knows angelic nature. Ye are grieved.
Ye sit here dull, disconsolate, and mute.
Come, tell your comrades of your hidden pain!
Disclose your wounded hearts, that we may heal them!
Lcsts. Ah, brothers, would ye ask the obvious?
Ye heard, as well as we, what Gabriel publish'd:
How we, through the new edict, from our state
Have fallen into slavery to Earth
And all the teeming progeny of Adam.
Wherein have we offended, by what fault,
That God a bubble, blown of wind and scum,
Has raised up to confound His sons, the Angels,
Honouring a bastard, form'd of filthy clay?
But now we had stood consecrated here
As pillars of His Court, fulfill'd our duties
As a true fellowship of officers,
And suddenly are banish'd and dash'd down
From all our honour, brutally oppress'd.
The privilege and right once given us
Were cancell'd, and instead of ruling here,
With God and under God, we find ourselves
Under the domineering rod of Adam,
Who triumphs in a race made infinite.
The Angels' sun is all too soon eclipsed.
Ah, comrades, join us in our sad distress.
Alas, alas, where had our joy departed!
Chorus. Are ye thus troubled at the charge of God
And Gabriel, His Herald? This were madness.
Who dares rebuke the word of the Most High?
Who would presume to strive against the Lord?
We are obliged to give Him right and honour,
In His law to abide. Who enters here
Into dispute with God's omnipotence?
His nod and word and will to us are law,
A measure and a rule. Who contradicts,
Transgresses the seal'd law of the Most High.
Obedience is more pleasing to our King
Than any frankincense and godlike music.
Be not so proud and high, for ye are made
To know subjection rather than to rule.

Ah brothers, cease this grievous lamentation!
Bow 'neath the yoke of God's authority!
Lcsts. Say rather, 'neath the yoke of swarming pismires.
Chorus. Whene'er it pleases Him, ye should be ruled.
Lcsts. What have we done amiss? Answer us that!
Chorus. What done amiss? Ye trouble God by grieving.
Lcsts. In sorrow and distress of soul we grieve.
Chorus. If ye seek peace, submit your wills to God.
Lcsts. We rest upon our rights, as due by law.
Chorus. It is your right to serve the will of God.
Lcsts. How can a greater serve a lesser master?
Chorus. By trusting God. To serve Him is to rule.
Lcsts. Willing are we, if man serves lower still.
Chorus. Man lives content, although his lot be humble.
Lcsts. To him a higher lot has been assign'd.
Chorus. Only through many ages will he rise.
Lcsts. An age on earth is but a moment here.
Chorus. It shall be as it must, as God ordains.
Lcsts. This mighty secret has been hid from us.
Chorus. God has reveal'd His heart as kind toward you.
Lcsts. But kinder still toward man; He sets him higher.
Chorus. Only when mix'd with Godhead wondrously.
Lcsts. Would God not mate with the Angelic nature?
Chorus. What pleases God Himself, is rightly praised.
Lcsts. How has He set man's level up so high?
Chorus. What God ordains is ever well and good.
Lcsts. But how will man bedim the Angels' crown!
Chorus. We shall behold and praise th' incarnate Lord.
Lcsts. Shall Angels worship thus a thing of dirt?
Chorus. Nay, we shall offer incense to God's name.
Lcsts. Rather, to man, under unfair compulsion.

Enter Apollyon and Belial.

Apol. Murmurs already? Here are tongues at strife.
Bel. What throngs lament here, grieving in their sorrow

With veils on breast and loins? No one would dream
That here, amid the Spirits that attend
The everlasting banquetings of Heaven,
Any could grieve, did we not see such numbers
Sitting disconsolate in dark distress.
What dire calamity has overcome them?
My brothers, how is this? What's your complaint?
Have ye been wrong'd? Your rights shall be protected.
What ails the Brethren? Speak, and let us hear!
Chorus. They grieve that the estate of man shall triumph,
As Gabriel proclaim'd, and rise above us,
That God should mix His Essence with man's nature
And place the Angels under man's dominion.
That is their grief's gravamen, short and clear.
Lcsts. So great a wrong is grievous to endure.
Bel. Almost beyond the soul's capacity.
Chorus. We pray your help, this trouble to compose.
Apol. How can they be content? They seek their rights.
Chorus. What rights? Who makes a law may change it too..
Apol. But how can Justice deal out unjust judgements?
Chorus. God's judgement doth transcend all common law.
Bel. The child is taught to trace his Father's steps.
Chorus. To do His will, that is to follow Him.
Apol. His change of will gave rise to this dispute.
Chorus. One He dethrones, and sets another up;
And either course will please a true son's heart.
Bel. Equality of favour would be best.
For now may darkness wax beyond the light
And children of the night defy the day.
Chorus. All that has breath may rightly thank the Lord
Who gave to each his being, low or higher.
When He shall please, the element of earth
Shall change itself to water, air, or fire,
Heaven to earth, an angel to a beast,
And man to brightness of transcendent wonder.
One Power rules: He casts the high ones down,
And what the low receive is utter grace.

Here free will serves not. Reason comes too late.
God's glory shines through inequality.
Thus we behold things differ in their weight
And beauty, colour separate from colour,
Diamond from turquoise-blue, and scent from scent,
Bright lights from faint, stars from the firmament.
For us to set in order would confound
The settled system of the Universe,
Embrangling all the Deity ordain'd.
We creatures would confuse in every part
All we attempted. Cease this murmuring!
God could dispense with the Angelic host.
He needs no service. His eternal kingdom
Is lordly, needing neither scent nor music,
No offering of incense or of praises.
Ungrateful Souls, be silent and blaspheme not!
Ye cannot know God's purpose. Be content
Beneath God's bidding, brought by Gabriel.
Apol. Have then the Angels an unstable lot?
On slippery ground, they are already wretched.
Chorus. Because a lesser rules? We keep our office,
Intact in honour. Where is our misfortune?
Bel. But man is next to God, his holy Refuge
And heavenly Father, resting on His bosom.
Chorus. To be aggrieved at others' happiness
Is a gross breach of love, and stinks of pride.
Let not this stain cling to the purity
Of angels, for 'tis pleasing to the Father,
Who has created all things in their place,
That ye should work together, each with each,
In harmony, fidelity, and love.
Bel. Grant that the orders stay as once they were:
They cannot yet endure to slave for man.
Chorus. That would be disobedience, transgressing
The bounds of duty. See the Host of Heaven,
Harness'd in gold and station'd in their place,
Keeping their watch as shining sentinels:
Among those stars set yonder in the sky,
The brightest dims the splendor of the least,
One has a smaller orbit, one a greater,
The lower parts of heaven move more quickly
The higher drift more slowly; even so,
Thou learnest in these inequalities
Of office, brilliance, orbit, path and pace

That there exists no discord, no, nor strife.
The voice of God directs that measured singing
And all repeat it straitly after Him.
Bel. The starry Host remain in that first state
In which God did create them, nor desire
The station of the Angels to disturb;
They rouse no stars from concord and from peace
Or trouble with lament our heavenly Palace.
Chorus. Take heed, not to augment this restlessness.
Apol. We wish to drive away this murky cloud
Before it bursts and sets the Heavens on fire.
Their numbers grow. What stills you now? Who comes?

Enter Beelzebub.

Lcsts. Alas, alas, where has our joy departed?
Beelz. (To himself). Things prosper. We increase.
Our angels gather.
They muster murmuring and full of grief.
(Aloud) What goads th' Angelic City to lament
In restlessness? Can God's blest flowers fade?
Can ye not be contented to possess
In quietness all that a Soul could wish
From God, the Bountiful? In your own light
Ye seem to stand, and pamper a vexation
The cause of which I neither see nor guess.
Cease from your lamentation. Rend no more
Your uniforms and standards. Rather, speak!
Speak cheerfully, with cheerful countenance.
Show foreheads fair with light, ye Sons of Light!
And let melodious throats thank God with song!
Be ye ashamed to mix discordant tones
And bastard measures with the hymns of Heaven.
Your grieving dissonance disturbs the music
Of the celestial Kingdom, whose high vault
Echoes your howls and caterwauls of woe
That roll along from arch to lofty arch.
Surely such discord offers foul offence
And hindrance to the glory of God's name.
Lcsts. General, at whose nod troops without number
Assume their skilful arms, in time thou comest
To soothe our griefs and ward off, through our power,
Hostile disdain and undeserved scorn.
Shall Gabriel set the holy Angels' crown

Upon the head of Adam, and beat down
God's first-born Sons through false inheritance?
'Twere better we had never been created
Ere the sun mounted in his chariot
And could give light to Heaven. God in vain
Selected Angels as the Household Guards
Of a fixed Court in which He would oppose
And raise Himself against the rights of Spirits,
Provoking them to innocent resistance.
Happy we were, bred up to offer praise
And worship Him with incense and obeisance,
Prostrate before Him. Heaven gave glad ear
To mounting voices, choir within choir,
Yea, melted at the grace of tongue and harp.
With Gabriel's edict came a sudden change:
This thunderbolt smote down amid our worship,
And lo, we lay abased, confounded, crush'd.
Our happiness expired; our throats were mute.
The youngest-born had gain'd the crown, the sceptre,
Yes, and the blessing; and the eldest son,
Cast off in scorn by his Almighty Father,
Was branded as a slave. Obedience
And piety and love and trust receive
This guerdon from the treasuries of God.
Here, partly plunged in grief, we burn with wrath
And righteous hate for man, desiring vengeance --
To choke his race out ere it overthrow
The state of Angels, and we, sorry slaves,
Be forced to run beneath his whip and will
As he now rules the hapless beasts of earth.
This downfall of the Spirits, General,
Thou canst prevent, and succour all their rights.
Protect us by thy power: for we are ready
To range beneath the standard of thy army.
Advance with us on Heaven! For 'tis good
To vindicate one's honour, crown, and right.
Beelz. Your error pains me. May the Lord of lords
Forbid it rather! Cease from mutiny
And discord; I beseech you cast no fuel.
On fires of revolt. What is my counsel?
I would appease both you and God himself.
Lcsts. The sacred rights of Angels have been wounded.
Beelz. To wound this right sets loyal hearts on fire
And spreads a blaze in which the skies might perish.

O wrong reward for pure fidelity!
How shall we best behave in this despair?
Lcsts. Trust all to chance, and mount the chariot.
Beelz. Why risk oneself? Go at a softer pace.
Lcsts. Here only might avails, revenge, and force.
Beelz. Where possible, a middle course is best.
Lcsts. Here, by delay, one will not win but lose.
Beelz. Concede this wrong some reasonable thought.
Lcsts. Reason assures us here that we are slaves.
Beelz. Ye might best gain your wish by flattery.
Lcsts. Discovery would mar that subtle business.
Beelz. Scarce can your plot be hidden from the light.
Lcsts. We grow in strength, and reach equality.
Beelz. Chance favours those who fight beside God's Marshal.
Lcsts. Nothing can be set right by dread and dotage.
Beelz. What says Apollyon to this case, and Belial?
Lcsts. They have avow'd our side and strengthen us.
Beelz. How has your cause advanced thus far so soon?
Lcsts. Heav'n, of its own accord, flows hither fast.
Beelz. Trust in no army full of waverers.
Lcsts. We see already more success than danger.
Beelz. He who starts rashly, glories in no profit.
Lcsts. All hangs upon the outcome of the venture,
And, before that is seen, all judgement errs.
The entire host wants thee as general
And leader in this march.
Beelz. Who's so bereft
Of sense as to defend your equity
And thus provoke the might of Michael's army.
'Twere better ye had pity on yourselves.
Excuse me from this charge. I choose no side.
Let this injustice be made good by treaty.
Chorus. Brothers, give ear! Continue here on high
To plead with God through chosen mediators.
One wins more easily by conference
Than by your stubborn way of raw revolt.
Deal coolly, with deliberated plans.
We likewise wish to guard your rights in Heaven.
Be calm: you vex the mighty Lord of lords.
Lcsts. And ye our rights! Go not beyond that fact.
Be thou our marshal, Prince Beelzebub.
Prepare our army. We shall follow thee.

Beelz. Think, think, ye zealots, further ere ye act!
I am prepared to go as intercessor
To the great palace Throne, and mediate
For these our rights, with voluntary peace
And mutual agreement, all unforced.
Chorus. Hold still, for Michael takes you unawares!

Enter Michael.

Mich. Where are we now? What uproar find we here?
This seems a court of quarrels, not of peace,
Duty, and trust. Come, Prince Beelzebub,
What reason dost thou give me, as a head
Of this rebellious wrath, that fain would rise,
Pregnant with sacrilegious treachery,
Against the God who here sustains us all?
Beelz. Pardon me, Michael, condescend to hear us
Before thou judgest us in angry zeal
For God's high honour. Charge us with no guilt.
Mich. With patience I shall listen to your plea.
Beelz. Th' assembling of so many thousand troops,
Confounded by the edict from the Throne
Proclaim'd by Gabriel's trumpet, now demands
Just mediation to put out the fire;
Wherefore I came to enquire of their cause
And check their mutiny in every way.
They were, however, all distraught and mad,
Driven to riot off the road of reason,
And sought to lay their quarrel's leadership
Forcibly on my shoulders. I have tried
To mitigate their frenzy (Let these choirs
Bear faithful witness to my loyalty!)
And bid them cast their grief before God's throne:
Alas, my zeal has been as fruitless here,
Amid the stir and roar, as if I sought
To calm a wind-tost sea. But now, thou'rt come,
God's Marshal, and we fain would follow thee
While thou dost mediate this dark dispute.
Mich. Who may oppose God and His holy will?
Who is so bold as to set up the flag
Of war in this, the kingdom of God's peace?
If ye through envoys will confer with God,
Your lots to warrant, I shall mediate

Your just propitiation with the Lord.
But keep your hands from violence, I warn you,
Or watch your heads! For ye shall not succeed.
Lcsts. Wouldst thou by force suppress our holy
rights?
Thou wert not sworn in Marshal for such ends.
Justice is bold, and we defend our rights.
Mich. To war on God is the least right of all.
Lcsts. We serve Him, as thou knowest, worthily,
While Heaven stands as it was first ordain'd.
But set no captains of our Fatherland
Beneath the earthly race! That servile station
The Hierarchies, Thrones, and Powers, high
And low Dominions among Spirits, Angels
And proud Archangels nevermore will hear!
No, not at all, ev'n though thy spear of lightning
Should pierce each breast and slay the faithful
heart.
We will not be defied by Adam's seed!
Mich. I bid each spirit, as I wave my hand,
To leave directly. Against God he sides,
Who sides, forsworn, against the Host of Heaven.
Return at once, each to his regiment,
As befits soldiers and obedient subjects!
What violence and wantonness are here!
He who shall fight, except beneath my banner,
Wars against God and is His enemy.
Lcsts. He who maintains his rights, yields not to
force.
Self-vindication is most natural.
Mich. Lay down your weapons straightway, I command
you!
This gathering is a breach of oath and honour.
Lcsts. We are united by a bond of Nature
To stand beside each other. Not alone
Is each offended in this grave dispute:
We have a strong community of grief.
Mich. Would ye disturb high Heaven with your arms?
Ye were not sworn in as the foes of God.
For this misuse of power, ye may fear Him!
Lcsts. The Governor is due at any moment.
He has been call'd and summon'd in all haste.
We all are of one mind, and would incite
War godlike against God, rather than yield

Our rights in face of force.
Mich. Such monstrous folly
I do not look for from the Governor.
Lcsts. It verges upon folly to have set
An elder and a firstling of Creation
Under the youngest's yoke in servile wise;
But that an Angel should bear arms against
His own angelic peers in kind and station,
That may be praised as verging upon honour!
Mich. Ye are a stiff-neck'd breed, no longer sons
Of God's own Light, but rather bastards bred,
That yield before no God, and so provoke
His lightnings in irrevocable scorn.
Keep on, keep on, and what a fall is due you!
Ye hearken to no counsel. We shall learn
What the All-Highest's voice shall bid in Heaven.
Come then, I wish the guiltless choirs at once
To separate from the rebellious throng.
Lcsts. Remove himself who will. We hold together.
Mich. Follow me, faithful choirs.
Lcsts. Go freely hence.
(Exit Michael)
Beelz. The Marshal goes to God, to make complaint.
Take heart! Prince Lucifer, I see, has mounted
His chariot and is escorted hither.
Brief counsel take: a military force
Without a head cannot expect to stand.
But as for me, the office is too heavy.

Enter Lucifer.

Luc. All Heav'n is moved and shaken by your quarrel.
God's legions stand divided, torn in twain.
Revolt sweeps all before it. We must counsel
With prudence, to avoid calamity.
Lcsts. Sir Governor, support of all the righteous,
We trust that thou wilt not, like Michael, grant
The neck of the Angelic race to be
A trampled footstool for man's progeny,
Nor gild and gloss such insult and affront
With specious show of reason, and encourage
The rise of men, a gross and earthy race.
What incense does this stranger bring to God?
Why are we charged to serve a vulgar worm,

Support his hand and hearken at his voice?
If God created Heaven and the Angels
Merely for him, 'twere better far that we
Had never been created. Pity us,
O Lucifer! Let not our Orders sink,
Thus guiltless, and be brought so low, while man
Above us shines in the inaccessible Light
Before whose Presence ev'n the Seraphim,
Trembling with blinded anguish, fade like shadows.
If thou wilt condescend to right this wrong
And champion our franchise in this Kingdom,
With one accord we promise to support thee.
Accept this battle-axe! Protect the right!
We swear to set thee, in full majesty
Upon the Throne assign'd by God to Adam.
With one accord we promise to support thee.
Accept this battle-axe! Protect the right!
Luc. My sons, on whose fidelity no blot
Of treason may be found, all that God wills
Or may demand of us is right. I know
No other right, and as His Governor
Support Him and His edicts with my power.
The sceptre that I bear, my hand received
From His Omnipotence, a pledge of favour
And mark of His benevolence towards us all.
If now His heart and thought have fall'n on Adam,
And He be pleased to set man in dominion
Above us all, crown'd on the Throne of Heaven,
Though we have never waver'd in our duty,
What shall we counsel? Who will speak against Him?
If Adam in the same magnificence
As the Angelic Orders had been set,
That could be borne by all the Sons of Heaven,
Sprung from God's stock. But now their grief were just,
If such displeasure were not guilt with God.
There's danger either way, howe'er you take it:
For we may either yield to Him through fear
Or rashly strive against His sov'ran Power.
I hope that He may pardon your offense.
Lcsts. Accept this baton, ay, Sir Governor,
And save the Right! We'll follow in thy wake.
Swoop swiftly forward on thy pinions now,
And we will perish or win victory!

Luc. 'Tis counter to our oath and Gabriel's word.
Lcsts. And that conflicts with God, and sets man higher.
Luc. Let God Himself defend His name and throne!
Lcsts. Do thou defend thine own! And we, as pillars,
Will uphold thee and Angels' honour too.
God's crown, and ours, no man shall tread upon.
Luc. The Marshal Michael, arm'd and bless'd by God,
Will meet us straightway now with all his host,
His forces against ours -- uneven warfare!
Lcsts. If thou gain not the half, yet canst thou draw
The third part of Heaven's army to thy side
If once thou art committed to this cause.
Luc. But we risk everything, our favour lost
To the Oppressors of your rights.
Lcsts. Yet courage,
And bravery, the sense of scorn and outrage,
Our rancour and despair, and martial skill,
These shall revenge the wrong that otherwise
Can ne'er be settled. With so much at stake
We shall be strengthen'd in our will to fight.
Beelz. The holy realm's already in our power.
In spite of all decrees strength lies in weapons,
Provided we but range ourselves for battle.
Those who still hesitate will join at once.
Luc. I agree then to answer force with force.
Beelz. So mount thy throne, thou bravest of the brave!
Sir Governor, that we may swear allegiance!
Luc. Bear witness, Prince Beelzebub, and you,
Ye most illustrious Lords, Prince Belial
And Prince Apollyon. Witness here that I
Accept this headship out of direst need,
To guard God's kingdom and ward off our ruin!
Beelz. Bring forth the standard now, that we may swear
Fidelity to God and Morning Star.
Lcsts. We swear alike by God and Lucifer!
Beelz. Now bring the incense, all ye loyal ranks
And wave your censers before Lucifer,
Your saucers full of fragrance; glorify

Our general with light and gleam of torches!
Exalt him now with poetry, and song,
And music, shawms and trumpets! We rejoice
Thus to escort him onward with all pomp.
Raise up a clearer tone
In honour of his throne!
Lcsts. Soldiers of Lucifer, come ye, running!
Follow his flag!
Gather together your strength and cunning!
None must lag!
Follow this god at his drum's brave beat!
Guard your rights and your country sweet!
Help him to trample on Michael's legions,
Brave in face!
Help to keep Adam from these high regions,
And his race.
Follow this hero with trumpet and drum.
Guard the crown of our angeldom.
See how his Morning Star now is shining!
At its light.
Soon shall the enemy's flag be pining,
Deep in night.
Lucifer proudly we'll crown as our king.
Incense we'll offer; his Star we'll sing.

CHORUS OF ANGELS

Whither has flamed this faction, (Strophe.)
That Heaven's rash dissents
Have rent the regiments
And bared the sword for action
In rude, insensate hands?
Who, though he win or perish,
Of all our Angel bands
Is happy? For we cherish
Our brethren, if they be
Victors in their endeavour,
Or, as the vanquished, flee
To exile, damn'd forever.
O sons of one great God,
Where have your rash feet trod!

Alas, and whither wander (Antistrophe.)
The Spirits? What pretext

Their calm delight has vex'd,
Seducing them to squander
Their powers without need
In this mad expedition?
Could Folly not take heed
Of Heaven's rich position?
Was Heaven not enough
To satisfy such cattle,
That Envy in a huff
Should sow this seed of battle
In our calm Fatherland?
By whom shall this strife be bann'd?

If this war-flame should not slacken (Epode.)
Through the might of higher Grace,
What will stand firm in its place?
Hot Ambition all will blacken:
Heav'n and earth and sea and shore,
Melted, will exist no more.
Fierce Ambition in one hour,
If in frenzy it should win,
Would destroy all heavenly power,
For it knows not God nor kin.

ACT FOUR

Enter Gabriel and Michael.

Gab. All heaven is aglow in one bright fire
Of treason and revolt. I, as God's envoy,
Do summon thee to rise immediately
And burn out, with a flame of zeal, these stains
Upon God's name and Heaven's purity.
Prince Lucifer in proud defiance calls
The rebels round with trumpet and with drum.
Mich. Alas, has Lucifer betray'd his trust?
Gab. A third of Heaven has already sworn
Allegiance to the faithless Morning Star,
Worshipp'd his throne with incense, as to God,
And, with the blasphemy of godless music,
Sung in his honour. Hither come they, throng'd
In ample power, and threaten terribly
To burst the doors of Heaven's arsenal

With violence. A wild, disorder'd noise
Of thundering roars fast, above, below.
It lightens, storms, and rages, in such pain
As almost shakes the pillars of our Court.
One hears no Seraphim, no antiphons
Of holy praise. Each sits in chill distress
Plunged to the ears and over. All the choirs
Of Paradise grow silent for a moment,
Then burst out wailing in their sympathy
Over the blind apostasy of Angels,
The blessed Host, and the Angelic nature.
'Tis more than time for thee to carry out
This day thy duty, by thy holy oath
Erst on the sword-point of the lightning sworn,
As Marshal, in God's Name.
Mich. But what has tempted
God's Governor to turn against his Lord
And serve as head for mad conspirators?
Gab. God knows with what reluctance I defend
His righteous cause to this extremity!
How bitterly will vengeance smite that crew!
For none can find a way of mediation
To lead this wretched, stray'd, and sightless race
Back to the highroad of their loyalty.
I have beheld God's rapture cloak itself
Within a cloud of grief; but in the end
Wrath lit a fire in the Eyes of Light
And He gave orders for His troops to march
And break the attack. There in defence I heard
God's Mercy and God's Righteousness maintain
Stark equipoise upon the scales of Reason.
I saw the Cherubim, how they fell down
Prostrate upon their faces and cried out:
"Grant mercy, mercy, and not justice, Lord!"
Thus for the heavy wrong there had been made
Propitiation, and the Deity
Seem'd almost ready to be reconciled;
When suddenly there mounted up a stench
Of incense, offer'd Lucifer below
With song of praise and trumpet. God withdrew
His holy face from such idolatry,
Accursèd to all Spirits here in Heaven.
Mercy has had its day. Put on thine armour.
God summons thee, ere the revolt surprise us.

Tame with thy weapons the wild Behemoths
And foul Leviathans that riot thus!
Mich. Swift Uriel, my Squire, fetch my lightning,
Harness and shield and helmet, and God's banner!
Now let the trump be blown! To arms, to arms!
Come, all ye Thrones and Powers that are true,
And bear your arms with us in righteousness!
Advance ye regiments, each in his place!
God gives the word, so let the trump be blown,
The hollow drums be beaten, and in zeal
Summon innumerable throngs in arms!
Strike up! I gird the weapons on, that guard
The Name of God: our courage now is high.
Gab. This harness fits as bravely on thy limbs
As if created with thee. Here's the flag,
In which God's name and weapon shine upon thee,
And a Sun rampant promises success.
The colonels come to greet thee, as the Head
Of all of Heaven's Host, beneath God's banner.
Courage, Prince Michael. Thou shalt lead His battle.
Mich. So shall I. Guard my interests in Heaven.
Gab. Our prayers and hopes go with thee in the fray.
(Exeunt severally)

Enter Lucifer, Beelzebub, and Luciferists.

Luc. How stands it with our army, and my cause?
Beelz. The army longs, directly, with thy blessing,
To fly against the van of Michael's host.
Lcsts. 'Tis even so. Each waits for thy command
To hasten up with arms and wings together,
To intercept the winds from our great foe,
And, as he lies confounded, chain him down.
Luc. How numerous are our troops? How great our strength?
Beelz. It grows each moment, foaming from each sphere
To join us, like a sea of light and fire.
I wager that a third of Heav'n supports us,
If not indeed the half; for Michael's tide
Is ebbing every instant everywhere.
Half of the Watch and the chief household Guards
Out of each Order, from each Hierarchy,
Forswear their lord, Prince Michael, as do we.
Here are seen Cherubim and Seraphim,

Bearing our banners. Paradise itself,
Compell'd by grief to languish, pales its verdure.
Where'er the eye turns, certain ruin shows.
Above our heads a dark cloud seems to hang,
Pregnant with rain. The omen spells success
For this our venture. We have but to grasp it.
The crown of Heaven is as good as yours.
Luc. I like these words much more than Gabriel's edict.
Hearken, before the staircase of my throne!
Hearken, ye generals! Give ear, ye knights!
And hear what I shall set forth, brief and plain!
Ye know how far already we have gone
In quest of condign vengeance against God.
'Twere folly to draw back, in hope of peace.
Nor may one think this stain indelible
To cleanse through pardon. Thus necessity
Must be for us a law, a certain refuge
From any thought of wavering or yielding.
Defend ye, therefore, with relentless power,
My standard and my Star, and our new State
Proclaim'd by Angels who aspire to freedom!
Let come what may! Great-hearted and ungrieved,
The immortal natures that ye once were given
Cannot be crush'd out by Omnipotence.
If you will fiercely thrust with your fell pikes
Into your foemen's hearts and come to triumph,
Then shall the tyranny of Heaven be changed
Into a Free Republic, in whose Court
No Son of Adam, crown'd in highest honour,
And flatter'd with an earthly retinue,
Shall set the chains of slavish servitude
Upon your necks, to sweat in service, bent
Beneath his iron yoke forevermore.
As you have sworn allegiance with one voice,
Utter the oath again, that we may hear it.
Lcsts. We swear, alike by God and Lucifer!
Beelz. But see how Raphael, alarm'd and full
Of mild compassion, with his olive-branch
Comes flying from above, to embrace thee here
In the soft hope of armistice and truce.

Enter Raphael.

Raph. Ah, Governor, chief representative

Of God's authority, what drives thee thus
Far from the path of duty? Shouldst thou strive
Against the great Creator of thy glory
And lightly totter in fidelity?
I never look'd for this from thee. Alas,
I swoon with grief, and hang upon thy neck,
Pallid and anxious.
Luc. Honest Raphael!
Raph. My happiness, my dearest friend, I pray thee,
Hear me!
Luc. Speak, and as fully as thou likest.
Raph. Pardon, O Lucifer! Ah, save thyself!
Draw now no weapon against me, who pine
In pain for thee. I come with medicine
And balm of mercy from the heart of God,
Who, in His council, once anointed thee,
Above His myriads of crown'd Dominions,
Upon thy lofty throne as Governor.
What madness is it that confounds thy thought?
He set His seal and likeness on thy head
And hallow'd brow, shining with beauty, grace,
And wisdom, and whatever richness flows
Unstinted from that Source of every blessing.
Then didst thou shine in Paradise, before
The sun's bright face, out of a cloud of dew
And fragrant roses, and thy festal robe
Was stiff with pearls, turquoises, emeralds,
Rubies and diamonds and purest gold.
A sceptre was entrusted to thy hands,
Heavier than all the rest; and thou didst rise
With trumpet and with music through the light
Of glowing stars in gemm'd magnificence.
And wilt thou rush in rashness from thy throne,
And hazard all that splendor and that beauty?
Why should thy radiance, that blazons Heaven,
Darken our light amid a mob of beasts,
A wanton crowd of monsters -- gryphon's claw
And dragon's head and other gruesomeness
Misshapen? And should Heaven's eyes, the stars,
See thee so low, so reft of all thy power
And rank and honour, through disloyalty?
May God forbid it, upon whose Face I gaze
Amid the holy Light where all we Seven
Serve Him before His throne and quake before

Such Majesty as shines upon our foreheads
And quickens all things that have life and breath!
Ah, Sir, may my petition move thy heart!
Thou knowest my pure purpose and my heart,
Concern'd for thee. Take this proud helmet off!
Remove this armour! Cast the battle-axe
Down from this hand, thy target from the other!
Not higher! Lay it down, ah, lay it down!
Thyself pull down that flag, and bow thy pinions
Before the glory of Almighty God,
Ere from the throne and topmost pinnacle
Of honour He shall smite thee down to dust,
Yea, shatter thee to powder, till thy race
Survives in neither root nor branch nor life
Nor any memory. An end like that
Were a distressful life if Death, Despair,
And the eternal gnawing of a worm
Might bear the name of living. Come, submit!
Halt now this march! I offer you God's mercy,
With this green branch. Accept, or 'tis too late!
Luc. Sir Raphael, I have not merited
Contempt or threats. My heroes here have sworn
Allegiance both to Lucifer and God,
And have set up this flag by Heaven's oath.
Let wantons gossip as they will through Heaven:
I do but wage this warfare, under God,
To guard the privileges of my choirs,
Their due and lawful birthright before Adam
Saw the sun rising and o'er Paradise
The primal daylight shone. No human rule,
No earthly yoke shall gall the necks of Spirits,
No Angel host maintain the throne of Adam
With its free shoulder like a useful slave,
Though the End be that God will bury us
Deep in the pit of hell forevermore
With all the sceptres, crowns, and glorious light
That He had lavish'd on us from His bosom.
Let all things break that may! I guard the Right,
Compell'd by paramount necessity,
And only after my remonstrances
Were silenced by a lamentable cry
From many thousand tongues. Go hence, and take
This message to the Father under whom
I bear this standard in our country's cause!

Raph. Ah, Governor, why wouldst thou thus disguise
Thy thinking before God's all-seeing Eye?
Thou canst not veil thine aim. His face reveals,
By its white radiance, that hidden thing --
The dark Ambition which thy pregnant soul,
Now ripe for travail, presently will bear,
A hideous monster. How my hairs rise up!
Truly I flee for terror. Lucifer,
Blind Morning-Star, spare thyself yet! Thou knowest
Deceit is hateful to Omniscience.
Luc. Thou talkest of Ambition. Have I fallen
Short of my duty here in any way?
Raph. What hast thou spoken in thine inmost heart? —
"I will mount upward to the highest Heaven,
Hence through all clouds, above the stars of God,
And, like God's self, shine upon none with mercy,
Till, at my throne, they offer gifts as vassals.
No majesty shall shine with crown or sceptre
Until I grant the right from my high throne."
Cover thy face! Fall down! Fold humble wings!
And learn a higher Power above us all!
Luc. What! Am I not the Governor of God?
Raph. Thou art indeed, but finite is the power
Thou didst receive from infinite Dominion.
Subordinate, thou rulest in His name.
Luc. Alas, how long? Until Prince Adam comes
To put us all to shame and take his place
Above the Angels, sitting next to God.
Raph. Though sovran Monarchy divide its power
With an inferior, yea, set the crown
Of kingship upon man and hallow him
As Head above all Spirits, and o'er all
That bear, or ever shall bear, crown and sceptre,
Yet must thou learn to bow to God's decrees.
Luc. That is the stone on which to whet this axe.
Raph. Thou dost but sharpen it for thine own neck.
Consider where we stand. God tolerates
No stain of jealous envy, hate, or pride.
His chastening will cleanse these blots away.
Here no dissembling helps thee, Lucifer.
Would that before that all-beholding Sun,
Those Eyes all-penetrating, I could shield
These faults of thine! Where is thy glory now?
Luc. My glory has long since been giv'n away

To Adam and his Seed. No more they call me
God's eldest heir and first-anointed son.
<u>Raph</u>. Lord Lucifer, beware, and save thyself!
Submit to the supreme authority!
Vouchsafe that I may bear the welcome tidings
Up to God's Court, where everyone awaits me!
See, I fall humbly at your Lordship's foot!
For God's sake, do not give your aid to rebels
Who turn upon your will as on an axis.
Ought you, opposing Heaven, to disturb
These highest realms of holiness and peace
With myriads in armour, to conduct
The battle-flag with drum and trumpet forth,
To turn against our God, the matchless Wrestler?
<u>Luc</u>. He turns against me first. If Adam's issue
Were giv'n the same estate and throne as Angels,
That would seem tolerable. But the sparks
From this dispute now fly indignant hence
Over all roofs. Let Angeldom be silent,
(That is thy plea!) and let us all concur
Respectfully in this award to man
Of all that we possess. To strive with man,
Forsooth, is sinful striving against God.
How could God find it in His heart to abase
So low, so deep, those whom He once created
For sov'ran empire? For a noble mind,
Once consecrated to command, can scarce
Humble itself to an inferior
Who rises from mean station to the throne
And strips all former dignities away.
Such foul humiliation stains the dawn
And glory of one's rising; better far
Had one remain'd in shadowy, colorless
And baseless non-existence. To be nothing
Surpasses this disgrace a thousandfold.
<u>Raph</u>. Rule that is lent is no inheritance.
<u>Luc</u>. I then refuse the loan, if such it be.
<u>Raph</u>. Stand by thine office! Or hast thou forgotten
The end to which thy wisdom has been pledged
As Governor of Heav'n, so that thou mightest
Hold all things in stability and peace?
And hast thou against God put on that cuirass,
The perjured head of blind conspiracy?

Luc. We armed ourselves but from necessity,
Little disposed to stand out against God.
But reason speaks, though shield and sword were mute.
We free our state. Dost grudge us victory?
Raph. No victory is noble, where within
A single realm, one kingdom's battle-hordes
Strive with their kindred. It is pitiful
When brothers of one Order in the end
Are vanquish'd by their brothers. For our sake,
For God's sake and his waiting penalties,
Ah Governor, dismiss thy regiments!
I hear the frightful sound of smithying
At chains, in order, after thy defeat,
To lead thee fetter'd through the air in triumph.
I hear a noise already as the host
Of Michael gradually marches near.
'Tis time, high time, to halt your mad campaign.
Luc. What profit's it at the eleventh hour
To save oneself? Here is no hope of peace.
Raph. I vouch for clemency, and pledge myself
As mediator to redeem thee yonder.
Luc. To drown my star in darkness and disgrace!
To see my foes triumphant on the throne!
Raph. Ah Lucifer, wake from insensate sleep!
I see the brimstone pit gape terrible
Near thee with yawning throat. Shalt thou indeed,
Fairest of all that God has yet created,
Become a prey for the insatiable
And ever-burning maw of Tartarus?
Nay, God forbid! Alas, accept our plea
And olive-branch! We offer thee God's peace.
Luc. Was e'er sad creature so perplex'd as I,
Standing between great terror and faint hope?
Vict'ry is hazardous, defeat half-sure.
Is it but folly against God to strive,
And first to set rebellious standards up
Against His high decree and plain command?
To lead a host of rebels against God
And set a counter-law against His law?
Sully myself with base ingratitude
And vex the mercy, love, and majesty
Of the all-bounteous Father, who bestows
All blessings present, past, and yet to be?
How I have wander'd from the path of duty!

Having forsworn my Maker, how can I
Before His brightness hide my blasphemies
And sacrilege? Alas, here no retreat
Profits at all. No, we have climb'd too high.
What plan were best in all this hopelessness?
Time grants no respite, and this instant now
Is no sufficiency of time, if one
May give the name of time to this brief moment
Between salvation and eternal doom.
It is too late. Our stain's past remedy.
Hope and device are gone. I hear God's trumpet.

Enter Apollyon.

Apol. Up, Governor! This is no time to tarry:
Michael with all his starry regiments
Draws near and summons thee to take the field.
The time requires thee to gird for battle.
Rise, rise with us! We see the conflict won.
Luc. Won? That's too early. Fighting's not begun.
Let none make light of battle's heavy onslaught.
Apol. I have beheld the fear in Michael's face,
And his pale troops will want to save their heels.
Doubt not that we shall here demolish all.
Here comes our standard, with our generals.
Luc. Each to his company and due division!
Now boldly sound the clarion and trumpet!
Apol. We wait thy word.
Luc. So follow, in this sign.
Raph. Alas, but now he waver'd, deep in doubt.
Despair's his leader. Into what a state
Of woe th' Archangel hurls his followers!
No more with joy in heaven may he shine,
Unless our God's compassion intervene.
Ye heavenly choirs, come, turn yourselves to prayer!
Meekness may ward this blow off even yet,
For prayer can break a heart of adamant.

CHORUS OF ANGELS

Father, whom no perfumeries
Nor gold nor psalm of praise can please
So much as trust in Thine ordaining, --
The mute humility of soul

That shapes itself to Thy control
And works thy will without complaining, --
Thou seest, Author of us all,
How he Thou didst as Chief instal
Has turn'd his arms against Thy pleasure,
And how with trumpeting and drum
And chariot he dares to come,
Led by Ambition beyond measure.
Have mercy on this blasphemy;
Avert the dreadful destiny
Of myriad comrades thus mistaken,
Who, wretchedly misguided, dress
In armor of rebelliousness;

Raph.
I pray Thee God of Mercy, spare
The Governor, who seeks to wear
The crown of crowns upon his forehead
And reign in triumph at Thy side!
Ah, who will cleanse him of this pride,
This foul offense, debased and horrid?

Chorus.
O suffer not the fairest one
Thine eyes of grace have gazed upon
To perish in contempt and terror!
Let him atone his thankless deed,
And to his duty still give heed.
Forgive in mercy all his error!

ACT FIVE

Enter Raphael, then Uriel.

Raph. The sky, from its foundation to the crown
Of highest heav'n, exults with Gabriel's trumpet
And swaying banner. Victory is won.
Our shimmering shields emblazon mimic suns,
And from each shield-sun streams triumphant day.
There, from the fight, comes Uriel, the squire,
Bearing the sharp, two-edged sword of flame,
Whetted by God's revenge and wrath to pierce
Breastplate and shield and helm of adamant:
And this, to left and right, hath swept through all

That would have thrust at God's Omnipotence.
O austere squire, Heav'n's executioner,
With righteous blow, upon defiant wrong
That raised itself against the eternal Right,
Blest be thy weapons that thus vindicate
And shield the honour of our Angel-town.
What glory thou hast won, in God's esteem!
But tell us of the fight and all the course
Of heaven's first battle, for we fain would hear.
Uriel. My heart, at thy desire burns to begin
And boldly tell the tale of that wild storm
In which God's army won the victory.
Our Marshal Michael (notified by God
Through heaven's messenger, sent flying down
Faster than falling star across the sky,
How Lucifer in arrogant revolt
Prepared to lead the hosts that worshipp'd him
And swore allegiance to his star and standard)
Put on directly, urged by Gabriel,
His scaly cuirass, and gave prompt command
To all his captains, chiefs, and generals
To set the troops in order in God's name,
So that, with power united, through the vault
Of heaven's pure blue, upon that perjured scum
They might sweep down and whelm those fiends in darkness
Ere they should triumph unexpectedly.
At this command, God's armies came in haste,
Array'd for battle, swiftly as an arrow
Shot from the bow-string. One saw countless troops
Drawn in a murmuring three-edged multitude
That shone triangular upon our face,
A unity of fierce, three-pointed light
Bright as a glass of polish'd diamond,
A battle-point fit for almighty God.
The Marshal, with hot lightning in his hand,
Stood by God's banner at the army's centre:
He who would triumph, with courageous mien,
Must above all guard and defend the heart.
Raph. Where lay the accursed host that would attack us?
Uriel. They came with bravery to the assault,
And had forgotten all obedience
And oath and honour in their wickedness,

Too arrogant to yield to God and us.
Swiftly their host wax'd like a crescent moon;
Sharp'ning its points, it set two horns against us,
As when the creatures of the Zodiak
And all the other monstrous beasts of heaven
The starry Bull assails with golden horns.
Upon their right was Prince Beelzebub,
With trusty guards, seeking to clip our wings.
Prince Belial held their left. One saw them both
Gleam in their armor; while the Governor,
Now recreant Field Marshal against God,
Secured the centre of the host, to guard
The midmost clasp that tied the troops together.
His proud flag, shining with his morning-star,
Was boldly borne behind him by Apollyon,
Full-panoplied in light from head to toe.
Raph. Alas, what dares th' Archangel undertake?
Ah, that I had in time persuaded him
To leave off his endeavour. None the less,
Describe for me the appearance of the fight
And in what guise the Prince led on his bands.
Uriel. Ring'd by troops uniform'd in green and sapphire,
He, moved by wrath and grudge implacable,
Dress'd in a golden coat of mail that shone
Above his purple tunic, mounted now
His chariot, with gold wheels, ruby-studded.
The Lion and fell Dragon were his team,
In harness all bepearl'd, ready for flight,
Sprinkled with myriad stars upon their backs,
And burning for the wild destructive strife.
He bore a battle-axe; his shimmering shield,
In which the morning star was wrought with art,
Hung on his left arm, ready for all hazard.
Raph. O Lucifer, thou'lt rue this arrogance!
Thou Phoenix, among all that give God praise,
How thou didst stand forth from among the host
With head and helm and shoulders! With what pride
And lordly dignity thou worest weapons
As if thy nature had been born for it!
O head of all the angels, stop, turn back!
Uriel. So stood they, ranged in ranks, squadron by squadron,
Each at his post along the battle-line

And ready at command; when clamorous drum
And the resounding trumpet mingle war,
The sound makes keen the weapons in their hands
And mounts into the holy vault of light --
A sound at which a pregnant thunder-cloud
Broke straightway, flash on flash, with flaming
hail,
A lightning-storm that frighted heaven, and shook
The pillars of God's court; the spheres and stars,
Bewilder'd in their round and orbit, swoon'd
Amid their circling, since they knew not where
To drive, to east or west, above, below.
Lightning alone is seen, and thunder heard.
Nothing can stand. The highest is struck down.
But when the roar of heav'n's artillery
Subsided, then the armies come to grips
With mace and halberd, sword, and spear and dagger.
They then proceed to slash and pierce each other;
And he who best can slay or maim makes haste,
And strikes and maims and slays. All brotherhood
Is over now, and no one recognizes
His fellow-citizen. One sees pearl'd hoods,
And tresses of bright hair, and pinions fly,
Scatter'd and scorch'd amid the lightning-fire.
One sees blue turquoise, gold, and diamond mix'd,
And strings of pearls and tresses' ornaments
And wings and broken arrows fluttering
Down through the gulf of air. A gruesome cry
Breaks from the army in green uniform,
Forced by necessity to seek retreat.
But Lucifer in rage renews the fight
In three assaults, and buttresses most proudly
The faintness of his regiments, as when
The noisy surges, seething on a cliff,
Halt, wave on wave, and move no farther on.
Raph. It calls for courage, in despair to fight.
Uriel. Brave Michael blew the trumpet, praised be
God!
And all our troops grew bold at that command
To mount aloft and gain advantage high
Over the enemy; who also rises
But, heavier, drifts to leeward. Even thus
A falcon, heavenward, on lusty pinions
Betakes himself before the herons spy him

And tremble in their meadow by the wood;
The herons cry to see that soaring flight,
And rear their beaks, seeking to shun
The hostile claws and pierce the falcon's breast
As from above he swoops upon his prey.
Raph. O Lucifer, what counsel in such straits,
Poised there, unfortified, in open field!
A horrid hurricane will soon befall thee,
And sink thee to the unplumb'd pit of Hell.
Uriel. That was a noble prospect to behold:
Below, a crescent; and above, three-edged,
A spear-point lunging! Thus the regiments,
Opening and closing ranks at nod of head,
Stood firm as walls of iron in their place,
As on an equipoise of air upheld
With all their siege tools and artillery.
One might imagine them a thunder-head,
A hanging cloud on which the sunlight plays
And gleams in checker'd and translucent rainbows.
The heavenly eagle, flown so steeply up,
Espied God's foe, a hawk's flight underneath,
And bravely clapp'd his wings, not apt to chase
In futile recklessness but resolute
To smite his foe and plunder his bright plume.
So rose hood'd beak and claw in ample air,
To seize the prey or drive him down the wind.
Then they come headlong from on high, in streams
As to the sea some Northern cataract
That foams and rages from the beetling rocks
And with its roaring frightens beasts of earth
And monsters of the deep in some sheer fjord,
Where water-jets descend the precipice
With stones and countless pine-trees, hurtling down
With irresistible compulsion. Thus,
The spear-point of the army fiercely smote
The navel of the half-moon, striking out
The ghastly flames of brimstone, red and blue,
In blow on blow and thunderbolt on bolt.
A cry ascends. The centre of the host
Slowly begins to yield in rancour back.
The bow of the half-moon nigh snapp'd and crack'd
Under the tension, for the ends held fast
But it must break asunder in the midst
Unless a breathing-space be giv'n straightway.

Now lordly Lucifer swoop'd here and there
And at that cry drew near, and show'd himself
Brave and great-hearted still to save the day
And by his prowess in his chariot
Give courage to the fainting. He wards off
The cruellest blows and arrows on the teeth
Of his wild team. Lion and Dragon fly
In fury, as he drives, with fearsome speed.
One roar'd and bit and tore; the other shot
Poison with his cleft tongue and kindled plague,
Filling the air with smoke from out his nostrils.
Raph. The fire from above will harry them.
Uriel. He swings his battle-axe, and seeks to fell
God's banner now descending, forth from which,
Out of God's name, a fairer light shines forth,
And pales the lesser glory of his face.
It seem'd that Lucifer begrudged the omen.
With battle-axe in hand, now here, now there,
He check'd the missiles and demolish'd them,
And cast them backward from his shield, till Michael
Appear'd to him in shining armaments,
Bright as a god amid a ring of suns.
"Dismount, O Lucifer! Grant God the field!
Surrender arms and standard! Yield to God!
Lead off this wicked host, this godless band,
Or else beware thy head!" Thus cried he downward.
But the Arch-enemy of God, stiff-neck'd and staunch,
Yea prouder at that word, renew'd the attack
And three times sought to sunder with his axe
The adamantine shield that bore God's name.
But he, provoking Heaven, felt Its wrath:
The axe upon the holy adamant
Rang loudly and was shiver'd into pieces.
Then Michael raised his hand, and with a bolt
Of thunder, strengthen'd by Omnipotence,
He smote the wicked one through helm and head
So pitilessly that he toppled back,
Hurl'd from his chariot, which overset
And soon with Dragon, Lion, and all else
Follow'd its falling master as he sank.
At that, the standard of the Morning Star
Lost all its brilliance; fleet Apollyon felt
My flaming sword, and gave the flag as prey
Amid the myriads that swarm'd to stay

The Head of those fell squadrons in his fall.
On one side still, Beelzebub was zealous;
And Belial defied us on the other;
But in the midst the forces were untied,
And with the Governor's heavy overthrow
The half-moon broke in pieces. Then Apollyon
Came to the rescue with as many monsters
As all the starry belt of heaven bears.
Giant Orion shouted till the air
Grew faint to hear him, boasting with his club
To bruise our army's front -- that does not yield
To wild Orion's club, or any giant.
The Arctic Bears rear'd up on their hind paws
To slay a hundred with their rending strength;
The Hydra gapes at us with fifty throats
And vomits venom: such a gallery
Of battle-pictures was ne'er seen before.
Raph. Praise be to God! Kneel and invoke His name!
Ah, Lucifer, where is thy treason now?
Under what aspect shall I see thy form?
Where is thy radiance, which out-did all light?
Uriel. As the clear day, turn'd to insensate night
When the sun sinks, forgets to shine with gold,
So all his beauty, in that dread descent,
Changed to deformity, accurst and vile:
The heroic visage to a brutish snout,
His teeth to fangs, able to gnaw through steel;
His feet and hands into four sorts of claws;
The skin of opal to an inky hide;
Out of his bristled back burst dragon's wings;
In short, the Archangel, reverenced but now
By all the angelic host, was changed in aspect,
And in most gruesome fashion, as we gazed,
He mingled seven animals in one:
A lion, arrogant; a greedy swine;
A slothful ass; a horn'd rhinoceros;
An ape, shameless alike and gross in front
And hinder parts, and lewd and hot of nature,
An envious snake; an avaricious wolf.
His beauty is a beast now, to be cursed
Ever by God, by spirits, and by men.
The monster shudders if one gaze upon him,

And hides his griesly form in fog and mist.
Raph. So fares Ambition that would thrust at God.
Where is Apollyon?
Uriel. When he saw the tide
Turn at the sinking of his Star, he fled.
All fled the heavenly cannon that above
Pour'd volley after volley, lightning-flash
And roll of thunder. Monsters that had crawled
Into the light were swept to join the rout.
Ah, what an eddy there of showers together!
And how the onslaught raged! What tides, what tides
Swept onward as our forces, blest by God,
Struck, and struck down whate'er our weapons met!
Our green-clad foes reel'd everywhere in flight
And wildest desolation -- changed in form
And limbs and stature! Lo, they roar'd and bark'd;
One yelp'd, another howl'd, What scowls we saw
On Angel-faces verging upon Hell
And hellish hideousness! Hark, I hear Michael
Coming to triumph with angelic spoil.
The choirs greet him now with songs and cymbals,
With shawms and tambours. They approach, and strew
Their leaves of laurel at the heavenly sound.

Enter Chorus of Angels and Michael.

CHORUS

Blest be that hero most
Who all the godless host
With standard and with power and with might
Hath cast down from their boast!

He whom God placed on high
Is hurtled from the sky,
Sunk in the night with all his perjured Power.
God's Name we glorify!

In flames the rebels fell;
Brave Michael knew right well
How to extinguish such a fray, and thrust
The guilty down to Hell.

God's honour he retrieves.

Crown him with laurel leaves!
The court of Heaven grows in peace, and here
No voice of discord grieves.

Now sing th' Almighty's praise
In halls Hell cannot raze;
Give laud and honour to the Lord of lords
Inspiring all our lays!

Michael. Now God be praised! The state in Heaven is changed.
The Arch-Fiend's vanquish'd, and has left his standard
And Morning-star and helmet, arms and shield,
These trophies of defeat, on heaven's axis.
Now with all jubilation, laud, and praise
And clarion and trumpet, hang aloft
The escutcheon of revolt that dared to rise
Against our God, the Stock invincible,
The Source and Well and Father of all things
That have known being and identity.
No more we'll see the radiance of His throne
Tarnish'd by mists of base ingratitude.
Deep, deep beneath our sight, and these high courts
The rebels hurtle in the abyss of air,
Darken'd and blind and horribly deform'd.
So may it be with him who wars on God!
Chorus. So may it be with him who wars on God,
And grudges Heaven's light to man, created
After the image of the Form Divine!

Enter Gabriel.

Gab. Alas, alas, how fortunes now have alter'd!
What fear's at hand! Our triumph is in vain:
'Tis vain to make display with spoil and standards.
Mich. What hear I, Gabriel?
Gab. Adam is fallen,
The stem and father of the human race,
Too lamentably, sadly, brought to ruin.
He's lost!
Mich. That is a thunderbolt to hear.
Yet I would haste to learn of his disaster.
Has the Accursed One attack'd Earth also?
Gab. After defeat, he drew his host together,

But first his Generals, who shudder'd much
To see each other's face. Then covertly
He set himself to shun th' all-seeing Eye
Within a hollow cloud, a den of murder
Dark with mists, that cloak'd their fiery glances;
And there surrounded by his hellish Council
He, from his seat, raged hellishly at God:
"Ye Powers, who so proudly, in just cause,
Have borne this wrong, now is it time to take
Revenge for all our grief -- in wrath and guile
To harry heav'n with grudge unreconciled
Against its chosen image, and seduce
The human race, right in its source and cradle
Before the power of its strength wax great
And triumph in the strong succeeding race.
I seek to ruin Adam and his seed,
And, through transgression of God's primal law,
To lay on them such stain past remedy
That, poison'd with their sad posterity,
They never shall inherit that high throne
From which we have been cast. Yet it may be
That some, a slender number, shall rise up,
And still, through thousands dead and toil and pain,
Mount to the crown'd estate that we have lost.
Straightway, on Adam's track, distress unending
Shall spread abroad throughout the whole, wide world.
Nature, thus harm'd shall almost be consumed,
And wish to turn to Nothing and to Chaos.
So I see man, who bears the stamp of God,
Debased and alienated from that Likeness,
Darken'd in will, temper, and understanding,
His inborn Light demolish'd or bedimm'd,
Mourning his life, till in the lap of Earth
He sate th' inevitable maw of Death.
I shall exalt my haughty tyranny,
And ye, my sons, shall be adored as gods
At altars in high temples without number,
Worshipp'd with cattle, frankincense, and gold, --
Thus shall more men than tongue can utter, doom
All Adam's race forever through foul acts
That offer proud affront to God's own name.
His triumph o'er my crown will cost him dear!"
Mich. Such proud defiance is a cursed sin!

We soon shall cure thee of that blasphemy.
Gab. Thus spake the Fiend, and sent Prince Belial
That he forthwith, might bring man to his fall.
Straight he assumed a guise of wickedness,
That of the serpent, craftiest of all beasts,
In order to adorn with gloss of words
The lure which thus the guileless creatures took
In simple faith as for the nonce he hung
Down from a branch upon the tree of knowledge:
"Has God forbidden you, on pain of death,
So solemnly, so sternly, here to taste
The freedom of this fruit, this best of trees?
No, simple Eve, by no means! Thou art wrong.
Gaze but upon this apple. How it shines,
And glows in blended grace of red and gold!
How much you need this banquet! Ay, my daughter,
Walk somewhat nearer, for no poison lurks
Amid the shade of these immortal leaves.
How tempting is this fruit! Ay, pluck! Pluck freely!
I promise thee the gifts of light and knowledge.
Come, why dost thou retreat, afraid of harm?
Taste, be like God Himself in sapience
And comprehension, praise, and majesty,
However much He may begrudge the favour!
So shalt thou grasp the difference in kind
And essence and identity in things."
At once the fair bride's heart begins to burn,
And kindles, yearning for the lauded fruit.
The fruit seduced the eye, the eye the mouth,
Desire moved the trembling hand to pluck.
She pluck'd and proved, and ate (her progeny
Will suffer for that sin!) with Adam too,
And soon their eyes are open'd and they see
Their nakedness and cover it with foliage,
Hiding their shame with fig-leaves in disgrace,
And seek for shelter in the shadowy wood,
Hiding, in vain, from God's all-piercing Eye.
The air grows slowly dark. They see the rainbow,
A messenger and omen of God's grief.
For Heaven mourns. No wringing of the hands
Nor lamentable outcry helps the pair.
It lightens, flash on flash; and blow on blow,
The thunder speaks. All that they hear and see

Is anguish, sorrowing, and mortal fear.
They flee their shadow, but can ne'er escape
The worm of guilty conscience in their hearts.
Foot after foot, they totter stumbling onward.
The countenance sees death, the eyes, deep drown'd
In tears, behold no light; All hope is gone.
But a short time ago they used to rear
Their heads most bravely in the sunny air;
And now a rustling leaf, a brook, a noise
However slight appals them; while a cloud
Descends beside them, and divides, and shows
A dawning Light, a Radiance, whence shines
The Most High, on their melancholy state,
And speaks in thunder, beating them to earth.
Chorus. Alas, 'twere better man had never been!
What pangs for doting on forbidden fruit!
Gab. "Adam, where art thou?" thunder'd God in anger. --
"Forgive me, Lord. Naked, I fled Thy face." --
"Whence didst thou learn thy nakedness and shame?
Are thy bold lips stain'd with unlawful fruit?" --
"Alas, my bride, my consort, tempted me!" --
"The cunning snake," said she, "beguiled me thus."--
Each on another laid the cause of sin.
Chorus. Mercy! What doom was pass'd on this offence?
Gab. The woman, by whom Adam was seduced,
God plagued with pangs of travail and subjection,
The man with work, sweat, care, and irksome toil;
The field, which at the last shall bury man,
With weeds and pestilence; the Snake, for guilt
With its sly tongue, shall creep upon its belly
And live in wretchedness on dust and earth.
But that the man might have firm consolation
In such distress, God promised faithfully
To raise up, from the woman's seed and blood,
The Mighty One, who through ancestral hatred
Shall bruise the Dragon and the Serpent's head,
And though the fell Beast bite Him near the heel,
The Hero shall be victor in this fray.
I come now in the name of the Most High
To publish this disaster. Set your ranks
In order straightway, ere they brew more trouble.
Mich. My squire, Uriel, most swift to guard

The holy Right and punish recklessness,
Take now thy flaming sword, fly down from hence,
And drive those out of Eden who thus blind
And reckless sinn'd against the primal law.
Guard thou the entrance of the Paradise
That they have desecrated; turn away
By force these exiles from the Tree of Life.
See that they pluck not its immortal fruit
And so misuse its harvest. Thou art set
On guard before the Garden and the Tree.
Outside let Adam wander, late and early,
And plough the stubborn clay from which God form'd
him.
Ozias, to whose hand God consecrated
The hammer of resounding adamant
And ruby chains and gyves and manacles,
Go hence, chain up that host of hellish beasts,
The Lion and fell Dragon, who have raged
Against our banners thus. Sweep clean the air
Of this accursèd herd, and fetter them
By neck and claw, and chain them fast forever.
This key to the abysmal pit of Hell
Is granted, Azarias, to thy care.
Go hence, and lock within its griesly gulf
All spirits that are hostile to our power.
Maceda, take this torch: the flame is thine
To kindle, in the bowels of the earth,
The brimstone lake, and torture Lucifer,
Who has been guilty of so many crimes,
With ever-burning fire and chilling frost;
That place shall Sorrow dwell, and Horror, Hardness,
Hunger and Thirst, Despair uncomforted,
And Conscience' sting, hid from the light of God,
Amid the murky haunt of wicked devils
That bear due witness to the doom of Heaven.
Meanwhile the promised Seed shall reconcile
The wrath of God, and shall restore with love
All that was lost in Adam's bitter fall.
Chorus. Redeemer that shalt bruise the Serpent's
head
And ransom fallen man from Adam's fault,
Op'ning a fairer Paradise above
To all the exiled progeny of Eve,
We count the ages -- year and day and hour --

Until Thy mercy dawn, and glorified
In body and in soul Thou shalt restore
Vigor to fainting Nature, and ascend
The holy throne from which the Angels fell.

ABRAHAM COWLEY

Davideis (1656)

Book I

Beneath the silent chambers of the earth,
Where the Suns fruitful beams give metals birth,
Where he the growth of fatal Gold does see,
Gold which above more Influence has than He . . .
There is a place deep, wondrous deep below,
Which genuine Night and Horrour does o'reflow,
No bound controls th' unwearied space, but Hell
Endless as those dire pains that in it dwell.
Here no dear glimpse of the Suns lovely face
Strikes through the Solid darkness of the place . . .
Here Lucifer the mighty Captive reigns;
Proud, 'midst his Woes, and Tyrant in his Chains.
Once General of a guilded Host of Sprights,
Like Hesper, leading forth the spangled Nights.
But down like Lightning, which him struck, he came;
And roar'd at his first plunge into the Flame.
Myriads of Spirits fell wounded round him there;
With dropping Lights thick shone the singed Air. . . .

Thrice did he knock his Iron teeth, thrice howl,
And into frowns his wrathful forehead rowl.
His eyes dart forth red flames which scare the Night,
And with worse Fires the trembling Ghosts affright.
A Troop of gastly Fiends compass him round,
And greedily catch at his lips fear'd sound.
Are we such Nothings then (said He) Our will
Crost by a Shepherds Boy? and you yet still
Play with your idle Serpents here? dares none
Attempt what becomes Furies? are ye grown

Benum'd with Fear, or Vertues sprightless cold,
You, who were once (I'm sure) so brave and bold?
Oh my ill chang'd condition! oh my fate!
Did I lose Heav'en for this?
With that, with his long tail he lasht his breast,
And horribly spoke out in Looks the rest.
The quaking Pow'ers of Night stood in amaze,
And at each other first could only gaze.
A dreadful Silence fill'd the hollow place,
Doubling the native terrour of Hells face;
Rivers of flaming Brimstone, which before
So loudly rag'd, crept softly by the shore;
No hiss of Snakes, no clanck of Chains was known;
The Souls amidst their Tortures durst not groan.
Envy at last crawls forth from that dire throng,
Of all the direful'st; her black locks hung long,
Attir'd with curling Serpents her pale skin
Was almost dropt from the sharp bones within,
And at her breast stuck Vipers which did prey
Upon her panting heart, both night and day . . .

Spend not, great King, thy precious rage (said she)
Upon so poor a cause; shall Mighty We
The glory of our wrath to him afford?
Are We not Furies still? And you our Lord?
At thy dread anger the fixt World shall shake,
And frighted Nature her own Laws forsake. . . .
Heav'ens guilded Troops shall flutter here and there,
Leaving their boasting Songs tun'd to a Sphere;
Nay their God too -- for fear he did, when We
Took rebel Arms against his Tyrannie,
So noble Arms, and in a Cause so great,
That Triumphs they deserve for their Defeat.
There was a Day! oh might I see't again
Though he had fiercer Flames to thrust us in! . . .

She spoke; all star'ed at first, and made a pause;
But strait the general murmur of applause
Ran through Deaths Courts; she frown'd still, and begun

To envy at the praise herself had won.
Great Belzebub starts from his burning Throne
To' embrace the Fiend, but she now furious grown
To act her part; thrice bow'd, and thence she fled;
The Snakes all hist, the Fiends all murmured.

Book II

An angel gives to David, in a trance, a vision of future events, down to and including the annunciation and the birth of Christ. At this stage he starts up out of his trance but is met by the Archangel Gabriel in visible form, who confirms the vision and all its hopeful promise.

Hither an Angel comes in Davids trance;
And finds them mingled in an antique dance;
Of all the numerous forms fit choice he takes,
And joyns them wisely, and this Vision makes. . . .

With sober place an heav'enly Maid walks in,
Her looks all fair; no sign of Native sin
Through her whole body writ; Immod'erate Grace
Spoke things far more then humane in her face. . . .
An Angel straight broke from a shining clowd,
And prest his wings, and with much reve'rence
bow'd . . .
Lo a new Star three eastern Sages see;
(For why should onely Earth a Gainer be?)
They saw this Phosphors infant-light, and knew
It bravely usher'd in a Sun as New. . . .
Angels peep round to view this mystick thing,
And Hallelujah round, all Hallelujah sing.
No longer could good David quiet bear,
The unwieldy pleasure which ore-flow'd him here.
It broke the fetters, and burst ope his ey.
Away the tim'erous Forms together fly.
Fixt with amaze he stood; and time must take
To learn if yet he were at last awake. . . .

When Gabriel (no blest Spirit more kind or
fair)
Bodies and cloathes himself with thickned ayr.
All like a comely youth in lifes fresh bloom;

Rare workmanship, and wrought by heavenly loom! . .

Thus drest the joyful Gabriel posts away,
And carries with him his own glorious day
Through the thick woods; the gloomy shades awhile
Put on fresh looks, and wonder why they smile.

SAMUEL PORDAGE

Mundorum Explicatio (1661)

I sing no Hero's douty gests in warrs,
Nor blazon forth some Warlike Champion's Scarrs:
I here no Prince's acts hyperbolize
With glozing prayses: Nor unto the Skies
Advance some common Justice in a King,
Nor the dread fury of the Wars I sing:
Nor with bewitching Layes advance above
The Sacred, the base toyes of wanton Love.
Nor praise the Courtly beauties of the times,
With Wine-inspired, and lascivious Rhithmes.
With Mars or Venus doth my Muse conjoyn,
She is *URANIA* and her Song's divine. . . .

Sad and deplorable's the state of man,
Whose day's a vapour, and whose life's a span;
Whose years a bubble, and whose bliss is pain,
Whose joys are trouble, and whose hopes are vain,
Should there indeed no other Worlds but this
Terrestrial be, in which he dwelling is.
Vain were the hopes of just and righteous men,
Than they none were more miserable then . . .

For I confesse I do believe there's four,
And never was, and never shall be more:
Three of these Worlds are infinite, but this
Grosse World both visible, and finite is.
It matters not unto Salvation,
Whether there be a thousand Worlds, or one . . .

A glorious study 'tis to study Nature,
To read the great JEHOVAH in the Creature,
To meditate his mighty wonders here,
And Trophies to his Name thereby to rear:
The great Creator made all things that be,
For profit, pleasure, and commodity
Of man alone, therefore His holy Name
He ought to praise, and thank him for the same. . . .

They therefore who acquainted are, with the
Internal Worlds, and their grand mysterie,
Whose sences are unlocked by that hand,
Which doth all sences, and all Worlds command,
Can Spirits see, and with Lincean eyes
Behold their Bodies, features, shapes, and guise:
Can also touch them, and their Bodies feel:
Can also tast them: and their scents can smell;
The Sulph'ry stinks, which from dark Spirits rise,
The sweet perfumes from those of Paradise . . .

This wily Serpent all his craft did use,
His poyson th'row this Earth for to diffuse,
Which he no way effect could: b' Adam's lapse
Only a way is made; He him intraps . . .

Adam thus made, perfect, and good, by God
In Paradise is plac'd, a bless'd abode:
Then was the golden age indeed, Earth gave
Nor Weeds, nor Thorns, but cloath'd in liv'ry brave
Had a perpetual spring; continual green
In ev'ry place, on ev'ry tree was seen:
No dainty Flower, which art makes now to flourish,
But then the Earth did naturally nourish.
A constant verdure it retain'd, and then
With thousand flowers spotted was the green:
Each tree at one time bore both fruit, and flower;
Each herb to heal, but not to hurt had power.

In this state ADAM stood; but God foresaw
The wo that he soon on himself would draw:
Therefore he thus forewarns him: New made Soul!
Work of my Hands, in whom no pheeces foul
Remain! a second Deity! O thou
For ay mayst live! Thou art immortal now;

Thou art an Angel, and I thee prefer
For to possesse the Throne of LUCIFER.
For this end did I thee Create, that the
Voy'd Throne of LUCIFER possess'd might be:
Thou shalt enjoy, and if thou stand'st upright,
Th' Eternal mansions of ne're fading Light.
Look to thy self therefore, for thou mayst guesse
LUCIFER envy will thy happinesse . . .
ADAM awakes, and views his new made EVE,
He knows she's part of's self; doth to her cleave,
And upon her his sole desire doth cast,
With her he joys, in her he takes repast.

In Paradise as yet they were, for sin
Actually had yet not enter'd in,
Nor was the vanity awak'd, as yet,
God's blessed Image in their souls was set,
Though much obscur'd: In great felicity
And Joy they liv'd, not knowing vanity,
Nor Good, nor Evil; Could they so have stood
They had been blessed, for their state was good.
Their pronity unto a farther Fall
God saw, therefore he thus to them doth Call.

Great Protoplast! and Prince of Paradise!
Take heed thou losest not these happy Joys
Once more I thee forewarn: already thy
Imagination in Earth's property
Did work: thou seest what thou thereby hast lost,
Thy Earthly Body did a better cost . . .
Look to thy self, let not the Devil thee
Provoke, to eat on this forbidden Tree
For if thou dost, thou wilt it soon repent,
For breaking this my just Commandement.

The Devil like a Gamester, who hath lain
All that he hath at stake, and is undone
If that he lose: or like some General
Encamp'd before some rich, strong City Wall,
In whose subversion he's assured to gain
A masse of Treasure, and eternal Fame,
Doth play his part, and useth all his skill
To win the Game, and conquer Adam's will . . .

Amongst the other Beasts that did resort
As humble servants unto ADAM'S Court,
There was a Serpent whose fine speckled hide,
And pretty features with rare colours dy'd,
Had gain'd EVE'S Love, and who it may be had
Entwin'd about her naked neck, and play'd
With her white hands; or favour'd in her lap:
This Sathan thought was best her to intrap.
Into this Beast he goes, and still doth lie
About the Tree forbid: Eve's longing eye
Full oft salutes that fatal Tree; desire
She doth to taste the fruit, approaching nigher
The subtle Serpent frisking on the Tree
She spies: The shaddow cannot hurt, thinks she.
Nearer she goes; thinking on God's Command
She feares for to proceed, then makes a stand,
But still the more she thought she was forbid,
The more she longs, the more desire she did,
(The same we still retain, for even thus
We most desire what is forbid to us)
She steps a little forward; then retires
Then moves again: tempted by her desires
She doth the Tree approach. God's stricter Law
Affright's her; she's about for to withdraw:
Sathan se'ing her the place about to leave,
Thus through the Serpent tempts our Grandame Eve.

Great Mistresse of this World, our gracious Queen,
Commandresse of this mighty Orb terrene,
Why so unwilling to approach this Tree,
Which I the best judge in this Grove to be?
Me thinks you seem'd to dread the shade thereof
When you unwilling to approach, aloof
Stood looking on't: As yet you seem to fear
The very shade; as if some hurt dwelt here.
Tell, what is in't that can displease you thus?
Eve answers then: The Lord commanded us
To please our tastes, with the variety
Of all those fruits which in this Garden be,
Only this Tree alone he bard us from
And charg'd us never near its shade should come.
For Death is harbour'd in this Tree, our last
And fatal day is come should we but taste

This tempting fruit: Great pity 'tis so fair
And lovely Apples should such poyson bear.
The subtle Serpent that he might beguile
The better, answer'd with a forced smile.

Pleasures are hardly left, when that our sence
Confirm'd by reason, and experience,
Find them both good, and just: I am too wise,
This Tree in truth hath opened mine eyes,
For to beguiled be; Think you to 'fright
Me, with your Bug-bears from my chief delight?
No, you would drive me from my happinesse
That you this fair Tree might alone possesse.
Say what you will, this Tree nor fruit I fear,
I by experience know no hurt dwells here;
And you know that; Not I say'd Eve, nor do
I now dissemble, I the truth to you
Declared have; God charg'd us not come nigh,
Nor tast this Tree; did we, we sure should dye.
The subtle Serpent thus reanswereth:
And speak you Truth? What this Tree bring you
Death?
God charg'd you thus? And told you you should dye
Did you but tast thereof? I now know why
He made you this believe: Lend me your ear,
I'le banish soon from you this vainer fear,
And let you know that in this Grove there's none
So beautiful, and Good, as is this one.
All what I have, this subtlety, this wit
I must acknowledge that I owe to it,
Which by frequenting of this better Tree,
Hath been I know not how, inspir'd in me.
You see more wit, and subtilty I have
Then all the Beasts beside; This Tree this gave;
Which doth increase, and whilst I here remain
More wit, and knowledge every day I gain.
Reflect a little; let your eyes but trace
Each Tree that grows in this Celestial place,
Consider all their beauties: look ag'in
And see is any like to this is seen.
Though all are full of Beauty, verdant, fair,
May yet there any with this Tree compare?
This Tree is Mistresse of the rest, and Queen
Of this same Grove, none hath such verdant green;

See how she in the midst is plac'd, each tree
Encompasse her, and as her servants be,
Bow their proud tops unto her lofty spire;
See how she mounteth than the rest far higher,
And threatneth with her waving tops (well neer
Unto the clouds) the rest who shrink for fear
Their humble heads. See what a length extends
Her interwoven Armes, which still befriend
The under-growing grasse with pleasing shades:
Look what soft mosse her mighty bole invades,
Like to a mantle of green plush, these be
Like Ornaments unto her Majesty,
As Queen of all the rest. Consider, and
Think if that he who this severe Command
Gave unto you, so would his works disgrace
By placing poyson in the happiest place:
All things he made are Good; where are your Eyes?
Think you that ill can be in Paradise?
Can this choyce Tree so great an ill contain?
Pish! don't believ't, for all such thoughts are
vain.
No, no, I'le tell you why he did forbid
You to come neer this Tree; such virtue's hid
Within its golden Fruit, should you but tast,
You'd be for ever happy, ever blest;
No longer then in stupid Ignorance
Should you enchained be; then happy glance
From brighter Light, would in your souls arise:
See then would your blind Soul; and dimmer eyes
Made bright, discern betwixt all good, and ill,
Transcendant knowledge then your brains would fill,
You should be wise, and like the Gods; this knew
They well, should happen (if you eat) to you:
Therefore they did prohibit you this Tree,
Lest you by eating like themselves should be.
Thus should you dye, fear not such feare-crows now;
See how the glit'ring Fruit doth lade each bow:
Look how they're painted with Vermilion dye
Like golden starres set in a verdant Skye,
Or like the blushing Roses, which are seen
New peeping forth thorow a verdant Screen.
Look how the Apples blush, see how they stand,
See how the boughs, bow down to kiss thine hand;
All's at thy choyce: which on this fair-spread Tree,

(Come tell me Eve!) most liked is by thee?
See, here's a fine one, this? or this best likes
Thee? do but look what many pretty strikes
Of red, and yellow paint; here's one that skipps
Unto thy mouth: here thine own Cherry lips
Are answered; thy softer skin thou mayst
Here find; but there's a mellow one whose tast
So sweet -- delicious that 'twil ravish quite
Thy looser sences with extream delight;
Thou hast such choyce thou knowst not which to
choose:
Come take this on my word, try what accrews
By this: here take it, prethee eat, and try
If thou a Goddesse art not by, and by.

Tempted by these fine words, and that fair
Fruit,
Fear holds her Hands, desire prompts her to't,
At last she takes the sugar'd bait, doth eat,
Findes it for th' present very pleasing meat,
Now on its pleasing hue her looks she cast,
Then with her tongue the sweeter Liquor tast
She doth: mean time her husband passing by
The place she thus attempts. Look here what I
Have got (said she) so fair an Apple, yet
Thou never saw'st: 'tis passing pleasing meat,
Melts in my mouth; I wonder'd much that we
So strictly were forbid this pleasing Tree:
As mortals here we shall not make abode,
I shall a Goddesse be, and thou a God;
We shall be wise as they: here eat thou this
I first have prov'd: me thinks it pleasing is.
Adam invited thus receives the fruit,
And without long delay falls rashly to't.

He that hath drunk the juice of Aconite,
Or the lethiferous Henbane, strait his sp'right
O'rfir'd, or too much cool'd, a punction feels,
With grievous smarting rage, his body reels,
His eyes grow dim, his sences stupid; stand
The blood doth in his Face, nor Feet nor Hand
Can he scarce wagg; the World turns round: his Head
Grows dizzy, by and by his spirits fled
From his swell'd Carcase, dead they leave him: so

These guilty couple 'gan to feel their wo;
Strait operates the Fruit, a shivering cold
Upon their naked Carcasses takes hold,
A sudden tremour shakes their Limbs; their Eyes
Close on a sudden and dark mists arise . . .

The Planets now forego their wonted Love,
Contrary'ng do in opposition move . . .
Then storms of Rain, and blustring Winds do make
Her Brooks o'reflow, her Trees, and Mountains
quake. . . .
Now Love is lost; no longer unity
But wrath, and hatred 'mongst the Creatures be:
The Lamb now fears the Wolf: The Lion tears
The Kid for food: Bees rob'd are now by Bears . . .

Wrath's mighty Monarch se'ing how he had wrought,
And the whole Orb under his power brought
By Adam's lapse, rejoyced much; and straight
He doth his Kingdom's Princes convocate,
With the whole Host of Hell: to whom he thus
Speakes. Princely vassals! Who is like to us? . . .
We left those Orbs, and did them all despise,
And did this mighty Kingdom colonize
Because we would be free; here we Command,
Are Kings; there servants, did obedient stand . . .
Mighty Baalzebub follow him, and be
Thou Lord of discords, plagues, discordancy . . .
Great Belial, with thousand Legions wend
Thou next into the Earth, thy Forces bend . . .
Next Python go with thy innumerable
Legions of Daemons, be thou strong, and able . . .
Ten thousand Legions I assign to thee
Abaddon Spirit of Impiety:
Take thou away all comfort: sicknesse, death,
Destruction cause to all that are beneath
Thy power. Mammon tho the last, not least,
For thy power reach shall from the West, to East . . .
The Stygian Princes bow their snaky heads,
And Joy their Captain in their Faces reads:
Io they hisse, and from their sulph'ry throats,
Belch out ten thousand loud confused notes.
Then from their Centre thousand Myriads go . . .
Black Death triumphing with a sable Bow,

The Earth with armes displayed marcheth too . . .

The Prince of Love, of Light, of Peace, of Truth,
Beholds poor Man, and his sad state with Ruth:
And tho Man's guilt brought down this sad distresse,
He love immense doth still to him expresse:
And left that mighty Wrath his Soul devour,
He will protect him with his mighty Power.
Heav'n's brighter Bands he therefore Convocates,
And thus his Royal Will to them relates.

Blest Princes of this lighter World! and ye
Vast Troops indu'd with immortality!
Know; Man for whom a Paradise we made,
By his own folly is to Wrath betray'd.
He hath deserted us: this happy Realm
Hath lost; now misery doth overwhelm
Him; and our Image in obscurity
Doth buried by the World's grosse Spirit lye. . . .
Shall we desert him? leave him to his Foe?
Strict Justice might, but Love cannot do so:
Can fier cool? or can cold Water burn?
No more can I from this my nature turn:
Nor his neglect, nor his strange follies move
May me to Wrath. O no! I still am Love. . . .
Arch-Prince of Angels MICHAEL; of all
Heavens brighter Legions be thou General:
Conduct our forces to Earths Orb, and there
Oppose the Dragon, bid man not to fear . . .
And thou Mittatron thy strong Legions place
In rank and order 'gainst Baalzebubs face . . .
Next Caphtiel 'gainst Belial thy foe,
With Myriads of brighter Angels go . . .
Go Jophiel and hinder Python's force,
Obstruct his vile infatuating source . . .
Next Haniel your Legions compleat,
Let your battalions 'gainst Abaddons meet . . .
Strong Gabriel, with courage meet thy Foe,
And with thy Troops, 'gainst mighty Mammon go . . .

(On pages 105-106, Pordage describes how sinners in Hell are carried by devils back and forth between the icy waters of the Styx and the fiery waves of

Phlegethon.)

When presently they are arriv'd upon
The burning Banks of fiery Plegeton.
In here they souse them: Crys, and shreeks they make,
But hard-heart Devils can no pity take:
Over, and over here they plunge them, then
To cold-stream'd Styx they bear them back agen,
And thus by turns these torments, with delight
They give, without a moment of respite. . . .

This said, they both together go: No flame
Or lighter blaze, from that dark fire came . . .
At th' upper end great Lucifer he saw,
(Whose frown keeps the Tartarean troops in awe)
Sit on an Ebon Throne, more black than Jet,
And round about him Hel's great Princes set,
According to their ranks. Great Lucifer
A sable Crown upon his head did bear . . .

(On page 117 is described the Tree of Death that grows in a dark valley in Hell.)

Thrice fifty Cubits scarce could close about
Its mighty bole: on every limb stretch'd out
Hung crawling Vipers, sucking with delight
The juyce of Henbane, and of Aconite
From off the leaves, which gave a filthy stink,
And were more black than Pitch, or blackest ink.
An horrid blast arrising from the ground
Concusse the leaves, which make a dryery sound
In their forc't kissing: Bitterer then soot
Mixed with Gall, and Wormwood's juyce, the fruit
Was, which thick sparsed here, and there did grow . . .

JOOST VAN DEN VONDEL

Adam in Ballingschap (1664)

ADAM IN EXILE[1]

Tragedy of all tragedies
"Prima malorum causa"

Argument

God placed Adam and Eve in Paradise, wedded together, and commanded them on pain of death, not to eat of the tree of the knowledge of good and evil; but the Serpent, craftier than all beasts and set on by Satan, first seduced Eve into tasting the forbidden fruit, and through Eve her husband. Then their eyes were first opened, and knowing their nakedness (for they both stood clad only in their innocence and righteousness), they wove fig-leaves to cover themselves. Meanwhile there appeared the stern Justice of the Most High, and punished them (who in vain blamed one another) and they were driven out of the Garden into exile.

The Scene is in the earthly Paradise. The tragedy begins before the hour of dawn, and ends with the hour of evening.

Dramatis personae

Lucifer, the Prince of Hell
Adam
Eve
Chorus of Guardian Angels

---

[1] Translated from the Dutch of Vondel by Watson Kirkconnell. Blank verse replaces the rhymed Alexandrine couplets of the dialogue in the original. Choruses retain their original pattern of strophe and rhyme.

Gabriel)
Raphael) Archangels
Michael)
Asmodeus) Hellish Spirits
Belial)
Uriel, Angel of Justice.

ACT ONE

Enter Lucifer, Asmodeus, and Belial.

Luc. I, consecrated at the first to wear
A crown of light, but now condemned to darkness,
Far from the eternal light, come thundering up
Out of the brimstone lake to haunt the earth,
Without transgression of my pale of doom;
For though my proud Foe has misshapen me
To this dark form of horror, I may still,
With you, my comrade Counsellors of Hell,
Rule o'er the realms of sea and earth and air.
It pleased me as a Prince of this ill World,
Disliking day and stronger in the darkness,
To choose the night for this black expedition;
But now the shades of dusk are disappearing
And he who hates the light will stoop in shadow
By cave and hedge, by shrubbery and tree.
Where am I now? The tuneful nightingale
Sings harbinger of sun and morning-shine.
A breeze is born amid the morning coolness
And rustles sweetly through the golden leaves.
We hear four streamlets from one single source
Gush babbling forth and spread to every part,
Falling from one green hill. From this we know,
Clearly enough, what soil it is we tread.
Here flows the Euphrates. And here Eden blooms,
The realm of Adam and his wedded mate.
Here must I hide, a sentry, in a wood,
In the dark bower of a myrtle glade,
And look behind, before, and to the side,
Considering how mischief may be wrought.
For I, estranged from good and under curse,

Desire to harm and foully desecrate,
Through His creation, Him whom naught can hurt
In His own nature. Thus there shall be built
The hellish kingdom of great Lucifer
That shall endure forever. In my sight
No onslaught is too bold, for naught forbids
My fierce attack on heaven. My revenge
Takes in this way the whole world in its teeth
And draws the universe from its alignment
Till heaven's axis cracks beneath my power.
It pleases me henceforth incessantly
To give them cause for labour, and though lightning
Has hurled me from my throne, to let them see
What I can compass, even in my fall.
We fail'd in heaven; but high Authority
Must yet consider we are left with power
To strive against the Despot through His works.
The title of Almighty is but vain, -
Ambition's feeble echo. If He knew
In any way how to destroy my essence,
I should be lost indeed, and little left
To the possession of Hell's lordship. There
His power lies too low, although mine own
Appears to lie a-lee. Yet if we luff,
It surely cannot fail that with the wind
We shall sail past the cape, and then drive on
With flying sheets into the wealthy haven
For which we steer. All hangs on the beginning:
As to the outcome, it were not in doubt.
Let Heaven's legions from their battlements
Mark that we do not sleep, while plunder waits.
Out of suspicion they have stationed here
To keep in check the Empire of the Dark,
A sentry-band of angels, who protect
The court of Adam and perform their part
In trouble and in danger. So must we,
Ere they suspect attack, work covertly.
The Garden's king, unarmed and innocent,
May sleep secure beneath th' angelic guard:
For without such a watch, it now were time
Fearless with violence to waken Adam
And his fair consort from their nuptial dream
And with a hellish blast of brimstone reek
To stifle them to death -- thus, thus to spite

Him who gave Adam life. So Paradise
Should serve them, not as a garden, but as grave.
I, crowned with wreaths of sulphur and of pitch,
Should dance with triumph round about their bodies
Under this very Tree of Life, and bellow
So that all earth and heaven would resound.
But that's a bit too early. Since at first
Our leap miscarried, we must move with caution
Seeking some subtle opportunity
Where best and how to strike at the Creator
Through any of His creatures, great or small.
We gain by every blow. One must begin
By gradual degrees, from low to higher.
He who climbs steadily arrives at last
Where he is victor. In well-ripened plans,
Each step is a step forward. Let us see
What favoring chance the dawning day will give.
The rising sun will give the Garden life
And vivid colour; Adam, with his mate,
Will wander hand in hand through his domain,
Which, planted with magnificence, seems blest
Close to the realm of the angelic host,
Sated in life and soul from God's full lap.
Here one may mark their converse from afar
And thence espy with cunning what may serve
For harm and injury. In corners hid,
Let me discern what is forbidden them
Or what commanded upon penalty
Of life and soul; for God is no one's friend
When he is proud for glory and advancement -
The reason you, my high confederates,
Have been thrust down to Hell as ruined rebels,
And so thrust down and so diabolized
That there is no return for evermore
To the celestial Gate from which we fell.
But let us hide before the light breaks forth
In the bright east; and from this vale of roses
Awakened Adam, with his bride, comes forth
And falling on his face adores the Lord,
The Liege who has bequeathed to him in feof
The messuage of Eden and its orchard.
Hold still, as if ye slept, and steal apart
Into this glade where shadows deepen most
To the fond couple's gaze, so glad to greet

The angels as they walk, their human limbs
Clad in white silk of innocence and virtue,
Woven so fine in thread that through the fabric
The beauty of the flesh can shine and glow
As we, through dew, see light become more lustrous.
One can best spy upon the Garden here,
Deep in these shadows. See, they come. Stoop down!
They cannot see us thus; but we can see
And eavesdrop quietly athwart the leaves
Upon their converse, port, and character.
He swings a myrtle-twig; she smells a rose,
Fresh-plucked and still in bud. The trees all bend
And curtsey with respect as they walk hither.
Even the sun shines down in pure devotion.

(Lucifer and Comrades conceal themselves.)

Enter Adam and Eve.

Adam. There rises the all-quickening light
That from the east, with ruddy mirth,
Drives from the countenance of earth
The shadows and the gloom of night.
Sweet bird-song, with the kindling dawn,
Begins a morning melody
To God's high praise, with rapture free,
From every leafy hedge and lawn.
Let us in turn take up the tune
Thus warbled from their matin throats,
And weave a song of dulcet notes
To grace the Deity Triune!
I will precede thee with my song,
And thou shalt follow, rich in praise.
What theme may best become our lays?
What shall our harmonies prolong?
Eve. Glory to God let us express -
The holy Source of everything!
What dearer subject could we sing?
He has bequeathed us happiness.
Give Him the praise; and I in turn
A song in sequence shall employ,
Until our antiphons of joy
The vales and trees and caves may learn.
Adam. To Thee we thus begin our praise,
O God almighty, good, and wise!

Thou Source of all beneath the skies,
Draw forth the sun that lights our days!
We see, we see that to our sight
Thou art far fairer than the sun,
Yea, bright beyond comparison,
A great eternal Well of Light!
And Thou art He that gave us being,
Out of red clay our forms did knit,
Inbreathed a soul, and honoured it
With lustre from Thine own bright seeing -
Humbling a high celestial spark
In human souls, that drew from Thee
Free will and immortality
And reason, never dimm'd or dark.
Eve. Praise be to God, who was, and is,
And shall endure forevermore!
In thee, His nature I adore
With what is earthy and not His.
The All-Wise God knows how to bind
Two unlike things with His firm hand, -
Both soul and body with a band
Unbreakable, in humankind.
Adam. This Garden by the Deity
Was planted as man's calm abode,
With all that heart could wish bestowed
And tilth for loving husbandry.
Here gushes forth, by His decrees,
That four-fold Stream the Garden thanks,
That flows along by blooming banks
And laves the roots of all the trees.
Here blooms the Tree of true delight
That still with Life our veins reprieves
Through fruit, bedecked with silver leaves,
That feeds man's ageless appetite.
The dews that in the morning fall
From heaven above are manna pure;
Here dainties for the tongue are sure.
We praise the Source of good things all!
Eve. Praise be to God, the Bountiful,
Who hath so satisfied man's heart
And given him this realm apart
That bears His mercies thick as wool!
His plenty in abundant measure
From a full horn He here hath poured

This Garden cometh from the Lord;
From Him is all its brimming treasure.
Adam. Now know I first the happiness
Of good companionship, and thou
Consortest gladly with me now.
Our friendship sweet delights possess.
My solitude is turned to joy
Since thou hast come to rapture me.
My helpmeet, should I part from thee,
Bereavement would my heart destroy.
My dear, what title shall I use? -
My sister, daughter, or my bride?
Before our feet in verdant pride
Nature her palms and flowers strews.
Eve. Only what pleases thee, my dear,
And naught else, shall delight my heart.
From that design the day shall start
And thither moves the solar sphere.
Obedient peace, intelligence,
A happy heart, a spirit gay
Befit the world's first bride to-day.
May God unite us, flesh and sense!
Adam. Begin, ye guardian angels likewise, and
proclaim,
In turn, in one glad choir, Him who creation wrought!
And Paradise shall echo as ye hymn His fame,
How the fair universe was fashioned out of naught.

Chorus of Guardian Angels

Strophe I

God first made Chaos, dark and blighted.
Nature was universal Night.
Formless it lay and all unlighted;
And then God said: "Let there be light!"
And straightway light was born, created
A disembodied glimmering,
But, though no eyes her beams elated,
Yet in a circumambient ring
Through twice twelve hours she wheeled, patrolling
The blind abyss of Chaos hence,
Where seeds of all the world lay rolling,
A primal mixture, crass and dense.

O Light, we come to greet thee, rainbow-shod,
As eldest daughter at the feet of God!

Antistrophe I

The self-same Hand that made light's lustre,
   Cleft heaven from the earth below,
And caused the floods of heaven to muster
   And strait within their bounds to flow,
So that mankind, beneath them, gazing
   Upon the watery welkin, oft
Might marvel at the vault amazing
   That through God's power wheels aloft;
An element unbound, unstable,
   Out of unfathomed deeps arose
Obedient to a Voice thus able
   A crystal heaven to enclose.
At last, in mighty circles, round it went.
Thus was His second day of labor spent.

Strophe II

As yet the earth lay deep and hidden
   In waves that cloaked her face from view.
Then wet from dry was sundered, bidden
   By the Most High. The flood withdrew.
So at the shore the wave stood halted.
   The moving waters there left free
The prairies vast, the hills exalted,
   And mountains founded on the sea.
Then with the fervor of a lover
   He sowed the earth with fruitful seed.
Above her form His strength did hover.
   He clothed her limbs with grace indeed.
In garments of sweet flowers we see her drest.
O matchless beauty, thus supremely blest!

Antistrophe II

The heavens also claimed their beauty
   When the Almighty's torch arose
The sun that in his path of duty
   With high imperial splendor goes
Forth from the east, the day enhancing;

At eve, the moon displays her light,
And from the dark the stars come dancing
To revel in the vault of night.
So men learned months and years to measure;
And earth in field and wood received
Celestial warmth with fervent pleasure
As the sun stooped and she conceived
New life in Nature. In this holy sign
One marks fulfilment of a plan Divine.

Strophe III

Now in the world hath God perfected
The elements that in it lay;
But what new work may be expected
Upon the fifth creative day?
The fish whose fin can cleave the ocean,
The bird that swims the sky's blue sea
With nimble wing and grace of motion
Received their playful ecstasy.
There crawls the whale, the dolphin dances;
Here eagles mount to heaven's height
And with their brave and piercing glances
Confront the sun's transcendent light.
With teeming life the air and ocean live:
Each for its sphere is formed definitive.

Antistrophe III

The sixth great day the beast arouses
That treads the bosom of the earth,
And on the grassy herbage browses;
And humankind, a higher birth.
These praise their Owner and Creator,
Who, for their sake, ordained His plan
And high angelic hosts that cater,
Thus bidden, to the good of Man.
Here in this Park the pair together
Are plighted by the primal Power,
Who meets them in the vernal weather
And weds them in a tender hour.
O happy couple, in Earth's courts of love,
Look for a fairer Court in Heaven above!

ACT TWO

Enter Gabriel and Raphael.

Gab. Down the white Milky Way we flutter'd softly,
On, past the sun, that shining from the sea,
Low to southeastward, in gold chariot
Mounted to crown the midday. Then we saw
This well-spring with four arteries supply
The earthly Paradise (from Heaven named).
Here shall the joys of primal troth be sung
By happy angel-tongues to groom and bride.
Hither forthwith we stretch our wings, and fly
Like some great eagle that from o'er the sea
Or from the stars to the high cedars' top
Swoops down, alights, and folds her cloak of
feathers.
How rare a Kingdom has God planted here!
How sweetly smells the fragrance of this land
Of milk and honey, lilies snowy-white,
And breathing buds of roses! How the shores
Here gleam with turquoise, bdellium, and rubies,
Bright onyx-stone and sparkling diamonds!
The ground is carpeted with flowers. No hand
Of angel could embroider it so richly.
What birds are here, in costly feathers dress'd!
There stands the unicorn, that in the spring
Mirrors himself. And here the sunflow'r turns,
Following the sun's face, kindled in her heart
With living rays. What angel-choruses
Gush from the birds' warm throats! How hangs the
fruit
Luxuriant! How swells this muscatel!
The orange-tree gives promise to the mouth
Of juice refreshing. The cattle prosper here
Upon a thousand kinds of fragrant herbs.
The glowing purple fleece of playful lambs -
The coat-of-arms of Adam's royal court -
Bears witness to the wonder of this meadow.
The tree gives honey-dew. Sweet cream and wine
Flow in the brook. The bark is cinnamon.
Here falls the sunlight with a temperate ray,
Neither too hot nor cold. Th' All-bountiful

Has poured his treasures out in beast and ore
And stone and plant and herb, and most to Adam,
Here in the noblest region of the world,
Earth's kingdom that has won the heart of God.
Raph. Archangel Gabriel, illustrious envoy,
This rarest pleasure-garden of the earth
Needs not, and quite surpasses, angels' praise.
Indeed, to laud it is to dim its beauty.
The Deity has wandered in the shade
Of its cool leaves, and has allowed Himself
To linger in this Garden. God has bless'd
The ground that He so blessedly has trod,
And called the region "Eden", or "Delight".
Here, to man's eye, no perfect thing is lacking.
Gab. O Raphael, my guide, who gained in Heaven
The highest consecration sevenfold,
Well worthy to attend the mouth of God
And to support His virtuous decrees,
It now is time for both of us to greet,
At the inauguration of Man's Kingdom,
The human king and queen, with courteous word
Wishing them health, with blessings on their love
From the Most High to crown them, glad of spirit.
Then shalt thou, at my side, array the feast
Of lavish bridal. Be in readiness
To crown them, at my bidding, with a wreath
Of everlasting laurel, from the hills
Of shining heaven, intertwined with gems.
With holy hands let angel choruses
Supply the banquet with the previous fruit
That feeds the life of man, stiffens his sinew
Against all weakness and maintains the blood
In all the vigor of its inmost pulse,
Even as oil maintains the burning flame.
The sun proceeds upon his way and marks
The time, the hour; and so this quickening fruit
Strengthens the essence of man's natural life
Throughout the centuries, arch-enemy
Of things corruptible; and so man lives
Immortal like the angels and like God.
God's marshal, Michael, meanwhile, on the watch,
At the command of Heaven's court, remains,
Over the godlike race of humankind,
So that no hellish guests may come unbidden

To mingle with the wedding, and unhelped
The bride and bridegroom may not drink of death
Out of some pearly shell in which the grape
Has pressed his mild, invigorating juice.
In short, let each upon his duty stand.

Enter Michael.

Mich. Envoy of Heaven, I appear in armor,
With helmet and with shield of adamant
And this two-edgèd sword from which fierce fire
Sprang forth when I o'erthrew proud Lucifer
And drove his army headlong down to hell,
Though from below they mounted bellowing,
There where the navel of the earth now holds
All whom God cursed and sundered from the light
That cherishes and quickens all that lives.
Before no power stand we terrified:
Give us the worst, and gladly will I start
With sword-point once again and soon hang up
Hell's weapon-trophies in the church of Heaven.
Gab. I pray thee, then, keep watch about the
Garden.
Yet follow us a little space, that Adam
May welcome us and we may crown the pair
With laurels and with never-fading praise.
They shall be wedded where the Tree of Life
O'ershades the crystal spring from which but now
There drank a lion and a lioness
And all the beasts that came at Adam's nod,
Named each by him with its own proper name.
Methinks I see the couple hand in hand
Approaching hither. Ah, how dear and pleasant
Is such devoted fellowship in troth!
Gladly, as bidden, shall I give God's blessing.
Behind them comes a choir of guardian angels
That woo their listening ears with joyful song.

Enter Adam and Eve.

Adam. My dearest, what good fortune shall be ours?
For heavenly creatures come on silver feet
That make the Garden's greensward dance with light.
They left a trail of gold as down they flew.
Ah, see their snowy pinions that in flight
Appear as streaks of white, so fast they haste

Athwart the wind and stars to do God's will!
Gifts they bring with them, and two laurel crowns.
What will the Almighty now disclose, who thus,
Already guarding us by angel bands,
Sends down still higher Spirits from the Stars?
God-consecrated messengers from Heaven,
Ye whom Himself knows best, be welcome here!
Is it your pleasure to fly down to see
Once, through and through, the region where men
    live,
In order to set higher against lower
And grasp more clearly the true difference
Between Heaven's treasures and Earth's lesser good?
Or has the Most High sent you from His throne
Upon some special mission? Doth He seek
To set His creature nearer to His will?
Welcome to us are ye, yea more than welcome.
The earth esteems your stainless fellowship.
If man's entreaty may move angels' minds,
We trust ye'll tarry somewhat with us both
To whom our fortune sends you, here to mingle
Light with our darkness, Paradise with Eden.
Gab. O Governor by God's high power appointed,
Greetings to thee, first offspring of the race
And stock of that one Child the worlds await:
O Prince, whom God holds as our sole liege-lord,
The Deity in whose high power thou trustest,
God, who hath wedded thee with this thy rib,
Thy flesh, thy mate, through His supernal favor,
Hath sent us down to wish thee, in His name,
Greeting, in this new state, that fairer dawn
Of the world's age may break upon you both,
And that due bridal, with attendance godlike,
May bind your troth in harmony, through bonds
Of mutual pledge, sealed surely, hand in hand.
And thou, O sister, bride, and daughter too,
Of thy protector, richly favored Eve,
Fair light of human maidens, and great mother
Of all the living issue of thy womb
That earth greets from afar, fairest bed-fellow
Of Nature's fairest bridegroom, morning-star
Among all women, how thy name and fame
Shall spread afar, since the All-Bountiful,
Who raised thee high and set thee thus to shine,

Is working out His purpose through this marriage!
Now let us crown you both, in His high name,
While all the heavens dance about in joy.
Receive these crowns, blest pair! A greater crown
Awaits your brows in God's eternity.
Adam. Timely ye come to honour us below.
Gab. God sent us to array your bridal feast
Under the shadow of the Tree of Life.
Adam. Praise be to God Most High, who stretches
out
His mercy farther than the sun's bright rays
Extend in radiance from their turquoise heights!
With gratitude your blessing we receive.
The Father on His subjects pours His heart
In lavish benefits innumerable.
The potent fruitage of the Tree of Life
Can nourish and delight us, heart and soul.
Now hath He joined this loving mate to me,
To joy me with her comfort and her help.
Thus can no solitude oppress or vex me.
In this, the heart of God lies open to us.
Gab. Live, therefore, happily with thy dear spouse,
Thou like a king, and she as queen of Eden.
Adam. Ye choirs, attend our path with festal song.
We'll tread the Garden. Birds before you sing,
And beasts attentive hearken to your voices.

Chorus of Guardian Angels

Strophe I

Who now can sate his greedy vision
Upon this pair, in bridal dress -
Sheer garb of innocence Elysian
And pure, transparent righteousness?
Dame Nature wrought not this attire,
Nay, verily, it could not be;
And fashion'd by a Hand far higher
Is its surpassing purity.
The garment from above was given,
A bridal treasure sent from God
Whose heart with tender love was riven
For these fair children of the clod.
No marring foulness may deride it.

No whiteness can be named beside it.

Antistrophe I

From no bright sun that daily rises
   This spotless purity proceeds,
But from the Source that light devises
   And all illumination breeds.
The Deity, in His compassion,
   Conceals His form in lordly light;
Omnipotence in kindred fashion
   Hath given Man apparel bright.
Now fades the fragrance of the roses,
   The purity of lilies yields:
More beauty in this pair reposes
   Than all the flowers of the fields.
Here we behold with admiration
The Deity's supreme creation.

Strophe II

Mankind, composed of flesh and spirit -
   Two elements unlike in kind -
Has felt no inner conflict fleer it,
   No need omitted can it find.
Each to the other's wants is gracious;
   The reason yields itself to God.
The flesh obeys the soul sagacious.
   But if man in his own strength trod,
Reft of his lot, God's gift that matters,
   Alas, he could not stand a day:
His bridal garb would hang in tatters
   And all that beauty pass away
Round which the Cherubim now wonder -
White radiance and white flesh thereunder.

Antistrophe II

As throat and harp-string sweetly blending,
   Intent upon the selfsame tones,
Create such music, soft-ascending
   That listening angels leave their thrones,
So is that unity of essence
   Where body has been blent with soul,

A loveliness of coalescence
   Eternal as the ages roll.
So upon earth man lives untroubled:
   Like to some god his state shall be,
With joys of youth and springtime doubled,
   If he obey the Deity.
So shall the union last forever,
And soul from flesh be sundered never.

Epode

Angelhood and beasthood mingle
   In the making of a man.
These to join in nature single
   Here on earth, the Father's plan
Has enriched them with one charter
   That each unlike essence draws,
Making each its freedom barter
   For repose beneath His laws.
Dear ones, let His charter charm you!
   Guard your Father's ordinance!
Thus no enemy can harm you.
   Ye are saved from evil chance.

ACT THREE

Enter Asmodeus and Lucifer.

Asm. Illustrious kaiser of the Pool of Woe
And of Earth's realm, at thy command I come
Here in the shadow of the Tree, bent down
With glorious fruitage through which knowledge grows.
Bid now thy servant anything thou wilt.
Luc. O Asmodeus, help us now to build
The Empery of Hell. We seek thy help
Through crafty counsels, for we wish revenge
For outrage undeserved and shameful wrong
Suffered in heaven above, when Michael strove
And hurled our armies with his thunderbolt
Out of their thrones and seigniory forever.
Now we as bandits shall incessantly
Assail the kingdom of our Ancient Foe,
Not in plain sight nor yet by open force,

Since in the world His military power
Prevails against us, but through fraud and guile,
For thus the smallest beast can plague the greatest.
The attack for once is taking proper form.
Asm. The plan is to attack Him craftily
In his well-shapen image, whose fair beauty
Sparkles divinely. If we darken this,
The image of the Father, He will turn
His face away in anger, for thou knowest
How stern is His forbiddance of this fruit;
And if at such transgression He is wroth,
Propitiation will not come by tears
Or prayers or aught that weeping man can do.
Luc. 'Twere an offence against God's Majesty
To harm His honour in the realm of earth.
Asm. With reason. If we sully this His image,
While on His lofty throne He sits secure,
The pearl of His imperial crown is snatched
And trampled in the mire and all befouled.
Luc. We shall consider it. But dost thou know
Yet other tricks, in order by degrees
And not too suddenly, to work our will?
For Heav'n has closed a circle with a guard
Of angels round this pair who now are mating
In happy nuptials. Through the foliage
We hear the bridal song and birds' clear piping
Echo from branch and hedge the angel choir.
The feast begins. They busily prepare
To deck the banquet. Guardian angels go
Beside the guests and happy bridal pair.
Here also Michael, God's chief Marshal, waits
Lest any grudge of hellish sprite disturb them.
In short, they are well guarded on all sides
And bandits would be easily betrayed.
Asm. Bandits must needs be watchful, hid from foes;
Shunning the light, they'll have no fixed abode.
Shadows and corners rather, glade and hedge
And pathless bush and cave may best conceal
The spectre of the night that in the day
Is seen unwillingly. We must take care.
Luc. How couldst thou work and not reveal thy nature?
Asm. One can assume the likeness of some beast.
Luc. A bird that beats the air with hurrying wings

Resembles spirits, who can likewise fly.
Choose then the eagle, prince among the birds,
More valorous in strife than all the rest,
He who with countenance and gleaming eye
Doth not refuse to front the noon-day sun.
Nevertheless, the eagle would reveal
His onslaught from afar: he must approach
Hotly to war with beak and rending claws.
Or choose an elephant. His form is huge
In which to hide for hostile mummery.
He is the cleverest of all dumb beasts
And mighty with his snout to uproot a tree
Or to toss Adam and upon his tusks
Impale him, did the Spirits not forbid.
Asm. That's true. The Deity keeps watch below
About this under-god, his governor,
The prince and regal ruler of the earth.
No beast is so like man in subtilty
Or quite so useful to our sly attack
As is a scaly serpent, sheeny-wing'd.
His tongue, if told to follow human speech,
Should haggle and deceive and lie with ease.
That were the proper falcon to let fly,
To grip these simple creatures in his flight.
Luc. Speak softer! Look around! Look yet again,
Lest any random air reveal thy voice
And they become aware of thy design.
For, win or lose, in secret must thou work,
And so depart before they dream of danger.
Asm. What of the serpent?
Luc. He is bold and sly,
Two traits of character most aptly chosen.
Asm. Slyness is born inherent in this beast,
And daring likewise. If these two go paired,
Our venture will succeed, and after it
Will draw a train of woes through all the ages.
Luc. We must not try both man and wife together.
Asm. One at a time we'll take them. That were wise.
Luc. Blessing and curse are common to them both.
They have one mind and but a single will.
Asm. If one of them should change in will and purpose,
The other in his mate's dark track will follow.
Luc. In such a case, the woman would consult

With her own husband. It were fruitless then
To launch our bold adventure with the woman.
'Twere better first to win her husband's heart,
And she would lightly follow after him.
Asm. Nay, one can win no profit from the man,
Luc. She will be slow to stain her lips with fruit.
Asm. A wanton love of dainties will undo her.
Luc. Transgression's taste is raw.
Asm. The fruit is ripe,
Sweet on the tongue, alluring to the eyes.
Thus feeling, taste, and sight at once are lured,
Three senses by one apple are seduced.
Luc. Then Madam shall be first, and next the master.
Asm. The wife comes first, as weaker of the two
She'll offer him the fruit.
Luc. But what if he
Refuse to sample the forbidden fruit?
Asm. If she unfold to him its promises,
How can he fail to put it to the test?
Luc. To grieve the Most High by a bite of apple
And through transgression of His strict command
To die a certain death, does that not teach him
That deadly poison should not fill his mouth?
Asm. If she beseech with tears, he'll not reject
So small a plea from his young bride. Besides,
Forbiddance and the threat of punishment
Kindle the appetite. Thou knowest that.
Luc. But by the angels' fall he'll warn himself.
Asm. He's too confused and eager for more knowledge.
Luc. But much is naturally known to him
By his own nature.
Asm. Yet he still falls short,
And wishes to resemble God in knowledge.
Luc. The source and only fount of our misfortune
Was to be insubordinate to God.
Asm. They'll yield to him who plies them craftily.
Luc. Begin. Fulfil thy plan. Prepare thy snares
In every corner lest our prey escape.
If ten assistant spirits are too few,
We shall bring hither a whole regiment.
Asm. Sly Belial, my squire, holds himself ready.
I shall instruct him how, to hunt for man,
We best may spread our nets and at one blow
Catch the whole human race in the first pair.

<u>Luc</u>. Hell's kingdom shall, with smoke and hymn
of praise,
Laud thee forever if thou do this deed.
All poised on bat-wings in the sulphurous air
Desire to share in this triumphant blessing,
And at the hellish trumpet-blast to go
So proudly to escort the victor home
That Heaven's throne shall totter at the sound,
Startled to find man fallen. But indeed,
I speak too soon: this court must first be stormed.
Begin with quiet confidence. Proceed.
Deceive the bridegroom first and then the bride.
Here now comes Belial, on fire for booty.
Exit <u>Lucifer</u>.

Enter <u>Belial</u>

<u>Bel</u>. My lord, I sought thee in this Garden's shade,
Where, after flight from Hell, thou sojournest.
What news now of our Grand Duke Lucifer?
What revel do I hear?
<u>Asm</u>. Not far from hence
They hold a wedding; but we aren't invited.
<u>Bel</u>. How fair this Garden blooms in full delight!
Into the mouth of its admirer falls
The fruit of Paradise. The air is sweet
With fragrant health from every bud and flower;
And, as their wont, the trees bloom all year through.
Earth smiles with four fair seasons in one spring,
As if they held eternal nuptials here.
<u>Asm</u>. The Gardener who built this pleasaunce fair
And planted it is pleased to linger here.
The present wedding is of His design.
We have considered routing all this joy
In His despite. Our Prince, who envies man
And mocks at Heaven's honour, has desired
That thou shouldst help to lure this pair of lovers
Boldly to pluck the fair forbidden fruit
Through their delight in dainties. Heaven's honour
And mankind's welfare thus shall go to wrack.
Upon this single branch the whole world hangs:
Its evil fate is hidden in this fruit.
<u>Bel</u>. How now? Is His creation not all good?
Did the Creator fashion aught that's evil?
<u>Asm</u>. By no means. All is good. Evil consists

But in transgression. To presume against
God's edict, that is evil. Human life
Must be maintained by eating; but to eat
Aught that He has forbidden will bring death.
Bel. I comprehend thy problem. Yes, but how
Can we approach them while they celebrate
The wedding feast with their angelic guests?
Asm. Thou shalt be hidden in a subtle serpent
And quietly gain access to their side.
Bel. If with so fair a mummery is honoured
The world's first wedding, sure the bride and groom
With sorrow will remember it forever.
And what is mummery? A whited lie,
One thing in semblance, other in the deed.
I shall mix poison in the bridal dish.
The color of the ruddy fruit shall proffer
A dainty bait and by its very brightness
Conceal the dark, vile worm that lurks within.
If either of the couple tastes this fruit,
Both will be caught securely on my hook.
Asm. Thou canst not take and tempt them suddenly.
They first must hear thy speech and specious plea.
Bel. The hearing must come first, so that my talk
May take away their scruples. Gradually
Nearer the tree they'll venture. foot by foot;
Then with the hand shall they approach the apple,
That charms the eye and lures the mouth to taste.
Thus Death is kissed unwittingly, before
The fires of lust for dainties are extinguished.
Asm. Thou canst direct thine aim upon one mark.
Bel. Then shall abasement shortly follow pride.
Asm. So Lucifer discovered in his fall.
Bel. We likewise, humbled in the brimstone pool.
Asm. The Prince thinks that the man should first
 be tried.
Bel. Nay, for man sees too keenly. Through our
 mask
He'd mark the lie. But womankind is weak
And simple as a dove. With ease we'll work
And get at Adam through the woman-creature.
Asm. That's the best way to hit him in the heart.
Bel. To waste our ammunition on a strong
And shot-proof hero were not practical.
Cunning avails, not force, in such a case.

We must make soft his stony heart by pleas
From woman's lips. Let moisture thus and clay
With warmth and damp be kneaded; Adam thus
Was fashioned by the Almighty out of earth.
Asm. Shall man be thus persuaded by his rib?
Bel. With reason: for his wife is next his heart,
Like his own rib. And if they talk together,
And she invites her lord, his heart, amazed,
Shall feel this pull and in his own despite
Shall please the appetite of his dear bride
Out of his overwhelming love for her.
Asm. Accommodation is the nurse of peace.
Bel. So shalt thou see all males in Eden act:
The cock obeys his hen, the hart his hind,
The lion the wood-lioness; for one
Is by the other drawn. Where does resistance
Fall with such ease as when a loved one tempts?
But ere we hide us in a serpent form,
What thinkest thou? Might we in angel guise
Intrude like wedding guests for whom the feast
By angels is prepared?
Asm. In angel guise?
Nay, that were wrong. Unlikely would it be
In angel guise to have thy way with Eve.
For could she not perceive that thy desires
Clash against Heaven's will and should be blamed?
No holy angel strives against the Court
From which he has been sent. Thy victory
Would thus be damaged ere thou hadst begun.
Bel. The serpent mask then suits our mummery.
Asm. If through that mask thou apest human speech
Devoid of error and with pleasing tone.
Bel. If they shall fail to mark my treachery,
My utterance shall not lack a sound sincere
Less like a human voice than like the chant
Of holy angels. Like a ductile string
To stretch the serpent-tongue and raise its pitch
To that of harmonies from out of Heaven -
That were to ravish ear and soul with art.
Asm. If thou succeedest, thou shalt charm the sense
And through the hearing conquer human hearts.
Bel. My warbling should subdue a hurricane
And hold a wild bear standing in amaze.
Soon shall I steal from man his heavenly source

And hinder him from triumphing on high
Or hoping for the throne from which Hate thrust us.
At our revenge, his seed will weep forever.
Asm. The wedding-guests who tread the Park with joy
Little expect to bear this news aloft.
Bel. And no one less than Seraph Gabriel.
Asm. The festal music sounds. The feast is honoured
With trumpet-play and song. Gladness is heard.
Thus far we see no chance for our design.
Bel. If it should happen that the bride and groom
During the banquet should retire a while
To wander through their Garden, and the bride,
Walking alone, should tarry for her spouse
Along this side, in a green gallery,
Then would it be the time to tempt her mouth
With Fruit forbidden upon pain of death.
Asm. Fortune agrees to this: the huntsman's art
Is still dependent upon time and place
And nature's disposition, lacking which
The oldest marksman shoots beside the mark.
Bel. If we should fail now, we can try again.
Asm. If it be possible amid this throng
And at this feast to snare them in our net,
That wins the highest prize. It pleases me
To desecrate and break the primal law
Through earth's first couple. Thus the peacock-tail
Of proud humanity is beaten down.
Let Gabriel announce this news on high!
Bel. What rending shrieks would rise in Paradise!
Oh, what a smoke to sully Heaven's light!
Asm. We are exulting ere our cause is won.
Bel. With hope we win already in this world.
Courage anticipates the victory.
Asm. But in the end the conqueror's word is law.
Bel. What thrilling sound is that?
Asm. The bridal song
Is to the lovers sung, while angel trumpets
Play their divine accompaniment. Be still,
And let us listen to what follows here.
Bel. The Garden is suffused with radiance.
Asm. The guests begin a dance of praise and honour

To Heaven, with the cornet, drum, and flute.
Here they approach. I'll hide. Behold our prize!

Exeunt _Asmodeus_ and _Belial_

Enter _Adam_, _Eve_, and _Chorus of Guardian Angels_.

Strophe I (Chorus)

Dance we now, God's honour praising,
As the lovers here are wed,
As devoted vows are said.
Let them both, their voices raising
In the midst of this our choir,
While the horn and shawm sing higher,
While sweet harp with flute rejoices
And the quivering organ-voices,
Turn in turn trip farther, nigher,
Mingling rounds of mazy pleasure
Streamwise and against the stream,
Quick of ear for time and measure;
Circling angels crown the scheme.
Let us, on our pinions soaring,
Weave festoons of buds and bays,
Let us dance with feet adoring
Till the floor of Eden sways.
Now before white feet go hasting,
Let us greet this handsome pair,
Seemly nuptial joys foretasting
In our sweet, respectful air.
Song and dance will surely ease them:
Let us now begin to please them.

Antistrophe I

Happy, happy pair of lovers -
Bridegroom fair with laurel crowned
And thou bride, whose graces round
All of earth and heaven hovers
With rejoicing for your sake,
Grant your guests to undertake
Here to dance, God's honour praising
And your happiness amazing.
Jubilation thus we'll make;
For no silence is befitting
Nuptial comrades at the feast.

God we please, in dances flitting.
   All the angels, most and least,
Soar in Heav'n, God's glory singing,
   Dance in pure eternal ways,
In His presence gladly winging,
   Everlasting in His praise.
Hear with pleasure our requesting;
   Tread before us, hand in hand;
As we all, your feast investing,
   Circle round you in a band.
Move to sound of harps before us.
Set the fashion to our chorus.

Strophe II (Adam sings)

Let us learn the festal measure
         And the plan
Of the Lord of Heaven's treasure,
Copying His ways with pleasure
         If we can.
Wandering stars and fixt aspire
         Each to do
In its path God's full desire;
Every star in Heaven's choir
         Thus is true.
Wheeled within the Empyrean
         As it burns,
Seven spheres chant one great paean,
Universal, hymenean,
         Each dancing turns.
I the Sun am representing;
         Thou, my bride,
Moonlight by thy dance inventing
Shalt entrance, my love cementing,
         Swell my pride.

Antistrophe II (Eve sings)

By thy dance, mine own I fashion.
         Follow me.
Be my moonbeams bright with passion,
Be they blotted out and ashen,
         Reft of thee,
I shall trust the absent lender

Till once more
I reflected beams shall render
From thy rich illumined splendor,
Light's true store.
When thy face shall shine upon me,
I shall burn,
Kindled with the love that won me,
Plighted nevermore to shun me,
Ne'er to spurn.
Go before me and entreat me;
Then deploy -
Parting but to come to meet me
Here where first thy soul did greet me,
Full of joy.

Epode (Guardian Angels)

Down, thou heavenly bride, who dancest
Round and round
This thy husband, laurel-crowned,
Circles of pure beauty weaving,
Splendor from his torch receiving
Near and far
Shining like the morning-star,
Or again like Hesper glowing,
At his coming, at his going
Following his heavenly way,
True and gay.
The dance is over; let us turn again
To share the feast in which God blesses men.

ACT FOUR

Enter Eve, Adam following.

Eve. Stand we in Eden, or among the stars?
What heavenly yearning ravishes my soul?
My feet can feel no earth: it sinks away.
The godlike sound of holy bridal song
Unties the bond that couples soul with body.
The soul, intent upon its heavenly nature,
Rejects the earthly and becomes a flame
That seeks the high, first Source of its own being.

Adam. Whither, my dear? Stop! Do not fly from me!
Eve. I'm driven towards the Source of all Salvation.
None else can cool my fire. Ah, let me go!
Adam. Here is thine element. Thy lover calls thee.
Eve. Now am I brought back to myself again.
Adam. The Cherubim and glowing Seraphim
May fitly sear where they with bended knee
Fall on their faces, fearing to approach
God's Majesty and honour him with incense.
Eve. Happy are they who fellowship with angels.
Our modest bridal dish is honoured here
With heavenly manna and with Eden's grapes
Whose flavor quite bedims all other fruits.
Ay, but the Angel's discourse hath surpassed
All of the bridal banquet. From the eyes
Of humankind he pushed aside the veil
And showed us what a city God has built,
High in the light of heaven, purged of rebels,
Where Reason, now infused in earthly flesh,
Expects, a spotless citizen, to dwell
And honour Him, after the law of souls.
Adam. Now is the City built, from base to top.
Eve. If all our bodies should be changed to eyes
Of heavenly eagles, on the sight of it
Our eyes, for yearning love, could not be sated.
Adam. From what side should the eye first gaze at it?
Eve. Let the Archangel make thy question clear.
Adam. One cannot build without a firm foundation.
Rich jewels give the ground magnificence:
Jasper and sapphire, emerald and beryl,
Sardonyx, sardius, and amethyst
Will not in that foundation yield in splendor
To chrysolyte, chalcedony, bold topaz,
Jacinth or any chrysoprase; for each
Is braver in its glory of display.
Adam. The lofty walls, four-square in perfect plan,
Are thickly riveted with purest jasper.
Eve. The gates are each a pearl, and each fair street,
Paved with pure gold, gives ready avenue

To all the spirits passing to and fro.
Adam. No fane is there nor vaulted temple-work,
For the infinitude of God's own Being
The sanctuary is where He is served
By innumerable spirits who at feasts
Hail Him eternally with Hallelujahs
And jubilantly roll His praises forth
With answering echoes of angelic song.
Eve. There moves no Sun on its majestic way
Nor does the fickle brightness of the Moon
Lighten the City where the eternal light
Of an all-sweet, all-satisfying Face
Bedims the fairest day that mortals know.
For that abode we yearn with all our hearts.
Adam. How sweetly in my ear the waterfall
Resounded that from God's high dais flowed,
Clearer than crystal, through the shining town,
And in the midst of it the Tree of Life
Hung all year round, from month to joyous month,
Its precious fruitage in the vital air!
Eve. In bridal style the Angel entertained us,
And hoped one day to welcome us above
In heaven, to a happier marriage feast.
Adam. Drawn meanwhile here below to mutual love
And unity of spirit, day by day,
Let us win upward, step by step, to Heaven,
Reaching the highest fortune from the lowest
Eve. Come, bid me what thou wilt. It seems no
yoke
To subjugate my will to thy commands.
Adam. Let offspring year by year be evidence
Of our fidelity. Through love alone,
Love kindles and awakens. Doves thou seest,
The male and female, fondly bill and coo.
We see how swan courts swan. The mighty lion
Grows gentle as he woos his lioness.
The ivy clasps the elm. Plant grafts with plant.
One touch of love prevails in everything.
All that feels life desires to mix itself
With a like mate, and Nature gives delight
In the warm act where each begets its kind.
The future of the world is in thy womb,
For thou, as mother of the human race,
Shalt bring forth patriarchs, law-givers, kings,

Heroes and heroines, yea, sons and daughters,
Who shall have teeming issue in their turn.
I see thy name in honour everywhere
When thou hast crammed the emptiness of earth
As full of children as the fields with flowers.
This is my wish. I trust it is thy hope.
Eve. So long as Earth enjoys the embrace of Heaven,
And, as his bride, receives her fruitfulness
From such a bridegroom, who o'ershadows her
And gloats upon her from the vault above
With thousands of star-eyes, so long my soul
Shall mate with thine and every kiss and favor
Can look for passionate return from me.
Adam. Permit me, at this point, to turn aside,
To speak with God and in my solitude
Give thanks to Him for thy companionship.
Excuse me, pray.
Eve. My dearest, go with God.
Exit Adam.

Enter Belial, in serpent form.

Bel. Good luck, O bride and mother of the race!
May all thy married life be happiness!
May Heaven ever guard thee! Let thy bridegroom
Be ever thy support! The rose and lily
Close up in shame before thy fairer feet.
O flower surpassing all earth's fairest flowers,
O paragon of all things beautiful,
Earth's glories strike their flag before thy beauty!
It were impossible to be more fair!
Eve. What voice draws near me from the leafy shadows?
Who could approach me with such warmth of love?
Whether thou be a spirit or a beast,
Unmask, declare thyself, and let me know
Who greets me with such charm. If thou dost float
On wings in air, or tread the earth with feet,
Disperse the clouds that hide thee from the sun,
Or if thou art a mortal, show thyself!
Bel. O fair young consort of a happy man,
I am a beast endowed with human speech.
All of the rest are mute and quite deprived
Of thy sublimer Reason. I acknowledge
I am far less than thou, O lofty one,

And yet beneath thy feet I am not timid.
Grudge not a serpent the true privilege
Of wishing thee the utmost happiness!
I love the conversation of mankind.
So nestle friendly birds about thee here
On branch and thicket; from the salty waves
The dolphin thrusts his head, by impulse driven
To worship the white body of a woman.
See how enamor'd birds about thee flutter
And how the dolphin with his tail and fins
Caresses here the shore with loving strokes
To win the favor of a woman's heart!
In thy pure maidenhood the unicorn
Should take delight and stand in utter peace
At the mere vision of thy perfect face.
That swift one does not let himself be caught
Save by a girl, but at the sight of thee
He smiles and weeps with longing at the thought
Such beauty is denied him. Thus a maid
Stirs tender love within the mighty beast.
Eve. And why dost thou, O creature, praise me thus?
Bel. Lest thou in shy confusion shouldst take fright,
As at the onset of a human lover.
But I from thee desire no enjoyment -
Only a trifling favor. Thou art worthy,
A bride most blessed and most beautiful.
My power is small, and yet my heart is ready
To serve as best it can. Thus I invite thee
To try this Tree, that bears the glowing prize
Of universal wisdom and all knowledge.
Eve. Silence! Take heed how thou invitest me
To fruit that holds this promise of all knowledge!
This apple is forbidden to my mouth
And God has warned me to avoid such fruit.
Said He: "Of all the trees within the Garden
Ye may partake indeed; but do not pluck
The Fruit of Knowledge or ye die the death,
With ruin to yourselves and all your seed!"
Bel. Can this be true? Should God, enthroned so high,
Almighty, good, and infinitely wise,
Say, of a truth: "Ye shall by no means eat
All things that grow within this Paradise"?

Eve. All sorts of fruits we pluck, and eat them
too.
But God commanded us to shun this Tree,
In the park's midst, like plague or very death.
What pleasure should I take in dissipation,
If I lay hold on death with hand and tooth?
Bel. O simple dove, this law is contradictory
To right and reason. Hearken to me now.
Why doth God show Himself so envious?
I bid thee, simple one, to turn thine ear
And shun not useful counsel or this Tree,
Rare as the Phoenix in its wondrous power.
Wisdom is lurking in these leaves. The reins
Should not be shortened for a fair young woman.
Grant her luxurious pastures for delight.
God is not wroth. These apples know no poison.
Upon the tongue they melt delightfully,
And they rejoice the heart like wine from heaven,
Holding humanity forever young.
This is a wedding where the choirs of God
Are happily enraptured by thy beauty.
For thee the fullest pleasure should be wished.
Why shouldst thou be so narrowly restricted?
Even this fruit's enamored of thy lips.
Eve. 'Tis wrong to dote on anything that's evil.
It is a sin to taste forbidden fruit.
Bel. Our Maker has created nothing evil.
How art thou now so narrowly beset?
'Tis superstition! Whither will it lead?
Be sure no food or drink can sully life,
And least of all the soul. Reach upward now,
And boldly pluck, and it will profit thee.
Eve. But tell me first, thou who hast dared invite
Me thus to eat, why is the Tree forbidden?
Why to the tasting of this pleasant fruit
Is death attached? Why has the Gardener
Forbidden us to touch it upon forfeit
Of life and soul? Hath he not then concealed
A fatal poison in so fair a semblance?
Bel. O simple dove, believe my honest word:
I swear to thee, thou shalt not surely die!
Make use of that which charms the eye and mouth!
And if thou'lt trust my oath, I'll tell thee true
The hidden purpose of this prohibition.

Eve. I shall be pleased to hear. Tell me God's
secret.
Bel. If all these leaves, perchance, were changed
to ears,
They might betray it; for it is forbidden
The secrets of the Most High to divulge.
Nevertheless, at peril of my life,
I shall reveal it to thee, but be sure
It rests with thee alone. Protect my fault,
And keep my true devotion from disgrace.
Envy forbids thy mouth this charming fruit
Lest thou should see with altered eyes of knowledge,
With understanding like to God Himself,
For thou into a goddess wouldst be changed
No whit inferior to God in wisdom.
Rich treasures in these apples are concealed,
Leading to knowledge and the power to judge
Both good and evil. This has been the cause
Of His strict prohibition. In this fruit
Divinity lies hidden. Taste, taste, taste,
Ere someone comes to spy upon the act!
I shake the tree, to cast into thy mouth
So fair a lot -- a nature all-divine.
Nay, sigh not! Stifle that unhappy groan!
Why wilt thou cast a shadow on thy pleasure?
Do thou but contemplate this heavenly fruit,
The golden apple, sweetly mild of juice;
For it shall give thee heavenly attributes.
Eve. O noble Tree, how dare I pluck thy fruit?
O Tree divine, by such a harvest hallow'd,
How my heart beats in fits of shuddering fear!
O rosy apple, I can see thee flash
With rays of silvan gold and living red.
I trust it is not sin to taste of thee.
Trembling, I draw yet nearer. How may death,
A livid worm, be hidden in thy bosom?
Cease, cease to tantalize my appetite!
Wherefore from fruit should I withhold desire?
What harm is in one bite, a venial fault?
Fondness for sweets is easily forgiven.
I pluck. And if I thus corrupt my hand,
Permit it patiently, O my Creator!
The offence is half begun. How fair it is!
Bel. Now, beauteous one, apply thy mouth to it.

O, try the apple! Art thou timid yet?
Eat, eat, that Heaven may bless thee in the act!
(She eats.)
Here comes thy bridegroom walking, and he seems
Happy in spirit. If to such a banquet
As this red apple, freshly pluck'd and sweet,
He were invited, how could he refuse
To prove its power if his bride should bid him?
I'll help thee in thy discourse so to speak
That, though the fruit entice him not, he shall,
In order not to grieve thy tender favor,
Follow thee and believe thee at the last.
Exit Belial.

Enter Adam.

Adam (soliloquizing). How sweet it is, in quiet solitude
And rapture, with the highest Majesty
To parley, face to face, and to receive
As token of His favor on my forehead
The reflex of His radiance as we talk,
So that my soul, charmed to another state,
Cries out: "O Lord, sustain me! I am filled
With Goodness all too generous and great.
Sustain me, and be gracious to Thy servant!"
Now to my bride, the half of my own soul,
I shall return. Where is she lingering?
What, in the meanwhile, hath she contemplated?
Here in the shade of this forbidden Tree
I see her sitting. What is this? What hand
Has brought her food? This omen, sure, is evil.
Eve. Draw near, my darling! What is this? Hast thou,
My bridegroom, lost thy passion for thy bride?
I have awaited thee with yearning here.
Adam. What art thou doing? What desire hath seized thee?
My dear, who hath invited thee to feast?
Eve. God's apple-tree vouchsafed me shade and food.
Adam. What food? A food so high, God bade us shun it. . . .
Eve. And therefore was I moved to seek it out
For prohibition did inflame desire.
My bridegroom and my comfort, do but gaze

Upon this apple! See how fair it blushes!
Since it thus outwardly can please the eye,
Think how delicious is the taste within!
Adam. The taste! Cold fever overruns my body.
My hair stands up. Where will this lead, my love?
How is my heart oppressed! Ah, would that God
Might cancel both the apple and the Tree!
Ah, woe and sorrow! Is this now the fruit,
The joy I looked for from the bridal bed?
Hast thou thus wickedly profaned God's law?
Eve. Husband, be calm! I understand His law
Better than thou. Why is thy narrow life
So much disturbed over one bite of apple?
That's naught but superstition!
Adam. Woe is me!
What do I hear? If I were dumb and deaf,
Or lacking eyes, yet would I hear and see,
In such a state, thy sorrowful performance.
Eve. Not so, my husband. Here no evil lies.
Accept thy bride's first gift, and taste this apple.
Believe and follow her, and prove by taste
A universal knowledge of all things.
Adam. Should I obey thee, showing scorn for God?
Heaven preserve me from such insolence!
One cannot break, unhurt, the laws of God.
Eve. What laws of God? This law's a breach of
Reason.
Adam. But God transcends the reach of human Reason.
Eve. Be not dumbfounded by an idle fear.
I know by taste the virtue of this food.
Adam. True knowledge has its source in fear of God.
He who is willing to obey His law
Is free from such a stain of calumny
As that by which the rebel angels fell.
Eve. I think an angel shook this apple down,
And as it fell I took it in my hand,
No dark abomination but a pledge
Of bliss and favor. Wherefore dost thou weep?
Wilt thou curtail the pleasure of thy bride
And flout her pleading with harsh contradiction?
That is too early, and is far from kind.
This was not thine intent when at the first
Thou didst behold me and didst clasp my hand
And Heaven set its seal upon our union.

I am thy flesh and bone; so bear thyself
More like a man, and let us live together,
Sharing one common lot. To God's own gifts
Would I invite thee. Let thy knowledge reach,
In proud asseveration, to the stars.
Thus shalt thou be in wisdom like to God.
Use thy free will, and in obedience
To this my first request, vouchsafe to me
Thy first true glance of love. Obedience
Will bring thee peace. I will have no refusal.
Adam. Oh, what a conflict and dispute is this!
Shall I resemble God Himself in knowledge,
And do the bidding of my own free will,
Partaking boldly of forbidden fruit,
Or shall I, like a slave, accept His laws
And bear His yoke, for fear of punishment?
Eve. Why dost thou tarry? Use what Heaven gives
us -
Thine own free pleasure and to-day's delights!
God rules on high, but here the gods of earth.
Adam. Oh, what a conflict! Here the woman stands;
There, God. Her bidding here entices me;
But there His stern command restrains me still.
Shall I now lose the favors of my wife,
Or turn God's favor into sore displeasure?
Within my soul a thunderstorm is raging.
Oh, what a choice, all sorrow either way!
Which shall I rather lose, my spouse's love
Or Heaven's favor? Dare I, in myself,
Sully this likeness that resembles God,
Tarnish my soul for such a wicked partner?
Nay, rather, let me, sundered from my wife,
Embrace in peace the Source of my well-being!
I have already, from His gracious hand,
Received too much and look for too much more.
Life would I rather choose than certain death.
My wife, why dost thou ask me? I refuse
To be misguided thus. I cannot bear
To part from God, and here, if choose I must,
I'd sooner part from thee. This much is certain.
Eve. So thus thou severest the bond of marriage
Against the will of Heaven, and for one apple
Wouldst dare to injure wedlock, showing clear
Thy faithless nature as a hard young rake.

Forsooth, that goes right well. Be off! Henceforward
Thou shalt be void of help and wifely comfort.
Go, live with beasts and know them, one by one,
Giving them names; for thou shalt have no wife.
No longer dost thou prize thy flesh and blood:
Thy heart is turned to ice, to frosty stone.
Alas, I suffer now; but if hereafter
Thou seekest for thy wife and canst not find her,
Then, though thou wail and curse, I swear to thee
Thou shalt not chance to see her, nor shall Eve
Hold thee as dear or offer thee her mouth.
I call upon the Garden and its beasts
To bear their witness to thy wicked heart.
The savage lion loves his lioness.
The tiger burns with passion for his mate
And finds her fairest; from one rill they drink,
They eat one food and wander side by side.
But Adam values not his loving bride.
Farewell! For thou shalt gaze on me no more.
Adam. Ah, whither art thou going? Stay a little!
My dearest, tarry yet.
Eve. We are estranged.
Why dost thou hold me? Let me go my way!
Go, love some other woman more than me.
Whilst thou wert sleeping, thou wert given a wife
To grace thy bed, and took her without love,
Even as now without regret thou partest.
A loveless meeting means a painless parting.
Another rib still lies below thy heart:
Let God then manufacture thee a wife
According to thy fancy! If He does,
Love her, I do beseech, and honour her,
More than thou lovest me. If that be irksome,
'Twere best thou shouldst be single as before,
Living unmated. Only so, perchance,
Shalt thou not darkly grieve a woman's heart.
Adam. Peace, dearest, peace! Ah, thou dost rack my heart:
How can I, in this case, please God and thee?
God finds no pleasure in a breach of troth,
He joined us twain. Let us then live together.
O Father, if Thou canst forgive Thy son
For one brief lapse, that I may please my spouse,

Pray overlook it as a passing fit.
One must be soft and gentle with the weak.
And Thou canst bless the apple and annul
The poison flowing from the prohibition.
Give me the apple. We shall share one lot.
(He eats.)
Eve. Thus does one learn with knowledge to distinguish
Both good and evil. But alas, my husband,
Why shakes thy head?
Adam. I heard the bridal chorus
Raise a lament that blots out every joy.
Eve. Why is thy cheek so pale? Be brave, my dear!
Thou needst not be afraid; for I alone
Have taken all thy guilt upon my soul.

CHORUS OF GUARDIAN ANGELS

Strophe I

Alas, what boots an angel guard,
If God's great Eye all-seeing
Holds not mankind from evil barr'd!
The father of the race is marr'd
And all who share his being -
Bereft throughout eternity
Of all the bliss that was to be!
O feast of a few hours,
High Heav'n itself has felt this blow!
Man's spiritual powers
Might have endured like ours,
But they have been too weak and low
To give their Maker pleasure.
O time of woe past measure!

Antistrophe I

Had Adam marked the sorry case
Of angel-hosts that proudly
Misused their day of light and grace
And climbed above their proper place,
Malignantly and loudly
Flouting God's mild, indulgent reign,
He might have lived without a stain.

   May Mercy interceding
Reach out to help the fallen pair
   Who heard, no duty heeding,
   The serpent's evil pleading
And now lie weeping in despair
   For all the Fall has lost them!
   How dear their lusts have cost them!

Strophe II

To seek for knowledge is not wrong.
   We angels press yet higher
And trace in speculation strong
The secrets that to God belong.
   To knowledge we aspire:
For, mirrored in the spheres of light,
God's world lies naked to our sight.
   There the Most High is showing
The shining shapes of things to come,
   Unborn but boldly glowing
   In semblance for our knowing.
Shall Adam, likewise venturesome,
   Find venomous damnation?
   This calls for explanation!

Antistrophe II

The Godhead knows itself, and first
   Its knowledge is then splendid,
And free from any stain accurst.
The souls that for such knowledge thirst
   With favor are attended.
This aspiration to abet,
A Tree of Knowledge hath He set.
   But this by means forbidden
Defiantly to bear away
   Is gravely to be chidden.
   Adam in shame lies hidden.
Prince Lucifer has won the day.
   O Adam, lofty cedar,
   In thee Earth lost its leader!

ACT FIVE

Enter Lucifer and Asmodeus.

Luc. The dirge begins. No song's of such a sort.
Asm. How wakefully this guard has done its duty!
Luc. Our wish is granted. We have passed the cape.
O Asmodeus, the dark realm of Hell
Will praise thee now and will escort thee home,
Marching to the hoarse clarions of night.
Our palace will be decked with tapestries
Of spider-webs, festooned with withered leaves,
To hold the feast of victory. We shall crown thee
Illustrious monarch of the Orient.
Thou hast confounded man's first festival,
And shalt, as Oriental god of marriage,
Inflame the bridal bed with lust by night
And shalt be strong to break the bridegroom's neck
As he lies folded in his bride's warm arms.
Asm That's more than I deserve. 'Tis by thy blessing
That zeal has crowned my head. Thou too art worthy.
Luc. Where now are the young bridegroom and his bride?
Asm. They've slunk away, o'ercome with shame and fear,
And slipped into a cave. Their nakedness
Appals them, for they now behold themselves
With other eyes, derided and deceived.
Blushing they weave, to cover up their shame,
A hasty kilt of fig-leaves for their loins;
For we through brambles and through hedge of thorn
Have dragged them by the hair and torn apart
The white silk of their primal innocence.
Thus are they all befouled, splashed black with mire
And sprinkled red with blood. They cry and wail,
Blaming each other for the dark misdeed,
And curse till Eden echoes pitiably.
Sad Adam tears his face and rends his hair,
With wild resounding outcry: "Whither, then
Ah, whither have I fallen? I gave ear,
Not to my bride but to an enemy.
Mine own flesh hath betrayed me. I have followed

Unholy paths. An evil love of dainties
Was the dark shaft that pierced both Eve and me.
This comes of love of woman. By my rib,
Yea, by my own flesh have I been betrayed.
Love of my wife hath cost me all too dear.
I wanted, in my pride, to rear my flag.
Upon the topmost pinnacle of being
And to resemble God Himself in knowledge.
Pride has deceived and ruined me. The Devil
Grapples and boards me from the fleet of Hell.
A fight already rages in my body:
One thing my soul desires, my flesh another.
Reason and will, touched by this sudden taste,
Feel all too late a catastrophic blow.
Sorrow I feel, without me and within.
How can such losses ever be restored?"
Luc. Thus my revenge is satisfied, and Hell
At last is victor. Let my Foe take heed
And set up laws to ward off such invasion.
No more are we restrained by dyke or dam
Of laws or promises or fearsome threats.
Nature lies violated, trodden flat;
The human race is mine inheritance.
God's promises and threats have lost their power.
The will has ferried over, from the Good
That God commanded, to the shore of Evil.
In God's despite, I shall sow fanes and altars
And men shall honour images of me
With human sacrifice and gold and incense,
And swear by all the deities of Hell
For fear of punishment. Thus plausibly
And falsely do I shift the cause of ill
From mine own shoulders to mine enemy's.
Though all the earth should crawl with Adam's heirs,
From sixty centuries He shall not save
More souls than a mere handful. By my fall,
I thus have mounted upon higher stairs.
This much has lust achieved -- and apple-juice.
But let us hide a while, and we shall hear
The close of this eternal tragedy
From Adam's lips. The sad role is played out.
He comes to know his guilt, through punishment
That treads upon the weak transgressor's heels.
On such a wicked monster God must gaze

And cry aloud, with pallid countenance:
"Yea, I repent that I created Man!"
Exit Lucifer and Asmodeus.

Enter Adam and Eve.

Adam. O shadowy cave, in this thy dismalness
I thought to hide my guilt and naked shame
From the all-piercing radiance of heaven,
But all in vain. No cave or thicket shields me.
For pricking conscience constantly betrays,
Convicting me of sin. It is a worm
That gnaws within my heart incessantly,
Devouring all my vitals. Where can I,
For peace from thoughts that burn me, set my foot?
Oh, what a restless load of guiltiness
Is in my breast, that staggers to and fro,
Swayed back and forward by its weight of sin!
How altered is my state! With groping hands
I seek my former rest and find it nowhere.
It flees continually, and will not stay.
Why do I grasp the air, that mocks my fingers?
Where are the glad angelic feast-companions?
The Watchers of the Garden? They are fled.
The bridal-song is silent. Birds are mute.
No choir rejoices over bride and groom.
The heavenly trumpet hails the feast no more.
Nay, horns of hell hold forth with horrid blare.
Eve. What hath possessed thee? Hast thou lost thy senses?
Adam. I see hobgoblins, and I hear their clamor
About me in the night. See, Furies climb
Up from the Pit and threat us with grimaces! . . .
The mist that cloaked my vision vanishes.
Spectres come marching in an endless line.
In spite of all the love thou hast unfolded,
The woe that thou hast brewed appals me still.
Eve. So thou wouldst cast thy fault upon my shoulders!
Adam. Cause of my downfall and all grief to come,
Are these the ways of women? Sure, our marriage
Was not established upon such conditions.
Eve. On what condition were our hands then plighted?
Adam. That thou, my helpmeet, shouldst uphold thy man.

Eve. A man should be a model to his wife.
Adam. Let this vile Tree bear witness who it was
First dared to sin and taste forbidden fruit!
Eve. Weak female nature through desire was lost.
Adam. Thy cursèd appetite hath cost me sore.
Eve. A man should still be resolute and firm
And hold his ground till woman's nature yields.
Adam. It was thy tongue that made me change my tack.
Eve. True piety and righteousness yield not
To all the wheedling and the threats of woman.
Be brave! I still am faithful 'mid our woes,
Even as once in our prosperity,
And nevermore shall fail thee in thy need.
Adam. Vain comfort, for we have no second chance.
Eve. What remedy? God made us fallible,
And fashioned us imperfect in our nature.
Adam. Thus does the pleasure of a moment draw
An endless chain of suffering and grief.
I care no more to taste this life. It seems,
Where'er I go or stay, pale forms of Death
Are glowering enviously. Open thy lap,
O Earth! Receive me, for all joy is lost!
Once more receive me, for I came from thee!
This body to thee comes. The soul removes,
And seeks far hence a secret habitation,
Whither a curse condign shall thrust it down,
For having made misuse of God's high blessings.
Why does Death tarry? Life's my enemy,
And dismal darkness dearer far than day.
Too naked lies my fault. I fain would die.
Prevent it not. Take pleasure in my death,
And raise no voice to wail the timely corpse,
For seasonably he dies whose hope is gone.
My life is short, but I have lived too long;
I've lost all bliss, and have no more to lose.
What stroke of death is readiest for me?
Shall I leap fearlessly from some high peak,
Or drown in the Euphrates, drifting on,
With current and with eddy, out to sea
As food for fishes? Woman, hold me not!
'Twere surely better far to let me go.
The sun has veiled its head and in the West
Anticipates my setting. Oh, unhand me!
Mine eyes would shun the light. I have outlived

The blessèd lot assigned me, and have striven,
Led on by pride, too recklessly and steeply,
After a mark set far above man's fate.
Hence must I cast myself in death to Hell.
Eve. Where fallest thou? Wilt thou abridge thy
life
And leave me a sad widow? Am not I
Thy flesh and bone indeed?
Adam. Ay, flesh that lied
And so misled me with its venomed tongue!
Eve. The serpent had deceived me with its cunning.
Adam. Thou art the serpent that hath brought me
death.
Eve. Where's thy high genius now, that once could
reach
To comprehend the stars? Where's the bright light
Of thine illumined reason? If my tears
And humble pleas can move thee not, permit me
To die together with thee, at thy side;
For without thee I do not care to live.
I'll not deny that I urged on this crime:
My appetite hath led thee to this woe.
So let us then, companions in dark guilt,
Atone together for an act of evil.
Content with such an end, most willingly
I'll learn to bear the punishment I merit.
Here is my hand. I'm reconciled to death.
Go forth, and mope no longer. Walk before me.
Stand by thy word: be resolute to die.
Me too no death shall fright, though it should be
To crash from some high rock or in the sea
To leap, thy hand in mine. I promise it.
Adam. Ah, dearest, 'tis my fault. Most precious
one,
I will prolong my life through love of thee.
Wipe off these tears that sprinkle thy pale cheeks,
And set thy noble heart at rest. Though here
No wish for life remains, it pleases me
To live to serve thy favor and thy face.
Thou shalt not, as a widow, here bewail
Earth's primal wedding-day, alone and pallid,
With hanging head, low seated on a stone,
Lamenting that thy man, o'ercome with grief,
Had laid his guilty hands upon himself.

I shall restrain dejection and in calm
Await the uttermost that shall ensue.
Eve. What do I hear? A storm begins to rise;
Tempestuously the dark and pregnant air
Breaks into tumult that tears loose the leaves
And rends the trees and bushes everywhere.
The trembling earth resounds with roars and wails.
It lightens, flash on flash; with deafening roll
The thunderbolts come hurtling, blow on blow,
To chase the dying day into the night.
Adam. How quakes the heart with fright! My body trembles,
Ridden by fever and the fear of death.
My hair stands up, and all my blood congeals.
The all-seeing Judge draws near, provoked to anger
By hideous transgression of His law.
Where shall we flee? He makes His coming heard.
Come, let us seek a thicket where the sun
Can never thrust its penetrating rays.
No fig-leaf web can clothe our nakedness.
For He who knows all hearts can look us through,
From top to toe, in body and in soul.
How quickly Heaven's punishment can tread
Upon Offence's heels! Stoop down, my dear,
And I shall shield thee closely with my shadow.
O lust! O apple-tree! O stain of sin!
Hide us, O bush, so far as yet thou mayest!
God's Justice comes. O woeful wedding-day!

Enter Uriel.

Uriel. O Adam, hearken! Whither runnest thou
To hide in dismal shadows? Dost intend
Thus to conceal thy sin and shame from God
And His all-seeing light? No cavern deep
In dark can hide thee from the Infinite
Who dwells in all the earth and sky and sea.
In God's name I arrest thee. Show thyself!
The God who made thee subject to His law
Arrests thee. Wherefore dost thou flee thy Maker?
Adam. O voice, I shall obey. Let me approach thee.
The herald of thy coming in the wood,
The thunder that declares thy majesty
Amazed those, who, made naked, must be shamed

Out of humility and veneration,
Emotion that befits our human duty.
Uriel Who hath revealed this nakedness to thee?
Hast thou then tasted of the Tree of Knowledge?
Confess the misdeed freely. Hide it not.
Make no excuse, for here no cloak avails.
O faithless one, daredst thou alone profane
The high command of God by eating fruit
Forbidden thee indeed on pain of death?
Adam. 'Tis not my fault: the coaxings of the woman,
Vouchsafed to me by God to be a help,
Enticed my ears and heart, my eyes and mouth,
Even by colour of the fruit to taste,
Alas, to my destruction and my doom.
Thus from the woman did my fall begin.
Uriel. O woman, chos'n as helpmeet of thy spouse,
What turned thy thoughts to this accurst defiance?
Eve. A serpent, God's own creature, tempted me
And led my simple heart to eat the apple.
Uriel. O serpent, subtle beast, thou now shalt feel
The highest wrath of Heaven. Thou henceforth,
Hated by every kind of beast, shalt creep
Upon thy belly, void of peace and rest,
And driven to thy cave shalt pass thy life
Consuming dust as food. Justice divine
Shall raise up inextinguishable hate,
Even between the woman's Seed and thee.
For He shall crush thy head, though in the strife
'Twill be thy lot to bite Him in the heel.
O woman who hast thus betrayed thy husband,
Endless shall be the pangs in store for thee
In pregnancy and childbirth, and as slave
To Adam as thy lord, to do his will.
And thou, O Adam, who hast given ear
To this weak woman's voice more than to God's,
In eating fruit and breaking His command,
Shalt sweat beneath the yoke of painful toil.
Cursed is now the earth, and shall repay
Thy ploughing and thy sowing many-fold
With weeds and straw and chaff. The thorn and thistle
Shall choke the proper harvest of the field

Until thou turnest to the earth again,
Sodden with sweat and buried in the womb
Of that terrestrial dam that gave thee birth.
But in the meantime, that thou mayest feel
How God has valued mercy more than justice,
Thy wife shall bear thee young, and God, to guard
Thy modesty and health, shall cover thee
With the warm fleece of sheep. But now, begone!
Depart forthwith! And you, ye Cherubim,
God's Garden-sentries, show your faithfulness
And chase this pair of exiled bandits hence,
Out of this Paradise! Be sure ye watch
The golden Tree of Life, to hold in check
With your sharp swords all wantoning delight!
Let those white sabres burn with heat and flame,
Lest any exile taste the Tree of Life.
Exit Uriel.
Eve. O what a fire kindles all the Garden
And browses off the trees! The bridal tune
Is silent now, and hushed all birds and beasts.
It is thy lot and mine to celebrate
Our marriage with these flaming angel-torches.
Whither, my dear, Oh whither shall we go?
Adam. This is no time for loitering. That Spirit
Appear'd not Uriel but God Himself,
Whose law we broke to climb above man's lot
Upon the roof of heaven and challenge Him
In plenitude of wisdom and of power.
A reckless move has brought about our fall.
Alas, who now supports my wavering steps?
My wife, support me in my dreary exile!
'Tis time to flee. My bones are shuddering.
We go, devoid of hope of e'er again
Beholding thee, O Garden of Delight!
What boots this fruitless gazing? We are bidden
To leave this gate and seek a thirsty land
Of drought and misery. O keen repentance!
O sweating toil, O endless wretchedness,
Escort me forth with all your band of sorrows!
Here summer's at an end; and winter's cold
Grapples and boards me. God's two-handed sword
Flames ruthlessly behind us. And we go.

PART TWO

--

DESCRIPTIVE CATALOGUE

PART TWO: DESCRIPTIVE CATALOGUE

Analogues are listed hereunder in chronological order. Where microfilms or photostats have been secured for purposes of more careful study, the source of the photographic material has been noted. Incipits and explicits have been omitted in a few cases, especially in translated works. Abbreviations: PL, Analogue of Paradise Lost; MPG, Migne's Patrologia Graeca; MPL, Migne's Patrologia Latina; Mi, microfilm; Ph, photostat; asterisk (*), item not located.

PL-1. (Sumerian)

Kramer, Samuel N. (tr.). Enki and Ninhursag: A Sumerian "Paradise" Myth. (New Haven, 1945).

This poem was hailed in 1915 by its first translator, Stephen Langdon, as an "epic of Paradise, the Flood and the Fall of Man." Subsequent scholars have been almost unanimous in rejecting this interpretation as baseless.

The original text was inscribed on a six-column tablet dug up at Nippur around 1900, but it has more recently been possible to collate part of it with a duplicate tablet in the Louvre. The results of the most recent scholarship are embodied in Dr. Kramer's transliteration, translation and notes.

Its nearest analogies to the Genesis story are as follows: (a) the idyllic land of Dilmun is described as free from sickness, old age and death, (b) Enki, the god-hero of the poem, is placed under a mortal curse because he has eaten certain plants, and (c) one of the goddesses born to heal his dying members is called "Nin-ti", which can be equally well translated as "the Lady of the rib" and "the Lady who makes live." In the Biblical story, Even combines these terms in her origin and in her name "Hawwah", which means "she who makes live"; but the original Sumerian pun is lost in the Hebrew.

Kramer suggests that the Nippur tablet dates from the 17th or 18th century B.C., but the age of composition may be far earlier.

PL-2. (Babylonian)

The Babylonian Epic of Creation. Possibly based on an earlier Sumerian poem is an epic in the Semitic speech of ancient Babylonia. In the form found about 1875 A.D. in the library of Assur-bani-pal at Nineveh, it was inscribed in the time of that monarch (688-626 B.C.) on seven numbered tablets; but there are evidences, internal and external, that it was composed many centuries earlier. In this epic, there is a "council in hell" of the gods of chaos and confusion, plotting against the gods of law and order. They marshal their forces of horrible monsters, including "monstrous serpents, sharp of tooth, merciless of fang, with bodies filled with venom instead of blood." Marduk, the divine son of the supreme god Anshar, is exalted by his father and acclaimed by all the host of heaven. He then goes out to the "war in heaven" and single-handed destroys Tiamat, the leader of the host of evil, and assumes supreme power. Slicing the dead body of Tiamat in two, he creates the firmament from one half and the earth from the other. On the earth he causes vegetation to spring up and finally creates man, to honour the gods in worship.

PL-3. (Babylonian)

The Gilgamesh Epic. Made known to the modern world, like PL-2, through the discovery at Nineveh of the royal cuneiform library of Assur-bani-pal, is the Gilgamesh Epic, in twelve clay tablets or books. In the 1st tablet, a wild man, Enkidu or Eabani, is created by Aruru. He lives peacefully among the gazelles and the beasts of the field until a woman comes into his life. In tablets II to VI, he accompanies Gilgamesh, the hero of the epic, on an expedition to Ishtar's forest of cedars. They slay its guardian, Khumbaba, and also a divine bull sent against Gilgamesh after he has repulsed the love of Ishtar. In tablets VII and VIII, Enkidu is smitten with a grievous disease and dies. In tablets IX and X, Gilgamesh, seeking to avoid the fate of his friend, journeys to find Ut-Napishtim, a sort of Babylonian Noah who following his escape from a Flood is granted immortality, dwelling with his wife in a terrestrial Paradise "in the distance at the confluence of the streams." In tablet XI, Gilgamesh is shown a Plant of Life, but just as he is about to eat it, a serpent, sent by the gods, snatches it away from him. In tablet XII, Gilgamesh, like Odysseus in Book XI of the Odyssey, obtains an interview with the ghost of his dead friend and learns from him of the sad fate of the dead. The discovery of fragments of the epic in the script of c. 2000 B.C. shows that it is at least that old.

PL-4. (Hebrew)

The Genesis story of the Creation and the Fall.

Incipit. Bereshith bara Elohim eth hashshamayim . . .
Explicit. . . . lishmor eth-derekh 'eç-hahayyim.

This account in chapters 1-3 of Genesis is the seminal nucleus from which Paradise Lost and all its literary kindred are ultimately derived. As will be noted later, the brief Old Testament narrative was in due course amplified to giant proportions in the hexameral literature and the commentaries, many of which, directly or indirectly, contributed source material to Milton's epic.

PL-5. (Hebrew)

The Book of Enoch, ed. by R. H. Charles (London, 1917). A composite work, with elements of various dates, the earliest before 161 B.C. Written originally in Hebrew or Aramaic, or part in each, and later translated into Greek, Latin and Ethiopic. Only the latter remains intact. The *Book of Enoch* was not accessible to Milton, but it exerted a great influence on New Testament thought.

The most relevant portions for students of Milton are (a) chapters vi-xi, describing the Fall of the Angels through lust after the daughters of man, and (b) chapters xvii-xxxvii, describing Enoch's journeys through Earth and Sheol. Strikingly like Milton's cosmogony are the descriptions of Chaos and the place of punishment for the wicked. In the demonology of this work, Satan rules a kingdom of evil, yet is subject to the Lord of Spirits. He led the angels astray; and it was an evil spirit, named Gadreel, that seduced Eve. The function of the evil spirits is to tempt, to accuse, and to punish.

PL-6. (Hebrew)

The Book of Jubilees or *Little Genesis* (*Λεπτὴ Γένεσις* or *Μικρογένεσις*) or *Apocalypse of Moses* or *Testament of Moses* or *Book of Adam's Daughters* or *Life of Adam*. *This is* the *oldest of the "Adam-books"*, *written* originally in Hebrew (now lost), before 105 B.C., but surviving in Greek (fragmentary), Ethiopic, Latin and Syriac.

"The effects of the Fall were limited to Adam and the animal creation. Adam was driven from the garden and the animal creation was robbed of the power of speech; but the subsequent depravity of the human race is not traced to the Fall but to the seduction of the daughters of men by the angels who had been sent down to instruct men, and to the solicitations of demonic spirits, the ghosts of their offspring. The evil engendered by the former was brought to an end by the Deluge, but the incitement to evil on the part of the demons was to last to the final judgement." - R. H. Charles, in *Apocrypha and Pseudepigrapha of the Old Testament*, *Vol. II, 8-9*, *in which volume a full translation* is to be found (pp. 11-82).

PL-7. (Greek)

The Book of the Secrets of Enoch or II Enoch. Written originally in Greek, by a Hellenistic Jew, in Egypt, about the beginning of the Christian era; but survives only in two Slavonic versions, one Ukrainian and the other Serb. These have been collated and translated by W. R. Morfill in Apocrypha and Pseudepigrapha of the Old Testament (ed. R. H. Charles), Vol. II, pp. 425-69).

In this work, the world is specifically created out of nothing. The details of each day's creation are given (cc. 25-30). The seven days are a symbol of 7,000 years of human history. All the souls of men were created from the beginning of the world. "Man's soul was created originally good, and while in the Garden he could see the angels in heaven (31,2). Free-will was bestowed on him, and the knowledge of good and evil. He was likewise instructed in the Two Ways of light and darkness, and then left to mould his own destiny (30,15). But the incorporation of the soul in the body with its necessary limitations biased its preferences in the direction of evil, and death came in as the fruit of sin." (Charles, op. cit.)

PL-8. (Greek)

Philo Judaeus (fl. A.D. 40), On the Account of the World's Creation, Given by Moses. Philo Judaeus, On the Cherubim, and the Flaming Sword, and Cain the first Man created out of Man.

Philo was the earliest great writer, in Greek, in a long series of allegorical commentators on the "hexameron" or six days of Creation. He combines an absolute faith in the inspiration of the Scriptures with absolute freedom in interpretation in the spirit of Greek philosophy. Thus he calls the literal story of Adam's rib being made into Eve a myth; and he then goes into an involved argument that Adam represents the human reason and Eve sense-perception, and that the reason is dormant while sense-perceptions are being formed. Philo's emphasis on the significance of certain numbers - an emphasis inherited from the Pythagoreans - also crops up frequently among later writers.

Philo's influence is marked in an allegorical school of hexameral writers associated with Alexandria, especially Origen (*De Principiis*, MPG, xi), and *In Genesim*, MPG, xii, Athanasius of Alexandria (*Hexameron*, MPG, xxvi), Cyril of Alexandria (*Hexameron*, MPG, lxix) and Anastasius the Sinaite (*Hexameron*, MPG, lxxxix). A school of sharply contrasted realism developed at Antioch and Edessa, and included the *Hexamera* of St. Ephrem, Cyril of Jerusalem, Severien of Gabala, St. John Chrysostom and Theodoret. Mid-way between the two schools, and tending to stress the scientific and encyclopedic aspects of the Genesis-story, was the work of the Cappadocian school of St. Basil and his successors (cf. PL-15 below).

PL-9. (Greek)

The Apocalypse of Adam, 1st century A.D. (a lost book, quoted in the *Epistle of Barnabas*, ii, 10), also known as *The Penitence of Adam* (mentioned in the Gelasian Decree) or *The Testament of Adam* or *The Testament of the Protoplasts*. Detailed discussion of this work may be found in *The Lost Apocrypha of the Old Testament*, by Montague Rhodes James, pp. 1-8. Apparently all of the titles quoted refer to what is substantially the same work. Considerable fragments survive through quotation, e.g. by Georgius Cedrenus, who quotes, in connection with Adam's repentance, a revelation vouchsafed to him in his 600th year, including a time-table of the prayers that ascend to God at the different hours of the day (the first hour, opening prayers in heaven; the second hour, the prayers of the angels; the third hour, the prayers of birds; the fourth hour, the prayers of domestic cattle; the fifth hour, the prayers of wild beasts, etc.).

PL-10 (Latin)

Vita Adae et Evae, ed. by Wilhelm Meyer in Abhandlungen der Münchner Akademie der Wissenschaften, 1878. A 1st century A.D. Latin version of the Greek Apocalypse of Moses (No. 7 above), with certain variations. The most noteworthy episodes are as follows: (1) Adam and Eve seek to show their penitence by standing naked for forty days, the former in the Jordan and the latter in the Tigris. The Jordan and all its fishes lament along with Adam; but Satan, disguised as an angel, persuades Eve to come out of the Tigris. (2) Adam, amid the aches and pains of old age, persuades Seth and Eve to go to the gate of Eden and ask for some of the oil of the tree of mercy. Michael tells Seth, however, that this oil will not be available for 5,500 years. Then Christ will come, and after his baptism in Jordan the oil of God's mercy will be granted. The bodies of Adam and the other dead will then be raised, and Christ will lead Adam to the Paradise of God. (This sequel appears again in the apocryphal Gospel of Nicodemus.)

*PL-11. (Greek)

The Gospel of Eve, a lost work, referred to in Epiphanius, Adv. Haereses, xxvi, 2,3. (Cf. M. R. James, op. cit., p. 8.) Apparently a Gnostic work. Eve is seduced by Satan, and bears him two sons, Cain and Abel. Cf. also Fabricius, Codex Pseudepigraphus Veteris Testamenti, I, 95.

PL-12. (Latin)

Victorinus Petavionensis, De fabrica mundi (MPL, v. 301-314). Mi: University of Chicago.

Inc. Cogitanti mihi, una cum animo meo conferenti, de fabrica mundi istius . . .
Expl. idcirca quia seniores sunt et aliis angelis et hominibus.

A fragmentary prose work on the Creation, stressing (like Philo) the symbolic significance of such numbers as seven and twelve. Victorinus (fl. A.D. 290) was a bishop of Petavio or Poetavio, in Pannonia, and suffered martyrdom under Diocletian.

PL-13. (Armenian)

An Armenian Life of Adam, tr. by Conybeare in The Jewish Quarterly Review, 1895, vii, 216-35. Apparently translated from the Greek Apocalypse of Moses (cf. PL-6 above), with some additions and alterations of a Gnostic character.

PL-14. (Greek)

Nazianzenus, Gregorius. Περὶ κόσμου . (MPG, xxxvii, 415-423.) Mi: Harvard.

Inc. Εἰ δ'ἄγε μεγάλοιο Θεοῦ κτίσιν ὑμνείωμεν,
Δόξαις ψευδομένησιν ἐναντία δηριόωντες ...
Expl. Κάλλεϊ τε μεγέθει τε, καὶ εἰκόνος ἐμβασίλευμα·
Πρῶτος δ' ὕστατός τε Θεοῦ μεγάλοιο λόγοισι.

A poem of 100 hexameter lines, being part iv of Gregory's Poemata Dogmatica. It is devoted to the theological aspects of the Creation and stresses the eternal contemporaneity of God. St. Gregory of Nazianzus (c. 329-c. 389) was one of the four great fathers of the Eastern Church. In his early literary work he was closely associated with St. Basil, his fellow-student at Athens.

PL-15. (Greek)

St. Basil the Great. Hexaemeron. MPG xxix, 3-207. Mi: Chicago.

Inc. Πρέπουσα ἀρχὴ τῷ περὶ τῆς τοῦ κόσμου συστάσεως μέλλοντι διηγεῖσθαι ...
Expl. δοξαζέσθω ὁ Κυριος, ᾧ ἡ δόξα καὶ τὸ κράτος

εἰς τοὺς αἰῶνας τῶν αἰώνων. Ἀμήν.

St. Basil (c. 330-379) was the chief hexameral writer of the Cappadocian school, imitated by all the rest and translated into Latin several times during his lifetime. His Hexameron was in turn the main inspiration of the hexameral poets of the 16th century. Thus the Italian scholar, Giuseppe Scopa, has systematically compared Tasso's Sette Giornate with St. Basil and finds that 3190 lines out of the 7667 lines dealing with the first six days are a literal translation of the Greek prose of St. Basil. Du Bartas's poem is much less crudely lifted from St. Basil, but numerous episodes and examples are drawn directly from him and there is even some close rendering of his language. More notable still is DuBartas's appropriation of St. Basil's very style: its oratorical tone, its swelling phrases, its occasional digression in a conversational tone, and its prompt return to the grand manner.[1]

Among the numerous contemporaries and successors who followed St. Basil's example in Greek were his brother Gregory of Nyssa (cf. PL-17), Gregory Nazianzenus (cf. PL-14), George of Pisidia (cf. PL-39), Eusthates of Antioch, James of Edessa, Procopius of Gaza, Joannes Philoponos, and Joannes Damascenus. Among his early emulators in Latin were St. Ambrose (cf. PL-18), St. Augustine and St. Jerome.

PL-16. (Greek)

St. Basil the Great. Orationes (MPG xxx, 10-72) Mi: Chicago.

Inc. Παλαιοῦ χρέους ἔκτισιν ἀποπληρώσων ἥκω...
Expl. ἡ δόξα εἰς τοὺς αἰῶνας τῶν αἰώνων. Ἀμήν.

The first and second of these three discourses deal with the creation of man, the third with the

[1] Cf. Maisières, op. cit., pp. 39-40.

earthly Paradise. They supplement his major work in the *Hexaemeron*.

PL-17. (Greek)

St. Gregory of Nyssa. *De hominis opificio*. Mi: Chicago.

Inc. Αὕτη ἡ βίβλος γενέσεως οὐρανοῦ καὶ γῆς ...
Expl. ᾧ ἡ δόξα καὶ τὸ κράτος εἰς τοὺς αἰῶνας τῶν αἰώνων. Ἀμήν.

St. Gregory of Nyssa (c. 331 - c. 396) was a younger brother of Basil the Great. He ranks as one of the four great fathers of the Eastern Church. For Renaissance writers, his *De hominis opificio* was a frequent source of material for the last day of the Creation. Like his brother, he also wrote a *Hexaemeron*.

PL-18. (Latin)

St. Ambrose. *De Paradiso liber unus*. Circa 375 A.D.

Inc. De paradiso adoriundus sermo non mediocrem aestum nobis videtur incutere, quidnam sit paradisus . . .
Expl. Si enim carnalia seminaverimus, quae carnalia sunt metemus; si vero spiritalia seminaverimus, metemus ea quae sunt spiritalia.

Saint Ambrose (340?-397), bishop of Milan, is the father of Roman hexameral writers and exerted a profound influence on the scholarly world of the 16th century. Erasmus, for example, hailed his hexameron as a literary masterpiece. In his *De Paradiso*, he describes Paradise as situated on a mountain and watered by a fountain fed by a subterranean river. Ambrose was a close imitator of Basil.

PL-19. (Latin)

St. Ambrose. <u>De Cain et Abel libri duo</u>. Circa 375 A.D.

<u>Inc</u>. De paradiso in superioribus pro captu nostro, ut potuimus, quod Dominus infudit, sensus invenit, digessimus, in quibus Adam atque Evae lapsus est comprehensus. . . .
<u>Expl</u>. Excusare posset quod se redemisset vel sera actione poenitentiae, nisi cum praematura poena rapuisset.

Commentary on the Murder of Abel.

PL-20. (Latin)

St. Ambrose. <u>De Dierum Creatione Hymni VI</u>. Circa 375 A.D.

<u>Inc</u>. Lucis creator optime,
Lucem dierum proferens . . .
<u>Expl</u>. Dissolve litis vincula,
Adstringe pacis foedera!

Though commonly attributed to St. Ambrose, these six hymns on the six days of Creation are thought by some critics to be the work of St. Gregory.

PL-21. (Latin)

St. Ambrose. <u>Hexaemeron libri sex</u>. Circa 389 A.D.

<u>Inc</u>. Tantumne opinionis assumsisse homines, ut aliqui eorum tria principia constituerent omnium Deum, et exemplar, et materiam, sicut Plato . . .
<u>Expl</u>. Ipse enim requievit, qui fecit: cui est honor, gloria, perpetuitas a saeculis, et nunc, et semper, et in omnia saecula saeculorum. Amen.

St. Ambrose's treatment of the seventh day served as a model for Renaissance writers, who found only six days in St. Basil's work.[1] In notes to DuBartas published in his own lifetime, the source-parallels in St. Ambrose are freely conceded. A manuscript of Tasso's *Sette Giornate* (cf. PL-169 below) discovered in 1920 *records in the* margin in Tasso's own hand[2] some 39 borrowings from St. Ambrose.

PL-22. (Latin)

Prudentius, Aurelius. *Hymnus ante cibum*. MPL, lix, 796-811). Ca. 400 A.D. *Mi: Harvard*.

Inc. O Crucifer bone, lucisator,
Omniparens, pie, verbigena . . .
Expl. Dux parili redivivus humo
Ignea Christus ad astra vocat.

This is in Part III of his *Cathemerinon* or "Hymns for the Day". It is a poem of *205 decasyllabic* lines, in which the fault of Adam and Eve is treated at some length, prior to a brief prayer for blessing on a modest meal. Prudentius also wrote a hexameral work, *De fabrica mundi*, now lost, of which Gennadius reports *"Commentatus est* et in morem Graecorum Hexaemeron de mundi fabrica usque ad conditionem primi hominis et praevaricationem eius" (cf. *De scriptoribus*, in Migne, *Patrologia Latina*, viii). *Prudentius (348-c*.410) seems *to have been influenced* by Ambrose in his hymnody.

PL-23. (Latin)

Prudentius, Aurelius. *Diptychon* (or *Dittochaeon*) *utriusque Testamenti*. *Circa 400* A.D.

---

[1]An earlier source was the *De hominis opificio* (MPG, xliv, 123), in which St. *Gregory of Nyssa* completed his brother's unfinished work.

[2]Maisières, *op. cit*., p. 26.

Inc. Eva columba fuit tunc candida; nigra deinde . . .
Expl. Et septem potuit signacula pandere solus.

A series of Latin epigrams, of four hexameter lines each, which run the gamut of the Scriptures from Genesis to Revelation. Only the first eight lines are closely relevant to Milton's theme.

PL-24. (Latin)

Prudentius, Aurelius. Hamartigenia, id est, De origine peccatorum. Circa 400 A.D.

Inc. Fratres ephebi fossor et pastor duo,
Quos foeminarum prima primos procreat . . .
Expl. Lux immensa alios, et tempora vincta coronis
Glorificent; me poena levis clementer adurat.

Beginning with the murder of Abel by Cain, Prudentius proceeds to discuss the origin of evil, dismissing the Marcionite heresy of a duality of gods, good and evil, and stressing the reality but inferiority of Satan. The ruling passion of the latter is portrayed as jealousy of the supremacy of God.

PL-25. (Latin)

Prudentius, Aurelius. Psychomachia. Ca. 400 A.D.

Inc. Senex fidelis prima credendi via
Abram, beati seminis serus pater . . .
Expl. Aeternum solio dives Sapientia regnet.

This, the most finished work of Prudentius, is an allegory in epic form, dealing with the "battle of the soul" against the forces of the Evil One. It is thus a forerunner of Bunyan's Holy War. Prudentius is able to mould his material into an artistic literary whole.

PL-26. (Latin)

Proba, Valeria Faltonia. Centones Virgiliani ad testimonium Veteris et Novi Testamenti. (MPL, xix, 804-818.) Mi: Harvard.

Inc. Jamdudum temerasse duces pia foedera pacis,
Regnandi miseros tenuit quos dira cupido . . .
Expl. O dulcis coniux: et si pietate merentur,
Hac casti maneant in religione nepotes.

A poem of considerable length in hexameters, most of which have been culled from Vergil but have been adapted ingeniously to deal with Biblical themes. The largest single section deals with the Creation and the Fall of Man. The author, Valeria (floruit A.D. 400, wife of the proconsul Adelfius) develops in her opening invocation the very same sort of appeal for heavenly, rather than earthly, inspiration that was to mark the opening lines of almost all subsequent poets of the Fall, including Milton:

Nunc, Deus Omnipotens, sacrum, precor, accipe
carmen,
Aeternumque tui septemplicis ora resolve
Spiritus, atque mei resera penetralia cordis:
Arcana ut possim vatis proba cuncta referre.
Non nunc ambrosium cura est mihi quaerere nectar,
Nec libet Aonio de vertice ducere musas . . .

PL-27. (Greek)

Ammonius. Enarrationes in opus sex dierum. A lost work, referred to by Anastasius Sinaita (MPG, xcii, 1388)

PL-28. (Latin)

St. Hilarius Arelatensis. Metrum in Genesim, ad Leonem Papam. (MPL, l, 1287-1292.) Mi: Harvard.

Inc. Paruimus monitis, tua dulcia jussa secuti,

Antistes Christi, quae dabas ore pio.
An ego non canerem tanti praeconia Patris,
Munus opusque Dei, dum mihi lingua foret? . . .
Expl. Attamen antiqui etiam nunc gutta veneni
Spargebat populos, et erant vestigia fraudis,
Quae bonus ablueret doctor melioribus undis.

A poem consisting of a 6-line dedication to Pope Leo the Great, in elegiacs, followed by 195 hexameter lines, giving a condensed summary, didactic in treatment, of the Creation, the Fall, and the evils that followed the Fall. St. Hilarius (403-449), bishop of Arles, was a Gaul of good birth and education. The poem, sometimes called a "Carmen heroicum", was formerly ascribed to St. Hilarius of Poitiers (300-367).

PL-29. (Latin)

Sedulius, Caelius. Carmen Paschale. Circa 430 A.D.

Inc. Quum sua gentiles studeant figmenta poetae
Grandisonis pompare modis, tragicoque boatu . . .
Expl. Nam si cuncta sacris voluissent tradere chartis
Facta redemptoris, nec totus cingere mundus
Sufficeret densos per tanta volumina libros.

A Latin poem in five books and 1,753 hexameter lines, dealing both with the Fall and with the Atonement. The author makes much of the guilt of Eve:

Noxia tu coniux magis, an draco perfidus ille?
Perfidus ille draco, sed tu quoque noxia coniux.

Sedulius was a Latin philosopher who embraced Christianity in the consulship of Theodosius and Valentinian. His floruit is about 430 A.D. Some authorities believe he was a Scot from Ireland.

PL-30. (Latin)

St. Prosperus Aquitanus. Carmen de providentia

divina. (MPL, lxi, 617-638.) Mi: Harvard.

Inc. Maxima pars lapsis abiit jam mensibus anni,
Quo scripta est versu pagina nulla tuo. . . .
Expl. Omnia quae fecit bona valde, ut non vitiorum
Incentiva, sed ut superas caperemus in illis,
Hic decertato virtutis agone, coronas.

The first 96 lines are a prologue in elegiac couplets, lamenting public disasters and calamities. The author himself was captured by the enemy and his city destroyed with fire. The remainder of the poem, written in epic hexameters, stresses the providence of God, from the Creation to the final defeat of Satan at the end of time. Prosperus, a disciple of Augustine, was a priest in Aquitaine, and died about A.D. 450. The authorship is disputed, for many scholars, finding its treatment of grace unorthodox, ascribe it to some heretic of the Pelagian group.

PL-31. (Latin)

Victor, Claudius Marius. Commentariorum in Genesin libri tres. (MPL, lxi, 937-970.)

Inc. Summe et sancte Deus, cunctae virtutis origo,
Omnipotens, quem nec subtili indagine rerum
Mentibus humanis sensu comprendere fas est . . .
Expl. . . . fortasse notabat
Luxuriae calidos ignes, fomentaque primi
Peccato contracta patris, coelestibus undis
Exstinctum quandoque iri: proque ignibus aeris
Justitiae, quibus illa olim lex dura vigebat,
Salvificis purgatum iri, et lustralibus undis.

The author was a rhetor of Marseilles (floruit A.D. 426) and one of the best poets of his century. His hexameter poem is a spirited and often original paraphrase, covering the Genesis story from the Creation down to the death of Abraham. He appears to have been steeped in the best secular literature and to have had no interest in the current allegorical interpretation of Scripture. In his version, Eve is a very human character who proposes to Adam that he kill the serpent with a rock.

PL-32. (Latin)

Salvianus, Hexaemeron (lost). Gennadius, De Scriptoribus (MPL, lviii, c.67), credits him with "librum unum in Hexaemeron, in modum Graecorum versu compositum". Salvianus was born at Cologne and became a priest at Marseilles.

PL-33. (Latin)

Andreas Lundensis, Hexaemeron, a lost poem in Latin hexameters. Cf. MPG, xciii, 1390: "Andreae archiepiscopi Lundensis ante annos 450 clari Hexaemeron MS. carmine heroico memorat Stephanius in notis ad Saxonem grammaticum, pag. 11."

PL-34. (Latin)

Dracontius. Carmen de Deo. MPL, lx, 679-901.) Mi: Harvard.

Inc. Qui cupiunt animis placidum rescire Tonantem,
Hoc carmen prae mente legant, dum voce recensent.
Agnoscent quod templa poli, quod moenia coeli
Auctorem confessa suum veneranter adorent . . .
Expl. Et grates exceptus agam de fasce malorum,
Additus insonti populo sub sorte piorum.

A 5th century poem in hexameters, totalling 2245 lines and arranged in three books. As the title indicates, it is largely a sermon treatise on the nature and works of God. A detailed description of Creation is incidental to Book I, and the Fall is brought into the general treatment of human depravity in Book II. Dracontius is the most distinguished Latin poet of Africa (in Christian times) and bears witness to the survival there of a cultured Christianity. His vivid description of Eden is as eloquent as that of Avitus.

PL-35. (Latin)

Avitus, Alcimus Ecdicius. _Poematum de Mosaicae historiae gestis libri quinque. First published A.D. 507. Accessible in MPL, lix,_ 325-382.

Inc. Quidquid agit varios humana in gente labores,
Unde brevem carpunt mortalia tempora vitam
Vel quod polluti vitiantur origine mores . . .
Expl. Nosque tubam stipula sequimur, numerumque tenentes
Petimus hoc tenui cymbae nunc littore portum.

The first really significant poem in the hexameral tradition, and one that was to have considerable influence in later centuries, was a Latin epic of 2,552 hexameter lines published in A.D. 507 by Alcimus Ecdicius Avitus, bishop of Vienne, a town on the Rhone in Central Gaul. Of Avitus himself, we know that his father Isicius was bishop of Vienne before him and that an elder brother Apollinaris was bishop of Valence, 35 miles farther down the Rhone. Both brothers were prominent champions of Trinitarian orthodoxy as against the Arian heresy of the Burgundians, who were the political masters of the region. Avitus was one of the chief writers of the time. Of his works, all in Latin, there are extant numerous letters, a number of sermons, some epigrams, a lengthy poem on chastity, and his sacred epic on the Fall.

A preface in prose, addressed to his brother, Bishop Apollinaris, stresses the point that the poem lacks final revision. It had been first drafted out many years before; the manuscript had been lost during the siege and capture of Vienne in 500 A.D.; and a part of it had been later rediscovered at the home of a friend. Avitus is reluctant to bring out a work that still requires long and arduous recasting, and blames its present publication on the affectionate importunities of his brother.

Analysis of the poem confirms its author's verdict all too well; for while it shows a poetic unity of intention, its integration is far from perfect. The single title for the whole work, Poematum de Mosaicae Historiae Gestis libri V is only vaguely descriptive, and there is no clear pattern in the sub-titles of its five books, viz.:

Book I.	The Beginning of the World.
Book II.	Original Sin.
Book III.	The Judgement of God.
Book IV.	The Deluge.
Book V.	The Crossing of the Red Sea.

The opening lines of Book I and the closing lines of Book V, however, make it clear that Avitus, like Milton, has in mind the one great theme of human depravity and ultimate redemption.

A brief summary will indicate the attempts of Avitus to organize his poem about this theme. Book I describes the creation of the world, including man and woman, who are placed in the Garden and warned by God against eating from the Forbidden Tree. In Book II, Satan assumes the form of a serpent and successfully tempts Eve. She in turn seduces Adam. In Book III, God passes judgement on the guilty pair and announces that the earth and all its creatures will rapidly deteriorate as the result of man's fall and will consequently suffer numerous punitive disasters, ending in general destruction. Book IV describes the Flood as one of these visitations on a wicked world; but the poet stresses also the idea that the deliverance of Noah is a symbol of human salvation to come. Book V tells of the rescue of the Israelites and the death of the Egyptians at the Red Sea. Avitus makes it clear that this event is symbolic of baptism, with its death of the old man and its saving of the soul, thus restoring the race that had been lost through the Fall. The inclusion, in Books IV and V, of subject-matter so unusual as the Flood and the Red Sea story, is explicable on at least two grounds: (i) that they lend themselves to vivid poetic treatment, and (ii) that by employing the allegorical method of scriptural interpretation inaugurated by Philo and further developed by Origen, Avitus can use these stories as symbols of Doom and Redemption, as a presentation of that great sequel to the Fall which completes and rounds out the Church's view of human history. It may be remembered that the Flood and the Crossing of the Red Sea are the chief episodes described by Milton in Books XI and XII respectively of *Paradise Lost*. Whereas Milton, however, keeps them within the framework of his action in Eden by having them revealed to Adam by Michael, Avitus presents them chronologically, as later historical developments issuing from the Fall. That he came close to the other, more dramatic device, is shown by his having God foretell to Adam, in Book III, such disasters as the murder of Abel by Cain.

The Latin style of Avitus, while not distinguished, is reasonably correct, and is strongly influenced by Vergil. This extends to the repetition of phrases, e.g., "O terque quaterque beati" (Avitus, V, 547, and Vergil's *Aeneid*, I, 94), and "Hic ver adsiduum" (Avitus, I, 222, and Vergil, *Georgics*, II, 149). Even a whole sentence, addressed by Meliboeus to Tityrus in the First *Eclogue*, - "Non equidem invideo, miror magis" - is lifted bodily and ascribed by Avitus to the Serpent in its speech with Eve (II, 157).

Two important questions may well be raised in connection with this poem: (1) To what extent does Avitus show originality in using the materials of the *Genesis*-story? (2) What evidence is there that Milton was familiar with Avitus?

As already intimated in analysing the structure of his epic, Avitus has shown considerable freedom of treatment. This is of three kinds: (i) straight expansion of Scripture by the multiplication of minor details; (ii) the imaginative addition of elements not in Scripture and sometimes even in contradiction to the Biblical version; and (iii) the intrusion of didactic passages. Good examples of extensive amplification are as follows:

(1) The formation of man from the dust of the ground is described in minute anatomical detail, both internal and external. (I, 73-127).
(2) There is an extensive description of the Garden of Eden. The river Gihon is identified with the Nile, and this serves as an excuse for an account of the annual inundation in Egypt. (I, 193-298).
(3) The dialogue between Eve and the Serpent is very much amplified. (II, 136-251).
(4) Pharaoh's army, in pursuit of the Israelites, is described in great detail. (V, 497-525).

There are still more numerous instances where Avitus uses his own imagination:

(1) He briefly touches on the nuptials of Adam and Eve, with the angels singing hymenaeal songs and with the stars as marriage torches. (I, 188-192).
(2) He brings Satan in person to the Garden, and gives him a long speech of bitter envy in which he resolves to make mankind share his punishment in hell. (II, 89-116).
(3) Satan, by supernatural power, assumes the form of a serpent. The serpent's deadly beauty is described in detail. (I, 118-135).
(4) After Adam and Eve realize their guilt, Satan, in serpent form, addresses them insultingly and vanishes through the clouds. (II, 408-423).
(5) God foretells to Adam the coming disasters of the world, including the death of Abel. (III, 177-194).
(6) The deterioration of the world through diseases, storms, warfare and civil strife is portrayed. (III, 311-361).
(7) Gabriel, rather than God, comes down and warns Noah to make an ark. (IV, 190-292).
(8) Men make fun of Noah's undertaking. (IV, 306-336).
(9) The animals voluntarily report for embarkation. (IV, 345-356).
(10) Gabriel, rather than God, battens down the hatches on the ark. (IV, 418-424).

(11) The failure of the raven to return to Noah is explained on the ground that it found plenty of floating corpses on which to perch and feed. (IV, 563-568).

Still more numerous are the didactic passages, often of great length, inserted by the poet-bishop:

(1) The sleep of Adam during the creation of Eve is compared to the sleep of Christ in death, during which his bride, the Church, issued from his side. (I, 160-169).
(2) A long passage is inserted on Lot's escape from Sodom, in order to compare Eve with Lot's wife and to point out how lucky Lot was that his wife hadn't time to persuade him to share her fate. (II, 276-407).
(3) The tree of the Cross is contrasted with the tree of the Fall and even with the figtree from which the first garments came. (III, 17-23).
(4) The serpent is contrasted with the brazen serpent and with the crucified Christ whom the latter symbolizes. (III, 24-26).
(5) The sense of guilt of Adam and Eve is compared to the sense of guilt on the part of man at the Judgement Day. This gives Avitus a good opening for a vivid description of the torments of hell. (III, 32-65).
(6) The story of Dives and Lazarus is brought in, in order that the unavailing repentance of Dives in hell may be cited as a warning. (III, 220-310).
(7) The symbolism of the Good Shepherd, the Good Samaritan, and the father of the Prodigal is elaborated in proof of God's readiness to restore man. (III, 362-425).
(8) The deafness of Noah's contemporaries to his warnings is contrasted with the ready repentance of Nineveh at the preaching of Jonah. (IV, 352-387).
(9) The floating ark is likened to the Church in an age of warfare and persecution. (IV, 352-387).
(10) The unreturning raven is compared to the Jews, who have not remained true to God's purposes.

(11) The rainbow is explained as a symbol of Christ as the intermediary between Heaven and Earth. (IV, 621-658).
(12) The blood of the Paschal Lamb is compared with that of the Atonement. (V, 247-259).
(13) The Red Sea episode is taken as a symbol of baptism. (V, 704-721).

Altogether, one may say that less than one-quarter of the total poem is a close paraphrase of the Old Testament.

Evidence that Milton was familiar with Avitus is either circumstantial or textual, and is not conclusive in either case.

The epic of Avitus was certainly accessible to him. It was printed as early as 1507, and had appeared in nine different editions[1] before Milton was born. It was popular with the grammar schools of the time. It may even have been studied at St. Paul's school while Milton was a pupil there; but this is only speculation.

Internal evidence from Milton's poems is more convincing, but even here one must be cautious. In the case of a poem that had been well known to Wester Europe for over eleven centuries, relevant details in its treatment of the Eden story might easily have been mediated to Milton through other intervening authors. Thus the envious speech of Satan in sight of Eden and the elaborate description of the serpent are both found in Grotius's _Adamus Exul_ (which is a certain source of _Paradise Lost_) and need not be referred back to Avitus. Two passages in Avitus seem echoed in Milton's early Latin poetry, written at the age of 16 (cf. _Elegy III_, 49-50, with Avitus, I, 193-195, and _In Quintum Novembris_, 7-23, with Avitus, II,

[1]The editions are as follows: Bologna, 1507; Paris, 1508; Cologne, 1509; Paris, 1510; Lyons, 1536; Paris, 1545; Lyons, 1562, 1589, 1604. There were still other editions in the 17th century.

56-76); but these again may be coincidental. The strongest evidence lies not in parallel conceptions but in a very close correspondence in phraseology, so close as to suggest verbal recollections on the part of the blind Milton. The three most striking of these happen to be among the most arresting of Milton's utterances:

(1) "All is not lost; the unconquerable will,
And study of revenge, immortal hate,
And courage never to submit or yield:"
(*Paradise Lost*, I, 106-108).
Cf. with Avitus (again Satan speaking):
Non tamen in totum periit; pars magna retentat
Vim propriam summaque cluit vitute nocendi.
(II, 95-96).

(2) "And heav'nly Quires the Hymenaean sung . . ."
(P.L., IV, 711).
Cf. with Avitus, I, 189-190:
Festivum dicebat hymen castoque pudori
Concinit angelicum iuncto modulamine carmen.

(3) "Greedily she ingorged without restraint,
And knew not eating Death . . ."
(P.L., IX, 791-792).
Cf. with Avitus, II, 231-232:
Adnuit insidiis pomumque vorata momordit.
Dulce subit virus, capitur mors horrida pastu.

One such correspondence might be accidental, but the force of their combined evidence is strong.

PL-36. (Latin)

Cyprianus Gallus. *Liber in Genesin*. (MPL, xix, 346-378.) Circa 550 A.D. *MI: Harvard*.

Inc. Principio Dominus coelum, terramque locavit:
Namque erat informis, fluctuque abscondita tellus
Immensusque Deus super aequora vasta meabat . . .
Expl. Nec minus interea Josephus munera mittit

Digna suis, magnumque duci dat ferre talentum,
Quo ditata fuit distractis frugibus aula.

The first 165 lines also appear as Incerti Auctoris Genesis (MPL, ii, 1087-8). Variously ascribed to Tertullian (ca. 155 - ca. 222), to Juvencus (fl. 329), and to Salvianus (cf. No. 32 above), it is most probably by Cyprianus, a 6th century bishop of Toulon. It is a rather close paraphrase, in hexameters, of Genesis, chapters 1-48. Its nearest approach to rhetoric is the oxymoron in the line: Quod propter gelida Cain incanduit ira.

PL-37 (Syriac)

The Cave of Treasures, accessible in Die Schatzhöhle (1883), edited by Carl Bezold, Syriac text with German translation. This prose narrative, written by a disciple of St. Ephraem, is closely related to the Apocalypse of Moses or Book of Jubilees (cf. PL-6). Unlike this work, it begins at some length with the story of Creation and the Fall. Its addiction to arithmetic savours of Jubilees, but it is not a mere translation. E.g. "In the third hour, they entered Paradise; and for the space of three hours their shame was uncovered; and in the ninth hour there occurred their departure out of Paradise."

The title of the work grows out of an incident early in its pages: "And when Adam and Eve had left Paradise, the door of Paradise was locked, and before it stood a Cherub, who bore a two-edged sword. And Adam and Eve climbed thence over the mountain of Paradise and they found a cave on the peak of a mountain; and they entered into it and sheltered themselves in it; and Adam and Eve were both virginal. And when Adam wished to know Eve, he took from the borders of Paradise gold and myrrh and frankincense, and placed them in the cave, and blessed it and consecrated it, so that it might be the bed-house of himself and his sons; and he called it 'The Cave of Treasures'."

In this cave, Adam's body was buried after his

death. At the time of the Flood, however, Noah took Adam's body on the ark, along with the gold, myrrh and frankincense. Shem later buried it on Mount Golgotha, beneath the very spot where Christ's cross was later erected. At the Crucifixion, when blood and water ran down from Christ's side, Adam was revived and ascended gloriously to Heaven.

The Cave of Treasures has a number of interesting variants of traditional stories. For example, Cain had a twin-sister Lebudha and Abel has a twin-sister Kelimath. Adam wants to marry Cain to Kelimath and Abel to Lebudha; but Cain wants to marry his own twin-sister, because she is beautiful and Abel's twin is not. This is the chief cause of the ill will between the brothers that results in the death of Abel. After his death, Lebudha goes into exile with Cain, leaving the homely Kelimath to wait one hundred years for Seth to be born as a prospective husband. Another novel detail is the arrangement prescribed before the Flood by Methusaleh, the father of Noah's daughters-in-law, that all of the four women on the ark are to be locked up in the west end of the vessel during the entire voyage - "for this sex has aroused God to anger, and they are not worthy to be neighbours of Paradise and to sing praises with the angels."

PL-38. (Ethiopic)

The Book of Adam and Eve, also called The Conflict of Adam and Eve with Satan, tr. from the Ethiopic by Rev. S. C. Malan (1882).

An apocryphal prose work of 207 pages, in three books, dealing with "the conflict of Adam and Eve, that befell them after they had come out of the garden". In Book I, Adam and Eve have their home in a "Cave of Treasures", stocked by God with gold, frankincense and myrrh. This book ends with the murder of Abel. In Book II, Adam, at his death, foretells the Flood, asks Seth to embalm his body and lay it in the Cave of Treasures, and leaves instructions for Noah to take it into the Ark, along with the gold frankincense and myrrh. In Book III, this is done; and later, Shem and Melchizedek bury Adam's embalmed body on Mount Golgotha. Ultimately, Christ is born, presented with gold, frankincense and myrrh, and, when a man, crucified on Mount Golgotha. Underlying the whole work is the conception of Satan's constant warfare against Adam and his race. The author is strongly celibate in his views, and has the righteous regard marriage with reluctance. Adam has intercourse with Eve only three times in 930 years. The book also includes the accidental killing of Cain by the blind Lamech, who thereupon, in rage, murders the youth who has misdirected his missiles.

PL-39. (Greek)

Georgios Pisides. *Hexaemeron sive Cosmourgia*. Circa 625. Accessible in *MPG, xcii, 1425-1578*. MI: Harvard.

Inc. Ὦ παντὸς ἔργου καὶ θεηγόρου λόγου
Καὶ γλῶσσα, καὶ νοῦς, καὶ τροφὴ καὶ καρδία ...
Expl. Ὡς ἐμεγαλύνθη τοῦ Θεοῦ τῶν κτισμάτων
Ἡ δημιουργὸς καὶ σοφὴ παντουργία!

This is a didactic epic on the Creation, running to 1,910 lines in the iambic senarius. The author, born in Pisidia but later a deacon in Constantinople, is distinguished from the other hexameral writers of classical Christianity by his free intermixture of pagan mythology and verbal echoes of Plato, Homer, Horace, Cicero and Seneca. The poem was very popular in Renaissance Europe and went through several editions in the 16th and 17th centuries.

Thibaut de Maisières (*op. cit*., pp. 23-24) cites Colletet, the first biographer of DuBartas, as giving Morelle, the publisher of DuBartas, as his authority that the *Hexaemeron* of George of Pisidia was a work "que DuBartas, qui n'ignorait pas les poètes latins ni les grecs, imita en tout et partout".

PL-40. (Latin)

Eugenius Hispanus, *De diei septimi opere carmen heroicum*, ed. by Jac. Sirmondus, Paris (1619). This poem also appears in MPL, lxxxvii, 370 et seq., as "Dracontii Hexaemeron a Sancto Eugenio jussu regis emendatum". It is a rather drastic recasting of the *Carmen de Deo* (PL-34, above) of Dracontius, made by St. Eugenius, a 7th century bishop of Toledo, at the request of Chindasvindus, king of the Visigothic realm in Spain.

PL-41. (Old English)

Anonymous. *The "Caedmonian" Genesis*. Edited by George Philip Krapp, New York, 1931.

Inc. Us is riht micel ðaet we rodera weard,
wereda wuldorcining, wordum herigen,
modum lufien! He is mægna sped . . .
Expl. onbleot þæt lac gode, sægde leana þanc
and ealra þara sælða þe he him sið and ær,
gifena drihten, forgifen hæfde.

This Anglo-Saxon poem on the Fall forms part of a unique manuscript (MS Junius 11), now in the Bodleian Library, Oxford University. The manuscript was discovered, sometime before 1650, by James Ussher (1581-1656), archbishop of Armagh and one of the greatest antiquarians of his time. By him it was given to the Huguenot scholar, Franciscus Junius the Younger (1589-1677), who lived in England from 1620 to 1651, and was librarian to Thomas Howard, second earl of Arundel. Junius, who was a pioneer in Anglo-Saxon studies, published the manuscript in Amsterdam in 1655 under the title *Caedmonis monachi paraphrasis poetica genesios ac praecipuarum Sacrae paginae Historiarum, abhinc annos MLXX Anglo-Saxonicè conscripta*. The work consists of four parts: (1) "Genesis" (2936 lines), (2) "Exodus" (590 lines), (3) "Daniel" (764 lines), and a poetic patchwork of a lament by the fallen angels, the harrowing of Hell, the Last

Judgment, and the Temptation of Christ, all usually grouped today under the caption "Christ and Satan" (729 lines). The story of "Paradise Lost" comprises the first 964 lines of the "Genesis" section.

To Junius and his contemporaries this old religious poetry seemed to correspond exactly with the verse ascribed by Bede in his Historia Ecclesiastica to Caedmon, an illiterate herdsman at the abbey of Streoneshalh (Whitby) on the east coast of Northumbria, who had the divine gift of turning into Anglo-Saxon verse all that the monks told him of the sacred story. Modern scholarship is agreed, however, on a multiple origin for the Junius manuscript and doubts whether any of it may be ascribed to Caedmon. So far as the "Paradise Lost" section is concerned, at least three begetters (two poets and a scholar) have been postulated, as follows: (i) a Northumbrian poet of about A.D. 700, who rendered faithfully into competent Anglo-Saxon (Northumbrian dialect) the Vulgate Genesis down as far as the offering of Isaac; (ii) a gifted Continental poet, of great originality and power, who composed in Old Saxon, about A.D. 830, a poem on the defeat of Satan and the rebel angels and their subsequent success in seducing Adam and Eve; (iii) a scholar of about A.D. 930, who transcribed both of these poems into the closely related dialect of the West Saxons and combined the two by substituting the second for the brief account of the Fall in the first. This interpolation was first advanced as a theory in 1875 by Professor Eduard Sievers, and was dramatically proven in 1894 when Professor Zangemeister of Heidelberg discovered among the manuscripts in the Vatican Library a fragment of the original Old Saxon poem. In the Junius MS, the old Northumbrian paraphrase, sometimes called "Genesis-A" or the "Elder Genesis", comprises lines 1 to 234 and 852 to the end; while the Old Saxon poem, known as "Genesis-B" or the "Later Genesis", occupies lines 235 to 851. Throughout the manuscript, there are a number of gaps, where medieval vandals have torn out pages for the sake of their pictures.

Two earlier debts may be indicated. The first

111 lines of Genesis-A constitute a prologue on the fall of the angels, the opening of which is an obvious imitation of the "Hymn" of Caedmon, as preserved by Bede. In the opening lines of Genesis-B, moreover, we find a close paraphrase of a passage from Avitus (cf. PL-35). It also follows Avitus in turning aside from the landscape of Eden to describe the fall of the angels and to introduce Satan speaking in person. Otherwise, however, both in matter and in emotional power, the Old Saxon poet is profoundly original.

As for Milton's relations to the Junius manuscript, we have little to go on except the inner resemblance between two defiant Satans. Masson quotes a letter, dated August 1651, in which a foreign visitor mentions both Milton and Junius among his intimates in London, and we know that Junius already had the Caedmonian manuscript; but there is no evidence to show that the two men ever met. Neither is there any hint that Milton ever showed the slightest interest in Anglo-Saxon studies.

The spirit of _Genesis-B_ is that of the old Teutonic feudal order. God is a _drihten_ or lord, and the war in heaven comes when some of His angel vassals break their pledged faith and fall away from their _giongorscip_. Satan likewise claims the loyalty of his vassals; and it is one of the latter, and not Satan himself, who successfully undertakes the dangerous expedition to Eden. Closely akin to _Paradise Lost_, Bk. I, is Satan's speech of irreconcilable defiance.

Peculiar to this version is the portrayal of Adam and Eve as simply deceived and not seduced. The infernal visitor in Eden claims to be a messenger from God with instructions that they are to eat the apple; and his plausibility at last prevails over the well-intentioned pair.

PL-42. (Old English)

Anonymous. _Christ and Satan_ (ll. 1-364). Ca. 790-

830 A.D.

Inc. þæt wearð underne eorðbuendum,
þæt meotod hæfde miht and strengðo
ða he gefestnade foldan sceatas. . . .
Expl. byrhtne burhstyde. Blæd bið æghwæm
þæm ðe hælende heran þenceð,
and wel is þam ðe þæt wyrcan mot.

This section of the Junius MS. is named by Wülker "Die Klagen der Gefallnen Engel". It is largely given over to dispirited lamentation by the fallen angels in Hell. The Satan that it depicts is utterly different from the defiant prisoner of *Genesis-B*.

PL-43. (Greek)

Syncellus, Georgius. *Ekloge Chronographias*. Circa 800 A.D. Mi: Harvard.

Inc. Ἐν ἀρχῇ ἐποίησεν ὁ Θεὸς τὸν οὐρανὸν ...
Expl. ὑπὸ τῆς κοσμικῆς ἀρχῆς ἐξελαύνεται
τῆς ἐκκλησίας.

A Greek prose summary of history "from Adam to Diocletian". The early pages tell of the Creation and the Fall. Syncellus is one of the earliest of the Byzantine chroniclers, represented also below in prose by Georgius Cedrenus (PL-54) and in verse by Constantinus Manasses (PL-58). The list could easily be extended by adding Malalas (6th century), Georgius Monachus, John Zonaras and Michael Glycas.

Syncellus is an important source of quotations from apocryphal works on the life of Adam. He gives the most elaborate detail as to the number of days taken for each act in the Genesis story, e.g. "On the 46th day of the Creation of the world, the 4th day of the 7th week, the 14th of Pachon and the 9th of May, the sun being in Taurus and the moon diametrically opposite in Scorpius, at the rising of the Pleiades, God brought Adam into Paradise on the 40th day of his creation." (Cf. M.R. James, *The Lost Apocrypha* of the Old Testament.)

*PL-44. (Syriac)

Emmanuel Syrus. De opere sex dierum. Ca. 800.

A poem in Syriac, extant in manuscript in the Vatican Library, cf. MPG, xcii, 1391: "Emmanuel, doctor Syrus, qui saeculo IX ineunte vixit, scripsit librum De opere sex dierum, carminibus Syriacis, ut testatur Ebed-Jesu in catalogo librorum Syrorum apud Assemanium Bibl. Orient. Tom. II, p. 499 et tom. III, p. 277, qui codicem in bibl. Vatic. exstantem describit."

PL-45. (Greek)

Ignatius Diaconus. Στίχοι εἰς τὸν Ἀδάμ. Drama de primi parentis lapsu. (MPG, vol. cxvii, 1163-1174.) Mi: Harvard.

Inc. Ἀγῶνας, ἆθλα καὶ παλαίσματα βλέπων,
Ἃ ταῖς γενάρχαις ὁ προσερπύσας ὄφις ...

Expl. (Deus loquitur):
Φαγῇ τὸν ἄρτον ἐν κόποις καὶ φροντίσιν,
Ἕως, ἐῶν γῆς γηγένης, παλινδρόμει.

In this, the earliest extant dramatic treatment of the Fall, 54 lines of narrative and descriptive prologue are followed by 89 lines of dialogue (in iambic senarii). The serpent addresses Eve and urges that she eat the fruit and become godlike. God, he says, is really jealous of mankind. She will be able to persuade Adam. She eats, enjoys, and urges Adam to eat. He demurs, scolds, and succumbs. Both feel qualms of pain, realize their nakedness, and clothe themselves with fig-leaves. God comes and questions them and passes judgement.

The author was a 9th century archbishop of Nicaea. His brief mystery play seems to have been performed in church.

PL-46. (Latin)

Wandalbertus Prumiensis. De creatione mundi. (MPL, cxxi, 635-640.) Mi: Harvard.

Inc. Simplex, purus et unus
Aeterni Pater atque
Summae fons bonitatis . . .
Expl. Aeterni hunc paradisi
Flos fructusque perennis,
Vitae fonsque fovebit.

A poem of about 260 lines in pherecratic trimeter. After a prologue expounding the one and triune God, it proceeds to a day by day description of Creation, ending with that of man, and closes with a dissertation on the mystic sense in which man is to understand the creation of the world. Wandalbertus (813-ca.870), a monk of West Frankish birth, was reared in the monastery at Prüm, in Lorraine.

PL-47. (Old Saxon)

Old Saxon Genesis. Circa 830. Fragment I (on the Fall) printed by Fr. Klaeber in The Later Genesis, Heidelberg, 1931, and by Wilhelm Braune in Althochdeutsche Lesebuch, Halle, 1921.

Inc. "Uuela, that thú nú, Eua, habas" - quad Adam -
"ubilo gimarakot
unkaro selbara sid! Nu maht thu sean thia
suarton hell . . .

One of the most dramatic episodes in modern scholarship was the affirmation of E. Sievers in 1875 by internal evidence that lines 235-851 of the "Caedmonian Genesis" (cf. PL-41 supra) in Old English must have been a translation of a hitherto undreamed-of Old Saxon original, and the subsequent vindication of Sievers by K. Zangemeister's discovery in 1894 of actual fragments of the Old Saxon poem among the manuscripts in the Vatican Library. Attempts have been made[1] to identify its author with the unknown author of the Heliand, but the identification is not accepted by all scholars.

PL-48. (Early Middle Irish)

Oengus Celi-De? Saltair na Rann. Ca. 987?

Inc. Moríse rí nime nair,
cenhuabur, cenimmarbaig . . .
Expl. imriadat cohéttlaide
mili bliadna 'sindlóo.
Il-lathiu indluain lainerda.

Saltair na Rann ("The Psalter of Quatrains"), ed. by Whitley Stokes (1883), is a collection of 162 poems, totalling 8393 lines. The metre throughout is deibidhe, a quatrain rhyming aabb, with the proviso that the final words in lines 2 and 4 must each have more syllables than the final words in lines 1 and 3. Alliteration is frequent but not systematic.

Three poems exceed all others in importance, viz., I, on the Creation, XI, on the repentance of Adam and Eve, and XII, on the death of Adam. These last two are based largely on the Latin Vita Adae et Evae (PL-10, above); and the first, while partially based on Genesis i-ii, includes a great deal of extra detail, e.g. the colours of the winds, the distance from the earth to the firmament, the seventy-two windows in the firmament with a shutter on each, and astronomical details for the calendar of a year.

Authorship is uncertain. It has been falsely attributed to Ængus mac Ængobann (floruit 800), but there are references in the poems to the great cattle murrain of A.D. 987, and possibly to Bishop Dub-dàlethe (d. 1061). Rudolf Thurneysen, in Die Irische Helden und Königsage (1921), p. 58, specifically

[1]Cf. W. Bruckner, Die altsächsische Genesis und der Heliand, das Werk eines Dichters. 1929.

assigns the work to Ængus Cele-De in 987, and Stokes records the name as above.

PL-49. (Arabic)

Menbidj, Agapius (Mahboub) de. Kitab al-'Unvan. In Patrologia Orientalis V, 565-691. Arabic text and French translation by Alexander Vasiliev.

Agapius de Menbidj was a Christian Arab historian of the 10th century A.D. In the early part of his "universal history" he gives the story of Adam and Eve, and tells how they mourned for one hundred years before Adam finally cohabited with Eve and begot Cain.

*PL-50. (Middle High German)

Ezzo von Bamberg. Der Sündenfall.

The author, a scholar of Bamberg, is supposed to have made a pilgrimage to Jerusalem in 1064. He is also alleged to have written a poem called Die Schöpfung.

PL-51. (Middle High German)

Anonymous. Die altdeutsche Genesis. Circa 1070 A.D. Edited by Viktor Dollmayr (1932). Mi: Yale.

Inc. Nv fer nemet, mine liebe,
ich wil in aine rede fore tŏn.
ube mir got der gŏte
gerŏchet senten ze mote . . .
Expl. daz muzze si sîn
nu unt in ewin.
AMEN. deo gracias.

The author is unknown, but from the evidence of language belonged to South Bavaria. Internal evidence places composition between 1060 and 1080. German researchers have proven the influence of Avitus.

The poem consists of 6062 lines of roughly rhymed verse and covers about the same period as the book of *Genesis*, ending with the death of Joseph. The part relevant to the Creation and the Fall covers only the first 1050 lines, and even this is no mere paraphrase of the Bible. It begins with a description of the angels and the names that God gave to their various orders (engele, hochengele, gestule, herscefte, gewalte, fursten, cherubin, seraphin). Lucifer voices his decision to rebel, and God tells this to the faithful Michael. "Then Michael lifted up his hand and hit the Devil such a blow that heaven broke under him and he fell forthwith into the abyss with as great a company as if a storm came with rain falling for three days and three nights". After consultation with the faithful residue, God creates heaven and earth, living things, and finally man. The creation of man is described, as in Avitus, in great anatomical detail. The temptation in the Garden follows the Bible closely. The style is strongly didactic.

PL-52. (Latin)

Hildebertus Cenomanensis. *De operibus sex dierum*. (MPL, clxxi, 1214.) Mi: Harvard.

Inc. Omnipotens in principio coelumque solumque
Fecit; principium ejus Filius erat. . . .
Expl. Nempe Deus mundum sola bonitate creavit,
Indiguit mundi non tamen ille bonis.
Et nec in his, sed ab his requievit, nullius horum
Indigus; et tribuens, non requiem accipiens.

Hildebert of Lavardin (1056-1133) was bishop of Le Mans and ultimately archbishop of Tours. He was one of the chief literary figures of the Middle Ages. His Latinity has a fine classical flavour and his verses were popular throughout Western Europe.

This poem, in elegiacs, deals with the Creation. The style is dogmatic and didactic rather than narrative.

PL-53. (Latin)

Hildebertus Cenomanensis. De ordine mundi. (MPL, clxxi, 1223.) Mi: Harvard.

Inc. Maxime sanctorum sitiunt quem vota piorum
Adventus cujus faex temporis exigit hujus
Comple quod de te sancti cecinere prophetae . . .
Expl. Gymnasii nudos fastidit cernere ludos:
Ad luctam tingui vult nemo lampade pingui.

This poem is in general rather complementary to PL-52. It begins with the Fall of Man and ultimately passes on to Christ and the establishment of His church. Its hexameters have inner rhymes.

PL-54. (Greek)

Cedrenus, Georgius. Synopsis Historion. Circa 1100 A.D. Mi: Harvard.

Inc. Πολλοὶ τῶν πρὸ ἡμῶν φιλοθέων ἀνδρῶν
καὶ φιλιστόρων τὴν ἐπιτομὴν . . .
Expl. Καὶ βασιλεὺς αὐτοκράτωρ Ῥωμαίων ἀναγορεύεται.

A summary of world history from the Creation down to the times of the Emperor Isaacius Comnenus. The early pages cover the Eden story.

PL-55. (Middle High German)

Anonymous. Die Bücher Mosis. Circa 1100 A.D. Accessible in Josef Diemer, Deutsche Gedichte des 11 und 12 Jahrhunderts (1849). Mi: Yale.

Inc. Getorste ich von minen funden
so wolde ich ev gerne chunden . . .
Expl. daz also maneger mvter barn
in die helle sol varn.

The first part of this is also known as the

"Vorauer Genesis". It is a bald verse paraphrase of Scripture in rhymed couplets of four-stressed verse.

PL-56. (Middle High German)

Anonymous. *Die Schöpfung*. Circa 1100 A.D. Also in Diemer, *op. cit.* *Mi*: Yale.

Inc. Got vat ewich ist daz an-
gengi. allir guten dingin.
der gibundin hat den diu-
uil. des man craft wonit . . .
Expl. widi bracht daz diz unsir ir lose-
ri alliz daz lobi. suaz dir ist undir
deme himili ioch dar obi.

This poem is also known as *Anenge* or *Gedicht von der Weltschöpfung*. It is a rugged old poem, in couplets of four-stressed lines, dealing rather tediously with the Creation.

PL-57. (Latin)

Abaelardus, Petrus. *Hymni nocturni*. (MPL, clxxviii, 1775-1780.) Mi: Harvard.

Inc. Universorum Conditor,
Conditorum dispositor,
Universa te laudant condita,
Glorificant cuncta disposita. . . .
Expl. Sit perpes Deo gloria.

Nine Latin hymns (ca. 1130) whose general background of thought is the Creation set forth in the sequence of *Genesis*.

PL-58. (Greek)

Manasses, Constantinus. Σύνοψις Χρονική. Circa 1150 A.D. Mi: Harvard.

Inc. Ἡ μὲν φιλόϋλος ψυχὴ ταῖς ὕλαις ἐπιχάσκει, ...
Expl. οὐ γὰρ περάσιμα τὰ τῶν Γαδείρων πέρα.

Some 6733 hexameter lines in Greek, covering human history from the beginning of time down to the Emperor Nicephorus Botaniates. Lines 26 to 341 cover the story of Creation and the Fall in the traditional hexameral style.

PL-59. (Greek)

Prodromus, Theodorus. Epigrammata. Circa 1150. Accessible in MPG, cxxxiii, 1101 et seq.

A sequence of brief Greek poems in various metres, arranged chronologically to cover the Old and New Testaments. There are 76 such poems dealing with events in Genesis, especially those of the Creation and the Fall. Their poetic value is slight.

PL-60. (Latin)

Comestor, Petrus. Historia Scholastica. Ca. 1170. Accessible in MPL, cxcviii, 1053-1722.

Inc. In principio erat Verbum, et Verbum erat principium,
In quo, et per quod Pater creavit mundum. . . .
Expl. et ita Paulus honorabiliori morte mortuus est, quia gladiatus. Gladio enim perimebantur nobiles,
et in loco magis honorabili, scilicet in catacumbis.

An extended version of history, from Adam to Paul, following the course of the Scriptures. Part I, "Historia Libri Genesis" (pp. 1055-1142), describes the Creation and the Fall at great length. Petrus Comestor (fl. 1169-1175) draws upon many sources for his material and his work represents a compendium of the traditions prevailing in his day. On his Latin prose narrative, many mediaeval poetic versions were based.

PL-61. (Latin)

Riga, Petrus de. Fragmenta ex Genesi. (Part iv of his Aurora, in MPL, ccxii, 21-23.) Mi: Harvard.

Inc. Mox Deus adduxit animantia singula terrae:
Praebeat ut cunctis nomina rebus Adam. . . .
Expl. Nunc etiam tales absorbet, eoque laborant,
Qui mundi regimen et loca summa tenent.

Some 84 lines, in elegiac couplets, chiefly given over to affirming various traditions, e.g. that Adam was created from the earth at Damascus, and that Adam set up pillars recording his prophecy of a twofold judgement, by water and by fire. Peter Riga (fl. 1191-1208) was canon in the abbey of St. Denis at Rheims. He seems to have written a great deal of very poor poetry on Scriptural subjects.

PL-62. (Norman-French)

Anonymous. Le Mystère d'Adam. XIIth cty. Mi: Cornell.

Inc. FIGURA: Adam
ADAM: Sire!
FIGURA: Fourmé te ai
De limo terre. . . .
Expl. EVE. Dieu nous rendant sa grace et sa présence,
Nous tirera d'Enfer par sa puissance.

This, the oldest surviving religious drama of France, was written in the dialect of Normandy. While most of it consists of four-stressed iambic lines, rhymed in couplets, there are passages in which quatrains of iambic pentameter lines are linked by a single rhyme. The style is not that of a novice, but shows marked clarity of phrase and rapidity of dialogue.

The first half of the play deals with the Temptation and Fall, and this is followed by the murder of Abel by Cain, but the rest of the play is largely a pageant of Old Testament worthies - Abraham, Moses, Aaron, David, Solomon, Balaam, Daniel, Habakkuk, Jeremiah and Isaiah - each of whom is duly led off to Hell by an escort of devils. Finally comes Nebuchadnezzar, testifying to the Fourth Figure in the "burning fiery furnace" and going on to describe for the audience the fifteen portents of the Doomsday that shall end our sinful world. Some scholars suggest that the prototype of the mystery play was such a pageant of prophets and patriarchs, beginning with Adam, and that the expansion of the Adam-story, as here, represents the first deviation from that rather simple sequence of figures. It may be that Gil Vicente's _Breve Sumario_ (PL-108 below) bears out this conception of a march-past of prophets.

The stage directions (in Latin) are quite full and often vivid, as for example when Adam and Eve leave the stage: "Then shall come the Devil, and three or four other devils with him, bearing in their hands chains and iron fetters which they shall place on the necks of Adam and Eve. And some shall push them, and others drag them, to hell. Other devils shall stand near hell to meet them, and shall dance greatly over their damnation; and other individual devils shall point at them as they come, and shall receive them and place them in hell. And they shall cause a great smoke to rise up from it, and they shall rejoice loudly together in hell, and shall clash their kettles and cauldrons together, so that the noise is heard outside."

PL-63. (Old Church Slavonic)

Slovo Adama ko Lazariu bo Adi ("The Discourse of Adam in Hades to Lazarus"), cf. _Slavonic and East European Review_, December 1931, pp. 244-252.

One of the few genuinely imaginative works of Old Russian literature. Written for the most part in rhythmic prose, reminiscent of the verse-structure of the Psalms, it portrays Adam in Hell giving Lazarus, during his four days sojourn in the underworld, a message of petition to Christ on behalf of himself and of the prophets and just men who are with him in Satan's domain. The work ends with the harrowing of Hell and the deliverance of Adam.

PL-64. (Middle High German)

Deutsches Adambuch, ed. by H. Vollmer (1908). Mi: Yale. A German equivalent of the Vita Adae et Evae (cf. PL-10 above), connected with a legend of the Cross.

*PL-65. (Middle High German)

Regensburger Prophetenspiel (ca. 1195). An early mystery play, presenting a sequence of prophets, beginning with Adam (cf. Le Mystere d'Adam, John Bale, Gil Vicente, etc.).

*PL-66. (Middle High German)

Rigaer Prophetenspiel (ca. 1204-5). A mystery play of the same type as PL-65.

*PL-67. (French)

Gossouin. L'Image du Monde. Completed 1245 (O.S.)

For English translation by Caxton, see PL-98. Originally a rhymed French poem of 6,594 octosyllabic verses, divided into three parts. The first of the "mirror" type of didactic poem, presenting in encyclopaedic form a wide range of such subjects as the creation of man, why God made man, the nature of angels' bodies, Ptolemaic astronomy, the trees of the earthly Paradise, the phoenix, the nature of free will, etc.

*PL-68. (German)

Rudolf von Ems. Weltchronik. Circa 1250.

An unfinished poem on universal history from Genesis to the death of Solomon.

PL-69. (Middle English)

The Story of Genesis and Exodus, An Early English Song, About A.D. 1250. Ed. by Richard Morris, E.E.T.S., London, 1865.

Inc. Man og to luuen ðat rimes ren,
ðe Wisseð wel ðe logede men,
hu man may him wel loken
ðog he ne be lered on no boken . . .
Expl. And in-to blisse wid seli men;
Wið muð and herte sey we, Amen!

A poem in the Southeast Midland dialect, consisting of 4,162 lines in four-stressed iambic verse, rhymed in couplets or quatrains of continuous verse. It is a typical verse paraphrase of Scripture, interlarded with homily and legend, in the hexameral tradition. The author states (ll. 13-14) that he has translated it from a Latin original. There is the usual appeal to God for inspiration in singing of the Creation, and there follows a day by day description of the process by which the divine Wisdom "made ilc ðing of nogt". The poet then inserts a brief narrative of the pride, envy and rebellion of Lucifer ("Ligber") and his malicious speech as he gazes at the happiness of Adam and Eve. Then he "wente in to a wirme and tolde eue a tale". She in turn tempted Adam. After the ejection from Eden, the Cherubim closed the gates of Paradise, which were not to be re-opened until Christ was crucified. The poem is probably based on the Historia Scholastica of Petrus Comestor (PL-60, above)

PL-70. (Italian)

Alighieri, Dante. La Divina Commedia. Written before 1321. First printed editions in 1472

Inc. Nel mezzo del cammin di nostra vita
Mi ritrovai per una selva oscura,
Che la diritta via era smarrita. . . .
Expl. Ma gia volgeva il mio disiro e il velle,
Si come rota ch'egualmente è mossa,
L'amor che move il sole e l'altre stelle.

While not a direct analogue of Paradise Lost in point of structure, the Divina Commedia has much more in common with it than many works that are closer to it in design. For similarities in style one may consult C. L. Barnes, "Parallels in Milton and Dante", in Papers of the Manchester Literary Club, xliii (1917), pp. 8-29; Antero Meozzi, "Paralleli Danteschi" in Il Giornale Dantesco (Firenze), xxvi (1923), pp. 123-127; and C. H. Herford, "Dante and Milton", in The Post-War Mind of Germany and Other European Studies (Oxford 1927, pp. 58-114. Fundamental differences are discussed by William J. Grace in "Orthodoxy and Aesthetic Method in Paradise Lost and the Divine Comedy", Comparative Literature, vol. I, (spring 1949), pp. 173-187.

PL-71. (French)

La Bible et le Nouveau Testament Moralisés et mis en Vers par Macés de la Charité sur Loire, Curé de Cinquoins. MS. dated 1343. Original in Bibliothèque Nationale, Paris. Microfilm from the Mediaeval Institute, Notre Dame University.

Inc. Dieu crea au cōmencement
Le ciel e la terre ensement . . .
Expl. Couche te tart, leve matin,
Soys curieux de ta besoigne,

Et donc tu trouveras ta soigne.

This is a famous old rhyming version of the Bible, in the same tradition as the Irish Saltair na rann and the English Cursor Mundi. The Creation and the Fall take their due place in the narrative, as does also the story of Samson and Delilah.

PL-72. (Icelandic)

Ásgrimsson, Eysteinn. Lilja. Terminus ad quem, 1361.

Inc. Almattigr Guð, allra stetta
yfirbjooandi engla og þjooa . . .
Expl. lof se þer um aldr og aefi,
eining sönn i þrennum greinum.

This is the chief poem of the Church in Iceland in pre-Reformation times. Written by a monk of the Augustinian cloister at Thykkvabaer, it consists of 100 stanzas in modified court measure and recapitulates almost the entire "celestial cycle", viz., the Fall of the Angels (stanzas 6-9), the Creation and the Fall of Man (10-21), the Annunciation, Birth and Baptism of Christ (22-38), the Temptation of Christ (39-45), His Passion and Death (46-60), the Harrowing of Hell (61-66), His Resurrection and Ascension (67-69) and the Last Judgement (70-74). All this is set in a framework of prayer to Christ and to the Virgin Mary (1-5, 75-99), whose honorific "The Lily" gives its title to the poem. It has been hailed as being perhaps "the greatest mediaeval religious classic of the whole of the north of Europe" (Charles Venn Pilcher, Icelandic Christian Classics, 1950, p. 20); but because of its brevity and lack of epic pretensions it offers no challenge to Milton's work.

PL-73. (Latin)

Anonymous. De creatione Ade et formatione Eve ex costa eius Et quomodo decepti fuerunt a serpente. 14th Century? Mi: British Museum.

A series of brief legends in Latin, from the Fall of Satan down to the death of Adam. Its closest resemblance is to the *Vita Adae* (PL-10).

PL-74. (Middle English)

Anonymous. *Cursor Mundi: A Northumbrian Poem of the XIVth century. Ed. by Richard Morris.*

Inc. (Cotton Vesp. A iii, British Museum):
Man yhernes rimes for to here,
And romans red on maneres sire . . .
Expl. And steres his cristendame fro
And livers him to þe find his foo. (11. 29546-7).

A very lengthy poem in octosyllabic couplets, covering the whole course of Scriptural history and a good deal else besides. Lines 271-1044 describe the Creation of the world, the Fall of the Angels, the Creation and Fall of Man, and his subsequent repentance. There are many apocryphal elements. Cain kills Abel with the cheekbone of an ass; and when he buries the corpse, the earth casts it up again. When Seth visits Paradise to ask for some oil from the tree of mercy (cf. No. 10), he sees a marvellous tree with bare branches. Its roots reach down to hell and its branches reach up to the sky. An adder is coiled about it and a newborn babe lies crying in the topmost branches. (This symbolic tree suggests influence from the Old Norse tree Yggdrasil.) Seth is given three seeds to place under Adam's tongue at his burial.

PL-75. (Old Church Slavonic)

Skazanie o Adami i Evi (14th century?). A Slavic version of the apocryphal life of Adam and Eve. Ed. by Jajić, along with a Latin translation, in *Denkschriften der Wiener Akademie der Wissenschaften*, xlii (1893).

PL-76. (Middle English)

York Plays. I. The Creation, and the Fall of Lucifer. XIVth Century. MI: Yale.

Inc. (Deus loquitur):
I am gracyus and grete, god withoutyn begynnyng,
I am maker vnmade, all mighte es in me . . .
Expl. And all þis warke lykes me ryght wele,
And baynely I gyf it my blyssyng.

One of the earliest surviving cycles of mystery plays are those of York, commonly regarded as taking form in the 14th century. Six plays of the series, listed here, are relevant to this survey. In general the York plays lack the vitality and broad humour that transform so many of the Towneley plays. Some critics find in them a close parallel to the scheme of the Cursor Mundi (PL-74).

PL-77. (Middle English)

York Plays. II. The Creation, to the Fifth Day.

Inc. (Deus loquitur):
In altissimis habito; in the heghest heuyn my hame haue I,
Eterne mentis et ego, withoutyn ende ay lastandly. . . .
Expl. (Deus loquitur):
My blyssyng haue ye all;
the fift day endyd es.

PL-78. (Middle English)

York Plays. III. God creates Adam and Eve.

Inc. (Deus loquitur):
In heuyn and erthe duly be dene
Of v. daies werke, evyn vnto þe ende . . .
Expl. (Deus loquitur):
Ye shalle lyff in likyng,

My blissyng with you be. Amen.

PL-79. (Middle English)

York Plays. IV. God puts Adam and Eve in the Garden of Eden.

Inc. (Deus loquitur):
Adam and Eve, this is the place
That I haue graunte you of my grace . . .
Expl. (Deus loquitur):
Adam, and Eve thy wyfe,
My blyssyng haue ye here.

PL-80. (Middle English)

York Plays. V. Man's disobedience and fall from Eden.

Inc. (Satanas loquitur):
For woo my witte es in a were,
That moffes me mykill in my mynde . . .
Expl. (Adam loquitur):
Allas! for sorowe and care!
owre handis may we wryng.

PL-81. (Middle English)

York Plays. VI. Adam and Eve driven from Eden.

Inc. (Angelus loquitur):
Alle creatures to me take tent,
Fro god of heuen now am I sent . . .
Expl. (Adam loquitur):
This tree vn-to me wille I ta,
þat me is sende.
He þat vs wrought wisse vs fro wa,
whare-som we wende.

PL-82. (Italian)

Anonymous. La legenda d'Adamo ed Eva sua moglie. Testo inedito del Secolo XIV. Bologna, 1870. Mi: British Museum.

A prose narrative, edited by Alessandro d'Ancona from a unique codex in the Florentine Library. It begins with Adam's expulsion from Eden and deals particularly with his later request for the oil of mercy. It would appear to be based on the Vita Adae (PL-10).

PL-83. (Middle English)

Anonymous. Clannesse. Circa 1375. Ed. Richard Morris, 1864. Mi: Yale.

Inc. Clannesse who-so kyndly cowþe comende,
& rekken vp alle þe resounz þat ho by riht askez . . .
Expl. þat we gon gay in oure gere þat grace he vus sende,
þat we may serue in his syht, þer solace neuer blynnez.
Amen.

Clannesse ("purity") is an anonymous 14th century poem of 531 lines, based on alliteration, with four principal stresses in each line. Its main theme is purity, in expounding which it tells the story of the Fall of the Angels, the Fall of Man, the Noachic deluge, the destruction of Sodom, and the fates of Nebuchadnezzar and Belshazzar. In this version, the angels fall from Heaven to Hell, as thick as snow, for the space of forty days.

PL-84. (Middle English)

Anonymous. Canticum de Creatione. MS. Trin. Coll. Oxf. 57, fol. 156. Composed 1375. Mi: Yale.

Inc. Jhesu Crist, heuene kynge,
And his moder, þat swete þyng . . .
Expl. þat Jhesu Crist, oure sauyour,
And his moder, þat swete flour,
Grante vs þe blesse of heuene.

A poem of 1200 lines, in 6-lined ballad-stanzas. Apparently based largely on the Vita Adae et Evae and possibly Petrus Comestor's Historia Scholastica. The penitence story is told thus:

Eve yede forþ to Tygre flod,
To done here penaunce wiþ carful mod,
   As Adam hadde here tauth;
And he him dede to Jordon,
And þerynne stod oppon a ston
   þe water his nekke rauth.

þe her of here hevedis þat was long
Spradde abrod on þe water strong -
   Ruthe hadde ben to se.
þanne seyde Adam to Jordon:
"Water, come and make þy mon
   And waymente here wiþ me!

Gadere alle þe fisches þat in þe be,
And do hem come aboute me,
   To helpen me make mone -
Nogt for yow, bote al for me:
For neuere yut senyyede ye
   Ne wraþþed youre god one. . . .
(lines 139-156).

PL-85. (Middle English)

Anonymous. Canticum de Creatione. Ms. Auchinleck, Edin. Advoc. Library. Circa 1375. Mi: Yale.

Inc. . . . Lihtbern, þat angel briht,
Answerd anon riht:
Expl. Gif ous grace for to winne
þe ioie pat Adam now is inne.

Although, like PL-84, it is based largely on the Vita, it is a fundamentally different poem, both in metre and in treatment. It comprises 780 four-stressed lines in rhymed couplets; and whereas the Trinity College Canticum starts with the expulsion of Adam and Eve, the Auchinleck Canticum gives first (1-64) the story of how Lightbern (i.e. Lucifer) rebelled in Heaven and later tempted Eve "in licknesse of an adder". Where the matter in the two poems is parallel, the Auchinleck poet is far more sparing in detail. For example, the penitence episode quoted under PL-84 is dismissed in four brief lines:

Eue in to Tigres wode
And vp to þe chin sche stode,
And in to þe flum wode Adam
And his penaunce vndernam.

Both poems are given in full in Horstmann's Altenglische Legenden (1878).

PL-86. (Middle High German)

Lutwin. Adam und Eva. MS. of 14th or 15th century. First printed Tübingen, 1881. Mi: Yale.

Inc. Wer die worheit gerne mynn(et)
Und sich guter dinge versynn(et) . . .
Expl. Got helffe uns zu siner ere
One alle swere. Amen amen.

A Middle High German poem of the 13th century, consisting of 3942 lines in rhyming couplets. Of its author, little is known, except that he is supposed to have been an Austrian. The poem extends from the Creation down to the death of Adam and Eve, and follows closely the Vita Adae et Evae (cf. PL-10 above), especially the penitence of Adam and Eve in the Jordan and the Tigris.

PL-87. (English)

"Creatio" in The Towneley Plays, ed. by George England and A. W. Pollard (1897). Original date about 1410.

Inc. (Deus loquitur):
Ego sum alpha et o,
I am the first, the last also,
Oone god in mageste . . .
Expl. (Lucifer loquitur):
And now ar thay in paradise;
bot thens they shall, if we be wise.

Four scenes of this play are extant. In Scene I, God declares His nature and His power, and proceeds to the creative work of the first five days. The cherubim then chant His praise, but mention that Lucifer has been created the brightest of them all. In God's absence, Lucifer proudly sits in His throne and asks the angels how he looks. In Scene II, the bad angels are in Hell, where they reproach Lucifer for their fall. He has left only nine orders where there were ten. Scene III shifts to the Earth and the creation of man and woman. God forbids them the tree of life and an angel instructs them. The fourth scene shifts to Hell, where Lucifer tells his companions of his plans against mankind. The original manuscript has apparently lost 12 leaves at this point, dealing with the Temptation and the Fall.

PL-88. (English)

"Mactacio Abel" in The Townley Plays, ed. by George England and A. W. Pollard (1897). Original date about 1410.

Inc. (Garcio loquitur):
All hayll, all hayll, both blithe and glad,
ffor here com I, a mery lad;
be peasse youre dyn, my master bad . . .
Expl. ("Caym" loquitur):
ffare well les, and fare well more,

ffor now and euer more,
I will go me to hyde.

Some 473 lines of rhymed verse in couplets and stanzas. The rude vigour of the play is increased by supplying Cain with a rowdy serving-man, "Garcio" or "Pyke-harnes", who gives his master as good as he gets conversationally. Cain tries to cheat God out of His tithes on his wheat-crop, and when God reproves him for reviling Abel, he makes fun of God:

Whi, who is that hob-ouer-the-wall?
We! who was that that piped so small?
Com go we hens, for perels all;
God is out of hys wit.

PL-89. (Italian)

Frezzi, Federico. Il quadriregio. Circa 1430. Mi: Johns Hopkins.

Inc. La dea, che'l terzo ciel volvendo move,
avea concorde seco ogni pianeto
congiunta al Sole ed al suo padre Love. . . .
Expl. e'l volto alzando al cielo, i' dico: -- Oh quando
sera, mio Dio, il di che a te retorni!

This poem was apparently composed about the beginning of the 15th century. There are thirty manuscript editions, the earliest dated 1430, and ten printed editions, the earliest printed in 1481 at Perugia. It is written in terza rima, totals about 13,500 lines, and is divided into four books: I, Del regno d'amore; II, Del regno di Satanasso; III, Del regno de' vizi; IV, Del regno delle virtu.

It is a symbolic work, akin to Dante's Divina Commedia in subject-matter and scope and to the Roman de la Rose in method. The element of far-fetched allegory is already being pushed so far as to detract seriously from the reality of the presentation. In the vision-allegory of Book I, the author is led by Cupid through the realm of Love. The goddess Minerva then takes over and leads him, in the three remaining books, through the realms of Satan, of the Vices, and of the Virtues respectively. Among the more vivid episodes in Book II are his glimpse of the temple of Pluto in Canto 17 and his meeting with Satan in Canto 19.

PL-90. (Middle English)

Furnivall, Frederick James (ed.). The Fall and Passion. 15th century?

Inc. þe grace of god ful of migt. þat is king an euer was:
mote amang us aligt. an give vs alle is swet grace. . . .
Expl. an after he steig to heuen aboue. þer ioi þat euer lest:
an þer he sal al vs loue. in his swet blisful fest. amen.

A brief rhymed version of the fall and redemption of man. In it we learn that a tenth of the angels fell from Heaven with Lucifer, and that they fell for seven days and nights (ll. 25-28), unlike the nine days mentioned in Paradise Lost (VI, 871).

PL-91. (Middle English)

Furnivall, Frederick James (ed.). þe Develis Perlament, or Parlamentum of Feendis. Lambeth MS. 853, circa 1430 A.D.

Inc. Whanne marye was greet with gabriel,
And had conceyued & boren a childe,
Alle þe deuelis of þe eir, of erþe, & of helle,
helden þer paralament of þat maide mylde . . .
Expl. Crist! kepe us out of harme and hate,
For þin hooli spirit so special!

In this very early version of a "great consult" of evil angels, we learn that Lucifer was made out of nothing by God the Son as the first of all created things (ll. 329-332), and that God Himself gave his seat to Lucifer for a while (ll. 339-344).

PL-92. (French)

Anonymous. Le Mistere du Viel Testament. XV Century. Published by Baron James de Rothschild, Paris, 1878. Mi: Cornell.

Inc. Dieu
Pour demonstrer nostre magnificence
Et decorer les trosnes glorieux,
Voulons ce jour, par divine excellence,
Produire faictz divins et vertueux . . .
Expl. Sera faicte, au près de sa femme;
Dieu leur face pardon a l'ame! (line 4291).

A remarkable sequence of 15th century French mystery plays, dealing with themes from the Old Testament. The verse rhymes progressively in quatrains: abab, bcbc, cdcd, dede, etc. The first seven mysteries are entitled as follows: (1) La Creacion des Anges; le Trebuchement de Lucifer; la creacion d'Adam et d'Eve; (2) La Transgression d'Adam et d'Éve; (3) Du Procès de Paradis; (4) Des Sacrafices Cayn et Abel; (5) De la Mort d'Abel et de la Malediction Cayn; (6) De la Mort d'Eve; (7) De la Mort d'Adam. A certain unity is given to the long sequence by recurring debates between Justice and Mercy (in No. 3, No. 7, etc.).

PL-93. (English)

Chester Plays. I. The Fall of Lucifer. Circa 1447. Mi: Yale.

Inc. (Deus pater loquitur):
Ego sum Alpha et w,
primus et nobilissimus;
It is my Will, yt sholde be soe,
yt is, it was, yt shall be thus . . .

<u>Expl</u>. (Deus pater loquitur):
My first day now have I wrought,
I geve yt fullie my blessing.

The Chester cycle of mystery plays, 25 in number, is apparently later than the York and Towneley cycles (cf. PL-76 and PL-87), but earlier than the Coventry plays (cf. PL-101). The following note is found on the cover of the original manuscript (MS. Harl. 2124): "The Whitsun playes first made by one Don Randle Heggenet, o monke of Chester Abbey, who was thrise at Rome before he could obtain leave of the Pope to have them in the English tongue. The Whitsun plays were playd openly in pageants by the Cittizens of Chester in the Whitsun Weeke. Nicholas the fift. then was Pope in the year of our Lord 1447." They are indebted to the <u>Mistére du vieil testament</u> (cf. PL-92); and lack the humour and pathos sometimes found in the other English mysteries.

In the first play, lines 1-208, Lucifer and Lightburne become proud, but the rebellious angels are driven out. In lines 209-280, they lament in hell.

PL-94. (English)

Chester Plays. II <u>De Creatione mundi et Adami et Evae, De eorumque tentatione</u>. Circa 1447.

<u>Inc</u>. (Deus loquitur):
I God, most in maiestye,
in whom beginning none may be . . .
<u>Expl</u>. (cayne loquitur):
Now I goe, to all that I see,
I graunt the same gifte.

In the second Chester play, the Creation (ll. 1-160) is followed by an envious speech by the Devil in Eden, represented as a sort of sphinx, "volucris penna, serpens pede, fronte puella". The temptation and expulsion finally end in the death of Abel. The play runs to 704 lines, chiefly in 8-line stanzas.

PL-95. (French)

Greban, D'Arnoul. Le Mystére de la Passion. Written before 1452; published in Paris, 1878. Mi: Harvard.

Inc. ADAM: O souveraine majeste,
bon Dieu qui en eternite
regnez sans jamès prendre fin . . .

A colossal mystery play, of 34,574 lines of 4-stressed iambic verse in couplets. The prologue (1740 lines) presents the Fall of Lucifer, the creation of man, the Fall of Man, and the sequel down to the death of Seth. On the first day of the Passion, Adam, Eve, Isaiah, Ezekial, Jeremiah and David speak in Hell, urging Christ to come and save them (1741-2071) then Mercy, Justice, Peace, Truth and Wisdom talk in Heaven with God the Father (2072-3394); etc., etc.

PL-96. (Cornish)

"Origo Mundi" in The Ancient Cornish Drama, edited by Edwin Norris, 2 vols., 1859. Circa 1450?

Inc. (Deus Pater loquitur):
En tas a nef y'm gylwyr
formyer pup tra a vyt gvrys . . .

Expl. (Rex Salomon loquitur):
a barth a'n tas . menstrels a ras
pebough whare.

The remains of Cornish literature consist of a 2072-line "epic" entitled Mount Calvary, a series of three mystery plays or Ordinalia, on the Creation (2846 ll.), the Passion of Our Lord (3242 ll.) and the Resurrection (2646), and a later play, written by William Jordan in 1611, entitled The Creation of the World with Noah's Flood (PL-191). The first Ordinale, listed here as "Origo Mundi" covers not only the Creation but the Temptation and Fall, the death of Abel, the death and burial of Adam, the Deluge, the story of Abraham, the story of Moses, the story of David and the story of Solomon. It presents no real points of difference from the mystery plays of English and French, and was probably adapted or translated from them. It contains such apocryphal elements as Seth's obtaining the oil of mercy from the Garden and placing three apple-seeds in the mouth of the dying Adam. The verse is trochaic tetrameter catalectic, in stanzas of 4, 6 or 8 lines.

PL-97. (Middle High German)

Immessen, Arnoldus. Der Sündenfall. Ca. 1475 A.D. (Edited by Otto Schönemann, Hanover, 1855.) Mi: Harvard.

Inc. Almechtige god, vel leve here,
Wy beden dek alle lof unde ere,
Umme dine mildicheit und gote. . . .
Expl. Nu singet mit my, wat juwer is,
Sancta maria virgo, succurre miseris.

A morality play of 3953 lines in rhymed couplets, written by Arnold Immessen, rector of Eimbeck. The first 929 lines correspond closely to Part I of the French Mistere du Viel Testament (PL-92). The characters include Justice and Mercy, who argue with the Creator (lines 3645-3719) but end by kissing together at his command. Much time is taken up with the lamentations of Adam, Eve, and the prophets in Hell. The devils use rather homely language, as when the "nonus diabulus" says to the wailing Eve: "Shut up, you old chaff-sack, and let your tears be!" A final time of rejoicing follows the annunciation to Joachim and Anna of the impending birth of Mary, who will be the mother of the Saviour. In the processus prophetarum in this work, twelve sibyls are included; and one gets the impression that there was more pageantry than drama in it.

PL-98. (French-English)

Caxton, William, Mirrour of the World. London, 1480.

Accessible in edition by Oliver H. Prior for E.E.T.S. (1913).

Inc. Here begynneth the table of the rubrices of this presente volume named the Mirrour of the world or thymage of the same. . . .
Expl. and after this short & transitorye lyf he bringe hym and vs in to his celestyal blysse in heuene. Amen.

A prose translation of Gossouin's L'Image du Monde (PL-67). It proved to be a very popular and influential work.

PL-99. (Latin)

Rupertus, abbas Tuitiensis. Opus originale de victoria verbi dei in tredecim libros divisum. Augsburg. 1487. Mi: Harvard.

Inc. Victoriam verbi dei effectum et opus dicimus propositum dei ad laudem ipsius omnipotentis et invicti . . .
Expl. Tanta tunc erit lux solis: quia tunc manifeste parebit quale sit verbum; per quod deus omnia sex diebus fecit: et in septimo requievit ut supra.

This Latin manuscript of 210 pages provides a summary of the action of the "celestial cycle" closely resembling that found in Paradise Lost, as for example Rupert's account of Satan's revolt (I, 8ff.). Both works have Michael conduct inconclusive warfare against the angelic rebels and have God the Son achieve final triumph in battle. There is, however, no cogent evidence to suggest that Milton borrowed from the Victoria Verbi Dei.

PL-100. (German)

Anonymous. Lucifers mit seiner gesellschaft val. Bamberg 1493. Facsimile, Harvard.

Inc. Als der almechtig got am anfang seiner geschöpff all creature erschaffen hat, so seind die engel die ersten vermiensstigen creatur gewesen. . . .
Expl. Also schreibe Nicolaus de Lyra über das puch der geschöpff da geschriben stet von dem val des ersten menschen. Desgleichen auch ander lerer.

A brief treatise on angels, beginning with an enumeration of their several orders and passing on to describe the fall of Lucifer and his angelic adherents. In an exemplum there is set forth the story of a fallen angel who served a mediaeval knight as his squire and cured his wife of an illness by bringing her, within an hour, a supply of fresh lioness's milk from Arabia to Germany.

PL-101. (English)

Ludus Coventriae. I. The Creation and the Fall of Lucifer. Circa 1500 A.D.

Inc. (Deus loquitur):
My name is knowyn god and kynge
My werk for to make . now wyl I wende . . .
Expl. (Lucifer loquitur):
Ffor fere of fyre a fart I crake
In helle donjoon . myn dene is dyth.

The most artistic and dramatic of the cycles of English mystery plays in Coventry series, edited in 1922 by K. S. Block as Ludus Coventriae or The Plaie called Corpus Christi. This is a collection of 42 plays, with themes extending from Creation to Doomsday. The first play, written chiefly in rhyming 13-line stanzas, covers the Creation of Heaven and the angels and the fall of Lucifer.

PL-102. (English)

Ludus Coventriae. II. The Creation and Fall of Man.

Inc. (Deus loquitur):
Now hevyn is made ffor Aungell sake
þe fyrst day and þe fyrst nyth . . .
Expl. (Eva loquitur):
Ye must delve and I xal spynne
in care to ledyn oure lyff.

The second play in the Coventry series portrays the creation of the Earth and of man, and the fall of man. Eve persuades Adam to eat the apple by describing this as the advice of "a ffayr Aungell", although she later describes her tempter as "a werm with An Aungelys face". Her grief after their expulsion from the Garden is so great that she asks Adam to wring her neck. He refuses, for fear of being sent to Hell for murder.

PL-103. (Latin)

Pontanus, Joannes Jovianus.[1] De Mundi creatione. Written about 1460, printed posthumously in Venice, 1513. Mi: British Museum.

Inc. Hoc coelum, quaeque obliquo distincta meatu
Sed certa ferri sydera lege vides . . .
Expl. Quodque decet bona cuncta Deo iustumque piumque
Ascribis, nostrae sed mala nequitiae.

Some 120 lines in Latin elegiacs. All was created well for man, and he has perverted the universe by his own act.

PL-104. (Latin)

Pontanus, Joannes Jovianus. Urania, sive de Stellis Venice 1513. Mi: British Museum.

---

[1]An Italian humanist and poet (1426-1503), born at Cerreto and educated at Perugia. He spent most of his life at Naples, as military secretary and chancellor to the ruling family.

Inc. Qui coelo radient ignes, quae sydera mundo
Labantur tacito, Stellis quibus emicet ingens
. . .
Expl. Proscripsitque crebro portisque inclusit ahenis,
Ociaque hesperias iussit regnare per urbeis.

An expository poem on the heavens running to over 6,000 hexameter lines. Its organization is encyclopedic rather than unitary.

PL-105. (Latin)

Pontanus, Joannes Jovianus. Meteorum Liber. Venice, 1513. Mi: British Museum.

Inc. Hinc, ego quae nubes causae, quis spiritus auras
Sollicitet, quae vis agitet liquida aequora ponti
Expediam, et salsae dicam sapor unde lacunae.
. . .
Expl. Mi sat erit si coeruleo Sebethus ab amne
Intractae Salicis fluviali munere donet,
Ac mihi pomiferis uacet Antiniana sub hortis.

An expository poem of about 1,800 hexameters dealing with the non-astronomical aspects of the sky.

PL-106. (Latin)

Quintianus, Joannes Franciscus. Theocrisis. Tragoedia de extremo iudicio. (In Christiana Opera, 1514. Newberry Library, University of Chicago.)

Inc. (Michael solus loquitur):
En ecce quanto murmure et quanto impetu
Fragore quove tremuit immensus polus.
Expl. (Chorus loquitur):
Mox sidereae lumina sedis
Nostris aperit tandem precibus:
Victo ut stygio principe tecum
Semper merita sede fruamur.

In this play on the Last Judgement, the chief partial analogues are a long debate between Michael and Lucifer and another between Lucifer and two lesser angels. Another parallel in poetic method is where St. John asks St. Peter to relate to him the manner of the Judgement, because he himself had on that occasion been absent (procul aberam), in attendance on the Virgin Mary - an argument similar to that of Raphael when he asks Adam to tell the story of his creation because he had been absent that day,

Bound on a voyage uncouth and obscure,
Farr on excursion toward the Gates of Hell.
(PL., VIII, 230-1).

PL-107. (Italian)

Cornazzano, Antonio. "De la creatione del mundo", being part II of his La vita e passione de Christo. Venice, 1518. Mi: British Museum.

Inc. Lanfinita virtu del maestro eterno
E labsoluta libera potenza
Che tien del mondo limmortal governo
Come creasse lhom: di qual semenza . . .

Expl. . . . Questo fun colpo troppo troppo acerbo
Allinimico nostro: che scacciato
Piobbe dal ciel per tanto esser superbo.
E mori el suo valor con Christo nato.

A passage of 178 lines in terza rima, summing up the Creation and the Fall, and linking them with the Atonement.

PL-108. (Portuguese)

Vicente, Gil. Breve sumario da história de Deos. Lisbon, 1527. Mi: Library of Congress.

Inc. ANJO. Ainda que todalas cousas passadas
sejão notorias a Vossas Altezas,
a história de Deos tem taes profundezas . . .

Expl. BELIAL. Crede vós, Rei, que tendes imigos;

porque estas doencas que trago comigo,
denotao perigos.

A religious play, apparently based on the familiar pageant of Old Testament prophets (cf. Mistere du Viel Testament), in which, beginning with Adam, they fall one by one under the power of Hell. Finally Christ comes, and with His triumphant resistance to temptation the play ends. The characters are as follows: Lucifer, the lord of Hell; Belial, the bailiff of his court; Satan, a noble of his council; the World, dressed as a king: Time, as his inspector; Death; Eve; Adam; Job; Abraham; Moses; David; Saint John the Baptist; and Christ. The drama was first played in 1527 before King John III of Portugal and Queen Catherine.

PL-109. (Latin)

Vida, Marcus Hieronymus. Christiados libri VI. Rome, 1527. Mi: Yale.

Inc. Qui mare, qui terras, qui coelum numine comples
Spiritus alme, tuo liceat mihi munere regem . . .
Expl. Christiados, toto surgit gens aurea mundo,
Seclorumque oritur longe pulcherrimus ordo.

This Latin epic on the life of Christ was one of the most famous poems of the Early Renaissance. Its first patron, Pope Leo X, hailed it with the couplet:

Cedite Romani scriptores, cedite Graii;
Hic scio quid majus nascitur Aeneide.

In relation to Paradise Lost, its most significant feature is probably the description of the Council in Hell, addressed by Lucifer, in Book I, a feature later to be copied by such men as Tasso, Clarke and Cowley. The standard English translations are those by J. Cranwell (Cambridge, 1768) and Edward Granan (London, 1771). Extracts from the latter version are given above, pp. 43-44.

PL-110. (Latin)

Palingenius, Marcellus. Zodiacus Vitae. Venice 1531. Mi: Newberry.

Inc. Scribere quid deceat, primus liber explicat apte:
Divitias summum esse bonum, negat ipse secundus . . .
Expl. Tu varios populos diversaque regna superstes:
Quaere: studeque meum late diffundere nomen.

An encyclopaedic poem, ostensibly on astronomy but combining a wide range of erudition with a style of pungent power. It is cast in the form of a dream-allegory, like the Roman de la Rose. In Bk. XI, named "Aquarius", the poet discusses many such fundamental problems as the eternity of the world, the infinity of the universe, and creation ex nihilo. Like Milton, he lays great stress on the freedom of the will and the importance of the right use of liberty. The relation of body and soul is treated with the widest range of detail. Palingenius is above all passionately concerned with the problem of evil.

The author was probably Pier Angelo Manzolli, of Stellata, near Ferrara. He was a Catholic and died in peace, but his bones were dug up and burned in 1558. His book was placed on the Index, but was reprinted some thirty times in Protestant countries in the next forty years.

PL-111. (Italian)

Folengo, Teofilo. Della Humanità del Figliuol di Dio. Venice, 1533.

Inc. Del' alma, et sempiterna Trinitade
L' alto, profondo, e incomprensibil senso . . .
Expl. Uccide Morte, e uscendo con gran voce
Lascio vittoriosa il corpo in CROCE.

A muddled and discursive Christiad, totalling 9,152 lines in ottava rima, by a monk from Mantua. PL-117 is by the same author. It dilates interminably on the plight of mankind "dal tempo che d'Adam l'ingordo dente morse 'l vietato pomo", and has no narrative merit.

PL-112. (English)

The Story of the Creacyon of Eve, with the Expellyng of Adam and Eve out of Paradyce. Composed before June 16, 1533. Privately printed, Norwich, 1856.

Inc. (Deus Pater loquitur):
Ego principium, Alpha et ω, in altissimis habito;
In the hevenly empery I am resydent.
Yt ys not semely for man, sine adjutorio,
To be allone, nor very convenyent. . . .

Expl. (Adam et Eva loquuntur):
Wythe dolorous sorowe we may wayle and wepe
Bothe nyght and daye in sory, sythys full depe.

This is the earlier version of the pageant of the Grocers of Norwich, England (vide infra, PL-145). The Serpent here claims to be an angel sent from God to ask Eve to eat the apple. The style is primitive and laconic.

PL-113. (Latin)

Palearius, Aonius.[1] De Animorum immortalitate, libri III. Lyons, 1536. Mi: Harvard.

Inc. Felices animae, coeli omnipotentis alumni,
Astrorum decus, et qui versicoloribus alis

[1] Aonio Paleario, of Veroli, in the Roman Campagna. (c. 1500-1570). In 1520, went to Rome. Later, a professor at Lucca and at Milan. Executed in Rome in 1570 by the Inquisition, on the charge of heresy.

Aethera tranatis liquidum, qui sydera, quique
. . .

Expl. Adspicite, obtutuque oculos defigite in unum,
Unus ego omnipotens, ego Rex hominumque Deumque.

A poem of approximately 1,840 lines, in Latin hexameters, being a highly erudite discussion of the nature of souls, both angelic and human, and of the nature of God himself; also of the spiritual laws of the universe, the punishment of the wicked and the rewards of the blessed. In the invocation to Book I, appears the traditional assertion of adventurous originality:

Vestra ego fretus ope, ingredior loca, nullius ante
Trita pede; et quoniam vestra haec, aequique bonique
Munera vos facite, et sancto aspirate labori.

PL-114. (English)

Bale, John. The Chief Promises of God unto Man. London, 1538.

Inc. PATER COELESTIS. In the begynnynge, before the heauens were create,
In me and of me, was my sonne sempyternall. . . .

Expl. IOANNES BAPTISTA. As wyll faythfullye receyue hym with good mynde.
Lete our voyce then sounde, in some swete musycall kynde.

John Bale (1495-1563) was bishop of Ossory, a very disputatious theologian, and the author of several plays. The present drama is in seven acts, written partly in Alexandrines, rhymed in couplets, and partly in rime royal. There is a prologue by Bale himself. Then the Pater coelestis announces his displeasure with man. Adam pleads for mercy, and is finally assured that though he must die, he will one day be raised again because of his true repentance. The first act ends with the angels singing hymns to the "eternal Sapyence" of God. There are successive interviews between God and Noah, Abraham, Moses,

David, Isaiah, and John the Baptist. There is a marked similarity in general plan with the French Adam (No. 62) and Gil Vicente's Breve Sumario (No. 108). As to the origin of this type, Schelling, Elizabethan Drama, i.8, says: "The Prophetae, for example, originated, not in a chant but in a lectio or narrative, the pseudo-Augustinian Sermo contra Judaeos, Paganos et Arianos de Symbolo of the sixth century. In it the prophets are cited to bear witness to Christ." It is possible that this may have been influenced by the Ludus Septem Sapientium, sometimes attributed to D. Magnus Ausonius (4th century), in which the Seven Wise Men of Ancient Greece come on the stage in succession and propound their aphorisms.

PL-115. (German)

Voith, Valten. Ein schön Lieblich Spiel, von dem herlichen ursprung: Betrübtem Fal. Gnediger widerbrengunge. Müseligem leben, Seligem Ende, und ewiger Freudt des Menschen aus den Historien heiliger schrifft gezogen gantz Tröstlich. Magdeburg, 1538. Mi: Yale.

Inc. ADAM. Do Gott vater als gschaffen het
Durch sein wort, den Son, mich vorstet,
Hetten ein gros gefallen dran,
Durch seinen geist, thet von ihn gan . . .
Expl. JESUS. Trewlich ich euch das alzeidt rath,
Hört mich, mein wort ans vaters stadt.

A poetic drama, in rhymed octosyllabic verse in couplets, totalling 3068 lines. Its author, Valten Voith (1487-1558?), was a citizen of Magdeburg and the author of several plays. He was a Meistersinger and had studied at the University of Wittenberg. The present drama is a mystery play, extending from the Fall of Man (Act I, scene 1) through the whole range of the Old Testament (Abraham, Isaac, David, etc.) down to the triumphant atonement for man by Christ (Act V, scene 10). The allegorical figures of Sin, Death, and the Law have prominent speaking parts.

*PL-116. (German)

Knausts, Heinrich. Tragödie von Verordnung der Stände. Wittenberg, 1539.

Cited in Johannes Winzer, Die ungleichen Kinder Evas in der Literatur des 16 Jahrhunderts, Greifwald, 1908, as the earliest dramatic treatment of this theme, based on Melancthon's legend.

PL-117. (Italian)

Folengo, Teofilo. La Palermitana. Circa 1540.

Inc. Or ch'io son posto a fren di quell' etade,
ch' altrui distempra per molt' anni e indura
. . .
Expl. e fra ramo d' ulivo, alloro e palma
trarrá noi suscitati al Padre eterno.

The author was born in Cipada, near Mantua, in 1491, and died in a monastery near Vicenza in 1544.

This poem of some 7,500 lines in terza rima was written while he was an abbot in Sicily. It remained in manuscript at his death but is included in his printed works today. It is a sort of expanded commentary on his earlier poem, La Umanità de Figliuolo di Dio (PL-111). It opens with a lengthy description of the creation of the angels, the world and Man; proceeds to the Fall and the lament of Nature; and ends with a long procession of sibyls, prophets, kings, queens and patriarchs, all announcing the ultimate coming of Christ. There follows a brief morality play, in Latin except for two Italian speeches by Human Nature.

PL-118. (German)

Sachs, Hans. Schöpfung, fal und erlösung Adam, Eva und gantzes menschlichen geschlechts. A.D. 1545.

Mi: Harvard.

Inc. Im anfang Got, der Herr, beschuff
Durch seins allmechtig wortes ruff
Himel und erden und das meer . . .
Expl. Da ewig freud uns blü und wachs
Nach dem elend, wüncht uns Hans Sachs.

A narrative poem of 126 lines in rhyming iambic tetrameter couplets. It gives the story of man's creation and fall and at the very end foretells his ultimate redemption.

PL-119. (Latin)

Zieglerus, Hieronymus. Protoplastus, Drama comicotragicum. Basel, 1547. Mi: Yale.

Inc. (Deus loquitur):
Coeli plagas postquam vagi creaveram,
Terram rudem mox fluminis cavi sinu
Circumdedi, et lucem produxi protinus . . .
Expl. (Cherub loquitur):
Et posterorum vox damnabit publica.
Haec est dies signandus atro calculo,
Quo generis humani periit miserè salus.

This is a Latin play of about 1850 lines in the iambic senarius. Since its rude simplicity forms an instructive contrast to the art of Grotius, a detailed summary is given hereunder. Its author (d. 1562) was a professor at Ingolstadt, Augsburg and Munich.

ACT I. Scene 1. God enters and describes in detail his creation of the universe and of all living things, by word alone. (He then makes the figure of a man out of clay and breathes into its face.) He tells man that he is making him lord of the earth, but warns him against pride. Scene 2. Raphael, Michael and Gabriel discuss with one another the wonders of the creation and the high lot of man. Scene 3. Conversation between God and Adam. God emphasizes Adam's privileges and Adam humbly acknowledges them. God says: "Vasallus es mihi, dominus feudi sum ego." The one condition laid down is that Adam must not eat the fruit of the tree of knowledge of good and evil. Adam promises obedience. Scene 4. Adam soliloquizes on his fortunate lot; then lies down to sleep on green grass, in the shade, beside a babbling brook.

ACT II. Scene 1. God decides that man needs a wife and helpmate, who may bear him children. Hence God has put Adam into a deep sleep. (He takes out a rib, turns it into Eve) then awakens Adam and explains the purposes of matrimony. Adam thanks God. Scene 2. Adam tells Eve that child-bearing will be painless, pleasant and very frequent. He also tells her of the command not to eat of the fruit of the one tree. Adam gives an eloquent description of the delights of the Garden. The pair walk through it. Scene 3. Lucifer, Belial and Satan confer. Lucifer tells of his grief and his desire for revenge. They decide to tempt, not the man (whose strength of character they fear), but the woman. Lucifer will use the help of the Snake: "Comes Serpens erit". Lucifer has overheard God warning Adam. Scene 4. The Serpent (with Lucifer in background) meets Eve alone, discusses the garden, and asks why the one fruit is not eaten. Eve explains. Scene 5. Eve comes to the tree and eats. Adam enters. He is at first horrified, but finally takes from her hand and eats. Then both perceive their nakedness and are in despair. They make themselves garments of fig leaves, and fear the coming of God.

ACT III. Scene 1. Lucifer, Belial and Satan rejoice. Scene 2. Raphael, Michael and Gabriel lament. Scene 3. God judges Adam and Eve. Scene 4. Raphael ejects the guilty pair. Scene 5. The Cherub guard of Eden describes the sequel.

PL-120. (Latin)

Betuleius, Xystus ("Sixt Birck")[1]. Eva: Mythologia Philippi Melanthonis redacta in actionem ludicrum. Basel, 1547. Mi: Yale and Folger.

Inc. GOD. Adibimus visuri quid rerum gerat
Nunc exul in mundi solitudine,
Adamus ille Protoplastus, omnium
Mortalium parens in terris gentium
Futurus. . .
Expl. EPILOGUE. . . . sic habes mysterium
Tam sacrosanctae fictionis splendidum
Hic fructus est huius sacri spectaculi.

This is the earliest that I have examined of several dramatic versions (cf. PL-116,140,142,150, 168,196) of a fable invented by Philip Melancthon. Eve has half finished washing her children in preparation for a holy day tomorrow. God comes to visit them. The clean children are lined up to meet him, while the dirty ones are hidden under the hay. God cross-examines the clean ones as to their catechism. Abel and Seth (both clean) reply well. The others, including Cain, are then brought out from under the hay. Cain is contumacious and is denounced by God.

PL-121. (German)

Sachs, Hans. Tragedia von schöpfung, fal und ausstreibung Ade auss dem paradeyss. A.D. 1548. (Mi: Harvard.)

Inc. CHERUB: Der götlich himelische segen

[1]Xystus Betuleius or Sixt Birck (1501-54) was a native of Augsburg, where he later became head of the St. Anna Gymnasium. He was a distinguished teacher of Latin and Greek and wrote several Latin school-dramas in the style of Plautus and Terence, based on Biblical themes.

Sey mit euch ietz und allewegen . . .
Expl. CHERUB: Das sein gÜt Über uns erwachs
Hie und dort ewig, wÜnscht Hans Sachs.

A play in 3 acts, written in rhyming couplets in iambic tetrameter, totalling 1,000 lines.

Act. I. God creates Adam. While Adam retires with God to receive instructions, three angels (Raphael, Michael and Gabriel) discuss man's estate. Adam returns and pledges obedience to God. Adam sleeps.

Act. II. Eve created. Adam warns her of the one prohibition. They retire. Three devils (Lucifer, Satan and Belial) enter and discuss their desire to overthrow man. The serpent persuades Eve, and she Adam. They make aprons of fig-leaves.

Act. III. The three devils dance with joy and depart. The three angels weep over the fall. God comes and judges the guilty. A cherub with a flaming sword drives them out and epilogizes.

PL-122. (German)

Elsaeszisches Adam und Evaspiel, 16th century folk-play, printed pp. 121-134 in Alemannia, Zeitschrift fÜr Sprache, Litteratur und Volkskunde des Elsaszes Oberrheins und Schwabens, Vol. xvii, Bonn, 1889.

Inc. ENGEL. Ich trit hinein wohl ohne Spott,
Ein guter Abend gew euch Gott . . .
Expl. ENGEL. Habt ihr das Spiel recht gÜät betracht,
So wÜnsche mir euch alle eine rÜthesame Nacht.

A brief Alsatian folk-play of 252 lines in rhyming couplets. It has been handed down by oral tradition, but seems to have been originally derived from Hans Sachs's tragedy on the Fall of Man (PL-121). There are only five characters: God the Father, an Angel, Adam, Eve, and the Devil. Action is largely limited to the creation of Eve (Adam remaining awake), the temptation by the Devil (without benefit of serpent), the enslavement of Adam and Eve by the Devil, and their expulsion from Eden.

PL-123. (German)

Anonymous. Das Oberuferer Paradiesspiel. Originating in 16th century?

Inc. Singen wil ich aus herzens grund,
weils gibt das gemüte mein . . .
Expl. ALLE. Ein jedweder das best betracht!
So wünschen wir von Got dem almächtigen eine
gute nacht.

This mystery play and the Salzburger Paradiesspiel (PL-124) are printed in K. J. Schröer's Deutsche Weihnachtspiele aus Ungern (Vienna, 1858). Oberufer is a village in the Grosse Schütt district, near Pressburg. The play associated with it consists of 348 lines in rhyming couplets, the greater part of it being almost identical with Hans Sachs's Tragedia von der schepfung, fall und ausstreibung Adae aus dem paradeis. The Oberufer play seems to be the oldest of a considerable group of folk-plays based on the work of Sachs (cf. PL-124, PL-125, PL-126, PL-127).

PL-124. (German)

Anonymous. Salzburger Paradiesspiel. Originating in 16th century?

Inc. ERZENGEL: Wir kommen daher mit grosser freud,
Wir wünschen euch al ein glückselige zeit. . . .
Expl. Wir dörfn uns nit saumen:
Got geb euch eine gute Nacht.

Printed along with the Oberuferer Paradiesspiel in K. J. Schröer's Deutsche Weihnachtspiele aus Ungern (Vienna, 1858). It consists of 256 rhyming lines, mostly in couplets. Much of the action is described in song by an archangel and there is a chorus that runs through the whole play, as in the

Oberufer drama. Schröer traces a close connection between Hans Sachs and the Gastein community (near Salzburg) where the MS. of this play was found in 1820. He leaves unsettled, however, whether Sachs gave artistic form to a folkplay already in existence or whether these communities began with Sachs's play, an original work, and altered it with variations of their own. The interspersed choral passages certainly seem to be of some other origin. Schröer compares this feature with the choral elements in the old 12th century Anglo-Norman *Adam* (PL-62) and suggests this as a separate survival reinforced by Sachs.

PL-125. (Czech)

Feifalik, Julius (ed.). *Paradeisspiel* (sic), in *Volksschauspiele aus Mähren*. Olmüz, 1864. Sixteenth century?

Inc. ENGEL: Vchazím ve jmenu Nejvyššiho,
dobry vecer vinsuji . . .
Expl. ENGEL: dobrou noc vam vinsuji
a za uděleni diskreci děkuji.

This Temptation-play in the Czech language is in part taken almost verbatim from Hans Sachs, although close comparison with the *Oberuferer Paradiesspiel* (PL-123) suggests that the borrowing has been through the folk-version and not directly from Sachs.

PL-126. (German)

Hartmann, August (ed.). *Laufener Adam- und Eva- Spiel*, in *Volksschauspiele in Bayern und Österreich-Ungarn gesammelt*. Leipzig, 1880. Originally 16th century?

Inc. ENGEL: Ich tritt herein wohl ane Spott;
Ein guten Abend geb euch Gott . . .
Expl. CHOR: Also ward Adam und Eva weis
Geschlagen aus dem Paradeis.
Gott loben wir schon

Im höchsten Thron.

Another play largely derived from the work of Hans Sachs. Hartmann finds, however, that the simple folk who perpetuate it have lost any awareness of its origin and have passed it down by word of mouth. Of the Laufen play, 157 lines are from Hans Sachs and the remaining 106 from some other source, later than Sachs yet comparatively far back.

PL-127. (German)

Hartmann, August (ed.). Das Kain- und Abel- Spiel, in Volksschauspiele in Bayern und Österreich-Ungarn gesammelt. Leipzig, 1880. Originally 16th century?

Inc. ABEL: Komm, herzallerliebster Bruder Kain!
Dies soll unser Opfer sein . . .
Expl. KAIN: Nimm hin! da hast dein rechten Lohn,
Weilsd' soviel giltst bei Gottes Thron!
(erschlägt ihn)

A brief folk-drama (81 lines in rhymed couplets) of the same provenance and character as PL-123.

PL-128. (German)

Weinhold, Karl (ed.). Das Paradeisspiel aus Vordernberg in Obersteier in Weihnacht-Spiele und Lieder aus Süddeutschland und Schlesien. Graez, 1853. Originally 16th century?

Inc. Ihr Kristen all zusammen
steht nur ein wenig still . . .
Expl. GOTT SON (sic): Nun Adieu, mein allerliebster himmlischer Vater, nun Adieu mein allerliebster heiliger Geist; sieh ich gehe in die Welt ins leiden, welches mir von Ewigkeit is zubereit. Nun Adieu ihr lieben Engelein! (geht ab.)
DER ENGEL: Gloria in excelsis deo.

The verse is in various metres, and there is

even a little prose, e.g. in the speeches of the Serpent. The setting is in the Garden and the main theme is the Fall. Three devils confer, viz., Lucifer, Satan and Belial. There are lengthy arguments between Mercy and Justice. A typical mystery play of the village sort.

PL-129. (German)

Ruff, Jacob. Adam und Heva. Zurich, 1550. Mi: Yale.

Inc. (Gross herold, am ersten tag):
Fromm, vest, fürsichtig, eersam herren!
dem höchsten gott vorab zuo eeren,
zuo lob und eer Zürych, diser statt,
die ein verrümpten nammen hat . . .

Expl. (HEROLD.)
. . . darby ich 's yetz wil blyben lon:
ir spillüt blaasst uf! wir wend darvon!

A mystery play in rhymed couplets of octosyllabic iambic verse, in five acts, totalling 6381 lines. Its author, Jacob Ruff (d. 1558), was a stonecutter in Zürich, Switzerland. It was apparently put on with great ceremony on June 9 and 10, 1550. The caste calls for no fewer than 106 persons; and the chief concern seems to be with the possibilities of pageantry.

The main interest lies in Act I and the first four scenes of Act II. This part of the play may be summarized thus: Act I, sc. i. Michael, Gabriel and other angels drive Lucifer and his crew out of Heaven and imprison them. Sc. ii. The devils lament loudly, but decide, on Satan's advice, to send a messenger to spy on God's actions with a view to spoiling His plans. Sc. iii. God creates man and places all things on earth under his dominion. Sc. iv. He plants a garden, puts Adam in it, but warns him, on penalty of death, against eating of the Tree of the Knowledge of Good and Evil. Sc. v. He brings all beasts to Adam to be named. Sc. vi. The creation of Eve and her marriage to Adam. Act II, sc. i. The infernal messenger reports back in Hell. Lucifer proposes to instigate the serpent to persuade Eve and her husband to eat the forbidden fruit. This proposal is passed unanimously. Sc. ii. The serpent seduces the pair; they clothe themselves with leaves. Sc. iii. Death appears and enters Paradise. Sc. iv. God arraigns Adam and Eve, clothes them in skins, and has Gabriel drive them out of Paradise.

The remainder of the drama is taken up with the murder of Abel, the corruption of Seth's innocent descendants by the wanton descendants of Cain, and the onset of the Noachic deluge. The play ends amid shrieking, the roar of waters, and the crashing of thunder.

PL-130. (German)

Adams und Evens Erschaffung und ihr Sündenfall. Ein geistlich Fastnachtspiel mit Sang und Klang: aus dem Schwäbischen in's Oesterreichische versetzt. 1783. (Circa 1550?)

Inc. GOTTVATER. Nichts ist nichts, und wird nichts werden,
Drum hab ich wöllen gebehren ein' Erden . . .
Expl. Jetzt habt ihr ein Komödie g'sehen;
Wie d'Erbsünd' auf der Welt sey g'schehen.

A diglott version, Schwabian and High German, of a simple mystery play of the Creation and the Fall. It presents no points of special interest. The authorship is unknown. Although printed as above in the 18th century, it probably belongs in the 16th.

PL-131. (Latin)

Major, Joannes. "Hortus Adamus." In Delitiae Poetarum Germanorum, vol. IV, pp. 107-122. Mi: London Library.

Inc. Quam bene vivebant antiquo tempore Patres,

Quorum compositus mentis convivia duxit
Filius ipse Dei nostrae sub imagine carnis . . .

Expl. Hei fugite hinc miseri, fugite hinc, latet anguis in herba,
Non hic certa piis statio, sed in aetheris horto,
Huc nos fata vocant, instat nunc tempus, eamus.

A poem of about 520 hexameter lines, in which the poet waxes eloquent over the glories of the home lost in Eden.

Joannes Major was born at Joachimsthal in Bohemia and became a professor at Wittenberg. He died 16 March 1600.

*PL-132. (German)

Kymeus, Johannes. Adams Klage.

*PL-133. (Italian)

Agnifilo, Amico. Il caso di Lucifero.

PL-134. (Latin)

Naogeorgus, Thomas. Satyrae, Bk I, No. 3. Circa 1550. Mi: London Library.

Inc. Expulsi Paradiso olim tectique ferarum
Pellibus ob tristem noxam incussamque pudorem . . .

Expl. Reddidit his animum dictis, semenque profundo
Firmiter infixit cordi, post arte movendum
Serpentis nulla, aut angusti turbine corde.

A Horatian discourse in hexameters, telling how Adam after the Fall recovered faith in the future of the race. About 240 hexameter lines. Narrative rather than satiric in the modern sense.

The name is a pseudonym for Thomas Kirchmayer or Kirchmair (1511-1563) one of the chief writers of Latin drama in Germany in the 16th century.

PL-135. (Latin)

Naogeorgus, Thomas. _Satyrae_, Bk. II, No. 2. Circa 1550.

Inc. Ediderat gnatum primos experta dolores
Humani mater generis, dixitque Cainum,
Grandia promittens pariter mundoque sibique.
Post alium peperit, nomenque illi indidit Abel. . . .
Expl. Concidit ille statim, superasque animam efflat in auras,
Humanumque bibit tellus invita cruorem.

A further discourse, giving the story of the death of Abel. About 270 lines.

PL-136. (Latin)

Naogeorgus, Thomas. _Satyrae_, Bk. III, No. 1. Circa 1550.

Inc. Quum Dominus coelum quondam terramque crearet,
Spiritibus coelum angelicis extemplo replevit.
. . .
Expl. Nullius et noxae veniam scelerumque precari,
Ut ne cocyti frustra mergantur in undis.

A narrative dealing with Satan's revolt and the Fall of the Angels. About 200 lines.

PL-137. (Latin)

Naogeorgus, Thomas. _Satyrae_, Bk. V, No. 1. Circa 1550.

Inc. Omnipotens postquam coelum terramque creasset,

Ornassetque polum stellis et sole corusco . . .
Expl. (Satanas loquitur):
"Maluit auscultare mihi diversa iubenti,
Estque mei iuris factum et sectabitur una,
Quae mihi cunque placent poenasque resolvet
easdem."

An eloquent description of the Garden of Eden, followed by a full account of the Temptation and the Fall. About 270 lines.

PL-138. (Latin)

Macropedius, Georgius. Adamus fabula Christianae pietatis plena. In qua ostenditur, quo pacto lapsus homo post multas multorum saeculorum calamitates et miserias per Christum ab initio promissum, tandemque mundo exhibitum, saluti restituitur. Utrecht, 1552. Mi: Univ. of Illinois.

Inc. (Prologus):
Vos plurimum salvere cupis quotquot huic
Theatro alacres advolasse conspicor.
Expl. (Epilogus):
Humanitas Christi atque Christo indigna mors
Contra offerant veniam, salutem, et gratiam.
Haec si probe egimus, et placuimus, plaudite.

A quaint morality play in five acts, running to some 3,000 lines in the iambic senarius or considerably more than the length of Shakespeare's Julius Caesar. Cain murders Abel in Act I, and thereafter in act after act Adam and Eve, without regard for chronology, meet successively with Abraham and Isaac (Act II), with Aaron and Moses (Act III), with the Prophets (Act IV), and finally with Simeon, Zacharias, Elizabeth, Joseph and the Virgin Mary (Act V). Their anxiety through the millenia is resolved into rapture as they hear Mary read from Isaiah of the coming Nativity of Christ. The play ends with the Magnificat.

Georgius Macropedius or Langhvelt (1475-1558),

member of the monastic order of St. Jerome, was rector of schools at Herzogenbusch, Leiden and Utrecht. He is spoken of by Karl Goedeke (*Geschichte der deutschen Dichtung*) as "the most distinguished Latin dramatist of the 16th century."

PL-139. (Latin)

Mizaldus, Antonius. *De Mundi Sphaera, seu Cosmographia, libri tres*. Paris, 1553. Mi: Brown Univ.

Inc. Primus libellus ostendit omnia providentia gubernari: probatque Deum rerum mundi universarum authorem . . .

Expl. Hanc, si forte leges astrorum captus amore:
Sis memor authoris, qui regit illa, Dei.
Et si quid nosti melius, vel doctius:
Candidus imperti: si minus, ista feras.

A Latin treatise on astronomy, partly in prose. In his verse introduction to Book III, he repeatedly invokes Urania:

Ergo, ades Urania, et facilem te trade roganti,
Urania, cui nota omnis penetralia coeli . . .

PL-140. (German)

Sachs, Hans. *Die ungeleichen kinder Eve, wie sie Gott, der Herr, anredt*. A.D. 1553. Mi: Harvard.

Inc. HEROLT: Heyl und genad von Gott, dem Herren,
Sey all den, so von nah und ferren
Versamlet seind ahn dieses ort . . .

Expl. HEROLT: Da ewig freud uns aufferwachs
Mit allen engeln, wünscht Hans Sachs.

This appears to be an expansion of Sixt Birck's Latin play (PL-116). Hans Sachs adds some details of his own: Cain and the other unwashed boys take counsel of Satan; Cain, when catechized, recites a wicked parody of the Lord's Prayer; and the play ends with the murder and burial of Abel.

*PL-141. (German)

Olinger, Paulus. Genesis. Strasburg, 1555.

A versification of Genesis, cited by Philipp Wackernagel (Bibliographie zur Geschichte des deutschen Kirchenliedes im XVI Jh.) as "meistersingerisch."

PL-142. (Latin)

Selneccerus, Nicolaus. Theophania, comoedia nova et elegans de primorum Parentum conditione et ordinum sive graduum in genere humano institutione. Wittenberg, 1560. Mi: British Museum.

Inc. (Eva sola):
Quam pessime de posteris egi meis,
Et de genere toto humana miserrima,
Seducta Diaboli persuasionibus. . . .
Expl. (Eva loquitur):
Nunc ingrediar expectatura mariti reditum, et filios
Monitura ad nova munera recte exequenda, quae imposuit Deus.

Still another dramatic version of Melancthon's fable. Eve mourns after the Fall. Cain increases her grief by refusing to let her wash him for a festal day, and by threatening his brothers. While she is scrubbing the other boys, Abel and Seth, God pays a call, accompanied by angels. Dirty Cain hides in the hay. The clean boys are praised and Cain, who is dragged out, insults God, and is blamed. As a result, God ordains different ranks for mankind, based on merit. God promises his aid to the pious and retires to heaven. The "theophany" is over.

The author was born in 1532 at Schellenecker and died in 1592 at Leipzig.

PL-143. (English)

Googe, Barnabe (tr.). _The Zodiake of Life_ by Marcellus Palingenius. (Translated from the Latin, 1560-1565. Reprinted in Scholars' Facsimile Reprints, New York, 1947.).

Inc. My minde with fury ferce inflamd of late I know not how,
Doth burne Parnassus hils to see, adournd with Laurel bow . . .
Expl. Through every country (thou alive) and realmes of sundry fame
Go passe, and seeke in every place to blase abroade my name.

This free translation from the Latin of Palingenius (cf. PL-110) became perhaps "the most popular astronomical poem of the English Renaissance". (F. R. Johnson, _Astronomical Thought in Renaissance England_, 1937).

PL-144. (French)

Sceve, Maurice. _Microcosme_. ca. 1562 A.D. Accessible in _Oeuvres Poetiques complètes_, ed. by Bertrand Guegan, Paris, 1927.

Inc. Le vain travail de voir divers pais
Aporte estime à qui vagabond erre . . .
Expl. Universelle paix appaisoit l'univers
L'An que ce Microcosme en trois livres divers
Fut ainsi mal tracé de trois mille, et trois vers.

A poem of 3,003 lines, in heroic verse, arranged in three books: (i) the Fall; (ii) a dream vouchsafed to Adam concerning the future of mankind; and (iii) Adam's narration of his vision to Eve as a source of hope. Its merits are encyclopaedic rather than narrative. Maurice Scève (1500? - 1564) was the leader of a Lyonnese group of writers who developed a literary theory of love from Platonic and Petrarcan sources.

PL-145. (English)

<u>The Storye of the Temptacion of Man in Paradyce, beyng therin placyd, and the Expellynge of Man and Woman from thence. Dated 1565. Privately printed, Norwich, England</u>, 1856.

<u>Inc</u>. (Deus Pater loquitur):
I am Alpha et Homega, my Apocalyps doth testyfye,
That made of nothinge for man his sustentacion;
And of this pleasante garden that I have plante most goodlye
I wyll hym make the dresser for his good recreacion. . . .

<u>Expl</u>. (Adam loquitur):
Therfor, myne owne swett spous, withouten cavylacion
Together lett us synge, and lett our hartes reioyse
And gloryfye ower God wyth mynde, powre and voyse. Amen.

The second version of the pageant of the Grocers of Norwich (PL-112) differs almost entirely from the first, being not simply an expansion to over twice its length, but a substantially new poem. They have in common the lie of the Serpent that he is a messenger from God. Whereas the first, however, ends with grief over the Expulsion, the second closes with joy over the promise of the atonement.

PL-146. (Latin)

Strasburgus, Jacobus. <u>Hypotyposis divini judicii contra lapsum hominem</u>, <u>in Orationes duae carmine heroico scriptae</u>. Leipzig, 1565. Mi: British Museum.

<u>Inc</u>. Flebile iudicium coeli, primosque parentes
Iusticia damnante reos, caussamque secutae

Mortis, et autorem nostrae dominumque salutis
Dicere conamur . . . .

Expl. Dirige conantem, facilesque in pectora motus
Frigida, divinis, lucis dator, injice flammis.

A discourse of some 800 Latin hexameters, delivered in the Academy at Leipzig on April 21, 1565, for the edification of the young students. It describes a debate in Heaven in the presence of God, in the course of which Justice and Mercy argue for and against the destruction of Adam and Eve, following the Fall.

*PL-147. (Italian)

Alfani, Antonio. La battaglia celeste tra Michele e Lucifero. 1568.

PL-148. (English)

Lyndesay, Sir David. The Monarche. Copenhagen, 1568.

Inc. Musing and maruelling on the miserie
Frome day to day in erth quhilk dois incres . . .

Expl. Quhilkis wold not that thare craftynes wer kend,
Latt God be Iuge: and so I mak ane end.

A dialogue between Experience (a priest) and a courtier as to the sad state of the present world. Much of the former's discourse is taken up with the evil fate of "Father Adam" from the time that he was created in "the Campe of Damassene". The metre is iambic pentameter in rhymed couplets. The length is 6,338 lines.

*PL-149. (Latin)

Candidus, Pantaleon. "Lapsus Adae" in Loci communes theologici. (1570).

PL-150. (German)

Stricken, Johann. _Ein geistlich Spiel, von dem erbermlichen Falle Adams und Even._ Eismar, 1570. Mi: Herzog August Bibl., Wolfenbüttel.

Inc. EVA. O Weh meines Elendes gros
Des jammers, und der schweren not . . .
Expl. Würd er denn damit schweigen nicht,
Ein bespotten er darzu krigt.

The edition here quoted from is one issued, sine loco, in 1602, but the title page of the play vouches for its having been performed on March 25, 1570. Its author is also referred to as Strick, Stricker and Stricerius. The drama is described in the prologue as "ein Comedie . . . aus dem Moise", but it is actually only another and still more prolix treatment of Melancthon's fable about the unlike children of Eve. The verse throughout is iambic tetrameter in rhyming couplets.

*PL-151. (German)

Roll, G. _Adam_ (1573).

PL-152. (French)

Saluste, Guillaume de, Seigneur du Bartas. _L'Uranie ou Muse Célèste._ Paris, 1573. Mi: Cornell.

Inc. Je n'estoy point encor en l'Avril de mon aage,
Qu'un desir d'affranchir mon renom du trespas
. . .
Expl. Je te donne ces vers, qui peut estre rendrent
De nostre amitie saincte eternel tesmoignage.

A poem of some 348 Alexandrine lines, arranged in quatrains rhyming abba. It is a tribute to Urania, not as the muse of Astronomy (as commonly found in earlier Renaissance works) but as the muse of sacred verse, revealing the spiritual mysteries of Heaven.

The author, a Gascon by birth and a Huguenot in religion, was not only a poet and a learned man but a soldier and a man of affairs who served as ambassador to England and to Scotland. Like Milton, he added an intimate knowledge of Hebrew and Italian to his mastery of Greek and Latin. The chief formative influences on his poetry were Homer, Vergil, Ariosto and Ronsard. His reputation was less at home than it was abroad, where he was regarded, especially among Protestants, as one of the great geniuses of poetry. His influence on Milton (cf. PL-153, PL-165) was very extensive.

PL- 153. (French)

Saluste, Guillaume de, Seigneur du Bartas. La Sepmaine, ou Création. 1578. Mi: Cornell.

Inc. Toy qui guides le cours du ciel porte-flambeaux,
Qui, vray Neptune, tiens le moitie fraen des eaux,
Qui fais trembler la terre, et de qui la parole
Serre et lasche la bride aux postillons d'Æole . . .

Expl. Ici ia tout nous rit: ici nul vent ne bat:
Puis c'est assez vogue pour le iour du Sabat.

A didactic "epic" of some 7,500 lines in heroic couplets, dealing with the Creation. For a detailed analysis of the paramount influence on Paradise Lost of this poem and its sequel (PL-165), especially through the English translation by Joshua Sylvester (PL-182-3), see George Coffin Taylor's Milton's use of Du Bartas (Harvard University Press, 1934), where hundreds of reminiscences in phrase and concept are traced and classified. Because of these analogies, extensive extracts from Sylvester's version are printed in this volume.

While Du Bartas derives his form chiefly from Homer, Vergil and Ariosto, he draws his subject-matter copiously from George of Pisidia (PL-39),

St. Basil (PL-15) and St. Ambrose (PL-18), as well as from the "Mirror literature" and from the whole tradition of patristic erudition and hexameral speculation. Thibaut de Maisières (op. cit., pp. 39-40) asserts that the very style of Du Bartas is essentially that of St. Basil, and even cites episodes and phrases that have been openly borrowed.

PL-154. (Latin)

Lermaeus, Gabrielis. Gulielmi Sallustii Bartassii Hebdomas. Paris, 1578. Mi: British Museum.

Inc. O Qui flammiferi cursus moderaris Olympi,
Et manibus fraenos tumidarum flectis aquarum
Telluremque quatis . . .
Expl. Hic sperata salus, hic nullus sibilat auster.
Et festa magnum nos luce peregimus aequor.

A rather hasty Latin translation of the epic of DuBartas (PL-153) by a French humanist.

PL-155. (English)

Danaeus, Lambertus. The Wonderfull Woorkmanship of the World ("Englished by T.T.") London, 1578.

Inc. What is naturall Philosophie? It is the true knowledge or discourse concerning the Creation . . .
Expl. Wee give thankes unto God, for that hee hath given us a minde and abilitie to write those things which wee have heere declared.

A philosophical discussion of various aspects of the Creation, what God created first, whether there is a plurality of worlds, why the waters covered all things, the origin of "poysons and hurtfull thinges", and so on.

PL-156. (Latin)

Monin, Joannes Edoardus du. Beresithias, sive Mundi Creatio, Ex Gallico G. Salustij du Bartas Heptamero expressa. Paris 1579. Mi: British Museum.

Inc. Flammiferi rapidos cursus qui flectis Olympi,
Spumea qui tetricae, Neptunus, fraena procellae
Dirigis, horrisonas Cereris qui concutis arces,
Qui nutu Aeolios solvisque premisque clientes
. . .

Expl. Hic iam cuncta favent, placidus stat flatibus aër,
Et cum Sabbata sint, sat longum adnavimus aequor.

Another Latin translation of La Semaine of Du Bartas.

PL-157. (Latin)

Vivarius, Jacobus. Redemptio nostra. Comoedia nova, in qua ostenditur maxime relictos et afflictos esse maiorem consolationem consequutos. Antwerp, 1579. Mi: Library of Congress.

Inc. Hic quotquot advenistis inclyti fide.
Favete linguis: Comicam non fabulam,
Nec ludicram, velut Poëtae plurimi,
Sed misticum vobis damus spectaculum. . . .

Expl. PETRUS. Quod huius est incommodo, vobis lucro.
Cantate Christo gloriam, atque plaudite.

A Latin play, 1320 lines in length, in iambic senarii. In the opening scene a Jew tells a Canaanite about the creation and about the wrath of God against guilty mankind at the time of the Flood, but hopes that mercy and salvation may yet come. In the course of the play, angelic messengers gradually divulge the coming of the Christ. The Creation story insists on the orthodox making of all out of nothing by fiat.

PL-158. (Portuguese)

Camoes, Luiz de. Da creaçao e composicao do homem. Ca. 1580. Read in Obras (Lisbon, 1861), iii, 267-324. Ph: Columbia.

Inc. Na mais fresca e aprazivel parte do anno,
A Venus dos antigos dedicada . . .
Expl. E a lingua em fim se me apegue à garganta.
Se eu nao louvar e amar merce tao santa.

A poem in ottava rima, in three cantos, totalling 1664 lines. It is laboriously descriptive and homiletic, and has little narrative interest. Canto I: In a pleasant April, the poet is shown by a spirit the making of man, distinguished from the brutes by his intellect and soul. A description of Eden. Canto II: All the ancient world's most glorious works of architecture and art cannot compare with the wonder created by God when He made the human body. The poet summarizes the anatomy of the body under an allegory of architectural terms. This body, though beautiful, is mortal. Canto III: The princess (i.e., the soul) who inhabits the palace (i.e. the body) is subject to death; but there is salvation in the blood of Christ.

PL-159. (Italian)

Tasso, Torquato. Gerusalemme Liberata. Ferrara 1581. Mi: Yale.

Inc. (Bk. IV). Tutti i Numi d'Inferno à se raccoglie
L'Imperator del tenebroso Regno . . .
Expl. (Bk. IV). S'ancor chi per GIESV la spada cinge,
L'empio ne' lacci suoi tal' hora stringe?

Tasso's romance of Christian chivalry parallels Paradise Lost largely in the Council of the devils in Hell portrayed in Book IV. His wicked angels, however, have been diabolized into foul and fantastic shapes and lack the heroic lineaments of the fallen host in Milton's opening books. Their forerunners are probably to be found in Vida (PL-109).

PL-160. (English)

Bartholomaeus Anglicus. Batman vppon Bartholome, His Booke De Proprietatibus Rerum. London, 1582. Mi: Harvard.

Inc. The Father, the Sonne, the holy Ghost, be three persons by personal properties, but the absolute properties be common to all three persons . . .
Expl. That is the high God, gloriously living and reigning evermore without end. Amen.

An encyclopedic work, comparable to Caxton's Mirrour of the World but on a much vaster scale, running to nineteen "books" and many hundreds of chapters. The whole of the second book is given over to a description of the several angelic orders, with their natures and properties.

The edition of 1582, here cited, gives the following explanation of its provenance: "Barthelmew Glantuyle descended of the noble familye of the Earles of Suffolke, he was a Franciscan Frier, and wrote this worke in Edward the Thirds time, about the yeare of our Lord 1366. In the year 1397, 31 years after, was this sayd worke translated into English and so remained by written Coppie; until Anno Domini 1471, at which time printing began first in England, the 37 yeare of the raigne of King Henri the 6. sithence which time this learned and profitable worke was printed by Thomas Barthekt, the 27 yeare of the reigne of King Henrie the 8. which was the yeare of our Lord God 1535. And last of all augmented and enlarged, as appeareth, for the commoditie of the learned and well disposed Christian, by me Stephan Batman, professour in Divinitie, and printed by Thomas East, Anno 1582."

*PL-161. (Italian)

Verallo, Giacinto. _La guerra degli angeli_.

*PL-162. (Latin)

Parifioli, Lorenzo. _De creatione Mundi_.

*PL-163. (Latin)

Henaeus, Andreas. _Satanomachia_.

PL-164. (French)

Du Monin, Edouard. _L'Uranologie, ou le ciel, contenant, outre l'ordinaire doctrine de la Sphaere, plusieurs beaus discours dignes de tout gentil exprit_. Paris, 1582. Mi: British Museum.

Inc. Au plus ardant midi de mon ieune prin-tems
I'oi braquer maint canon contre mes passe-tems . . .
Expl. Soit au cercueil, Ô Dieu, mon corp mis en depos,
Pour par si douce mort gaigner si dous repos.

A mediocre work on astronomy, intermingled with much literary lore in the Bartassian tradition.

PL-165. (French)

Saluste, Guillaume de, Seigneur du Bartas. _La Seconde Semaine_. 1584. Mi: Cornell.

Inc. Grand Dieu, qui de ce Tout m'as fait voir la naissance,
Descouure son berceau: monstre moy son enfance . . .
Expl. Triomphe de toy-mesme, et, denot, brave et sage,

Confirme de mes vers l'eternel tesmoignage.

In this unfinished but extremely lengthy sequel (16,000 lines) to La Sepmaine (PL-153), Du Bartas goes on to versify the Fall and the subsequent history of sinful mankind through the ages. Parallels are especially evident with Books IX, XI and XII of Paradise Lost. As compared with Milton's poem, Du Bartas' work is formless and pedestrian but it marks a convergence of all the numerous elements in the hexameral tradition and enjoyed a phenomenal influence in most of the countries of Western Europe, with scores of translations and imitations.

PL-166. (Spanish)

Hera y dela Varra, Bartholome Valentin dela. Repertorio del mundo particular de las Spheras del Cielo, y de las significaciones correspondientes a su luz y mouimiento. Madrid, 1584. Ph: Biblioteca Nacional, Madrid.

Inc. Estando Dios gozando de la gloria de su deydad, en si mesmo como agora la tiene . . .
Expl. pues el que tuuiere necessidad deste punto sabra buscale por otra via, sin esta regla.

A prose work on the universe, especially in its astronomical aspects. It begins with a prayer to God for strength and illumination. The first section deals with "La creacion de quatro substancias, siendo las primeras las dos del Cielo Angelico". Length 254 pp.

PL-167. (Italian)

Valvasone, Erasmo di. L'Angeleida. Udine, 1590. (A reprint of 1825 is in the Harvard College Library.)

Inc. Io canterò del ciel l'antico guerra,
Per cui sola il principio, e l'uso nacque . . .
Expl. Così disse Michele, e dalle pure

Ciglia di Dio refulse un chiaro lampo,
Che gli die segno del divino assenso,
E tutto il Ciel fu pien di gaudio immenso.

One of the most important of the minor analogues of Milton is "The epic of the angels", by the Italian poet Valvasone[1]. This is an epic written in ottava rima, arranged in three cantos and totalling 2,982 lines. Canto I announces Valvasone's theme as the war in heaven. All was calm and joyful in the universe until Lucifer broke the peace by wishing to usurp the throne of God. As war is impending, Nature appeals to the Deity against the coming destruction. The divine Justice foretells the Fall of Man, the confusion and pain of earth, and much future history. The opposing forces array themselves. Lucifer proudly addresses his followers, while the faithful express their devotion to God. Canto II brings on the main battle. The wicked angels are diabolized into hideous shapes, with beaks, horns, wings, hooves and tails. The forces of Lucifer invent cannons and gunpowder. Michael arranges his army in the form of a cross. The climax of the battle comes in single combat between Lucifer and Michael. After the victory of the latter, the evil spirits are cast down into Hell. In Canto III, the defeated rebels decide to establish a new kingdom in the lower world. Michael and the victorious army are welcomed back into Heaven. The poem closes with a sonnet in honour of Michael.

Some Italian critics (e.g. the Abate Angelo Feruglio, in an edition of 1825) have attempted to identify *L'Angeleida* as "the source" of *Paradise Lost*.

---

[1]Erasmo di Valvasone (1523-93) was the son of Modesto, lord of the castle of Valvasone. His first literary works were translations into Italian verse of the *Electra* of Sophocles and the *Thebaid* of Statius. His first original poem was one on hunting, *La Caccia*. In 1580, he published four cantos of an unfinished Arthurian epic, *Tavola rotonda*, with Lancelot as its hero. His last and greatest poem, *L'Angeleida*, was published at Udine in 1590.

This is obviously an excessive claim for a poem that deals with only one phase of Milton's great theme. There are, however, a number of passages in which there are such marked similarities of treatment as to make it very likely that Milton knew Valvasone's work and drew on his memories of it in drafting certain parts of his own poem. No other analogue except the *Adamus Exsul* of Grotius exhibits so many points of resemblance. Some of the more relevant passages are given above in translation.

*PL-168. (German)

Quiting, Arnold. *Kinderzucht*. Dortmund, 1591.

Cited by Johannes Winzer, op. cit., as borrowing heavily from Sachs's treatment of the unlike children theme.

PL-169. (Italian)

Tasso, Torquato. *Le sette giornate del mondo creato*.

Inc. Padre del Cielo, e tu del Padre Eterno
Eterno Figlio, e non creata prole,
Dell' immutabil mente unico parte . . .
Expl. Così ragiona 'l mondo. E sorda è l'alma,
Che non ascolta i suo' rimbombi, e'l canto,
E seco non conguinge'l pianto, e i preghi.

This product of Tasso's broken last years is little more than a pedestrian versification of St. Basil's *Hexameron* (cf. PL-15), with additional borrowings from Ambrose and other Fathers. Thibaut de Maisières (*op. cit*., p. 55) finds specific borrowings from Du Bartas as well. The total poem runs to 8,808 lines of blank verse. It is chiefly interesting as demonstrating, much more crudely than most, the contribution of the Greek and Latin Fathers to the hexameral poetry of the 16th and 17th centuries.

PL-170. (Latin)

Thuanus, Jacobus Augustus Aemerius. Parabata vinctus, sive triumphus Christi, Tragoedia. Paris, 1595. Mi: British Museum.

Inc. PROL. Per multa veteres seu poetae seu sophi
Finxere amoenis involuta fabulis . . .
Expl. Iustam infelix iusti experior
Iudicis iram.

This is a full-length Latin drama, modelled on the Prometheus Vinctus of Aeschylus (ex Aeschylo novata vel parodia) but with Lucifer as the fettered "transgressor". The Archangel Michael is somewhat reluctant to bind his old comrade, but is goaded into the task by Justice. The Greek chorus of sea-nymphs is replaced by one of angels. The captive Lucifer in the depths of Hell is interviewed in turn by Job, Moses, Elijah, John the Baptist and the Archangel Gabriel. This last warns the angelic Chorus to leave betimes, lest they be caught unawares in the impending terrors of the Harrowing of Hell, and the play ends with Lucifer admitting the justice of his punishment.

*PL-171. (Latin)

Mollerus, Fredericus. De creatione et lapsu angelorum. 1596.

The author (b. 1528) died in 1567 as rector of the gymnasium at Danzig.

PL-172. (English)

Sabie, Francis. Adams complaint. London, 1596. Mi: Huntington.

Inc. New formed Adam of the reddish earth,
Exilde from Eden, Paradice of pleasure . . .

Expl. Fight manfully, trust in the promisd seed,
And be most sure thou shalt arrive the port,
Port full of joy and heavenly blessedness,
Free from all cares, and worldly wretchedness.

A poem of 86 six-line stanzas, rhyming ababcc, and setting forth the grief of Adam after the Fall. He rebukes himself for his own pride and folly and deplores the blood and suffering that have overtaken the living things of Earth.

PL-173. (English)

Middleton, Chrystopher. The Historie of Heaven: Containing the Poeticall fictions of all the starres in the firmament: gathered from amongst all the Poets and Astronomers. London, 1596. Mi: Bodleian.

Inc. When from a chaos of confused things
Was framed the compasse of this christall skie,
The subject which my home-borne muse now sings,
Though farre unfit to reach a note so hie . . .
Expl. So was the first world blest with heavenly favours,
And the last curst with painfull hellish labours.

A sequence of 124 six-line stanzas, expounding the astronomical and mythological lore of the heavens.

PL-174. (English)

Spenser, Edmund. "An Hymne of Heavenly Love", in Fowre Hymnes. London, 1596.

Inc. Loue, lift me vp vpon thy golden wings,
From this base world vnto thy heauens hight,
Where I may see those admirable things,
Which there thou workest by thy soueraine might . . .
Expl. Th' Idee of his pure glorie, present still
Before thy face, that all thy spirits shall fill

With sweet enragement of celestiall loue,
Kindled through sight of those faire things
aboue.

A poem of 287 lines (41 stanzas in rime royal) expounding the theme of Paradise Lost in brief compass. Here is the creation of the Angels, their fall to Hell through pride, the lapse of their successor, Man, and the miracle of atoning Love that descends to suffer and redeem the lost. This poem (printed in full on pp. 87-95) figures largely in Edwin Greenlaw's argument[1] that Spenser was a primary influence in the shaping of Milton's work. It is worth noting, however, that many of the alleged Spenserian originals could have been borrowed from Du Bartas by both Spenser and Milton.[2]

PL-175. (Latin)

Zanchi ("Zanchius"), Girolamo. De operibus Dei intra spatium sex dierum creatis opus. 2nd ed., Hanover, 1597. Mi: Harvard.

Inc. Quae duae sunt priores Christianae Theologiae partes . . .
Expl. ad gloriam Dei, & ad salutem Electorum, planum, ut confidimus, perspicuumque faciemus.

An encyclopaedic work, running to 1,081 double-column pages, devoted to a detailed discussion of all conceivable questions arising out of the Creation as described in Genesis. Thus Part I, Bk. IV, is devoted to the theme "De Angelis malis".

[1] Studies in Philology, XIV, 196-217; XVII, 320-359.

[2] George C. Taylor, Milton's Use of Du Bartas (Cambridge, 1934), pp. 25-37.

PL-176. (English)

Fairfax, Edward. Godfrey of Bulloigne: or the Recoverie of Jerusalem. London, 1600. Mi: Yale.

Inc. (Bk. IV). Sathan his feends and sprites
assembleth all,
And sends them foorth to worke the
Christians woe . . .

Expl. (Bk. IV). Since these true champions of the
Lord aboue
Were thralles to beautie, yeelden
slaues to loue.

The standard Elizabethan version of Tasso's Gerusalemme Liberata is that by Edward Fairfax. For comment on the original see PL-159.

PL-177. (Italian)

Peri, Giovandomenico. Il Caos: overo la guerra elementale. Circa 1600. Mi: Biblioteca Nazionale, Firenze.

Inc. Canto il primo moto, e la cagione
Di questa immensa machina del Mondo . . .

Expl. Fal nell' orrenda ed' oribil mistura
Fran l' alti Eroi campion della Natura.

The author of this poem (cf. also PL-193 and PL-194) was born in 1564 at Arcidossa, diocese of Chiusi, the son of a poor peasant family. His education was limited and he remained a rustic poet to the end of his days. His first major effort, here listed, was a hexameral poem in five cantos of ottava rima, written to glorify God's part in the creation of the world. Creation is represented as bringing peace out of the warring chaos of the elements:

Ond' al celesti' segno ultima guerra
Bolle; e cade nel' Centro l' ampia Terra.

Tradition has it that he decided in 1600 to go to

Florence with his poem beneath his arm, but that he was vilely received by everyone and never got within a hundred yards of Prince Cosimo dei Medici, the patron that he sought.

A special study of the works of Giovandomenico Peri in his possible relation to Milton is being undertaken by Miss Molly Mahood, of St. Hugh's College, Oxford.

PL-178. (Latin)

Grotius, Hugo. Adamus Exsul. Tragoedia. 1601. Ph: British Museum.

Inc. SATHAN. Sacri Tonantis Hostis, Exsul patriae
Coelestis, adsum! Tartari tristem specum . . .
Expl. ADAM. Labor! dolorque! et cumulus instantis mali!
Vos ite mecum! tristis exsilii duces!

This adolescent drama by Grotius (Huig van Groot) was so poorly thought of by him that he did not include it in his collected works. The translation given above (pp. 97-220) is based on a photostat of a rare copy in the British Museum Library. It is not a great literary work, in spite of its undoubted vitality and freshness. Structurally, there are five acts, preceded by a brief prose argument and divided by lyrical choruses. The metre of the dialogue is the iambic senarius, or, in modern terminology, blank verse in Alexandrines, a measure used with effective freedom by Robert Bridges in his Testament of Beauty. The choruses, sung by guardian angels, are in various metres - anapaestic, sapphic, asclepiadean, and the like. The dramatis personae are limited to Satan, Adam and Eve, an angelic mentor, and the Voice of God. Of these, the most convincing character is Eve, whose self-possession and resolute courage after the extent of their disaster is revealed, are in pleasant contrast to the frenzied panic of her husband. "No one is so far lost", she urges, "that he should not still hope for deliverance." That Milton should have been familiar with the play is rendered externally probable by his personal acquaintance with Grotius, whose guest he was in Paris in 1638.

Internal evidence is convincing. After eliminating those elements which both might have drawn from *Genesis*, we find certain features in *Adamus Exul* that are woven into the ampler pattern of *Paradise Lost*:

(i) Satan's arrival in Eden after his flight from Hell; his prospect of the Garden; and his soliloquy in terms of hatred and revenge.
(*A.E.*, Act I, *P.L.*, BK.IV.)

(ii) An angel, sent as mentor to Adam, discusses with him the details of Creation and of the heavenly bodies. In *Paradise Lost* this angel appears as Raphael; and the warning with regard to Satan, implied in Grotius, is expanded at some length.
(*A.E.*, Act II, *P.L.*, BK.V.)

(iii) There is a chorus of angels on duty in the Garden. These are merely vocal in Grotius, but take part in the action in Milton's epic.
(*A.E.*, *passim*; *P.L.* Bk. IV, lines 776 *ad fin.*)

(iv) Satan, having entered into the serpent, approaches Eve with alluring coils of colorful splendor. He accosts her, and argues at great length the advantages of her eating the fruit. In his successful argument in *Paradise Lost*, there are possible echoes of Grotius, e.g. "Or is it envie, and can envie dwell in heavenly breasts?" (*Tanta quae menti sedet invidia?*) Even these passages may, however, represent only natural parallels in arguments necessarily similar.
(*A.E.* Act IV, *P.L.* Bk. IX.)

(v) Adam consents to eat, out of passionate love for Eve. Guilt is later followed by despair, complaint, and violent counsels. These are ended by divine intervention.
(*A.E.* Act V; *P.L.*, Bks. X-XII).

The debt of Milton to Grotius appears to be general rather than specific. This seems the more natural when we remember that when Milton began serious work on his great epic in 1658, he had already been blind for six years. As has been pointed out by Christopher Charles Love, however, in his *The Scriptural Latin Plays of the Renaissance and Milton's Cambridge Manuscript* (Typed MS. of doctoral thesis, University of Toronto), there are marked parallels between the careers of the two men. Each wrote a poem on Adam (*Adamus Exsul* and *Paradise Lost*), a poem on Christ (*Christus patiens* and *Paradise Regained*), and a poem on an Old Testament character (*Sophompaneas* and *Samson Agonistes*) with autobiographical overtones; each wrote a Latin work (*De Veritate Religionis Christianae* and *De Doctrina Christiana*) setting forth his theological position; each was a Christian humanist, a rationalist and an Arminian; and each played a considerable part in public affairs. That Milton, twenty-five years the younger, should have taken Grotius as a sort of Renaissance model is at least a plausible sort of theory.

*PL-179. (Latin)

Lernutius, Janus. *De creatione mundi*. 1603.

PL-180. (Latin)

Taubmannus, Fredericus. *Bellum Angelicum*. Leipzig, 1604. Mi: Newberry.

Inc. Bella per aetherios dicam civilia campos:
Ut stetit hinc Michael, illinc Draco Miles in armis . . .

Expl. Tympana tenta tonant! Taratantara rauca fragorem
Horrificum ingeminat! . . .

This is an unfinished epic, breaking off abruptly in line 72 of Book III. It contains many familiar concepts. Lucifer is described as beautiful beyond the rest of the angels. The revolt is provoked by the exaltation of the Son. At the end of Book I, Satanas, a lieutenant of Lucifer is preparing an ambush to catch the army of loyal angels unawares, but the beginning of Book II, like the beginning of Milton's Book VI, finds the armies of Heaven alert and well informed: "Clam Satanas sua furta putat; scit totus Olympus." There is likewise an interchange of challenging speeches between Michael and Lucifer (*alias* Draco).

The author (1565-1613) was professor of poetry at Wittenberg.

PL-181. (Italian)

Soranzo, Giovanni. *I duo primi Libri dell' Adamo*. Genoa, 1604. Mi: *British Museum*.

Inc. L'Innocenza perduta, ed Adamo io canto,
Che seminò nel mondo con la moglie,
Che fù prima cagion de nostro pianto . . .
Expl. E l'effesa a Dio fatta, e'l ben perduto
Membrò gran tempo in suon flebile, e muto.

A poem in *ottava rima* on the Fall of Man. It comprises two *books and runs* to approximately 1440 lines. The style is sometimes rather precious. The sun, for example, becomes "il sommo Argo Celeste", and the devils are "Tartarei Numi". The treatment, however, is on the whole traditional, with considerable space given to the enmity. Book I begins with a brief summary of the Creation, with its climax in the fashioning of Eve. Then follows the Temptation and the Fall. Book II tells of the condemnation of the guilty pair and their expulsion from the Garden.

PL-182. (English)

Sylvester, Joshua. Du Bartas His Divine Weekes and Workes. Composed 1592-1604. The first complete edition is dated 1608.[1]

Inc. Thou glorious Guide of Heav'n's star-glistring motion,
Thou, thou (true Neptune) Tamer of the Ocean
. . .

Expl. Excell thy selfe; and, brave, grave, godly Prince,
Confirm my Song's eternall Evidence.

This huge work runs to some 23,500 lines in heroic couplets, or more than twice the length of Paradise Lost. It was through this English translation of Du Bartas that John Milton became early acquainted with the French epic of Creation and the Fall. It is significant, for example, that in 1621 the book-seller, Humphrey Lownes, a close friend of the Milton family, brought out, in Bread Street, a few steps from the home of the 15-year-old John Milton, an edition of Sylvester's Du Bartas and that Spenser and Sylvester were at this time his favorite poets.[2] George Coffin Taylor has made a monumental analysis of the correspondences between Sylvester's text and that of Paradise Lost. He even notes[3] one entire line that has been carried over verbatim from line 45 of The Divine Weekes to line 373 of Paradise Lost, Book III:

Immutable, Immortal, Infinite.

There is a second such borrowing, not noted by Coffin, namely

---

[1]Cf. George Coffin Taylor, Milton's Use of Du Bartas, p. 7, footnote.

[2]Cf. David Masson, The Life of Milton, I, p. 89; H. Ashton, Du Bartas en Angleterre, p. 239.

[3]Taylor, op. cit., p. 71.

And thou, O moon, i' th' vale of Ajalon, which is transferred from Week II, Day III, Part IV of The Divine Weekes to line 266 of Paradise Lost, Book XII.

Extracts embodying the most striking parallels between the two poems are printed above (pp. 47-79).

PL-183. (English)

Sylvester, Joshua. Urania, Or, The Heavenly Muse. Same provenance as PL-182. Text of 1641 Folio.

Inc. Scarce had the Aprill of mine Age begun,
When brave desire t'immortalize my Name . . .
Expl. Where, your great worth, and my good-will
shall stand
Inrowld for ever with Urania's hand.

The standard English translation of PL-152.

PL-184. (Italian)

Murtola, Gasparo. Della creatione del mondo. Venice, 1608. Mi: Univ. of Michigan.

Inc. Di nulla il Ciel creato, e gli Elementi,
E l'Huom primiero, e la Natura io canto,
Alhor, che d'Oro il Sol raggi lucenti
E la Luna spiego d' Argento il Manto . . .
Expl. E sottile, e leggiero in ogni loco,
Comme viua passar Fiamma di Foco.

A poem in the heavy didactic tradition of Du Bartas's La Semaine and Tasso's Mondo Creato, to both of which he pays tribute in his preface. He describes his own work as "poema narrativo, e non epico". One might claim that it is not even narrative but merely expository. Its classical parent is the Georgics and not the Aeneid. It consists of sixteen cantos, written in Alexandrine lines in ottava rima. Totalling 12,240 lines, it is considerably longer than *Paradise Lost*.

The sixteen cantos treat of the following themes: Canto I: The creation of light and of the angels, the war in heaven. Canto II: Description of the elements and of fire, air, echoes, water, lightning, comets, etc. Canto III: Seas, rivers, lakes and islands. Canto IV: The earth, mountains, valleys, continents and countries. Canto V: Praises of Italy, Rome, Liguria, Piedmont. Canto VI: Praises of the earth, including precious stones and gems. Canto VII: Description of plant life, trees, loves and hates of plants, plant perfumes, the fig-tree and the vine, praise of wine. Canto VIII: Praises of grain and flax, gardens, melons, roses and rural life. Canto IX: The fixed stars, the zodiac, the various constellations, the Milky Way, the planets, the sun, moon and tides. Canto X: Fish, whales, dolphins, squids, shells, the invention of purple dye, etc. Canto XI: Birds, concluding with the Phoenix and its funeral rites. Canto XII: Higher animals, horse, elephant, bull, etc., and their characteristics. Canto XIII: Serpents, basilisks, spiders, mosquitoes, snails, ant armies, crickets, cicadas, the republic of the bees. Canto XIV: The creation of Adam, described in minute anatomical detail, ending with the brain and its attributes (common sense, fancy, reason, memory and the soul). Canto XV: The earthly paradise, the state of innocence, the display of all the animals, the creation of Eve, praises of marriage, Eve and the apple, Adam's sin, their flight from Eden and subsequent misery. Canto XVI: God's providence, the order of nature, predestination, death, hell and judgement.

The least pleasant feature of the poem is Murtola's unbounded flattery for his patron, the Duke of Savoy, and all his house. In Canto I, for example, his anticlimax to a long and eloquent description of the angels is to turn to Prince Thomas, son of the Duke of Savoy, and tell him that he has the eyes and forehead of an angel ("D'Angelo hai gli occhi, e d'Angelo la fronte"). In Canto II, he turns aside from Castor and Pollux to celebrate the return from

Spain of the princes Vittorio and Filiberto of Savoy. In Canto V, his panegyric on Italy ends with "Lodi del Sig. Duca di Savoia, suo Signore". Or again, in Canto VI, a passage in praise of pearls shifts to a eulogy of the princess Margherita of Savoy.

Murtola has unflagging metrical facility but no narrative interest and no power of dramatic imagination. For example, the Fall, in Canto XV, is scarcely dramatized at all. Eve is moved by pride and perverse will to take the apple and the motivation is vaguely referred to the guile of a serpent, but there is no conversation recorded between the two and it is not even clear that the serpent puts in an appearance.

> The woman saw the apple, that it was
> Most beautiful and marvellously charming;
> On it she turned her gaze in mute applause;
> Nearer she walked with recklessness alarming;
> Its rosy radiance did not give her pause -
> To try its sweetness did not seem like harming.
> Alas, she stretched her hand to pluck the fruit!
> What will, o fool, makes you so resolute?
>
> Eve, stay your hand! What are you doing, Eve?
> Do you not see, alas, you are beguiled
> By serpent stealth, eternally to grieve
> Because your will is impious and wild?
> To match yourself with God - would you conceive
> A plan so furious and so defiled?
> And by what frail excuse can you begin
> To justify so terrible a sin? (Stanzas 51, 52).

Milton owes nothing to this poem.

PL-185. (Italian)

Passero, Felice. L'Essamerone, overa l'opera de sei giorni. Venice, 1609. Mi: Univ. of Chicago.

Inc. La bell' opra di lui, che gia di nulla
Il Ciel sublime, l'ampia terra, e quanto

Il giro e'l grembo lor nutre, è raccoglie . . .
Expl. Pur la lode sia tua, ch' à te si debbe,
Si l'inchinai, ma se dall' opra Ei cessa
La stanca mente ancor prenda riposo.

A copious imitation of Du Bartas's La Sepmaine in Italian verse by a monk of Monte Cassino. It is didactic rather than epic in quality.

PL-186. (French)

Gamon, Christofle de, La Semaine ou Création du monde contre celle du Sieur du Bartas. Paris (?), 1609. Mi: British Museum.

Inc. Toy qui du Ciel doré tends la courtine ronde,
Qui mis le Monde au jour, qui mis le Jour au Monde,
Qui peux à un seul clin d'oeil escrouler l'Univers,
Et soustiens sans soustien ses estages divers
. . .
Expl. Mon ame, à qui l'Espous dans le Jardin de vie,
Fonde un beau pavillon d'eternelle verdour,
Y loge de pensée, attendant l'heure et l'heur
Que des gluans mortels, despestré, je desloge,
Pour voler au Repos où Christ fonde ma loge.

A Catholic counterblast to the Huguenot poem of Du Bartas. It runs to 8,228 lines in heroic couplets.

PL-187. (Spanish)

Caxes, Juan. Auto de los dos primeros hermanos. First printed in Revue Hispanique, Paris, 1901, pp. 139-160, from an autographed manuscript, dated 1610, in the Biblioteca Nacional, Madrid.

Inc. PROVIDENCIA. El terrenal paraiso
es este, do el mismo Dios
que daros vida y ser quiso . . .
Expl. MUSICA. en el valle del llanto,

de ella saldra triunfante el justo y santo.

This is a mystery play in verse, rhymed in quintains. Its peculiarity is that all characters except Adam, Eve, Cain and Abel are personifications. Providence, in Eden, warns Adam not to eat of the fruit of the Tree. Guilt and Envy (not Satan or a serpent) plot successfully against the pair, and they are driven out of the Garden. Adam has a reassuring dream. Abel's offering is preferred to Cain's, and Cain murders his brother. Enter Death, with scythe and crown. Justice and Providence sentence Cain.

PL-188. (Italian)

Marini, Giambattista. La Strage degli Innocenti. Venice, 1610. Book I, "Sospetto d'Herode".

Inc. Musa non piu d'Amor cantiam lo sdegno
Del crudo Re, che mille Infanti afflitti . . .
Expl. Pianti le trombe; i suoi destrier son due
Pigri animali, un Asinello, un Bue.

The original of Crashaw's version (PL-231), chiefly notable for its description of an infernal council in Hell.

PL-189. (Spanish)

Anonymous. Misteri de Adam y Eva. Appendix to Altes und Neues aus Spanien, by Julius Freiherr von Minutoli, Berlin, 1854, vol. ii, pp. 221-231.

Inc. DEU: Puix ya he creat los cels y la terra,
lo sol, la lluna, ab lo firmament . . .
Expl. ADAM Y EVA: Domine Deus noster, in te
sperantes non despicies.
Eruisti nos ex inferno inferiori.

A naive miracle play, covering the creation and the Fall.

PL-190. (English)

Fletcher, Giles. Christ's Victory in Heaven being Part I of Christ's Victory and Triumph. London, 1610.

Inc. The birth of Him that no beginning knew,
Yet gives beginning to all that are born . . .
Expl. So down she[1] let her eyelids fall, to shine
Upon the rivers of bright Palestine,
Whose woods drop honey, and her rivers skip
with wine.

Some 85 eight-line stanzas (ababbccc) present a debate in Heaven, in the presence of God, between personified Justice and personified Mercy. The poem is thus a partial analogue of the debate in Heaven in P.L., Book III, although in form and content it rather anticipates the interminable arguments in Salandra's Adamo Caduto.

PL-191. (Cornish)

Jordan, William. Gwreans an bys. Written before 1611. Edited by Whitley Stokes, Berlin, 1863.

Inc. DEUS PATER: Ego sum Alpha et Omega
heb dallath na dowethva
pur wyre me ew . . .
Expl. ny ve udn mabe dean sparys
menas noy y wreag hay flehys.

A mystery play, running from the Revolt of Lucifer to the Flood, written in Cornish in 1611 by William Jordan. The MS. ends "Heare endeth the Creacion of the world with noyes flude wryten by William Jordan: the XII of August 1611." Stokes, in his preface, states, however: "We may remark that the author imitates and often copies the ordinale called 'Origo Mundi', which stands first in

[1] Mercy.

Mr. Norris's Cornish Drama. Some parts, however, are his own; for example the fall of Lucifer and his angels, Cain's death, Enoch's translation, Seth's prophecy, and the erection of the pillars. Who the author was remains uncertain. The William Jordan mentioned at the end may well have been only the transcriber, and the occurrence in the stage-directions of such forms as sortis, beastis, every ch-on 'every one' and car(i)eth 'they carry' seems to indicate a date prior to 1611, when Jordan completed his manuscript."

PL-192. (English)

(Savile, Thomas). Adams Garden. A Meditation of thankfulness and praises unto the Lord, for the return and restore of Adam and his posteritie: planted as flowers in a garden, and published by a Gentle-man, long exercised and happilie trained in the schoole of God's affliction. London, 1611, Mi: Bodleian.

Inc. Oh my most mercifull Lord, who hast enforced my returne, after my running away from thee . . .

Expl. thou sustainedst thy hell heere, the fathers wrath, agonies and bloudie sweate, that I might appeare in Thy presence blamelesse and without spot, to the praise of thy everlasting grace, for evermore Amen.

A devotional work, 28 pages in length, adequately described by the title.

PL-193. (Italian)

Peri, Giovandomenico. Adamo cacciato del Paradiso. Before 1612. Mi: Biblioteca Nazionale, Firenze.

Inc. PECCATO. Questo crin rabbieffato, questa Carn' Squalida, e negra mia, questo Serpente . . .

Expl CORO. Donque vechi Mortali

Ergete al Ciel per trovar Pace l'Ali.

Another play by the rustic poet Peri, amounting to some 3,120 lines in largely unrhymed verse. It may conceivably have been influenced by Andreini, but never shakes itself free from the morality play tradition. The prologue is spoken by Sin. Adam's soul appears as a speaking character before its incarnation in Adam, and his guardian angel is also on hand. In addition to the principals (Adam, Eve, God the Father, Lucifer, the Serpent), there are numerous personifications: Innocence, Felicity, Life, Death, Guile, Fraud, and Envy, along with choruses of angels and demons and an Avenging Angel. There is apparently a tradition that this play and PL-194 were acted in Florence at the theatre of the Court at roughly the same time as Milton's visit, but the matter is hard to certify. Miss Mahood cites E. Lazzareschi's footnote reference to Francesco Trucchi, _Poesie Italiane tradite_, 1847, vol. iv, pp. 194 et seq., but has not been able to check. In some ways this play seems closer to Milton than is Andreini's play, e.g. in its characterization of Lucifer, its quiet close and its verse, but its dramatis personae are farther than Andreini's from the Cambridge MS.

PL-194. (Italian)

Peri, Giovandomenico. _La guerra angelica: tragicommedia celeste_. Before 1612. MI: Biblioteca Nazionale, Firenze. (MS - Magliab. VII. 273).

Inc. Di colà, dov' in Trono ampio, e sublime
Siede di Dio l'onnipotenza eterna . . .
Expl. CORO. In te raggio di vita
Si speuri ogn' alma a tè restand' unita.

This is a five-act play dealing with the revolt of the angels. That it is wholly in the morality play tradition is shown by the dramatis personae. With the exception of Lucifer and Michael, almost all are personifications: Pride, Envy, Wickedness, War, Discord, Ingratitude, Peace, Concord, Power, Providence,

Vigilance, Prudence, Divine Vengeance and Divine Justice (Astraea). There is a chorus of faithful angels and another of wicked angels. At the beginning of Act V, Astraea tells how she has sealed all of the evil rebels in Hell.

PL-195. (Latin)

Husanus, Henricus. "Elegia de Angelis" in *Delitiae Poetarum Germanorum* part III, pp. 586-617. *Frankfurt, 1612. Mi:* London Library.

Inc. Nunc de spiritibus, primi sub fine libelli,
Pauca, sed e multis optima lecta, canam.
Expl. Quicquid erit, placide superabimus omne ferendo:
Cui Deus auxilio est, huic onus omne leve est.

About 930 lines in elegiac couplets. Not an elegy in theme, but a treatise on angels written in elegiac verse. The first part deals with the Fall of the Angels and the Fall of Man.

The author was born in 1533 at Eisenach and died at Luneburg in 1587.

*PL-196. (German)

Ketzel, Wolfgang. *Lapsus et reparatio hominis. Ein geistlich Spiel von Adams und Evas betrübten Jammerfall*. Schmalkalden, 1613.

Only known copy in the Staatsbibliothek, Berlin (Soviet sector), and report in 1947 as inaccessible. Johannes Winzer, *op. cit.*, describes it as plagiarized almost entirely from Balthasar Schnurr's German translation (1597, 1607) of Nicolaus Selneccerus's *Theophania* (PL-142).

PL-197. (Italian)

Andreini, Giambattista. L'Adamo. Milan, 1613.

Inc. PROL. A la lira del Ciel Iri sia l'arco,
Corde le Sfere sien, note le Stelle . . .
Expl. ANGELI. Primavera gioconda
Le promette nel Cielo il gran cultore
Piagato, ferito, avvampato, infiammato
Fulminato per l'uom d'eterno amore.

Andreini's Adamo has little that is based on the Genesis-story except the actual Temptation and the expulsion from Eden. The stage is monopolized by spiritual personalities and personifications, and Adam and Eve spend long pages in tedious discussion with the Seven Deadly Sins, and with the World, the Flesh, and the Devil. An alleged parallel with Paradise Lost is found in the dialogue (Act I, scenes 3-6) where Satan, Lucifer (the two are distinct), Beëlzebub, and other evil spirits approve of the proposal to seduce mankind by means of the forbidden fruit. There is little conceivable resemblance, however, to the "great consult" of Paradise Lost. The discussion in Adamo is an informal one, held in the Garden of Eden; there is virtually no characterization or dramatic value; and there are no obvious correspondences in language.

For over two centuries, many Italian scholars have regarded Andreini as a martyr from whom a great but wicked Milton stole his Paradise Lost. An a priori argument sometimes adduced in favor of Milton's knowledge of Andreini, is the fact that there exists in the library of King's College, Cambridge, Milton's draft outline of a tragedy on the theme of Paradise Lost, made in 1641-42, soon after his return from Italy. The hasty assumption is therefore that he had just read Andreini's drama or had seen it acted; but the argument is inconclusive. On this same European journey, he had, as we have noted, been the congenial guest of Grotius, an English translation of whose passion play, Christus *patiens*, by George Sandys in 1640 was an event of some literary importance. According to F. E. Schelling (*Elizabethan Drama*, I, 44), Milton was himself then busy on an English translation of George Buchanan's Latin tragedy on *John the Baptist*, which he published in 1642. The dramatic interest had, moreover, predominated thus far over the epic in his work, as *Arcades* and *Comus* bear witness, although there had intervened, in his Latin epistle to Giovanni Manso, the recorded project of an Arthurian epic.

Those who regard Andreini as a source for Milton point out that all four variants of the King's College draft provide for allegorical personifications comparable to those in *L'Adamo*. This argument, however, is not conclusive. Thus the mute personifications of Sin, Disease, Famine and Death, on which its proponents lay great stress, are addressed as present phantoms by Adam in Act IV of *Adamus Exul* and need not have been borrowed from Andreini. On the other hand, the abstractions given speaking parts in Milton's draft, viz. Conscience, and Faith, Hope, and Charity, are not in Andreini at all, and seem to be Milton's own invention. His suggested titles, "Adam Unparadised" or "Adam's Banishment", are obvious equivalents for *Adamus Exul* by Grotius; and virtually every correspondence cited in favor of Andreini can be deduced from the earlier Latin play.

Giambattista Andreini (1578-1650) is chiefly interesting on his own account. His father and mother were both actors of note and he himself was an actor and a man of letters. He is regarded as the chief Biblical poet in 17th century Italy and was the author of upwards of thirty plays. His *L'Adamo* has great interest as an analogue and is mostly notable for the ways in which it differs from *Paradise Lost*. Thus there is no account of the Creation, except that of Adam and Eve, which takes place on the stage; there is no divine messenger and no description of Hell; and the devils, instead of being "archangels ruined", are uncouth monstrosities with cloven hooves, snaky hair, and the beaks and talons of eagles.

PL-198. (English)

Ralegh, Sir Walter. The History of the World. London, 1614. Mi: Harvard.

Inc. God, whom the wisest men acknowledge to be a Power ineffable, and Virtue infinite; a Light by abundant clarity invisible . . .

Expl. . . . whose unspeakable and never enough lamented loss, hath taught me to say with Job, Versa est in luctum cithara mea, & organum meum in vocem flentium.

In the tradition of the earlier chronicles by men like Syncellus (PL-43) and Cedrenus (PL-54), Ralegh devotes his first four chapters (pp. 1-71) to the Creation and the Fall. His chapter-headings reveal the character of his disquisition: I, Of the Creation and Preservation of the World; II, Of Man's estate in his first Creation, and of God's rest; III, Of the place of Paradise; IV, Of the two chief Trees in the Garden of Paradise.

PL-199. (English)

Alexander, Sir William. Doomes-Day, or, The Great Day of the Lords Judgement. Edinburgh, 1614.

Inc. Thou of whose Power (not reach'd by Reasons
hight)
The Sea a Drop, we Earth a Mote may call . . .

Expl. And that my Spirit may be refresh'd that way,
It must a space amidst dombe Pleasures stray.

A poem of some 3,760 lines in ottava rima dealing with the Judgement Day. In the first book, there is an extensive treatment of the Fall of the Angels (stanzas 38-56) and the Fall of Man (stanzas 57-71).

PL-200. (Spanish)

Acevedo, Alonso de. Creacion del mundo. Rome, 1615. Mi: Columbia.

Inc. Inspire ardor del fuego inaccessible
En mis versos y estilo el Padre Eterno . . .
Expl. Oh dia de descanso y de dulzura,
Dia alegre, en el cual el gremio santo,
Del enemigo alcanzara victoria,
Y tendra premio de reposo y gloria!

This poem was once regarded as one of the more notable analogues of Milton in the Bartasian tradition. More recent research has shown it to be a wholesale plagiarism from Du Bartas, via the Italian translation by Ferrante Guizone (La Divina sentimana, Venice, 1592). Where Acevedo departs from Guizone's Du Bartas, it is usually to interpolate still other thefts from Tasso's Il Mondo Creato. Full documentation of the case may be found in Thibaut de Maisières, Les Poèmes Inspires du Debut de la Genese a l'Epoque de la Renaissance, pp. 61 et seq. James Fitzmaurice-Kelly insists[1] that "the Spanish Catholic has avoided the verbal extravagances of the Gascon Huguenot, has improved the framework and added many descriptive passages of considerable beauty"; but this judgement probably mistakes as original the plagiarisms from Tasso.

PL-201. (Latin)

Mellius de Sousa, Joannes. De miseria hominis deque reparatione humana carmen. Lisbon, 1615. Accessible in Corpus Illustrium Poetarum Lusitanorum qui Latine scripserunt. Lisbon, 1745. Mi: British Museum.

---

[1]A New History of Spanish Literature, Oxford, 1926, p. 342.

Inc. Quis satis humani casus miserabile damnum
Expediet? Variis quae foeta doloribus et nos
Heredes primae teneant contagia culpae . . .
Expl. Sicut enim Dominum, famuli, vidistis euntem,
Sic iterum veniet, justissimus Arbiter orbis,
Omnibus aequa suis factis ut praemia reddat.

This Latin epic of some 8,600 hexameter lines is comparable to Paradise Lost in its dimensions. At the same time it offers a most significant contrast to Milton's epic, both in theological emphasis and in structural plan, and would repay detailed comparative study in these terms.

Whereas Milton, the Puritan humanist, is concerned primarily with man and the problem of free will issuing in an evil choice, Mellius de Sousa, the Catholic, is almost wholly taken up with the dogma of divine grace manifested in the Incarnation and the Atonement. For the Portuguese poet, the central figure in the epic is not Adam but Christ - with his Virgin Mother continually in the background.

The plan of the epic follows largely from this emphasis. Books I and II, "De Miseria Hominis", are a preliminary discourse on the deadly consequences of the Fall and the horrors of Hell: "Sulphureis Cocytus aquis, puteusque profundus, ignis ubi sine luce." Action proper begins with Book III, "De Lapsu Adae" and here too comes the clear statement of his typically Catholic argument and his appeal for divine inspiration:

> Quae genus humanum tulerit dispendia vitae
> Vipereis illata dolis, foecundaque Virgo
> Germine Divino reparavit alma, canamus.
> Te supplex, Aeterne, voco, te deprecor o qui
> Ardua non linquens, mortales induis artus
> Virgine clausus Homo, lux o clarissima Coeli,
> Nos arcana doce, primaeque exordia causae . . .

This book gives an idyllic picture of Eden, harmonious with the songs of the nightingale, the swan and the phoenix. Disease and pain are unknown.

The scene then shifts to a Council in Hell, where Satan delivers a speech from the throne. The infernal plot issues in the Temptation and Fall of Man. In Book IV (as in Paradise Lost, Book X) Satan goes back to Hell and exultingly reports to the Council of Hell that he is the victor. There are bloody sequels on earth in the death of Abel and the rise of war. From this point on, Mellius de Sousa and Milton part company. Books V and VI deal with the conception and the birth of the Virgin Mary, and Books VII and VIII with the Incarnation and the Birth of Christ. At this point a "Shepherds' Eclogue" is introduced and a Book dealing with the visit of the Magi. Books X, XI and XII tell of the Crucifixion, the Resurrection and the Ascension of Christ. From the plan of the poem, the hexameral Creation story and the War in Heaven have been omitted as major episodes. The Council in Hell is the only fully developed action anterior to the Temptation. One's impression from the last eight Books is that Mellius de Sousa is interested in the fall of Adam and Eve only as a convenient reason for the ultimate manifestation of the Divine Love.

PL-202. (French)

D'Aubigné, Agrippa. "Au désert" in Les Tragiques. Paris, 1616. Mi: Bibl. Nationale, Paris.

Inc. Ouvre tes grands thresors, ouvre ton sanctuaire,
Ame de tout, Soleil qui aux astres esclaire
Ouvre ton temple sainct à moy, Seigneur, qui veux
Ton sacré, ton secret enfumer de mes voeux:

Expl. Ores aux derniers temps et aux plus rudes jours
Il marche à la vengeance et non plus au secours.

A poem on the vengeance of God on evil. It expatiates at some length on the story of Cain and Abel.

PL-203. (Italian)

Laparelli, Marcantonio. La Cristiade, poema heroico. Rome, 1618.

Inc. Vorrei del mio Signor l'opre leggiadre,
Cantar con alto stil soave, e grato . . .
Expl. A te mi tira, ond' io resti sepolto
In te nel grembo al mio Giesù rascolto.

This poem of 16,000 lines of ottava rima, organized in 24 books, differs from the Christiads of Vida, Ross, Clarke and Mellius de Sousa in starting with the Incarnation rather than with the Fall and in invoking the latter only incidentally rather than as a structural element in the epic.

PL-204. (English)

Peyton, Thomas. The Glasse of Time in the First Age. London, 1620. Mi: Harvard.

Inc. The author first, doth Gods assistance crave,
Throughout the worke that he his help may have:
The sacred Sabbaoth, Satans envious gall,
The woman fram'd, and mans most dismal fall . . .
Expl. Of all the world hath sung the first beginning,
Told Adams faults and Eves offensive sinning
Their seede defac't in breaking of thy lawes,
And heere I'll stay, and sit me downe and pause.

This is a poem of about 2450 lines in heroic couplets, subdivided into strophes of varying length. Less than one-third of the "epic" is devoted strictly to the story of the Fall. The rest is given over to incessant divagations into history and theology, with harangues against Roman Catholics and "Puritants". Its author, Thomas Peyton (1595-1626), was educated at Cambridge and at Lincoln's Inn. A single copy of his original edition survives in the British Museum, but his works were reprinted in New York in 1886.

PL-205. (English)

Peyton, Thomas. The Glasse of Time in the Second Age. London, 1623, Mi: Harvard.

Inc. Urania soveraigne of the muses nine
Inspire my thoughts with sacred work divine
Come down from heaven, within my Temples rest,
Inflame my heart and lodge within my breast . .
Expl. Meane time deare Muse, with Noahs sacred Pile,
Let us but stay and rest ourselves awhile.

This is a sequel to PL-204. It runs to 2,900 lines and carries human history from the Fall down to the Flood. Peyton describes the apocryphal wanderings of Adam and his penitential stand in the Ganges:

Until his flesh from top to toe was seene
With cold and froath, all overgrowne with greene.

Eve meanwhile had been wandering in Nubia and the two meet again in Arabia. Cain is drawn to murder by the horrid spirit Medusa, not unlike Sin in Milton:

Whose cursed hair about her shoulders falls,
Powdered with Serpents full of poisoned galls,
Hissing and crawling round about her head,
Hatched by a viper in her wombe that bred . . .
(vv. 65-67).

PL-206. (Latin)

Valmarana, Odorico. Daemonomachiae: sive, de Bello Intelligentiarum super Divini Verbi incarnatione, libri XXV. Sine loco, 1623. Mi: Bibl. Centr. Naz., Florence, Italy.

Inc. Ausa manus superum summo certare parenti
Carmen erit, totumque genus mortale coactum
In caedes, horrenda malo quo foedere Ditis . . .
Expl. Delitias superum, ridentes carpere flores
Et senium renovare meum longumque per aevum.

This lengthy epic in Latin deals with the

continued Revolt through the ages of the wicked Angels against the Incarnate Word. Its author was a priest of Vicenza, Italy. His treatment differs greatly from that of Milton. Thus instead of naming his devils after pagan deities, he gives Greek names to the Seven Deadly Sins in diabolical form: Typhoeus (Pride), Plutus (Avarice), Asotus (Lechery), Laemurgus (Gluttony), Tisiphonus (Wrath), Phthonerus (Envy), and Acedus (Sloth), and adds Pantolatria (Superstition), Philarchus (Ambition) and Micropsicus (Pusillanimity). The original warfare in Heaven, ending in Lucifer's defeat, is covered in Book I. Michael is a leading warrior but the Almighty Word finishes off the battle. Then follows presently Lucifer's fatal visit to Eden, where Michael had been assigned as guard and mentor:

> Haec Michael (Hominum generis cui credita cura est)
> Mandarat novisse Hominem praesagia Veri.

Here Michael judges the guilty pair but also protects them from the warlike violence of Hell. The Book ends with Uriel, with drawn sword, guarding the gates of the forfeited Garden.

PL-207. (Portuguese)

Rolim de Moura, Francisco Child. Os novissimos do homem. Poema em Quatro Cantos. Lisbon, 1623. Mi: Columbia.

Inc. Eu que cantei profanos pensamentos,
Memorias em meu damno eternisadas . . .
Expl. Aonde vê que só chorar peccados
Sao gostos cá na vida bem fundados.

A narrative poem of 2,856 lines in ottava rima, planned in four cantos entitled Death, Judgement, Hell and Paradise respectively. In Canto I, an infernal Council is held in Hell to discuss plans against mankind. After a speech by Satan, the evil spirits set out for Earth. The temptation, fall and expulsion from Eden are traditional in treatment. In Canto II, Adam is moved by a vision of the Crucified Christ and of the Last Judgement. In Canto III, he is conducted through Hell, Limbo and Purgatory by the ghost of his son Abel. As only Abel has yet died, the sheer emptiness of the dread realm is felt as devastatingly awful. In Canto IV, Adam is consoled by a final vision of Paradise.

All this is somewhat reminiscent of the _Book of Enoch_, chapters 17-22, in which Enoch is conducted through Hell by Uriel; but the author is more probably influenced directly by Dante. Child Rolim de Moura (1572-1640) was a Portuguese of good family and classical education.

PL-208. (Spanish)

Vega Carpio, Lope de. _La creación del mundo y primera culpa del hombre_. Madrid, 1624. Mi: Univ. of Chicago.

Inc. SAN MIGUEL. Qué atrevidos pensiamentos,
Loco, revolviendo estás?
Nos ves que con ellos das
Precipicio á tus intentos?
Expl. ADÁN. Esta es, Senado, la historia
De aquel antiguo pecado,
Primera culpa del hombre,
Principio de males tantos.

A verse drama, in various metres. It is organized in terms of three days, each with its own characteristic action: Day I, the Creation of the World and the sin of Adam; Day II, the murder of Abel; Day III, the death of Cain at the hands of Lamech. These three actions are unified by the conception of Adam's original sin and its consequences. Saint Michael is the only representative of Heaven throughout, and Luzbel is the only devil. The play opens effectively with a sharp interchange between these two. Michael challenges the presence of Luzbel in Eden, and the latter says that he has come to admire the view.

PL-209. (English)

Stradling, Sir John. Divine Poemes. London, 1625. Mi: Huntington.

Inc. The Theame propos'd, the heav'nly ayde implor'd:
Mans fall. Messias of the Womans seede
promis't, by whom Mankinde should bee restor'd
. . .

Expl. Affects to be perspicuous and plaine,
Shunning of purpose an heroike vaine.

This is a discursive religious poem of nearly 9,000 lines in 6-line stanzas. The exposition at the beginning of Book I shows, as has been noted by Dr. Malcolm Ross of Queen's University, some resemblance to Milton's exordium in the pattern of ideas into which obvious phrases from Du Bartas are assembled, thus implying that Milton "found in Stradling the skeleton upon which to shape the scattered Du Bartas material" (Huntington Library Quarterly, xiv, 2, pp. 129-140).

PL-210. (Latin)

Fletcher, Phineas. Locustae, vel Pietas Jesuitica. Cambridge, 1627. Mi: Harvard.

Inc. Panditur Inferni limen, patet intima Ditis
Ianua, concilium magnum, Stygiosque Quirites
Accitos, Rex ipse nigra in penetralia cogit
. . .

Expl. Carmina diffundet fluvio; coelum audiet omne,
Audiet omne nemus: resonabilis accinet Eccho.

836 lines of Latin hexameters. Describes a council in hell, addressed by Lucifer, in rage at the peaceful spread of Protestantism, especially in England. He vows undying hatred against God, and finds apt allies in the Roman church and above all in the Jesuits. The poem ends with a summons to the ruler of England to oppose the Romanists. In the

debate there is only one other speaker, Equivocus by name.

PL-211. (English)

Fletcher, Phineas. *The Locusts or Apollyonists*. Cambridge, 1627. Mi: Harvard.

Inc. Of men, nay Beasts: worse, Monsters; worst
 of all,
 Incarnate Fiends, English Italianat . . .
Expl. Thus shall thy name in Earth and Heaven
 renowne,"
 And add to these three here, there a thrice
 triple crowne.

Bound under the same cover with *Locustae*, but with separate title-page. Not strictly an English translation of the Latin poem, but an English improvisation on the same theme of a Council in Hell, addressed by Satan and by Equivocus, as head of the Jesuits.

PL-212. (Dutch)

Cats, Jacob. *Gront-Houwelick, dat is: Beschryvinge van d'eerste bruyloft, gehouden in den Paradijse tusschen Adam ende Eva, eerste voor-ouders aller menschen*. Amsterdam, 1627. Mi: Harvard.

Inc. Op, droeve Sinnen, op. Waerom aldus geswegen?
 Waerom soo langen tijdt in uwen rouw gelegen?
Expl. Hoe vreemt is uw bedrijf! hoe wonder uw beleyt!
 Uw lof zy hoog geroemt tot in der eeuwigheyt!

A poem of 1044 lines in heroic (Alexandrine) couplets, being the opening instalment of a poem of some 30,000 lines on the history of human matrimony. It is given in the framework of a pastoral dialogue between Philogamus, a bachelor, and Sophroniscus, an aged widower. Philogamus reads his new poem, describing the beauty of Eden, the creation of Adam and Eve, their amorous conversation, the idyllic peace among the conjugal beasts in Paradise and finally an epithalamium sung by the angelic hosts.

PL-213. (English)

Fletcher, Joseph. The Perfect-Cursed-Blessed Man. London, 1629. Mi: Harvard.

Inc. Whenas by cursed disobedience
Man first did fall from perfect innocence . . .
Expl. To save my soule, Lord Jesus no time spend,
Spend, though to 'gin that time, Time cannot end.

A poem of 1518 lines in heroic couplets. Its plan is as follows:

(a) The argument.
(b) "The Author's Preamble upon it." (Appeal to God for inspiration.)
(c) Part I. "Man's Excellencie by his Generation." Largely a quasi-psychological discussion of creation and the nature of human personality.
(d) Part II. "Man's Miserie by his Degeneration." The story of the Fall and of its consequences.
(e) Part III. "Man's Felicitie Consulted-of." A debate in Heaven, by such personified elements as Pity, Mercy, Justice, Wrath and Reason. God approves of their assent to Man's redemption.
(f) Part IV. "Man's Felicitie Procured." A summary of the birth, life, death and resurrection of Christ.

Joseph Fletcher (1577-1637) was probably educated at St. John's College, Cambridge, and became rector of Wilby in Suffolk in 1609.

Other books with comparable divisions were written by Henry Holland (Historie of Adam, 1606), Henry Arthington (Principal Points of Holy profession touching these three estates of Mankind, etc., 1607), and William Smith (New Creation, 1641); but none of these can be classed as literary analogues of Milton.

PL-214. (English)

Austin, Samuel. _Austins Urania, or The Heavenly Muse_. London, 1629. Mi: Huntington Library.

Inc. I that had sate neere famous Isis shore
The space of twice twelve moones, and somewhat more . . .
Expl. And to the Lambe for euermore: Till when,
Cease not to pray, _Lord Jesus, come_. Amen.

A poem of some 5,000 lines in limping iambic pentameter couplets, aptly described by their author as "The heauie plunges of my sorry Muse." Book I deals with the Fall of Man and Book II with his Redemption; but the style is homiletic and hortatory rather than narrative.

PL-215. (Latin)

Gazaeus (Angelin Gazet). "Lacrymae Adami" in _Pia Hilaria_ (1631), pp. 261-263. Ph: London Library.

Inc. Immortalitatis eram, morboque impervius omni,
Hoc fortunatus nomine Iustus Adam. . . .
Expl. Disce Adam, vosque o venturi discite nati,
Quam nocuit subdi non voluisse Deo.

A poem in elegiac couplets, in which Adam, shortly after the Fall, tells the story of his offence and laments the evil consequences of disobedience. The most vivid hardships are those suffered from insect life: "It is sultry. I sit down under a cone-bearing terebinth. A fly smites me on the forehead with his stiff beak. . . . I who was formerly lord of earth and prince over beasts and (as even Heaven is my witness) almost a god, am harassed by a stinging wasp or the snout of a mosquito - so speedily have they come to hate the face of their prince. O lion, what will you not dare;

O bear, how will you not rebel; when a vile fly wages such wars against me?"

PL-216. (English)

Fletcher, Phineas. The Purple Island, or The Isle of Man. Cambridge, 1633.

Inc. The warmer Sun the golden Bull outran,
And with the Twins made haste to inne and play . . .
Expl. With Lilies set, and Hyacinths around;
And Lord of all the yeare, and their May-sportings crown'd.

A poem that combines the pastoral form of the Shepheardes Calendar with the allegorical tradition of the Faerie Queene. In its twelve cantos, shepherds rehearse the creation and spiritual destiny of mankind. That its range of subject-matter parallels much of that in Paradise Lost will be evident from the extracts printed above (pp. 277-284): The more obvious comparisons concern the invocation of divine help (P.I., VI, 24-27; P.L., I, 1-26), the discourse on psychology (P.I., VI, 41 et seq.; P.L., V, 100-113), and the figures of Sin and Despair (P.I., XII, 27-32; P.L., II, 648-670; cf also the figure of Error in Spenser's Faerie Queene, canto I).

PL-217. (Latin)

Ramsey, Andrew. Poemata sacra. Edinburgh 1633. Mi: Huntington.

Inc. Quae massae dedit orsa rudis vis diva creatrix,
Distribuitque locis, discludens Nerea terris,
Visque opifex eadem ut sinuatis orbibus orbés
Arcuat, et coeli camerat fastigia summa . . .
Expl. Tandem etiam iudex sontes lachrymabilis Orci
Addicet tenebris, nos coeli luce beabit.

This is a poem of about 1,600 hexameter lines,

divided into four books, as follows: Book I, the Creation; Book II, man's innocence in Eden, with an encomium on marriage; Book III, the Fall of Man; and Book IV, the redemption of man through Christ. The range of Ramsey's theme is comparable to Milton's, but his plan is less artistic, and the scale of his work much smaller.

Andrew Ramsey (1574-1659) was a Scottish divine, educated at St. Andrew's and in France. At Edinburgh he became professor of divinity and rector of his college.

PL-218. (English)

Heywood, Thomas. The Hierarchie of the blessed Angells. Their names, orders and offices. The fall of Lucifer with his Angells. London, 1635. Mi: Harvard.

Inc. Inspire my Purpose, favour mine Intent,
(O thou All-knowing and Omnipotent)
And give me leave, that from the first of daies,
I (Dust and Ashes) may resound thy praise . . .

Expl. And in thy Kingdome hoping for abode,
Freely surrender
Our Soules and Bodies. Whilest we live, when die,
Protect us with thy heav'nly Hierarchie.

This volume of over 600 pages deals in prolix detail with all the traditions of Christianity concerning the angels, both good and bad. It is organized in nine books, one for each celestial order as follows: I, Seraphim; II, Cherubim; III, Thrones; IV, "Dominations" (Dominions); V, Virtues; VI, Powers; VII, "Principats" (Principalities, Princedoms); VIII, Archangels; IX, Angels. Each book deals in verse (heroic couplets) with aspects most relevant to its order, and is supported by observations in prose and a final "meditation" in verse.

The sections most interesting to readers of

Paradise Lost are the classification of celestial beings in Book IV, the primacy and rebellion of Lucifer in Book VI, and the character of the demonic government in Hell in Book VII. Quotations are given above (pp. 287-290).

Thomas Heywood (1570-1641), educated at Cambridge, was probably the most prolific of all the Shakespearean and Jacobean dramatists. His didactic poem on the angels is notable for quantity rather than for quality.

PL-219. (English)

Swan, John. Speculum mundi or a Glasse Representing the Face of the World, shewing both that it did begin, and must also end: The manner How, and time When, being largely examined. Whereunto is joyned an Hexameron, or a serious discourse of the causes, continuance, and qualities of things in Nature; Occasioned as matter pertinent to the work done in the six dayes of the Worlds creation. Cambridge, 1635. Mi: Huntington.

Inc. The Philosophers of ancient times were diversly transported in the stream of their own opinions, both concerning the worlds originall and continuance . . .

Expl. For then they likewise freedome have,
No longer kept in pain:
Come therefore quickly (Lord) we crave,
Renew this world again:
And in its kinde (it being free)
"Twill praise thy name as well as we.

A lengthy hexameral treatise, discussing in systematic sequence the various questions arising out of the six several days of the Creation. It is one of the best examples of the "Mirror" literature. (Cf. PL-98).

PL-220. (German)

Felgenhauer, Paul. Das Büchlein Adam. Das ist, Offenbahrung des Menschens. Sine loco, 1635. Mi: British Museum.

Inc. Also spricht das Buch der Weiszheit: Alle Menschen seind Eytels die Gott nicht erkennen . . .

Expl. Die Gnade unsers Herren Jesu Christus des Eynigen Gottes und wahren Menschens sey mit Allen denen die seine Erscheinung liebhaben. Amen.

A devotional work, in prose, on man's spiritual destiny as a result of the Fall.

PL-221. (Latin)

Anonymous. "Protoparentum Crimen et Poena".[1] Milan, 1638?

Inc. ADAM. Quocumque fert ocellus,
Tui luminis favillam
Mei Creatoris Numinis,
Sit unda, sive tellus,
Recordor . . . .

Expl. ADAM. Oh virtus magna lacrymae dolentis!
Mollitur Coelum stilla poenitentis.

Published in No. 196 of the Monthly Magazine, London, in 1810, with the following explanation: "The following Latin Oratorio has been copied from an ancient manuscript, found, some years ago, in the library of Marquis Scati at Milan. It was performed for the first time at Milan while Milton was there; and is the famous original so much talked of by the learned, which gave him the hint of his Poem."

---

[1]Photostat supplied through the courtesy of Prof. J. H Hanford, Western Reserve University.

Unfortunately for this assurance of contact with Milton, the performance is dated March 21st ("decimo secundo Kal. Aprilis"), and we know that Milton's only visit to Milan was in late May or early June, 1639, on his way from Venice to Geneva. The entire month of March was spent in Florence, where the extant minutes of the Svogliati club record his presence at meetings on the 17th, the 24th and the 31st. (Cf. Masson, Life of Milton, I, 821-31).

The oratorio consists of 254 lines of rhymed Latin verse. There are three singers: Adam, Eve and Lucifer. In Part I, Adam and Eve indulge in declarations of love and piety, while Lucifer watches them, unseen and unheard. Part II presents the Temptation and the Fall, the Triumph of Lucifer ("Nobis parta est victoria") and the repentance of Adam and Eve ("Oh virtus magna lacrymae dolentis! Mollitur Coelum stilla paenitentis.").

PL-222. (Latin)

Ross, Alexander.[1] Virgilii evangelisantis Christiados libri XIII. In quibus omnia quae de Domino nostro Jesu Christo in Utroque Testamento, vel dicta

---

[1]Alexander Ross (1591-1654). Educated at King's College, Aberdeen. Schoolmaster at Southampton, 1616. Chaplain, circa 1622, to Charles I. He is mentioned in Hudibras, Pt. I, canto ii:

There was an ancient sage philosopher
That had read Alexander Ross over . . .

Milton was clearly indebted to three of Ross's prose works: (i) The New Planet no Planet (1646), on which Milton draws heavily in the dialogue on astronomy in P.L., Book VIII; (ii) his Pansebeia: or A View of all Religions in the World (1653), which Milton follows rather extensively in his catalogue of heathen deities in P.L., Bk. I; and (iii) his annotated translation of Johan Wolleb's Abridgement of Christian Divinitie, on which Milton leaned heavily in his De doctrina Christiana.

vel praedicta sunt, altisona Divina Maronis tuba suavissime decantantur. London, 1638. Mi: Harvard.

Inc. Ille ego qui quondam gracili modulatus avena
Carmen, et Aegypto egrestius per inhospita saxa . . .
Expl. Quod superest, oro liceat dare tuta per undas
Vela tibi, liceat collestem attingere portum.

A poem of approximately 11,000 hexameter lines pieced together in a huge patchwork quilt of actual or slightly adapted passages from Virgil. The source of each line throughout is painstakingly printed in the margin.

PL-223. (Italian)

Loredano, Giovanni Francesco. Adamo. Venice, 1640.

Inc. Apprendi, o Ambitioso, la tua prima origine. . . .
Expl. Mentre tutti i Secoli pagheranno una perpetua pena in riguardo all' errore d'Adamo.

This is a 76-page prose romance dealing with the story of Adam and Eve. Its style is sometimes rhetorical, as when the temperate climate of Eden is described as an "autumnal spring". The author is far from sentimental, however, as he comments thus typically on the hardships endured by Adam during Eve's first pregnancy: "Much less do I wish to tell of Adam's suffering; for obviously, to have a wife, and a pregnant wife at that, is a species of martyrdom." The book was so popular that it had been reprinted fifteen times by 1660.

*PL-224. (Latin)

Molinaeus, Petrus. In symbolum apostolorum hymni tredecim. London, 1640.

These Latin poems by Pierre du Moulin are

alleged to include a striking one on the Creation, embodying the figure of the Holy Spirit as a dove brooding over the Abyss.

PL-225. (Italian)

Malipiero, Federico. L'Eva. Venice 1640. Mi: Firenze, Biblioteca Nazionale Centrale.

Inc. So' ben' io, che devrei con stille di lagrimar rigar la candidezza di questi fogli . . .
Expl. . . . e la piacevole consonanza, che deve tramischiarse nella concordia, ed unione delle di loro volontà.

A prose discourse on the significance of the Fall, with detailed contrasts between Adam and Christ, Eve and the Virgin Mary, etc.

PL-226. (Italian)

Lancetta, Troilo. La scena tragica d'Adamo ed Eva estratta dalli primi tre capi della sacra Genesi et ridotto a significato morale. Venice, 1644. Mi: Harvard.

Inc. (Deus loquitur):
Posciache io creai le Zone del Cielo errante, indi nel seno della terra rude circondai un fiume cavo . . .
Expl. (Cherubim loquuntur):
. . . questo e giorno da notarsi con penello fosco, ò con ichiostro, per esser memorando nella perditione dell' humana salute.

A prose drama of the fall, in which every detail is adapted to the terms of a highly rationalistic symbolism. God is "the rationality that proceeds from a well regulated intellect"; Paradise is "the habit of a tranquil mind"; Adam is "an untutored human spirit with free choice for good and evil"; the Cherub is "minister of Reason for justice"; Eve is "the sensual part, which, when ill controlled, leads man into the Hell of disgrace"; the Serpent is "undue and irrational appetite"; the Devils are "thoughts of concupiscence and anger, at variance with reason and law"; the Angels are "thoughts in harmony with reason and law, acquired by right education"; while the Apple is "the heart of Adam". This somewhat tedious insistence on symbolizing destroys almost all dramatic value in the work.

Among the familiar elements in the play are a council of devils, led by Lucifer, Belial and Satan; the temptation by the Serpent (distinct from Lucifer); and the expulsion of Adam and Eve from the Garden by Raphael.

PL-227. (Latin)

Barlaeus, Caspar. *Paradisus, sive Nuptiae primorum parentum Adami et Evae*. Amsterdam, 1645. Mi: Harvard.

Inc. Humanum genus ex uno, populumque potenti
Prognatum genitore canam, thalamosque faces-
que . . .

Expl. Stellantes depicta sinus, tangensque jacentes,
Omina perpetuo genitalia foedere sanxit.

A Latin translation from the Dutch of Jacob Cats' *Gront-Houwelick* (PL-202). This poem contains a detailed description of the creation of the world and of man. God points out the universal operation of sex in the animal and vegetable world, and feels that Adam must be given a mate. Eve is created. Long speeches follow between bride and groom, Adam with interminable eloquence inviting her to intercourse and she, with equally prolix volubility, concurring in its naturalness. The poem ends with an epithalamium sung by massed choirs of seraphim and cherubim. In it, praise of the Deity culminates in tribute to God as the creator of man and the author of "the laws of the innocent marriage-bed".

Caspar "Barlaeus", or van Baerle (1584-1648), was a prominent Dutch scholar and man of letters, educated at Leiden and Caen.

PL-228. (Latin)

Barlaeus, Caspar. De Creatione Mundi. Amsterdam, 1646. Mi: Harvard.

Inc. Sidera cum terris digestaque corpora mundi,
Claraque ter magni numinis orsa canam. . . .
Expl. Iamque opifex magno dedit intervalla labori,
Et lux inceptis septima finis erat.

Some 140 lines in elegiac couplets, giving a day by day description of the Creation.

PL-229. (Latin)

Barlaeus, Caspar. Adamus Peccans. Amsterdam, 1646. Mi: Harvard.

Inc. Cernite me, me degenerem spectate nepotes,
Principium miserae posteritatis ero . . .
Expl. Ipsaque posteritas fatis innexa parentum
Flagitio debet velle perire meo.

A soliloquy by Adam, in elegiacs, bewailing his guilt and its consequences.

PL-230. (Latin)

Barlaeus, Caspar. Oratio Caini, occiso fratre Abele. Amsterdam, 1646. Mi: Harvard.

Inc. Peccavi, Superum rector, primique parentis
Crimina flagitio deteriore sequor. . . .
Expl. Dum superesse sinor, sinor huic superesse dolori,
Longius ut vivo, longius ut moriar.

In 88 lines in elegiacs, Cain speaks to God

regarding his sin and expresses his sense of long-enduring guilt.

PL-231. (English)

Crashaw,[1] Richard. "Sospetto d'Herode" in Steps to the Temple. Sacred Poems, with other Delights of the Muses. London, 1646.

Inc. Muse, now the servant of soft Loves no more,
Hate is thy Theame, and Herod, whose unblest
. . .

Expl. So much? rude Shepheards. What his steeds? alas
Poor Beasts! a slow Oxe, and a simple Asse.

A very free rendering of Book I of Giambattista Marini's religious epic, La Strage de gli Innocenti (1610). The analogy with Milton lies in the extensive description of Hell, "Belowe the Botome of the great Abysse", and an infernal Council there, Satan's speech of defiance, and the sending of a deadly emissary to Earth. In extracts printed above (pp. 220-226), close verbal parallels may be found to Paradise Lost I, 48, 105 et seq., 542-3, 548-9, 601-2, 653-4, II, 927-8.

PL-232. (English)

More, Henry. "A Platonick Song of the Soul". In Philosophical Poems, Cambridge, 1647. Available in Complete Poems, ed. Alexander B. Grosart, London, 1878. Mi: Harvard.

Inc. Nor Ladies loves, nor Knights brave martiall deeds
Gwrapt in rolls of hid Antiquitie;
But th' inward Fountain, and the unseen Seeds . .

[1]English religious poet, born in London 1613 (?), died in exile at Loreto, Italy, in 1649. Educated at Cambridge, ejected from a fellowship at Peterhouse in 1644. Went abroad and became a Roman Catholic.

Expl. Leave off your dance: For Plotin my dear friend
Thus much I meant my golden harp should sound.

A lengthy series of poems, almost entirely in Spenserian stanzas, dealing with the nature and destiny of the soul. Many of the problems raised in Paradise Lost are discussed here as well, but there is no evidence of influence. A typical extract from the poem "Antipsychopannychia" runs:

Has then old Adam snorted all this time
Under some senseless sod with sleep ydead?
And have these flames, that steep Olympus climbe
Right nimbly wheeled or'e his heedlesse head . . .

More was a younger contemporary of Milton at Christ's College, Cambridge.

PL-233. (Italian)

Salandra, Serafino della. Adamo Caduto, Tragedia Sacra. Cosenza, 1647. Ph: Harvard.

Inc. BONTA. Quell' io, che istupiditi qui mirate;
E l'un curioso si rivolge a l'altro . . .

Expl. BONTA. Con morte mai piu ingiusta, mai più cruda;
Ed in oltre l'addita.
Frà mille morti, sempiterna Vita.

A morality play of 251 numbered pages, plus 18 unnumbered preliminaries. It is the sole known work of its author, a Franciscan friar described on the title-page as "Preacher, Lector and Definitor of the Reformed Province of Basilicata". Two copies are known to exist, one in the Biblioteca Nazionale at Naples and the other in the Library of Harvard College. It is from a complete photostat of the latter that I have worked.

Salandra's play has achieved considerable notoriety through an excited article by Francesco Zicari, "Sulla scoverta dell' originale italiano da cui Milton trasse il suo poema da paradiso perduto" (Album scientifico-artistico-letterario, Naples, 1845, pp. 245-276), which was made current through an article by Bliss Perry, who was in turn quoted in extenso by Norman Douglas in a popular volume *Old Calabria* (New York, Modern Library, 1928, cf. chapter xxi, pp. 213-230, "Milton in Calabria"). Perry, who had handled Salandra's volume in Naples, supported Zicari's identification of it as the one great original on which Milton had based his epic and from which large parts of it were actually translated.

Having not only read Salandra's work several times but translated the entire play into English (printed above in large part, pp. 290-349), I have come regretfully to the conclusion that the Zicari-Perry argument is worthless.[1] Salandra's book was published eight years after Milton had left Italy, at a time when Milton's time was absorbed in public affairs and his eyes, "overply'd in libertyes defence", were soon to go dark. The onus of proof that in the brief remaining interval of sight he drafted out his epic on the work of an obscure fifth-rate Italian poet with whom he had no known contact is surely on those who advance such a theory. Unfortunately for Zicari and Perry, every detail that they seize on as borrowed from Salandra is to be found in many other analogues much more accessible to Milton. Some details go as far back as Avitus, who records, for example, the sad deterioration in Nature that succeeded the Fall.

Worse still, the plot analysis given by Zicari-Perry to show the parallel structure of *Adama Caduto*

---

[1]The spreading ripple of error finally touches the shores of nonsense in the solemn statement of Burton Rascoe (*Story of the World's Great Writers*, 1932, p. 281) that "Milton had stolen the whole scheme of *Paradise Lost* from a little-known Italian contemporary and had translated or transliterated (sic!) passage after passage almost word for word until (sic!) Professor Bliss Perry happened to examine the text of a unique (sic!) copy of *Adamo Canuto* (sic!) by Serafino della Salandra in the library of the University."

and *Paradise Lost* is disingenuous and misleading. For example, the following outline is given of the early part of the play:

"Salandra at the opening of his poem (the Prologue) sets forth his argument and dwells on the creative Omnipotence and his works. The same with Milton. Salandra then describes the council of the rebel angels, their fall from heaven into a desert and sulphurous region, their discourses. Man is enviously spoken of and his fall by means of stratagem decided on. It is resolved to reunite the Council in Pandemonium or the Abyss, where measures may be adopted to the end that man may become the enemy of God and the prey of hell. The same with Milton."

The assumption is that after a brief statement of the argument, one passes to Hell and the Council there. On the contrary, the whole first Act, itself longer than the first three acts of *Macbeth* together, is taken up with tedious morality play discourses of Goodness, Omnipotence, Mercy and the Four Elements, as well as conversations between God and Adam and Eve, and it is not until Act II, Scene 1, at line 1332, that the scene finally shifts to Hell, and there we find, not a solemn "Council" but an ugly squabble between Lucifer and Belial, which ends in Lucifer knocking Belial down and stamping on his face. Anything less like Milton would be hard to imagine. A council is finally called in Act II, Scene 3, but there is no mention of "Pandemonium".

A second example of Zicari-Perry misstatement runs (Douglas, *op. cit.*, p. 216): "Salandra's chief personages are God and His Angels; the first man and woman; the serpent; Satan and his angels. The same with Milton." On the contrary, apart from Adam and Eve the chief speakers in the play are personified Mercy and Omnipotence, while Innocence, Simplicity, Guile, Sin, Death, Life, Goodness and the Four Elements, together with the foregoing probably account for more than half of the dialogue.

Still more misleading is the declaration of Zicari-Perry as to the close of Salandra's drama: "Salandra describes the passion of Jesus Christ and the comforts which Adam and Eve receive from the angel who announces the coming of the Messiah; lastly, their departure from the earthly paradise. The same with Milton." When we turn to the original, however, we find that Adam and Eve are driven out of the earthly paradise in Act III, Scene I, less than half way through the play! There remain 8 scenes in Act III, 12 in Act IV and 8 in Act V, all taking place after the expulsion, even to the death of Cain as an old man (Act IV, sc. 12). In Salandra an announcement as to the Messiah is not made to Adam and Eve by "an angel". The first intimation of it comes from Mercy (Act III, Sc. 6) and the full details are given by God Himself (Act V, Sc. 7).

Details of resemblance were manipulated at every turn by the industrious Zicari. Salandra's Megaera is said to be like Milton's "grisly Terror", threatening Satan. But Megaera is not Death but a mere Fury in Hell; she does not threaten Lucifer but amiably cooperates with him in disciplining his lieutenants; she cuts off Benemoth's tongue and gouges out Belial's eyes; and only at the end of Act III, Sc. 3, places, without warning, a crown of fire on Lucifer's head. Or again, the symptoms of grief in Nature which Zicari assumes to be original in Salandra and stolen by Milton are a commonplace of the long hexameral tradition, going back at least as far as Avitus, and are in any case treated by Milton with complete originality of phrase. Salandra's vacillo la terra means simply "the earth shook"; Milton's phrase "Earth trembled from her entrails" is magnificently his own. Of all Milton's alleged translations from Salandra, there is not one that will hold water for a minute.

Zicari's mare's nest is more understandable when one realizes that his sole standard for comparison with Salandra was Paradiso Perduto (Venice 1818), Rolli's Italian translation of Paradise Lost, and that he has scarcely any inkling of the scores of earlier poets who had dealt with the theme. Neither was he aware of Milton's patristic and rabbinic erudition and the profound acquaintance with several literatures that has been naturally assimilated into the very tissue of his poetry. Salandra's style is sackcloth; Milton's is a Gobelin tapestry; and Zicari cannot tell the difference.

Since, however, Salandra's Adamo Caduto has some intrinsic interest of its own as a belated expansion of the morality play, and since the notorious claims of Zicari, Perry and Douglas call for detailed examination, the play, in major part, will be found above in English translation.

PL-234. (English)

Anonymous. Hell's triennial Parliament, Summoned five yeeres since by King Lucifer. (Oxford ?), 1647. Mi: British Museum.

Inc. Lucifer, God of this World, Prince of Darkenesse, King of Styx and Phlegeton, Lord of Gehenna . . .

Expl. He should be next to Lucifer, in the governing of his Infernall Kingdome. And so the Court adjourned.

This political pamphlet may be taken as typical of a whole genre that in the period 1642-60 was published again and again to represent one's enemies - Royalist or Roundhead - as associated with the Devil in the councils and plots of Hell. The present document is "Signed at our Court of Gehenna, August 30, in the 5666 yeere of our reigne" by "Lucifer Rex", and opens with a long verbatim report of "Lucifers Speech at the beginning of his last Infernall Parliament" Other pamphlets of the same type are A Declaration of Great Lucifer, Prince of the Ayre (Westminster, 1648) and A Discovery of Some Plots of Lucifer and his Council (London, 1656). If Milton's "great consult" were construed politically, it would have plenty of forerunners.

PL-235. (English)

Beaumont, Joseph. *Psyche, or Love's Mystery, in XXIV Cantos: Displaying the Intercourse Betwixt Christ and the Soul*. London, 1648. Mi: Yale.

Inc. Enrag'd at Heav'n and Psyche, Satan laies
His projects to beguile the tender maid . . .
Expl. That She, unable to contain its Tide,
With three deep sighs cry'd out O LOVE, and dy'd.

With its closest affinity to be found in the work of Henry More (cf. PL-232) is this long-winded poetic allegory on the soul. In subject-matter it touches on Milton's theme at many points as in the court in Hell (Canto I, 8), the Dove brooding on the abyss at Creation (VI, 107), the Temptation (VI, 222-259), and Satan's defiant address to the Sun (XVIII, 25). Extracts will be found on pp. 350-357.

PL-236. (French)

Soucy, François du. *Le project du plan de la creation du monde. Ou l'on verra quantite de curiositez inouïes; Et plusieurs merveilles du Paradis terrestre*. Paris, 1653. Mi: British Museum.

Inc. Si je suis assez heureux pour apprendre que ce commencement du Plan de la Création du Monde . . .
Expl. Ainsi que nous ferons voir clairement dans la premier partie de mon *Thresor* de la *vie Humaine*.

An extensive prose analysis of the various theological problems involved in the Creation story - how light is material, why Eve was formed from a rib, why God cursed the earth (and not Adam) for the sin of Adam, and so on.

PL-237. (Latin)

Clarke, Robert. Christiados libri XVII. Completed 1650, published 1670. Mi: Harvard.

Inc. Bis genitum Caeli regem, qui morte perenni
Damnatos, roseo divini sanguinis imbre,
Dite triumphato, tenebrosi e faucibus Orci . .
Expl. In coelum revocate animos: de nomine CHRISTI
Nomen habens, toto surgat gens aurea mundo!

Robert Clarke, a native of London, became a Carthusian monk at Douai in 1620. His real name was Graine. In due time he became professor of poetry in his monastery. He lived in the Carthusian community at Nieuport from 1632 until his death in 1675. His Latin epic, The Christiad, running to 14,000 hexameter lines in seventeen books, is reported by his Order to have been completed in 1650 and published in 1670. While its action opens in the Garden of Gethsemane, the epic then turns back to the Garden of Eden and spends most of Book I in recapitulating the War in Heaven, the Fall of the Angels, the infernal plot that issues in the Fall of Man, the Deluge, and the ultimate machinations of Hell against the Virgin and Christ Himself. Book X describes the death on the Cross, Books XII and XIII, Christ's descent to Limbo and Hell; while Book XVII ends the poem with His ascension to Heaven.

PL-238. (Dutch)

Vondel, Joost van den. Lucifer, Treurspel. Amsterdam, 1654.

Inc. BELZ. Myn Belial ging hene op lucht en vleugels
drijven,
Om uit te zien waer ons Apollion magh
blijven. . . .
Expl. CHORUS. Herstell', verheerelycke, in lichaemen,
en zielen;
Stoffeerende den troon, daer d'Engelen uit

vielen.

Vondel is to the Netherlands what Shakespeare is to England, although in dramatic and poetic rank he is closer to Dryden than to Shakespeare. To quote the late Sir Edmund Gosse: "This venerable and illustrious person, the main literary glory of Holland through her whole history. . . . is the typical example of Dutch intelligence and imagination at their highest development. Not merely is he to Holland all that Camoens is to Portugal and Mickiewicz to Poland, but he stands on a level with these men in the positive value of his writings."

He left behind him thirty-two tragedies in verse, most of them written for the great public theatre at Amsterdam at a time when its European reputation had succeeded to the expiring glories of the London stage. All of them observe the classical unities of time and place and are written on the fixed model of five acts (in Alexandrine couplets, alternating masculine and feminine rhymes), with choral interludes between the acts. They thus give scope for his lyric as well as his dramatic gifts.

The greatest of his dramas is Lucifer (1654), in which, with striking originality and a strength that at times approaches the sublime, he describes the rebellion of the Archangel Lucifer (the Governor of Heaven, under God), following the abrupt proclamation that all the angelic host are henceforth to be ministering servants to Man, God's newly created favorite and destined partner on the throne of heaven. Clear and convincing characterization is given not only to Lucifer but to his lieutenants (the crafty Belial, the gay dare-devil Apollyon, and the fire-eating army colonel Beëlzebub) and to the "loyalist" leaders (Gabriel the glib herald, Uriel the battle-loving squire, Raphael the tender-hearted emissary of God's mercy, and Michael the rigid, unimaginative "brass-hat" Field Marshal of God's troops). The absence of any Scriptural tradition of events left Vondel free to invent situations and motivations at will. The language is vigorous throughout, and in more ways than one. Thus Lucifer, referring contemptuously to Adam as "an earthworm creeping from a clod of clay" and as "a bubble, blown of wind and scum", reminds us that Vondel, in addition to being a dramatist, was the chief satiric poet of his time. On the other hand, something approaching epic power is manifested in Uriel's description (Act V) of the great battle in heaven, where Michael's air force swoops implacably from a superior height upon the air-squadrons of Lucifer. The most obvious parallels with Milton are:

(i) The description of Apollyon's flight, on a journey of reconnaissance through the abysses of space that lie between Heaven and Earth. This resembles in outline, but not in detail, the flight of Satan across the gulf of Chaos. (*Luc*. I, 10 et seq.; *P.L.* V, 266 et seq.).
(ii) The elaborate description of the battle in Heaven, culminating in decisive personal combat between Lucifer and Michael. In Milton, this combat ends the first of three days warfare, on the third of which God the Son routs the enemy. (*Luc*. 1708-1981; *P.L.* VI, 56-405.) The details differ in many further respects: Milton's two armies are in two long ranks, Vondel's are in the shape of a half-moon and of a triangle respectively; Milton's armies fight on the level like infantry, while Vondel has Michael's winged forces manoeuvre like an air-fleet for a higher position from which to shatter the enemy; Milton's bad angels in their rout retain something of their angelic attributes, though darkened and blasted, while Vondel's bad angels, as they fall headlong towards Hell, are diabolized into a horrid synthesis of lion, swine, ass, rhinoceros, ape, snake, and wolf.

There are occasional correspondences in phraseology, as where the declaration of Milton's Satan

"Better to reign in hell than serve in heaven"

resembles that of Vondel's Lucifer:

" Better it were below
To be the Monarch of a lesser Court
Than be a servant in the Courts of Light."

The probable relationship between the two poets is carefully worked out by George Edmundson in his Milton and Vondel (London, 1885). That Milton knew Dutch is proven by a letter written by Roger Williams, of Providence, on July 12, 1654, to his friend John Winthrop (given in full in Knowles's Life of Roger Williams, pp. 261-264), in which he states: "The Secretary of the Council, Mr. Milton, for my Dutch I READ him, read me many more languages." In the period 1649-54, moreover, Milton was closely in touch with all events in Holland (a) through his controversies with Salmasius and Morus, (b) through his supervising editorship of Needham's Mercurius Politicus, which had its regular Dutch correspondents, and (c) through his contact with the Hague bookseller, Ulac, who sent him single sheets of Regii Sanguinis Clamor wet from the press. The storm of Calvinist church criticism that forced the withdrawal of Vondel's Lucifer from the Dutch stage after two days in January 1654 - and caused the first edition to sell out almost immediately could not have failed to arouse Milton's keen interest. The scores of parallels that Edmundson finds between Vondel's play and Milton's epic become in most cases, however, less plausible when we consider the full range of prior analogues on which Milton might have drawn; but there are enough close resemblances to make his familiarity with Vondel reasonably assured. Avitus, Valvasone, Grotius and Vondel are the most likely forerunners of Milton's epic work.

Some of the chief interest in Lucifer lies in the overtones with which it is charged. Thus Lucifer can bear comparison with Cromwell, whom Vondel, a Catholic royalist, hated and denounced bitterly. He has also been plausibly compared with Wallenstein, who envied the emperor's son, Ferdinand III (to whom Vondel dedicated the play) of Austria, and coveted the crown of Hungary for himself. Most notable of all, however, are the analogies between the play and the history of the Low Countries, e.g., (a) Lucifer can be equated with William of Orange, God with Philip II, Michael with Alva, and Adam with Cardinal Granvelle; (b) the lion and the dragon that draw Lucifer's chariot are blazoned on the crests of the two provinces, Holland and Zealand, that most supported Orange; (c) the medley of seven beasts into which Lucifer was changed can be assigned to the seven northern provinces that became the Dutch Republic, while the southern provinces, nearly two-thirds of the whole, are the faithful angels; (d) the battle-scene simile of the sea dashing on a rock recalls Orange's motto, "Saevis tranquillus in undis"; (e) the crescent-array of the rebels recalls the slogan of the Water-beggars, "Rather Turk than Papist"; and (f) Lucifer accomplished the fall of Adam, even as the Stadtholder brought about the expulsion of Granvelle. All this is an extra attraction in a play whose primary significance lies in its poetic and dramatic power.

PL-239. (Latin)

Masenius, Jacobus. Sarcotis. Cologne, 1654. Mi: Harvard.

Inc. Principium culpae, stygiaeque Tyrannidis ortum,
Et quae fera premant miserandos fata nepotes
. . .

Expl. Sarcothea aeternum, dignis obnoxia votis,
Serviet, et tanti statuet monumenta favoris.

A work sometimes alleged as a source for Paradise Lost is "the epic of Sarcothea", a Latin poem by Jacobus Masenius, professor of rhetoric and poetry in the college of the Jesuits at Cologne. It consists of 2,486 epic hexameter lines, arranged in five books. Its author does not claim for it the dignity of an epic; and it is rather a sequence of descriptions in the heroic style. In fact, one may say that it is a blend of one part classical epic to two parts of heroic romance in the worst 17th century tradition. Typical of the latter genre is its array of nymphs and warrior-maidens. Even the primal pair, Adam and Eve, are replaced by a single female figure, Sarcothea; for the heroic romance preferred a heroine to a hero as the central character in the plot. Typical, again, is the plethora of personifications, both good and evil

The poem may be summarized as follows: Book I. Sarcothea is the beautiful female embodiment of mankind (Adam and Eve combined). In the Garden of Delights, she is attended by Virtue, Love, Justice, Hope and Reason, all charming female figures. Antitheus (Lucifer as "God's adversary") regards her with envy and resolves to ruin her. He assembles an army of demons, notably Diseases, Old Age, Toil, Poverty, Guile, Hunger and Death, and with them leaves Hell for the Garden. Book II. Guile, disguised as a Cupid-like youth, leads Sarcothea to the Forbidden Tree, where Antitheus lurks in serpent form. Self-love wounds Sarcothea with one of his arrows and Reason urges the advantage of eating the apple. At the moment of Sarcothea's guilty disobedience, Nature suddenly changes for the worse and Devils and Evils everywhere possess the world. Antitheus wishes to carry Sarcothea at once to Hell, but Virtue and Providence fight against him. Justice retires to Heaven; Reason changes her name to Repentance; Love and the other nymphs are wounded and driven out. Wretched Sarcothea barely finds a refuge with Earth, who condemns her to servitude. Book III. Antitheus divides the universe among his devils, who become the pagan gods. Sarcothea, by union with Philautus (Self-love), has seven daughters: Pride, Avarice, Envy, Wrath, Gluttony, Sloth and Lechery. The appearance and character of Pride; her splendid palace with its brittle foundation; her arrogant rule over mankind. Book IV. The life and works of Avarice. Virtue, having tried in vain to reform Avarice, seeks the Garden of Pleasure and makes many converts among the young people there. Book V. Envy and Wrath stir mankind up to war. Here the poem ends abruptly. It is obvious that the pious author intended to provide full length portraits of all the Seven Deadly Sins, but the sketches of Gluttony, Sloth and Lechery were never completed.

Comparison with Milton is most valid in three passages: (i) the opening invocation of Book I; (ii) the description of Eden; and (iii) the warlike speech of the Devil to his hosts (see above pp. 358-360). The opening lines of Masenius bear a striking resemblance to those of Milton in general thought (the declared theme of "Man's First Disobedience" - *Principium culpae*; the appeal for divine inspiration rather than for the aid of the classical Muses; the confidence that "Heav'n hides nothing from thy view"- *omnia namque te ductrice patent*; and the resolve to soar "with no middle flight" - *nimborum domos et fulminis aulam transgredior*); but on the whole the likeness is one of ideas rather than of detailed phraseology. Resemblance is more remote in the other passages.

PL-240. (Italian)

Pona, Cavalier (Fran.) *L'Adamo*. Verona, 2nd ed., 1654. Mi: British Museum.

Inc. Era sù'l di penultimo la Settimana Divina, c' hauea tenuto nello impiego amoroso della universal Creatione tutta la Deità. . . .
Expl. . . . mando fuori lo spirito, e dormi il sonno gelidissimo della Morte.

A somewhat high-flown prose romance, covering the legendary story of the Fall, from the First Sabbath to the death of Adam. Length 61 pages.

PL-241. (English)

Cowley, Abraham. *Davideis*. London, 1656.

Inc. I sing the Man who Judah's sceptre bore
In that right-hand which held the crook before
. . .
Expl. But, lo! they arriv'd now at the appointed place,
Well chosen and well furnish'd for the chase.

This is a scriptural epic on the life of King David. It was originally composed (circa 1637) in

Latin hexameters, of which one book still survives; but he finally published it in 1656 in four books of heroic couplets in English. Its chief claim to be included in the present galley consists of the portrayal of an infernal council in Book I, and the alleged influence of the work on Milton in several minor points. Cowley's Lucifer, however, is crudely melodramatic beside the dark majesty of Milton's Satan.

PL-242. (Latin)

Harderus, Henricus. Epigrammatum Libri Tres. Copenhagen, 1660.

A collection of epigrammatic poems in Latin, dealing with Biblical subjects. Those most relevant here are Book I, No. 2, "Creatio mundi", No. 3, "Lapsus Adami", No. 4, "Hevae mors", and No. 5, "De Caino desperante." The author, Hendrik Harder (1642-1683), was a Danish scholar.

PL-243. (English)

S(amuel) P(ordage) Armig(er)[1], Mundorum Explicatio or, The Explanation of an Hieroglyphical Figure. London, 1661. Mi: Columbia.

Inc. I sing no Hero's douty gests in warrs,
Nor blazon forth some Warlike Champion's
Scarrs: . . .
Expl. But yet accept my Labour and my Pains;
My Heart examine, not my duller strains
For if they any shall with Light befriend
I joy: for that of writing is
THE END.

This 13,000-line didactic epic in heroic couplets expounds the story of Adam and Eve in terms

[1] Esquire.

of a threefold world: external, internal and eternal. Adam began with an angelic nature but he forfeited this when he became more interested in Eve than in God; this earthbound innocence passed on to positive guilt when he broke God's commandment regarding the forbidden fruit. The poem is saturated with speculations on hundreds of matters of theology discussed in the Fathers, the hexamera and the Mirror literature; and Pordage's mere index of such points runs to 16 pages. Along with his theorizing on the spiritual nature of man and the universe goes a great deal of vivid description and narration, e.g. his account of the Temptation and the Fall, and of the subsequent organized march of the Devils to take over the Earth. Of relevance to Milton's similar description in _Paradise Lost_, Book II, is Pordage's narrative of how the sinners in Hell are shifted back and forth between the icy waters of the Styx and the flaming waves of Phlegethon. A striking anticipation of the deceptive Tree in hell in Paradise Lost, X, 547-570, is found in Pordage's infernal Tree of Death (p. 117), on whose branches everywhere vipers crawl, sucking the bitter fruit. Significant extracts are given above (pp. 424-433).

PL-244. (Dutch)

Vondel, Joost van den. _Adam in Ballingschap_. Amsterdam, 1664.

Inc. LUCIFER: Ick, eerst geheilight om de Kroon
van't licht te spannen,
En nu van't eeuwigh licht in duisternis
gebannen . . .

Expl. ADAM. Hier heeft de zomer uit. de winter
Klamptme aen boort.
Godts slaghzwaert volght ons op de hielen.
spoenwe voort.

Vondel's _Adam in Ballingschap_, based, by his own statement, on Grotius's _Adamus Exul_ and dealing with the temptation and fall of man, was never staged during its author's lifetime, owing perhaps to the reluctance of that Calvinistic generation to present Adam and Eve on the stage in their primordial nakedness. Modern Amsterdam, however, has got bravely over these scruples, and a silk-diapered performance in 1900, directed by Dr. Willem Royaards, played for two hundred and fifty nights to crowded and enthusiastic houses.

Although it derives its central conception from Grotius, Vondel's play is essentially a new creation, original in phraseology and characterization and much better adapted to stage purposes. It even approaches opera at the close of Act III, where the Guardian Angels, as they sing, engage in a marriage ballet to which Adam and Eve contribute solo dances. As compared with _Lucifer_, _Adam in Ballingschap_ is much homelier in diction. Not least in interest is the use of many metaphors derived from navigation, naval warfare, and the dykes of Holland. For a careful, but overly optimistic, analysis of Milton's debt to this analogue, see George Edmundson's _Milton and Vondel_, pp. 136-157.

PL-245. (English)

Dryden, John. _The State of Innocence and Fall of Man. An Opera._ London, 1674.

Inc. LUCIFER. Is this the Seat our Conqueror has given?
And this the Climate we must change for Heaven?
These Regions and this Realm my Wars have got;
This mournful Empire is the Loser's Lot. . . .
Expl. RAPHAEL. But, part you hence in peace, and having mourn'd your sin,
For outward _Eden_ lost, find _Paradise_ within.

This is a dramatic poem of some 1480 lines, arranged in five acts and written in heroic couplets except for an occasional passage in blank verse (e.g. Lucifer's soliloquy in Act II) and a few Alexandrines. It was never acted. As to its origins, Dryden himself has stated, in "The Author's Apology for Heroique Poetry and Poetique Licence", prefixed to it, that "I cannot without Injury to the deceas'd author of _Paradise Lost_, but acknowledge that this POEM has _receiv'd its_ entire Foundation, part of the Design, and many of the Ornaments, from him". The setting of Act I is in Hell; Act II opens in "a champaign country", shifts to a far region of the sky, and then passes to Eden; while Acts III, IV and V all take place in the Earthly Paradise. The poem should be of special and perhaps embarrassing interest to those who argue that Milton's original draft of _Paradise Lost_ was dramatic, not epic.

PL-246. (German)

Dedekind, Constantin Christian. _Versündigte und begnadigte Aelteren, Adam und Eva, nach Ahrt eines Musicalischen Schau-Spiels, eingerichtet_. Dresden, 1676. Mi: Univ. of Göttingen.

Inc. JEHOVA. Ich, Jehova, der Einige, in dem Wäsen, und dreifache an Personen . . .
Expl. Er werde von Männschen auf Erden besungen, im Himmel gerühmet von Englischen Zungen.

This is an oratorio in three acts plus an epilogue. Singing parts are assigned to Jehovah the Creator, Christ the Judge, Adam, Eve, Justice, Mercy, Truth, Azarias the Herald, a Cherub-sentry, the Serpent, Satan, and an Angel chorus. Act I deals with the Temptation and the Fall, Act II with interjected hopes of an ultimate Saviour, and Act III with the condemnation and expulsion of the guilty; while the epilogue gives choral assurance of God's ultimate mercy. The adaptation of this theme to oratorio is a sign of the times.

*PL-247. (German)

Richter, Christian. _Der geschaffne, gefallne, und aufgerichtete Mensch_. 1678.

*PL-248. (Italian)

Semenzi, Giuseppe Girolamo. Il Mondo creato. Milan, 1686.

A later satellite of Du Bartas and Tasso.

PL-249. (English)

Blackmore, Sir Richard. Prince Arthur. An Heroick Poem. London 1695.

Inc. I Sing the Briton, and his Righteous Arms,
Who bred to Suff'rings, and the rude Alarms
Of bloody War, forsook his Native Soil,
And long sustain'd a vast Heroick Toil . . .

Expl. So by Prince Arthur's Arms, King Tollo slain,
Fell down, and lay extended on the Plain.

An epic of some 9,000 lines in heroic couplets, dealing with the wars of Prince Arthur against the pagan invaders of his Christian kingdom. The enemies are sponsored by Lucifer himself, who hopes through their victories to reclaim Albion for the powers of Hell. In Book I the anger and fierce ambition of Lucifer are portrayed. Thor and Odin are represented (like Moloch and Beelzebub in Paradise Lost) as former lieutenants of Lucifer in the War in Heaven. Raphael and other angelic messengers are part of the epic "apparatus". There is a full Council in Hell of "th' Infernal Thrones and Powers". In Book II, Prince Arthur narrates to Hoel, a converted pagan, the story of Creation in full hexameral measure, with the Fall of Man, the interposition in Heaven of the Son for mercy, and the subsequent story of the Atonement - virtually the whole theme of Paradise Lost compressed into one book. In Book III, he goes on to describe the Last Judgement and the lot of mankind in Heaven or Hell. Book IV, rehearses the story of the barbarian invasions. In Book V, there is a naval battle between the fleets of Arthur and Octa the Saxon King, and Arthur is victorious. Arthur in a dream is shown a series of subsequent monarchs by the ghost of his father Uther, reaching its climax in William of Orange. In Book VI there is a further Council in Hell, with the chief speech by Asmodai. Megoera infects the Br. camp with disease and the dead are everywhere. Raphael stays the plague. In Book VII both sides mobilize for war. Episodes of battle fill the last three books, ending with the death of the Saxon leader Tollo at Arthur's hands. The poem is clearly indebted both to Vergil and to Milton.

PL-250. (French)

Perrault, Charles. Adam, ou la création de l'homme, sa chute, et sa reparation. Poème chrestien. Paris, 1697. Mi: Library of Congress.

Inc. Chantons du Tout-puissant la sagesse profonde,
Dans l'ouvrage accompli des merveilles du Monde;
Chantons comment sa main de l'argile forma
L'Homme que de son soufle ensuite il anima . . .
Expl. L'Ange ayant de la sorte acheve son discours,
Prit soudain son essor vers la source premiere,
Et son vol fut suivi d'un long trait de lumiere.

A poem of some 1800 lines, in heroic couplets. The contents are as follows: Book I. Creation; Book II. The Fall; Books III and IV. At God's bidding, an angel messenger instructs Adam and Eve as to the ultimate Atonement.

PL-251. (English)

Blackmore, Sir Richard. Creation, a philosophical Poem in seven books. London, 1712. Mi: Yale

Inc. No more of Courts, of Triumphs, or of Arms,
No more of Valour's Force, or Beauty's Charms
. . .
Expl. Grateful to Heav'n, I'll stretch a pious Wing,
And sing His Praise, who gave me Pow'r to sing.

A didactic epic, in harmonious but dull couplets, intended to demonstrate the existence of a Divine Eternal Mind. The proofs of God's existence are adduced from natural and physical phenomena. Blackmore surveys the systems of the Epicureans and the Fatalists and concludes with a devout hymn to the Creator. The general effect is tedious and commonplace.

PL-252. (Latin)

Noel, Manz. "Lucifer," In *Opuscula poetica in quatuor partes distributa* pp. 339-391. Frankfort, 1717. Mi: University of Göttingen.

Inc. SAP. Nunquam otiosa praescii virtus Dei
Jam constitutos mente in aeterna bonos . . .
Expl. Haec tota mundi machina in nihilum ruat.
Aeternitas! Aeternitas! Aeternitas!

The setting of this Latin drama is in Heaven. As the play opens, the divine Wisdom is explaining to the recently created angels that the terms on which they may enjoy eternal glory, and avoid eternal pain, is that they must serve God and God-in-man. Lucifer refuses and seduces the loyalty of man. The play ends in the exile of the rebel angels to Hell. The metre of the dialogue is the iambic senarius. The Chorus consists of Ambition, Envy, Impiety, Dishonesty, Justice, Love, Piety, Honesty and Reason.

PL-253. (Portuguese)

Soledade, Felix Joseph da. *Auto da Vida de Adam.* Lisbon, 1727.

Inc. Deos Optimo, Maximo, querendo manifestar por huma obra exterior a sua infinita Omnipotencia . . .
Expl. cujo nome, e cuja militante posteridade durará tanto, como o mesmo Mundo.

An indifferent prose treatment of the theme.

PL-254. (German)

Haller, Adalbert von. Ueber den Ursprung des Uebels. 1734. Accessible in Fritz Brueggeman's Das Weltbild (1930). Mi: Columbia.

Inc. Auf jenen stillen Höhen,
Worans ein milder Strom von steten Quellen rinnt . . .
Expl. Und kündig Deines Rats, den blinde Spötter schmähn,
In der Gerechtigkeit nur Gnad und Weisheit sehn.

A metaphysical poem of the period of the Aufklärung, instigated by the Theodicy of Leibniz and other discussions of the place of Evil in the best of all possible worlds. The problem dealt with by Milton is here expounded with a minimum of concrete poetic realization. It is really closer to Pope's Essay on Man.

PL-255. (Italian)

Campailla, Tommaso. L'Adamo, ovvero il mondo creato: Poema filosofico. Rome, 1737. Mi: Columbia.

Inc. Canto de la Natura, e di Natura,
Opra del gran Fattor, l'opre, e i portenti . . .
Expl. E imprendono, di esempio a mutue gare,
Di lor Salvezza Eterna il grande Affare.

A philosophical treatise on the nature of the created universe, expounded in the course of conversations between the newly created and well informed Adam and the Archangel Raphael. The author prides himself on having incorporated all the findings and terminology of "metaphysics, mechanics, astronomy, hydrostatics, chemistry, metallurgy, meteorology, botany, optics, anatomy, medicine, pharmaceutics, moral philosophy and theology", and to have overlaid and interfused these with a very intricate and detailed allegory. The verse is ottava rima, running to 19,224 lines, organized in 20 cantos. The book is a tour de force of expository erudition, rather than a poem.

PL-256. (French)

A.D.V. (pseud. for Alexandre Tannevot). Adam et Eve. Tragédie Nouvelle. Amsterdam, 1743.

Inc. URIEL. Archange Gabriel, choisi par le Seigneur,
Pour conserver ici la paix & le bonheur,
Je ne scais quel Esprit, trop suspect de mystère,
Du Soleil que j'habite, a traversé la sphere?
. . .
Expl. ADAM. Vous, Ministre de Paix, qui me l'avez appris,
Patrons, Que mon exil sera doux à ce prix!

A five-act play in French, showing obvious indebtedness to Milton.

PL-257. (German)

Klopstock, Friedrich Gottlieb. Der Tod Adams. Leipzig, 1757. Mi: Harvard.

Inc. SELIMA. Wie schön ist dieser glückselige Tag der Liebe! Wie hell ist er! . . .
Expl. ADAM. Richter der Welt! ich komme! (Indem der Fels krachend einstürzt.) O Tod! - Du bists! Ich sterbe!

A prose tragedy in three acts and 20 scenes. Adam lives in a hut whose inner room is built around Abel's stone altar, which, after all these years, is still stained with Abel's blood. Beside this altar, Adam now digs a grave for himself and informs Seth that he (Adam) is to die before sunset. In the Second act, Cain comes to seek revenge on Adam for his coldness; and he leaves, thinking that he has harmed his father. Adam sends Seth after him to announce his forgiveness. In the final act, Adam, having blessed Eve and some of his assembled descendants, dies at sunset amid the tremors of an earthquake.

The brief play seems to owe little to any source and is apparently a mildly romantic creation of Klopstock himself. The matrimonial felicities of Adam's grandchildren are woven sentimentally throughout the drama.

PL-258. (German)

Gessner, Solomon. Der Tod Abels. Zürich, 1758. Mi: Harvard.

Inc. Ein erhabnes Lied möcht' ich izt singen, die Haushaltung der Erstgeschaffnen nach dem traurigen Fall . . .

Expl. Sie giengen izt beym Mondschein, oft zurükweinend, von den Hütten weg, hinaus in öde Gegenden, wo noch keines Menschen Fusstritt gewandelt hatte.

A prose-poem in five strophes. A somewhat sentimental Romantic narrative. The story of the expulsion from Eden is told in retrospect by Adam to his grown-up family. In due course, Abel is murdered. The poem ends with Cain and his sister-wife Mehala going into exile: "They left the huts by moonlight, often gazing back, and went out into desert places where no human foot had ever wandered."

PL-259. (German)

Zachariä, Friedrich Wilhelm. Die Schöpfung der Hölle. Altenburg, 1760. Mi: Harvard.

Inc. Also, (schloss Raphael) hab' ich dir, Adam, nach deinem Verlangen,

Dinge, die sonst dem Menschengeschlechte verborgen geblieben . . .
<u>Expl</u>. Plötzlich ein Strom von Thränen; doch fasst er in seiner Seele
Nochmals den festen Entschluss des Schöpfers Gebote zu halten.

A poem of about 500 lines in dactylic hexameters. Zachariä goes back to the Miltonic episode in the Garden of Eden where Raphael is instructing Adam as to the universe and its history. At Adam's express petition, Raphael goes on to tell of the building of Hell in three nights as a prison for the rebellious armies of Satan. Zachariä wrote directly under the influence of Milton, of whose Paradise Lost he issued a 2-volume translation in German hexameters in this same year (1760).

PL-260. (English)

Byrom, John. On the Origin of Evil. In Miscellaneous Poems (published posthumously), Manchester, 1773.
Mi: Harvard.

Inc. Evil, if rightly understood,
Is but the Skeleton of Good,
Divested of its Flesh and Blood. . . .
Expl. And when the Life of Christ in Men
Revives its faded Image, then,
All will be Paradise again.

A poem of 36 lines in octosyllabic triplets dealing with good and evil, the Revolt in Heaven, the Fall of Man, etc., from the optimistic viewpoint of 18th century Deism.

*PL-261. (German)

Bodmer, J. J. Der Tod des ersten Menchen. 1776.

PL-262. (German)

Müller, Mahler. Adams erstes Erwachen und erste seelige Nächte. Mannheim, 1778. Mi: Harvard; Fabre du Faur Library.

Inc. Jetzt winkt Adam der Vater der Menschen allen, aufs Moos nieder; er aber bereitet sich auch . . .

Expl. Jetzt reicht Cain der brauen Melboe die Hand. Sie gehn Arm in Arm geschlungen über die mond-dämmernde Aue am Hügel hinunter im stillen Entzücken der Liebe. Abel aber begleitet Tirza bis an die Hütte, und steigt dann sorgsam wieder den Hügel hinan, unter seiner Heerde zu schlafen.

An idyll in rhythmic prose, 120 pages in length, written under the influence of Gessner. Adam tells Eve and his children the emotions of his earliest days. There follow various imaginary adventures of the Adam family. It is a sentimental work, ending in love and moonlight.

PL-263. (Danish)

Ewald, Johannes. Adam og Eva eller Den ulykkelige Pröve, et dramatisk Stykke. Preface dated July 2, 1779. In Samtlige Skrifter, Copenhagen, 1851.

Inc. IRMIEL. Saa staerk er Venskabs Magt! Velsig-
nede blant Dage,
Du som min glade Aand tör önske sig tilbage!

Expl. CHORUS. Evig, evig gode Gud!

A verse drama in five acts, about 3500 lines in length, written in heroic couplets (alexandrine couplets, with masculine and feminine rhymes alternating). While Adam and Eve and the Fall are the central theme, at least three-quarters of the dialogue is carried on by good angels (Eloah, Michael, Raphael, Gabriel, Uriel, Irmiel, Ithuriel, Zephon, Obaddon, and a chorus of good spirits) and wicked angels (Baal, Moloch, Satan, Abdiel Abbadona, and a chorus of evil spirits). The whole play takes place in Eden. In Act I, the good spirits discuss man's destiny; in Act II Adam and Eve fear God's injunction; in Act III Satan overhears their conversation and plans their overthrow; Act IV sees their successful seduction; and in Act V Satan claims his prey. At the very close, the Atonement is revealed to Adam, who exclaims: "My God! My Saviour!" In an epilogue, Adam and Eve kneel gratefully at the foot of God's holy hill and worship Him.

PL-264. (German)

Lavater, Johann Caspar. _Adam, Fragmente einer unvollendeten Epopée_. Leipzig, 1779.

Inc. Aller Sterblichen frühsten, der Väter Vater, den Ahnherrn . . .
Expl. Deiner Söhne wird Einer Euch, Fürsten der Hölle, zerschmettern.

Fragments of a Romantic treatment of the Eden-story, written in epic hexameters but without integration into an artistic pattern.

PL-265. (Dutch)

"Schasz, J. A." (pseud. for Pieter 't Hoen). _Lucifer en Beëlsebub, of het drommelsche committe van Raadgeeving. Klugtig blyspel_. The Hague, 1796.

Inc. LUCIFER, _zijn klaauwen over een vuurtestje warmende_: Burger Beëlsebub! ik bedroef mij hoe langer hoe meer over onzen rampzaligen toestand. - Daar zitten wij, als twee oude Druilöoren, elkander aantegaapen; konde en ongemak lijdende, en bij niemand op de waereld meer gerespecteerd, dan bij de zodanigen, die in ons gelooven, om ons te verachten en te vervloeken. . . .

Expl. BEËLSEBUB. Gij groote en kleine Drommels! Deelgenooten van ons geluk en van onze vreugd! Komt, vieren wij deezen dag overeenkomstig deszelfs grootheid. Er word een Duivelsballet gedanst, dat met een vervaarlijk donderen en bliksemen eindigt.

This three-act comedy, with its setting in Hell, is a satire on the French Revolution, with its slogan of "Vrijheid, Gelijkheid, Broederschap".

PL-266. (Italian)

Alfieri, Vittorio. Abele, tramelogedia. Florence, 1796. Mi: Columbia.

Inc. PECCATO. Imperàtor del doloroso regno,
Al negro abisso io torno . . .

Expl. Ah quai terrori e quanti
Al cor materno misero fan guerra!

A "tramelogedia" or lyric tragedy; 1557 lines of verse, in five acts. The tragic, human characters (Adam, Eve, Cain, Abel) use blank verse chiefly; while the fantastic characters, (Lucifer, Beelzebub, Mammon, Astaroth, Sin, Envy, Death, Chorus of Angels, Chorus of Devils, and Voice of God) use rhymed lyric measures. The drama opens with a council in Lucifer's palace, plotting more evil for Adam's children. As in morality plays, the personifications have a large part in persuading Cain to commit murder. The drama ends with Adam and Eve worshipping God over the corpse of Abel.

PL-267. (Spanish)

Reinoso, Félix José. La Creacion. Seville, 1797. Accessible in Obras, Seville 1872, vol. i, 20-26.

Inc. En qué furor sagrado ardiendo el pecho
algun númen que ignoro
tras sí me lleva? . . .

Expl. cual un Rey destronado,
guardando en su interior, el que perdiera
antiguo imperio recobrar espera.

An ode, in varying rhymed metres, on the subject of the Creation, tracing ecstatically the various stages of the process, culminating in the making of man. Reinoso closes with the thought that man's sin leaves him in ruined majesty, like a dethroned king.

PL-268. (English)

Coleridge, Samuel Taylor. "The Wanderings of Cain." Dated 1798 in the poet's MS. First published in the collected edition of 1828.

Inc. "A little further, O my father, yet a little further, and we shall come into the open moonlight."
Expl. And they three passed over the white sands between the rocks, silent as the shadows.

A prose-poem of 176 lines (Oxford edition, pp. 288-292), originally written as part of a projected joint work with Wordsworth, who did not write his share. Coleridge's fragment deals with the attempt of an evil spirit in the shape of Abel to lure the exiled Cain into offering the blood of his innocent child Enos to "the God of the dead". A piece of fantasy in the Romantic tradition.

PL-269. (Spanish)

Reinoso, Félix Josef. La Inocencia Perdida. Madrid, 1804. Mi: Biblioteca Nacional, Madrid.

Inc. Recibe el plectro ya, profana Clio,
Que de Bétis me diste en las riberas . . .
Expl. Salen ay! la mansion de la alegría,
Donde; infelice yo! nacer debia.

An epic poem in two cantos, written in 808 lines of ottava rima. Canto I describes the Council in Hell, headed by Luzbel, in which the decision is for war. In Canto II, after the Temptation in the Garden and the Fall, the Son (el sacro Verbo) offers himself for the Atonement.

PL-270. (English)

Stephens, G. The Death of Cain. Portsea, 1810. Mi: British Museum.

Inc. After Adam, through his disobedience and transgression of the divine command, was turned out of Eden . . .
Expl. They were equally addicted to avarice, pride and other vices and outrages.

A sentimental account of the return and pious death of Cain. Its inspiration is found in Klopstock and Gessner, English translations of whose Tod Adams (cf. PL-257) and Tod Abels (cf. PL-258) are printed in the same volume.

PL-271. (English)

Stephens, G. A. Cain's Lamentations over Abel. Portsea, 1810. Mi: British Museum.

Inc. "Be calm, be serene; let an awful silence reign throughout the wounded face of nature! . . .
Expl. With one smiling groan, he gave up the ghost, and - died!

Over 200 pages of rhapsodic sentimentality in the Klopstock-Gessner tradition.

PL-272. (Dutch)

Bilderdijk, Willem. De ondergang der eerste wereld.

Leeuwarden, 1820. Mi: Columbia.

Inc. Ik zing den ondergang van d'eersten Wereldgrond,
En 't menschdom dat, met Hel en Duivlen in
verbond . . .
Expl. En kleure uw zon heur licht in onzen regendrop.

A long poem in rhymed Alexandrines, beginning with the Fall but passing on in Romantic fashion to deal with the tender emotions of some of Eve's daughters and the primordial wars of Adam's sons.

PL-273. (English)

Byron, George Gordon. Cain: A Mystery (1821).

Inc. (Adam loquitur):
God, the Eternal! Infinite! All-wise! -
Who out of darkness on the deep didst make
Light on the waters with a word - all hail!
Expl. Cain: And might have temper'd this stern
blood of mine,
Uniting with our children Abel's offspring!
O Abel!
Adah: Peace be with him!
Cain: But with me! -

This 3-act Romantic drama is written in blank verse. In Act I, in the region outside of the Earthly Paradise, Cain's discontent is answered by a visit from Lucifer, who glorifies to him a spirit of revolt against God: "Nothing can quench the mind, if the mind will be itself And centre of surrounding things - 'tis made to sway." In Act II, Lucifer conveys Cain first to the luminous abyss of space and then to the vast dim world of Hades, professing at all times to be a spirit of truth in opposition to the false tyranny of Jehovah. In Act III, back on earth, Cain murders Abel, repents bitterly, is cursed by Eve and cast off by Adam, and departs into the wilderness along with his sister-wife Adah and their two small children. The most powerful concept in the drama is the symbol of freedom-loving revolt presented in the character of Cain.

PL-274. (German)

Baggesen, Jens. Adam und Eva, oder die Geschichte des Sündenfalls. Ein humoristisches Epos in zwölf Büchern. (Leipzig, 1827).

Inc. Es war einmal im Anfang eine Zeit,
Da gar nichts war auf Erden weit und breit,
In Lüften und in Meeren und in Landen,
Als blosser Platz zu Allerlei vorhanden . . .
Expl. Wer weiss, ob mir vielleicht entblüht der Menschheit Krone? -
Wir wissen's achtzehnhundert Jahre lang.

In about 7,500 lines of rhyming verse, Baggesen gives a mock-epic account of the Eden-story. When Adam comes to name the animals, he calls the camel "Gross-Zwillings-Buckel-Thier" and the mammoth the "Wandelberg" or "Schnabel-Riesenstier". When Adam and Eve have to leave the Garden, Adam gets the Lord's permission to take along his favorite hound-dog and Eve to transplant some of her favorite flowers. In the dialogue between Eve and the Serpent, both fall back temporarily on French for purposes of flirtation; and the Serpent cunningly assumes that Adam is Eve's father. The genial levity is maintained throughout.

PL-275. (English)

Pollok, Robert. The Course of Time. London and Edinburgh, 1827. Mi: Columbia.

Inc. Eternal Spirit! God of truth! to whom
All things seem as they are; thou who of old . . .
Expl. Time gone, the righteous saved, the wicked damned,
And God's eternal government approved.

A blank verse poem of approximately 9,000 lines, as compared with the 10,565 lines of Paradise Lost.

The setting is in Heaven, eons after Doomsday. In the first book, three younger spirits rashly apply to an "ancient bard" for information; and the remaining nine books are taken up with his almost interminable attempt to "sketch in brief the history of man". Part of Book II is devoted to an exclamatory account of Creation and the Fall. By the end of Book X, Pollok reaches Doomsday, the burning of the Earth with fire, and the creation of a new earth in which the just may dwell. The narrative elements of this alleged epic are lost in floods of ejaculatory piety and Romantic sentiment.

PL-276. (French)

Lamartine, Alphonse-Marie-Louis de. La chute d'un ange. Paris, 1828. Mi: Paris, Bibliothèque Nationale.

Inc. Vieux Liban! s'écria le céleste vieillard
En s'essuyant les yeux que voilait un brouillard,
Pendant que le vaisseau courant à pleines voiles
. . .

Expl. Et sur son front levé vers la céleste voûte,
L'homme sentit pleuvoir une première goutte.

Very marginal to the whole Miltonic theme is Lamartine's grandiose failure, La chute d'un ange. Starting from the record of angelic-human miscegenation in Genesis vi, 2, he traces the fate of an angel named Cedar who forsook the marvels of Heaven for the charms of a woman. The idyllic first part of the almost interminable poem has its setting among a pastoral tribe on the banks of the Orontes; a melodramatic second part takes place among sadistic Titans in the city of Babel. Between these two episodes is set a philosophical discourse, "The Eighth Vision", in which, on the summit of Lebanon, the aged Adonai reads fragments of the Primordial Book to Cedar and his beloved Daïdha - advocating universal pacifism and vegetarianism and the abolition of capital punishment. The general theme of the vast Romantic "epic" is that the errant angel Cedar, by a series of expiations in successive incarnations, will ultimately regain his original estate.

PL-277. (English)

Reade, J. E. Cain the Wanderer. London, 1829. Mi: British Museum.

Inc. CHORUS. Thou, who art hid from sight,
Ingenerable Essence! who dost dwell
Above us throned invisible . . .
Expl. Lo, the fulfilment - thou hast slain thy
father!

A full-length verse drama, with openly acknowledged tributes to Byron and Goethe. The human characters are Adam, Eve, Cain, Enoch, Adah, Zillah and Heilel: the spirits are Lucifer, Beelzebub, Moloch, Mammon and Azaziel, as well as God, Michael and the host of Heaven. In conversation with Michael, Lucifer complains that God was to blame for the Temptation in Eden: "They plucked and were deceived - but not by me." The action proper begins with Cain, the murderer, a fugitive in the desert, accompanied by his wife Ada and his little son Enoch. He deserts them and, as in Byron, has long rationalistic communion with Lucifer, who takes him to view the central Abyss and the void of Space. He also gives him a vision of a world at war and a world suffering from the Deluge, and leads him to the Paradise of Heilel and even to Pandaemonium, where the ghost of Ada, now dead, comes to warn her husband. He returns home, only to be shot in mistake by Enoch.

PL-278. (English)

Montgomery, Robert. Satan. A Poem. London, 1830.

Inc. Awake, ye thunders! let your living roar
Exult around me, and a darkness shroud
The air, as once again I greet . . .
Expl. Mine hour is come, and I am wreck'd of all,

All, save Eternity, and *that* is mine.

A monologue by the Prince of Darkness, extending through some 5,000 lines of blank verse. The Creatiòn, the Fall and man's ultimate redemption receive only incidental treatment. The work is divided into three books: (i) a survey of the inhabited world, with appropriate comments; (ii) a sermon on crime and its consequences; and (iii) the seamy side of modern English life.

PL-279. (English)

Barham, Francis Foster. *The Adamus Exul of Grotius, or the Prototype of Paradise Lost. Now first translated from the Latin*. London, 1839.

Inc. SAT. The sacred Thunderer's foe, exiled from
Heaven
My birthright and my home, I come,
Urging my desolate disastrous flight
From that Tartarean den, and the grim curse
Of dawnless midnight. . . .
Expl. ADAM. Where shall we wander? Whither shall we
bend
Our weary steps? Where choose our place
of rest
And find a home in exile, and a hope?

For over a century this has been assumed by the un-Latined to be, as its author affirmed, a translation of the *Adamus Exul* of Grotius. A comparison with the Latin of Grotius shows the claim to have very little foundation. For example, the 40 Latin lines, Grotius, 150b-190a, are roughly represented by 44 lines in the English of Barham. Of these, however, 14 lines are pure invention, not found in the Latin at all; 8 lines of the Latin, on the other hand, have been omitted from the translation; 27 lines of Barham are an adulterated and distorted version; and only 3 English lines are a straightforward rendering of the Latin. This is typical of his entire work. It is really not a translation at all but a piece of turgid Miltonese, paralleling the thought of Grotius at a distance of several miles. It has, however, some interest as an English poem in its own right, and is included here as such.

PL-280. (French)

Soumet, Alexandre. La Divine Epopée. Paris, 1840.
Mi: Bibl. Nat., Paris.

Inc. Un aigle qui planait sur un ciel nuageux,
Veut savoir s'il est roi de l'empire orageux
. . .

Expl. Lorsqu'ébloui d'amour, se fixant sur toi-meme,
Ton oeil au triangle supreme
En lettres de soleils lit: SALUT ETERNEL.

An inflated epic of 14,500 lines in heroic couplets, dealing with the ultimate triumph of Christ over the spirit of the Antichrist, Idaméel, earlier the spirit of Cain, which had come to rule in Hell more potently than Lucifer himself. On Christ's descent into Hell, he undergoes all over again the insults, agony and crucifixion already endured on Earth. When his blood flows in Hell, all its inhabitants, including Lucifer, adore the sacrifice, all with the exception of Idaméel, whose hatred vanquishes the love of Christ. The lightnings of God then intervene and seem to obliterate the citizens of Hell, but the prayers of the loving Sémida for Idaméel prevail and all Hell, including the Antichrist, are redeemed and transformed.

PL-281. (English)

Browning, Elizabeth Barrett. A Drama of Exile.
London, 1844.

Inc. LUC. Rejoice in the clefts of Gehenna,
My exiled, my host!
Earth has exiles as hopeless as when a
Heaven's empire was lost. . . .

Expl. CHOR. Waiting for that curing
Which exalts the wounded,
Hear us sing above you -
Exiled, but not lost!

A verse drama of about 2,600 lines. Mostly blank verse, with lyric choruses. Adam and Eve, after leaving the Garden, are full of grief. They are given further evil advice by Lucifer, but are strengthened by a vision of the Christ, who speaks to them.

PL-282. (Serb)

Njegosh, Petar Petrovich. Lucha Mikrokozma. Belgrade, 1845. Mi: Library of Congress.

Inc. Teshke li se u polet pushtati
Na lachitsi krilakh raspetijekh
Bez kormila i bez rukovoche . . .
Expl. Voskresenyem smrt si porazio,
Nebo tvojom khvalom odjekuje,
Zemlya slavi svoga spasitelya!

An epic, "The Rays of the Microcosm", in six books of blank verse by the chief religious poet of the Southern Slavs, a bishop of the Orthodox Church in Montenegro. While Njegosh (1813-51) was acquainted with Milton's Paradise Lost in a Russian prose translation, he shows great originality of his own. With him, Adam is a fallen angel who revolted along with Satan and then abandoned the latter on the third day of the War in Heaven, while the battle was still in doubt. God regards him as too black for Heaven and too white for Hell, and so creates the Earth as a purgatorial prison for him - a world combining elements of both Hell and Heaven - in which he may work out his punishment and purification. Man's tragic lot on earth is thus not due to the eating of forbidden fruit but rather to the misbehaviour of an angelic Adam before the Earth was ever created. In Njegosh, there is scarcely any idealization of Satan (as with Milton) and his portrayal of God is much less clearly anthropomorphic. The poem is an unusual one and deserves to be better known.

PL-283. (French)

Cailleux, Ludovic de. Le Monde antédiluvien. Poëme biblique en prose. Paris, 1845. Mi: Bibl. Nat., Paris.

Inc. Il était soir, temps où les jeunes filles ont coutume de sortir de la ville Hénochia, pour puiser de l'eau.
Expl. Mais la vengeance suivait la Créateur, Et l'espérance de Celui qui doit venir n'etait pas, Et cela fut fait.

A very lengthy Romantic narrative (376 pages) in poetic prose. The story opens at the time when the sons of God and the daughters of men had intermarried. Méthousaël is tormented by the ghost of his ancestor, Cain, who urges him to journey to Eden and avenge his race. He finds the ruins of the terrestrial Paradise. Its four rivers are silent, its foliage is yellowed in eternal autumn, birds have forsaken it, a single tree bears fruit, dark and poisonous, and round its trunk are wrapped the moist coils of a great serpent. The air of the place is deadly. At the end of the story, he perishes in the Deluge.

PL-284. (English)

Aird, Thomas. "The Devil's Dream", in Poetical Works, Edinburgh and London, 1848, pp. 90-96.

Inc. Beyond the north where Ural hills from polar
tempests run,
A glow went forth at midnight hour as of
unwonted sun . . .
Expl. 'Twas He that gave the Fiend a space, to prove
him still the same;
Then bade wild Hell, with hideous laugh, be
stirred her prey to claim.

Satan, wandering through the Universe, has a vision both of the past consequences of his seduction of mankind and of the eternal penalties that await his guilt in the unchanging lethargy of Hell. He awakes and in desperation soars to attack Heaven, but falls from among the untroubled stars back to Tophet without a blow being struck. The poem consists of 38 six-line stanzas in rhymed fourteeners.

PL-285. (German)

Hartmann, Moritz. Adam und Eva. 1851. Mi: Columbia.

Inc. Glücklich in solcher Zeit und dreimal glücklich ist Jeder,
Dem ein Winkel gehört, dahin er vermag sich zu flüchten . . .
Expl. Und sie sahen sich um - dort stand der theuere Vater,
Segnend streckte er aus seine Hand und lächelte: "Amen!"

This poem in classical hexameters is subtitled "Eine Idylle in sieben Gesänge", viz., The Creation, Paradise, The Serpent, The Tree of Knowledge, The Tree of Life, And He Shall be thy Master, Out of Paradise into Life. It deals, however, not with the original Eden-theme but with the simple love-story of a 19th century peasant couple, cast into the mould of the older narrative forms.

PL-286. (French)

Leconte de Lisle, Charles Marie René. Qain. Paris, 1852. Mi: Bibl. Nat., Paris.

Inc. En la trentième annee, au siecle de l'epreuve,
Étant captif parmi les cavaliers d'Assur . . .
Expl. Et ceci fut ecrit, avec le roseau dur,
Sur une peau d'onagre, en langue khaldaïque,
Par le Voyant, captif des cavaliers d'Assur.

In the days of the Hebrew captivity in Assyria, Thogorma the Seer has a dream, and sees Henokhia, the City of Anguish and Solitude, where the tomb of Cain is. A Horseman of Hell comes riding to announce its overthrow in the Deluge, and Cain, although ten centuries dead, rouses himself to confront the bitter intruder and defiantly foretell a time when Jehovah's evil priests will be brought to scorn, and little children will laugh in their cradles because they no longer know Jehovah's name. The Deluge commences and as the mountains sink beneath its waters, the Seer sees the grim figure of Cain, the Enemy and Avenger, walking through the storm towards the Ark.

PL-287. (French)

Pommier, Amédée. L'Enfer. Paris, 1853. Mi: Bibl. Nat., Paris.

Inc. La grande echeance est venue;
Les vastes cieux se sont ouverts . . .
Expl. Le cadran, sans chiffre inutile,
N'offre qu'une aiguille immobile
Et le seul mot: ÉTERNITÉ.

Some 1524 jingling lines, describing with gay malice the tortures of the damned in hell. One gains the impression that the poet does not take the matter very seriously.

PL-288. (French)

Hugo, Victor. La fin de Satan. Circa 1855?

Inc. Depuis quatre mille ans il tombait dans l'abîme.
Il n'avait pas encore pu saisir une cime,
Ni lever une fois son front demesure. . . .
Expl. DEUS. Et j'efface la nuit sinistre, et rien
n'en reste.
Satan est mort; renais, ô Lucifer celeste! -

This elaborate poem of nearly 8,000 lines,

mostly in rhymed Alexandrines, was largely composed between 1850 and 1860 but remained still unfinished when its author died in 1885. It was planned as a succession of odes, beginning with the fall of the vanquished Satan through infinite space and ending with his pardon and restoration to Heaven at the end of time. Between those limits lies the whole course of human history, in which he is at once an active agent in the human mind and a vast symbol of the individual will in rebellion against eternal law. The climax of the poem comes in the Crucifixion, in which, according to Hugo, the divine love is so potent that even the hatred of Satan's heart is exorcised. Liberty is also a motif, and blends with that of love as Satan is persuaded that freedom is found in surrender to the infinite love of God.

PL-289. (French)

Hugo, Victor. "Le sacre de la femme." In La Légende des siècles, Paris, 1859, vol. I, pp. 25-42.

Inc. L'aurore apparaissait; quelle aurore? Un abîme
D'éblouissement, vaste, insondable, sublime . . .
Expl. Et, pâle, Ève sentit que son flanc remuait.

Two themes are developed: (a) the primeval beauty of the earthly paradise, and (b) a lyric apologia for love and Eve's maternity. Hugo opposes the conception that Eve knew love and pregnancy only after the Fall, and makes the climax of his poem the awareness of the innocent Eve that the life of an unborn child is stirring in her womb.

PL-290. (French)

Hugo, Victor. "La conscience". In La Légende des siècles, Paris, 1859, vol. I, pp. 47-51.

Inc. Lorsque avec ses enfants vetus de peaux de betes,
Échevelé, livide au milieu des tempetes,
Caïn se fut enfui de devant Jéhovah . . .

<u>Expl</u>. Quand il se fut assis sur sa chaise dans
l'ombre
Et qu'on eut sur son front ferme le souterrain,
L'œil etait dans la tombe et regardait Caïn

The fugitive Cain, wherever he goes, sees in the sky above him the unsleeping eye of God. His children build a city and hide him in a tower in the midst of it, but still he sees the eye. At his request, they dig a grave and he descends into it, but still he sees the eye. This last phase is based on a Vulgate reading of Psalm 139, verse 8: "The eye was in the grave and looked at Cain."

PL-291. (German)

Anonymous. <u>Adam, Ein dramatisches Gedicht</u>. Berlin, 1862. Mi: <u>British Museum</u>.

<u>Inc</u>. (Gott, als Stimme)
Ich war . . . ich bin . . . ich werde unaufhörlich:
Der ew'gen Allmacht ungetrübte Kraft. . . .
<u>Expl</u>. (Adam Evae loquitur):
Fort, fort, befehle ich! . . .
Von nun an sei Dein Loos,
Was ich gebiete
Zu vollbringen:
Was ich befehle
Zu vollziehen.
(Schleudert sie vor sich hin. Der Vorhang fällt rasch.)

An anonymous drama in verse, apparently influenced both by Goethe and by Milton.

PL-292. (Magyar)

Madách, Imre. <u>Az ember tragédiája</u>. Budapest, 1862. Mi: Columbia.

<u>Inc</u>. (Chorus angelorum):

Dicsoseg a magasban Istenünknek,
Dicsérje öt a fold es a nagy eg,
Ki egy szavával hiva letre mindent
S pillantásától függ ismét a veg. . . .
Expl. ADAM: Gyanitom én is, és fogom Követni.
Csak az a vég! csak azt tudnám feledni!
DEUS: Mondottam ember: küzdj és bizva
bizzál!

This is the greatest of all Hungarian dramas. The play is one of sombre magnificence, a great philosophical presentation, in verse, of the vanity of man's search for happiness in this world. The author, though steeped in Milton and Goethe, is profoundly original.

After a Prologue in Heaven, Lucifer meets with Adam and Eve, tempts them successfully, and then seeks to prove to Adam that life, for which God has created him, is not worth living. Adam is defiantly optimistic. Lucifer then causes him, in a dream, to live through many successive stages of human history, each of which he is compelled to acknowledge as bankrupt in human happiness, yet with an unconquerable hope that some other type of civilization might not be so. Thus Adam finds himself a Pharaoh in Egypt, with Eve as a slave girl and Lucifer as grand vizier. He recoils from the brutal tyranny of Egypt and longs for Democracy. The scene shifts to Greece, where the fickle rabble of democratic Athens exiles him because of his very virtues.

In the next scene, a life of prodigal dissipation is vanquished by contact with the austere beauty of early Christianity; but after a brief black-out, Adam, as Tancred, in the time of the Crusades, finds the Church racked with theological dissension and finds himself separated from the woman he loves (Eve) by her vows as a nun.

Yet again, Adam, as Kepler the astronomer, finds his intellectual freedom strangled by Church and State. He clamours for "Liberty", and the scene suddenly shifts to the lawless liberty of the French

Revolution, where, at the hands of Lucifer, he ends his life on the guillotine. Wealthy London as a heartless "Vanity Fair", the deadly uniformity of a modern Socialist state, and the soul-freezing squalor of an Eskimo's igloo (a million years hence, on a frozen sea at the present equator) - these complete the devastating proof by Lucifer. Adam awakes, and contemplates suicide. Eve, about to become a mother, persuades him to live. The voice of God then denounces Lucifer and calls on Adam and Eve to face life with Stoic fortitude.

The only other related Hungarian poem appears to be A lelek halhatatlansága (Debrecen, 1805) by Vitéz Mihaly Csokonai. This is a dissertation, chiefly in blank verse, on the immortality of the soul. It has been influenced by Milton and by Rousseau, but can scarcely be classed as an analogue.

PL-293. (French)

France, Anatole. "La Fille de Caïn". Dated July 1864, published in Poèmes Dorés, 1873.

Inc. Un matin de ces temps où des hymens étranges
Aux filles de Caïn mêlaient les pâles anges . . .
Expl. L'ange flottait, splendide et triste, dans le vent,
Las d'offrir à la foudre un front toujours vivant.

A narrative poem of 72 lines in Alexandrine couplets, telling of the tragic love of Oholibama, daughter of Cain, for the angel Azraël.

PL-294. (Italian)

Carducci, Giosuè. "A Satana". Pistoia, 1865.

Inc. A te, de l'essere
Principio immenso,
Materia e spirito,

Ragione e senso . . .
Expl. Sacri a te salgano
Gl' incensi e i voti!
Hai vinto il Geova
De i sacerdoti.

This defiant hymn, in 50 tense lyric quatrains, salutes Satan as the vital principle of existence, the triumphant self-vindicating spirit of a rebellious, rational human life.

PL-295. (English)

Rossetti, Christina Georgina. "Eve". Dated 30th January, 1865, in Poetical Works ed. by W. M. Rossetti, at page 374.

Inc. "While I sit at the door
Sick to gaze within
Mine eye weepeth sore
For sorrow and sin . . ."
Expl. Only the serpent in the dust
Wriggling and crawling
Grinned an evil grin and thrust
His tongue out with its fork.

This 70-line poem expresses the grief of Eve over the death of Abel and states that all creatures except the serpent grieved in sympathy with her.

PL-296. (Portuguese)

Macedo, Jose Agostinho de. A creação. Poema. Lisbon, 1865. Ph: Lisbon, Bibl. Nac.

Inc. Canto o Ente Immortal, e esta pasmosa
Obra fatal do seu saber profundo . . .
Expl. Elles mostrando estao com evidencia
Tua gloria, teu saber, tua existencia.

This little volume, consisting of 108 stanzas in ottava rima, is a belated representative of the hexameral school of poetry. There is an opening declaration of his theme (the Creation) and a more lengthy appeal to God for inspiration and illumination. There follows a somewhat Romantic description of the created universe. The poet's avowed debts, however, are to Aratus, Manilius, Lucretius and Seneca, rather than to Du Bartas or Basil.

This is a posthumous publication of a very learned and splenetic priest, Jose Agostinho de Macedo (1761-1831). In his youth, he was thrown out of six Augustinian seminaries and finally out of the Order itself. His poetry is dull and turgid.

PL-297. (Portuguese)

Eça de Queiroz, José Maria de. "Adão e Eva no Paraiso". In Obras, Lisbon, 1922, vol. I, pp. 121-133. Original date 1865.

Inc. E' o mar. Nosso Pai transpoe as palidas dunas - e diante dele está o Mar!

Expl. . . . êsses Sóis, êsses Mundos, essas esparsas Nebulosas, que, inicialmente fechedas, como nós, na mão de Deus, e feitas da nossa substância, nem de-certo nos amam - nem talvez nos conhecem.

This vivid prose narrative paints the difficulties of Adam in becoming adapted to the primeval world. For example, the Father of Mankind is attacked by the big black Father of Bears and kills him in desperate fight. After many vicissitudes he is moved to appeal to God: "I'm much obliged, my sweet Creator, but give the government of the Earth to some better choice, to the Elephant or the Kangaroo . . . !

José Maria de Eça de Queiroz (1843-1900) is the greatest Portuguese novelist of the realistic school; but this sketch from his youth is a blend of the exotic and the whimsical.

PL-298. (English)

Cranch, Christopher Pearse. Satan. A libretto. Boston, 1874.

Inc. CHORUS OF WORLD-SPIRITS: Ye interstellar spaces
serene and still and clear,
Above, below, around! . . .
Expl. CHORUS: He who hath made us will lift us,
though stained and deformed and degraded,
Lift us and love us, though drowned in the
surges of darkness and death!

Blank verse dialogue between Satan, Raphael and various spirits, together with many lyric choruses. The Spirits ask Satan if he were not guilty of seducing mankind in Eden, and he remonstrates:

No personal will am I, no influence bad
Or good. I symbolize the wild and deep
And unregenerated wastes of life . . .

PL-299. (Spanish)

Topia y Rivera, Alejandro ("Crisófilo Sardanápalo"). La Sataniada, grandiosa epopeya dedicada al Principe de las Tinieblas. Madrid, 1878. Mi: Harvard.

Inc. Del hombre triste la mortal caída,
La de su yugo redención felice . . .
Expl. Los Jefrys de Satán aprestan yugos,
de Pilatos haciendo ó de verdugos.

This is an epic in thirty cantos in ottava rima, which cost its author, the chief poet of Puerto Rico, sixteen years of unnecessary labour. Its theme is that this world is really hell, ruled over by Satan. The poem is ostentatiously dedicated to "the Prince of Darkness", who is greeted with extravagant praise and appealed to (as Milton appeals to a "Heav'nly Muse") to inspire the poet to verses worthy of his Infernal Majesty.

PL-300. (Italian)

Rapisardi, Mario <u>Lucifero, Poema</u>. Mi: Columbia.

<u>Inc</u>. Dio tacea da gran tempo. Ai consueti
Balli movean gl' ignari astri, e con dura . . .
<u>Expl</u>. D' adamantino cor figlio di Temi:
Lèvati, disse, il gran tiranno è spento!

A poem of approximately 9,200 lines, organized in 15 cantos. Mostly in blank verse, but with some passages in terza rima, ottava rima, canzone-measure, and other forms. A philosophical poem by a modern free-thinker, hailing the victory of free thought over religion. Satan, the hero of the poem, is encouraged by the silence of God in modern times to attempt His overthrow, and divulges his purpose to Prometheus, who at first is rather pessimistic. After various experiences in Greece, France, the United States and Italy, Lucifer attacks Heaven, where the saints and angels have been behaving scandalously. God dies, and Lucifer goes in triumph to the Caucasus to report to Prometheus. The temper of the poem is aggressively antireligious.

PL-301. (English)

Meredith, George. "Lucifer in Starlight".

<u>Inc</u>. On a starred night Prince Lucifer uprose.
Tired of his dark dominion swung the fiend . . .
<u>Expl</u>. Around the ancient track marched, rank on rank,
The army of unalterable law.

A sonnet portraying the discomfiture of Lucifer, when, in a "hot fit of pride" he soars aloft and views, in the marching stars, "the army of unalterable law".

PL-302. (French-English)

Gallet, Louis (tr. Francis Hueffer). Eve, a mystery in Three Parts. London, sine dato. Music by J. Massenet.

Inc. HEAVENLY VOICES:
Man in the palm shade sleeps at even,
Sweetest odour floats on the breeze . . .
Expl. CHORUS. Ye are accurst!

The brief libretto of an opera by Massenet, dealing with the Garden of Eden story.

PL-303. (Ukrainian)

Franko, Ivan. Smert' Kayina. Lwów, 1889. May be found in his collected poetry, Z vershyn i nyzyn, Kolomiya and Winnipeg, 1920, pp. 553-581.

Inc. Ubyvshy brata, Kayin mnovo lyit
Blukav po svityi. Mov bychi krivavi,
Yovo honylo shchos' iz krayu v kray . . .
Expl. Pokryv sya; kynenyj izblyz'ka kamin'
Rozbyv vsyu chashku, splyushchyv do zemlyi,
Pokhoronyv na viky pid soboyu.

Having translated Byron's Cain from English into Ukrainian, Franko (1856-1916) went on to write an original poem in the same tradition. Smert' Kayina ("The Death of Cain") consists of about 900 lines in blank verse, shot through with the symbolism of a deeply religious message. The aged, exiled Cain, after the death of his wife, has an unconquerable nostalgic desire to gaze on Eden again. After appalling sufferings, he reaches a hilltop from which he can look down into the Garden. There thousands of frantic human forms crowd around the Tree of Knowledge and only grow more brutal in their quest while very few seek the Tree of Life, and these are butchered by their fellows. By deep meditation, Cain concludes that human intellect and human impulse can be reconciled by love. He seeks to preach this new gospel to his descendants, but is shot to death by the blind Lamech, symbolizing the unreasoning masses.

PL-304. (French)

"France, Anatole." Lucifer, being item III, pp. 71-80, in Le Puits de Sainte Claire (Paris, 1895).

Inc. Le Tafi, peintre et mosaïste florentin, avait grand peur des diables . . .
Expl. Il languit encore quelques jours dans la fièvre, et puis mourut.

This is a modern version of an old legend. A painter, Spinello, who has been painting a mural in which Lucifer is represented as hideous in countenance, is angrily rebuked in a dream by Lucifer, who is as beautiful as Michael though sad and proud. Lucifer threatens to pull Spinello's ears. The latter awakes in a panic, then lapses into a fever, and soon dies.

PL-305. (French)

Bleau, Edouard. Le Paradis Perdu. Drame-Oratorio en quatre actes. Montreal, 1897. (Laval).

Inc. ("Chœur des Séraphins"):
Aux profondeurs étherees
Pleines de frissons,
Louons le Seigneur, disons,
Disons nos hymnes sacrées. . . .
Expl. ("Grand chœur final"):
Que ta grandeur soit proclamee,
Que ton saint Nom soit béni!

This is a libretto of some 450 lines, almost entirely in lyric measures. Act I presents the Revolt and War in Heaven, following the exaltation of the Son; in Act II comes the Council in Hell; Act III portrays the Temptation, with Satan invisible but audible throughout; while Act IV concludes with judgement on the guilty. God the Father takes no part in the oratorio, but God the Son announces his atoning purpose a few lines from the end and is greeted by the final chorus. Eve is a soprano; an Archangel is a mezzo-soprano; Adam and Uriel are tenors; Satan, the Son and Belial are baritones; while Moloch is a bass.

PL-306. (English)

Santayana, George. Lucifer or The Heavenly Truce. A theological tragedy. Cambridge, 1899.

Inc. HERMES. What star art thou and by what god beguiled
To wander in this heaven
Far from the serene and mild
Circle of the sisters seven? . . .
Expl. LUCIFER. For, knowing grief, I have forgot to grieve,
And, having suffered, without tears receive
The visitation of my kindred stars.

In this poetic drama, the most profoundly philosophical of modern treatments of the Lucifer theme, there are three circles of dramatis personae: The Infernal group, consisting of Lucifer (self-conscious rationality), Mephistopheles (inveterate malice), Azazel, Belial, etc.; the Celestial group, consisting of the Risen Christ, Michael, Saint Peter, etc.; and the unselfconscious Olympians - Zeus (political cares), Hera (domestic cares), Hermes (gracious care-free youth), Ares, etc.

Hermes, astray in the Universe, finds a lodging for the night with Lucifer in a mountain cave on a remote star. Lucifer comes to love the lad and finds new springs of tenderness running in his heart. He is deposed in Hell by his unsympathetic followers, headed by Mephistopheles; but proceeds to Heaven to intercede with Christ the King for the happiness of his new friend. Christ proclaims his own triumph in this spirit of love, and Lucifer admits that if

Hermes
"believe and enter through the gate
His faith has opened, I will follow him,
Resume my throne and wear my old estate . . ."
but he declares that faith is beyond him, since he lives by truth and not by religious illusion. The Olympians perish and the play ends with Lucifer facing eternity in a spirit of agonized fortitude.

Santayana in the preface to his second edition (1924) describes this Lucifer as "a purged and sublimated spirit, an atheistical saint" who "must fall back, wretched but self-justified, on the absolute claims of his living thought".

PL-307. (English)

Shaw, George Bernard. Man and Superman. London, 1901, 1903.

A considerable portion of Act III (about 2400 lines of prose) is taken up with Hell, and a discussion of the spirit world by the Devil, Don Juan, Doña Ana, and the Statue. The Devil explains that "the strain of living in heaven is intolerable. There is a notion that I was turned out of it; but as a matter of fact nothing could have induced me to stay there. I simply left it and organized this place." As for the alleged gulf between Heaven and Hell, the Devil explains that "the gulf is the difference between the angelic and the diabolic temperament".

Much of the dialogue savours of a flippant parody of Milton: "You are a lady; and wherever ladies are is hell. . . . Nothing is real here. That is the horror of damnation. . . . Our souls being entirely damned, we cultivate our hearts. . . . do not be alarmed: there is plenty of humbug in hell (indeed there is hardly anything else); but the humbug of death and age and change is dropped because here we are all dead and all eternal."

PL-308. (English)

Binyon, Laurence. The Death of Adam. London, 1904.

Inc. Cedars, that high upon the untrodden slopes
Of Lebanon stretch out their stubborn arms
Through all the tempests of seven hundred
years . . .
Expl. Their burning deep unquenchable desire
Shall be their glory, and shall forge at last
From fiery pangs their everlasting peace.

A narrative poem of some 687 lines of blank verse, regarded by Mr. Binyon himself as his most memorable work. Adam, at the end of extreme age, sends his youngest children to look for Cain, so that he may be reconciled to him. They search in vain and Adam realizes that the curse is irrevocable. Calling his family about him, he grieves over the sorrows, unsuspected by them, that will yet overtake them and their children's children. As his hour of death approaches, he has them carry him in a litter to a cave from which he can see the far-off shining gates of Eden. There he dies, dreaming of the trials and triumphs of his descendants.

PL-309. (English)

Doughty, Charles M. Adam Cast Forth. London, 1908.

Inc. (Satan solus):
Am I not that great SAMMAEL, he that was
Before the Stars? Beside me only was
The EVERLASTING. . . .
Expl. (Adam loquitur):
Under the covert of HEAVEN FATHER'S WINGS,
Thou and our Children sleep. Thou HAWWA hast
Need thou to sleep: sleep! whiles I bete
our hearth.

A remarkable poetic drama, in five acts called "songs" but really in dialogue, written almost entirely in blank verse. Doughty borrows from The Dynasts (1904, 1906, 1908) of Thomas Hardy the device of the dramatic comment of supernatural intelligences. His style, however, is a deliberately archaic type of English, both in vocabulary and in syntax, seeking with some success to create a sense of primeval strangeness and newness of experience on the part of the first man and the first woman - called by him Adam and Adama. In the first act, Adam and his wife, separated by a desert storm after the Fall, meet again in the Land of the Lord's Curse. In the second "act", they are restored to health in the Valley of the Lord's Rest. In the next two acts they almost perish in a God-directed pilgrimage through waste places, but pass through Earth's Gate to the Lord's Field. In the final act, they achieve peace in work and parenthood. After Adama gives birth to triplets - Kayin, Habel and Noaba - her husband renames her Hawwa (Eve).

*PL-310. (German)

Nocken. Adam und Eva. 1909.

PL-311. (English)

Stephens, James. "The fulness of time". In The Hill of Vision, 1912, p. 30.

Inc. On a rusty iron throne
Past the furthest star of space
I saw Satan sit alone . . .
Expl. And they seated him beside
One who had been crucified.

Satan, at the end of the ages, is brought back to Heaven by God and welcomed by Gabriel, Uriel and Raphael.

PL-312. (English)

Stephens, James. "Eve". *Op. cit.*, pp. 100-103.

Inc. Long ago in ages grey
I was fashioned out of clay . . .
Expl. Sun and moon and I are true
To the work we have to do.

Eve is described as the cosmic embodiment of the eternal feminine.

PL-313. (English)

Stephens, James. "In the cool of the evening." *Op. cit.*, p. 108.

Inc. I thought I heard Him calling. Did you hear
A sound, a little sound? My curious ear . . .
Expl. He may not come . . . what? listen, listen, now -
He is here! lie closer . . . *Adam, where art thou?*

The lines are supposed to be spoken by Adam to Eve as they cower from the inquisition of God after their disobedience.

PL-314. (English)

Stephens, James. "The lonely God". *Op. cit.*, pp. 117-129.

Inc. So Eden was deserted and at eve
Into the quiet place God came to grieve. . . .
Expl. And say "'twas worn by Eve." So, smiling fair,
He spread abroad His wings upon the air.

The poem describes the loneliness of God after the fall of those who had been his friendly daily companions.

PL-315. (German)

Lipiner, Siegfried. Adam. Vorspiel zur Trilogie "Christus". Stuttgart, 1913. Mi: Library of Congress.

Inc. EVA Dort war's.
ADAM. Lass ab!
EVA. Tief, tief im Osten liegt es;
Vom fernsten Himmel blickt das Licht darein.
. . .

Expl. KAIN. Und keine Hand, die's von mir nimmt?
Niemand im Himmel? Niemand auf der Erde?
Niemand - Niemand -
(Er verschwindet im Geklüft.)

Siegfried Lipiner (1856-1911) was a Galician Jew who ultimately embraced Christianity. He was educated at the universities of Vienna and Leipzig. His doctoral thesis on "Homunculus, a Study of Faust and the Philosophy of Goethe" was typical of a life devoted to philosophy, religion and poetry.

His Adam, while intended as a prelude to a trilogy of philosophical dramas entitled Christus, is a 64-page, three-act verse tragedy, complete in itself. It is a new and profound treatment of the Genesis-theme, centring about the murder of Abel. Abel is a character of deep inner joy, at peace with the animal creation; while Cain desires only to kill the wild beasts and birds. After the murder, Adam, wishing to punish Cain, calls down the wrath of Heaven on him and invokes the wild beasts to tear him apart. A pack of wild animals then appears, but it is Adam that they slaughter, while Cain, in a moment of desperate self-forgetfulness, wishes that he could die for his father. Both Adam and Cain represent a tragic wrestling with the problem of man, as, hemmed in by natural instincts, he strives to achieve the light of knowledge. Abel, whose character is a foreshadowing of that of Christ, finds inner peace in a Consciousness of the presence of God.

PL-316. (English)

Howard, Katharine. Eve. Boston, 1913.

Inc. Adam! Adam! What followeth thee?
Adam! Adam! Why is the earth red about thee?
. . .
Expl. She calleth her children to rest in her branches.
She calleth to Adam to rest in her shade.

In this free-verse dithyramb, Eve, prompted by "the Inscrutable One" (the serpent) tells Adam to clean himself for an aeon or two before he is fit to be the father of her children. After the prescribed lapse of time he accepts her as ruler and under her sway all is well with the world. Apparently a feminist outburst.

PL-317. (French)

France, Anatole. La Révolte des Anges. Paris, 1914.

Inc. L'hôtel d'Esparvien dresse, sous l'ombre de Saint-Sulpice, ses trois étages austères . . .
Expl. SATAN. Nous avons été vaincus parce que nous n'avons pas compris que la victoire est Esprit et que c'est en nous et en nous seuls qu'il faut attaquer et détruire Ialdabaoth.

A cynical novel of a "phoney war" of Satan against God in more recent times. A group of apostate angels who have been living in modern France decide that the time is ripe for a new assault on Heaven. They call on Satan to lead the enterprise and that night he has visions of victory. In the morning, however, he changes his mind and harangues his legions accordingly. To triumph over God would merely interchange their roles and he has come to prefer Hell and Earth to the realms above. They will gain a truer victory by vanquishing the fear and ignorance in their own souls. There is a good deal of mock-Miltonese in the style of the book.

PL-318. (Polish)

Kobylanski, Idzi Faustyn. Adam i Ewa. Milwaukee, 1914. Mi: Library of Congress.

Inc. A na poczatku, jak to sami wiecie,
"Nic" tylko bylo na tym marnym świecie. . . .
Expl. Wali kazdego kto wejść usiluje -
Na tem sie konczy ta moja pieśń czwarta.

An 1800-line poem in four parts, dealing respectively with (a) the creation of the world, (b) the creation of Adam and Eve, (c) the first sin, and (d) the expulsion from Eden. Each section is made up of continuous verse but the prosodic sub-units in the respective sections are (a) heroic couplets, (b) sapphics rhyming aabb, (c) and (d) iambic pentameter quatrains rhyming abab. The author is a Polish-American priest.

PL-319. (French)

Peguy, Charles. Eve. Paris, 1914.

Inc. (Jesus parle.)
O mère ensevelie hors du premier jardin,
Vous n'avez plus connu ce climat de la grâce,
Et la vasque et la source et la haute terrasse,
Et le premier soleil sur le premier matin. . . .
Expl. Et l'autre est morte ainsi d'une mort solennelle.
Elle n'avait passé ses humbles dix-neuf ans
Que de quatre ou cinq mois et sa cendre charnelle
Fut dispersée aux vents.

A poem consisting of some 1915 rhymed quatrains. The eternal Jesus addresses the eternal Eve, full both of a nostalgic wistfulness for the charm of a lost primordial spring and of a sense of anxious dismay at the depravity of European civilization on the eve of World War I.

PL-320. (English)

Hodgson, Ralph. "Eve", in Poems. London, 1917.

Inc. Eve, with her basket, was
Deep in the bells and grass,
Wading in bells and grass
Up to her knees. . . .

Expl. Picture the lewd delight
Under the hill tonight -
"Eva!" the toast goes round,
"Eva!" again.

An exquisite little poem on the Fall, being 66 lines in dactylic dimeter, occasionally catalectic, which capture the sense of Eve as a simple country maid in the morning of time.

PL-321. (English)

Shaw, George Bernard. Back to Methusaleh. London, 1921.

Inc. ADAM. Eve! Eve!
EVE'S VOICE. What is it, Adam?
ADAM. Come here. Quick. Something has happened.

Expl. LILITH. . . . And for what may be beyond, the eyesight of Lilith is too short. It is enough that there is a beyond.

In this cycle of five plays, the first one, entitled "In the Beginning" presents Adam, Eve and the Serpent in the Garden of Eden. The Serpent explains the meaning of death and the means of propagating life. In a second Act, set in an oasis in Mesopotamia, Adam makes clear to Cain the meaning of the Eden experience: "Be thankful to your parents, who enabled you to hand on your burden to new and better men, and won for you an eternal rest; for it was we who invented death." At the close of the fifth play, "As far as thought can Reach", placed in 31,920 A.D., the ghosts of Adam, Eve, Cain, the

Serpent and Lilith discuss the evolution of mankind. Adam and Cain are dissatisfied but Eve, the Serpent and Lilith feel that the onward movement of life is justifying itself.

PL-322. (English)

Wolfe, Humbert. Requiem, London, 1927.

An elaborate pattern of lyric poems, setting forth a varied human approach to the experience and significance of death. The stories of the fall of the Angels and of Man are invoked from time to time as part of the imaginative background of the work (cf. pp. 15, 25, 63, 92), but they do not emerge as central to its plan until the penultimate section, entitled "Losers and Winners", when the struggle of men and women with their destiny is caught up and generalized in terms of the old cosmic strife of "principalities and powers".

PL-323. (English)

Anderson, Olivia Cushing. Creation and Other Biblical Plays. Geneva, 1929.

Inc. VOICE OF GOD: Glory be to the new world
In which I give free life to all. . . .
Expl. CHILDREN OF GOD: Light! Who will give us light?

A modern mystery play by an American author. Man is portrayed as a harmonious spiritual being in the beginning, but as coming to enthrone material interests and so to lose his spiritual birthright.

PL-324. (Italian)

Properzi, Daniele. Adamo ed Eva. Aquila, 1930.

Inc. EVA. Diletto Adamo mio, queste ghirlande

han più vaghezza e grazia
dell' altre.
Expl. ADAMO. Taci! Taci!
E' nostro figlio!
EVA (cadendo a terra):
Ed io l'ho maledetto!

This "mystery play in three acts" is written in unrhymed verse, with generous stage descriptions. Act I, covers the Fall and the expulsion from Eden; Act II God's preference for Abel; and Act III the murder of Abel by Cain. The play ends with Eve's curse on the murderer.

PL-325. (French)

Goll, Ivan. Lucifer Vieillissant. Paris, 1934.

Inc. Je m'éveille d'un rêve qui se ferme sur moi
comme une grande grille dorée, sans que je
puisse rien pour la retenir. . . .
Expl. Et dans le ciel, au-dessus des lettres de sang:
VOUS NE SAVEZ PAS
l'Étoile du Soir annonciatrice est apparue.

A completely cynical treatment of man's spiritual plight. Lucifer, defeated in the primordial War in Heaven, chose as his punishment a life on earth in human form. In the stage reached by the book, the ages of faith have yielded to the age of liberty, nihilism, and futility. Man knows nothing, believes nothing, respects nothing, and at death hopes for nothing. Lucifer announces: "Je suis au bout du monde."

PL-326. (Spanish)

Lorca, F. Garcia. "Adam". In Poems, tr. by Stephen Spender and J. L. Gili, London, 1939.

Inc. Morning by tree of blood is moistened
Where the newly-delivered woman groans. . . .

Expl. But another obscure Adam sleeping
dreams neuter seedless stone moon far away
where the child of light will be kindling.

A modernistic sonnet, enigmatic as to sense.

PL-327. (Afrikaans)

Louw, W. E. G. Adam en ander gedigte. Johannesburg and Pretoria, 1944.

Inc. Hy het hom opgebeur vit daardie slaap
waarme die nanag eindelik sy drome
soos swane van verre en steile kuste keer. . . .
Expl. Die diepe rus van 'n voleindiging
het in die slaap vir hulle saam gevind.

Some 192 lines of blank verse, giving Adam's impressions of the created world round about him.

PL-328. (French)

"Hertel, François" (pseudonym for R. P. Rodolphe Dubé). Cosmos: poèmes. Montreal, 1945.

Inc. Il fut un temps où il n'y avait rien. Rien
que Dieu, seul en Lui-même, se pensant et s'aimant.
Pas un seul atome qui bougeait hors de Dieu.
. . . .
Expl. Que notre destinée soit à jamais en la votre
fondue et confondue
Pour l'éternelle réviviscence du monde en la
source de vie!

This free verse poem, in a style of piquant modernism, ranges roguishly from the Creation to the Last Judgement, with a wink of novelty at every turn. Thus it envisages God's feelings as he watches the sons of Noah grow busy after the Flood: "My God!" says God, "I shall never be done with this mud! And do these little vertebrate worms make pretensions to creation too?" Or he portrays thus the human attitude at the Last Judgement: "There is an end of embracing this world that they hoped to possess and that is now going to tumble in dust. There is nobody left in the pool-rooms, and the race-track is deserted. Only the red-light district is making a last minute profit. . . ."

PL-329. (French)

Valéry, Paul. Lust, la demoiselle de Cristal. Paris, 1946.

Inc. FAUST. Assez, Lust! Finissez-en! Ici l'on ne rit pas! . . .
Expl. DISCIPLE. Vous me rendez au diable!

This fragmentary comedy, printed as part of the volume Mon Faust Ebauches, comes in some respects closer to the central pattern and problem of Paradise Lost than it does to that of Faust, of which it is nominally an analogue. Faust, on a soft summer night in a Garden, has discovered personified Tenderness - at once a childlike rapture of pure existence and a type of the original relationship between Adam and Eve. But Mephistopheles is lurking in the form of a green snake in a tree in whose shade Faust and his secretary, "Lust, la demoiselle de Cristal", share a peach under his infernal auspices. From his comments, one gathers that Faust-Adam will turn from Tenderness to Lust, and will find in the brief physical brutality of sex a realization that life's essence is of the Devil. With Valéry, the far-off rivers of Eden flow at last in despair into the Dead Sea of Existentialism. Man's only means of escaping the inherent evil of life is to refuse to live.

INDEX

INDEX

(Arabic numerals refer to the listing in the Descriptive Catalogue; minuscule Roman numerals to the Introduction. The pagination of translations and extracts is given in Arabic preceded by "text pp. ".

A

C

D

E

F

G

H

I

J

K

L

M

N

O

P

T

U

V

W

Y

Z

www.ingramcontent.com/pod-product-compliance
Lightning Source LLC
LaVergne TN
LVHW082005060826
844660LV00028B/1238
9781487592363